BACKPACKERS
GUIDE
TO
AUSTRALIA

Little Hills Press

Backpackers Guide to Australia

ISBN 1 86315 223 7

Maps by MAPgraphics
and Little Hills Press
© Little Hills Press, 2004

Editor: Dan Homillosa
Designers: Darren Holt, Dan Hormillosa
Publisher: Charles Burfitt

Printed in China by Colorcraft, Hong Kong S.A.R.

Little Hills Press
Sydney, Australia
www.littlehills.com
lhills@bigpond.net.au

Contents

New South Wales

Australian Capital Territory

Queensland

Northern Territory

Western Australia

How to Use This Book

The chapters of this book are laid out firstly by state, and then by region. The chapters work around Australia's states in a circle, beginning in New South Wales, including the ACT, and ending in Tasmania. You can access information on chosen locations easily, regardless of which direction you are heading, or what part of Australia you are covering.

From regional characteristics, how to get there, where to stay, and what to see, we have approached in detail every way a visitor might occupy his or her touring time, with the intention of helping to make the most of that limited time. The headings are clear for ease of use, and our comprehensive Index will assist you in locating your area of interest.

Accommodation and Eating Out

The Accommodation (Let's Stay Here) and Eating Out (Let's Eat) sections contain by no means an exhaustive list of what Australia has to offer. We have tried to give you a starting point with budget accommodation given with prices in most population centres. They are designed to give you a basis for comparison and to act at the very least as a starting point for the planning of your holiday.

Note that most of the major budget accommodation listed can accept all major credit cards. Inquire at the desk before or while making bookings. American Express, Diners Club, Visa, Bank Card and MasterCard are widely accepted and usually signposted at participating outlets.

With regard to eating out, remember that there are always cheaper meals available at fast food outlets and in the food courts of most shopping complexes though we have focused on listing only popular and recommendable but cheap restaurants. Again, the GST is excluded from any prices listed. However, if you are prepared to wear shirt, shoes and socks you can always get a good meal for a very reasonable price at any licensed services club, RSL, Leagues, Soccer in the local area. Ask the manager of the hostel where you are staying for information. Then you can always buy food and cook your own.

Points of Interest

There are a million places to see in Australia. From historical monuments, botanical gardens and modern scrapers that define this country and unique own. In every city and town covered, detail on anything that might be of interest for every kind backpacker is listed. In highlights, it mentions the place, a brief description of its attraction and an address and contact number for further details. The Tourist Centres in the area are very helpful in obtaining more information.

Facilities

This section mainly lists the available sporting recreational centres in each town, to cater for those who have exhausted visiting the sites and are after for some fun activites.

Festivals

Festivals occur in each regions at different times throughout the year. Knowing when, where and which festivals are on might help better plan your itinerary.

Symbols

Throughout the text you will find that symbols have been used to denote the information that follows, whether it be an admission price, opening times, phone numbers, web or e-mail addresses. This will aid you in locating the specific details you desire more quickly.

Here is a list of the symbols used with an explanation of each:

☎ indicates a phone number
✪ indicates a price
☉ indicates opening times
▉ indicates a web site
✉ indicates an email address

Australia: An Overview

Australia is an island continent in the South Pacific Ocean. It is the smallest continent and the largest island in the world with a coastline of 19,650km. Its nearest neighbours are New Zealand and Papua New Guinea, while East Timor and Indonesia are a little further away, off the north-western coast.

The country has an area of 7,682,300 square kilometres and is divided into six states - New South Wales, Queensland, Western Australia, South Australia ,Victoria and Tasmania - and two territories - Northern Territory and Australian Capital Territory.

The capital of Australia is Canberra in the Australian Capital Territory (ACT). The capital cities of the states are as follows:

New South Wales - Sydney
Queensland - Brisbane
Western Australia - Perth
South Australia - Adelaide
Victoria - Melbourne
Tasmania - Hobart

The capital of the Northern Territory is Darwin.

History

It was generally accepted that the continent was first settled by Aborigines around 20,000 years ago, until recent discoveries suggested that they may have arrived much earlier. They were Stone Age people, and as the country had virtually no indigenous plants that could be cultivated for crops,

and no animals that could be domesticated, they neither grew nor bred their food, but survived by hunting and gathering. In the interior of the country, this necessitated a nomadic way of life, but in the coastal areas they led a more settled lifestyle because of readily available food from the sea.

Their diet consisted of animals, snakes, birds, birds' eggs, fish, insects, berries and fruits. Their main weapons were the spear and woomera (a sort of spear launcher) and the boomerang. In the hot weather, they didn't bother with clothes, but in the colder regions they wore cloaks of possum or kangaroo skin.

The Aborigines were a peaceful race, and were deeply religious. Their mythology described the creation and explained the reasons for most human behaviour. It was passed from generation to generation in stories, songs and dances, as they had no written language. The dances were called corroborees, and there was one for every special occasion from praying for rain, to mourning death or celebrating a successful hunt.

Aboriginal art was mostly linked with their religion, but sometimes it was only a form of self-expression and not meant to be permanent. Intricate bark paintings were often made for a corroboree, and when it was finished they were simply thrown away.

European Discovery

Many Europeans visited Australia from the early 1600s, but the

honour of discovering the continent goes to Captain James Cook, who in the ship *Endeavour* sailed into Botany Bay on April 29, 1770. Two boats went ashore, and tradition says that the first man to set foot on the land was Isaac Smith.

Cook and his party continued sailing northward, naming bays, capes, mountains and islands as they went, and reached a small island off Cape York where they went ashore on August 22, and took possession of the whole eastern coast in the name of King George III. Cook called the land New South Wales, and the island Possession Island.

European Settlement

The American War of Independence in 1783 was directly responsible for the settlement of Australia, as Britain then had nowhere to send her convicted criminals. In 1779, Joseph Banks, who had sailed with Cook, suggested that New South Wales would be a good place for a penal settlement, but nothing was done about it. By 1786 the situation was critical; old ships that had been converted into prison hulks were bulging at the seams, and the government decided to act. New South Wales was proclaimed a Crown Colony and Captain Arthur Phillip, RN, was appointed its first governor with orders to establish a penal settlement at Botany Bay.

The First Fleet sailed from England on May 13, 1787, and comprised *HMS Sirius*, the armed tender *Supply*, three storeships and six transports, with food clothing and other supplies sufficient for two years. They carried 1,044 people, comprising 568 male and 191 female convicts with 13 children, 206 marines with 27 wives and 19 children, and 20 officials. The ships moored in Botany Bay, but found the area unsuitable for settlement because of a lack of fresh water.

After exploring further north, Philip found the entrance to a large harbour, and decided the best spot for the new settlement was in the area he called Sydney Cove. In the afternoon of January 26, 1788, he and a party of officers and marines raised the Union Jack on the foreshore, drank toasts, fired volleys, and gave three cheers. The rest of the fleet arrived later in the day, and work on the new settlement began in earnest the following morning.

Expansion

The infant colony was not without its problems. The soil, except for a small area around Sydney Cove, was found to be of inferior quality. The majority of the convicts were city people, and so had no experience in farming or agriculture. The government in Britain was very good at giving orders about what should be done, but not very good at understanding the colony's problems and giving assistance to implement solutions. They simply kept sending more convicts, putting more strain on supplies.

Nevertheless the settlement survived and grew. Intrepid explorers discovered new areas, and other settlements were established - Parramatta in 1788, Newcastle in 1803, Hobart in 1804, Brisbane in 1824, Perth in 1829, Melbourne in 1835, Adelaide in 1836, and so on.

The last convict ship to reach Australia arrived in Fremantle on January 9, 1868.

In the 1850s, the discovery of gold brought a huge influx of migrants from all over the world in search of their fortune. Australia's population increased from a little over 400,000 to more than a million in ten years.

Federation

The campaign to form a federation of the colonies began on October 24, 1889, with a speech by Sir Henry Parkes, known as the Father of Federation, at Tenterfield. The movement grew rapidly under his leadership, and there was a meeting of colonial leaders early in 1890 and a convention in March 1891 in Sydney. Parkes died in April, 1896, and the reins were taken over by Edmund Barton, barrister and statesman. A second convention was held at Adelaide in March 1897, and a third conference in January 1898, when a draft constitution was accepted. The next step was to hold referendums in the various colonies. The first, in 1898, was defeated. The second, in 1899, saw the five eastern colonies vote in favour of federation and Western Australia abstain.

Barton then headed a delegation to London, where various objections raised by the Colonial Office were overruled. Western Australia agreed to join in after receiving a promise that a transcontinental railway would be built to link Perth with the east coast. On July 9, 1900, Queen Victoria gave her assent to the act which would unite the six colonies into a Commonwealth.

The Commonwealth of Australia was proclaimed and the first Governor-General, the Earl of Hopetoun, was sworn in at a ceremony in Centennial Park, Sydney, on January 1, 1901. About 60,000 people were present. On May 9, in the Exhibition Hall, Melbourne, the Duke of York (later King George V) officially opened the first parliament. The first Prime Minister was Edmund Barton.

In 1910, competitive designs were invited for the federal capital, to be built on a site of 2356 sq km, about 240km south-west of Sydney. The competition was won by Walter Burley Griffin, and after much discussion, it was decided to call the capital Canberra, an Aboriginal name for 'meeting place'. The first Parliament House, which was always considered to be a temporary building, was opened by the Duke and Duchess of York (later King George VI and Queen Elizabeth) in 1927. The present Parliament House was opened by Queen Elizabeth II in 1988.

Australians fought in World Wars I and II, Korea and Vietnam. The nation has lost over 100,000 in war this century, and of these, 60,000 were casualties of the first World War.

The legal system, public service and government structure of Australia are English-based.

Population

During the 1950s and 1960s,

people wishing to migrate from Europe and the United States were provided with assisted passage by the Australian government. However, it was not until the late 1960s that restricted entry to Australia from Asia was eased. In the last 40 years Australian society has undergone a tremendous change with now one in four people being a migrant or the child of a migrant.

Australia since the 1970s has become aware of its presence in South-east Asia. The countries of the region are starting to have more of an impact on Australian life. Many new migrants are Asian, and society reflects this blend of European and Asian cultures.

Approximately 85 per cent of the 19 million inhabitants live in urban areas. The east coast of Australia is the most populous because of the fertile plain east of the Great Dividing Range of mountains. The major cities are the state capitals, and the most populous state is New South Wales with 6,173,000 people, followed by Victoria with 4,533,300 people.

The social environment is heavily influenced by the US media and movies. California has a lot in common with Australia's east coast.

Language
Australians speak English, although due to the many people from other countries that have come to live in the country, it is not unusual to hear conversations in other languages when travelling by public transport.

Melbourne, for instance, has the second largest Greek population of any city in the world, surpassed only by Athens.

Like the English, Australians call 'gas' petrol and 'fries' chips; but you will find links to the US are perhaps stronger, with McDonalds, Pizza Hut and KFC firmly established in every suburb. There are a few words and phrases that are unique to Australia and in common usage, and dictionaries of Australian slang are available at local bookshops. Australians do say "G'Day", and if stressing authenticity or the truth of a statement, they might say that something is "fair dinkum" or "dinky-di".

There is not much difference between the accents of people from different states, although the pronunciation of particular words sometimes makes the distinction clear. For example, New South Welshmen say the place where a king lives is a 'carsel', but Victorians say it is a 'cassel'. People who live in the cities tend to speak much more quickly than those in isolated areas, and this becomes quite noticeable when travelling in the Outback.

Religion
The vast majority of Australians belong to the Christian Churches. There is only a slight margin between Roman Catholics and Anglicans, whose numbers hover around 26% each, reflecting the influence of migrating Irish and Italian Catholics, and the steady flow of English Anglicans into the country. All other religions and sects are present in Australia.

Jews, Hindus, Moslems and Buddhists are all represented strongly on account of the post World War II influx and other political developments since, which opened access to Australian shores. By and large there is peaceful coexistence, and the multicultural composition of society is typically celebrated and embraced.

Holidays
Christmas, New Year and Anzac Day (April 25) are the only holidays that are held at the same time throughout the country. Easter is a moveable feast that can fall in either March or April. Australia Day is accepted by all as January 26, but some states have their public holiday on the exact day, and others choose the closest Monday, so as to have a long weekend break.

The whole of Australia stops for five minutes on the first Tuesday in November for the running of the Melbourne Cup horse race, but only people living in Melbourne have the day off work.

In addition, school holidays are different in each state, although the long Christmas break is the most popular holiday time, and runs roughly from the end of the second week in December to the end of January.

It is a good idea to check with the Visitor Information Centres in the cities and towns before or upon arrival, as prices and availability of services will be affected on public holidays.

Overseas Visitors

Entry Regulations

All travellers to Australia need a valid passport, and visitors of all nationalities, except New Zealand, must obtain a visa before arrival. These are available at Australian Embassies, High Commissions and Consular offices listed in local telephone directories. No vaccinations are required. Or if you are planning a short stay you can apply for an ETA (Electronic Travel Authority) which does not involve in having your passport stamped and can be applied for over the web. the address is: ■www.eta.immi.gov.au/ETAAus3En.html

The citizens of the following countries can apply for an ETA -

Those Eligible:

You are only eligible to apply for an ETA while you are outside of Australia. To apply through this site, you must also hold one of the listed ETA-eligible passports. If you do not meet these criteria, then you should contact your nearest Australian visa office for further options.

What is an ETA?

According to the web site `An ETA is equivalent to a visa, but there is no stamp or label in your passport and there is no need for you to visit an Australian diplomatic office to submit an application. Applications for ETAs can be submitted through travel agents or airlines.

Now, you can also submit applications directly through this web site by clicking on the *Apply for ETA* button and, in most cases, they will be able to approve your ETA in less than 30 seconds. You can also check your ETA status, if you applied through this site, by clicking on the *Check your ETA* button.

The ETA is issued electronically by a computer system operated for the Department of Immigration and Multicultural and Indigenous Affairs (DIMIA) of Australia.

When an application for an ETA is submitted through this site, all you need to do is enter the details from your passport and your credit card information. The application is processed immediately. Approved applications are electronically recorded on Australian Government systems.

When you arrive at an airport for check-in on a flight to Australia, the airline check-in staff can electronically confirm that you have authority to board the flight to Australia.'

Travellers holding the following passports may now apply for an ETA through this site:

Andorra , Austria , Belgium, Brunei , Canada, Denmark, Finland, France, Germany, Greece, Hong Kong SAR, Iceland, Ireland, Italy, Japan, Liechtenstein, Luxembourg, Malaysia, Malta, Monaco, Netherlands, Norway, Portugal, San Marino, Singapore, South Korea, Spain, Sweden, Switzerland, United Kingdom, United States Of America, Vatican City

Holders of Hong Kong British National (Overseas) (GBN) passports are not eligible to apply for ETAs through this site. They must present at an Australian Overseas office.

The cost of the ETA is AUS$20.00. Payment is by credit card only. The cards accepted are Amex, Diners Club, JCB, Mastercard and Visa.

The Conditions of the ETA are the following*:

● It is valid for visits to Australia for tourism or to visit friends or relatives

● It is valid for multiple visits within 12 months from date of issue

● The maximum length of each visit is three months

● You may not work while in Australia

*Taken from the Immigration Depts web site.
If you wish to stay longer and you want to do some part time work then you will need a Working Holiday Visa

Working in Australia while you travel around

Working Holiday Maker Visa

For information see the Australian government web site: ■www.immi.gov.au/faq/whm/#what. Remember you can only use this visa once in coming to Australia.

Who is eligible?

You must be aged between 18 and 30 years without dependent children. Australia has reciprocal WH arrangements with the following countries - the United Kingdom, Canada, the Netherlands, the Republic of Ireland, Japan, the Republic of Korea, Malta, Germany, Sweden, Denmark, Norway, Finland, the Hong Kong Special Administrative Region of the People's Republic of China and the Republic of Cyprus.

Where can you apply?

The visa is not granted in Australia. All visa applications must be made overseas. However if you are from the United Kingdom, Canada, the Netherlands, the Republic of Ireland, Sweden, Denmark, Norway and Finland you can apply for a Working Holiday visa at any embassy or on line in any country (except Australia). Applicants who hold a valid passport from Japan, the Republic of Korea, Malta, Germany, or the Hong Kong Special Administrative Region of the People's Republic of China, and the Republic of Cyprus, must apply in their own country - ie the country of their passport.

How do you apply?

Downloading from the web the form 1150 (PDF File) Application for a Working Holiday Visa.

Quotas and costs

There is a quota which varies but you are talking about almost 90,000 people being admitted under this scheme each year in recent years. The cost of the visa is AUS$65.00.

You may be required to sit for an interview but this is rare, though you MUST have a return ticket and you must give evidence of sufficient funds for the initial stage of your travel. Medical examinations are really only required if you are from a high risk `medically speaking' area. You can also leave Australia during the 12 month period and return (say going off to New Zealand) but the Visa is 12 months from when you started your trip and time away is not discounted from the 12 month period.

Type of Work

There is no restriction on the type of work you can do but you cannot be employed by the same employer for more than 3 months unless you have written permission from the Secretary of the Immigration department prior to the conclusion of ther 3 months.

Employment Agencies

There is no problem using the services of an employment or recruitment agency.

They can also make sure you are paid the appropriate wage and you are not an excuse for cheap labour. For general information of wage rates you can access the following government web site: ▪www.wagenet.gov.au;

With regard to employment agencies - all the backpacker magazines you come across will have heaps of this information in them. Or all you need to do is go to ▪www.google.com.au and type in

Australia backpacker jobs.

When we did it some 8,100 leads came up. So it looks as though you are covered.

You are not permitted to work for the whole 12 months - what sort of holiday are you after anyway!! You can undertake study for up to 3 months if you wish on this visa - eg learning a language. Try the universities for this as they always have english courses.

Health Insurance

You are not covered by the government health insurance scheme - Medicare, so you should take out private health cover for the year before you leave.

Extending the Stay

If you want to extend you stay in Australia you may be able to change to a normal visitor's visa but you have to contact the Department of Immigration and possibly go in for an interview. Phone 131 881 to see how you should proceed.

US citizens who may want to apply for some short term work

You must between the ages of 18 and 30 to even contemplate this one and it is only valid for 4 months. This visa is granted no more than 3 months before departure date. The validity is based on your departure date so you must ensure you have confirmed flight bookings, otherwise you will be guarenteed a real hassle if you overstay.

See the following web site ▪www.austemb.org/DIMA/TempRes/416.htm for the

Australian embassy in Washington.

Sub Class416(B) is what you are after.

It is necessary to be preselected by one of the following organisations

Work Experience Down Under 1-888-449-3872

BUNAC (IEP) 1-800-462-8622

Council on International Education Exchange (CIEE) 1-888-Council

The VisitOz Scheme 1-212-924-0446

Get in contact with one of these companies for more information.

One you have been prese-lected you must do the following:

1. Fill out a form 147 on the web site ■www.austemb.org which covers it in detail
2. Pay a nonrefundable fee of US$97.00. You can pay with a credit card - Amex, Visa, Mastercard, plus another US$13 for delivery of the approval within the USA.
3. Present a valid passport.
4. Have a letter from the youth exchange program approved by the secretary of the Department of Immigration and Indigenous Affairs confirming your enrolment in the program. Work out the procedure to follow to obtain this through the agency in the US with whom you have been preselected.
5. Copy of your flight itinerary (return ticket).
6. Proof of funds, normally in the form of a recent bank statement.

If you have any other queries then it would be best to contact the library at the Australian Embassy in Washington whose details are as follows;

1601 Massachusetts Avenue, NW-Washington DC, 20036-2273, ph 202-797 3000, fax 202-797 3168, ■www.ausemb.org

Entry Regulations
Before you land you will be given immigration forms as well as Customs and Agriculture declarations. You must declare all goods of plant or animal origin. Quarantine officers will inspect these items and return them to you if no disease or pest risk is involved. Even if they are not prohibited, some may need to be treated before being allowed entry. Even chocolates that you have purchased on the other side of duty free have to be declared. The government have beefed up the customs and quarantine officials ever since the outbreak of foot and mouth disease and mad cow disease in Britain and Europe, and September 11.

Each incoming traveller over the age of 18 years is allowed duty free goods to the value of $400, plus 1125mL of liquor and 250g of tobacco products. These items must not be intended for commercial purposes and you must carry them with you through customs.

Exit Regulations
There is a Passenger Movement Charge or Departure Tax of $38 for everyone over the age of 12 years, but this is generally prepaid with inclusion in the price of an airline ticket. People

taking money out of the country, above the value of A$10,000 in Australian and/or foreign currency, must file a report with Customs. For more information on Customs or Quarantine Regulations, visit the following web sites:
■www.aqis.gov.au for Quarantine
■www.customs.gov.au for Customs

GST Refund
Overseas visitors qualify for a part refund of any GST they pay for items bought in Australia, if the total purchases made at any one business exceeds $300, and the purchases were made no more than 30 days before the date of departure.

Present the goods, a tax invoice, your passport and a boarding pass at the TRS (Tax Refund Scheme) booth in the international airport you are leaving from. The items on which you are allowed to claim back GST are only the hand-held items you intend to carry with you onto the plane, or those you are wearing. A refund will be made either directly into a bank account or credit card. Foreign currency will also be accommodated in this transaction. Note that any general consumption purchases made within Australia (for example, hotel accommodation or meals) do not qualify for a refund claim.

Be aware that there is no GST imposed on duty-free items sold in duty-free stores.

For further details and enquiries, phone the Australian Customs Information Line on ☎ *1300 363 263.*

Embassies

Nearly seventy countries have diplomatic representation in Canberra. Some missions are called Embassies, and others who represent countries belonging to the Commonwealth, are called High Commissions. There are also Consuls in the State capitals, and their addresses can be found in the local White Pages telephone directory.

Following are the addresses of a few diplomatic missions in Canberra: The area code is (02).

New Zealand: Commonwealth Avenue, Canberra, ☎6270 4211. ▄www.passports.govt.nz

Canada: Commonwealth Avenue, Canberra, ☎6270 4000.

Britain: Commonwealth Avenue, Canberra, ☎6270 6666. ▄www.uk.emb.gov.au

USA: Moonah Place, Yarralumla, ☎6214 6600. ▄usembassy-australia.state.gov/embassy/

Singapore: Forster Crescent, Yarralumla, ☎6273 3944.

Japan: Empire Circuit, Yarralumla, ☎6273 3244. ▄www.japan.org.au

Money

The Australian Currency is decimal, with the dollar as the basic unit. Notes come in a colourful array of $100, $50, $20, $10 and $5 denominations, with minted coins for lesser amounts - gold $1 and $2 coins, and silver 50c, 20c, 10c and 5c.

Currency exchange facilities are available at International airports, and most banks and large hotels.

The Australian dollar tends to fluctuate quite frequently, but approximate rates of exchange at the time of writing, which really must be used as a guide only, are:

NZ$1 = A$0.87
CAN$1 = A$1.01
EURO1 = A$1.68
UK£1 = A$2.39
US$1 = A$1.35
SGD$1 = A$0.79
Baht1 = A$0.03

For the most accurate and up-to-date currency conversions, it is recommended that you use the simple and easy facility at ▄www.xe.com/ucc

Travellers cheques are one of the most convenient ways of carrying money when travelling, and these can be exchanged at any bank, large hotels, and in large department stores.

ATMs

Automatic Teller Machines are another possibility. These machines are widely available in Australia, both in the cities and in country towns, and most are open 24 hours a day. Some banks allow access to overseas savings accounts via networks such as Cirrus and Plus, but it's best to check with your bank before departure to see if this is available in Australia.

Or you can put money into you VISA card/Mastercard account before you leave home and access the money here via the ATM. The conversion rate and extra charges are minimal compared to going into a bank.

If you are intending to stay for any great length of time, you might consider opening a local bank account. Different banks have different withdrawal limits, but it is generally about $1000 per day. All Australian banks operate this type of account.

Travel Information

How To Get There

To reach Australia from overseas, visitors must come either by air or sea. Information on arrivals is contained in the *How To Get There* sections of the various cities that accept international flights. Contact details for a number of major airlines is included at the beginning of every state chapter, including web addresses which will allow you to access current schedules and fares.

Before booking a flight, it is best to shop around for any cheaper fares that may be available. Your travel agent will be able to advise. You may also be able to find a Package Tour that meets all your requirements. These save you money because the companies that organise them can obtain cheaper fares and accommodation prices, as they are booking for groups. Again, your travel agent is the best person to ask.

Air Travel Within Australia

The major interstate carriers are **Qantas**, ☎13 1313 and **Virgin Blue**, ☎13 6789. Both airlines offer reduced fares and 'specials' as a matter of course on the web.

If you book in excess of a month ahead you are sure to get a price one way to Melbourne from Sydney for around $100. It is a use it or loose it operation.

Qantas have a Boomerang Pass that must be purchased outside Australia. This is independent of who you choose to fly with on the long haul to Australia. They are also valid on Air Pacific and Air Vanuatu.

You can access the UK web site of Qantas to find out:
🖳www.qantas.co.uk

The USA website is
🖳www.qantasusa.com

You can purchase a minimum of 2 and a maximum of 10 sectors. The sectors are divided into Zone 1 and Multizones. You have to book and pay for at least 2 sectors before you arrive in Australia and then you can buy others when you are here. Prices may vary from $300 to $400. It may be cheaper to go on the web or over the phone for instant fares and you may get a better deal that way

Zone 1 from £100 (USD$260)

Multizone fares from £125 (USD$330)

From Hayman Island £145 (USD$445)

UK Contact: Travel Agent or Qantas 020 8600 4307

In the US you can contact Qantas on 1 800 227 4500

These are the zones.
West Zone
Broome, Kalgoorlie, Karratha, Perth, Paraburdoo

Central Zone
Alice Springs, Ayers Rock, Darwin

East Zone
Adelaide, Blackwater, Brisbane, Bundaberg, Burnie, Cairns, Canberra, Coffs Harbour, Devonport, Emerald, Gladstone, Gold Coast, Gove, Grafton, Hamilton Island, Hayman Island, Hobart, Launceston, Mackay, Maroochydore, Melbourne, Newcastle, Proserpine, Rockhampton, Sydney, Townsville

New Zealand Zone
Auckland, Christchurch, Dunedin, Hamilton, Nelson, Queenstown, Rotorua, Wellington

South Pacific Zone
Apia, Honiara, Nadi, Noumea, Nukualofa, Port Vila, Suva

To check out where you want to go and if Qantas flies there go to the web site route map.

Virgin Blue has its own website and is a nofrills airline. Though it strives to appear hip and cool the fact is you do not get fed unless you pay for it, and you have little leg room. But the prices are good and they keep Qantas `honest' so to speak.
🖳www.virginblue.com.au

They fly to the major capital cities plus Alice Springs, Darwin, Launceston and a myriad of towns on the Queensland coast in the Great Barrier Reef area. With regard to booking outside

of Australia you just access their web site and book your flights no matter where you are and you are invoiced in Australian dollars with payment being by credit card. So it will be converted depending on what currency you credit card is related to.

By Rail
Train travel is possible between Brisbane, Sydney and Melbourne, and from Sydney to Canberra. Most towns in between are also linked, as well as those in popular outlying areas of each state. **Rail Australia** offers two rail passes that can only be purchased outside of Australia:
🖳www.railaustralia.com.au/rail_passes.htm

Austrail Flexipass 8 (✪$550), 15 (✪$800), 22 (✪$110) or 29 (✪$1440) days travel in 6 months with unlimited stopovers, in economy class.

Austrail Pass 8 Day Pass $559.50 15 Day Pass $862.40 22 Day Pass $1210.00 29 Day Pass $1569.70 for travel in Australia, including metropolitan services, in economy class.

Passes that are available within Australia include:

East Coast Discovery Pass travel one-way with unlimited stopovers in a six month period: Brisbane to Cairns (✪$225); Sydney to Brisbane/Gold Coast (✪$94); Sydney to Cairns (✪$312); Melbourne to Sydney (✪$94); Melbourne to Brisbane/Gold Coast (✪$176); Melbourne to Cairns (✪$394). Note that the above rates apply to travel in the opposite direction.

Countrylink Backpacker Pass

- unlimited use of Countrylink trains and connecting coaches for 14 Day Pass ✪$217.80, 30 Day Pass ✪$250.80, 90 Day Pass ✪$272.80, 180 Day Pass ✪$382.80.

Queensland Road Rail Pass

- unlimited use of Queensland Rail services (long-distance) and McCaffertys Coaches for any 10 days over a 60 day period (✪$286) or any 20 days over a 90 day period (✪$374).

To get the latest prices, visit the Rail Australia web site at ▧www.railaustralia.com.au/pass_rates.htm

Discovering Australia By Bus

The major interstate coach companies have combined - Greyhound PioneerMcCafferty's. Tickets for both companies are now interchangeable.

McCafferty's, ☎ 13 1499, ▧www.mccaffertys.com.au/

Aussie Passes: a pre-selected travel route along which you can stop off at designated points.

Here are some intineraries:

All Australian

Validity: 365 days
Cost: ✪$2403 full fare, ✪$2163 concession.

Aussie Highlights

Route: Melbourne - Sydney - Brisbane - Cairns - Uluru (Ayers Rock) - Adelaide - Canberra and many other outback, rural and coastal destinations in between.
Validity: 365 days

Cost: ✪$1434 full fare, ✪$1291concession.

Sunseeker (ex Sydney)

Validity: 183 days
Cost: ✪$374 full fare, ✪$337 concession.

Best of the West

Validity: 365 days
Cost: ✪$1444 full fare, ✪$1300 concession.

Best of the East

Validity: 365 days
Cost: ✪$1173 full fare, ✪$1056 concession.

Coast to Coast - Sydney to Perth

Validity: 183 days
Cost: ✪$485 full fare, ✪$437 concession.

Western Explorer

Validity: 183 days
Cost: ✪$674 full fare, ✪$607concession.

Reef & Rock - the Rocker Cairns to the Rock

Validity: 183 days
Cost: ✪$512 full fare, ✪$460 concession.

Rock Track

Validity: 90 days
Cost: ✪$455 full fare, ✪$410 concession.

Outback & Reef Explorer Pass ex Sydney

Validity: 183 days
Cost: ✪$830 full fare, ✪$747 concession.

Concession - YHA member, VIP, ISIC, Nomads, Australian Student University and High School, Euro26.

An Aussie Kilometre Pass, valid for 12 months, allows you to 'bulk buy' the distance you think you will need to cover for your holiday, at a rate designed to increase your value for money with every kilometre purchased. Prices range from ✪$321 (Concession $289) for 2000km ✪$1231 (Concession $1108) for 10,000km to ✪$2258 (Concession $2032) for 20,000km.

Discovering Australia By Road

Australians drive on the left-hand side of the road, and the speed limit in built-up areas is 50km/h or 60km/h, and on the open road up to 110km/h.

In an effort to cut the number of road fatalities, Australia has random breath testing which is carried out by police officers either from a standard police car or from what are known locally as 'booze buses'. The allowable blood alcohol level varies from state to state, but is generally around 0.05, or two standard drinks in the first hour and only one during every subsequent hour. But since body tolerance levels differ, it is best simply not to drink if you expect to drive soon after.

General Information

Time Zones

Australia is divided into three time zones: Australian Eastern Standard Time, which covers Queensland, NSW, Victoria and Tasmania, is GMT plus 10 hours;

Australian Central Standard Time, which covers South Australia and the Northern Territory, is GMT plus 9.5 hours; and Australian Western Standard Time, which covers Western Australia, is GMT plus 8 hours.

During summer, some of the states operate on daylight saving, putting their clocks ahead one hour on a designated Sunday morning in October, and back one hour on a Sunday in March. For NSW, Victoria and South Australia, it is the last Sunday in October and the first Sunday in March, but Tasmania remains on Summer Time until the end of March. Western Australia, Queensland and the Northern Territory do not have daylight saving, so at those times there are five different time zones in the country.

Telephones

If you are calling any Sydney number from overseas, dial 61 for the country code and 2 for the area code, then the eight digit number. Area codes refer to states rather than districts. If calling from interstate, use the following prefix before any number you dial to:

New South Wales - (02)
Australian Capital Territory - (02)
Victoria - (03)
Tasmania - (03)
Queensland - (07)
South Australia - (08)
Western Australia - (08)
Northern Territory- (08)

Public telephones are easy to find in the cities and suburbs on street corners, in hotels, shops, cafes, and so on. A local call costs 40c from a phone box, but

may be dearer from the privately leased phones outside shops. Emergency calls are free. For international calls, you can dial direct to nearly 20 countries from almost any hotel, home, office or public phone in Australia. Simply dial 0011 + country code + area code + local number. Country Direct is the easiest way of making international telephone card and reverse charge (collect) calls. Upon dialling your Country Direct number, you are immediately put in touch with your own country's operator who will then connect the call. To find out your country's number ☎1800 801 800 (free call).

Instant Access with the Handhelds

Now with handheld information sources from mobile phones to palm pilots it is easier just to plug into a phone line and have your emails down loaded. Phones can be adjusted with a new sim card for Australia. Just ask the phone company you use for your current mobile. Australia uses the digital rather than the analog network for mobile phones.

For phone numbers nationwide, go to:
▇www.whitepages.com.au
▇www.yellowpages.com.au
▇www.colourpages.com.au

Post

Australia has an efficient postal service, and postcards sent by airmail to overseas countries cost $1. To send a letter by Air Mail (weighing up to 50g) to the Asia Pacific Zone costs $1.10 and to the Rest of the World, $1.65.

Newspapers

Morning and afternoon newspapers are available everywhere, with each state having their own press, as well as selling the national paper *The Australian*. There are also several local papers in city and suburban areas which have local news and advise on local events, such as *The Sydney Morning Herald* in Sydney and *The Age in Melbourne*.

Radio and Television

There is a national radio station and a national television channel, both of which are run by the Australian Broadcasting Commission (ABC). The capital cities have many AM and FM radio stations, and several free-to-air television channels. The television channels are: 2 (the national channel), 7 (commercial), 9 (commercial), 10 (commercial) and 0 (SBS, which is government sponsored and has mostly foreign language programs, with English sub-titles). Regional areas broadcast programs on these networks, so their may be slight differences in programming (eg. WIN (9) in Wollongong and Prime (7) in Newcastle). Cable television is also available.

Videos

Australia uses the PAL system of videos. For the US market, tapes must be the NTSC system.

However, many people are switching to DVDs 4 zones therefore they are becoming more popular.

Electricity

Domestic electricity supply throughout Australia is 230-250

volts, AC 50 cycles. Standard three pin plugs are fitted to domestic appliances. 110v appliances, such as hairdryers and contact lens sterilisers, cannot be used without a transformer.

Internet General Information Sources

For general information on Australia, the best site to explore is ■www.australia.com which is the official web page of the Australian Tourist Commission.

The Internet
Cafes

These abound though less so now than in previous years when it was such a hassle to cart around a laptop. However, it is best to find out who the specialist are in this area rather than going to a bar which also has web facilities that will be second best. You will end up spending more money. How do you find out the specialist, again go to the web or ask when you arrive at your destination.

Asking questions does not cost you a thing but can save a packet both in time and money.

Accommodation

This book is solely dedicated for the use of budget style accommodation all over the county. From backpacker hostels, motels and caravan parks.

Australia has well-developed motel accommodation in cities, resorts and rural areas. A typical room is usually spotlessly clean and has air-conditioning or fans, a private bathroom, tea

and coffee making facilities, a telephone, television, and a small refrigerator. Because of the climate, many motels have small outdoor swimming pools.

Motels often provide a bar for paying guests and invited friends, although they are not obliged to do this. Most hotels and motels have a dining room or restaurant.

Motels have generally been developed to meet the needs of travelling motorists and are located in cities, towns and resorts, and along the major highways.

The majority of motels offer accommodation on a room-only basis, but some include one or more meals in their tariff. Enquire about any meals that might be automatically included in the room price and check whether you can pay just for the room, if this suits your travel schedule better. For example, there is no point paying for lunch if you plan on leaving before daybreak, or for a dinner if you know you won't reach your destination until late.

Youth Hostels in most parts of the country offer an inexpensive alternative for budget conscious travellers. Membership of the Youth Hostels Association is required, *9261 1111*, to take advantage of discounts. They have a comprehensive internet site showing all the hostel locations at ■www.yha.com.au and an email service at ✉yha@yhansw.org.au It is also becoming apparent that some of the major chains are getting into

this form of accommodation such as Nomads and others. Accor Hotels have Formule 1 motels which charge around $50 for the night without breakfast but space is at a premium,

Most towns and holiday resorts have caravan parks and camping grounds with shower and toilet facilities, at very reasonable rates. Caravan parks usually have some cabins or on-site vans available for overnight or longer stays. This is a comparatively inexpensive form of accommodation, but it usually means that you have to have your own bed linen, blankets and pillows.

Goods and Services
Tax

The prices quoted in this book include Australia's 10% GST. It should also be kept in mind that many products are exempt from the tax, including basic food items.

Shopping

Toy kangaroos and koalas are high on everyone's shopping list, and are available everywhere. Everything Aboriginal is popular, and although it seems more appropriate to buy them in the Outback regions, they are available in the big cities in specialty shops.

Probably the most sought after articles, though, are opals. Australia produces more than 90% of the world's opals, and the three main areas where they are found are Lightning Ridge in western NSW, which produces the Black Opal; Quilpie, where the Queensland Boulder Opal originates; and Coober Pedy in

South Australia, which has the White or Milk Opal.

When buying opals there are a few terms you should know:

Solid Opal this is the most valuable, and good for investment purposes. The more colourful and complete, the greater its value.

Doublet these are slices of opal glued together, and are of medium value. The Opal has no investment value.

Triplet these are slices of opal covered with quartz, perspex or glass, and are the least expensive. The Opal has no investment value.

If your pocket can't stretch as far as a solid opal, but you still would like a piece of opal jewellery, remember that anything that is glued can come unstuck, and that condensation can form under perspex or glass. The less expensive types of opal are not suitable for rings, unless you are going to remember to take it off every time you wash your hands.

Eating Out
In every town and city in this guide we have included a selection of restaurants. Restaurants can vary from either being licensed or unlicensed (BYO). Just to confuse everyone, some restaurants are both, so if you are unsure, check when reserving your table. Without going into the licensing laws of why this is so, here is a short explanation of how it will affect patrons.

A licensed restaurant has a wine list, and can provide beer, mixed drinks, ports, liqueurs, etc. Patrons are not allowed to provide their own drinks.

A BYO restaurant does not have a licence, so you Bring Your Own wine or beer or whatever. Glasses are provided, and a corkage fee (for opening the bottles!) may be charged, which is usually around $1.50 per bottle. The restaurant usually has a selection of soft drinks, mineral water and fruit juices.

A restaurant that is licensed and BYO can provide alcohol, but you have the choice of bringing your own wine (which works out cheaper), but you are not allowed to bring your own beer or mixed drinks.

Liquor stores in Australia are called 'bottle shops'. Rarely do hostels have one, but there's bound to be one around the shops and shopping centres.

We have also advised the distance to the nearest food store from you accommodation.

New South Wales

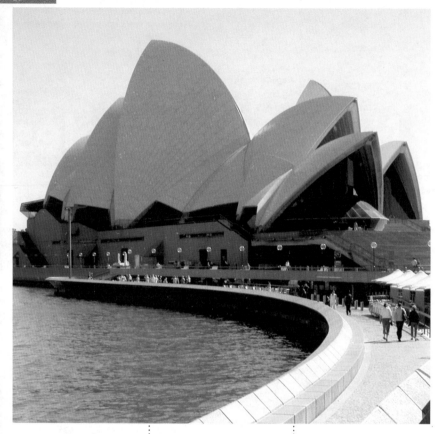

Sydney

Population over 3,900,000
Sydney is the capital city of
the State of New South Wales,
the birthplace of the Nation of
Australia, and the largest city in
the country. It is located on the
south-east coast of Australia,
latitude 33' 53" south, longitude
151' 13" east, on the shores
of Sydney Harbour, arguably
the most beautiful harbour
in the world. Circular Quay,
between the Harbour Bridge
and the Opera House, is the
ferry terminal, known locally

simply as 'The Quay'. The area
is always crowded with people
arriving or departing on ferries,
buskers competing for space, and
culture buffs strolling towards
the Opera House. Australia's
oldest city, Sydney began as a
penal settlement clustered around
what is now Circular Quay. The
present city sprawls about 55km
east-west from the Pacific Coast
to the Great Dividing Range, and
roughly 70km north-south.The
distance along the actual
coastline, allowing for all the
bays, is 350km, and in fact there
are so many bays and beaches
that even Sydneysiders who have

lived here all their lives don't
know every one by name, and
probably haven't visited more
than half of them. The ocean
beaches have beautiful white
sand and rolling surf. Life in
this cosmopolitan city is geared
to outdoor activities, taking
advantage of the sunshine and
the moderate climate

Climate
Sydney has a temperate climate,
and the average temperatures are:
January max 26C - min 19C; July
max 17C - min 8C.

The Seasons are:
Summer - December through February
Autumn - March through May
Winter - June through August
Spring - September through November.

Sydney does not experience snow and only rarely sleet, and quite often the temperature on a winter's day is higher than that of London or San Francisco in the middle of their summers. Lightweight clothing is necessary for the summer months, and medium to heavy for the winter months. A raincoat, or at least an umbrella, should be included in your suitcase whatever the season.

How to Get There
By Air
Airlines in Australia
Sydney is the major gateway to Australia from overseas, and all overseas airlines servicing Australia fly into Kingsford-Smith International Airport. **Qantas,** ☎ 13 13 13, is the major internal Australian airline, and there are a number of smaller ones servicing the country towns and some interstate destinations, Rex or Regional Express ☎ 13 1713.

Virgin Blue, ☎ 13 6789, are the latest carriers flying to major centres.

Airport Facilities
Kingsford-Smith is situated in the suburb of Mascot, 10km from the city centre. The Domestic Terminals are 3km to the east, and taxis and express buses connect them with the International Terminal. The large green and gold **Airport Express** bus runs every 10 minutes, 7 days a week and costs ✪$3 adults. The Airport Express also operate

services between the Airport and City (route 300), Kings Cross (route 350), and Darling Harbour and Glebe (route 352), from all passenger terminals to Central Railway and return.

Bus Route 300 travels between the Airport and Circular Quay, stopping at specially-identified places along George Street, and in Eddy Avenue near Central Railway.

Bus Route 350 travels between the Airport and Elizabeth Bay, · passing through Kings Cross. Buses run every ten minutes to and from Central Railway Station and every twenty minutes to the city and Kings Cross. No reservations are needed. Services run every day between, 6am and 11pm, ☎9667 3221 or ☎9667 0663. Fares are ✪$7 one way, $12 return.

Other Sydney Buses routes that travel via the airport are Route 100 (Dee Why-Airport, every 30 minutes Mon-Fri), Route 305 (Railway Square-Airport, every 30 minutes Mon-Fri) and Route 400 (Bondi Junction-Airport-Burwood, every 20 minutes Mon-Fri, every 30 minutes Sat-Sun).

Major rental car companies have desks at the international and domestic terminals, but it is a good idea to book your car in advance -

Hertz, ☎ 13 30 39;
Avis, ☎ 13 6333;
Budget, ☎ 13 27 27;
Thrifty, ☎ 1300 367 227.
Europcar ☎ 1300 13 1390

Taxis are readily available at the airport for transfer to the city, and the fare is at least ✪$25.

City Rail established a link between Sydney Airport and

Central Station. It provides an efficient alternative method of transportation to the city. The line comprises four stops, running northwards from the International terminal to the Domestic terminal, then to Mascot and Green Square before joining the City Circle. Travelling southwards it connects with Wolli Creek. A single ticket to Central costs ✪$15 one-way from the domestic terminal and $20 from the international terminal. Trains operate at fifteen minute intervals between the four stations.

Sydney Airport has all the facilities expected of an international airport - money changing, information, hotel bookings, car hire, shops, cafes, bars, restrooms/showers.

International Airline Offices
Following is a selection of airline reservation and flight confirmation telephone numbers.

Qantas - ☎ 13 1313.
Air New Zealand - ☎ 13 2476.
Canadian Airlines - ☎ 1300 655 767.
British Airways - ☎8904 8800.
Cathay Pacific - ☎ 13 1747.
Singapore Airlines - ☎ 13 1011.
United Airlines - ☎ 13 1777.

For further details of airline companies, refer to the Internet Information section at the back of the book.

By Bus
Following is a list of some of the bus companies that travel to/from Sydney and other cities and town in Australia. Many also offer day tours and package deals for touring the entire country.

Travelcoach Australia - Greyhound Pioneer McCafferty's - ☎ 13 2030 (see also Internet

Information) and - ☎ *13 1499* (see also Internet Information).
AAT Kings - ☎ *9666 3899.*
Interline - ☎ *9605 1811.*
Firefly Express - ☎ *9211 1644.*
Murrays - ☎ *13 22 59.*

By Rail
The **State Rail Authority's Countrylink** branch, ☎ *13 22 32*, has **XPT** services between Sydney and Brisbane, Melbourne and Murwillumbah. The XPTs are fast, smooth and comfortable with air-conditioning, aircraft style seats and big panoramic windows.There are overnight and daylight interstate services from/ to Melbourne, frequent services to Canberra, an overnight service from/to Brisbane, and a motorail service from/to Murwillumbah with bus connection to the Gold Coast and Brisbane.

A Countrylink East Coast
Discovery Pass may be a viable option if you plan to make rail your primary means of transport on your east coast holiday. This ticket offers travel one-way with unlimited stop-overs in a six month period from:
Brisbane to Cairns ✪$160;
Sydney to Brisbane/Gold Coast ✪$94;
Sydney to Cairns ✪$248;
Melbourne to Sydney ✪$94;
Melbourne to Brisbane/Gold Coast ✪$176;
Melbourne to Cairns ✪$330.

Note that the above rates apply for travel in the opposite direction. Other extended travel passes are available, and the website is 🖳www.*countrylink.nsw.gov.au*

Visitor Information
The Travellers Information Service at the Airport can make accommodation bookings, and also has a telephone information service that operates seven days a week between ⊕8am and 6pm, ☎ *9669 5111.*

First stop in Sydney for all visitors should be the Travel Centre of New South Wales, 11-31 York Street, ☎ *13 20 77.* The office is ⊕open Mon-Fri 9am-5pm, and has numerous brochures, maps, etc., and a large and very helpful staff. Pick up copies of all the current city information guides and you will have plenty of reading material, and good tips on what to see and where to go.

The Sydney Tower Visitors Information and Booking Service is located at the top of the tower, ☎ *9229 7430.* It is ⊕open seven days 9.30am-9.30pm (Sat till 11.30pm), and is a minefield of information for those people brave enough to take the lift to the top.

The Sydney Convention and Visitors Bureau has an information kiosk in Martin Place that is ⊕open Mon-Fri 9am-5pm, ☎ *9235 2424.* The Sydney Visitor Information Centre, 106 George Street, The Rocks, is ⊕open seven days, 9am-5pm, ☎ *9255 1788.* The website is 🖳www.tourism.nsw.gov.au There are three recommended websites that will give you additional information about Sydney's highlights, from obscure clubs and pubs to major attractions and current events.
🖳www.sydneyvisitorcentre.com 🖳sydney.citysearch.com.au 🖳sydney.sidewalk.com.au 🖳www.cityofsydney.nsw.gov.au

Independent Traveller Information
The Youth Hostels Association Membership and Travel Centre is at 422 Kent Street, ☎ *9261 1111.*

For information and travel advice, there is a Backpacker Travel Centre in Shop P33, Imperial Arcade, Pitt Street Mall, ☎ *9231 3699.*

The website for the Youth Hostels Association Australia is 🖳www.yha.com.au email ✉yha @nswyha.com.au

Lets Travel Australia - specialising in Australia, 175 Victoria St, Kings Cross, Sydney ☎ *93582295*, fax 93585220 ✉info@lets-travel-australia.com.au. The staff will be a great help. They also have an internet cafe on the premises.

⤶ Let's Stay Here
Sydney has a wide range of accommodation, from luxurious 5-star hotels to small budget-priced establishments offering the basics. Something to keep in mind though: even if you opt for the lower-priced accommodation, you are still going to pay a significant amount for the quality you receive, as is common in major cities. Caravan parks, are rare, and the closest you will find is in North Ryde, about half-an-hour's drive from the city centre. Simply put, if you wish to stay in the heart of Sydney you are going to have to pay for it - there are very few short-cuts. Though we have some good deals with the cheaper accommodation specifically for backpackers in here.

If you are after something a little different, "Staying in Sydney" by Sam Lynch and Chris Baker provides comprehensive details of those 'tucked-away'

establishments in Sydney which offer a unique alternative to mainstream chains and well-known accommodation venues. Rates are listed and assessed by the author so that you have a good idea of the places with facilities, service-levels and an ambience to match their price tag. The information gives a valuable insight into this niche market. However, this is if you want to splash out one night.

The following is a selection of backpacker styled accommodation. Considering that prices increase frequently and without notice, listing these places in this way will at least give you the best foundation for comparison. The telephone area code is 02. All prices are in Australian dollars.

Beaches
Bondi
Biltmore on Bondi,
110 Campbell Parade, ☎ *9130 4660,* 🖥 *www.bondibackpac kers.com* Set in a very very old building. This is probably the best located out of all the hostels in Bondi, having it only across the beach and close to everything else. There is a sink and fridge in every room. Facilities includes a fully equipped kitchen, internet access, laundry and a TV lounge. On site restaurant and bar. There's also free use body and surf boards. Weekly activities are organised by the hostel like an Aussie BBQ, quiz night and pub crawls and there are always special events happening. *Dorms ✪$19; single $40; double $45; twin $40* (breakfast included)

Bondi Beach Guest House,
11 Consett Ave, ☎ *9300 9310* An old looking house hostel situated on a quiet residential street not too far from the beach and shops. It caters a lot to long stayers. Very basic facilities including a kitchen and a barbecue area. *Dorms ✪$20; double/twin $50*

Bondi Beach YHA,
Corner Dellview and Fletcher Sts, ☎ *9365 2088,* 🖥 *www.yha.com* Quite a big art deco establishment compared to the other hostels around Bondi. Located not too far from the beach in the south and very close to the nearest foodstore. Some

rooms have en suites. The facilities includes a kitchen, laundry, two TV rooms, a study room, internet access, a barbecue area and the ever rare spa. There's also a nice balcony that overlooks the beach. Meals available. *Dorms from ✪$23; single $60; double/twin $35pp ($40pp with en suite) BC MC VA EFTPOS*

Bondi Sands,
252 Campbell Parade, ☎ *9365 3703 or 1800 026 634,* 🖥 *www.bondisands.com* Set in a nice old building that looks over the beach. Just newly refurbished. Note that there are no dorms here, only

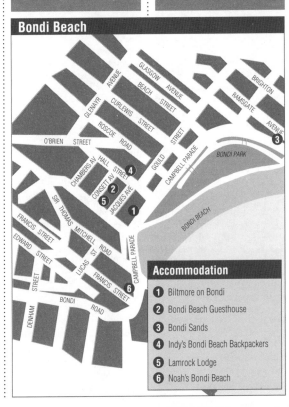

Bondi Beach

Accommodation
1. Biltmore on Bondi
2. Bondi Beach Guesthouse
3. Bondi Sands
4. Indy's Bondi Beach Backpackers
5. Lamrock Lodge
6. Noah's Bondi Beach

doubles, yet backpackers still flock here especially couples. Some rooms have TVs. Facilities includes a small kitchen, laundry, internet access and another TV lounge. The barbecue area is located on the rooftop terrace with great views of the beach. There's also free use of boogie boards. *Double ✪$37.50pp ($45pp with ocean views)* (price includes breakfast)

Indy's Bondi Beach Backpackers,

35A Hall St, ☎9365 4900 or 1800 150 971, 🖳www.indysbackpackers.com Located closely to the beach. A really party venue in terms of atmosphere. Facilities includes a kitchen and TV lounge with heaps of movies to watch, a Nintendo 64, plus cable. They offer a lot of free to use sports equipments like body boards, snorkeling equipment, fishing rods and wet suits. There are also mountain bikes, roller blades, soccer and rugby balls, volleyballs and nets, cricket, basket ball and baseball gear which you can use on the beach or in local parks. The only thing that is not free are the surfboards which are for hire. There are also board games and internet access to keep you busy. They offer employment assistance and have heaps of free passes to Sydney's best hotels pubs and nightclubs at the front desk. *Dorms ✪$26; twin $55*

Lamrock Lodge,

19 Lamrock Ave, ☎9130 5063 or 1800 625 063, 🖳www.lamrocklodge.com Located very close to the

beach and just a few blocks from the shops. Popular with the surfy crowd. Rooms have their own microwaves and TV. Other facilities includes a kitchen, laundry, common areas. 5 internet outlets and loads of vending machines which pretty much has everything. There are roller blades, bikes and boards for hire. *Dorms ✪$20; doubles $50*

Noah's Bondi Beach,

2 Campbell Parade, ☎9365 7100, 🖳www.noahsbondibeach.com Located just across the beach and very close to the centre and public transport. Double and twin rooms have fridges and TV. Other facilities includes a kitchen and a TV lounge. There is also the rooftop terrace with a barbecue area and great views of Bondi plus an on site bar with happy hours and cheap meals. They can also assist you with employment and travel info. Free airport pick up. *Dorms from ✪$20; double/twin $50 ($55 with beach views)*

Sinclairs of Bondi Budget Accommodation,

11 Bennett St, ☎9744 6074 Sinclairs Bondi is situated in an Art Deco 1920's house that has been completely renovated. Single and double rooms have en suite facilities. Some rooms have TVs, fridges, fans, heaters and electric blankets. With a communal kitchen on each floor, laundry facilities, a small TV lounge and internet access. *Dorms from ✪$25* (price includes breakfast)

Coogee
Indy's Coogee Beach Backpackers,

302 Arden St, ☎9315 7644, 🖳www.indysbackpackers.com "Indy's for Boarders" is an original Victorian mansion located only 200 meters from the beach. Not too far off from their sister place at Bondi. But this one mainly caters for long stayers and working travellers, so don't just turn up expecting a room. Great atmosphere though. Just your usual facilities of fully equipped kitchen and dining, laundry, TV lounge with cable plus the free sporting equipments like boogie boards and bikes. *Weekly dorms ✪$125*

The Castle Backpackers,

272 Clovelly Rd, Clovelly Beach, ☎9665 1824 or 1800 857 004, 🖳www.castlebackpackers.com Located closer to a shopping mall than the beach which isn't too far. It has a feel good atmosphere. All dorms have en suite bathrooms and most have their own TV and fridge. Other amenities includes kitchen with TV and laundry facilities. There are 5 rooftop sundecks which has nice views of the sea. The hostel usually organises events like BBQ, wine and cheese nights. They also offer free use of boogie boards, surfboards and snorkeling gear. *Dorms from ✪$17; double $55*

Surfside Backpackers,

186 Arden St, ☎9315 7888, 🖳www.surfsidebackpackers.com.au Located nicely in Coogee, just above McDonalds and very very close to everything. Some rooms are just next to the common rooms with it's own kitchenette, TV and bathrooms. Offers your basic accommodation and facilities like kitchen and TV lounge but the views from most rooms makes up for it. They also have beach volleyball equipments and free barbecue nights. Free pick up service. *Dorms from ✪$25; double/twin $31*

Wizard of Oz Backpackers,
172 Coogee Bay Rd,
☎*9315 7876,* ▆*www.wizard ofoz.com.au* Situated close to the supermarket, shops and not too far off the beach. Clean and well kept. Rooms are all fanned. Facilities includes fully equipped kitchen, laundry, TV lounge with widescreen and a nice garden out the back with a barbecue area. The staff organises weekly barbecue nights and can assist you with work. There's also free pickup service. *Dorms from ✪$23; double/twin from $50*

Darlinghurst and Woolloomooloo
Australian Backpackers,
132 Bourke St, Woolloo-mooloo, ☎*9331 0822,* ▆*www .australianbackpacker.com.au* Located not far from both city and Kings Cross. Really good atmosphere. All rooms have fridge, TV and lockers. Other facilities includes a kitchen, laundry, internet access, dining room with TV and cable. The rooftop terrace has good views. The staff also organises free barbecue nights on Fridays with free beer, followed by a pub crawl. They also of-

fer employment assistance. Watch out for the free surf lessons during summer. Pickup from airport or Central Station service offered. *Dorms ✪$22; double/twin $27.50pp* (prices includes breakfast)

Boomerang Backpackers,
141 William St, Darlinghurst,
☎*8354 0488,* ▆*www.boom erangbackpackers.com* Located just a short walk to the Opera House and city centre, and not far from the train station and supermarket. Facilities includes kitchen, laundry, internet access (free on arrival), cable TV and lounge area. The rooftop sundeck has the barbecue area and there's also job assistance offered. On site is a travel shop, a 24 hour convenience store and cafe, plus some fast food shops. *Dorms from ✪$20; double/twin $55*

Captain Cook Hotel,
162 Flinders St, Paddington,
☎*1800 655 536,* ▆*www.capt aincookhotel.com* Accommodation situated above a pub. Very close to Oxford St, the cricket ground (SCG) and the Aussie stadium. Popular with working travellers. All dorms are single sexed with lockers and linen is supplied. There's also a kitchen, laundry, TV lounge and an internet kiosk. The bar is downstairs with on site restaurant. *Dorms from ✪$18; single $40; double/ twin $50*

City Resort Hostel,
103 Palmer St, Woolloo-mooloo, ☎*9357 3333 or 1800 688 335,* ▆*www.backpackersn etinn.com* Located just behind

the Westfield Tower in between the city and Kings Cross, in a very busy street. Not much to look at in terms of atmosphere. They have more double rooms than dorms. All rooms have a kitchen, TV and fridge. There's also laundry. Nice views of the city can be obtained from the rooftop where the barbecue area is. *Dorms from ✪$18; single $40 double/twin $45 ($50 with en suite)* (free bread and coffee and all day rice)

Forbes Terrace,
153 Forbes St, Woolloo-mooloo, ☎*9358 4327,*
▆*www.g-day.com.au/index_ forbes.html* Located in the historic inner city suburb within walking distance to the heart of the city and Kings Cross. Set in a beautifully restored Terrace. All rooms have fridges and TV. Other facilities includes a kitchen and dining, laundry and games room with a pool table. There's a nice shady courtyard at the back with outdoor dining. Free pick up service from the airport. *Dorms ✪$19.80*

Harbour City Hostel,
50 Sir John Young Crescent, Woolloomooloo, ☎*9380 2922,* ▆*www.harbourcityh otel.com* Located in one of Woolloomooloos main roads. Not too far from shops, the Art Gallery, city centre and Kings Cross. This is a huge hostel, even with lifts and two TV lounges with cable and the other with a video. Kept very clean and well maintained. Other amenities includes kitchen and laundry. Great security. *Dorms ✪$21; double/*

twin $30pp (prices includes light breakfast)

Hotel Altamont,
207 Dalinghurst Rd, Darlinghurst, ☎ *9360 6000,* 🖥 *www.altamont.com* This used to be a really chic boutique hotel that has been transformed in a very posh backpackers place. Very trendy in nature with modern designs and decor. Many rooms remains as double rooms. All rooms have en suite and TV. Facilities includes a big kitchen, internet access and a nice sundeck on the roof. They also offer free pick service. *Dorms* ✪ *$20 ($2 breakfast offered)*

The Wood Duck Inn,
49 William St, ☎ *9358 5856 or 1800 110 025,* 🖥 *www.woodduckinn.com* Located close to the Australian Mu-

seum and very close to the city centre and Kings Cross. Though the place is small, the atmosphere is great, with polished wooden floors and fresh flowers. Accommodation is set in genders with fans in each room. Facilities includes a fully equipped kitchen, laundry, lounge with cable TV, internet access and a very nice sundeck with a barbecue area. The view from the top is superb. There's also an on site bar with happy hour (cheap drinks) every night, pool tables and juke box. The staff also organises activities including quiz nights, Aborginal dancing, surfing, cruises, Aussie BBQ nights and plenty more. Employment services also offered. **Recommended.** *Dorms* ✪ *$20; double/twin $55* (prices includes breakfast)

Other city areas:
Backpackers Headquarters,
79 Bayswater Rd, Rushcutters Bay ☎ *9331 6180,* 🖥 *www.backpackershqhostel.com* Located at a quiet spot at the Rushcutters Bay end of town and about 5 mins to Kings Cross station. Really good accommodation. Kept clean and well maintained. Facilities includes a fully equipped kitchen, laundry, a rooftop sundeck with a barbecue and great views. The TV lounge is pretty cool, nice and bright, with a big screen TV and a DVD player. There is free internet access and they help you with your job hunt. They also offer a pick-up service from the airport, coach and rail. *Dorms from* ✪ *$17; double/twin $55.*

Bernly Private Hotel,
15 Springfield Ave, ☎ *9358 3122,* 🖥 *www.bernlyprivate*

Darlinghurst and Woolloomooloo

Accommodation

1. Australian Backpackers
2. Boomerang Backpackers
3. City Resort Hostel
4. Cooee Travellers Accommodation
5. Forbes Terrace
6. Harbour City Hostel
7. Hotel Altamont
8. Wood Duck Inn

hotel.com Located minutes away from the station, close to Hungry Jacks, through a small alley way. Close to a lot of things. This is a very nice hotel that caters to budget backpackers and those that can afford the deluxe suites. Their facilities includes a small kitchen, guest lounge with cable TV and a sun deck that has really good views of the city. They have a daily housekeeping service plus the odd photocopy service. *Dorms ✪$20; single $50; double from $55 ($40pp for deluxe)*

Blue Parrot Backpackers,
87 Macleay St, Potts Point,
☎ *9356 4888 or 1800 252 299,* 💻 *www.blueparrot.com*
Located at Potts Point, known as the 'Manhattan or Upper East Side' of Sydney with beautiful tree lined streets, restaurants, cafes, bars and deluxe hotels close by. Really nice. Kept very clean and well maintained, and quiet. Rooms are fanned. Facilities are quite new - the laundry and the TV lounge with cable and open fire and a small fully equipped kitchen. The courtyard is nice with a barbecue place and a garden plus picnic tables. *Dorms ✪$22*

Challis Lodge,
21 Challis Avenue, Potts Point NSW 2011, ☎ *9358 5422,* 💻*www.channels.nl/ 35102b.html* Located in a quiet area, close to the City and harbour with buses and cafes outside the front door. Train station is about 10 minutes away. All rooms are different and will differ in price.

Some have their own en suite, balcony, fridge, TV and tea and coffee facilities. Laundry facilities are also available and also room service. *Dorms from ✪$45*

Coee Travellers Accommodation,
107-109 Darlinghurst Rd,
☎ *9331 0009 or 1800 200 793,* 💻 *www.cooeetraveller s.com* Located centrally in Kings Cross and is very close to the train and bus station. It's a fairly new hostel, very clean and a lot of the furnishing are pretty new from the Olympic Village. One third of the rooms have en suite bathrooms. Dorms have reading lamps for each bed and all bathrooms have the ever rare hairdryers. Facilities include a nice kitchen and dining, two laundries, pool table, TV lounge and a sundeck with three levels. They can assist you if you're looking for work. Free 10 minute internet each day. They also offer free dinner almost every night (except Sunday) and pick up service from the airport. Security is excellent. Ask about their privilege card to get discounts out and about. Recommended. *Dorms from ✪$22; double/twin $30pp (twin with en suite $32.50pp)*

Cross Road Backpackers,
174 Victoria St, ☎ *9356 4551*
Located again in central Kings Cross close to everything. Station just minutes away. Atmosphere is mostly gathered from the neighbouring backpacker places packed into one street. Like most rooms

in hostels in Kings Cross, a number of selected rooms have en suite bathrooms. Your normal facilities of small kitchen, laundry and a courtyard at the back. *Dorms ✪$18; double $50*

Eva's Backpackers,
6-8 Orwell St, ☎ *9358 2185,* 💻 *www.holidayonline.com.au*
Located close to everything. The area is kinda seedy, but the place is kept well clean and people are friendly. All rooms are fanned and are maintained daily, and some have en suites. There is a fully equipped kitchen and dining areas, comfortable TV room and private internet area. Full laundry facilities (free washing powder) is set on the beautiful roof top garden where you are invited to sit, enjoy the barbecue facilities and spectacular views of Sydney. The staff goes out of their way to organise BBQs and night outs. They also do wake up calls and airport transfers. *Dorms ✪$24; double/twins $30pp* (price includes breakfast)

Funk House Backpackers,
23 Darlinghurst Rd, ☎ *9358 6455 or 1800 807 130,* 💻 *www.funkhouse.com* This hostel has really great atmosphere with funky and colourful decor and friendly staff. Location is still in the seedy area but close to everything else. Twins and double rooms have their own fridge and TV. All rooms have fans. Facilities includes kitchen, laundry, large common areas, internet access and a nice barbecue

area on the rooftop. They also assist you with work and have an on site travel agent. *Dorms ✪$23; double/twin $58*

Hancock Dury House,
48A Darlinghurst Rd, ☎9357 2255 or 1800 778 282, ▤*www.duryhouse.com* Compared to the more lively hostels in the Cross, this will be probably be more suited for those looking for a quieter atmosphere. Popular with Asian backpackers. Rooms have en suite bathrooms. Your standard facilities including kitchen, laundry, common rooms and the nice views from the rooftop of the city and even the Opera House. *Dorms ✪$17; double/twin $50* (prices includes breakfast and free rice)

Jolly Swagman Backpackers,
27 Orwell St, ☎9358 6400 or 1800 805 870, ▤www.*jollys wagman.com.au* Pretty much located close to the vicinity of everything else like most of the hostels in Kings Cross. Quite lively and there is a feel good atmosphere. Rooms are fairly modern. It has your normal facilities including internet access and a rooftop sundeck. A weekly BBQ is held in the courtyard garden. Free beer on arrival and they also offer employment assistance. There is a pick up service also available. *Dorms ✪$21; double/twin $56*

Kanga House,
141 Victoria Street, ☎9357 7897, ▤www.*kangahou se.com* A newly refurbished establishment in a convenient location. Rooms at the back

have great city views. Facilities includes cable TV in the lounge room, kitchen facilities, 24 hour security and a sunny courtyard with a barbecue area. *Dorm ✪$16.60; double/twin $55*

Kings Cross Palace,
34B Darlinghurst Rd, ☎1800 688 336, ▤www.*backpacke rsnetinn.com* Located close to everything. Most rooms have en suite, fridge and TV. Due to this, the communal area including the kitchen is fairly basic. Security is good though and there are lockers in every room. *Dorms ✪$15; single $40; double/twin $50; triple from $60*

Montpelier Private Hotel,
39A Elizabeth Bay Road, ☎9358 6960 This lovely budget hotel is extremely close to transportation to the city and station. All rooms have TVs and fridges. There are separate men's and women's common bathroom, a rooftop garden, laundry and kitchen facilities, tea and coffee facilities and will very soon boast a large common area downstairs. *Single ✪$45; double/twin $55*

Potts Point House,
154 Victoria Street, Potts Point, ☎9368 0733 Potts Point House is situated in the heart of everything and extremely accesible. Only a 5 minute walk to Kings Cross Station and 10 minute walk to the City. You can see the City skyline from the door. All room have a TV and most

have fridges. There are 3 bathrooms, laundry and kitchen facilities and a common room with a lounge area just off the kitchen. *Dorms ✪$15-$20; doubles $35-$45*

Sydney Central Backpackers,
16 Orwell St, ☎9358 6600, ▤www.*sydneybackpackers .com* Like most, this one is also centrally located and has a nice reception. It has your normal facilities of a kitchen and TV lounge room with cable and playstation. Up on the sundeck upstairs is where you'll find the laundry, pool tables, picnic tables plus the view of the gorgeous city. *Dorms ✪$21; single $45; double/twin $55*

The Globe Backpackers,
40 Darlinghurst Road, ☎9326 9675 Having been fully re-furbished, re-painted and re-carpeted, The Globe is an ideal place to stay. Facilities includes a TV lounge, courtyard and fully equipped kitchen and laundry. Free internet access. There is a tour desk service available, as well as j ob assistance if you're looking for employment. There are also weekly activities, such as BBQs and cinema nights. Full security is ensured and a safe is available to stow away valuables. *Dorms ✪$21; double/twin $50* (breakfast included)

The Original Backpackers Lodge,
160-162 Victoria St, ☎9356 3232, ▤www.*originalbackp ackers.com* This is the one of the original and longest

establishments to call itself a 'backpackers' place way back in 1982. Kept clean and tidy. All rooms have fridges and TVs and beds are from the ex-Olympic village. Facilities includes a big kitchen, laundry, TV lounge, internet access and a nice courtyard with a barbecue area. *Dorms from ✪$21; double/twins $35pp*

The Palms,
23 Hughes St, ☎9357 1199, 📧www.thepalmsbackpacker s.com All rooms have their own fridge and most also have their own TV. All the dorm rooms have an en suite bathroom. Facilities includes two kitchens, laundry, internet access and a courtyard with a barbecue area. Security is good with lockers. *Dorms ✪$18; double/twin $50*

The Pink House,
Barncleuth House, 6-8 Barncleuth Square, ☎9358 1689 Close to the city and the beach, this hostel boasts a laundry and kitchen facilities, cable TV, free internet and job assistance and courtyards with a barbecue area. A safe is available to stow away valuables. There are also guest phones for the visitors. *Dorms from ✪$23-$24 per night; double/twins $30pp (with en suite $32pp)*

V Backpackers,
144 Victoria St, ☎9357 4733 or 1800 667 225, 📧www.vbackpackers.com Located at the heart of Kings Cross minutes away from everything. This funky place is just newly renovated. Facilities includes a kitchen, laun-

dry, cable TV, lounge room. There's also foosball and an internet access. Free BBQ dinner for guests on Monday and Friday nights. Cafe on site with cheap meals. They have job hunting services and organise activities. Free pickup service from the airport available. *Dorms $J24; double $65*

North Side of the Harbour
Kirribilli
Glenferrie Lodge,
12A Carabella Street, Kirribilli, ☎9955 1685, 📧www.glenferrielodge.com Within walking distance to buses, trains and ferries and close to everything. Some rooms have a private balcony while others have spectacular views. Facilities includes kitchen, laundry, common and TV room with cable, internet access, vending machines and a sunny courtyard. Meals available. *Dorms ✪$30; single $42; double/twins $32.50 (price includes breakfast)*

Kirribilli Court,
45 Carabella Street, ☎9955 4344 Situated in a safe neighbourhood, Kirribillli Court is close to all transport, bus, train or ferry. Caters mostly to long stayers and those working in Sydney. Not suitable for those wanting to stay for less than a week. It has laundry and kitchen facilities and cable TV in the common room. *Dorms ✪$20; single $40; double/twin $50*

Tremayne Private Hotel,
89 Carabella St, ☎9955 4155

Located about 15 mins to the city centre in a quiet residential area. More of a boarding house than a hostel, they ask that you stay a minimum of a week. Each room has a fridge, clock radios, iron and board and coffee making facilities. There are some rooms with a really nice view. Other facilities you'll find is a small kitchen and a TV lounge with cable. Parking available. *Dorms weekly rates ✪$140; double weekly rates $280 (prices includes breakfast and dinner on Mon-Fri)*

The Stratford Manor,
24 Goodchap Road, Chatswood, ☎9410 2982 This fabulous Tudor mansion has off street parking available and if you don't have a car is close to all transport. Share kitchen, dining and bathroom are available and rooms come in single, double and triple. All rooms come with a television, fridge and linen. *Dorms from ✪$45*

South/West of the City
Newtown
Billabong Gardens,
5-11 Egan Street, Newtown, ☎9550 3236 or 1800 806 419, 📧www.billabonggarden s.com Awarded 5 Backpacks for service and facilities by the NRMA. Situated in Newtown, close to the station and just 10 minutes from the city centre. Cheap food halls and shops are just close by. Accommodations vary from en suite motel-style to your normal dorms. Facilities include

a modern kitchen, indoor and outdoor dining areas, laundry, TV common room with internet facilities, games area with ping pong, billiards and the ever rare gym. There's also a solar heated pool and spa and tropical garden courtyard. Parking available. *Dorms from ☉$20; 4 to a motel style room from $40pp; double/twin $33pp; double/twin motel style $44pp*

Cooper's Arms Hotel,

221 King St, Newtown, ☎*0417 687 475,*💻*www.co opersarms.com.au* Central to the city minutes from the airport and Sydney's Central train station. Close to everything in Newtown. Accommodation above a pub in single sex dorms. Rooms are clean and fanned. Basic facilities includes a kitchen, laundry, TV room and 2 courtyards and a barbecue area. Special backpackers night on Thursdays with sausage sizzle BBQ and happy hour at the bar downstairs. They have cable TV too. *Dorms ☉$17; double $20 ; twin $18*

Sydney Summer YHA,

St Andrews College Carillon, Newtown, ☎*9557 1133,* 💻*www.yha.com* A relaxed and friendly hostel, Sydney Summer Hostel is located within Sydney University grounds. With it's leafy, green surrounds, it's close to Newtown with it's pubs, cafes and restaurants. The hostel boasts parking, TV common room, internet access, and BBQ facilities. It's close to the centre of Sydney, as well as the Footbridge Theatre, where

you can enjoy various plays offered throughout the year. Parking available. *Dorms from ☉$26; double/twin $56 BC MC VA EFTPOS*

Manly
Boardrider Backpacker,

63 The Corso, (entrance on Market Place) ☎*9977 6077,* 💻*www.boardrider.com* Located at the very heart of Manly and consisting of 4 floors. Very close to everything. Clean and well maintained. The fantastic facilities includes common room with a barbecue area that joins the kitchen and dining area. There is also laundry facilities and a TV lounge and a large open terrace that overlooks the ocean and the Corso. Security is great with lockers in the rooms. Recommended. *Dorms ☉$28; double/twin $37.50pp (42.50 with en suite)*

Manly Backpackers Beachside VIP,

28 Ralgan Street, ☎*9977 3411,* 💻*www.manlybackpac kers.com* Located 50 metres form the beach and within easy reach of the shops, cafe's and bars. Some rooms have en suites. With 2 kitchens, 2 laundries, and 4 bathrooms, there is really no need to line up for a shower, or go hungry in unwashed clothes. There is a lounge room with a large TV with a DVD player and cable and also pool table. There is a sundeck where you can relax and enjoy an alfresco breakfast, lunch or dinner. *Dorms ☉$24; doubles $50; twins $48*

Manly Beach Resort VIP,

6 Carlton Street, ☎*9977 4188* Just seconds from the beach. *Dorms* with en suites and double rooms are available. With 2 kitchens stocked with modern appliances, laundry facilities, TV lounge and a BBQ area. The courtyard is quite nice. Be warned about the minor traffic noise in some rooms. *Dorms ☉$24; double $55*

Manly Bunkhouse,

35 Pine Street, ☎*9976 0472 or 1800 657 122,* 💻*www.bunkhouse.com.au* The Bunkhouse is only metres from Manly beach and a short walk to the ferry and shops. Each room has an en suite, TV, fridge and a personal secure locker. Kitchen facilities are available, as is the internet. There is a TV and VCR in the lounge room and a vending machine plus the common rooms which are mainly downstairs. The courtyard at the back has a nice barbecue area with tables and your surrounded with banana trees. *Dorms ☉$25; double/twin $32.50pp*

Manly Cottage Inn VIP,

25 Pittwater Road, Manly, ☎*9976 0297,* 💻*www.users.bigpond.com/ Manlycottage/* This lovely family-run hostel is friendly and welcoming. It only accommodates 30 people. Newly renovated, it boasts laundry facilities, a lounge room with cable TV, a mini library and outdoor area with barbecue where you can relax. There is also an outdoor shower for those who have been surfing. Parking available. *Dorms from ✪$22; double from $50*

Manly Guesthouse,
6 Steinton Street, ☎ *9977 0884,* 💻 *www.manlyguesth ouse.citysearch.com* Only 70 metres from the surf and beaches. A friendly, welcoming place. It is only a short walk to the shops. Features a cable TV, laundry facilities, 2 squeaky clean kitchens, security safe for valuables and clean linen is provided. Offers on site job assistance if you require any. *Dorms ✪$25;*

single $40; double/twin $30 pp

Steyne Hotel,
75 The Corso, ☎ *9977 4977* Accommodation situated above a pub. Located close to the beach and shops. Quite a good quality accommodation for a pub and has a hotel feel. There are twin beds, TV and sink. Credit card a must. *Dorms ✪$29; twin $39* (price includes breakfast)

The Wharf Backpackers,
48 East Esplanade, Manly, ☎ *9977 2800* Located right

in the centre of Manly, The Wharf Backpackers offer dorm rooms with share bathroom, kitchen and laundry facilities. It is right opposite the ferry port, so you can cruise Sydney's coast and only 2 minutes from the beach. There is also a huge garden area out the back. *Dorms ✪$20*

South
Cityside at the Excelsior VIP, *64 Foveaux Street, Surry Hills,* ☎ *9211 4945 or 1800 000 549* Just your basic accommodation which is situated above a pub in a quiet

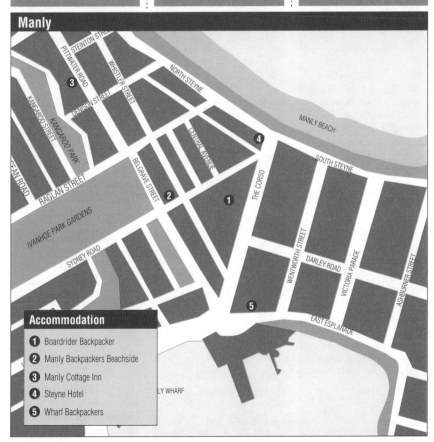

Manly

Accommodation

1. Boardrider Backpacker
2. Manly Backpackers Beachside
3. Manly Cottage Inn
4. Steyne Hotel
5. Wharf Backpackers

area of Surry Hills. Not far from Central station. Clean, comfortable beds and there's live entertainment every day at the pub downstairs. You get a free beer on arrival and there are laundry, kitchen facilities and TV room. Good security. *Dorm ✪$18; double/twin $24*

Gracelands,

461 Cleveland Street, Redfern, ☎*9699 1399 or 1800 804 795,* 🖥*www.kangaroobakpak.com.au* Run by the same family as Kangaroo Bak-Pak, Gracelands is a bright blue, antique building accommodating longer term residents. Being family-run, Gracelands is a small, personal place with an intimate atmosphere. Facilities includes large fully equipped kitchen, TV, video and lounge area, internet access and a nice outdoor barbecue area. They also offer work assistance and free airport pick up. Parking Available. *Dorms ✪$22; double/twin; $50*

Kangaroo Bak-pak,

665 South Dowling Street, Surry Hills, ☎*9319 5915 or 1800 804 795,* 🖥*www.kangaroobakpak.com.au* A restored Victorian style terrace, Kangaroo Bak-Pak is only 15 minutes to Coogee and Bondi Beach by bus. It offers 24 hour security, kitchen facilities, a TV and video lounge, free tea and coffee making facilities, a barbecue area, internet access, work assistance and a tour desk. *Dorms ✪$20-$22; double/twin $45-$50*

Kriskindl Hotel,

22a Hillcrest Street, Tempe, 9558 3322 or 1800 646 013 Only 7 minutes to the City, Kriskindle Guesthouse is family run, making it small and personal. There are kitchen and laundry facilities and internet access and the gym and pool are only 100 metres away. Clean, quiet and comfortable, you can stay for as long (or as short) as you want. *Dorm ✪$22; single $35; double/twin $25* (breakfast included, and if you stay for a week, you will receive a free, 3 course dinner for five nights)

Moore Park View Hotel,

853 South Dowling Road, Waterloo, ☎*9310 2875* Moore Park View Hotel has tea and coffee facilities as well as use of the guest kitchen and laundry. Breakfast is available and there is a TV room where you can watch the latest Aussie dramas. The BBQ area is perfect for meeting new people, or you could try the hotel bar and play a game of pool. Hotel parking is also available. *Dorms ✪$35; double $52; twin $31pp*

City

Alfred Park Hotel,

207 Cleveland St, Redfern, ☎*9319 4031,* 🖥*www.g-day.com.au/getting_here_alfred.htm* Located just across the Prince Alfred park close to Central Station. A place that would suit someone who's looking for a more quiet and private accommodation. All rooms have TV and fridge

and some dorms are en suite. Your basic facilities of kitchen, laundry, internet access and a nice courtyard outside. There is an annex building with extra accommodation next door. *Dorms from ✪$18; twin $44pp*

City Central Backpackers,

752 George Street, ☎*9212 4833 or 1800 249 91,* 🖥*www.ccbackpack.com.au* City Central Backpackers has recently been renovated with funky murals all over the stairs. There are kitchen and laundry facilities available and all the rooms are sunny, spacious and secure, using the keycard security door system and lockers. There is a TV room and games room with ping pong as well free internet access. Job assistance is offered and there is free pick up from the airport. *Dorms ✪$22; twin $55;* (price includes breakfast)

Downtown City Backpackers,

611 George Street, ☎*9211 8801 or 1800 248 815,* 🖥*www.downtowncity.com.au* Run by the same people who have brought you City Central Backpackers. Fantastically located at the heart of the city. Funky murals are again on the walls. There are kitchen and laundry facilities available and all the rooms are sunny, spacious and there is a balcony. Good security. There is also a TV room and games room for your convenience as well as free internet access. Also free pickup from the airport. *Dorms ✪$22; twin $55* (breakfast included)

Forbes Terrace Hotel,

153 Forbes Street, ☎*9358*

4327, ▇www.gday.com.au/index_forbes.html Within walking distance to all Sydney attractions and has beautifully restored terrace. Each room had its own linen supplied, TV, fridge, modern furniture, heating and cooling and is extremely clean. There is a super clean kitchen, laundry facilities, indoor and outdoor dining areas and a nice courtyard. They also offer free pick up from the airport. *Dorm* ✪*$18; single $44; twin $33pp*

Footprints Westend,
412 Pitt St, ☎ *9211 4588 or 1800 013 186,* ▇ *www.footprintswestend.com* Located at the centre of the city. This is a modern looking hostel, quite huge with over 13 floors. Very good atmosphere and caters for a lot to working travellers. You can locate the common areas on the first floor, and it has a fully equipped kitchen, the TV lounge with a huge screen and a pool table. There is also an on site cafe, travel agent and job hunt assistance. Has security with lockers under each bunk. *Dorms from* ✪*$30; double $38pp; twin $35pp* (prices includes breakfast)

Harbour City Hotel,
50 Sir John Young Crescent, Wolloomooloo, ☎ *9380 2922 or 1800 822 922,* ▇ *www.harbourcityhotel.com* Located close to stores, some food halls and the Art Gallery of NSW. Rooms are clean and spacious, fanned, heated and there are reading lights. Facilities includes a kitchen, laundry, cable TV, videos and

a book exchange. The staff are willing to help in your job hunt. Place is secure. There is also free pick up from the airport and free beer vouchers. *Dorms* ✪*$20; double/twin $65*

Hyde Park Backpackers,
88-90 Wentworth Ave, ☎ *9282 9266,* ▇ *www.hydeparkbackpackers.com* Located only minutes walk from train and coach station and Hyde Park. It's only a small hostel with fans in all rooms. Facilities includes full kitchen facilities, laundry, TV lounge with cable and internet access. An all girls dorm rooms is also available. *Dorms* ✪*$20; double $32.50pp; twin $58*

Indys City Backpackers,
198 Elizabeth St, ☎ *9211 4200,* ▇ *www.indysbackpackers.com* This is a newly renovated old building located in the city close to everything. It's only a small hostel with your basic facilities of kitchen and laundry. Their TV lounge is their asset with a big screens, movies and cable. All rooms have fans and heating plus a fridge. Take advantage of the free internet access. On site bistro downstairs that serves cheap meals. There are also trivia nights, pub treks and the ever popular free beer and wine night, where everyone has a chance to win great prizes. *Dorms* ✪*$23; double $32.50pp* (free breakfast included)

Maze Backpackers,
417 Pitt St, ☎ *9211 5115 or 1800813522,* ▇www.mazebackpackers.com This big old

heritage building is located at the very heart of the city, close to the Central Station and everything else. Great atmosphere and caters a lot to working travellers. Facilities includes a small kitchen and dining, laundry, TV room with a pool table and cheap internet access. The staff also organises free activities like wine and cheese nights, quiz nights and even movie marathons. Free Airport Transfers. *Dorms from* ✪*$23; single $49; double $27.50pp; twin $27.50pp*

Noah's City Central,
240A Elizabeth St, 9211 9111, ▇*homepages.ihug.com.au/⊠noahscc/content.html* Located in the heart of Sydney City on the main street, just a short walk to all the major attractions and food stores. Set in two buildings and is decorated with murals. There is a fully equipped kitchen, laundry, TV lounge with cable, internet access and an open roof deck covered with plants. Take advantage of the complimentary free internet access whenever you want the web, free weekly BBQ dinners with live music, free trivia nights and the free movie nights. They also assist you in looking for employment. Bike hire, airport pick up service and parking available. *Dorms* ✪*$20; double $47* (free breakfast each day)

Royal Albert Hotel,
140 Commonwealth St, Surry Hills, ☎*9281 2580 or 1800 259 010,* ▇*www.whereisthepub.org* Accommodation located above a

GOAT ISLAND

PORT JACKSON

McMAHONS POINT

Blues Point

Blues Point Reserve

Kirribilli

Milsons Point

Olympic Dr

Sydney Harbour Tunnel

Sydney Harbour Bridge

Hickson Road

Walsh Bay

Dawes Point

DAWES POINT

Darling Street Wharf

Illoura Res

BALMAIN EAST

Weston St

William St

Edward St

Peacock Point

Millers Point

MILLERS POINT

Merriman St

Hickson

High Street

Kent

Street

Observatory Park

Observatory

Windmill St

Argyle Pl

Argyle

Bradfield Highway

Pottinger Street

Lower Fort Street

George St

Playfair St

Cumberland St

Gloucester St

Harrington

Street

Street

Street

Street

THE ROCKS

Circular Quay W

Sydney Cove

Ferry Wharves

Circular Quay

Cahill Expressway

Circular Quay East

Opera House

Government House

Farm Cove

Royal Botanic

Conservatorium of Music

Alfred Street

George Street

Grosvenor St

Gloucester St

Dalley St

Loftus St

Albert St

Young St

Street

Gresham Street

Bridge Street

NORTH

0   200   400m

DARLING

KINGS CROSS

WOOLLOOMOOLOO

DARLINGHURST

East Sydney Institute of Technology

Woolloomooloo Bay

Cowper Wharf Roadway

Nicholson Street

Harmer St

Cathedral Street

Dowling Street

Farrel St

Hardie St

Victoria Street

Darley St

St Peters S

Forbes Street

Bourke Street

Young C.

Plunkett St

Street

Street

Sir John

Broughton St

Kennedy St

Robinson St

Palmer Street

Liverpool Street

Burton

L. Oxford St

Campbell

Street

The Domain

Art Gallery Rd

Cahill Expressway

Parliament House

Macquarie Street

St Mary

Cathedral St

Haig Av

Boomerang St

Riley Street

Riley Street

Riley St

Seale St

Yurong

Stanley Street

Francis Street

Oxford Street

Brisbane Street

Poplar St

Waine St

Palmer St

Street

Street

Prince Albert Rd

William Street

College Street

Avenue

Goulburn Lane

St James Rd

St James

Phillip St

Bligh Street

Phillip Street

Macquarie Street

Martin Place

Elizabeth Street

Martin Street

Hunter Street

Pitt Street

Hyde Park

Park Street

Museum Street

Nithsdale St

Street

Street

Street

Wentworth Av

Foster Street

Elizabeth

Castlereagh

Castlereagh St

SYDNEY

Wynyard S

Carrington S

Wynyard St

Barrack St

George Street

York Street

Market Street

Druitt St

Bathurst

Town Hall

Liverpool Street

Goulburn Street

HAYMARKET

Campbell St

Parker St

George Street

Erskine Street

Clarence Street

Kent Street

King Street

Sussex

Street

Harbour St

Day Ave

Dixon Street

Little Hay St

Hay

Street

Quay

Harris

George Street

7

8

China Twn

1

HARBOUR

PYRMONT

Jones Bay Rd

Foreshore Road

Casino

Gateway

Maritime Museum

Sydney Aquarium

Pyrmont Bridge

Cockle Bay Wharf

Harbourside

Cockle Bay

Convention Centre

Darling

Union St

Murray Street

Harwood St

Burn St

Edward St

L Edward St

Bridge St

Pyrmont

Gipps St

Allen Street

Wattle

Quay

Flg

Bay

Mbalong Park

Chinese Gardens

Harbour Street

Entertainment Centre

ULT

Na♦

Street

pub. Very basic facilities but clean and well maintained. There is a bar and bistro downstairs that serves food. *Dorms ❍$25*

Sinclairs Surry Hills,
510 Cleveland St, Surry Hills, ☎ *8399 2518*
🖳www.*sinclairs.com.au/*
Located close to shops and restaurants and not far from the city and Chinatown. Public transport is easily accessible. Just newly re-furbished. Remote colour TV and fridge in room plus heaters, fans and electric blankets. Other amenities includes light cooking facilities, laundry and internet access. *Dorm ❍$25; single $49.50; double $56* (free breakfast buffet, tea and coffee)

Sydney Backpackers,
7 Wilmot St, ☎ *9267 7772 or 1800 887 766,* 🖳www.*sydneybackpackers.com* This is probably the most centralised hostel in the city, being very close to Town Hall station and everything else. Accommodation set in an old building. All rooms have their own lockers, fridge and TV and are air conditioned. Other facilities includes a small kitchen, lounge room, TV room with cable, internet access and a nice sundeck on the roof top with a barbecue area and some great views of the city. *Dorms ❍$23; twin $40pp*

Sydney Central YHA,
11 Rawson Pl, ☎ *9281 9111,* 🖳www.*yha.com.au* This hostel is huge and has fantastic facilities. Very close to everything, and Chinatown isn't far either. Everything feels brand new, clean and very well

maintained. There is your normal fully equipped kitchen, laundry, games room with a pool table and video games, lounge rooms in each floor and the rare Sydney hostel heated swimming pool and spa. There is also internet access and an on site bar called 'Scubar', bistro and minimart downstairs and a barbecue area. Meals available. Limited parking available. *Dorms from ❍$25; double with en suite $44pp; twin $39pp BC MC VA EFTPOS*

Wake Up!,
509 Pitt St, ☎ *9264 4121,* 🖳 www.*wakeup.com.au* Just next to Central Station, very convenient for travelling around the city. Kept clean and well maintained. Very modern and each floor is colour coded. The hostel consist of nine floors, having the kitchen, laundry, TV lounge rooms and internet access on the lower floors. There is also an on site bar, bistro and cafe. Good security. *Dorms from ❍$25; double/twin $39.50pp ($44 with en suite)*

Wanderers On Kent,
477 Kent St, ☎ *9267 7718 or 1800 424 444,* 🖳 www.*wanderersonkent.com* Probably one of the best hostels to stay at in Sydney. Has a really feel good atmosphere to it. Located conveniently in the city close to everything. Everything feels brand new and is clean and very well maintained. *Dorms* are big and spacious and an all girls dorm is also available. Facilities includes a small kitchen, laundry, TV

room with pool table, internet access on two floors, and the never-to-be-expected-in-a-hostel solarium. Each floor also has a kitchenette. There is an on site travel agent, bar and cafe that serves affordable meals. Recommended. *Dorms from ❍$24; doubles $42*

Y on the Park Hotel,
5-11 Wentworth Avenue, ☎ *9264 2451 or 1800 994 994,* 🖳www.*ywca-sydney.com.au* Right at the heart of Sydney, Y on the Park Hotel offers comfort on style. En suites, TVs, fridges and telephones are included in the deluxe rooms and there is air conditioning and heaters in all rooms. Linen in supplied and there are kitchen and laundry facilities available for the guests. If you don't want to cook, you can visit the cafe/restaurant for some delicious meals. There is 24 hour reception and a tour desk as hand and lifts to take you to any level. *Dorm ❍$32; single $70; double $85*

Glebe
Alishan International Guest House,
100 Glebe Point Rd, Glebe, ☎ *9566 4048,* 🖳www.*alishan.com.au* Located nicely in a quiet area next to Glebe's main shopping lane. Very homely and relaxed atmosphere. Set in a beautiful renovated 100 year old Victorian Mansion that has very tasteful decorations. The facilities includes a kitchen, a common room with internet access and a barbecue area with picnic tables at the back. Upstairs is also a balcony that

overlooks the street. *Dorms from � $27; double from $49.50pp*

Glebe Point YHA Hostel,
262 Glebe Point Rd, Glebe, ☎ *9692 8418,*
🖳 *www.yha.com.au* Located very close to shops, and city is only minutes away by public transport. All rooms have their own reading light and sink. Facilities includes large kitchen, laundry and TV lounge. The common rooms have all the gaming equipments such as the pinball machines and pool tables. The rooftop provides a view of town and has the barbecue area. Staff also organises BBQ nights and activities. *Dorms from ☺$26.50; double/twin from $36.50pp BC MC VA EFTPOS*

Glebe Village Backpackers,
256 Glebe Point Road, ☎ *9660 8133,* 🖳 *www.bakpak.com/ glebevillage* Glebe is located close to many shops and restaurants in this lively area, Sydney central is only 10 minutes away by bus. Facilities includes a fully equipped kitchen, TV lounge rooms, garden courtyard with barbecue area. The staff also organises wine and cheese nights, pubcrawls and barbecues. *Dorms from ☺$25; double/twin $37.50pp*

Wattle House,
44 Henford St, Glebe, ☎ *9552 4997,* 🖳 *www.wattleho use.com.au* Set in an old beautiful building with a nice garden at the front. Small and quaint. Located in the historic inner-city suburb of Glebe

close to cafes and shops. Detail is placed as a priority with towels, linen and duvets on all beds and bathrobes in twin and double room. Beds have their own reading lamps, shelving and plenty of storage space for personal items. Facilities includes a fully equipped kitchen, laundry, a reading room, TV lounge and a nice backyard garden with their own tables. There is also complimentary soup, coffee, tea, hot chocolate, sugar and milk. *Dorms from ☺$25; double/twin from $37.50pp*

Northern Beaches
Avalon Beach Hostel,
59 Avalon Parade, Avalon Beach, ☎ *9918 9709* Located a good hour drive from the city. Close to shops and the beaches. Pretty relaxed atmosphere. Facilities includes the usual kitchen and an internet access. There's also a nice balcony and courtyard. *Dorms ☺$20; double $50*

Sydney Beachhouse YHA,
4 Collaroy St, Collaroy Beach, ☎ *9981 6897,* 🖳 *www.sydn eybeachhouse.com* Winner of the 2000 NSW Awards for Excellence in Tourism. Located close to the bus station, foodstore and not far from the beach at all. Quite a modern hostel fitting to the beach lifestyle with tones of facilities. Features a kitchen, laundry, TV lounge with open fireplace, internet access, games room with pool table and video games. There's also a sundeck with a heated swimming pool and 3 barbecue areas. Meals provided. Bike hire, surfboard and

sports equipment plus parking available. *Dorms from ☺$20; double/twin from $30pp BC MC VA EFTPOS*

Other Areas
Balmain Backpackers,
675 Darling St, Balmain, ☎ *9555 6436 or 1800 888 640,* 🖳 *www.backpackersydney.co m* Located close to everything and about 10 mins by bus to the city centre. Caters a lot to working travellers. Features a number of kithennetes, laundry, TV lounge, internet access and a barbecue area with a sundeck. BBQ nights are part of their activities. They offer job hunt assistance and a free pick up service. Parking available. *Dorms from ☺$17; single $30; double/twin $50*

Cronulla Beach YHA,
Level 1, 40-42 Kingsway, Cronulla Beach, ☎ *9527 7772,* 🖳 *www.cronullabeachyha.com.* Located at the centre of town close to the shopping mall and not far off the beach. Kept clean and well maintained. Facilities includes a large kitchen, laundry, TV lounge room, pool table, internet access and a barbecue area at the back. There is free use of body boards. Bike hire and parking available. *Dorms from ☺$21; double/twin with en suite from $30pp BC MC VA EFTPOS*

Dulwich Hill YHA,
407 Marrickville Rd, Dulwich Hill, ☎ *9550 0054,* 🖳 *www.yha.com* Set in a two storey Victorian terrace. Located closely to a shopping centre. The city is still pretty accessible. Accommodation

extends to the annex building at the back. Features a kitchen, laundry, TV lounge with cable, internet access, games room and a courtyard with a barbecue area. TVs and fridges are available for hire in rooms. They also offer employment assistance. Parking available. *Dorms from ✪$18; single from $25 BC MC VA EFTPOS*

Nomads Forest Lodge Hotel, *117 Arundel St, Forest Lodge,* ☎ *1800 688 815,* ▣*www. forestlodgehotel.com.au/ accommodation.html* This is another one of those above-the-pub lodging located next to the University of Sydney. Bus services are very frequent in this area and it's not too far from the city if you catch the bus. Clean with old looking decor. Just your basic facilities including a kitchen and TV lounge. Bar is downstairs with on site bistro and coffee shop which has basic meals. They also offer a free pick up service from the airport and the city. *Dorms from ✪$19; single $45; double/twin $55*

Pittwater YHA, *Ku-ring-gai National Park Lodge, via Halls Wharf, Morning Bay via Church Point,* ☎ *9999 2196,* ▣ *www.yha.com* This is a pretty secluded part of Sydney for those wishing to really get away from it all. You even have to bring all your food. Nearest food store is at Church Point a ferry ride away. Very basic facilities including a kitchen, laundry and a barbecue area. Enjoy a bit of canoeing to secluded beaches or meet some of the native

wildlife. Parking available. Call first for bookings. *Dorms from ✪$19; double/twin from $25 BC MC VA*

The Lodge, *96-98 Johnston Street, Annandale,* ☎ *9660 4600,* ▣*www.sydneycity.com.au/ backpack.html* Located close to the City centre, and just minutes away from Darling Harbour and Star City. Rooms have en suite bathroom and are fully furnished. Facilities includes a TV lounge with cable and a nice courtyard with barbecue area. *Dorms ✪$20*

Caravan Parks
These tend to be in the outer suburbs, but are generally good value for money.

The Grand Pines Tourist Park Ramsgate Beach, *289 The Grand Parade, Sans Souci,* ☎*2529 7329.* (No pets allowed), 73 sites, unlicensed restaurant, barbecue - *powered sites ✪$25-35 for two, on-site vans $50-60 for two.*

Lakeside Caravan Park, *Lake Park Road, Narrabeen,* ☎*9913 7845.* (No pets allowed), 368 sites, playground, barbecue - *powered sites ✪$20-22 for two, park cabins $70-135.*

Lane Cove River Caravan Park, *Plassey Road, North Ryde,* ☎*9888 9133.* (No dogs or cats allowed), 216 sites, playground, pool - *powered sites ✪$20 for two, park cabins $65-75 for two.*

La Mancha Cara-Park, *901 Pacific Highway, Berowra,* ☎*9456 1766.* (No pets allowed), 196 sites, sauna, squash, pool, playground - *powered sites ✪$20-22 for two, park cabins $64-69 for two.*

Local Transport
Sydney has an efficient public transport system, with buses, ferries and trains covering the city and the suburban areas. For information on all public transport contact the Infoline, ☎*131 500,* J6am-10pm, 7 days.

Train
The railway network is the backbone of the Sydney transit system and is operated by State Rail. There are ten route systems, each with a different colour code, and all services travel on part of the City Circle underground system.The main station is Central (Railway Square). All country trains begin their journey from here. All suburban trains pass through Central and Town Hall stations, and you can change either to link up with the City Circle; to cross over the Harbour Bridge; or to board the train for Bondi Junction, which passes through Martin Place, Kings Cross and Edgecliff.

The stations in the City are: Town Hall, Wynyard, Circular Quay, St James, Museum and Martin Place. These stations are all part of the underground network. The first five form the City Circle.

Town Hall Station has two entrances on each side of George Street. St James Station has entrances in Elizabeth Street and Queens Square.

Museum Station has entrances

on both sides of Liverpool Street and one in Elizabeth Street.

Martin Place Station is well sign-posted, as is Circular Quay Station.

Bus

Details of the routes and schedules of Sydney Buses can be found by calling the **Public Transport Infoline** on ☎ *13 1500* or visiting the web-site at ▪www.sydneybuses.nsw. gov.au Sydney Buses services radiate from the city, ferry wharves and railway stations, and connect the Sydney central business district with the suburbs.

Generally speaking, buses from the Eastern Suburbs terminate at either Central Railway or Circular Quay; those from the North-western and Western Suburbs terminate at York Street (near the Queen Victoria Building) or Circular Quay; and North Shore and Northern Suburbs bus routes end at Wynyard Park, near Wynyard Station, or outside the Queen Victoria Building.

Bus no. 888 runs between Wynyard Station, in George Street, and the Art Gallery of New South Wales in east Circular Quay every 10 minutes, Mon-Fri.

The Sydney Explorer Bus

The red Sydney Explorer bus is a great way to get around the city. It travels a 35km (21 miles) circuit to 22 different stops from 9am-5.25pm, beginning at Circular Quay, every day except Christmas Day. You can get on anywhere along the route where there is a distinctive Sydney Explorer bus stop sign. Passengers can get off at any stop, stay as long as they like, then pick up the next bus that arrives. The buses run every

20 minutes, and the fares are ✪$30 adults.If you miss the last Explorer bus, don't worry because your ticket is good on any State Transit bus running along the Explorer route until midnight.

The Explorer stops are:
1. Sydney Cove (Circular Quay)
2. Sydney Opera House
3. Royal Botanic Gardens/
              Museum of Sydney
4. State Library/The Mint
5. Mrs Macquarie's Chair
6. Art Gallery of NSW
7. Hard Rock Cafe
8. Kings Cross
9. Macleay Street
10. Elizabeth Bay House
11. Potts Point
12. Woolloomooloo Bay
13. Wynyard Station/Martin Place
14. Queen Victoria Building/
Sydney Tower/Planet Hollywood
15. Australian Museum
16. Central Station
17. Chinatown/Powerhouse
       Museum
18. Darling Harbour/National
       Maritime Museum
19. The Chinese Gardens/
       Powerhouse Museum
20. Sydney Aquarium
21. Campbell's Cove/Dawes
       Point
22. The Rocks Visitors Centre

Tickets can be purchased when boarding the bus, or beforehand from the NSW Travel Centre, *11-31 York Street*; Australian Pacific Tours, *102 George Street, City*; CountryLink Rail Travel Centres; *11 York Street, City*; or from a local travel agent.

Bondi and Bay Explorer Blue and White buses clearly marked Bondi and Bay Explorer operate on a 35km circular route from the city centre through the eastern harbour and bay-side areas. They run at 30 minute intervals from

9am-4pm every day, departing from Circular Quay. The fares are ✪$30 adults.

Bondi and Bay buses stop at the following destinations:
1. Circular Quay
2. Kings Cross
3. Top of the Cross
4. Rushcutters Bay
5. Double Bay
6. Rose Bay Ferry
7. Rose Bay Convent
8. Vaucluse Bay
9. Watsons Bay
10. The Gap Park
11. Bondi Beach
12. Bronte Beach
13. Coogee Beach
14. Royal Randwick Racecourse
15. SCG/Football Stadium/
       Paddington
16. Oxford Street
17. Hyde Park
18. Martin Place

If it suits your itinerary you can purchase twin tickets for both buses: ✪$50 adults.

Olympic Explorer

This service departs from the Homebush Bay Visitors Centre between 9.20am and 5pm daily, at 10-15 minute intervals. This is the most efficient way to explore the sporting facilities, with ten stops along the route at which you can disembark, and join a later bus after viewing the attraction at your leisure. A ticket costs ✪$10 for adults, but the higher cost will come from making your way out to the Olympic site to take the tour. If you are in the city, the best choice is to take the River Cat from Circular Quay and purchase an Olympic River Cat Ticket for ✪$22 adults - included in the price is access to the Olympic Explorer bus service.

Ferry

Providing undoubtedly the most scenic way to travel, Sydney's ferries and River Cats ply the magnificent harbour.

Full information on routes and schedules can be obtained by phoning ☎131 500 or visiting the same site as for Sydney Buses (see above).

Ferry services operate daily, 6am-11pm, from Circular Quay up-harbour to Balmain, Long Nose Point, Hunters Hill and Greenwich.

Across-harbour ferries travel to Kirribilli, Neutral Bay, Cremorne, Mosman and Taronga Zoo. Ferries and turbo powered catamarans service Manly. The wharves at Circular Quay are well sign-posted to indicate which area they service, but on weekends there are changes, and it is best to check before putting your ticket into the automatic turnstiles. Tickets can be purchased from machines on each wharf, or from the kiosk underneath the Circular Quay Station. This kiosk also sells tickets to harbour cruises run by Sydney Ferries, which leave at 10am daily, 1pm Mon-Fri, Sat-Sun 1.30pm, and 8pm Mon-Sat; and river cruises which leave at 10am daily.For information on times, connections and fares for all government and private bus, rail and ferry services in Sydney, contact the Infoline on ☎131 500 (daily 6am-10pm) - they can also advise on Sydney Discovery Tours tickets. Alternatively, visit the website listed above.

Sydney Pass

If you are going to be in the city for at least a week, it will pay you to invest in a Sydney Pass. It costs adults ✪$90 for 3 days, $120 for 5 days and $140 for 7 days. The Pass gives you unlimited use of the Sydney Explorer Bus, Manly ferries, harbour cruises run by Urban Transit, and all jetcat, ferry and bus services. These passes are available from the Travel Centre of NSW and State Transit ticket offices displaying the Sydney Pass sign.

The Monorail

The monorail system runs anticlockwise and has seven stations - Harbourside (Darling Harbour), Convention Centre, Haymarket, Garden Plaza, World Square (Liverpool Street), Galleries Victoria (Pitt Street, near Park Street) and City Centre (Pitt Street, near Market Street). It is the best way to get from the city centre to Darling Harbour. The fare for the monorail is ✪$3.50 for everybody 6 and over, whether you are going one stop or the complete circuit. You are not permitted to stay aboard for more than one circuit.An unlimited travel Supervoucher Day Pass can be obtained if you plan to use the monorail several times to make your way around the city (it also contains discount coupons for nearby attractions). The ticket costs $8 per person (there is no adult/child distinction) and is valid until closing on the same day. The alternative is the Supervoucher Family Pass, which costs $24 for 2 adults and 2 children (or 1 adult and 3 children).The monorail runs 7am-10pm Mon-Thu, Fri-Sat 7am-midnight and 8am-10pm on Sundays, ☎9552 2288 for further details. There is a website at ▣www. metromonorail.com.au

Sydney Light Rail

This tram service begins at Central Station and takes you through Haymarket to Darling Harbour, up to Pyrmont, Star City, Fish Market, Wentworth Park, Glebe, Jubilee Park, Rozelle Bay and finally Lilyfield. It runs 24 hours a day and generally at 10 minute intervals. There are two zones for fares - Zone 1 (Central to Darling Harbour) and Zone 2 (Darling Harbour to Lilyfield). Fares per person are from ✪$2.50 to $4.80. A ticket for unlimited weekly trips costs ✪$19 per person. This form of transport may prove useful as a quick and relatively cheap alternative for sightseeing. For further information, ☎9660 5288 or visit the web page at ▣www.metro lightrail.com.au

Taxi

Sydney is well served by taxis, and charges are set by the Department of Motor Transport. The main cab companies are:

> Taxis Combined Services, ☎83328888;
> RSL Cabs, ☎13 22 11;
> Legion Cabs, ☎13 14 51;
> ABC Taxis, ☎13 25 22;

Specially outfitted cabs for people in wheelchairs are available, and must be booked in advance.Taxis may be hailed in the street, hired at a taxi rank, or arranged over the phone for a pick-up, though there will be an extra fee. This service has vastly improved in recent years.Taxi ranks in the city include Central Station, Circular Quay, Park Street opposite the Town Hall, and outside all the major hotels.If you hire a taxi in the city to take you over the bridge, ✪$3 will be added to the bill even though there is no toll for travel south to north. This extra fee is added because the taxi driver has to pay the toll to travel over the bridge when returning to the city, and may not get a fare going back that way. Be aware of this for other destinations whose routes involve toll roads.If you are travelling to the airport from the northern side of the Harbour Bridge, it is safest to predict a $7 surcharge on your fare to cover all tolls and rates.

Water Taxi

Several companies operate on the harbour, including Taxis Afloat, ☎9955 3222; Quay Water Taxis, ☎9922 4252; and Water Taxis, ☎9755 4660. They will take you from one landing point to any other landing point on the harbour, and also offer scenic cruises.

Car

Renting a car is relatively cheap if you are travelling in a group, but driving in the city is not really recommended. The one-way streets take a bit of getting used to, and parking is a problem. Street parking is extremely hard to find, and the parking station fees add considerably to the cost of your day out. However, for travelling in the suburbs and outlying areas, a car is definitely the way to go.

Here we give you the names of the major rental car companies as they have branches throughout the country and though they may be more expensive than some real budget operators, if anything goes wrong you are covered and can be looked after. If you come across a budget operator that has just been

brilliant in an emergency then let us know in the next edition. Here are a few names of rental companies and their reservation phone numbers:

Avis, ☎13 63 33;
Budget, ☎13 27 27;
Hertz, ☎13 30 39;
Thrifty, ☎1300 367 227.
Europcar ☎1300 13 13 90

International and overseas drivers licences that are in English are accepted, and a deposit, or credit card details, are required before pick-up.

Other car rental companies are found in the A-K Yellow Pages Telephone Directory.The National Roads and Motorists Authority (NRMA) has reciprocal arrangements with overseas and interstate automobile associations. The head office is located at 151 Clarence Street, Sydney. The phone number for enquiries is ☎13 2132, and for road service, ☎13 1111.

Let's Eat

Sydney has a plethora of restaurants offering every type of cuisine imaginable. The harbour foreshores are liberally sprinkled with eating establishments, for there are not too many experiences that surpass, or for that matter match, a leisurely brunch on a sunny weekend with the harbour and all its craft as a backdrop. Unfortunately, though, you often have to pay top prices for this indulgence. With so much competition, you would expect that prices would have to be kept to a minimum, but there are apparently enough people to ensure that each restaurant is well-patronised, and indeed

bookings are essential when a water view is offered.

Restaurants are classified as Licensed or BYO. Licensed means that the establishment has a licence to sell alcohol. BYO means 'bring your own' wine, etc., because the restaurant does not have a liquor licence. Some restaurants, although licensed, allow patrons to supply their own wine (not beer or spirits), which is usually less expensive than paying the mark-up on the wines that the restaurant is legally allowed to add. In this case a corkage fee may be added, which will be per bottle or per person, but the end result is usually still less expensive. Alcohol can be purchased from one of the many bottle shops that abound in every suburb. It is reasonable to say that the price of a bottle of wine in one of these shops would be less than half the price of the same wine in a restaurant.
Following is a list of recommended restaurants, rated:

- Moderate (main course ✪$15-$23)
- Budget (main course under ✪$15).

Not included here are the restaurants in the 5-star hotels nor those that are classed as expensive, as everyone knows that they exist and are much the same the world over with regard to menus and prices.
Credit card abbreviations are:

Amex = American Express;
BC = Bankcard;
DC = Diners Club;
MC = MasterCard;
V = Visa.

There is Sydney landmark that

has been around a very long time: **Harry's Cafe de Wheels**, Cowper Wharf Roadway, Woolloomooloo, ☎9357 3074. It is not a restaurant, not even a cafe, just a roadside stall - but everyone knows Harry's. Their delicious real Aussie meat pies, peas and more, are handed to you on a paper serviette. Eating a pie in this fashion requires complex synchronisation of hand and mouth - an ability with which most Sydneysiders are already born, or one they develop with rapid evolution at weekend football matches. So, when in Rome...

The City and The Rocks

Casa Asturiana, *77 Liverpool Street, City*, ☎9264 1010. Licensed, Mediterranean cuisine, budget, ☾open daily from 6pm and Tue-Fri noon-3pm, Amex, DC, MC, V.

Rossini Rosticceria, *Shop W5, Circular Quay*, ☎9247 8026. Licensed, good views, outside tables, Italian, cafeteria style, budget, ☾open daily 7pm-10.30am, 11am-4pm, 5-10.30pm, no credit cards accepted.

Sailors Thai, *106 George Street, The Rocks*, ☎9251 2466. Licensed, Thai cuisine, budget, ☾open daily noon-2pm and 6pm-10am, Amex, BC, DC, MC, V.

Phillip's Foote, *101 George Street, The Rocks*, ☎9241 1485. Licensed (it is actually a pub), cook-your-own steaks, good salad bar, outdoor tables, budget, ☾open daily for lunch and dinner, Amex, BC, DC, MC, V.

Chinatown (Haymarket)

Golden Harbour, *31 Dixon Street*, ☎9212 5987. Licensed and BYO (corkage fee per bottle), Cantonese, budget, ☾open Mon-Fri 10am-4.30pm, 5.30pm-11pm and Sat-Sun 9am-4.30pm, 5.30pm-1am, Amex, BC, DC, MC, V.

House of Guang Zhou, *76 Ultimo Road*, ☎9281 2205. Licensed, Chinese, budget, ☾open Mon-Fri 11.30am-3pm, Sat-Sun noon-3pm and daily 5.30pm-2am, Amex, BC, DC, MC, V.

Malaya, *761 George Street*, ☎9211 0946. Licensed, Malaysian cuisine, budget, ☾open daily noon-3pm, Mon-Sat 5-10pm and Sun 5-9pm, Amex, BC, DC, MC, V.

East Sydney

No Name, *2 Chapel Street, Darlinghurst*, ☎9130 4898. BYO, Italian pasta and minestrone, budget, ☾open for lunch and dinner, no credit cards accepted. There are a few No Name restaurants around Sydney, but this is the original and most people think it is still the best.

In case you are wondering about the availability of a Big Mac, be reassured that there are 14 **McDonald's** in the city. **Pizza Hut** has two city branches; and **KFC** has one in the city and one at Darling Harbour.

Often you will find restaurants that we have not listed in the same street as the ones included above. Our list gives you somewhere to start and an idea of what is on offer. On weekends, it is a wise idea to phone ahead and book a table.

Entertainment

As mentioned in the Introduction chapter, the Friday edition of The Sydney Morning Herald has 'Metro', and the Thursday edition of the Daily Telegraph has '7 Days' which list what's on at all of Sydney's night spots.

Jazz Venues

The Basement, *29 Reiby Place, City*, ☎9251 2797. Open ☾open nightly for dinner, Mon-Fri for lunch. Features modern local and international artists and serves contemporary Australian food. Excellent music and food. Guaranteed to have a good time. For jazz lovers.

Soup Plus, *383 George Street, City*, ☎9299 7728. Open ☾Mon-Thu noon-midnight, Jazz 7:30-midnight; Fri-Sat noon-1am; Jazz 8pm-12.30am.Strawberry Hills Hotel, 453 Elizabeth Street, Surry Hills, ☎9698 2997. Open ☾Mon-Thurs 11am-midnight. Fri-Sat 11am-12.30am. Sun noon-10.30pm.

The Classics

The **Sydney Opera House** is the venue in Sydney for opera, ballet, and performances by the Sydney Symphony Orchestra.The newly refurbished Sydney Town Hall is also the scene of musical evenings. The 'Metro' lift out magazine from the Sydney Morning Herald has the information on programs, locations and times every Friday.

Theatres

Sydney has a vibrant theatre scene, and the local talent compares favourably with the rest of the world.The large theatres have cocktail bars for pre-show or intermission drinks, and most of them have banned smoking in these areas, as well as in the auditoriums themselves. Some theatres have restaurants attached, where service is geared to getting patrons into the theatre on time. Then there are the small theatre groups, and local dramatic and musical societies, whose performances are quite professional and you may see a star in the making. For example, **NIDA**, the National Institute of Dramatic Art (where Mel Gibson learnt his craft) presents plays at The Parade Theatre at 215 Anzac Parade, Kensington, ☎*9697 7613*, opposite the main entrance to the University of New South Wales. Prices vary according to the production but range from ♦$17 to $20, not much more than you pay to see Mel in a movie.

Half-tix

Speaking of prices, Sydney has a Half-tix booth in Darling Park, 201 Sussex Street, at the base of the IBM building, and it sells tickets to major venues at half price on the day of the performance.It is ⊕open between 9am and 5pm Monday to Friday, and 10am-3pm Saturday. The phone number for selections and reservations is ☎*9286 3310* and for the head office, ☎*9966* 1723. All major credit cards are accepted. They have a website at ▇www.halftix.com.au

Major Theatres

The **Sydney Opera House** has two theatres - the Drama Theatre, which seats 544, and the Playhouse, which seats 398. The Box Office is ⊕open Mon-Sat 9am-8.30pm, and charge

telephone bookings may be made, ☎*9250 7777*. There are several eateries at the Opera House itself, or you can choose from those in the area of Circular Quay.

Her Majesty's Theatre, *107 Quay Street*, ☎*9212 3411*, is close to Central Railway Station and within walking distance of the restaurants of Chinatown.

Capitol Theatre, *13 Campbell Street, Haymarket*, ☎*9320 5000* for recorded show information, or ☎*9266 4800* for bookings. The theatre is in Haymarket, near Chinatown.

The Theatre Royal, *MLC Centre, King Street*, ☎*9231 6111*, is in the heart of the city.

The Ensemble Theatre, *78 McDougall Street, Milsons Point*, ☎*9224 8444*, is situated in the Lower North Shore and has its own restaurant.

The Wharf Theatre, *Pier 4, Hickson Road, Millers Point (The Rocks)*, ☎*9250 1700*, also has a restaurant, ☎*9250 1761*.

Belvoir Street Theatre, *25 Belvoir Street, Surry Hills*, ☎*9699 3444*, doesn't have a restaurant, but does have a licensed bar offering light snacks before and after the show.

Seymour Theatre Centre, *Cnr Cleveland Street and City Road, Chippendale*, ☎*9531 7940*, has three theatres - the York, Everest and Downstairs, and a very good restaurant, ☎*9692 4138*. There is also a coffee and snack bar in the upstairs foyer.

The Footbridge Theatre, *Sydney University, Parramatta Road, Glebe*, ☎*9692 9955* or *9266 4800* (bookings), is actually in the grounds of Sydney University. It doesn't have a restaurant of its own, but there are plenty in nearby Glebe.

Small Theatres

Stables Theatre, *10 Nimrod Street, Kings Cross*, ☎*9361 3817*.

Bay Street Theatre, *75 Bay Street, Glebe*, ☎*9692 0977*.

New Theatre, *542 King Street, Newtown*, ☎*9519 3403*.

Pilgrim Theatre, *262 Pitt Street, City*, ☎*9261 8981*.

Enmore Theatre, *116 Enmore Road, Enmore*, ☎*9550 3666*.

These small theatres may not have a current presentation when you are in town, and others not mentioned here may have something that you would be interested in seeing. Check 'Metro' for details. More live cinemas are found in the suburbs.

Cinemas

The main cinema area in the city is in George Street, between Park and Liverpool Streets.Here you will find:

George Street Cinemas (Hoyts C and Greater Union), *505 George Street*, ☎*1902 26 3456*. There are also many cinemas in the large suburban shopping areas.

Three independent cinemas in the city are **Dendy**, *Opera Quays, Circular Quay*, ☎*9247 3800* and *261 King Street Newtown*, ☎*9550 5699* and then there's **Reading Cinemas**, *Level 3, Market City, Haymarket (at Chinatown)*, ☎*9280 1202*.

As a general rule, Tuesday is half-price night at all cinemas, although some offer discounts on other nights.

Shopping
The City

Sydney has a large shopping area in the city, stretching from Park Street in the south to Hunter Street, with shops along George, Pitt, Castlereagh and Elizabeth Streets, which run south-north, and Market, King and Hunter Streets, which run roughly east-west. The section of Pitt Street between Market and King Streets is a pedestrian mall, with many arcades connecting it to both Castlereagh and George Streets. The closest railway stations to the shopping areas are Town Hall, Wynyard, St James and Martin Place. If on the day you have set aside to shop, the heavens open and the rain pours down, remember it is possible to walk from Town Hall Station to the MLC Centre in Martin Place without venturing out of doors. It is rather a convoluted route, but there are signs pointing you in the right direction. Basically, from the station take the arcade under the Queen Victoria Building to Grace Bros, then from the first floor of Grace Bros take the overpass to Centrepoint, then travel across the Imperial Arcade, Glasshouse and Skygarden shopping centres to the King Street overpass, and, voila, you are in the MLC Centre. Of course, if the weather is warm and sunny, forget this option and stroll through the Mall.

Shops are normally ☺open Mon-Wed 9am-5.30pm, Thurs 9am-9pm, Fri 9am-6pm, Sat 9am-5pm, Sun 11am-4pm, but this is not a hard and fast rule. Some open earlier and close later, particularly on Sunday, and many suburban supermarkets are open until late at night six days a week, and until around 6pm on Sunday.

The shops in the tourist areas are open every day, usually with extended hours.

Souvenirs

If you are only interested in buying souvenirs, such as cuddly koalas and kangaroos, T-shirts, etc.., it is probably best to head for the tourist areas, such as The Rocks, Darling Harbour or Circular Quay. Other 'typically Sydney' souvenirs are found in the range of goods at the Done Art and Design Shops at The Rocks, Darling Harbour, Queen Victoria Building and the departure level of the International Airport. Ken Done is a local artist who produces very colourful works of art featuring the harbour, the bridge, the opera house, koalas, kangaroos, etc... These paintings are reproduced on material and his wife, Judy, designs a spectacular range of sportswear, swimwear, homewares, bags, stationery - in fact, just about everything you can think of can be found in their shops.

Department Stores

There are a several department stores , chief among them being David Jones which has two stores diagonally opposite each other in Market Street. It is an upmarket store where bargaining does not happen unless you have found a product cheaper in another shop - but you must have proof. Grace Bros owned by the retail giant Coles Myer also has a shop on Market Street. There is another department styled complex off Argyle Street in The Rocks.

The city abounds with arcades with lots of small stores - Town Hall Arcade that links Wynyard Station with the Queen Victoria Building. Then off Pitt Street there is Centrepoint where you can get a lift to view Sydney from the tower, Glasshouse on the Mall, Imperial Arcade that boasts an excellent bookshop in Angus and Robertson that goes the length of the Arcade on the lower ground floor.

Also running off Pitt Street Mall is the Strand Arcade which has a rather quaint air about it. The best thing going for it is the Darrell Lea sweet shop at the George Street end. Clothes here cost a bomb. Then there is mid city centre where the food hall is relatively inexpensive. Further south is the MLC centre which is really a destination shop for an expensive latte and jewellery. The Theatre Royal makes up part of the complex. Wynyard Arcade has been renovated and is situated inside the station and has specialty shops of its own as well as access to Westpac Plaza and the Hunter Connection. Chifley Plaza situated on Hunter, Elizabeth and Phillip Streets is home to, among other not-so-well-known names, the local branch of Tiffany's. In case you want something to put in your rucksack.

The Queen Victoria Building has become quite a landmark. It has gone from being an eyesore in the 70s to being a grand byzantine styled building with layer upon layer of boutiques, shops. The main entrance facing the Town Hall and the intersection of Park and George Street has a gross statue of Queen Victoria. It was a bicentennial gift of the Irish Government. When they had the uprising in the 1920s and Ireland became a republic rather than smash this statue that faced their parliament, the Irish had it put in storage for a rainy day when they could give it to someone. Well, Sydney town got it! That requires imagination.

The building has a royal theme with replicas of the Crown Jewels on the top level and the Royal Automata Clock performing on the hour between 9am and 9pm daily.

Darling Harbour also has the Harbourside Festival Marketplace with 200 shops from boutiques to souvenirs, sportswear to art, and restaurants, cafes and bars. It is a bazaar for overseas visitors rather than for Sydneysiders, and the refit was no doubt pitched at attracting the Olympic crowds. You may want to mozy down there for a look.

Markets
The Rocks Market

Every Saturday and Sunday, at the end of George Street in The Rocks, a sail-like canopy transforms the area into a Portobello Road. It is not an exceptionally large market, but it has many interesting articles for sale, and the Victorian terraces, pubs and old warehouses that surround it contribute to a holiday atmosphere year round. Nearby there are plenty of cafes, outdoor food stalls and restaurants.

Paddy's Markets

There are two locations: The original Paddy's is in Haymarket, on the corner of Hay and Thomas Streets, near Chinatown. It is open Fri-Sun 9am-4pm.The other is on Parramatta Road, Flemmington, and it is open Fri 10am-4.30pm and Sun 9am-4.30pm. There are over 1000 stalls in each location selling fashion garments, footwear, jewellery, household and electrical goods, takeaway foods, fresh fruit and vegetables,

poultry, seafood, and heaps and heaps of souvenirs.

Paddy's is the biggest market in Australia, and for further information, phone the Hotline - ☎ 1300 361 589.

Other areas
Paddington Bazaar, corner of Oxford and Newcombe Streets, Paddington, ☎ 9331 2646.
Balmain Saturday Market, corner Darling Street and Curtis Road, Balmain, ☎ 0418 765 736 (mobile). **Glebe Markets,** cnr Glebe Point Road and Derby Place. See Toruism office for more details.

City Sights

It is not possible to see the sights of the city of Sydney in one day on a walking tour, even if you are super-fit. Apart from the distance, Sydney is not a flat city, and the hills would slow you down. By taking advantage of The Sydney Explorer bus (see Local Transport) you could catch a glimpse of everything, but you still wouldn't have time to appreciate what you saw. It is best to allot at least a few days for the city itself before you spread your wings to the outer attractions. So this guide is set out in areas, perhaps you should allow one day per area. Note that all museums are closed on Christmas Day and Good Friday.

The grid references shown below refer to the colour map of Sydney (pages 34-35).

Circular Quay Area
Sydney Harbour Bridge E11

Affectionately known to Sydneysiders as 'The Coathanger' the Sydney Harbour Bridge dominates the city skyline. It is

503m long, and was completed in 1932 after nine years of construction. It was built from either shore, and when the two halves met they were only 7.6cm (3 inches in the old measurements) out of alignment! The Bridge opened with a piece of drama. The dignitaries were lined up, the Premier, Jack Lang, stepped forward to cut the ribbon, and up rode Captain de Groot on a noble steed. He slashed the ribbon with his sword, and all and sundry stood speechless, at least for a few seconds. The miscreant was apprehended, the ribbon was rejoined, and the ceremony continued. In August, 1992, came the opening of the long-awaited harbour tunnel, which has lived up to its expectations in reducing peak hour traffic snarls on the bridge. You can't walk through the tunnel but you can walk over the bridge, and you can climb up the south-east pylon for some of the best harbour views. The pylon is ☉open daily 10am-5pm and admission is around ✪$2 adult.

A popular endeavour is offered by Bridge Climb, *5 Cumberland Street, The Rocks*. Included in the three hour package is a safety briefing and a magnificent walk up and across the great steel span. From the top of the bridge, spectacular views of Sydney by day or night are the reward for making it to the top, ☎ 9252 0077 for tickets, ☉7am-7pm, 7 days a week.From the bridge there is a good view of Sydney's newest crossing, the Glebe Island Bridge with its many suspension cables. The bridge has improved the traffic flow into the city from the west.

Sydney Opera House G10
This magnificent performing arts

complex is situated on Bennelong Point, which was named by Governor Phillip after an Aboriginal he befriended, taught English, and actually took back to England. This spot is apparently where Bennelong resided in his humpy. Shrouded in controversy during its construction, Sydney Opera House was finally completed in 1973, and has since become almost the symbol of Australia. Instantly recognizable anywhere because of its unique architecture, this extraordinary building can only really be appreciated when acknowledged as part of its surroundings. The design encapsulates the concept of architecture mimicking its environment: the white sails give the vague impression that the building is a cluster of vessels on the waters of Port Jackson. The Opera House has four theatres, four restaurants and six bars, and is surrounded by wide walkways. Details of current programs are published in the daily newspapers, and the Box Office is ⊙open Mon-Sat 9am-8.30pm and two hours prior to the start of a Sunday performance. Phone bookings may be made up to seven days prior to the performance, and the booking clerk will advise when payment must be made, or you can use your credit card. Front of House tours are held ⊙daily from 9am-4pm, departing every 30 minutes, and cost ✪$15 adults, $10 concession, ☎9250 7111. There are also tours on some Sundays that take visitors backstage and cost ✪$23 per person with no concessions. The availability of the backstage tours depends on whether there are rehearsals in the house. It is best to contact Guided Tours, on the Saturday before you would like your tour, on the above number. Bus no 438 travels down George Street to the concourse. Circular Quay Railway Station is the closest stop for train passengers. Surely one of the world's greatest marine backdrops, the combination of Sydney's premier icons, the Opera House and the Sydney Harbour Bridge, must be appreciated at every angle. On any crystal morning, the white roof of the House is resplendent in the sunlight. Nearby, the impressive span of the Bridge arches over passing yachts and small cruisers carving their white trails across the harbour. The source of Sydney's beauty in a nutshell.

Circular Quay   F8

It doesn't seem to matter when you visit the Quay, there are always lots of people around, but it is on weekends and holidays that you have the added colour and noise of all the buskers. From men playing classical pieces on violins, to little kids belting it out on a range of brass instruments, to Aborigines and (non-Aborigines) playing didgeridoos and teaching people to perform kangaroo and emu dances - it's all captivating entertainment. The Quay is the heart of the Sydney Ferry network. At any given time, at least one of these green-hulled vessels will be visible at the docks, either accepting passengers or waiting for them to disembark. They then make their way slowly to and from the middle harbour on routes that stretch north-east to Manly and west towards Parramatta River. It is a real mezcla of people milling in anticipation of their ferry; people hurrying to catch their train at the railway station; some buying tickets for harbour cruises; some fishing in the doubtful water near Wharf 5; others, the well-dressed ones, beginning their walk around to the Opera House for a ballet or opera matinee. A fairly recent and certainly controversial development has been established along the eastern promenade, stretching most of the way to the forefront of the Opera House. It is lined with up-market cafes, restaurants, shops and a movie cinema. The top levels are exclusive apartment residences. This imposing complex was initially dubbed 'The Toaster' by protesters who demonstrated on the steps of the Opera House in December 1996, during its construction, hoping to preserve the aesthetic quality of this landmark area. You can judge for yourself the final result. Circular Quay Railway Station, although not underground, is part of the City Circle, and the Cahill Expressway on top of the railway takes traffic from the Bridge to the Eastern Suburbs and Macquarie Street.

Museum of Sydney F7

Situated on the corner of Phillip and Bridge Streets, on the site of First Government House, this modern museum is ⊙open daily 10am-5pm and admission is ✪$7 adults, ☎9251 5988. It has an excellent cafe and a good bookshop, both of which can be visited without entering the museum. The bookshop specialises in architecture and design titles. There are also exhibits in the forecourt, and in the entrance foyer the foundations of Australia's first Government House are visible.

Other attractions:

Justice and Police Museum, for those interested in phrenology or medieval-style weaponry. 9 Phillip Street, ☎9252 1144.
Museum of Contemporary Art (MCA) For details of current exhibitions phone ☎9252 4033 or the Infoline on ☎9241 5892.

The Rocks

The Rocks   E9-E10
The Rocks nestles on the western edge of Circular Quay, the initial point of colonial settlement. Preservation of the area's heritage was the subject of conflict during the 1970s, but eventually common sense prevailed and the region has undergone restoration and improvement to become popular with both locals and tourists. The architecture transports the visitor to a previous era, and even products of modern consumerism attempt to blend in with the nostalgic theme.

The Sydney Visitor Centre E9

Steps beside Cadman's Cottage lead up to George Street, and if you turn right at the top of the steps you will come to the old Sailors' Home which now houses The Rocks Visitor Centre, ☎9255 1788. The Centre is ⊕open daily 9am-5pm, and has a very good video presentation on the first floor, of the growth of Sydney from a small penal colony to a thriving modern city. They carry brochures and maps for tourist attractions all over Sydney.

George Street   E9-E10

Continuing along George Street, there are many old historic buildings and pubs, and on the weekends the Bridge end of the street is closed off and The Rocks

Markets are held (see Shopping section). In the building on the right hand side of the markets there are some interesting craft displays and shops.

The Rocks Square   E9

The square is in the middle of Playfair Street (which is closed to traffic) and this area has many outdoor eateries, little shops, jazz or rock bands, and several lanes sprouting in all directions. Following Playfair Street to its end brings you to Argyle Street.

Other attractions:

Cadman's Cottage, is the oldest remaining house in Sydney. Presently an information centre for Sydney Harbour National Park, ☎9247 5033. Bars and restaurants are plentiful around this area. **Westpac Museum,** 6-8 Playfair St, ☎9763 5670, traces the history of the bank from 1817 as the Bank of NSW, to the present day of technological banking. **The Rocks Puppet Cottage, 77** Kendall Lane, ☎9241 2902. Displays hundreds of puppets and shows. **Susannah Place,**58-64 Gloucester Street, Susannah Place, ☎9241 1893, is a museum of the lifestyle from the 1840s. **Argyle Stores,** 18-24 Argyle Street, ☎9251 4800, around 5000 square metres of upmarket shopping. **Clocktower Square,** corner of Argyle and Harrington Streets with the clocktower, with several souvenir shops, a Japanese restaurant, and The Rocks Opal Mine, ☎9247 4974. **Millers Point,** the suburb on the opposite side of the Harbour Bridge to The Rocks. **Holy Trinity (Garrison) Church,** Argyle Street, built in 1848. **Argyle Place**The little park just

up the street, is Sydney's oldest village green

Sydney Observatory   D8

Watson Road, Observatory Hill, ☎9217 0485, has a regular program of exhibitions, films, talks and night viewings, and a hands-on exhibition. Great for star gazing.

S.H. Ervin Gallery   D8

National Trust Centre, almost next door to the Observatory. Was home to one of Sydney's leading girls' high schools. ☎9258 0173.

The Royal Botanical Gardens and Macquarie Street

The Gardens are a popular lunchtime spot for city workers, and weekends see many family picnics. They are situated on the edge of Farm Cove, where the early colonists first tried to grow vegetables. As you enter through the gate near the Opera House and climb the slight slope, the astonishing building to your right is Government House. It is the state's finest example of sophisticated Gothic Revival and took eight years to build, finally completed in 1845. Although the battlements, turrets and arches present it for all intents and purposes as a castle, defence was not one of the building's intended functions, and it was instead given over to the administration of colonial affairs. Surrounded by scenic gardens in one of the city's finest corners, it now acts as a pleasant welcoming venue for the Governor's official receptions. It is ⊕open to the public Fri-Sun 10am-3pm, ☎9931 5222. The garden belonging to the House is ⊕open every day 10am-4pm. The building at the end of the driveway leading from Government House is the Conservatorium of Music, which was originally the Governor's stables. Signposts point the way to Mrs Macquarie's Chair, a rock outcrop where the Governor's wife apparently sat to watch for ships arriving from England.

The small remote island you can see in the centre of the harbour is Fort Denison. For a short time it was regarded notoriously among early convicts as the most inescapable gaol of the colony and the destination of wayward miscreants. The nickname 'Pinchgut' evolved from the starvation men unlucky enough to spend time on the island experienced. Poorly treated and unfit to attempt a fleeing swim, these criminals were naturally inappreciative of their otherwise superb location. Feared and despised in those times, the fort is now a prime location commanding one of the best views of the city and harbour. It was built as part of Sydney's defences, and has come under the jurisdiction of the National Parks and Wildlife Service, as part of Sydney Harbour National Park. Tours of Fort Denison leave from Wharf 6, Circular Quay, but must be booked in advance, ☎9247 5033 (NPWS at Cadman's Cottage). The tour costs ✪$16 for adults.

Back on land, the footpath by the sea wall leads to the Visitors Centre and shop, a kiosk, and a restaurant; and signposts show the way to the herbarium, the pyramid glasshouse and other exhibits. There are two exits near the pyramid, one on to Macquarie Street, the other leads to the Art Gallery. The Royal Botanical Gardens are ⊙open daily 8am to sunset, ☎9231 8125.

Art Gallery of New South Wales   G5

The Art Gallery is in Art Gallery Road, in the Botanical Gardens, and faces The Domain. It is a spectacular building, housing a vast contemporary collection of Australian, European and Asian Art, and a fine collection of Aboriginal paintings and artefacts. The names of famous artists are set in stone on the front of the building, upon the tier just below the roof level. Two statues of mounted horseman grace the patches of lawn on either side of the entrance. Many special exhibitions are held at the Gallery, and for recorded information on current exhibits, ☎9225 1744 or ☎9225 1790. Free guided tours of the Gallery are available - check at the information desk on your left as you walk into the gallery through the vestibule. There is no charge for admission to the Gallery and its permanent collection, but a fee is levied for special exhibitions.There is a restaurant and a coffee shop, and the Gallery is ⊙open daily, 10am-5pm. In this enriching environment, you can immerse yourself in culture and history before relaxing and reflecting among the flora of the Domain across the road or in the Botanical Gardens nearby.

The Domain   G5

The Domain is the large grassed area between the Art Gallery and the Public Library. It is a peaceful park setting for soap box orators on Sundays, and the venue for a number of Sydney'sfree summertime open-air concerts, such as Opera in the Park and Symphony in the Park.

Parliament House   F6

Situated in Macquarie Street, Parliament House has experienced several additions, removals, renovations and upgrades since its initial construction in 1816. It is a combination of styles - from Georgian to Victorian to contemporary - which have been carefully designed over the years to blend the variety and preserve the pleasant small scale of the building despite necessary expansions. The most recent challenge was the attachment of a twelve-storey office block to the existing framework, and its relative obscurity was accomplished by setting part of it underground, so that the new floors are only visible from the Domain at the rear rather than spoiling the Macquarie Street frontage.The House is open to visitors, and they can even attend a session. Parliament generally sits from mid-February to early May, and from mid-September to early December, on Tues, Wed and Thurs. ⊙For information on hours, ☎9230 2111.

St Mary's Cathedral F4

The Cathedral, on the corner of College Street and St Mary's Road, ☎9220 0400, is a magnificent example of revival Gothic architecture in Hawkesbury sandstone, out-matched in its style only by Government House. Outstanding stained-glass window, depicts scenes from the life of the Blessed Virgin Mary, and the early days of the Catholic Church in Australia. Under the Cathedral is a crypt where the Catholic Archbishops of Sydney are interred, and there is also an exhibition on the background of the Cathedral and the plans for its future. The Chapter Hall is the earliest building on the site. Built in Gothic Revival style between 1843 and 1845, it was to form part of a Benedictine Monastery planned to include the original cathedral. The monastery was never completed. Another attraction of the Cathedral is its world-famous choir which sings every Sunday at the 10.30am Mass. Daily Masses Monday to Friday are 6.45am, 1pm, 5.30pm

Hyde Park   F5-F2

Here you'll find the impressive Archibald Fountain. Its fanning peacock-spray captures the attention of people strolling through the northern section of Hyde Park. Hyde Park is bounded by Queen's Square, College Street, Liverpool Street and Elizabeth Street. The Anzac War Memorial, with the tomb of the Unknown Soldier and the Pool of Reflection, is in the southern section. Protruding from its lush surrounds, this enormous monument commemorates those Australians who gave their lives in wars.

Sydney Tower   E5

Now burdened with the most overbearing advertisement visible, AMP Sydney Tower soars over 300m above the city, and is the highest public building in the Southern Hemisphere. It is located above the Centrepoint Shopping Complex, bounded by Pitt, Market and Castlereagh Streets. From the Market Street foyer take the lift to the Podium Level, then board one of three double-decker lifts that will

take you to the Observation Level (Level 4). Here there are high-powered binoculars, an illuminated display of Sydney Harbour's water traffic, a tourist booking and information service, audio and guided tours. Level 3 has the highest coffee lounge in Australia; Level 2 has a self-service revolving restaurant; and Level 1 has an a-la-carte up-market restaurant. The Observation Level is ☉open daily 9am-10.30pm Sun-Fri and 9.30am-11pm on Saturday. A general tour is available, lasting between 30 and 45 minutes. The 76-floor ascension costs adults ✪$20, ☎9229 7444.

Chinatown   D2

Continue down George Street, turn right at Goulburn Street, and the first turn on the left will bring you to Chinatown, which has the usual amount of restaurants, delicatessens and herbalists. From here it is a short walk to Paddy's Markets, the Entertainment Centre and the restored Capitol Theatre.

Darling Harbour

Darling Harbour is Sydney's newest area, and is nearly half the size of the Sydney Business District at 54ha (133 acres). The Conference Centre, Exhibition Centre, Maritime Museum, Aquarium, IMAX Theatre, Chinese Gardens and Sega World can all be found here. A short distance away is the Entertainment Centre, the penultimate venue for concerts. On weekends families can be seen strolling along the walkways, picnicking on the grass and having a pleasant time. There is always something on at Darling Harbour. Every weekend there

is a program of entertainment, and almost every yearly festival or show has changed its venue to this central area - the Home Show, the Boat Show, Navy Week, Music Festivals, Book Fairs, Antique Fairs, and the list goes on. For information on special events when you are in town, phone the Darling Harbour Infoline on, ☎1902 260 568. Alternatively, you can visit the Darling Harbour Information Centre, situated between the IMAX Theatre and Sega World, or phone them directly on, ☎9286 0111. Their web site is at ▨www.darlingharbour.com.au

Darling Harbour Super Ticket

Several of the attractions at Darling Harbour have banded together to offer reductions in the form of the Darling Harbour Super Ticket, which can be purchased at any of the information booths at Darling Harbour, the Sydney Aquarium, the Monorail, the Chinese Garden, or at Matilda Cruises. The cost is ✪$45 adults, which may sound a bit expensive, but this is what you receive: A two hour Matilda Harbour Cruise, entry to Sydney Aquarium, discount entry to IMAX theatre, discount entry to the Powerhouse Museum, a ride on the Monorail, a visit to the Chinese Gardens and lunch at the Shark Bite Restaurant at the Aquarium. When you add all that, the ticket is definitely worth considering. Also, all sections of the ticket can be used on the one day, or you can use some sections on that day, and the rest are good for one month from the date of issue. The ticket also has a few optional extras, such as discount on the People Mover and on the bus fare to Homebush Bay.

Sydney Harbour Bridge

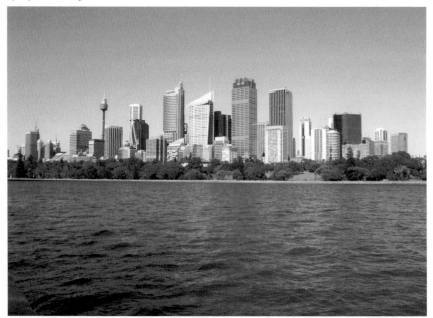

The City Centre from Farm Cove

Cockle Bay Wharf   C4

Located on the city side of Darling Harbour, this is the area's latest development. Modern, innovative and precise architecture is a feature of the construction, complemented by the space-age IMAX Theatre hovering at its southern end. Cockle Bay is worth visiting for its photogenic appeal alone, but there is much more. During the lunch hour and in the evening, corporate types stream from their multi-windowed offices in Sussex Street, behind the wharf, to patronize the many cafes, bars and restaurants found along this trendy strip. At night, an influx of people eager to participate in the atmosphere ensures the area bustles with life. Both a nightclub and a pub can also be found along the promenade, and the restaurants are outstanding. It is definitely a recommended place to dine, and two excellent choices are Coast, ☎9267 6700, and Nick's, ☎9264 1212, if you don't mind lightening your wallet.

Sydney Aquarium   C5

The Aquarium is located near the city end of Pyrmont Bridge, and is one of the largest and most spectacular in the world. The numerous tanks and tunnels allow the visitor to experience life on the ocean floor, surrounded by hundreds of different species of marine life. There are also displays of river systems, crocodiles, rocky shores, and the Great Barrier Reef. A touch pool allows you to get your hands onto some rough and spiky creatures. The Aquarium is ☉open daily 9.30am-9pm, and admission is ✪$22 adult, ☎9262 2300. The Shark Bite Restaurant has plenty

to tempt your taste buds while you are here.

Australian National Maritime Museum   B5

The museum, at the western end of Pyrmont Bridge, is dedicated to helping people understand and enjoy Australia's ongoing involvement with the sea. Among the craft moored at the museum are yachts, warships, tugboats, and a refugee boat. Free guided tours of the Museum building are available at regular intervals throughout the day, and a booking must be made at the Information Counter on arrival. Audio tours are also available from the Information Counter - ✪$3 adults, $5 for 2 adults sharing. The museum has a program of changing exhibitions, and information can be obtained by phoning the recorded information line on, ☎1900 962 002, or for general information, ☎9298 3777. There is also a library, a kiosk on the waterfront, and a shop with a wide range of nautical gifts. The museum is ☉open daily 9am-5pm (closes at 6pm in January), and minimum general admission is ✪$10 adult. There are extra charges for special exhibitions.

The Powerhouse Museum B2

While you are in Harris Street, you continue in the direction away from the water until you arrive at Australia's largest museum, The Powerhouse Museum, on your left. Created from the shell of an old Sydney power station, the museum is alive with dynamic exhibitions, hands-on fun and special performances. There is so much to see that some people spend the whole day wandering

through this incredible exhibition. Tours, talks, films, performances, demonstrations and workshops are continually in progress, and there is the Ken Done Restaurant (painted by, guess who?) and a kiosk when you need sustenance. As always, there is a souvenir/book shop, but this one offers some unusual merchandise. The Powerhouse Museum is ☉open daily 10am-5pm. Admission is ✪$8 adults, and the first Saturday of every month is free, ☎9217 0100. Back at Darling Harbour proper, the Exhibition Centre is the next group of buildings, and information on current shows is available from the Infoline. In front of the centre is Tumbalong Park, and from there it is a short walk to the next attraction.

The Chinese Garden C2

The Garden is the largest and most elaborate outside China. ☉open daily 9.30am-5pm and admission is ✪$4.50 adults. Across Pier Street from the Chinese Garden is the Sydney Entertainment Centre. Chinatown is opposite the main entrance to the Centre.

IMAX Theatre   C3

There is no way you could miss this building - it is the strangely-shaped monolith painted with yellow and black squares. The theatre has a 900m2 movie screen, the largest size in the world, and seating for over 500 people. Programs have varied from documentaries on Antarctica and the Ocean to concerts, virtual roller-coaster rides and 3-dimensional cartoon features. Current showings are advertised in the daily newspapers on the same pages as the more conservative cinemas, or you can contact IMAX on ☎9281 3300. Admission is ✪$17.50 adults.

Star City Casino   A5

An $867 million testament to the Aussie love affair with luck and misfortune, Star City coaxes punters inside with its glittering neon lights and extravagant surrounds. The exterior looks as if it has been airlifted to the site directly from Vegas; you will either be disgusted by its tackiness or impressed with its dazzling lavishness. A mecca for the nocturnal, this enormous complex sprawls over almost three-and-a-half hectares and consists of a five star hotel, an apartment complex, a huge gaming room, the Lyric Theatre, the Showroom, 20 bars and restaurants, shops and a nightclub. If you are going to lose your money, you might find some comfort in doing it here in style - and knowing you are not alone. The casino is at 80 Pyrmont Street, Pyrmont, a short stroll from Darling Harbour, and its doors are open 24 hours, ☎9777 9000.

Other attractions
State Library of New South Wales, commonly referred to as the Mitchell Library, contains the nation's finest collection of Australiana and an amazing wealth of historical records. Corner of Macquarie St, ☎9230 1414. **The Mint,** it was here that the gold sovereigns were coined in 1816. ☎9217 0311. **Hyde Park Barracks,** ☎9223 8922, houses an impressive collection which showcases the lives of the early convicts. **The Australian Museum,** 6 College Street,

☎9230 6000. The Australian Museum is recognised as one of the foremost museums of its type in the world. **Martin Place,** is a wide pedestrian mall that stretches for five blocks from George Street to Macquarie Street. **Sydney Town Hall,** corner of George and Druitt Streets. Built between 1868 and 1889 in French Renaissance style. Its concert hall houses a pipe organ which ranks with the biggest and best in the world. The steps of Town Hall are often crammed with people. ☎8223 3815 for further information.

St Andrew's Cathedral, the oldest cathedral in Australia, south of Town Hall. **Harris Street Motor Museum,** Level 1, 320 Harris Street, ☎9552 3375. where you will find a spectacular array of classic machines from the earliest to the latest, with lots of hands-on exhibits. **Sydney Jewish Museum,** corner of Darlinghurst Road and Burton Street, Kings Cross (Jewish Holidays). ☎9360 7999.

⚓ Sydney Beaches

Sydney's coastline stretches for approximately 65km, from Palm Beach in the north, to Cronulla in the south. Most Sydneysiders have their 'favourite' beach, which is not necessarily the closest to their homes. Some people grew up living near one beach, then moved as an adult to another, but you will usually find them returning to their original haunt. The people who live here have a connection with the ocean that develops from a very early age; sand between the toes and watery foam lapping at the ankles are not cliches but sensations simply indicative of a way of

life. Most of the ocean beaches are patrolled during the summer months on the weekends and during school holidays. The lifesavers, who know what they are doing, erect flags in the safest part of the beaches, and people are requested to make sure they swim between these flags. If they don't, and get into difficulties, the lifesavers are not going to let them drown, but under reasonable circumstances it should not come to this point. If the beach is considered unsafe, perhaps because of a strong undertow or a very high tide, the lifesavers will close it and erect a sign warning people not to enter the water. Take notice of such signs and decide to spend the day somewhere else. Board riders are given their own stretch of beach, so that they don't interfere with swimmers, and swimmers should keep out of designated board areas.

On weekends, Lifesavers in this country are not paid for the hours they spend on duty. They are willing volunteers who give freely of their time to keep our beaches safe. Harbour beaches are not patrolled. It must not be assumed that the harbour is one giant swimming pool. There are several places where shark-nets have been strung across inlets, and these are the only places where you should venture into the water. You won't see one, but there are sharks in Sydney Harbour. It is generally believed that old sharks, unable to fend for themselves in the open sea, come into the harbour for easy feeding - and what could be easier than a human thrashing around? Of course, there are also sharks in the open ocean, but the surf patrols on these beaches keep a sharp lookout, and sound alarms if a shark is sighted. You may not have caught a wave all day, but if a shark alarm sounds it is incredible how quickly you can get yourself back on the beach. Having said all that, there has not been a shark attack in Sydney since 1963, when two children were taken whilst swimming in Middle Harbour.

🚗 Ocean Beaches

Listed below are the beaches stretching from Palm Beach in the north to Bundeena in the south, with the closest main road, and the public transport that gives access.Also included is the following information for each venue:
• Dressing Shed - usually will include showers and toilets.
• Patrolled - in summer on weekends and during school holidays, ie from the first weekend in October to Easter the following year.
•Pool - rock pool suitable for children.
• Board - surf is suitable for board riders.
• Surfers - surf is suitable for body surfers.
Usually beaches back onto a park or a reserve, and there are clear directions on the major roads indicating the way to the beach. Most beaches tend to have some topless sunbathers during the hottest parts of the day

North of the Harbour

Palm Beach, off Barrenjoey Road, was once mainly frequented by the wealthy and yuppy set. It has now become very popular with British tourists because it is the setting for the TV series Home and Away. Dressing shed, patrolled, surfers and board, pool south end. About one-and-a-half hours drive from the city centre. Bus no 190 from Wynyard.

Whale Beach, off Barrenjoey Road. Dressing shed, patrolled, surfers and board, pool south end. Bus 190 from Wynyard, Bus 193 from Avalon (infrequent service).

Avalon Beach, off Barrenjoey Road. Dressing shed, patrolled, surfers and board, pool south end. Bus 190 from Wynyard.

Bilgola Beach, off Barrenjoey Road. Dressing shed, patrolled, surfers and board. Bus 190 from Wynyard.

Newport Beach, off Barrenjoey Road. Dressing shed, patrolled, surfers and board. Bus 190 from Wynyard.

Bungan Beach, off Barrenjoey Road. Patrolled, board. Bus 190 from Wynyard.

Mona Vale Beach, off Barrenjoey Road. Top end not patrolled (Bongin Bongin). Dressing shed, patrolled south end, surfers south end, board north end. Bus 157 from Manly, Bus 184 from Wynyard (peak hour).

Warriewood Beach, off Pittwater Road. Dressing shed, patrolled surfers and board. Bus 157 from Manly.

Turimetta Beach, off Pittwater Road. Not patrolled, board. Buses 155 and 157 from Manly.

Narrabeen Beach, off Pittwater Road. Dressing shed, patrolled, surfers and board. Buses 182 and 190 from Wynyard, Buses 155 and 157 from Manly.

Collaroy Beach, off Pittwater Road adjoining Narrabeen Beach. Dressing shed, patrolled, surfers and board, pool at southern end. Buses 182 and 190 from Wynyard. Buses 155 and 157 from Manly.

Collaroy Basin, off Pittwater Road. Surfers, little swell. Via Collaroy Beach.

Long Reef Beach, off Pittwater Road. Dressing shed, patrolled, surfers and board. Bus 182 and 190 from Wynyard, Bus 155 and 157 from Manly.

Dee Why Beach, Howard Street, off Pittwater Road, adjoins Long Reef Beach. Dressing shed, patrolled, surfers and board, pool south end. Bus 178 and 180 from Queen Victoria Building, Bus 190, 182, 184 from Wynyard.

Curl Curl Beach, Oliver Road, off Pittwater Road. Dressing shed, patrolled, surfers and board, pool south end. Bus 136 from Manly.

Freshwater (Harbord) Beach, Oliver Road, via Pittwater Road. Dressing shed, patrolled, surfers and board, pool north end. Bus 139 from Manly.

Queenscliff Beach, off Pittwater Road. Dressing shed, patrolled, surfers and board, pool north end.Bus 136 and 139 from Manly.

North Steyne Beach, off Pittwater Road, adjoins Queenscliff Beach. Dressing shed, patrolled, surfers and board. See Manly Beach for travel information.

Manly Beach, off Pittwater Road, adjoins North Steyne Beach. Dressing shed, patrolled, surfers and board. Bus 169 from Wynyard or Buses 143 and 144 from Chatswood, ferry from Circular Quay, Jet Cat from Circular Quay. Peak hour bus services available from Wynyard.

Shelly Beach, off Darley Road. Sheltered area with little swell, suitable for swimmers. Between Shelly Beach and Manly Beach there is a pool at Fairy Bower. Via Manly Beach.

South of the Harbour

Bondi Beach, via Bondi Road off Old South Head Road. Dressing shed, patrolled, surfers and board, sanctioned topless area south end, pool at south end. Bus 380 and 389 from Circular Quay, 365 from Edgecliff. An internationally famous beach, Bondi can attract more than 40,000 people on a sunny Sunday afternoon.

Tamarama Beach. Off Bronte Road. Dressing shed, surfers and board. Bus 360 and 361 from Bondi Junction.

Bronte Beach, off Bronte Road. Squeezed between Tamarama and Clovelly it can experience some rough surf at times. Dressing shed, patrolled, surfers and board, pool south end. Bus 378 from Railway Square.

Clovelly Beach, off Clovelly Road. Dressing shed, patrolled. Bus 339 and 340 from Millers Point. Although Clovelly has a sandy foreshore, it is more like a swimming pool than a beach.

Coogee Beach, off Coogee Bay Road. Dressing shed, patrolled, surfers and board, pool south end. Bus 372 from Railway Square, Bus 373 from Circular Quay (Pitt Street).

Maroubra Beach, Fitzgerald Avenue, off Anzac Parade. Dressing shed, patrolled, surfers and board. Bus 395 from Railway Square, Bus 396 from Circular Quay.

Wanda Beach, off The Kingsway. Dressing shed, patrolled, surfers and board. Catch a train to Cronulla and then make the short walk to beach.

Elouera Beach, adjoins Wanda Beach. Dressing shed, patrolled, surfers and board, pool south end. Train to Cronulla, walk to beach.

North Cronulla Beach, adjoins Wanda and Elouera Beaches, off The Kingsway. Dressing shed, patrolled, surfers and board, pool south end. Train to Cronulla, walk to beach.

South Cronulla Beach, off The Kingsway. Dressing shed, patrolled, surfers and board, pool north end. Train to Cronulla, walk to beach.

Shelly Beach, off Cronulla Street. Dressing shed, patrolled, surfers and board, pool south end. Train to Cronulla, walk to beach.

Harbour Beaches

There are hundreds of coves and bays around the harbour, but we are only including those that have shark-proof nets, changing facilities, takeaway food outlets, and picnic areas. Obviously the beaches on the harbour do not have waves.

Clifton Gardens, Chowder Bay. The bay is two bays north-east of Taronga Park Zoo. See your host for advice on this place.

Balmoral, Hunter's Bay. This is quite a pretty beach and is divided into two by Rocky Point. Bus 238 from Taronga Zoo, Bus 257 from Chatswood, or Bus 233 from Mosman Wharf.

Manly Cove, Manly. The swimming enclosure is adjacent to Manly Wharf, where the ferry from Circular Quay docks. Travel by Ferry, or Bus 144 from Chatswood.

Nielsen Park, between Vaucluse Road and Greycliffe Avenue, Vaucluse, in the eastern suburbs. Go to ▇www.littlehills.com for more info.

Taronga Park Zoo

The Zoo, ☎9969 2777, has Australia's best collection of native and exotic animals. Its main entrance (for car and bus access) is on Bradley's Head Road, but it is only a pleasant 12 minute ferry ride from Wharf 4 Circular Quay (leaving every half hour). Admission prices are ✪$21 adults. Taronga is ◔open every day, including Christmas Day, 9am-5pm, ☎9969 2777.

From **Mosman**, it is also a short bus ride, to Balmoral Beach. There's also the Spit Bridge, which opens to allow tall-masted boats to pass through into Middle Harbour, where they moor.

Manly

The Manly Visitor Information Centre, ☎9977 1088, is at North Steyne, on the beach opposite the Steyne Hotel. There are two websites to visit for this locality: ▇www.pcn.com.au and the official website of Manly Council, which is ▇www.manly.nsw.gov.au with an email address at ✉vic@manly.nsw. gov.au Probably the most popular attraction at Manly is Oceanworld, West Esplanade, ☎9949 2644. You have three options for getting close to the sea creatures: viewing them through the safety of glass, handling them in touch pools or - for the fearless - rubbing skin against scale with the sharks in the diving tank. Seals perform at 11.45am and 2pm. Oceanworld is open ◔10am-5.30pm and entry fees are ✪$16 adults.

Travelling to the inner eastern suburbs may seem that you have never left the city. The reason for this is that you really haven't. It is just that most of the streets have changed their names.

How To Get There
By Train

The Eastern Suburbs line runs to Kings Cross, Edgecliff and Bondi Junction.

By Bus

Buses to the eastern suburbs leave from Circular Quay and Railway Square.

By Ferry

Ferries travel from Circular Quay Wharf 4 to Double Bay, Rose Bay and Watsons Bay.

Attractions

The first suburb on this trip is **Kings Cross**, probably one of the best-known Sydney areas. The Cross is sleazy, of that there is no doubt, with its strip joints, sex shops and ladies of the night. But, if you drive through during the day mid-week, it may seem like any other suburb. It is when the sun drops that it comes into its own. There are some excellent restaurants and night spots, and there are some places where you have to be brave to enter. It is not the type of place where you talk to strangers, and believe me, there are some strange people walking the streets. Nevertheless, there are people who would think they had not seen Sydney if they hadn't been to the Cross. It is a haven for backpackers because of the number of cheap hostels, and it is certainly a central area. There are a couple of landmarks. The **El Alamein Fountain**, on the corner of Darlinghurst Road and Macleay Street, was built to commemorate the men of the Australian 9th Division who fought in North Africa during World War II. It is an unusually shaped ball of a fountain, and there are always hundreds of people in the park surrounding it.

A short walk away, although in a different suburb, is **Elizabeth Bay House**, at 7 Onslow Avenue, Elizabeth Bay, ☎ 9356 3022. It was built for the Colonial Secretary, Alexander Macleay and his wife Eliza, and is presently furnished to the period, 1839-1845. In its day it was considered to be the finest house in the colony, and its views over the harbour would have been even more impressive then than they are now. It is a two-storey house with a grand winding staircase, and is maintained by the Historic Houses Trust. It is ☺open Tues-Sun (Monday when a public holiday) 10am-4.30pm (except Christmas Day and Good Friday) and admission is ✪$7 adult.

Paddington is another suburb that seems to be part of the city, but it is a charming part. It has many crooked streets lined with pretty terrace houses that are decorated with Paddington Lace, a distinctive wrought-iron trimming. The original village was established in the 1840s and housed the workers building the Victoria Barracks. Parts of the original little town can be seen in the area bounded by Shadforth, Prospect and Spring Streets.

Darlinghurst Road links Kings Cross with Paddington, or you can follow **Oxford Street** from the city. Attractions in the area include numerous antique shops along Queen Street, and art galleries sprinkled along Oxford Street and the side streets. The **Paddington Village Bazaar** is held in the Uniting Church grounds every Saturday (see Shopping). **Victoria Barracks** in Oxford Street, next to the Town Hall, ☎ 9339 3170, is a Georgian-style building (1841-1848) and a living history of Australia's military. **The Army Museum** is ☺open on Sunday 10am-3pm. The **Sydney Cricket Ground** is a little further south, in Driver Avenue, Moore Park, ☎ 9360 6601. This famous and historic site continues to play host to many notable sporting events. A Sportspace Tour is available, guiding visitors through the complex and its memorabilia for ✪$20 adults, ☎ 9380 0383 (bookings essential).

Centennial Park in Oxford Street, was founded in 1888 to celebrate the centenary of the colony. The park is open daily sunrise-sunset, and there are facilities for hiring horses and bikes (see Sport). **Double Bay,** one of the most up-market suburbs in Sydney, is reached by bus from Elizabeth Street; or by train to Edgecliff and walking down New South Head Road. Known by Sydneysiders who can't afford to shop here as 'Double Pay', it is the most exclusive shopping area in Sydney, and all the well-known, top-class designers have outlets. The surrounding areas of **Darling Point, Point Piper, Vaucluse,** etc., are populated by people who can afford to shop here, and it is worth a visit. New South Head Road continues through **Rose Bay** and on to Vaucluse where it is worth visiting **Vaucluse House**, which dates from 1803. It was the home of William Charles Wentworth, one of the intrepid trio who first crossed the Blue Mountains, and the father of the

Australian Constitution. He, and his wife Sarah and their children, lived here from 1829 to 1853, and it's furnishings still recall that period. The house is set in 11ha with gardens, bushland and a harbour beach frontage, and has out-buildings and stables. The house is ⊕open Tues-Sun 10am- 4.30pm and Monday if it is a public holiday. Admission is ✪$6.50 adults. There are tearooms in the grounds, and they serve a-la-carte lunches, and Devonshire teas that you would die for. Bus 325 from Circular Quay stops at the front gate.

The end of New South Head road is **Watsons Bay**, which is on the Harbour, near South Head and the Harbour entrance. The area's most famous landmark is not, as some would say, the pub, nor is it Doyle's restaurant - it is **The Gap**, a cliff from which there are great views, and from where people have committed suicide by jumping into the ocean below. When things are not going too well for them, it is common for Sydneysiders to say that they are going to throw themselves off The Gap, although fortunately not many do. Nearby is the anchor from the ill-fated **Dunbar**, a barque which was to carry passengers and goods on a regular basis between Sydney and England, but was wrecked on the rocks of The Gap on its second voyage in August 1857. It was Sydney's worst shipping disaster, with 121 lives lost and only one survivor. From Watsons Bay you can follow Old South Head Road to Bondi Junction, or turn off Old South Head Road left onto Military Road and head for **Bondi Beach** and the other beaches to the south.

Bondi Junction is about 2km from the beach, and is the main bus/train link for public transport throughout this area. It is also quite a good shopping centre, and its branches of David Jones and Grace Bros are linked by the Oxford Street pedestrian Mall, which has many specialty shops. Bus no 280 runs between Bondi Beach and Bondi Junction.

South

The southern suburbs are for the most part either industrial or residential, and if you arrived by air, you have already travelled through parts of them. However, there are a few places that are historically interesting on the shores of Botany Bay. The two main areas are La Perouse, on the north head of Botany Head, and Kurnell on the south head.

How To Get There
By Train
There is no direct train route to La Perouse. To get to Kurnell, take the train to Cronulla, then local Bus 67 from the depot opposite the station, near Munroe Park.

By Bus
Bus no 398 runs from Circular Quay to La Perouse. The best transportation route to Kurnell is detailed above.

Attractions
La Perouse
Famous for it's snakepit and boomerang throwing. The **La Perouse Museum**, ☎ *9311 3379*, is housed in the Cable Station, inside a circle formed by the end of Anzac Parade. It contains many artefacts from the wrecks, as well as relics from their time in the Bay.

Kurnell
Kurnell has **Captain Cook's Landing Place,** an historic site of over 400ha. Cook landed at 3.00pm on April 28, 1770, and tradition maintains that the first person to step ashore was his wife's young cousin, Isaac Smith. The spot where he scrambled onto dry land is marked with a small obelisk, and there is a larger one dedicated to the discovery nearby. The site is also a monument to the Gwiyagal People, the Aboriginal tribe who inhabited the area at the time of European discovery. The **Discovery Centre**, in *Captain Cook Drive*, is ⊕open Mon-Fri 11am-3pm and 10am-4pm on weekends and public holidays, ☎ *9668 9111*. It is one of the major features of the site, with exhibits detailing Cook's life, exploits and achievements, including his notes and opinions on the country he had discovered. There are also scenic walks, picnic and barbecue areas, and an historic walk, and the visitor centre has maps and leaflets on everything you can see and do. The **Inner Western Suburbs** were settled in the early days of the colony and therefore have many buildings and homes from a bygone era.

How To Get There
By Bus
Buses 438, 440, 470 travel south along George Street and pass the beginning of Glebe Point Road, Glebe, but the buses that actually drive down Glebe Point Road are 431, 433, and 434. Bus no 433 continues on to Balmain. Bus 440 connects the city with Rozelle, passing through the suburbs of Camperdown, Annandale and Leichhardt.

By Ferry

Sydney Ferries travel between Circular Quay and three wharves in Balmain - Darling Street, Thames Street and Elliott Street.

Attractions

Glebe was first settled in the late 1700s as a church-owned estate. In a full turnaround, Glebe has become a trendy place to live again, and it has a small shopping centre with lots of art galleries and heritage shops. If you are here on a Saturday or Sunday, you might like to visit the **Glebe Markets**, held in Glebe Public School, on the corner of Glebe Point Road and Derby Place, ☎ 9660 4181.

Leichhardt has a large Italian population, and consequently a large number of Italian restaurants are found in the main streets of Parramatta Road and Norton Street. **Leichhardt Park**, at the end of Mary Street, has several football ovals, acres of parkland, and an attractively sited public swimming complex, ☎ 9555 8344, with views over Iron Cove.

Trendy **Norton Street's** newest addition is the Italian Forum. Most residents used to think that the closest they would ever come to Italy on their own doorstep was to venture into **Norton Street** and absorb the atmosphere of its Italian restaurant-lined sidewalk. Developers decided to go one step further. **The Italian Forum** is accessed through a narrow alley where buildings tower above and charming Tuscan flourishes grace the architecture. The end of the alley opens onto a stunning courtyard, surrounded by apartments, shops and restaurants, all mimicking something similar

to the typical image of a quaint Italian village (except for the commercialism). This is no down-market immitation - the restaurants are top-class, the boutiques are expensive and the apartments exclusive. A statue of Dante, ornate waterscapes and a bright selection of flowers help to round off the European feel, and transport you - at least temporarily - out of Sydney's lifestyle and into another. The Forum is located 100 metres from the intersection of Norton St and Parramatta Road on the eastern side.

Balmain is a trendy area now, rivalling Paddington with its quaint terraces, art galleries and alternative lifestyle shops, but it wins hands down in the restaurant department.

Wonderland Australia

Located near the M4, in outer western Sydney, **Wonderland** is 219ha (540 acres) of landscaped grounds in *Wallgrove Road, Eastern Creek,* and has Australia's longest wooden roller coaster, the Bush Beast. Other rides include The Demon, Space Probe and Snowy River Rampage. There are also many different kinds of theme shops, live shows and picnic spots. It is ⊙open 10am-5pm every day, ☎ 9830 9100 or ☎ 9830 9106 (recorded information). Admission is adults ✪$39. The Australian Wildlife Park, ☎ 9830 9187, also at Wonderland, is ⊙open daily 9am-5pm. Entry fees are ✪$18 adults. Shuttle buses run to the fun park from Mt Druitt, Fairfield, Blacktown and Rooty Hill train stations.

Also in Eastern Creek is the **Eastern Creek Raceway,** Brabham Drive, ☎ 9672 1000.

This venue has accommodated the 500cc Motor-bike Grand Prix, and hosts other races around the year.

Hawkesbury River

The River is 45km (28 miles) north of Sydney, and is dotted with historic towns such as Windsor, Richmond, Wilberforce, Pitt Town and Wisemans Ferry. It winds around Sydney's western outskirts through a natural forest area until finally meeting the sea at Brooklyn. One of the best ways to see it is to join the **Riverboat Postman** near the Hawkesbury River Railway Station in Brooklyn. This four hour cruise includes commentary and snacks. The cost is ✪$35 adults, ☎ 9985 7566. An alternative is to hire a house boat from the many on offer at Brooklyn, at the southern end of the Hawkesbury Bridge. Two such companies are Holidays Afloat Houseboats, ☎ 9985 7368, and House Boats Prestige, ☎ 9985 7744.

South of Sydney

Royal National Park

History

It is some 29km from the centre of Sydney, and covers 16,000ha of vegetation and landscape typical of the Sydney Basin sandstone. The original inhabitants of the area were the Aboriginal people of the Dharawal tribe. There are waterfalls at Wattamolla, Curracurrong, Uloola and National Falls.

How to Get There

By Rail

Trains on the Illawarra-Cronulla line stop at Loftus, Engadine, Heathcote, Waterfall and Otford, and from these stations there are walking tracks into the Park.

Water Taxi

Sydney Opera House

By Ferry

Cronulla National Park Ferry Cruises, ☎ 9523 2990, have a service from the wharf near Cronulla railway station to Bundeena, and the trip takes 25-30 minutes. The first ferry from Cronulla leaves at 5.30am Mon-Fri on the hour to 6.30pm, 8.30am Sat-Sun and public holidays on the hour to 6.30pm. The last ferry leaves Bundeena daily at 7pm (summer), 6pm (winter). It should be noted that Bundeena is not within the Royal National Park.

Visitor Information

A Visitor Centre and Wildlife Shop is on Farnell Avenue, Audley. Call into the centre for advice on all aspects of your park visit. Permits for camping are obtained here. It is ⊙open daily 8.30am-4pm, ☎ 9542 0648. The shop sells books, film, maps, posters, gifts and souvenirs.

Park Entrance Fee

Bus - ◎$3.00 per adult. Must display pensioner card. There is no charge for people who hike into the park for the day.

Park Regulations

All fauna, flora, Aboriginal sites and rock formations are protected. Wildfires can destroy lives and property, so be careful, especially during the bushfire danger period (normally October to March). Use only the fireplaces provided and observe Total Fire Bans. Portable fuel stoves are required for camping. Pets and Firearms are not permitted in national parks.Vehicles, including motorbikes must keep to formed public roads. Drive carefully. Please use rubbish bins if

provided; or take rubbish with you when you leave the park.

Camping

Caravans and car camping are permitted at the camping ground at Bonnie Vale, off Bundeena Road. For reservations, ☎ 9542 0648. For site fees, you can expect to pay about ◎$10 per person for the first two people, and a couple of dollars per extra person. There are lots of places for bush camping throughout the park, however.booking and obtaining permits are essential.

Festivals

The **Festival of Sydney** is held during the entire month of January each year, and features include twilight and open-air concerts in the Domain, contemporary music at Hyde Park and Darling Harbour, outdoor movies at the Opera House, bike rallies, street theatre, and classical theatre performances at the Opera House, the Belvoir Theatre and the Seymour Centre. **Australia Day**, January 26, sees the city come alive, especially around the harbour, with all kinds of displays, and a Ferrython in which all the Sydney ferries compete.

The **Gay Mardi Gras** is organised by representatives of the gay and lesbian community, and is held on the first Friday in February each year. For visitors who are new to this scene, be aware that the parade's participants are often very expressive. Nudity and sexual insinuation are always prevalent here.

The **Royal Easter Show** is now held at Homebush Bay, the venue of the 2000 Olympics.The Show begins on the Friday before Good

Friday and finishes on Easter Tuesday. Advertised as "when the country comes to town", there's something for everyone, with displays of horticulture, livestock, crafts and hi-tech machinery. For kids, there are rides and sample bags, and for all ages there is non-stop entertainment in the show ring with livestock judging, trotting races, equestrian events, the Grand Parade, bands, sky divers, clowns, rodeos, and fireworks displays. The Show is well patronized by Sydneysiders with attendances on the public holidays reaching 100,000.

Anzac Day commemorates the actions of Australian and New Zealand troops involved in the conflict of the First World War, and the lives they sacrificed. The day falls on the 25 April, the same date that the soldiers landed on the shores of Gallipoli in 1914 and were overwhelmed by the Turkish resistance. Originally conceived as a lightning campaign, the conflict soon developed into an 8 month conflict during which time both sides sustained heavy casualties. Anzac Day services are held around the country and involve parades, marches, laying wreaths, minutes of silence, playing The Last Post and reciting the poem, For the Fallen. The opportunity is taken to reflect on all military losses since WWI. It remains a solemn and important day of remembrance in the Australian psyche.

The National Folkloric Festival is an annual multicultural event featuring dancers and musicians from many ethnic backgrounds. It is held in June, and begins with a Sunday parade that terminates at the Opera House, the scene for the many events of the following weekend.

St Patrick's Day seems to be gaining momentum every year. On the 17 March, thousands don a green item of clothing, grab a clover in one hand, and trot down to the nearest pub for a few pints or more of Guiness. The day is intended to mark the death of Ireland's patron saint and to commemorate his lifetime work of converting the country's entire population to Catholicism, but how this ties in with flagrant alcoholism remains something of a mystery. There is plenty of fun and good cheer, though halos are in scarce supply and the behaviour is often less than saintly!

The Biennale of Sydney is an international exhibition of contemporary art held every two years. Since its inception in 1973, the Biennale has brought the world's leading artists to Sydney, and more than 800 of them from over 45 countries have been exhibited. The Biennale is not only confined to Sydney as visiting artists travel giving lectures, workshops and artist-in-residence programs, and special lectures and displays are organised.

The Sydney to Hobart Yacht Race can hardly be classed as a festival, but it does generate a lot of excitement. Every Boxing Day thousands of people line the vantage spots around the harbour to watch the mini and maxi yachts set off on their adventure, and there are so many boats of all sorts on the harbour, farewelling the entrants, that it is a wonder they ever get through the Heads. The race is closely monitored by news crews in light aircraft, and

hourly reports are given on TV and radio as to who is in the lead, and by how much. Meanwhile, the people in Hobart get ready for the big welcoming party.

The City to Surf Fun Run is another annual event. Held every year in August, thousands of people of all ages assemble for the start of the run to Bondi Beach, and as the starting gun goes off, Park Street becomes a sea of people. Of course, the race is always won by a professional marathon runner, but winning is not really what the spectacle is all about. Everyone who finishes receives a certificate, and their names are listed in the newspapers. Even those who don't finish are congratulated for entering, and there is a real spirit of comradeship as you watch people helping each other along the way.

In addition to the above, each municipal area of Sydney has its own festival, and there are other special annual events, such as the blessing of the fishing fleet.

Public Holidays

Christmas, Boxing Day, New Year and Easter are obviously celebrated at the same time as everywhere else in the world. Other holidays that are enjoyed in Australia are: Australia Day - January 26. Anzac Day - April 25. Queen's Birthday - the second Monday in June. Labour Day - the first Monday in October. Another day is Bank Holiday, which is held on the first Monday in August, but only banks, government offices, insurance companies and the like are closed.

Sydney Olympic Park

Situated roughly in the geographic heart of metropolitan Sydney, the Olympic Park is 14km from the CBD, in the suburb of Homebush. Facilities include Stadium Australia, Bicentennial Park, the Sydney International Aquatic Centre, the State Sports Centre, as well as Tennis, Hockey and Archery facilities. Other features include a major metropolitan park, called Millennium Park, a golf driving range and an Olympic Village which accommodated 15,000 athletes which has now become a suburban dormitory suburb called Newington. A concentration on modern architecture is the definitive element of the Olympic site. From a distance the domes, arcs and cylindrical shapes of the venue seem to make it spring like a spaceport from science fiction out of its green surrounds.

Stadium Australia

This enormous stadium was the venue for the Opening and Closing Ceremonies, and will host many other notable competition events into the future. It has a seating capacity of 80,000 people.

State Sports Centre

The Centre is a multi-purpose venue designed to present a full spectrum of events. It has seating for 5000, and a clear floor area of 57m x 38m. Also in the Sports Hall is the Hall of Champions which honours Australia's champs in many sports. The State Softball Centre has two floodlit fields, warm-up facilities and accommodation for 3000 spectators. The State Hockey Centre has two synthetic pitches, flood lighting, and accommodation for 8000 spectators. There are also outdoor netball courts, training centres and plans for many more sporting facilities. For information about current programs at the Centre, phone the information line on, ☎9763 0111. Transport to Homebush Transport to the Olympic Site is by car, bus, river cat or rail (Olympic Park station). Guided tours of the Olympic Site are available, and perhaps the best way to explore this venue and all of the others in close proximity, is on the Olympic Explorer Bus (see under Local Transport).

Central Coast

Going to this area, just north of Sydney, assumes you have a car or bike to get around as the real attraction are the myriad of beaches with their golden sand that litter this part of Australia's coastline. If you do not have a car - then organise yourself to go to one spot getting the train to Gosford and then book into a cheap hotel or B&B near the sea, or caravan park, and get the people with whom you are staying to organise your transport. Take in this local area - like Terrigal or Avoca and enjoy for a couple of days. Then head somewhere else, unless the sea really gets to you.

The Central Coast is located north of Sydney. It begins at the Hawkesbury River and stretches northwards to the southern shores of Lake Macquarie, and westwards to historic St Albans.

The area is roughly divided into two - the City of Gosford with Brisbane Waters, and the Shire of Wyong with Tuggerah Lakes.

Within these two districts there are many seaside and holiday centres.

Gosford City
Population 129,000
The City of Gosford is 88km (55 miles) north of Sydney. The natural beauty of the district and its close proximity to the major cities of Sydney and Newcastle has made it an attractive living and recreation area on the east coast of Australia. There are many popular surfing beaches and the Brisbane Waters are legendary for fishing, sailing and other recreational pursuits. Although for many years, it has been a popular holiday and retirement area, many young families are now settling in the district as an alternative to living in the outer suburbs of Sydney and Newcastle.

Climate
Average temperatures: summer max 25C (77F) - min 18C (64F); winter max 17C (63F) - min 10C (50F). Average annual rainfall is 1300mm (51 ins), average ocean temperature is 20C (68F).

How to Get There
By Bus
Interstate coachlines call at Gosford.

By Rail
There is a good electric train service from/to Sydney, and the State Rail Authority has mini-fares, family fares and combined rail/coach fares, ☎131 500.

Visitor Information
The Gosford Visitor Information Centre is in *200 Mann Street, Gosford*, ☎4385 4430 or ☎1800 806 258, ◷open Mon-Fri 9am-

5pm, Sat-Sun 9am-2pm. Their email address is ✉thecoast@cctourism.com.au and the web page is at ▣www.cctourism.com.au

If you are in Terrigal, the Visitor Information Centre is in Rotary Park, Terrigal Drive. It is ◷open 9am-5pm Mon-Sat and 9am-3pm on Sunday during summer. They share contact details with the Gosford Centre.

provided. Facilities includes big kitchen, laundry, iron, lounge room, reading and TV room, internet access and a barbecue area. Free use of body boards and surfboards. On premises parking. *Dorms ❷$20; single $40; double/twin $49 BC MC VA EFTPOS*

Let's Eat

No matter which locality of the Central Coast you choose to stay in, you will find excellent restaurants. Here is a brief list, and the Information Centre can advise you further if you desire.

Gosford

Gosford Shoreline, *Masons Parade,* ☎*4325 0644.* Fully licensed seafood restaurant with an a-la-carte selection. Open midday-2pm and 6pm-8.30pm Mon-Sat, and until 9.30pm Friday and Saturday nights, lunch only on Sundays, closed Public Holidays.

Gee Kwong Chinese Restaurant, *197 Mann Street,* ☎*4325 2489.* Open 11.30am-3pm and 4.30pm-9pm Mon-Sat, and until 10pm on Friday and Saturday nights, closed Sunday and Public Holidays.

Tohn Oor Sian Classic Thai, *26 Adelaide Street, Gosford East,* ☎*4324 2887.* Take-away available, dine-in BYO wine only. Open midday-2.30pm and 5.30pm-10.30pm 7 days.

Jaceys, *45 Imperial Centre,* ☎*4324 2558.*

Da Vincis, *1-2 Brisbane Waters Drive, Gosford West,* ☎*4322 8000.*

Saltwater, *Shop 6 Brisbane Waters Drive, West Gosford,* ☎*4323 7744.*

Curry House, *104 Mann Street,* ☎*4322 0223.*

Peking Garden, in the *Central Coast Leagues Club, Dane Drive,* ☎*4324 3788.*

Surrounding Areas

Paceys, *172 Avoca Drive, Avoca Beach,* ☎*4382 3588.* Seafood, a-la-carte. Open 6pm-9pm 7 days and midday-3pm weekends and Public Holidays.

Sirens, *1 Kurrawyba Avenue, Terrigal,* ☎*4385 2602.* Open 5pm-midnight every day.

Pizza One, *80 Ocean View Drive, Wamberal,* ☎*4385 3311.*

Ghandi Indian Restaurant, *189 Ocean View Road, Ettalong,* ☎*4341 1994.*

The Don's Italian Restaurant, *28 Kincumber Village, Avoca Drive, Kincumber,* ☎*4363 1900.*

Fishermans Wharf, *The Boulevarde, Woy Woy,* ☎*4341 1171.*

For **Pizza Hut** deliveries, ☎*13 1166.* Branches of **McDonalds** and **KFC** are found in all the major towns.

Points of Interest

The majority of people visit the area for the surf, sun and sand, but there are quite a few attractions worth visiting.

The Australian Reptile Park was the first major tourist attraction on the Central Coast, and is a popular science exhibit. Crocodile feeding in the impressive crocodile enclosure is by far the highlight of the day. The park supplies venoms to countries all over the world for antivenins and other research. There are picnic and barbecue facilities, but note that the place is overrun by kangaroos, and the joy of their company can quickly turn into despair if one bounds up and pinches your lunch while you pat her! The park is ☺open daily 9am-5pm, ☎*4340 1146,* and is on the Pacific Highway, Somersby. Admission prices are ❷$16 adults.

Other attractions

Henry Kendall Cottage and Historical Museum, 218 Gertrude Street, Gosford, ☎*4325 2270.* A historical museum with displays of various items from the past.

The **Starship Cruise and Ferry Service,** *100 John Whiteway Drive,* ☎*4340 1146,* has two venues for cruises to cruise the Brisbane Waters, and the Tuggerah Lakes and Wyong River.

The Fragrant Garden, 25 *Portsmouth Road, Erina,* ☎*4367 7322,* has a very large collection of fragrant plants, crafts, pot-pourri in an old-world garden. **Central Park Family Fun Centre,** *The Entrance Road, Forresters Beach,* ☎*4386 2466,* has something for everyone.

Festivals

Gosford's **Australian Springtime Flora Festival** is held in September.

Facilities

Fishing, swimming, boating, diving, wind-surfing, water skiing, horse riding, ten-pin bowling, squash, lawn bowls, golf and tennis. The Visitor Information Centre will give you all the information for directions and bookings.

Outlying Attractions
🏖 Beaches
The coastal beaches in the Gosford area are Killcare, McMasters, Copacabana, Avoca, Terrigal, Wamberal and Forresters. They each have their own attractions, and all are patrolled on weekends from October to April, with daily patrols during the school holiday periods. Apart from McMasters and Forresters, they have a choice of takeaway food outlets close to the beachfront.

The crystal clear waters right along the Central Coast offer some of the best diving in Australia, and there are fascinating wrecks off Terrigal in reasonably shallow water. If you are interested in learning how to dive, the Terrigal Diving Centre, The Haven Terrigal, ☎4384 1219, or Pro Dive, 96 The Entrance Road, The Entrance, ☎4334 1559, are the places to visit. They teach diving, and after 5 days tuition, which costs around $450, you are awarded a C card. If you are already a qualified diver and have your certificate with you, a diving charter can be arranged instead. Fishing tours are also available for those who prefer to catch fish rather than rub noses with them (unless you are one of those fanatics who performs this ritual after catching a fish); one option is **Haven Fishing Charters**, *12 Lexington Parade, Green Point, ☎4369 5673.*

The Blue Bead Arabian Horse Stud, *☎4382 2346*, is located at Razina Park in Picketts Valley Road, 5 minutes from Terrigal and Avoca Beaches. They have mountain trails for the experienced, and instruct beginners and improvers. Bookings are essential, and the stud is open 7 days.

Tuggerah Lakes
The administrative centre of the Tuggerah Lakes district is Wyong, 22km (24 miles) north of Gosford on the banks of the Wyong River. The Lake system extends from Killarney Vale in the south to the township of Lake Munmorah in the north, and consists of three lakes - Tuggerah, Budgewoi and Munmorah. The biggest lake is Tuggerah Lake, and it has the only opening from the ocean, appropriately enough, at The Entrance. There are no sharks in the lakes.

Characteristics
One of the most popular holiday places in New South Wales, Tuggerah Lakes has grown like Topsy. Once it was strictly a fisherman's paradise with basic fishing shacks. Now there are first class motels, hotels, restaurants and sporting facilities.

How to Get There
By Rail
There is a regular electric rail service from Sydney to Wyong, and local buses from the station to the other areas.

Visitor Information
The Entrance Visitor Information Centre has its office in Marine Parade, and is ☺open daily 9am-5pm. It shares its contact details with the Gosford Visitor Information Centre.

↪ Let's Stay Here
As with any holiday centre, there is a great deal of accommodation to choose from in the Tuggerah Lakes district. Here is a selection of budget accommodation which should be used as a guide only. The telephone area code is 02.

The Entrance
Lake Front Motel,
16 Coogee Avenue, ☎4332 4518. 14 units, swimming pool, barbecue - *from* ☻*$55.*

Sapphire Palms Motel,
180 The Entrance Road, ☎4332 5799. 20 units, swimming pool, spa, barbecue - *from* ☻*$55.*

Tienda Motel,
309A The Entrance Road, ☎4332 3933. 30 units, swimming pool, spa - *from* ☻*$55.*

Caravan Parks
Dunleith Caravan Park, *Hutton Road, North Entrance, ☎4332 2172.* 180 sites - *powered sites* ☻*$18-35 for two, cabins from $65 for two.*

Blue Bay Camping and Caravaning Park, *cnr Bay Road and Narrawa Avenue, ☎4332 1991.* (No dogs allowed), 48 sites - *powered sites* ☻*$23-30 for two, on-site vans from $50 for two, cabins from $60.*

Long Jetty
Buccaneer Motel,
398 The Entrance Road, ☎4334 3100. 14 units, swimming pool, barbecue - ☻*$68-120.*

Jetty Motel,
353 The Entrance Road,
☎4332 1022. 22 units; swimming pool, spa, barbecue *from ☉$60.*

The Coachman Motor Inn,
33 Gordon Road, ☎4332 3692. 7 units, swimming pool, barbecue - *from ☉$50.*

Bateau Bay
Bateau Bay Hotel/Motel,
The Entrance Road, ☎4332 8022. 6 units, licensed restaurant - *from ☉$60.*

Palm Court Motel,
61 Bateau Bay Road, ☎4332 3755. 10 units, unlicensed restaurant, swimming pool - *from ☉$60.*

Sun Valley Caravan Park,
Bateau Bay Road, ☎4332 1107. (No pets allowed), 342 sites - *powered sites ☉$21-30 for two, holiday flat from $65 for two.*

Budgewoi
Budgewoi Tourist Park,
Weemala Street, ☎4390 9019. (Pets allowed on leash), 380 sites, barbecue - powered sites ☉*$12-18.*

Hibiscus Lakeside Motel,
2 Diamond Head Drive, ☎4390 9100. 13 units, barbecue - *from ☉$65.*

Sunnylake Caravan Park,
2 Macleay Drive, ☎4390 9471. 130 sites - *powered sites ☉$15-30 for two.*

Noraville
Sea'n'Sun Motel,
115 Budgewoi Road, ☎4396

4474. 12 units, mini golf, barbecue - *from ☉$55.*

Toukley
Toukley Motor Inn,
236 Main Road, ☎4396 5666. 13 units, swimming pool - *from ☉$56.*

Twin Lakes Motor Inn,
57 Main Road, ☎4396 4622. 11 units, swimming pool - *from ☉$50.*

Let's Eat
The district has several licensed RSL and bowling clubs, and these usually offer reasonably priced meals. There are also many takeaway and fast food outlets, both in the towns and on the beachfronts.

Beach Point, *19 Point Street, Bateau Bay,* ☎4334 5070.

Cactus Blues Mexican Restaurant, *245 Main Road, Toukley,* ☎4397 1557.

Carmelos Italian Restaurant, *61 Bateau Bay Road, Bateau Bay,* ☎4334 5155.

Jans Chinese Malaysian Restaurant, *Shops 5-6, 227-229 The Entrance Road, The Entrance,* ☎4334 1333.

Jetty Indian Tandoori, *509 The Entrance Road, Long Jetty,* ☎4334 2477.

Pizza Pit, *65 Scenic Drive Budgewoi,* ☎4399 1035.

Rus Chinese Rendevous, *120 Railway Street, Wyong,* ☎4353 2494.

Silver Moon Chinese Restaurant, *105 Scenic Drive, Budgewoi,* ☎4390 0489. Licensed, open 5pm-9pm 7 days and for lunch midday-2pm every day except Monday.

Sounan Thai, *27 The Entrance Road, The Entrance,* ☎4332 8806. Fully licensed restaurant with waterside views. Open 6pm-11pm 7 days and midday-3pm Wed-Sun, closed Public Holidays.

Wyong Golf Club Restaurant, *Pacific Highway, Wyong,* ☎4352 1999.

Points of Interest
The **Forest of Tranquility,** *Ourimbah Creek Road, Ourimbah,* is the home of Willy Wombat's rainforest walk, the best walk in a rainforest in the Sydney environs. There are gas barbecues, a playground, and picnic area, and rainforest plants are for sale. ☉open Wed-Sun 10am-5pm and all public holidays, ☎4362 1855.

Crackneck Lookout, in *Hilltop Avenue, Bateau Bay,* offers sweeping views of the coastline to Norah Head and Bungary Point, over the three lakes and the three power stations.

Bateau Bay Golf Practice Range, *468 The Entrance Road,* ☎4332 3277, is the largest golf range on the Central Coast, and venue of Australian Golf Schools. Practice facilities include grass tees, target greens, bunker and distance markers. ☉open 7 days.

Long Jetty Catamaran Hire, *cnr Tuggerah Parade* and *Pacific Street, Long Jetty,* ☎4332 9362, hires out catamarans, sailboards, canoes and pedal boats. They also have lessons in water skiing, and sell fishing tackle and bait.

The Entrance Aquaslide, ☎4334 3151, adjacent to the Lakeside Plaza carpark, 19 Taylor Street, The Entrance, has The Space Spiral, Outer Orbit and Cosmic Crusher rides, and the good news is, the pool is heated.

Each afternoon at 3.30pm, near the playground in the **Memorial Park,** *The Entrance,* everybody gathers to feed the pelicans.

The pelican has been adopted as the symbol of the tourist industry on the Central Coast, and the daily feeding ensures that this symbol doesn't disappear. There is no doubt that they are fascinating creatures, with wing spans up to 2m, and those incredible beaks, but there are many locals who are not exactly enamoured of them. To start with, they eat fish and are not well mannered enough to limit themselves to the afternoon meals supplied by humans, but tend to fish for themselves in the lakes. And, they are much better at it than those people sitting in boats and on the shore with hooks and lines. Then they have lice, which they shed in the water to bite anyone who dares to swim in the area. It is not that the pelicans do this on purpose, but try selling that to a kiddy who is suffering from itchy bites. Of course, the pelicans came before people starting feeding them, but not in such large numbers.

At **Dunleith Caravan Park**, Hutton Road, North Entrance, ☎4332 2172, there is a Shell Museum, with an extensive display of shells and early photographs of the area, along with models of aquatic animals.

Norah Head Lighthouse, circa 1903, is open for visitors only by arrangement with the Visitor Centre. At Cabbage Tree Bay, the tiny settlement where the road to the light house commences, there are steps leading down to a lovely little rock pool, which is very popular with children. You can also drive down the steep road before the steps, but parking is usually a problem. There is a surfing beach alongside, but it is not patrolled, and there is a dangerous riptide.

Edward Hargraves Homestead, in *Elizabeth Drive, Noraville,* is not open for inspection, but can be viewed from the road. Edward Hargraves discovered gold near Bathurst in 1851, causing the first gold rush in Australia.

Toukley has a good-sized shopping centre, and the Toukley and District Senior Citizens Club in Hargraves Street, has loads of entertainment and things to do. **Toukley RSL** is also a very busy club, and visitors are always welcome, as they are at Toukley Bowling Club.

Warnervale Airfield, near the expressway (follow the road through Toukley, crossing the Pacific Highway) offers joy-flights every Sunday, and other days by appointment. Contact Central Coast Helicopters, Lot 1, Sparks Road, Warnervale, ☎4352 2222, or Warnervale Air, Jack Grant Avenue, ☎4392 5174.

Smokey Mountain Steam Railroad, in *Mountain Road, Warnervale,* offers a different day out for all the family with steam train rides through the surrounding picturesque valleys ⏱between 11am and 4pm. It operates on Sundays and public holidays from Boxing Day until the last Sunday in October, except Good Friday and days of total fire ban. For further information, contact them on, ☎4392 7644.

⛱ Beaches

The coastal beaches in the Tuggerah Lakes area are: **Bateau Bay; Shelly Beach; Toowoon Bay s; North Entrance; Soldiers Point; Cabbage Tree Bay; Jenny Dixon; The Lakes Beach.**

Jenny Dixon Beach and **Cabbage Tree Bay** are not patrolled, and Jenny Dixon has some nude bathers, but the other beaches are patrolled every weekend, and all through the school holidays, and have handy food outlets. From the Lakes Beach, miles of sand and surf stretch northwards, but it should be remembered that the site of the beach club was chosen because it is the safest part of that stretch.

Newcastle

Population 470,610
Newcastle is situated on the Hunter River, 171km (106 miles) north of Sydney, and 827km (514 miles) south of Brisbane.

Climate

Average temperatures: January max 27C (81F) - min 18C (64F); July max 17C (63F) - min 6C (43F). Average annual rainfall: 1134mm (45 ins), and the rain falls evenly throughout the year.

Characteristics

Newcastle is the second largest city in New South Wales, and the sixth largest in Australia. The site was discovered when Lt Shortland was searching for convict escapees in the late 18th century, and discovered coal, which together with steel dominated Newcastle to the mid-1960s.

Newcastle is a city with international-style hotels, motels and shopping centres. It is an ideal base for visiting the holiday areas of Lake Macquarie, Port Stephens and the Hunter Valley.

The city was hit by a shocking earthquake on December 28, 1989, with the loss of lives and many buildings. A swift Novocastrian recovery has meant that few signs of the disaster remain.

How to Get There
By Air
The Newcastle Airport is at Williamtown, 23km from the city, and there are plenty of taxis available for transport to the city centre.

Qantas, ☎ *13 1313* have regular flights to Newcastle.

By Bus
Greyhound Pioneer, ☎*13 2030*, and **McCaffertys**, ☎ *13 1499*, are among the coach companies that stop at Newcastle.

By Rail
Newcastle is on the Sydney/ Murwillumbah line with regular services, and connections from Murwillumbah to Brisbane and the Gold Coast, ☎ *13 2232*.

Visitor Information
The Visitor Information Centre is located at 363 Hunter Street, ☎*4974 2999* or ☎ *1800 654 558*. ⏱opening hours are 9am-5pm Mon-Fri and 10am-3.30pm on weekends. The internet references are ✉newtour@hunterlink.net.a u or ✉mail@ncc.nsw.gov.au for email, and ■www.ncc.nsw.gov.au for the website.

⤴ Let's Stay Here
As with any large city, moderately-priced accommodation places are in the suburbs, and the Tourist Office has a complete list of what is available. Here is a selection of budget accommodation which should be used as a guide only. The telephone area code is 02.

City
Backpackers by the Beach, *34-36 Hunter St,* ☎*4926 3472* Located close to the station and the Shortland Esplanade at Newcastle Beach. Two floors, one having the TV room, kitchen and dining room with big windows that face the street and the park across the road. You will find the second TV lounge and Internet access downstairs. There are lockers in rooms and has good security. *Dorm bed* ❂*$22; Double room $51*

Backpackers Newcastle, *42-44 Denison St,* ☎*4969 3436 or 1800 - 33 34 36,* ■*www .newcastlebackpackers.com* Located a few blocks away in a quiet side street between the Hunter St and Newcastles trendy eat-street called Beaumont Street. 24 hour supermarket nearby. Hostel setting is in two old houses. Rooms have fans in every room and it is gas heated for the cool winter months. Facilities includes kitchen, big common room with pool table and there's a courtyard with swimming pool and a table tennis table. Watch out for the free surf lessons and the free dinners and free drink four times a week

with the visit to local pubs. Free pickup and drop off to the bus and train terminals. Parking available. *Dorms from* ❂*$15; Single room $38; Double room $50*

Newcastle Beach, *30 Pacific St, Cnr King St,* ☎*4925 3544,* ■*www.yha.com.au* Located just across from Newcastle Beach and metres away from shops restaurants and the train station. A newly restored heritage building which has a ballroom with chandeliers, leather armchairs and open fires. Facilities includes a very modern kitchen, laundry, TV lounge room, pool table, internet access and a fantastic courtyard with palm trees and a barbecue area. There is an 'Irish Pub Night' which is held 3 nights a week and a weekly all-you-can-eat pizza. Free use of surf and boogie boards. Parking available. *Dorms from* ❂*$23; single from $42, double/twin from $29pp; BC MC VA EFTPOS*

Stockton Beach Backpackers, *68 Mitchell Street, Stockton,* ☎*4928 4333,* ■*www.stockto nbeachbackpackers.com. au* Stockton is situated only a 2-minute ferry ride from Queens Wharf Ferry terminal on Newcastle Harbour and close to the Newcastle's train and coach terminal. Only a 5 minute walk to the surf beaches, city centre and entertainment. A huge hostel with 3 floors of accommodation. Facilities includes kitchen, laundry, lounge areas and a barbecue area. There is also a roof

Newcastle

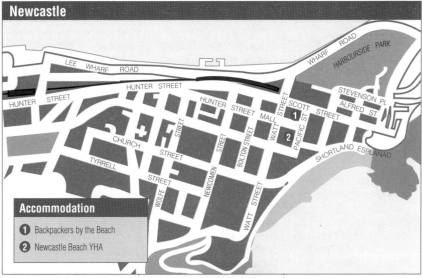

Accommodation

1 Backpackers by the Beach

2 Newcastle Beach YHA

---

top deck and a spa and sauna. *Dorm* ✪*$25; single $25; double $31.50pp*

West End Guest House, *775 Hunter St,* ☎*4961 4446* Located at the busy corner of Hunter Street and Stewart Avenue, about a ten minute walk to the centre of town. Newcastle Museum and a 24-hour shopping centre are located nearby. Accommodation set in an old pub that was renovated into a hostel. Basic facilities that includes a kitchen, small TV lounge and barbecue area plus a nice balcony. Cafe on site. *Dorm bed* ✪*$30; Double/twin room $65*

Caravan Parks
Tomago Village Van Park, *Pacific Highway and Tomago Road, Tomago,* ☎*4964 8066.* (No pets allowed) - *powered sites* ✪*$19 for two, cabins $45-70 for two.*

Redhead Beach Holiday Park, *1A Kalaroo Road,* ☎*4944 8306.* (No pets allowed) - *powered sites* ✪*$19-25 for two, cabins $45-95 for two, on-site vans $45-55 for two.*

Stockton Beach Tourist Park, *Pitt Street, Stockton,* ☎*4928 1393.* (No dogs allowed) - *powered sites* ✪*$16-20 for two, cabins $35-60 for two.*

Let's Eat
Finding somewhere to eat in Newcastle is not a problem. There are the licensed clubs (Newcastle Workers, Western Suburbs Leagues Club, Tubemakers Recreation Club, etc..) which all offer restaurants, bistros and snack bars. There are also some hostels and motels, which may have their own licensed or BYO restaurants, and coffee shops and takeaway food outlets. The Visitor Information Office has a complete list of restaurants, but here are

some you might wish to try.

Delaney Hotel, *134 Darby Street,* ☎*4929 1627.* Open 10am-midnight Mon-Sat and Sunday midday-10pm.

Elizas, *Shortland Esplanade,* ☎*4929 5576.*

Hawaiian Sunsets, *171 Darby Street,* ☎*4926 1264.* International menu, licensed. Open 6pm-midnight 7 days, closed Public Holidays.

Harry's on Hunter, *672 Hunter Street,* ☎*4926 2165.*

Lans, 146 Darby Street, ☎*4929 1565.* Open 5pm-10pm every day except Mondays and Public Holidays (closed).

Maharaja Indian Restaurant, *653 Hunter Street,* ☎*4926 1665.*

Mercury Cafe, *Mercury Hotel, 23 Watt Street,* ☎*4929 2025.*

Newcastle Happy Gardens Chinese Restaurant, *133 Scott Street,* ☎ *4926 2707.*

San Marco on the Park, *10 Pacific Street,* ☎ *4926 3865.* Fully licensed, open 12pm-3pm and 6pm-9pm Mon-Sat, closed Sunday.

Taco Bills Mexican Restaurant, *80 Darby Street,* ☎ *4929 2971.*

Thara Tong Thai, *541 Hunter Street,* ☎ *4929 6722.*

McDonalds are on the corner of King and Steel Streets. **KFC** is at 227 Hunter Street and **Pizza Hut** is located at 500 Hunter Street, ☎ *13 1166* for delivery.

Points of Interest

City Hall, in *King Street,* is the office of Newcastle's Lord Mayor, and is an impressive sandstone building with a tall clock tower opened in 1929.

Civic Park, opposite the City Hall, is a large park that has The special trees planted at the eastern and western ends are gifts from Newcastle's Sister City, Ube in Japan.

The Captain Cook Memorial Fountain forms a backdrop to Civic Park. It was built in 1966, and is illuminated at night.

The Newcastle Regional Art Gallery, in *Laman Street,* ☎ *4974 5100,* was opened in 1977 by Her Majesty, Queen Elizabeth II. It houses the city's Art Collection plus another gift from Ube, a stai-nless steel sculpture, 'Space Two'.

Christ Church Anglican Cathedral overlooks the city from the top of the hill, and can be seen from harbour, sea and

suburbs foundation stone laid in 1817.

Hunter Mall became a pedestrian arcade in 1980, and is framed by fine Victorian and Edwardian buildings. As well as David Jones department store, it has many specialty stores.

Fort Scratchley, on Nobbys Road, is one of two remaining 19th century closed fort complexes in NSW. The fort houses the **Newcastle Region Maritime Museum.**

The **Ocean Baths,** located at Newcastle Beach and at Merewether Beach, are the two largest saltwater baths in the Southern Hemisphere.

The Obelisk, up the hill just to the south of the city, marks the site of Newcastle's first windmill. The mill was erected in 1820 and became a navigational mark for ships approaching Newcastle.

The multi-million dollar **Queen's Wharf and Harbour** is a pleasant attraction. From the top of the tower in the complex one has a view of the city, harbour and beaches north up to Port Stephens, and west to the Watagan Mountains.

At **Harbourside Markets,** *cnr Wharf Road* and *Merewether Street,* there's everything to buy, in the classic market style.

William the Fourth was the first Australian-built coastal steamship, and is now anchored at Queen's Wharf. See the Visitor Information Centre for all the details.

Newcastle Regional Museum, *787 Hunter Street,* ☎ *4962 2001,* is the leading Regional Museum in the country. It features exhibits about the industrial and technological heritage of the surrounding region, its social

history, lifestyle and environment. The museum is ⊙open Tues-Sun and public holidays 10am-5pm.

Supernova, Newcastle's Science and Technology Fun Centre is housed within the Regional Museum. It is hands-on science, a museum where kids are encouraged to touch the displays.

Nobbys Head was a "small clump of an island" that was connected to the mainland by the breakwater in 1846. On top of Nobbys is a lighthouse signal station, and Nobbys Beach is a popular surfing beach with the Novocastrians.

The Heritage Centre, ☎ *4925 2265,* next door to the Post Office in *Hunter Street,* is Newcastle's former Police Station (1859), and is operated by the Hunter Region National Trust. The centre features an environmental Gift Shop, ⊙open Mon-Fri 9am-5pm.

🏖 Beaches

Newcastle Beach offers safe swimming from the rocks at the northern end to the front of the club pavilion, and surfboard riding to the southern end. Surfest, one of the world's leading surfing events takes place here every November. The floodlit and patrolled Ocean Baths are here also.

Nobbys Beach is an excellent family beach. There is good surfing on the reef, at the northern end and at Cowrie hole to the south (patrolled). Horseshoe Beach is Newcastle's only harbour beach, and is popular with trainers and their racehorses. It is also a good fishing spot.

Stockton Beach, is opposite the city, and offers safe swimming from the breakwater to Hereford

Street, and good surfing from there to the north. The main beach is patrolled. Here you can check out the wreck of the Sygna (1974).

Bar Beach to the south of Newcastle Beach and the Bogey Hole, is also a good family beach with safe swimming from the northern end (Bar area) to the front of the pavilion, and surfboard riding from there to the southern end. There is plenty of parking. The beach is patrolled and floodlit.

Susan Gilmore Beach, is accessed from the extreme northern end of Bar Beach, via a path down the cliff face, or over the rocks at low tide. The beach was named after an American ship that was wrecked here. It is a nudist beach, and is not patrolled.

Merewether Beach is an excellent swimming beach with good beachbreak surfboard riding south of the club house. The beach is patrolled and floodlit. There are Ocean Baths here too.

Dixon Park Beach offers safe swimming in front of the clubhouse, and is good for surfing, board and ski, in front of the cliff. The beach is patrolled.

Burwood and **Dudley Beaches** are excellent for swimming and board riding, but these nudists beaches are not patrolled.

Out-of-City Attractions
Shortland Wetlands Centre.
The Centre is situated on 65ha (160 acres) of wetland along Sandgate Road, Shortland on the edge of Hexham Swamp. More than 170 species of birds have been recorded here, with at least 30 of these breeding. During the summer months, several thousand egrets nest

in the paperbark trees in one of the shallow swamps. Facilities include a Visitors Centre with static and live animal displays and a souvenir shop that provides light refreshments; picnic tables; walking trails; and a bird observation tower. Canoes can be hired for exploring the 7km of waterways around Hexham Swamp. The Wetlands Centre is located less than 1km from the Shortland Shopping Centre along *Sandgate Road*, Shortland, and a 10 minute walk away from Sandgate Railway Station. The centre is ☺open daily 9am-5pm, with extended hours during holiday seasons.An small admission price applies. Phone ☎*4951 6466* for more information. The Information Centre in Newcastle can arrange half day tours and twilight walks to Shortland Wetlands.

Blackbutt Reserve. A reserve of approximately 180ha, Blackbutt is situated in the middle of Newcastle's suburbia. It consists of open forest land intersected by four valleys running from west to east. One of the area's greatest attractions, apart from vegetation, animals and uncommon birds, is its seclusion from the City around it. The Reserve is a popular spot with the locals and a source of interest for overseas tourists keen to observe the exhibition of Australian indigenous wildlife, including wombats, koalas, kangaroos, emus, wallabies and native birds. Families can prepare a meal, relax or play in the grounds with the barbecue facilities, children's playground, several quaint ponds and marked bush-walking tracks available. It is ☺open all year, 10am-5pm for the wildlife exhibits, and there is

no admission fee. The **Maritime Model Club** launch their ships on the biggest pond every Saturday. The Tourist Office has a leaflet setting out the various bushwalks and all the attractions, or you can call direct on ☎*4952 1449*.

Tours
The Tourist Office has details of tours in and around Newcastle, and of Hunter River and harbour cruises that are available. Here are two worth enquiring about: Australian Scenic Tours, 50 Hunter Street, ☎*4929 4333*. Free Spirit Charters, *Level 4, 175 Scott Street*, ☎*4929 1908*.

There are several helicopter flights over the city, the surrounding coastal areas, and further afield to the Vineyards and to Moffats Oyster Barn at Swan Bay. Scenic Helicopter Flights, *cnr Hannel* and *Cowper Streets, Wickham*, ☎*4962 2240*, is one company operating in the area.

Daily departures from Newcastle, Maitland and Cessnock to the Vineyards are available, visiting a range of wineries from small family-owned to large commercial, with numerous tastings. Two of these tours are Hunter Vineyard Tours, ☎*4991 1659*, and The Wine and Cheese Tasting Tour, ☎*4938 5031*.

Festivals
The **Matarra Festival** is held each September.

Facilities
Newcastle has all the facilities you would expect of a city its size. Theatre and cinema programmes are in the daily newspapers, and the Yellow Pages Telephone Book has details of all sporting

facilities. The Visitor Information Centre has all the details.

Outlying Attractions
Forster - Tuncurry

North of Newcastle, about 161km (100 miles), are the twin towns of Forster and Tuncurry, which are the major tourist areas of the Great Lakes, and are renowned for their beaches, fishing, seafoods and temperate climate all year around.

On land there is the Booti Booti National Park to explore, and the Cape Hawke Bicentennial Walk with its panoramic viewing platform. The popular beaches and lakes provide ample opportunities for swimming, fishing and sailing.

Forster has the Great Lakes Visitor Centre located in Little Street, ☎ *6554 8799* or ☎ *1800 802 692*. It is ☺open Mon-Fri 9am-5pm. They have a web page at ▤*www.greatlakes.org.au* and an email address at ✉*tourglc@tpgi. com.au*

⤵ Let's Stay Here
Dolphin Lodge,
43 Head St, ☎ *6555 8155,* ▤*www.yha.com.au* Located so close to the beach and not far from the shops and bus terminal. All rooms have en suite bathrooms. Facilities includes 2 kitchens, laundry, iron, lounge room, reading and TV room, internet access, pool table and a barbecue area. Free use of boogie boards and games. Bike hire available. Parking available. *Dorms* ✪*$23; single $36; double/twin $52 BC MC VA*

Barrington Tops

The Barrington Tops National Park is about 110km (68 miles) north-west of Newcastle, travelling through Raymond Terrace and Dungog. The area is on the World Heritage List.

The fabulous Barrington Tops landscape is the drawcard. It is very mountainous country, with many 4WD and hiking tracks, but care should be taken as many people have become lost wandering off the beaten track. There are many excellent places to spend a few days in this marvellous setting, suiting a wide range of budgets and tastes.

A wonderful website covers this area in great depth: ▤www. barringtons.com.au

Dungog Visitors Information Centre is on the corner of *Dowling* and *Brown Streets, Dungog,* ☎ *4992 2212*, or email: ✉dungogvc@ midac.com.au. It is ☺open Mon-Fri 9am-5pm and Sat-Sun 9am-3pm.

The Gloucester Visitor Information Centre is on the corner of *Church* and *Denison Streets, Gloucester,* ☎ *6558 1408*, or email: ✉glosinfo@tpg.com.au. It is ☺open 7 days 9.30am-4.30pm.

Port Stephens

Port Stephens is a 45 minute coastal drive north of Newcastle, and is regarded as one of the most attractive and unspoilt waterways anywhere in Australia. It proclaims itself as the 'Dolphin Capital of Australia', since more than 140 bottlenose dolphins reside in the port, which is more than twice the size of Sydney Harbour. Further upstream from where the Myall River flows into the Port are the Broadwater and the Myall Lakes systems with lovely waterways, tiny uninhabited islands, abundant bird life, a national park, and unpolluted beaches stretching north to the Smith's and Wallace Lakes systems.

What were once isolated fishing settlements around the Port's foreshores, have become connected with the influx of residents and tourist facilities. The main centres are Shoal Bay, Nelson Bay, Salamander Bay and Soldiers Point, and the smaller, and somewhat newer areas are Lemon Tree, Mallabula, Tanilba Bay and Oyster Cove.

On the waterway's northern reaches are the holiday centres of Tea Gardens and Hawks Nest, both offering good accommodation, beaches and facilities.

Lying only a couple of hours away from Sydney, this is a booming tourist area that bustles with visitors in the peak summer season. Nelson Bay is the Port Stephens service centre, with a variety of shops, a movie cinema, a supermarket, restaurants, banks, a pub, and plenty more. People flock to the scenic Marina for shopping, dining and entertainment.

There is no shortage of activities to occupy your time in Port Stephens, from all manner of watersports to a number of Hunter Valley wine tours.

The area also has theme parks catering for children, including **Toboggan Hill Park** in Salamander Bay, ☎ *4984 1022*; **Tomteland Australia** in Williamtown, ☎ *4965 1500*; and **Oakvale Farm** and **Fauna World** in Salt Ash, ☎ *4982 6222*.

The Port Stephens Visitor

Information Centre is on *Victoria Parade, Nelson Bay,* ☎*4981 1579* or ☎*1800 808 900*. It is ⊕open 9am-5pm Mon-Fri and 9am-4pm Sat, Sun and Public Holidays. You will find it at the drive-way entrance to the Marina. Email them at ✉tops@hunterlink.net.au or find the website at ⬛www.port stephens.org.au

↪ Let's Stay Here
Samurai Beach Bungalows Backpackers,
Robert Connell Circle, ☎*4982 1921* Set in 3 acres of bush land with cabins placed around the place. It's a nice quiet stop before you head up the coast. Facilities includes an outdoor kitchen with a bar-becue area, a volley ball court, a campfire area and indside you'll find the games room with a pool table and other small things to keep you oc-cupied. It's such a big place and hours away from the big city that you might just liter-ally find a native koala on the trees. Free use of sand boards, surf boards and they hire out bikes for free. *Dorms from* ❂*$22; doubles $58*

Shoal Bay Backpackers YHA,
59-61 Shoal Bay Beachfront Rd, Shoal Bay, ☎*4981 0982,* ⬛*www.yha.com.au* Located just in front of Shoal Bay on the beautiful Port Stephens Harbour. Centrally located in town and in built with the Shoal Bay Motel as a wing. Close to the bus station. Fa-cilities includes kitchen, laun-dry, TV lounge and a barbecue area. On site cafe. Parking available. *Dorms from* ❂*$19; double from $56   BC MC VA*

Hunter Valley
The beauty of the Hunter, with its rolling hills covered in rows of grapevines and surrounded by tall mountains, surprises many visitors. There are over 1500ha (3705 acres) of vineyards under cultivation in the Lower Hunter-Pokolbin district near Cessnock, and more than 1600ha (3952 acres) planted in the Upper Hunter, centred around the towns of Muswellbrook and Denman.

Renowned for the production of top quality table wines, the Valley's wineries range in size and production from small family affairs, where their entire vintage goes in their own tastings and cellar door sales, to large famous brand company bottlers whose award-winning labels have become household names.

In the last few decades, the rising popularity of the Hunter has produced a rapid development in ancillary visitor amenities with restaurants, craft shops, galleries and children's playgrounds becoming parts of many of the wineries.

Even if you are not in the grip of the grape, a day at Pokolbin Estate Vineyard, or Hungerford Hill wine village, is good fun for all the family.

The main Visitor Information Centre for the area is in Cessnock, but there is another in Maitland, in *King Edward Park, Banks Street East,* ☎*4933 2611.*

The Hunter Regional Tourism Organisation has a web page at ⬛www.huntertourism.com/ Online/ home/main.html

Murrurundi
The town of Murrurundi on the Pages River occupies the northernmost point of the

Hunter Valley, and has historic old buildings, many classified by the National Trust. Tales of bushrangers are intertwined with the region. Ben Hall was born here, and Thunderbolt roamed in the area in the latter part of the last century.

Sheep, cattle and horse breeding are the major interests, and the mountain scenery of the Liverpool Ranges, at the town's doorstep, gives an unparalleled view of the valley.

The Visitor Information Centre is at *113 Main St,* open Monday to Friday from 10am-5pm. Email ✉rayh@murrurundi.nsw.gov.au, ☎*(02)6546 6446*

Scone
Scone was first settled during the 1830s by Scottish settlers who likened the countryside to their homeland, and named many spots after their birthplaces. The town is now a thriving commercial centre supporting important rural industries, and is well known for its thoroughbred horses, cattle and sheep from stud properties in the area. Scone is also the inland gateway to the Barrington Tops region, via the Scone-Gloucester Road.

Nearby Glenbawn Dam is well stocked with freshwater fish, and is ideal for boating, yachting, water skiing and swimming.

The Burning Mountain, off the New England Highway between Scone and Murrurundi, turn-off just north of Wingen, has been burning for thousands of years. According to Aboriginal legend, a tribesman was lighting his fire on the mountainside when he was carried off into the earth by the evil one. Unable to escape, he used his fire sticks to set the mountain alight so that the smoke might warn others to keep away. Today the mountain is easily reached via a two kilometre walking track.

Travelling south through Aberdeen, which once housed a thriving abattoir, one comes to Muswellbrook.

Scone has a Visitor Information Centre on the corner of Susan and Kelly Streets, ☼open daily 9am-5pm. Email them at ✉stic@scone .nsw.gov.au or phone them on ☎6545 1526.

⤳ Let's Stay Here

Scone YHA Hostel,
1151 Segenhoe Rd, ☎*6545 2702,* ▉*www.yha.com.au* Two acres of grounds in the middle of thoroughbred country is the setting for this hostel. Built in an old school building. It is well facilitated, which is good since it's a fair way from a lot of things. These facilities are a self catering kitchen, laundry, lounge room, reading and TV room, internet access and a barbecue area. Basic food supply and meals available at the hostel. Bike hire available. On premises parking. *Dorms from* ✪*$18; double/twin $36;*

Muswellbrook

The Muswellbrook area has benefited in recent years with the growth of the mining and power industries, and as well, the wine industry. The major rural activity, though, is dairy farming. Produce is supplied through the Hunter Valley Co-operative Dairy Company's processing plant at Muswellbrook.

The area boasts a number of Art and Craft Galleries, and the

Rainbow Zone Fun Centre in Industrial Close, ☎*6541 4279.*

For more information, the Muswellbrook Visitor Information Centre is in *87 Hill Street,* ☎(02) 6541 4050. ☼open 9am-5pm daily. A web page lets you explore the area at ▉www.muswellbrook. org.au

Denman

Situated in one of the most fertile areas of the Hunter Region, some 15km south-west of Muswellbrook off the New England Highway. Denman has many fine horse and cattle studs, and has become an acknowledged quality wine producing area. Vineyards in the area are: Arrowfield, ☎*6576 4041,* one of the largest in Australia; Rosemount Estate, ☎*6549 6400;* McGuigan Wines, ☎*6547 2422;* and Horseshoe Vineyard, ☎*6547 3528.*

The nearby Widden Valley is considered to be second only to America's famous Kentucky Blue Grass region for the breeding of racehorses.

Singleton

Back on the New England Highway we come to the geographical heart of the Hunter Valley, Singleton. It has the Hunter River flowing past its doorstep and irrigating the surrounding rich grazing land.

Nearby Lake St Clair offers boating and fishing, and maps of the waterways are available from the Information Centre.

The Singleton Army Camp includes the Royal Australian Infantry Corps Museum, which is ☼open to visitors 9am-4pm Wed-Sun.

On the New England Highway, between Singleton and Muswellbrook, are the Liddell (☎*6542 1611*) and Bayswater (☎*6542 1611*) Power Stations, which are two of the biggest thermal power stations in the Southern Hemisphere. Visitor tours are available at certain times by arrangement.

The Singleton Information Centre at the southern entrance to the town, in the Shire Council, Civic Centre on Queen Street. They are ☼open Mon-Fri 8.30am-4.30pm, ☎*6578 7267.* The website is: ▉www.singleton. nsw.gov.au and the email address is ✉ssc@ singletoncouncil.nsw .gov.au

Cessnock

The town of Cessnock is 52km (32 miles) from Newcastle and 185km (115 miles) from Sydney. It is the gateway to the wineries, with approximately 30 in the area. Cessnock is the major town in the area, but the satellite district of Pokolbin provides the real accommodation treats.

The historic village of Wollombi, 31km (19 miles) south-west of Cessnock, has a few interesting buildings worth visiting - the Court House, St John's Anglican Church and the two-storey Post Office.

The Visitor Information Centre is in *Turner Park, Aberdare Road,* and ☼opens 7 days, Mon-Thu 9am-5pm, Fri 9am-6pm, Sat 9.30am-5pm and Sunday and Public Holidays 9.30am-3.30pm. The Information Centre has a list of all the attractions in the town, and of the wineries which are open for tours and cellar door sales. They can be emailed at ✉info@winecountry.

com.au or visited at the website
🖳www.winecountry.com.au

North Coast of Newcastle
Taree
Population 16,700
Taree is located on the banks of the Manning River, 330km (205 miles) north of Sydney.

Characteristics
Taree is the commercial centre of the Manning Valley, which offers a diversity of natural attractions from scenic lookouts and waterfalls that plunge deep into a box gorge, to some of the cleanest, whitest beaches on the east coast of Australia.

Climate
Average temperatures: January max 29C (84F) - min 17C (63F); July max 18C (64F) - min 6C (43F). Average annual rainfall: 1171mm (46 ins).

How to Get There
By Air
Qantas, ☎13 1313, has flights from/to Sydney.

By Bus
McCaffertys, ☎13 1499, and **Greyhound Pioneer**, ☎13 2030, stop at Taree on their Sydney/ Brisbane runs.

By Rail
There is an *XPT Countrylink* service from Sydney to Taree and the trip takes 5 hours, ☎13 2232.

Visitor Information
The Manning Valley Visitor Information Centre is on the Old Pacific Highway, Taree North, 3km north of the Taree Shopping Centre, ☎6552 1900 or ☎1800 801 522. They are ⊙open 7 days a week 9am-5pm, and the complex includes a restaurant, public toilets, and a 70-seat theatrette showing an audio-visual presentation. The email address is ✉manningvic@ gtcc.nsw.gov.au and the web address is 🖳www.gtcc.nsw.gov.au/tourism

⤵ Let's Stay Here
Taree has many motels, a few caravan parks, and house-boats for hire (available from Manning River Holidays Afloat, 36 Crescent Avenue, Taree, ☎6552 3162.
Here is a selection of budget accommodation with prices that should be used as a guide only. The telephone area code is 02.

Agincourt Motel,
9 Commerce Street, ☎6552 *1614.* 21 units - ❂$45-65.

Chatham Motel,
Pacific Highway, ☎6552 *1659.* 10 units - ❂$40-45.

Jolly Swagman Motel,
1 Commerce Street, ☎6552 *3511.* 21 units, barbecue - ❂$55-90.

Arlite Motor Inn,
cnr Bligh Street and Pacific Highway, ☎6552 2433. 20 units, swimming pool - ❂$50.

Caravan Parks
Twilight Caravan Park,
Pacific Highway, ☎0500 854 *448.* (Pets allowed under control), 65 sites - *powered sites* ❂$17-20 for two, on-site vans $30-40 for two, cabins $35-70.

Riverside Caravan Park,
Reid Street, Croki, ☎6556 *3274.* (No pets), 38 sites, barbecue - *powered sites* ❂$15-18 for two, on-site vans $35 for two, cabins $35 for two.

Let's Eat
The local licensed clubs also have dining rooms and bistros. Here are some restaurants you might like to try.

East Court Chinese Restaurant,
73 Victoria Street, ☎6552 2465. Licensed, salad bar, banquets, open 7 nights 5pm-10pm. Silhouettes, Shop 5, 103 Victoria Street, ☎6552 1393.

Il Colosseo, *32 Oxley Street,* ☎6552 6289. BYO, Italian, also offers free pizza delivery within a 10km radius. Open 6pm-10pm every day except Monday, and until midnight Fri-Sun.

Jin Hong Chinese Restaurant, *91 Victoria Street,* ☎6552 7199. Seafood on Victoria, 166 Victoria Street, ☎6557 8111.

Kowin Chinese Restaurant,
22 Chatham Avenue, ☎6552 *3482.* Licensed, open 7 nights 5pm-9pm.

Laurents, 33 Victoria Street, ☎6552 5022.

Pelican, *Old Pacific Highway,* ☎6552 2122.

Shades, *23-25 Oxley Street,* ☎6552 1455. Fully licensed restaurant with an international menu. Open every day except Sunday 6pm-midnight.

Thai Tarni, *Albert Street,* ☎6552

2366. BYO dine-in or take-away. Open 5.30pm-9.30pm every day except Monday and for lunch 11.30am-2pm Tue-Fri.

McDonalds is on the corner of the *Pacific Highway* and *Manning Street*. You will find **KFC** at *38 Victoria Street*. **Pizza Hut** is in *Manning Mall, Manning Street*, ☎ *13 1166*.

Points of Interest

Taree is, as we have mentioned, a holiday town, and there is not a great deal of sightseeing, just plenty of places to relax and take advantage of the river.

The riverside **Fotheringham** and **Queen Elizabeth Parks** offer the opportunity to feed the pelicans and seagulls, and to observe the river.

Manning River Cruises, ☎ *6557 4767*, have a cruise boat on the Manning, with informative commentary to accompany your charter. There are regular departures during school holidays.

The Big Oyster, Pacific Highway, North Taree, is like the other striking and largely ludicrous 'Bigs' in the country.

Facilities

An 18-hole golf course, several tennis courts, 4 bowling clubs, BMX track, Olympic swimming pool, basketball stadium, indoor cricket stadium, squash courts, ten pin bowling, greyhound racing and horse racing, and facilities for rugby league, rugby union, soccer,

hockey, and netball.

The Manning Entertainment Centre, ☎ *6551 0555*, has a 505 seat auditorium, and local clubs have top local and interstate bands throughout the year. There is also a twin cinema.

Outlying Attractions
Crowdy Head

4km (2 miles) north-east of Harrington is the quaint village of Crowdy Head, the home of the local fishing fleet.

There's good fishing from the headland, and a co-op if you don't have any luck yourself. The lighthouse is easily reached by a sealed road, and gives excellent views of the coastline, both north and south.

Crowdy Beach sweeps in a long arc through to Diamond Head in the National Park, and offers safe swimming.

The Harrington Crowdy Visitor Information Centre is at 85 Beach Street, Harrington, ☎ *6556 1188*.

Wingham

Situated 13km (8 miles) west of Taree, Wingham has a feeling of 'olde England', with its town common that is also the local cricket pitch. There are also about 13 buildings which have been classified by the National Trust for their historical significance, and most have been carefully reconstructed. They include the School of Arts, the Police Station and Court House, the Bank Building, Gibson and Skinner Butchery and the Australian Hotel.

Manning Valley Historical Society's Museum, *corner Farquhar and Bent Streets*, ☎ *6553 5823*, ⏰ open 10am-4pm, is also located within the town square area, and displays include

Jimmy Governor's cell, together with various items relating to the history of the area.

Wingham Brush, located 500m from the shopping centre on Farquhar Street, is 7ha (17 acres) of coastal rainforest, with birds and native marsupials. The Brush is adjacent to the Manning River and has picnic tables, barbecues and boat launching facilities.

Use the resources of the Taree Information Centre to obtain further details of Wingham, ☎ *6552 1900*.

Forestry Drives

Bulga Forest Drive is a scenic tour through timbered country north west of Wingham, passing the Ellenborough Falls near Elands. The round trip from Wingham takes visitors through three State Forests - The Bulga, Dingo and Knorrit.

Kiwarrak State Forest is 5km (3 miles) south of Taree, adjacent to the Pacific Highway. Highlights include the Pines picnic area and Breakneck Lookout.

Coopernook highlights includes Vincents Lookout, Newbys Creek Walk, Newbys Lookout, Starrs Creek, Big Nellie Mountain and Wautui Falls.

Middle Brother Forest surrounds Middle Brother Mountain (556m -1824 ft). Several walking trails have been established within the Forest, and attractions include the largest Blackbutt trees in the State.

Hallidays Point – Diamond Beach

Midway between Taree and the Great Lakes region is the coastal area of Hallidays Point - Diamond Beach. The Lands Department has established a rainforest walk encompassing the coastal landforms as well as rare tracts of coastal rainforest. The walk takes in two headlands, Black Head and Red Head, and is joined by Black Head Beach. The Visitor Information Centre in Taree has brochures on the Walk.

Nine Mile Beach stretches southwards.

Port Macquarie
Population 33,700
Port Macquarie is situated at the mouth of the Hastings River on the North Coast of New South Wales, 423km (263 miles) north of Sydney.

Climate
Average temperatures: January max 25C (77F) - min 18C (64F); July max 18C (64F) - min 7C (45F). Average annual rainfall: 1563mm (62 ins). The CSIRO suggests that Port Macquarie has the most ideal climate in Australia. A warm off-shore current combines with the surrounding barrier of hills to form a pocket, and produce this small range of temperature.

Characteristics
A major coastal tourist resort and retirement area, Port Macquarie is the most historically significant town along the coast between Newcastle and the Queensland border.

In October, 1818, John Oxley reached the mouth of the Hastings River and described the area as "... a beautiful point of land, having plenty of good water and grass, and commanding a fine view of the interior of the port and the surrounding country". He named the inlet Port Macquarie in honour of the Governor of the Colony of New South Wales.

In 1821, the settlement of Port Macquarie was established by a pioneer party of soldiers and convicts.

How to Get There
By Air
Qantas, ☎ *13 1313* provide flights from Sydney, Melbourne, Brisbane, Newcastle, Taree, Coffs Harbour, Lismore, Ballina and Coolangatta.

By Bus
Greyhound Pioneer, ☎ *13 2030*, and **McCaffertys**, ☎ *13 1499* stop at Port Macquarie.

By Rail
The **XPT** service from Sydney stops at Wauchope and a coach service connects with Port Macquarie, ☎13 2232.

Visitor Information
The Port Macquarie Visitor Information Centre is on the corner of Clarence and Hay Streets, ☎(02) 6581 8000 or ☎1800 025 935. Their ⊕opening hours are 8.30am-5pm Mon-Fri, 9am-4.30pm weekends. Their web page is at ▣www.portmacquarieinfo.com.au and they can be emailed at ▣vicpm@midcoast.com.au

↶ Let's Stay Here
There is a lot to choose from in Port Macquarie itself, and their neighbouring towns. It is still advisable to book well in advance during the Christmas and school holiday periods. The prices listed here should be used as a guide only.

Airlie Palms,
50 Pacific Drive, ☎ *1800 242 992.* 6 units, air conditioning, comfortable facilities, barbecue, undercover parking - *From* ✪*$55.*

Beachside Backpackers,
40 Church St, ☎*6583 5512,* ▣www.*yha.com* Located only minutes away from town and the beaches. Includes your basic facilities of a kitchen, laundry, TV lounge room, internet access and a barbecue area. There are BBQ nights and free boogie board lessons on mornings. Ask about the camel rides at reception. Bike hire and parking available. *Dorm from* ✪*$20; twin from* $45 *BC MC VA*

Blue Pacific Holiday Flats,
37 Pacific Drive, ☎*6583 1686.* Self-contained units, undercover parking - ✪*$45-80.*

Golden Sands Apartments,
☎*6583 2067.* 5 self-contained suites, barbecue, undercover parking, centrally located - ✪*$50.*
Lime Burners Lodge,
353 Shoreline Dr, North Shore, ☎*3583 3381* Two story accommodation. Access by vehicle ferry. Rooms have en suite plus TV, video, radios and heating. Other facilities includes a kitchen, swimming pool and a barbeque area. Meals available. *Dorms* ✪*$24; double $28pp*

Lindel Port Macquaire,
2 Hastings River Dr, ☎*6583 1791 or 1800 688 882,* ▣www.*lindel.com* A quaint hostel with a nice verandah that has views of town. Facilities includes a kitchen, laundry, TV lounge with cable,

Pelicans at Batemans Bay

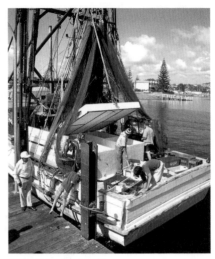

Fishing Boat on Hastings River

North Wollongong Beach

Vineyard, Hunter Valley

pool table, internet access, swimming pool and a barbecue area. Parking available. *Dorms ⊘$20; single $30; double/twin $42*

Narimba Lodge Motel, *4 Narimba Close,* ☎*6583 3839.* Five units with en suites and a range of facilities - ⊘*$55-80.*

Ozzie Pozzie Backpackers, *36 Waugh St,* ☎*6583 8133,* ▇www.nomadsworld.com A nice small purpose built hostel. Located within 5 minutes walk from shops, cafés and nightclubs. Facilities simply includes a large well equipped kitchen, laundry, internet access and a nice common room. Outside you'll find hammocks and the barbecue area with some picnic tables out in the courtyard. Cereal is served with the complimentary tea and coffee. There are also great BBQ nights. Free pick up service from the bus staion. Take advantage of the free use of boogie boards and bikes. Parking available. *Dorm ⊘$24; single $60; double/twin $30pp ($32.50pp with en suite)*

Caravan Parks
Sundowner Breakwall Tourist Park, *1 Munster Street,* ☎*6583 2755.* Swimming pool, games room, guest lounge, no pets allowed - p*owered sites ⊘$19-32 for two, cabins $50-140 for two.*

Hastings River Caravan Park, *268-270 Hastings River Drive,* ☎*6583 3387.* En suite cabins, tent area, powered sites, barbecue, swimming pool - p*ow-*

ered sites from ⊘*$18 for two, cabins from $45.*

Lighthouse Beach Holiday Village, *50 Hart Street,* ☎*6582 0581.* 24 self-contained cabins, 91 powered sites, no pets allowed - pow*ered sites ⊘$16-30 for two.*

Melaleuca Caravan Park, *128 Hastings River Drive,* ☎*6583 4498.* Budget to luxury accommodation, swimming pool and slide, barbecue, central location, no pets allowed - *81 powered sites ⊘$18 for two, on-site vans $35-60 for two, cabins from $55-115.*

Let's Eat
There are many restaurants in the town, offering local seafood, French, Italian, Thai, Mexican, Chinese, Vegetarian and Aussie fare. Here are a few you might like to try.

Al Dente, *74 Clarence Street,* ☎*6584 1422.* Licensed Italian restaurant on the waterfront, lunch and dinner.

Cafe 66, *66 Clarence Street,* ☎*6583 2484.* BYO, Italian fare, from snacks to meals, open late. Toro's Mexican, 22 Murray Street, ☎6583 4340. BYO, dine in or take away.
Filou Restaurant, *Mercure Sandcastle Motor Inn, 16-24 William Street,* ☎*6583 4646.* Licensed, French cuisine, breakfast, lunch and dinner daily.

Pancake Place, *cnr Clarence and Hay Street,* ☎*6583 4544.* BYO, open seven days from 10am, take-away and home delivery.
Scampi's on the Marina, *Park*

Street, ☎*6583 7200.* Seafood, dinner 7 days after 6pm, BYO, 'Seafood to Go' quality takeaway available for dinner 7 days.

Spinnakers Resort, *Sails Resort, Park Street,* ☎*6583 3999.* A la carte dining, licensed, breakfast, lunch and dinner.

Zephyrs on Clarence, *2 Clarence Street,* ☎*6583 6822.* Authentic Australian foods including crocodile, kangaroo and barramundi, licensed, open from 6pm.

McDonalds is on the corner of *Bay* and *Park Streets, opposite Settlement City* and on the corner of the *Pacific Highway and Oxley Street.* **KFC** is on the *corner of Horton and Hayward Streets.* The phone number for **Pizza Hut** deliveries in the area is ☎*13 1166.*

Shopping
Two major shopping centres in the town are:
Port Central Shopping Centre, *Horton Street,* ☎*6584 2988;* and **Settlement City Shopping Centre,** *Bay Street,* ☎*6581 7377.*

Points of Interest
Peppermint Park, *cnr Pacific Drive and Ocean Street (near Flynn's Beach),* ☎*6583 6111,* has landscaped parkland with water slides, pools, mini golf, aviaries, monkeys, 'Twista' Dodgems and roller skating. Barbecue facilities, a milk bar, and a fitness trail are other attractions. The Park is ⊙open Tue-Sun, and every day during school holidays. Adults ⊘$14.
Sea Acres Rainforest Centre, *Pacific Drive,* ☎*6582 3355,* has a 1.3km boardwalk within 6.2ha (15

acres) of coastal rainforest. There is also a theatre with continuous shows, a restaurant, gift shop and picnic area. The centre is ☺open daily 9am-4.30pm. Adults ✪$10.

The Church of St Thomas the Apostle, *cnr Hay and William Streets,* was built by convicts, completed in 1828, and has the original box pews made from local red cedar. In the church grounds is the old hospital dispensary, now a simple chapel. For a donation of a couple of dollars, two-hour tours are available on weekdays. The hospital was across the road, where St Agnes' Catholic Church now stands.

Fantasy Glades, Port Macquarie's Fantasy World, is in *Parklands Close, off Pacific Drive,* ☎*6582 2506.* Situated in 2.5ha (6 acres) of rainforest gardens, the Glades have ghosts, castles, dragons, witches, dwarfs, mini-cars and train rides. There are also barbecue and picnic areas and a coffee shop. A wonderful attraction for families. ☺open daily from 9am-5pm. Adults ✪$9.

Kingfisher Park, *Kingfisher Road, off the Oxley Highway,* has a large collection of Australian fauna and farm animals. There is also a coffee lounge and barbecue facilities. ☺open daily from 9am, ☎*6581 0783.* Adults ✪$9.

Billabong Koala and Aussie Wildlife Park, near the intersection of the *Pacific and Oxley Highways,* ☎*6585 1060,* is another place where you can cuddle a koala or pat a kangaroo. There are also indoor and outdoor displays and activities, a souvenir and gift shop, a barbecue courtyard, and Matilda's Restaurant. The Park is ☺open every day 9am-5pm. Adults ✪$9.

The **Hastings District Historical Museum,** in *Clarence Street near the corner of Hay Street,* ☎*6583 1108,* won the Museum of the Year Award way back in 1981 and 1982. Its 14 rooms are ☺open Mon-Sat 9.30am-4.30pm, Sun 1.30-4.30pm.

Port Macquarie Observatory, in *Rotary Park, William Street,* allows visitors to observe the Solar System with the aid of a Planetarium and telescope. ☺open Wed and Sun 7.30-9.30pm (8.15-10pm during Daylight Saving).

Both the **Historic Cemetery Gardens** and *Kooloonbung Creek Nature Park* are situated at the southern end of Horton Street. The cemetery has many old graves dating back over 150 years, and the nature reserve has landscaped gardens and walks along the creek.

Tacking Point Lighthouse, at the end of Lighthouse Beach Road, is the third oldest in the country.

Macquarie Nature Reserve, Roto House off Lord Street, has an historic visitors' centre, and in the grounds you can picnic, spy on some healthy koalas, or visit some sick ones in the yard of the Koala Hospital a short distance away (the public is not permitted inside the complex itself). The koalas are fed daily at 8am and 3pm. The Koala Preservation Society of NSW is a voluntary organisation and your support will help save the koalas in Port Macquarie.

Old World Timber Art, *120 Hastings Drive,* ☎*6583 2502,* is where you can watch craftsmen creating hand-crafted woodware and souvenirs from beautiful

Hastings timbers. The complex is ☺open Mon-Fri 8.30am-5pm, and the showroom is open Sat-Sun 10am-4pm.

Thrumster Village Pottery, is a pottery and craft centre situated 9km (6 miles) west of Port Macquarie on the Oxley Highway. Pottery, leatherwork, copper enamelling, hand made glassware and hand crafted works are on display. ☺open daily during school holidays, otherwise Thurs-Sun 9am-5pm, ☎*6581 0885.*

Cassegrain's Hastings Valley Winery, Pacific Highway, is ☺open daily 9am-5pm, ☎*6583 7777.* They offer winery inspections, wine tasting and cellar door sales. There are also picnic and barbecue facilities, a children's play area, cooperage and souvenirs.

Surfing beaches are part of the city atmosphere. The best known is **Lighthouse Beach,** which has magnificent surf for boards and body surfing.

Tours

The Visitor Information Centre has details of many river cruises, boat hire outlets and deep sea fishing charter boats. They can also advise on bush and forest safaris. Here is a selection:

Port Explorer Bus, ☎1800 025 935 for details. Town Tour, ✪$15 adults, $12 children, $13 pensioner.
Eagle Iron Motorcycle Tours, ☎1800 025 935 for details. From ✪$34 for half an hour to $290 for a full day (7 hours).
At the southern end of Lighthouse Beach, Camel Safaris, ☎6583 7650, offer camel rides lasting from 20 minutes (✪$14 adult, $9 child) to overnight camping safaris ($195pp).
Everglades Waterbus, ☎6582

5009. 5 dolphin-spotting cruises on offer, from adult ✪$22 to $50. Fantasea, ☎015 256 742. Adults ✪$19, children $8, pensioners $17, family $48.

Macquarie Mountain Tours, ☎1800 025 935 for details. Full day, adult ✪$85, child $50; River and Mountain Escape, adult ✪$80, child $40, Wine Tasting Tour, ✪$23.

Mansfield's Aussie Beach and Bush Tours, ☎1800 025 935 for details. Full day with two meals provided, ✪$80.

Port Macquarie Canoe Safaris, ☎1800 025 935. Short day tour, ✪$55 adult, $33 child. All day tour including lunch, ✪$85 adult, $45 child.

Port Macquarie River Cruises, ☎1800 025 935 for details. A number of choices including a 2hr scenic cruise, ✪$17 adults, $17 child, $9 pensioner.

Queens Lake Cruiser, ☎1800 025 935 for details. 2hr scenic cruise, adult ✪$16, child $8; 4hr lunch cruise, ✪$23 adult, $12 child.

Seaplane Joy Flights, ☎1800 025 935 for details. From ✪$45 adult, $22 child.

Wingaway Air Scenic Flights, 18000 025 935 for details.

Festivals

Port Macquarie has **The Carnival of the Pines** over the Easter period, and Wauchope (see separate entry) has **Colonial Week** in September.

Facilities
Horse Riding
Cowarra Homestead Forest Trails, ☎1800 025 935 for details. 1hr ✪$28, 2hrs $45, several routes to choose from.

Watersports
Port Macquarie Kayak Adventures, ☎1800 025 935 for details. Half-day ✪$33.
Port Water Sports, ☎1800 025

935 for details. Parasailing ✪$50, coastal tour $39.

Golf
Supa Putt Golf, ☎1800 025 935 \for details. Adult ✪$7, child $5 for 18 holes.

Outlying Attractions
South West Rocks
The largest seaside resort in the Kempsey Shire is South West Rocks, 32km (20 miles) north-east of Kempsey, near the mouth of the Macleay River. The town was so named because the pilot officer at Grassy Head, the old entrance to the river, advised masters of vessels to anchor in Trial Bay, south-west of the rocks to ensure their ships would be in deep water with room to manoeuvre under sail.

There are many beaches in the area, and two interesting places to explore: **Trial Bay Gaol** and **Smoky Cape Lighthouse.**

Trial Bay Gaol, overlooking Trial Bay, was opened as a prison in 1886, and later during World War I was an internment centre for 500 Germans. Guided tours are available through the gaol, or you can browse through the complex, with its museum pieces and restored cells. The gaol is ⏰open 9am- 5pm daily, ☎6566 6168.

Smoky Cape Lighthouse, on the border of Hat Head National Park, is the highest lighthouse on the NSW coast, standing 128m (420 ft) above sea level, and was opened in 1891. Visitors are welcome on ⏰Tuesdays and Thursdays, and you can chat to one of the light-keepers, and admire the outstanding views.

On the shores of the beaches around South West Rocks there are many wrecks of vessels dating back to 1816.

Kempsey
Situated 48km (30 miles) north of Port Macquarie, Kempsey straddles the Macleay River and is the heart of a fast growing valley renowned for its natural beauty and stress-free lifestyle.

Attractions include: The **Macleay River Historical Societies' Museum,** which can be found in the Information Centre complex on the Pacific Highway, South Kempsey, ⏰open daily 10am-4pm; The **Kempsey Shire Library** and **Les Graham Art Collection**, Elbow Street, West Kempsey, ⏰open Mon-Fri 10am-6pm, Sat 9am-noon; and Kempsey Saleyards, Kemp Street.

There are many bushwalks and drives in the Macleay Valley. The area has facilities for every kind of sport imaginable on land and water.

The beaches in the Kempsey Shire offer safe, patrolled sections for families. The village of Stuarts Point is the focal point for the beaches that stretch north from the mouth of the Macleay River to the Shire's boundary above Middle Head.

The coastal village of **Hat Head** is regarded as one of the top fishing spots on the coast of NSW, because of its close proximity to the continental shelf. Hat Head is situated in the heart of the Hat Head National Park, and is the perfect base for a quiet family holiday, a fishing trip or a nature-lover's excursion.

The Kempsey Visitor Information Centre is on the *Pacific Highway, South Kempsey*, ⏰open Mon-Fri 9am-5pm, weekends 10am-4pm. ☎6554 8799 or ☎1800 642 480 or email at ✉ktic@midcoast .com.au

Wauchope

Wauchope is 19km (12 miles) west of Port Macquarie on the Oxley Highway. At the centre of the region's timber industry, this historic town draws visitor mainly to its Timbertown theme park.

The main attraction is Timbertown, ☎6585 1866, an entire village recreated to demonstrate the struggles and achievements of the pioneers. It has a steam train, timber sawing, a bullock team, a woodturner and a general store selling the finished goods plus lollies from glass jars and licorice by the yard, amongst other things from 'the good old days'. There is also a bakery offering freshly baked damper with home-made jams, and Devonshire teas. The houses and the church have been faithfully reproduced in the manner of the era (1880-1910), many with fine furniture and utensils brought out from the home country. You should allow 4 hours minimum for a visit, maybe more if it's a hot day and you spend some time in the Maul and Wedge Hotel. Timbertown is ☉open daily from 9am. It is 3km from Wauchope on the Oxley Highway.

Another attraction is the **Big Bull** in Redbank Farm, 50 Redbank Road, ☎6585 2044, just over the river. The Bull is 14m (46 ft) high, and in the complex there is a working dairy farm, an animal nursery, an educational display, hay rides, a restaurant, and a souvenir shop. It is ☉open daily 9am-5pm.

The Wauchope Information and Neighbourhood Centre is in Shop 3 Roland Plaza, 33 High Street, ☎6586 4055.

Coffs Harbour

Population 22,170

Coffs Harbour is situated on the coast of New South Wales, 578km (359 miles) north of Sydney and 427km (265 miles) south of Brisbane.

Climate

Average temperatures: January max 26C (79F) - min 19C (66F); June max 19C (66F) - min 9C (48F). Average annual rainfall: 1759mm (69 ins); wettest six months October to March.

Characteristics

Coffs Harbour is a popular year-round tourist destination. On one side there are the blue waters of the Pacific Ocean, while the western border area is the Great Dividing Range. The combination of golden sands, high mountains, dense luxuriant rainforests, steep banana plantations, clear rivers and streams make it a superb holiday area.

Coffs Harbour was originally called Korff's Harbour, named after Captain John Korff, who sheltered here in 1847. The harbour, being halfway between Brisbane and Sydney, was an extremely busy port facility for the many vessels plying the coastal trade. It was considered a dangerous port, however, and after a boycott by many ships' captains, the lighthouse was eventually built in 1878.

The surrounding lowlands and rolling hills were once a source of red cedar and other valuable timber when discovered some 150 years ago. The pastoralists followed in the tracks of the timber cutters and the area was given to cattle, dairying, vegetable growing and, of course, banana plantations.

How to Get There
By Air

The following airlines fly regional services into Coffs Harbour: **Qantas**, ☎13 1313 and **Rex**, ☎13 1713.

By Bus

Interstate coach lines operate daily in Coffs Harbour. Contact **Greyhound Pioneer**, ☎13 2030, or **McCaffertys**, ☎13 1499.

By Rail

XPT services operate daily from Sydney and overnight expresses operate from Sydney and Brisbane, ☎13 2232.

Visitor Information

The Coffs Harbour-Tourism Holiday Coast Information Centre is located at the corner of Rose Avenue and Marcia Street, Coffs Harbour, ☎6652 1522 or *1300 369 070*. It is ☉open 9am-5pm daily. Email them at ✉tourism@coffscoast.com.au or check out the website at ▧www.coffs.net

---

↪ Let's Stay Here

Hostel, pub, caravan and cabin/lodge accommodation is plentiful. Here is a selection with prices which should be used as a guide only. The telephone area code is 02.

Aussitel Backpackers,
312 High St, ☎*6651 1871 or 1800 330 335,* ▧www.*aussitel.com* Located close to the Jetty area opposite the Coffs Creek. Close to beaches, food, entertainment and the International Marina. Facilities includes kitchen, laundry, TV, video, pool table, games, volleyball, darts, a large heated swimming pool

and a barbecue area. There are loads of free stuff for use like canoes, boogie boards, bikes, scuba diving in their pool, golf and tennis equipment and fishing rods and reels. Plus free BBQ. They also have an excellent range of planned social activities every night of the week and they can assist you in finding work. Parking available. *Dorm* ✪*$24; double/twin $30pp*

Barracuda Backpackers, *19 Arthur St,* ☎ *6651 3514 or 1800 111 514,* 🖳*www.bac kpackers.coffs.TV* Located close Park Beach Plaza shopping centre and the beach. All rooms have fridges and comes with linen plus towels. Facilities includes kitchen, laundry, TV lounge, internet access and there's also a swimming pool with spa. Staff are very helpful with the local

info and the things to do. Ask for the drink vouchers. Free scuba lessons in the pool, free use of fishing equipment and games equipment like volleyball, football, surf and boogie boards. Parking available. *Dorms* ✪*$20; double/ twins $50*

Coffs Harbour Backpackers Resort, *110 Albany St,* ☎ *6652 6462,*

Coffs Harbour

Accommodation

1 Aussitel Backpackers
2 Barracuda Backpackers
3 Coffs Harbour YHA
4 Hoey Moey Backpackers

🖳www.*yha.com.au*
Located closely to the city centre, the bus stop and to the shops. A nice and friendly hostel and kept clean. A pretty well equipped hostel in terms of facilities. They are your normal fully equipped kitchen and dining, laundry, lounge room, TV room with video, internet access, a games room with a pool table, a swimming pool and a barbecue area. There are also barbecue nights. Bike, boogie boards and surf boards available for hire. For information on other activities, like kayaking, at the reception. Parking available.*Dorms from ✪$21; twin from $46; double from $50 BC MC VA*

Emu Park Backpackers,
77 Coast Rd, Cabarita Beach, Tweed Head, ☎*6676 1190*
The lodge is only minutes away from the beaches, shops, restaurants, hotel and club. Facilities are a fully equipped kitchen, laundry, games and common rooms, internet acces and barbecue area. There is also free use of sporting equipment like surfboards, boogie boards, fishing gear. Free airport pick up service. Bike hire and parking available. *Dorms ✪$21; doubles $55*

Hoey Moey Backpackers,
Ocean Parade, ☎*6652 6462,*
🖳*www.parkbeach.uss.net.au/ hoeymoey/hostel.htm* Located right at the beach of Coffs Harbour and only minutes away from Park Beach Plaza. Formerly a motel transformed into a hostel, all rooms have

their own fridge, TVs and en suite bathrooms. Other facilities includes your basic kitchen, laundry, internet access and a TV lounge. Beer garden on site with live entertainment. Parking available. *Dorms ✪$20; double/twin $43* (ask for the special prices if you intend to stay longer)

Pacific Lodge,
2 Pacific Ave, ☎*6652 2266,*
🖳*www.ghostlovers.com.au/ pacific.htm*
Located in centre of Coffs Harbour Tourist area only minutes walk away from Park Beach and Park Beach Plaza. Fully equipped and basic facilities. *Rooms ✪$50.*

Caravan Parks
Coffs Village Caravan Park,
215 Pacific Highway, ☎*6652 4633.* (No pets allowed), 52 sites - *powered sites ✪$17 for two, on-site vans $25 for two.*

Bananacoast Caravan Park,
Pacific Highway, ☎*6652 2868.* (Dogs allowed by arrangement), 105 sites - *powered sites ✪$17-26 for two, cabins $35-105 for two.*

Split Solitary Caravan Park,
Split Solitary Road, ☎*6653 6212.* (No pets during holiday period), 125 sites - *powered sites ✪$15-20 for two, cabins $40-75 for two.*

Let's Eat
Coffs Harbour has many restaurants and fast food outlets, particularly down on the Marina. The restaurants range from many international cuisines to the

family type catered for by the local clubs. Some of the motels and hotels have restaurants and bistros, and here is a taste of what else is available.

Ocean Oyster and Steak Grill,
394 High Street, ☎*6650 0444.*

Sands, *cnr Park Beach Road* ☎ *Ocean Parade,* ☎*6652 2666.*

Sawan Thai Restaurant, *376 High Street, Coffs Jetty,* ☎*6652 9699.* Vegetarian food is a speciality, Open 5.30pm-10.30pm Mon-Sat, closed Sunday and Public Holidays.

Star Anise, *93 Grafton Street,* open 6pm-9pm Wed-Sun, 11.30am-2pm Thursday and Friday, closed Monday and Tuesday with selected hours on Public Holidays.

Stetsons Steakhouse and Saloon, *cnr Pacific Highway and Bray Streets,* ☎*6651 9166.* Open 5.30pm-10pm 7 days, closed Public Holidays.

Taruah Thai Restaurant, *360 High Street,* ☎*6652 5992.*

Tequila Mexican Restaurant,
224 High Street, ☎*6652 1279.* Fully licensed open 5.30pm-8pm every day.

The Dragon, *108 Grafton Street,* ☎*6652 4187.* Cantonese cuisine with a seafood emphasis.

The Fishermans Katch, *394 High Street,* ☎*6652 4372.* Seafood platters and steak. Open 6am-8pm daily, closed Public Holidays.

The Village, *97 Park Beach Road,* ☎ *6652 2055.*

McDonalds have a branch on the corner of the *Pacific Highway and North Boambee Road* and one in the *High Street Mall.* There is a **Pizza Hut** on the *corner of High and Gordon Streets,* and you can call them for delivery on ☎ *13 1166.*

Points of Interest
The Big Banana, *Pacific Highway,* ☎ *6652 4355* is the landmark of Coffs Harbour, and is 3km north of the town. There you will find an audio-visual theatrette, Aboriginal Dreamtime Cave, historical exhibits, hydroponics glasshouse, banana packing shed, Triffid Forest, Time Tunnel, Future Culture Space Station, Greenhouse Food Fair/Souvenir complex, display gardens, machinery museum/ocean lookout, and a farmers' market.

Pet Porpoise Pool, ☎ *6652 6133, in Orlando Street,* has performing dolphins and sea lions, native fauna, marine animals, live sharks and reef tank, a kiosk and souvenir outlet. It is ☺open daily 9am-5pm. Shows are at 10.30am and 2.15pm.

North Coast Regional Botanic Garden, ☎ *6648 4188,* in *Hardacre Street* in the centre of town, has 19ha (47 acres) featuring native and exotic plants, ☺open daily.

Within an hour away of Coffs Harbour, and covered with magnificent rainforest, is **Dorrigo National Park,** which has many walking trails.

There are seven State Forests in the area. **Sealy Lookout** is a must when visiting **Bruxner**

Park Flora Reserve, as it offers panoramic views of the city, Pacific coastline and banana-clad hillsides. The **Dorigo National Park** and **Rainforest Centre** is on the corner of *Dome Road and Lyrebird Lane,* ☎ *6657 2309.*

Several art and opal galleries are in and around the town. The Visitor Information Centre in *Hickory Street, Dorrigo,* ☎ *6657 2486,* can provide you with details if you are interested in browsing through these places.

Joy flights over Nambucca Heads, Bellingen, Orara Valley, Woolgoolga and the Solitary Islands, are available (Skylink Helicopters, Aviation Drive, ☎6658 0899; Wingaway Air, Airport Drive, ☎ *6650 0655),* as are deep sea fishing trips (Adriatic Fishing Trips, Shop 5 International Marina, ☎ *6651 1277;* Cougar Cat 12 Fishing Trips, ☎ *6651 6715).*

Storyland Gardens, ☎ *6653 1400,* 10km south of Coffs Harbour on Lyons Road, Sawtell, has a giant Old Woman's Shoe, surrounded by popular fairytale settings such as Snow White and Little Red Riding Hood. It is ☺open 10am-4pm Thu-Sun and every day during school holidays.

And of course, there are the beaches. Coffs Harbour has many, and they range from those with full-blooded rolling surf that boardriders and body surfers love, to the sheltered, lagoon-type that are perfect for toddlers, to some secluded beaches used for nude bathing.

Festivals
The **Agricultural Show** is held in May.

Facilities
Two golf courses, five lawn bowling clubs, three surf clubs, a yacht club, a deep sea fishing club and racecourse. Tennis, squash, ten-pin bowling, croquet and indoor cricket facilities are available. An indoor stadium caters for basketball, badminton, indoor hockey and many other indoor sports.

Outlying Attractions
Woolgoolga
Situated 25km north of Coffs Harbour, Woolgoolga has a large Sikh community and they have built a lavish temple, called **Guru Nanak.**

The **Raj Mahal Emporium,** ☎ *6644 1149,* an Indian Theme Park on corner of Pullen Street and the Pacific Highway, has Indian artefacts and food.

The **Woolgoolga Art Gallery,** *Turon Parade,* ☎ *6654 1064,* has a treasure trove of fine art, pottery, batikwork and woodcraft, and is ☺open daily 10am-4pm.

Whitewater rafting on the Nymboida River is available for the adventurous.

George's Gold Mine, ☎ *6654 5355, 782 Moleton Road, Moleton,* is ☺open Wed-Sun 10am-5pm, and has inspections of the Bayfield gold mine and original equipment. There are picnic and barbecue areas, and food is available.

Valery Trails, 758 Valery Road, Valery, ☎ *6653 4401,* offer escorted trail rides through the Pine Creek State Forest, catering for both experienced and inexperienced riders.

Nambucca Heads
Situated 114km (71 miles) south of Coffs Harbour, Nambucca

Heads is another popular holiday resort, and has a wide range of accommodation from premier hotels to flats and caravan parks.

It is a farming and timber district, and there are facilities for boating, lawn bowls, fishing (river, rock, beach and deep sea), golf, surfing and tennis. Attractions include the **Nambucca Historical Museum; Mary Boulton's Pioneer Cottage; The Pub with No Beer; Taylor Arm** - venue for the Easter Country Music Festival and Fair; the historical **Star Hotel; Kew House Toy and Doll Museum;** and the **Worm Farm**, Valla Road, Valla, which has worm picking, packing and racing.

The Nambucca Valley Visitor Information Centre can be found at *4 Pacific Highway*. They are ☼open 9am-5pm daily, and have all the information you will need, ☎*6568 6954* or ☎*1 800 646 587*.

�753 Other Areas to Stay
Bellingen Backpackers YHA, *2 Short St,* ☎*6655 1116,* ▬*www.yha.com* A great hostel with a feel good atmosphere, perfect for a few days off. They give you an option of using mosquito nets on your bed which is a rarity. There are also optional secluded campsites in the garden. Facilities includes the kitchen, laundry, internet access and a pool table. There's also the music room where you can chill, listen to your cd or try their musical instruments. Outside you'll find a barbecue area, hammocks, a volleyball court and campfires. Verandahs and balconies abound. There's also canoeing and bike hire available. Nearest

foodstore is close by. Rainforest tours are organized by the hostel. Parking available. *Dorms from ☻$22; double/twin from $56; camping $10 BC MCVA EFTPOS*

Grafton
Population 16,500
Grafton is situated on a bend of the Clarence River, 660km (410 miles) north of Sydney, 320km (199 miles) south of Brisbane, and 160km (99 miles) east of Glen Innes.

Climate
Average temperatures: January max 32C (90F) - min 19C (66F); July max 17C (63F) - min 7C (45F).

Characteristics
Grafton, the Jacaranda City, has tree lined streets and graceful old buildings. The district was originally discovered by the escaped convict Richard Craig in 1831. For a pardon and one hundred pounds, he brought a party of cedar getters to log the huge cedar stands. The stories of the 'red gold' spread, and John Small arrived in 1838 and first occupied land on Woodford Island.

The settlement was established shortly after, and the first sale of town blocks took place in 1851. Governor Fitzroy officially named the town after his grandfather, the Duke of Grafton, and it was proclaimed a city in 1885.

How to Get There
By Bus
Greyhound Pioneer and McCaffertys stop at Grafton on the Sydney/Brisbane routes.

By Rail
There are daily **Countrylink** services from Sydney to Grafton.

Visitor Information
The Clarence River Tourist Association is on the corner of *Spring Street* and the *Pacific Highway*, ☎*6642 4277*. They can give tips on the best parts and offer you directions on how to access them, and whether road conditions require 4WD at your time of visit.

�753 Let's Stay Here
For a holiday with a difference, visitors can hire a houseboat accommodating up to eight adults in comfort, and cruise up and down the Clarence River, stopping at many of the 100 islands. No licence is required to operate local houseboats. For more information contact **Clarence River Boats**, *Clarence Street, Brushgrove,* ☎*6647 6232*. As for more conventional budget accommodation, Grafton has motels, hostels, and caravan parks. Here is a selection which should be used as a guide only. The telephone area code is 02.

Hi-Way Motel, *Pacific Highway,* ☎*6642 1588.* 31 units, playground, pool - ☻$55-75.

Roches Family Hotel, *85 Victoria Street,* ☎*6642 2866.* 14 rooms, licensed restaurant, barbecue - ☻$40.

Caravan Parks
The Gateway Village, *598 Sum-merland Way,* ☎*6642 4225.* 90 sites, pool, practice golf, barbecue - *powered sites*

✪ *$20 for two, cabins from $60, on-site vans $40-45 for two.*

Grafton Sunset Caravan Park, *302 Gwydir Highway,* ☎6642 3824. (Pets allowed by arrangement) 70 sites, barbecue, kiosk, pool - *powered sites* ✪*$15 for two, on-site vans $30-35 for two, cabins $40-45 for two.*

Let's Eat

Most establishments are open for counter lunches and counter teas from Monday to Saturday, and the Bowling Club, in Kemp Street, is open for lunch and dinner Mon-Fri, while the District Services Club in Mary Street, is open for lunch and dinner daily. In South Grafton, the Golf Club is open for dinner Wed-Sat. Here is a selection of restaurants you might like to try.

Clancys Restaurant and Bistro, *Grafton Hotel, 97 Fitzroy St,* ☎6643 3411.

Jarmers Restaurant, *85 Victoria St,* ☎6642 2866.

Kuppazz Family Restaurant, *Shopping World Shop 40,* ☎6643 1003.

Lea-Mar's Bistro, *93 Prince St,* ☎6643 2290.

New Oriental Chinese Restaurant, *127 Prince St,* ☎6642 7888.

Points of Interest

Grafton has a bus service operating hourly tours that pass many of the historic buildings and points of interest (no service Sun or after noon Sat), ☎6642 3111.

Buses leave Market Square at 20 minutes past the hour. There are also regular bus services to Yamba, Maclean, Ulmarra, Lismore and Glen Innes.

Clarence River Ferries, ☎6646 6423, have a fleet of three passenger ferries with individual capacities up to 160 people, servicing the needs of residents and visitors from Grafton to the river mouth, during special events like the **Jacaranda Festival**. Every day a minimum of four return trips connect Iluka and Yamba. The 30 minute river crossing is a popular scenic alternative to the lengthy road journey. The services from Yamba are met at Iluka by a courtesy bus provided by Iluka's Sedger's Reef Hotel, where passengers can enjoy a top seafood luncheon.

Regular river cruises also operate from Yamba and Iluka including a weekly visit to Maclean (Monday) and Harwood Island (Wednesday and Friday). There are plans to have regular river cruises and ferry services to Susan Island from the wharf at the river-end of *Prince Street*, beginning in 1991.

Susan Island is situated in the Clarence River, with its tip almost opposite Prince Street. The northern end of the island has a rainforest with walking tracks, and the largest fruit bat colony in the southern hemisphere. It is a spectacular sight when the colony departs at dusk each summer evening. The southern section of the island has barbecues, picnic and toilet facilities.

Grafton Regional Art Gallery, *158 Fitzroy Street,* occupies the restored Prentice House (1880), and has a variety of exhibitions from many notable artists and

crafts people. It is ⊙open 10am-4pm Wed-Sun.

Schaeffer House Museum, *192 Fitzroy Street,* is in another fine old homestead, and has exhibits tracing the history of Grafton and the Clarence Valley. ⊙open 2-4pm, Tues, Thurs and Sun.

Christ Church Cathedral (1884), is designed along Gothic lines with towering arches and a spacious interior. The Cathedral is ⊙open 7am-5.30pm daily.

Saraton Theatre in Prince Street, is a restored traditional picture theatre which also hosts live shows, conventions and community functions.

The National Parks of the Clarence Valley are Yuraygir, Bundjalung, Gibraltar Range and Washpool. Yuraygir and Bundjalung are coastal parks, and Gibraltar Range and Washpool to the west offer a variety of scenic drives, camping areas and walking tracks.

Grafton is very proud of its trees, and 7000 of them line the avenues and shade the 24 well-maintained parks. The Visitor Centre has a brochure on trees and parks, but the most popular parks are: **Market Square**, adjacent to the clock tower in Prince Street; **Memorial Park and Boulevarde**, river end of *Prince Street*; **South Grafton Boulevarde**, *Through Street*; **See Park Arboretum**, *Pound Street.*

Festivals

The **Jacaranda Festival** was first held in 1935, and is Australia's longest running festival. The Jacaranda Queen is crowned on the last Saturday in October each year, heralding the start of the major festival week. On the first Saturday in November there is a spectacular street parade for the close of the Festival, but not the end of festivities. People flock for weeks before and after to view the trees, exhibitions and events.

Facilities

Horseback trail rides can be taken through the coastal forests; the Grafton racetrack has over 40 meetings a year, with the **July Racing Carnival** rating as the richest country carnival in the nation; the July Carnival at the nearby greyhound track is also a major event; lawn bowls are catered for at four licensed clubs; the Big River Squash and Fitness Centre, *Hoof Street*, ☎6642 6633, has a gym, swimming pool, sauna, aerobic classes, masseurs and Tae-kwan-do training; Grafton Squash Centre, *39 Queen Street*, ☎6642 2989, welcomes visitors; tennis courts are in *Prince Street*, ☎6642 5666; the Grafton Olympic Pool in *Oliver Street* has a waterslide, and there is a heated pool in Armidale Street; Big River Ski Lodge at Seelands caters for skiers and hires out boats, ☎6644 9324; and the Visitor Centre can advise on local sailing clubs.

Outlying Attractions
Maclean

"The Scottish Town in Australia," Maclean, 34km (21 miles) north of Grafton, was first settled by Scottish immigrants, and the town's annual Highland Gathering over the Easter period, and Free Presbyterian Church (the oldest in Australia) are legacies of this past.

During September, the Cane Harvest Festival is celebrated with a Queen Crowning, a street parade, and plenty of fun. A local cane farm can be inspected every Friday, throughout the year.

The Clarence River is one of only two NSW rivers trawled for prawns, and the river fleet works from the Ulmarra ferry to the river mouth using Maclean as its base.

For Visitor Information look out for places displaying the blue "I" sign, or call in at Scottish Corner souvenir shop in River Street. Attractions include **Maclean Lookout, The Pinnacle Rocks,** and the **Bicentennial Museum,** all in Wharf Street, and a number of historic buildings. Water skiing, sailing and fishing are popular pastimes.

The Lower Clarence Visitors Centre is in *Ferry Park, Pacific Highway,* ☎6645 4121, email ✉crta1@nor. com.au. It is ⊕open 9am - 5pm daily.

Lismore
Population 27,200
Situated between rainforest and sea, Lismore is in northern New South Wales, inland from Ballina on the Bruxner Highway.

Climate
Average temperatures: January max 30C (86F) - min 19C (66F); July max 20C (68F) - min 6C (43F). Average annual rainfall, 1349mm (53 ins); wettest months December-May.

Characteristics
The commercial, cultural and sporting capital of the North Coast region. Lismore is the administrative centre for Federal and State Government and has a university, as well as being the commercial and retail hub of the region. The surrounding countryside is extremely fertile and all types of agriculture are found in the region. Tropical fruits, such as bananas, avocados, pineapples and macadamia nuts, are widely grown. Dairying is also popular and the hills away from the coast are still timbered. There has been much controversy in past years over logging.

How to Get There
By Air
Rex, ☎13 1713, fly to/from Sydney.

By Bus
Greyhound Pioneer, ☎13 2030, stop at Lismore on their Sydney/ Brisbane Pacific Highway route. **Kirklands Coaches**, ☎1300 367 077, provide daily services to/from Brisbane and nearby regional centres.

By Rail
There is a regular Countrylink service from Sydney to Lismore, ☎13 2232.

Visitor Information
The Lismore Visitor Information Centre, *cnr Ballina and Molesworth Streets* (the main street), ☎6622 0122 or ☎1300 369 795, has literature, maps, souvenirs and accommodation booking services, and is ⊕open 9.30am-4pm Mon- Fri, 10am-3pm weekends and 9.30am-4pm on Public Holidays. The online references for more info are: email ✉tourism@liscity.nsw. gov.au and website 🖥www.liscity. nsw.gov.au

↪ Let's Stay Here
Here is a selection of accommodation available in Lismore, with prices that should be used as a guide only. The telephone area code is 02.

Lismore Backpackers (Currendina Lodge), *14 Ewing St,* ☎ *6621 6118,* Located close to the shops. Set in a big old wooden building. Facilities includes a well equipped kitchen, laundry, TV lounge and a barbecue area. Parking available.There is also a little balcony. *Dorms* ✪ *$22; single $35; double $47*

Caravan Parks
Lismore Tourist Caravan Park, *Dawson Street,* ☎ *6621 6581.* (Pets allowed by discretion), 92 sites, barbecue - *powered sites* ✪*$17 for two, on-site vans $30-35 for two, cabins $40 for two.*

Lismore Lake Caravan Park, *Bruxner Highway,* ☎ *6621 2585.* (Pets on application), 138 sites, pool, barbecue - *powered sites* ✪*$13 for two, cabins $35-45 for two.*

Road Runner Caravan Park, *Caniaba Road,* ☎ *6621 6705.* (No pets allowed), 133 sites, tennis, pool - *powered sites* ✪*$14 for two, cabins $40 for two.*

Let's Eat
For tasty and reasonably priced meals, try the Golf Club and the local RSL Club. A few additional suggestions are:

Bangkok Lismore, *44 Ballina Street,* ☎ *6621 3375.*

Giorgios Vegetarian Italia, *73 Magellan Street,* ☎ *6622 3177.*

Lismore Seafood Inn, *25 Eggins Lane,* ☎ *6621 3736.*

Mandarin Palace Chinese Restaurant, *153 Keen Street,* 11.30am-2pm and 5pm-8pm 7 days, closed Public Holidays.

Mexican Magic, *6 Carrington Street,* ☎ *6621 8206.*
Paupiettes, *56 Ballina Street,* ☎ *6621 6135.* Open 6.30pm-9.30pm Tue-Sat only.

Thai Lotus Classic, *207 Ballina Street,* ☎ *6622 0062.*

The Loft, *6 Nesbitt Lane,* ☎ *6622 0252.*

The Tempted Palate, *34 Molesworth Street,* ☎ *6621 6566.*

For real budget **McDonalds** is on the corner of *Laurel Avenue and Brewster Stree*t or call **Pizza Hut** on ☎ *13 1166.* Otherwise try another of the several take-away establishments in the city, most of which are on Keen, Ballina and Union Streets.

Points of Interest
Lismore was the queen of the river towns last century, as it was as far up river as the trading schooners could reach. The red cedar and other rainforest timber logs from **'The Big Scrub'** were floated downstream to Lismore.

Cedar Log Memorial - a giant cedar log is displayed in the small park behind the City Hall as a permanent memorial to the first cedar loggers of the Richmond Valley.

Claude Riley Memorial Lookout, 3km north-east along the New Ballina Cutting, offers a fine view of the city.

Robinson's Lookout, also called Girard's Hill Lookout, is 2km south of the city centre. It

offers views of the city, the river and the surrounding countryside.

There is a walking track that joins onto Wilson's walk, which starts at Albert Park and is 6.5km (4 miles) long. It takes you through Wilson's Park, a rainforest remnant with many trees identified by plaques where you can spot local bird life.

The Lismore Visitor and Heritage Centre, ☎ *6622 0122,* established during the Bicentennial Year, features an unusual walk-through, indoors 'rainforest experience'. Also incorporated in the centre are 'hands on' displays, models and photographic features of Lismore's history.

Lismore Lake is 2.5km from Lismore on the Casino road. There are gas barbecues and a swimming pool, a playground and a BMX track. It is popular with water skiers.

Heritage Park, near the Visitors Centre, has toilets and gas barbecues.

The Richmond River Historical Society Museum, *165 Molesworth Street,* ☎ *6621 9993,* contains a fascinating collection of Aboriginal artifacts and pioneer relics, as well as geological specimens.

The Regional Art Gallery, *131 Molesworth Street,* ☎ *6622 2209,* houses fine collections of paintings, pottery and ceramics.

An Aboriginal Bora Ring adjoins **Tucki Tucki Cemetery**. The Ring overlooks the Steve King's Plain and the mid-Richmond valley. It is one of several tribal ceremonial grounds in the district, and has been fenced and marked with a description board.

Historic River Cruises aboard

MV Bennelong, a fully licensed cruise boat, sail regularly from Lismore. For bookings, call into their office in Boat Harbour Road, Ballina, or ☎0414 664 552 (mobile).

At Alphadale, on the eastern edge of the city, Cowlong Road, is **Macadamia Magic.** This is a macadamia nut processing complex where factory inspections are welcome. The tourist annex specialises in macadamia products and provides refreshments and souvenirs daily, ☎6624 2900. It is ☺open 9am-5pm weekdays and 10am-4pm open weekends.

Festivals

September is the month when it's all happening: **The Spring Orchid Show; The Lismore Cup,** which is the highlight of the racing calendar in Lismore; **The Cedar Guitar Awards; The Spring Greyhound Racing Carnival** and the **Annual Spring Garden Competition.**
The **North Coast National Show** is held in the third week of October each year.

Facilities

Rolling skating at Summerland Skate Centre, North Lismore; Lismore Grand Prix, South Lismore, is a racing circuit where you are the driver, or where you can enjoy mini-golf.

You can learn to water ski at the Lismore Lake Ski School; The Lismore Bowl is ☺open daily 9am-midnight for ten-pin bowling.

Lawn bowls, tennis, swimming, squash and golf are all catered for, as well as the traditional spectator sports and seasonal activities, such as the Speedway and Karting programmes.

Outlying Attractions Murwillumbah Region

If you wish to visit the Murwillumbah region, drop into the World Heritage Rainforest Visitor Information Centre Murwillumbah, cnr *Pacific Highway* and *Alma Streets,* ☺open Mon-Sat 9am-4.30pm, Sun 9.30am-4pm. They share a web page with Tweed Heads Information at ▇www.tactic.nsw.gov.au, and you can email them here at ✉info@tactic.nsw.gov.au Mt Warning, 1157m (3796 ft), which towers above the Tweed Valley behind Murwillumbah, dominates the scenery for . miles around. It was named by Captain Cook in 1770. The area is a National Park, and a walking track winds its way to the top for panoramic views of the Tweed Valley and the coast. The lower slopes are rainforest with heathlands higher up. Ask at the Information Centre about where to start and the current conditions of the climb.

↵ Let's Stay Here
Murwillumbah Hotel,
13 Wharf St, ☎*6672 1139,* ▇*www.murwillumbahhotel.com* Situated in the main street of Murwillumbah, heart of the Tweed Valley. A fully renovated modern equipped country hotel. Accommodation located above a pub. Basic facilities, with a common room, TV and the kitchen with a toaster, microwave and fridge. They also have function facilities, great food at the on site restaurant and the best cold beer in town. Pool tables are in the pub. *Dorms ✪$15; double $40*

Riverside YHA Backpackers,
1 Tumbulgum Rd, ☎*6672 3763,* ▇*www.yha.com* Located at the banks of the Tweed River. A warm and friendly atmosphere built within a 90-year-old Sea Captain's house. Plenty of character. 250 metres to nearest foodstore, nearby railway station and bus stop and some restaurants are in the area. The facilities are kitchen, laundry, TV room and barbecue area. If you stay two nights, you are entitled to free transport to Mt Warning plus use of canoe. Bike hire available. *Dorms from ✪$23; double/twin from $50; BC MC VA EFTPOS*

Nimbin
Situated inland, in the centre of an area where the 'hippy' approach to life is very popular. One could say Nimbin was the birthplace of alternative lifestyle in Australia in the late 1960s. It is 30km from Lismore.

It is not quite so 'lovey-dovey' now with not a few gaunt addicts roaming the streets and dope openly offered.

Nimbin Rocks, or Needles, are unusual rock formations 3km on the Lismore side of Nimbin. They are a sacred site of the Bundjalung Aboriginal Tribe.

The Tuntable Falls, 13km (8 miles) from Nimbin, can only be reached by a three hour return hike along the creek bed, and it is a walk only for the fit and healthy.

The website at ▇www.nimbin.net will give you an idea of the limited facilities the town offers and a taste of the prevailing attitudes of this small rural community. The email address is: ✉thecrew@nimbin.net.au

Cape Byron Bay

Whales at Byron Bay

Flynns Beach, Port Macquarie

⤳ Let's Stay Here

Granny's Farm Backpackers,
*Cullen St, ☎6689 1333, ✉w
ww.nimbinbackpackers.com*
Situated on the edge of the
village, bounded by a shady
swimmable creek, full of wildlife. Watch out for the platypus. Set in a huge 10 acre
rural land. Very clean and well
maintained. Your normal accommodation with big dorms,
and there is also a dorm inside an old train carriage. Facilities includes a large kitch-
en and TV room, plus two
swimming pools, an outdoor
area with a common area with
pool table, fire and barbecue
place. The staff organises
movie nights and meal nights
at the nearby theatre. Camping also available. *Dorms
♻$20; double $48; camping
$10 (one person), $18 (two
people), $25 (three people)*

**Nimbin Hotel and
Backpackers,**
55 Cullen St, ☎6689 1246
Most conveniently located, at
the very centre of town, just
next door to Hemp Embassy.
Another accommodation situated above a pub with clean
dorms. Basic facilities that includes a small kitchen owning
a microwave. There's also the
common room with a TV and
the balcony that overlooks the
street. *Dorms from ♻$15.*

Nimbin Rox YHA,
*74 Thorburn St, ☎6689 0022,
✉www.yha.com* Set in an
amazing hilltop that overlooks
the Night Cap Ranges and
Nimbin Rocks sacred site. A
km to nearest foodstore and
bus depot. Facilities includes

kitchen, laundry, TV lounge,
internet access and a barbecue area. There are also lush
tropical gardens and swimming holes around. Parking
available. *Dorms from ♻$22;
BC MC VA EFTPOS*

Rainbow Retreat,
75 Thornburn St, 6689 1262
Located outside of town, but
only a short walk back to the
village. Very Nimbin atmosphere. Accommodation set in
a number of buildings with
your normal hostel facilities.
Cafe on site. If you're after
some hippy experience,
the you've found the right
place. *Dorm bed ♻$15;
double/twin room $40;
camping $8pp*

The Channon

This is a charming village on
Terania Creek, 20km (12 miles)
north of Lismore.

On the second Sunday of every
month, the famous **Channon
Craft Market,** the original country
market in the area, is held. Only
hand-made articles and produce
are sold. There is always a
colourful crowd with buskers
and street theatre, pony rides and
games for the kids.

Terania Creek, about which
there was so much controversy
in the 1970s, is now part of the
Nightcap National Park, in which
there are many walking tracks
through tropical rainforest and to
Protesters' Falls.

The **Wyymara Protea
Plantation**, *8 Cooks Lane,
Dalwood, ☎6629 5270*, has 2000
protea shrubs in production, with
many different varieties of fresh
and dried protea flowers.

Byron Bay

42km (26 miles) from Lismore
is idyllic Byron Bay - New South
Wales' worst-kept secret. More
than 500,000 tourists flock
here each year, making it the
most visited destination outside
Sydney. The city is renowned for
its relaxed, peaceful atmosphere,
though it is getting harder with so
many visitors.

The focus here is on
recreation and relaxation, so
most of the town's services fall
into one of these categories.
Visit or contact the Information
Centre to find the interests that
most appeal to you.

Cape Byron is the most easterly
point of Australia, topped by an
extremely powerful lighthouse
built in 1901. The Lighthouse is
⊙open daily 8am-6.30pm.

For further details, the Byron
Bay Visitor Information Centre
is located at the Old Railway
Cottage, Johnson Street,
☎6685 8050. It is ⊙open
9am-5pm daily. You will find
a useful internet reference at
✉www.byronbayvbo.com

⤳ Let's Stay Here

Due to the popularity of this
town, top quality budget accommodation is plentiful.
Take your pick.

Acquarius Backpackers,
*16 Lawson St, ☎6685
7663 or 1800 028
909, ✉www.aquarius-
backpack.com* Right in the
heart of Byron Bay. This is
backpacker luxury with motel
style accommodation. Great
atmosphere. Dorms have en
suites and linen is supplied
in all rooms. The facilities

includes a kitchen and laundry. There is a pool table, book exchange, internet access, an inground pool and a large barbecue area. Licensed cafe/bistro on site with good food at affordable prices and free entertainment. Boogie boards for hire. There's also a free pick up service. *Dorms ✪$22; doubles $55*

Arts Factory Lodge VIP,
Skinner Shoot Rd, ☎*6685 7709,* 🖳*www.artsfactory.com .au* Located not too far from the centre of Byron Bay. The Arts Factory is one place that won't have you bored. With an on site cinema, a tour desk, cafe open for breakfast and lunch and Piggery's Supernatural Restaurant open for dinner, Wednesday night BBQs, yoga, drumming and dancing workshops and free didgeridoo lessons, you'll

have enough to keep you occupied. The Arts Factory also features regular dorms as well as Teepee, Wagon, Island Huts and a Campground and a Nunnery girls only and Pentagon. Other facilities includes a big kitchen, laundry, internet access, a games room with pool tables, pinball machines and video games, plus a swimming pool and sauna. There's also a volleyball court. Bike, boogie board and surfboard are also available for hire. Shuttle bus service available to and fro town. Parking available. Recommended. *Dorms from ✪$25; tepee dorm and pentagon from $25; nunnery (girls dorm) from $30; island retreat and hippy bus double room from $30pp; camping from $15*

Backpackers Inn on the Beach VIP,
29 Shirley St, ☎*6685 8231,* 🖳*www.byron-bay.com/ backpackersinn* Located just a short stroll to shops, pubs, entertainment and a selection of eating places. Nicely designed hostel set within tropical gardens. Very clean and well maintained. Rooms have fans. Facilities includes kitchen, TV lounge, common room with a pool table and sofas, and outdoors is a swimming pool, barbecue area and a volleyball court. There is also an on-site shop. Free courtesy bus to and from stops. Bike hire and boogie boards available. *Dorms ✪$25; double/twin $34pp*

Belongil Beach House VIP,
Childe St, ☎*6685 7868* Located close to the beach.

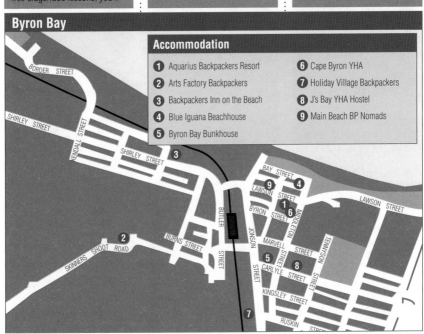

Byron Bay

Accommodation

1. Aquarius Backpackers Resort
2. Arts Factory Backpackers
3. Backpackers Inn on the Beach
4. Blue Iguana Beachhouse
5. Byron Bay Bunkhouse
6. Cape Byron YHA
7. Holiday Village Backpackers
8. J's Bay YHA Hostel
9. Main Beach BP Nomads

Beautifully designed dorms, with stained glass windows, polished timber floors and ceiling fans. Facilities includes kitchen, laundry, TV room, internet access, games room and a barbecue area. On site Balinese style cafe and restaurant. Free courtesy bus to pick you up from station. Parking available. *Dorms* ✪*$28; double/twin $35pp ($40pp en suite)*

Blue Iguana Beachouse,

14 Bay St, ☎*6685 5298* One of the last remaining old funky beachouses. Blue Iguana is a beachouse offering 20 beds and no rules. Newly renovated. It has a relaxed and friendly atmosphere and is situated right on the beach and just off the town centre. Facilities includes a small kitchen and a barbecue area outdoors. With BBQs and friendly staff. *Dorms* ✪*$25; doubles $32.50pp*

Byron Bay Bunkhouse,

1 Carlyle St, ☎*6685 8311 or 1800 241 600,* ■*www.byronbay-bunkhouse.com.au* Just minutes to the beach. Bunkhouse is for the budget minded. There is a kitchen, laundry, a huge common room, games room with darts, pool table and video games and internet access and facilities. Meals are also available. Activities are also organised for the guest for a bit of fun. Offers free pickup from the nearest town, free bike and board hire. *Dorms from* ✪*$19; doubles $56* (breakfasts included)

Cape Byron Lodge,

78 Bangalow Road, ☎*6685 6445,* ■*www.capebyron lodge.com* This is a excellent value accommodation for international travellers with loads of atmosphere. Located not too far from town. Facilities boasts of a swimming pool at the front, a barbecue area, TV lounge, pool table, kitchen and laundry facilities. There is free bike, boogie board and snorkeling equipment hire as well as a free shuttle bus that provides pickups and drop offs to the town and beaches. *Dorms from* ✪*$16; twin $50; double $40; camping $10* (free pancakes, tea and coffee every morning)

Cape Byron YHA,

Corner of Byron and Middleton St, ☎*6685 8788,* ■*www.yha.com* Located very close to beach, bus stop, train station and shops. Facilities includes kitchen, laundry, TV and reading room, games room, internet access, heated swimming pool and a barbecue area. On site cafe and dive centre. There is also BBQ nights twice a week. Bike hire and free use of boogie boards available. Parking available. *Dorms from* ✪*$22; double/ twin $30 (from $35pp per en suite room) BC MC VA EFTPOS*

Holiday Village,

116 Jonson Street, ☎*6685 8888* This family owned and operated hostel has two kinds of accommodation: hostel style (share accommodation) and self contained apartments (mostly 4 share and some doubles). Right in the centre of town, you are only minutes away from the shops. There is a tour desk available, free bike and board hire, barbecue area, swimming pool, volleyball and basketball for the athletes, a TV common room where you can meet new friends and kitchen and laundry facilities. *Dorms* ✪*$24; self contained $24 per per person night; double $32.50pp*

J's Bay YHA,

7 Carlyle St, ☎*6685 8853 or 1800 678 195,* ■*www.yha.com* Located very close to the beach and in the town centre. All rooms are fanned and open out unto large decks. The communal area and kitchen leads to the swimming pool and the barbecue area. Everything is surrounded by palm trees. The TV and lounge room are separated, and there is also internet access. Bike hire and parking available. *Dorms from* ✪*$22; double/twin $30 (from $35pp per en suite room) BC MC VA EFTPOS*

Main Beach BP Nomads,

Cnr Fletcher and Lawson Sts, ☎*6685 8695 or 1800 150 233,* ■*www.nomads.com* Ideally located at the centre of town and very close to Main Beach. Facilities includes kitchen facilities, laundry, internet access, pool table, a swimming pool and spa, a fabulous sundeck, and a barbecue area. Meals also available plus there are BBQ nights. Free board hire and free pickups. Parking available. *Dorm* ✪*$22; double $35pp*

Other Areas:
Lennox Head Backpackers,
2-3 Ross St, ☎6687 7636,
🖳*www.yha.com* Located
very very close to Seven Mile
Beach and Tea Tree Lake
Ainsworth. Nearest foodstore
is about 200m away and bus
and train station not too far
either. Clean and well maintained. Facilities includes
kitchen, TV lounge, internet
access and a barbecue area
outside with a courtyard. On
site natural theraphy. Bike,
boogie board and surfboard
hire available including tennis
racquets, golf clubs and paddle skis. Try canoeing, windsurfing or sail a catamaran.
Parking available. *Dorms from
✪$22 ; double/twin from $25;
BC MC VA EFTPOS*

Alstonville
An attractive village that boasts a
nice little bookshop, Alstonville is
19km (12 miles) from Lismore on
the way to the coast.
Near the village is the Victoria
Park Nature Reserve, a remnant
of the **'Big Scrub'** which once
covered most of the district.

The **Summerland House
With No Steps,** *Wardell Road,*
☎*6628 0610,* is a unique project
providing job skills and training
for the handicapped. It also has
avocados, macadamia nuts,
tropical stone fruit, custard
apples, lychees and citrus fruits
growing in plantations, and on
sale, as well as a craft cottage,
retail nursery and fruit packing
house. Devonshire teas and light
lunches are available ⊙daily
9am-5pm.

At **Bexhill**, 10km north-east of
Lismore, is an open-air cathedral.
The pews are fashioned from

logs, whilst behind the stone altar
and cross are magnificent views
of the Corndale Valley.

Ballina
A resort town, Ballina has all the
usual tourist facilities. Take the
coast road for a more pleasant
drive to/from Byron Bay, rather
than rejoining the Pacific Highway.

The **Big Prawn** can be seen
several kilometres from town.

The **Maritime Museum,**
Regatta Lane, ☎6681 1002,
records the maritime history of
the Richmond River and features
the Las Balsa Raft which voyaged
from South America to Ballina
in 1973.

Shaws Bay Hotel, next to the
caravan park, *2 Brighton Street,
East Ballina,* has a beautiful red
cedar dining room and staircase
which were carved in Spain,
⊙open daily 10am-10pm, ☎*6686
2034.*

The **Broadwater Sugar Mill**,
19km (12 miles) south of Ballina,
has tours during the crushing
season (June to December).

The Ballina Visitor Information
Centre is on the corner of *La
Balsa Plaza* and *River Street.*
They have a startling range of
literature on tourist interests
and should be your first point
of contact. The centre is ⊙open
9am-5pm Mon-Fri, 9am-4pm
on weekends. Phone them on
☎*6686 3484* or email them at
✉balinfo@balshire.org.au

⤸ Let's Stay Here
Ballina Travellers Lodge,
36 Tamar St, ☎6686 6737,
🖳*www.yha.com* Located at
the heart of town where everything is accessible. A modern
purpose built hostel with quiet
and comfortable accommo-

dation. Facilities includes
kitchen, laundry, TV lounge,
swimming pool and a barbecue area. Free courtesy pick
ups available. Bike hire and
parking available. *Dorms from
✪$19; twin/double from $22
(from $29 with en suite) BC
MC VA EFTPOS*

West Sydney
Blue Mountains
Population 70,800
The City of the Blue Mountains,
comprising 26 towns and
villages, stretches from Penrith,
53km (33 miles) from Sydney, to
Mount Victoria, 122km (76 miles)
from Sydney. The drive up to the
region's major centre, Katoomba,
only takes about an hour and a
half, making this scenic area a
comfortable distance from Sydney
city for day trips or a weekend
retreat.

Climate
The area has distinct seasons and
is cooler than Sydney all year
round. Occasionally snow falls in
winter, usually July, but it does
not last.

Characteristics
The Blue Mountains derive their
name from the perpetual haze
draped over them. Miniscule
drops of eucalyptus evaporate
from the leaves of the dense forest
and are struck by the sunlight to
produce this effect.
It was not until twenty-five years
after the arrival of the First Fleet
that the Blue Mountains were
crossed in search of grazing
land. The intrepid explorers who
performed the feat in 1813 were
Blaxland, Wentworth and Lawson,
and three mountain towns bear
their names.

Blue Mountains

Katoomba

In the 1920s and '30s, the Blue Mountains was the Holiday Capital of New South Wales, then it declined in popularity, as people travelled further afield. In recent years there has been a revival, and the Blue Mountains is once again a popular tourist centre.

How to Get There
By Rail
Electric trains depart from Central Station in Sydney every day with stops at Lapstone, Glenbrook, Blaxland, Warrimoo, Valley Heights, Springwood, Faulconbridge, Woodford, Hazelbrook, Lawson, Wentworth Falls, Leura, Katoomba, Medlow Bath, Blackheath and Mt Victoria.

CityRail have special off-peak fares to Katoomba - any train after 9am on weekdays, or any time at the weekend, with return before 4am the next morning, for ✪$11.80 adult. For further information ☎*(02) 4782 1902.*

By Bus
AAT Kings, ☎*9666 3899,* **Newmans,** ☎*1300 300 036,* and **Australian Pacific Tours,** ☎*9247 7222,* have daily tours departing from Sydney Day Tour Terminal, Circular Quay West at 9am.

Fantastic Aussie Tours, ☎*9938 5714* (Sydney) or ☎*4782 1366* (Katoomba) have three hour tours which connect with trains from Sydney at Katoomba Railway Station.

They also have full day tours of Jenolan Caves departing daily from Katoomba Station in the morning. The Blue Mountains Explorer Bus also operates daily and picks up and drops off in Katoomba and Leura at the main attractions and restaurants. It meets most trains from Sydney,

and connects with trains returning to Sydney. On Wednesdays only, they offer trips to Australia's Wonderland, as well as Darling Harbour and the Olympic Site combined.

Visitor Information
Echo Point Information Centre, ☎*1300 653 408* and Glenbrook Visitor Information Centre, *Great Western Highway, Glenbrook,* ☎*1300 653 408,* are ✪open Mon-Fri 9am-5pm, Sat-Sun 8.30am-4.30pm. Contact them by email on ✉info@bluemountainstourism.org.au

The official website of Blue Mountains Tourism, ☎*1300 653 408,* is 💻www.bluemountainstourism.org.au but another one to visit is 💻www.bluemts.com.au

---

↵ Let's Stay Here
Though there are plenty of places to stay here, back-packer budget style is quite a rarity. It's best to head to Katoomba or the neighbouring towns for those.

Let's Eat
If you would like a superb meal, try:
Cecil, *108 Katoomba Street, Katoomba,* ☎*4782 1411.*

Clarendon, *68 Lurline Street, Katoomba,* ☎*4782 1322.*

Felton Woods Manor, *Cnr Lurline Street and Merriwa Streets, Katoomba,* ☎*4782 2055.*

Grand View, *174 Great Western Highway, Wentworth Falls,* ☎*4757 1001.*

Mountain Heritage, *Cnr Apex and Lovel Streets, Katoomba,* ☎*4782 2155.*

St Mounts, *194 Great Western Highway, Blackheath,* ☎*4787 6111.*

The Imperial, *Station Street, Mt Victoria,* ☎*4787 1788.*

The Swiss Cottage Restaurant, *132 Lurline Street, Katoomba,* ☎*4782 2281.* Undoubtedly one of the best restaurants in the Blue Mountains, The Swiss Cottage offers excellent meals in a warm atmosphere. The steaks and fish are superb, the soup is thick and rich, and, for dessert, the melted-Lindt-chocolate-soaked pudding is unbeatable (look for 'Death By Chocolate' on the menu). Your lively host Monique will make you feel welcome and keep you chuckling as she serves up each course.

The Victoria and Albert, *19 Station Street, Mt Victoria,* ☎*4787 1241.*

For a touch of nostalgia make sure you visit the National Trust classified **Paragon Cafe** at *65 Katoomba Street, Katoomba,* ☎*4782 2928,* which is fully licensed and is the home of the famous Paragon Chocolates.

Local Transport
Bus
Pearce Omnibus, ☎*4751 1077,* have services connecting Faulconbridge and Penrith; Springwood and Winmalee; Blaxland and Mt Riverview. **Katoomba Woodford Bus Company,** ☎*4782 4213,* operate services between Katoomba, Leura and Wentworth Falls; Bullaburra and Lawson; Hazelbrook and Woodford; Katoomba Falls, Scenic Railway and Skyway. (No service on public holidays) **Katoomba Leura Bus Service,** ☎*4782 3333* links

Leura, Katoomba, Echo Point, North Katoomba, Blackheath, Medlow Bath and Mt Victoria. (No service Saturday afternoon, Sunday or public holidays)

Car Hire

Thrifty, *80 Megalong Street, Leura,* ☎*4784 2888.*

Taxi

Taxis Katoomba, ☎*4782 1311;* Springwood Taxis, ☎*4751 1444;* Blue Mountains Taxi Cabs, ☎*4759 3000;* Lawson Taxis, ☎*4759 3000.*

Points of Interest
Penrith

Situated on the Nepean River, less than an hour's drive from Sydney, Penrith is one of the most rapidly growing regions in Australia. The biggest tourist attraction is **Panthers**, set in 81ha (200 acres), where bona fide visitors are most welcome. The club has two cable water ski lakes, a miniature car racing track, swimming pool with water slides, tennis complex and a lake with canoes, windsurfers and paddle boats. It also has a motel, six restaurants, a huge variety of poker machines, cocktail bars and a Cabaret Room. It is located in Mulgoa Road, ☎*4720 5555.*

Other major attractions Penrith offers are the **Nepean Belle Paddlewheeler** (☎*4733 1274*), the **Museum of Fire** (☎*4731 3000*), **Warragamba Dam** and **Wonderland Sydney** (☎*9830 9100*). For more information on these and other places contact the Visitor Information Centre in the carpark at Panthers, *Mulgoa Road,* ☎*4732 7671.* If you are in the mood for a show, there are two places you may wish to

contact to find out what is on - the **Q Theatre**, ☎*4721 5735* and the **Joan Sutherland Performing Arts Centre,** ☎*4721 8832.*

Lower Blue Mountains
Lapstone-Blaxland

Lapstone Zig-Zag Walking Track begins behind the RAAF base at Glenbrook, and follows the original railway cuttings with views of the arches of Knapsack Viaduct.

Blue Mountains National Park, Glenbrook Area, has bushwalking, picnicking and camping. Information and advice plus publications are available from the Visitors Information Centre, *Great Western Highway, Glenbrook,* ☎*1300 653 408.*

Lennox Bridge, *Mitchell's Pass Road, Glenbrook,* was built in 1833 and is the oldest bridge on Australia's mainland. The bridge is well sign-posted from the Great Western Highway.

Wascoe Siding, *15 Grahame Street, Blaxland,* ☎*4739 9701,* has a miniature railway and picnic area, and is open on the first Sunday of each month, except January.

Springwood

Two extremely good bushwalks originate in Springwood: the first, an easy 90 minute walk to Birdwood Gully, starts from Bednall Road; the second, to Sassafras Gully, is rated medium, and access is either from Holmdale Street, Sassafras Gully Road or Bee Farm Road.

The **Local History Centre** and a **Community Art Gallery** are in Braemar, an early Federation home which is classified by the National Trust, as are the Frazer Memorial Presbyterian Church and Spring-wood Railway Station.

In the cemetery is the grave of Sir Henry Parkes, the Father of Federation.

Faulconbridge

Norman Lindsay Gallery and Museum, *Chapman Parade,* ☎*4751 1067,* is the home of this famous Australian artist and writer. There are displays of his paintings, etchings, ship models and family mementos, and a special Magic Pudding room. The house is set in delightful gardens with dozens of statues, some of which are also 'delightful'. There is a shop and a good coffee shop. ☺open Fri-Sun and public holidays 10am-4pm.

Central Blue Mountains

Bull's Camp, *Great Western Highway, Linden,* was used as a camp for convicts working on the road across the Blue Mountains. It is now a good picnic spot.

Selwood Science and Puzzles, *41 Railway Parade, Hazelbrook,* ☎*4758 6235,* is a mid-Victorian house which has been classified by the National Trust. It is ☺open Thurs-Mon 9am-5pm, and has a fine collection of art and science features.

There are two interesting bush-walks emanating from Lawson: one begins at South Lawson Park, Honour Avenue, and goes to Adelina, Junction, Federal and Cataract Falls - 90 minutes, easy; the other starts in North Lawson Park, Bernards Drive, and walks along Dantes Glen and Lucy's Glen to Frederica Falls - 180 minutes, easy.

Wentworth Falls

Yester Grange, *Yester Road,* ☎*4757 1110,* is a 19th century house with a collection of 19th century water colours, Victoriana and ceramics. The house is set in bush and parkland and Devonshire teas and light lunches are available. ⊙open Wed-Fri 10am-4pm, Sat-Sun and public holidays 10am-5pm.

Wentworth Falls Lake, *Sinclair Crescent,* is a pleasant picnic spot with a playground and tame ducks. Row boats are available for hire.

There are several walks with good views in this area. From Falls Road to Fletcher's Lookout, Undercliff Walk, to Den Fenella - easy walk with views and wildflowers, 90 minutes. To Princes Rock with views of Wentworth Falls and Jamison Valley, 20 minutes. To the top of the Falls, 30 minutes. To Undercliff Walk, Den Fenella, Overcliff Walk to Valley of the Waters with panoramic views, 150 minutes.

Upper Blue Mountains
Leura
Sublime Point, at the end of *Sublime Point Road,* has great views of the Three Sisters and the Jamison Valley.

The Everglades Gardens, *37 Everglades Avenue,* ☎*4784 1938,* is classified by the National Trust as one of the Great Gardens of Australia. There are unique sandstone terraces, magnificent mature trees and native flora, and a grotto pool, ⊙open daily 10am-5pm during spring and summer, and closing an hour earlier during the colder seasons. Admission is ✪$5 adults.

Leuralla, *36 Olympian Parade,* ☎*4784 1169,* is an historic art deco mansion with a collection of 19th century Australian art and a Memorial Museum to Dr H.V. Evatt, first President of the United Nations Organisation. There is also a toy and railway museum.

Gordons Falls Reserve is

a pleasant picnic area with playground and toilets, and from it there is a walk to the Pool of Siloam and Lyrebird Dell.

Leura Cascades on Cliff Drive is another picnic area, and there are a number of bushwalks that start from this point, with the Round Walk taking about 40 minutes.

⤳ Let's Stay Here
Caravan Parks
Leura Village Caravan Park, *cnr Great Western Highway and The Mall,* ☎*4784 1552* (no pets) - *powered sites ✪$13 for two, on-site vans $31-33 for two.*

Katoomba
The best way to see the attractions of Katoomba is to follow Cliff Drive. From the Railway Station, take *Lurline* and *Merriwa Streets* to the Drive around the Jamison and Megalong Valleys. Along the drive there are many lookouts, all sign posted, the most famous of which is undoubtedly **Echo Point,** from where there are the best views of The Three Sisters, Mennhi, Wimlah and Gunnedoo. These rock formations are very important in Aboriginal legend, and are floodlit at night. From the point you can also see the **Ruined Castle** and **Mount Solitary,** and it is possible to pick out many animal shapes on the mountains on the other side of the valley.

From Echo Point the **Giant Stairway** of almost 1000 steps leads to the floor of the Jamison Valley and the Federal Pass, and the **Prince Henry Cliff Walk** leads left towards Leura or right towards the Scenic Railway Complex.

The Point has picnic facilities, a restaurant and a takeaway food outlet.

Katoomba Falls Reserve is another picnic spot because the cascades, and several walking tracks begin behind the kiosk.

The Scenic Railway and Skyway on *Cliff Drive,* ☎*4782 2699,* offer a ride down to the Jamison Valley, which is not for the faint-hearted, or a ride over the valley in the Skyway. The complex also has the cafeteria-style restaurant, a fun parlour and a souvenir shop, and is ⊙open daily 9am-5pm. Fares are ✪$5 for adults.

Also on Cliff Drive is **Cahill's Lookout,** another picnic spot, this time with views of escarpment and valley, and of Boar's Head Rock. The Drive ends at the *Great Western Highway,* at Katoomba Holiday Caravan Park.

Explorers' Tree, on the highway 2km west of Katoomba, commemorates the crossing of the Blue Mountains by Blaxland, Wentworth and Lawson. From behind the tree a Katoomba to Jenolan Caves walk begins, which takes 2-3 days. More information is available from the Visitor Information Centres.

⤳ Let's Stay Here
Blue Mountains Backpackers VIP,
190 Bathurst Rd, ☎*4782 4226,* 🖳*www.backpackers.com.au* Small and clean and built within an old house and close to the station. Huge fresh food market and super-market almost right next door. Just your usual facilities in-cluding a kitchen, laundry, TV room, lounge and the good old fireplace and a barbecue area. Campground on site with equipment hire. Staff are great with local info. Free

courtesy bus. Parking available. *Dorms* ✪*$19; double/twin $54; tent hire $13*

Blue Mountains YHA,
207 Katoomba St, ☎*4782 1416,* 💻*www.yha.com.au* Located in the heart of Katoomba, built in a historical 1930's building. Formerly a Cabaret Club, it kept it's huge ballroom floor. Close to the bus and train station. Great atmosphere. Facilities includes a kitchen, laundry, pool table, game machines, open fireplace, TV lounge, internet access and a barbecue area.

Parking available. *Dorms from* ✪*$19; double/twin from $31pp; BC MC VA EFTPOS*

Hawkebury Heights YHA, *836 Hawkesbury Road, Hawkesbury Heights, 4754 5621,* 💻*www.yha.com.au* Purpose built bush YHA opened mid 1999. Fantastic views in a bushland setting. Eco-friendly design with solar electricity and hot water and wood fire. The YHA is on the same site as the former hostel known as North Springwood, with shops 4 kms away. It is close to the Blue Mountains Na-

tional Park with waterfalls and terific lookouts. Your basic facilities includes kitchen, laundry and a barbecue area. Parking available. *Dorms from* ✪*$18 BC MC VA*

Katoomba Mountain Lodge,
31 Lurline St, ☎*4782 3933,* 💻*www.bluemts.com.au/ kmtlodge/default.htm* Situated in the heart of the Blue Mountains. Basic accommodation, but the great atmosphere should just make up for it. Some rooms have AM/FM clock/radio, coffee maker, iron/ironing board, microwave oven and fridge. Facilities includes a small kitchen, internet access, games room, two TV lounges with an open fireplace, outdoor patio and barbecue. There is also a balcony at the front of the building. Bike and car hire available. Parking available. *Dorms* ✪*$17; single $42; doubles $58;*

Number 14,
14 Lovel St, ☎*4782 7104,* 💻*www.bluemts.com.au/no14/* Located just five minutes walk from Katoomba railway station, in the heart of Blue Mountains. "No 14" is an old guesthouse which has been restored with polished wooden floors and nice old features. Facilities includes a big kitchen, a fire place and a nice verandah. *Dorms* ✪*$20; double/twin $55 (30pp with en suite)*

Caravan Parks
Katoomba Falls Caravan Park, *Katoomba Falls Road,* ☎*4782 1835.* (No pets), 68 sites, barbecue - *powered*

Katoomba

Accommodation

1 Blue Mountains Backpackers VIP
2 Blue Mountains YHA
3 Katoomba Mountain Lodge
4 Number 14

sites ❂*$25-30 for two, cabins $60-84 for two.*

Blackheath

Evans Lookout, *Evans Lookout Road,* offers superb views of the Grose Valley.

Govett's Leap, *Govett's Leap Road*, also has views of **Grose Valley** and of **Bridal Veil Falls**, the longest single drop fall in the Blue Mountains.

⤳ Let's Stay Here
Caravan Parks
Blackheath Caravan Park, *Prince Edward Street,* ☎ *4787 8101.* (No pets), 74 sites, - powered sites ❂*$20-22 for two, cabins $38-55 for two.*

National Parks and Wildlife Service Heritage Centre, Govett's Leap Road, ☎*4787 8877,* has an exhibition on natural features of the Blue Mountains, and nearby Fairfax Heritage Track is suitable for disabled people.

Blue Mounts Rhododendron Garden, Bacchante Street, is set in native bushland. It is ⊙open 9am-5pm and admission is by a donation. There are easy walking tracks and picnic facilities.

From Anvil Rock and Wind-eroded Cave, Hat Hill Road, Blackheath, you can get good views of the Grose Valley.
Mount Victoria

A visit to the village of Mt Victoria is like taking a step back in time, with buildings of sandstone and iron lace, and others of colonial weatherboard housing antiques, crafts and tearooms. Attractions include the Post Office, Toll House and Railway Station, the Scenic Drive and **Mount York** where explorers Blaxland, Lawson and Went-worth

realised they'd crossed '**The Impenetrable Barrier'. Victoria Falls, Mount Piddington** and **Pulpit Rock Reserve** are also worth a visit.

The Mounts Area

Rich volcanic soils and high rainfall produce the lush vegetation for which the Mountains are renowned. A beautiful area with famous gardens, lookouts and walks.

Cathedral of Ferns, Mount Wilson, is a beautiful rainforest with nearby picnic area.

Mount Tomah Botanic Garden, Bells Line Road, ☎*4567 2154,* was a Bicentennial project of the Royal Botanic Gardens, Sydney. It features cool-climate planting with sections representing specific geographic areas of the world. There are panoramic views and picnic areas, and the gardens are ⊙open 10am-4pm March to September, and until 5pm during the other months.

Festivals

Lawson Festival - March;
Wentworth Falls Autumn Festival - April;
Yulefest - June/July;
Springtime in the Blue Mountains - September thru November;
Leura Gardens Festival - October;
Leura Village Fair - October;
Blackheath Rhododendron Festival - November;
Glenbrook Festival - November. For dates and attractions for these festivals it is best to contact the Glenbrook Visitors Centre.

Facilities

Lawn bowls, bush walking, golf, horse riding, scenic drives,

swimming pool, tennis, cinemas, squash, art galleries and craft shops.

Outlying Attractions

Hartley Historic Site, Hartley, ☎*6355 2117* includes the old Courthouse, churches and inns. The site consists of a relatively small cluster of mid-nineteenth century buildings preserved by the NSW National Parks and Wildlife Service. Hartley is about 35km (22 miles) west of Katoomba.

Zig-Zag Railway

Situated about 7km east of Lithgow, the Railway is an engineering feat. It is a system of tunnels, cuttings and stone viaducts built 1866-69 to overcome the steep descent from the Blue Mountains to the Western Plains beyond. There are picnic areas, and rides are available on an old world steam train. Trains run ⊙daily and the cost of a return journey is ❂$13 adults.

Jenolan Caves

Probably the best-known limestone caves in NSW, the Jenolan Caves were discovered in the 1830s when the victim of a bushranger tracked his attacker to this hideout. The entrance to the caves is in a narrow gorge accessed through the Grand Arch, about 24m (79 ft) high. The view from Carlotta Arch, which overlooks the Blue Lake, is superb. Nine of the twenty-two caves are open for inspection, and guided tours are available. Phone the Jenolan Caves Reserve Trust on ☎*6359 3311* for more information.

Caves House, ☎*6359*

3322, right at the caves complex, is a charming hotel, with a restaurant, bar and accommodation. There are several bush walks in the area, and daily tours are run from Sydney and Katoomba.

Bathurst

Population 26,500

Bathurst is situated on the fertile western slopes of the Great Dividing Range, 208km (129 miles) west of Sydney.

Climate

Average temperatures: January max 27C (81F) - min 13C (55F); July 11C (52F) - min -1C (30.2F). Average annual rainfall: 629mm (25 ins); drizzle rain in winter and storms in summer.

Characteristics

Bathurst is Australia's oldest inland settlement and the centre of a large grain and pastoral district with many historic and distinctive buildings. When gold was discovered in the hills around Bathurst, many towns such as Hill End, Sofala and Hargraves sprung up. Most of them have either disappeared or are now ghost towns.

How to Get There
By Bus

Greyhound Pioneer all have daily services to Bathurst from Sydney.

By Rail

There is a Countrylink service from Sydney to Bathurst and Orange.

Visitor Information

The Bathurst Visitor Information Centre is at 28 William Street,

Bathurst. They have a website, ▇www.bathurst.nsw.gov.au, and an email address, ▭visitors@ bathurst.nsw.gov.au, ☎ *1800 681 000.*

↴ Let's Stay Here

Here are some budget accommodation with prices that should be used as a guide only. Some other pubs will have accommodation at reasonable prices. Check with the information centre. The telephone area code is 02.

Bathurst Motor Inn, *87 Durham Street,* ☎ *6631 3568.* 53 units, licensed restaurant, swimming pool, spa, gym, room service - ✪*$55-150.*

Caravan Park
Easts Bathurst Caravan Park, *Sydney Road,* ☎ *6331 8286.* (No pets) 145 sites, pool, tennis - *powered sites* ✪*$18 for two, cabins $50-85 for two.*

Let's Eat

Many of the motels have restaurants, either licensed or BYO, and the licensed clubs have dining rooms or restaurants/bistros. There are also the usual number of takeaway food outlets, and the Tourist Office will have a complete list.

Points of Interest

The Visitor Centre has trained guides available to provide a commentary on historic buildings in Bathurst for tour groups, and makes brochures available to individuals.

The Victorian Renaissance Court House, with its double-storey portico and large octagonal

central dome, faces Kings Square. It has two wings and the verandahed wing was built as a telegraph office.

The Historical Museum is in the East Wing, and is ☉open Mon-Fri 9am-4.30pm, Sat-Sun 10am-4pm.

The Bathurst Regional Art Gallery, *70 Keppel Street,* is ☉open Tues-Sat 10am-5pm, Sat-Sun 2-5pm.

Abercrombie House, built in the 1870s and classified by the National Trust, is ☉open for inspection on Sundays at 3pm, except in winter.

Ben Chifley's Cottage, the home of the former Prime Minister, is ☉open Tues-Sat 2-4pm, and Sunday 10am-noon.

Old Government Cottage, behind *no. 1 George Street,* is where Macquarie stayed during his farewell visit to Bathurst in 1821. It is ☉open Sundays 1.30-3.30pm.

Miss Traill's House, *321 Russell Street,* is also a National Trust property and is ☉open Tues-Sat 1pm-3pm and Sun 10am-3pm.

The Holy Trinity Church at Kelso was completed in 1835 and is the oldest consecrated Anglican Church in Australia.

St Michael and St John's Catholic Cathedral was completed in 1861. **St Stanislaus' College** has taken pupils since 1873, and is Australia's oldest Catholic Boarding School.

Ohkuma Japanese Garden is on the corner of *Stanley* and *George Streets.* Okhkuma is the sister-city of Bathurst, and this garden was laid out in 1998 as a symbol of the link.

Macquarie River Bicentennial Park is a popular spot for a picnic.

The 35 bells of the **Carillon** in *Kings Parade* plays every day at noon and 1pm. Also located within the park are three war monuments which commemorate the sacrifice of men from the Bathurst district.

Outside the Visitor Centre is the **Victors' Walk,** where brass plaques have been embedded in checker-board concrete to commemorate winners of the Bathurst 1000.

At Mt Panorama is the **Motor Racing Circuit** which is used for the annual Bathurst 1000 motor race. Experience the excitement, disappointment and enjoyment that is motor racing in Bathurst at the **National Motor Racing Museum**, which is on *Murray Corner* and is ☉open daily 9am-4.30pm. It has a selection of memorabilia associated with the big race, collected over the years, from cars and trophies to souvenirs.

Located on Mt Panorama is the **Sir Joseph Banks Nature Park,** which has koalas, kangaroos and wallabies in a 41ha (101 acres) park, ☉open daily 10am-4pm.

The **Bathurst Sheep and Cattle Drome,** Rossmore Park, *Limekilns Road, Kelso,* is only an eight minute drive from the centre of town. There visitors can milk a cow or sit back in air-conditioned comfort and enjoy an 80 minute show of sheep shearing and wool classing. If the weather is fine, there will be a sheep dog in action. The newest addition to the Sheep and Cattle Drome is their Golf Practice Driving Range, open daily.

Bathurst Rotalactor is a modern rotary dairy that milks over 300 cows, situated in the picturesque Dunkeld Valley. There is a large, well-appointed, indoor viewing area, a cafe specialising in dairy products, and many educational displays on various aspects of the dairy industry.

Festivals

The **Bathurst 1000 Motor Race** is held during the October long weekend (first Monday in October), with activities organised during the week leading up to the Race.

Facilities

There is an olympic swimming pool and water slide. Bathurst also has all the usual sporting facilities you would expect in a large town, including lawn bowls, golf course, tennis courts and squash courts.

Orange

Population 38,000

Situated 55km (34 miles) from Bathurst, Orange is a larger town than Bathurst, and the area produces 10% of Australia's apples, as well as cherries and other stone fruit, on the rich volcanic soil slopes of Mt Canobolas. The upper slopes of the extinct volcano are a flora and fauna reserve with picnic areas and walking trails. There is a lake in the crater, and canoeing, sailing and fishing are popular.

The Ophir gold find gave the early settlement a firm foundation, and it has grown into the largest town in the district. **Bowen Terrace** is a perfect and rare example of its period. The row of ironwork-decorated houses was built in 1876 by the owner of the first tannery. Endsleigh House, built in 1858, is thought to be the oldest house. The golf club is housed in the 1876 Duntryleague mansion.

A.J. (Banjo) Paterson, perhaps Australia's most popular poet and writer, was born along the Ophir Road in 1864 and an obelisk marks the spot. It is inscribed with a verse from Clancy of the Overflow.

Orange is the headquarters of the **Ministry of Agriculture,** and has a large agricultural college.

The Orange Visitor Information Centre is on corner of Byng and Peisley Streets, ☎*6393 8226*, email ✉tourism@oran ge.nsw.gov.au. The website is 🖳www.orange.nsw.gov.au

Outlying Attractions
Ophir

Gold was first discovered in Australia in 1951 at Ophir, approximately 40km (25 miles) from Orange. Today the area is a reserve, and trails lead to old tunnels, sluices and other relics among the hills. The reserve is, naturally enough, popular with fossickers.

Abercrombie Caves

On the Goulburn Road, 72km (45 miles) from Bathurst, is one of the smaller but most spectacular limestone cave systems in Australia. The reserve has a camping/caravan park with picnic facilities, and cave inspection times and tours vary. For more information phone ☎*6368 8603*, visit 🖳www.jenolancaves. org.au or email ✉abercrombie@ jenolancaves.org.au

Sofala

Set amongst the steep hills of the Turon Valley, Sofala is one of the old gold rush towns. It has a quaint store and some faded old-time buildings.

The Royal Hotel is the only hotel remaining of the forty which were operating during the gold rush era.

Hill End

The Parks and Wildlife Service have declared Hill End an historic site, and they publish an excellent information sheet 'Exploring Hill End Historic Site' which has a map on one side and an excellent walking tour on the other. Only a small community remains today. Miners dug up 701,000 ounces of gold here. Panning and fossicking are still popular, and gold pans may be hired in town. Hill End is 84km (52 miles) from Bathurst.

Mudgee

Situated 69km (43 miles) north of Hill End, Mudgee is the second oldest town west of the Blue Mountains, and was laid out in 1838. A score of handsome buildings, classified by the National Trust, dot the town, the oldest being the Catholic Presbytery, built in 1852. The church, St Mary's, was commenced five years later, and has an exceptional iron screen and stencilled decorations.

The **Court House, St John** the **Baptist's Church,** the **Police Station** and **Post Office** were all built in the early 1860s. The **Colonial Inn Museum,** *Market Street,* is ⊙open Sat 2-5pm, Sun, school and public holidays 10am-5pm.

Mudgee is renowned for its honey, and visitors are able to watch honey processing at two factories.

There are also many wineries in the district, and all have cellar door sales. Mudgee is well known for its fine wines, and is gaining fame for its beautiful rose gardens. There is a **Days of Wine** and **Roses Festival** each year in September/October.

Mudgee Gulgong Tourism is at *84 Market Street,* ☎ *6372 1020,* email ✉tourist@mudgee.nsw. gov.au. It is ⊙open 9am-5pm Mon-Fri, 9am-3.30pm Sat and 9.30am-2pm Sun.

Gulgong

Gulgong, 29km (18 miles) from Mudgee was, until the advent of plastic currency, the 'Town on the Ten Dollar Note'.

It has narrow streets which wind between quaint clapboard and iron buildings, complete with verandahs and iron lace. **The Pioneers' Museum,** in *Medley Street,* covers .4ha (1 acre) and includes an astonishing array of Australiana. The **Henry Lawson Art Gallery** is open during school holidays. **The Phonograph Parlour,** *69 Lee Street,* has recorded sound equipment dating back to 1889. Gold is still found around Gulgong and panning is popular.

New South Wales – West
Dubbo
Population 38,000
Dubbo is situated in mid-western New South Wales on the Macquarie River, at the junction of the Newell and Mitchell Highways. The city is 416km (258 miles) from Sydney; 862km (536 miles) from Brisbane; 818km (508 miles) from Melbourne; and 1207km (750 miles) from Adelaide.

Climate
Average temperatures: January max 32C (90F) - min 18C (64F);
July max 15C (59F) - min 3C (37F). Average annual rainfall - 584mm (23 ins); height above sea level - 262m (859 ft); average number of rainy days per year - 74.

Characteristics
Dubbo is known as the Hub of the West. It is a prosperous service centre for the fertile farmlands around it.

How to Get There
By Bus
Pioneer and Greyhound stop at Dubbo on their Melbourne/ Brisbane/Gold Coast runs.

By Rail
There a **Countrylink** service from Sydney to Dubbo.

Visitor Information
The Dubbo Visitors Information Centre is on the corner of *Macquarie* and *Erskine Streets,* ☎ *6884 1422,* email ✉tourism@ dubbo.nsw.gov.au. It is ⊙open daily 9am-5pm, but closed Christmas Day.

railway station. It also adjoins parklands to river. Facilities includes a kitchen, laundry, lounge room, TV area, internet access and a barbecue at the back. Bike hire and paking available. *Dorms from ☾$19; double/twin $40; BC MC VA*

Matilda Motor Inn,
231 Darling Street, ☎6882 3944. 38 units, licensed restaurant, swimming pool - *from ☾$60.*

Caravan Parks
Dubbo City Caravan Park,
Whylandra Street, West Dubbo, ☎6882 4820. (Pets allowed) 128 sites, good facilities, pool - *powered sites ☾$18 for two, on-site vans $28 for two.*

Poplars Caravan Park,
Lower Bultje Street, ☎6882 4067. (Pets allowed) 69 sites - *powered sites ☾$12 for two, on-site vans $26 for two.*

Windmill Caravan Park,
cnr Mitchell Highway and Sheraton Road, ☎6882 4583. (Pets allowed on application) 78 sites, pool, barbecue, playground - *powered sites ☾$14 for two, on-site vans $25 for two.*

Midstate Motor Park,
21 Bourke Street, ☎6882 1155. 53 sites, barbecue, golf, pool - ☾*$16 for two, on-site vans $35 for two.*

Let's Eat

As mentioned in the Accommodation section, several of the motels and hostels sometimes have restaurants. Here are some others you might like try.
Blue Lagoon, *81 Cobra St, ☎6882 4444*.

Darbar Indian Restaurant, *215 Macquarie St, ☎6884 4338*.

Golden Dragon Restaurant, *36 Victoria St, ☎6882 6663*.

Hing Wah, *143 Talbragar St, ☎6882 4401*.

Jules Crepes Restaurant, *195 Macquarie Street, ☎6882 9300*, is fully licensed, and serves a wide variety of crepes in an old world atmosphere. It is open Mon-Sat noon-2.30pm, 6.30pm onwards.

Rose Garden Thai Restaurant, *208 Brisbane St, ☎6882 8322*.

Safari Lounge Restaurant, *78 Whylandra St, ☎6882 1600*.

Settlers Restaurant, *Newell Hwy, West Dubbo, ☎6882 4777*.

The Dubbo RSL Club, *Wingewarra Street, ☎6882 4411*, welcomes visitors.

McDonalds is at *22-24 Cobra Street.*

Points of Interest

The city is best seen by following the sign posted Tourist Drive, which starts at the Civic Centre, *Darling Street.*

Heritage Walk commences at the Museum and takes in many historic buildings around the city.

The **Old Dubbo Gaol,** *☎6882 8122*, in Macquarie Street between the State and Commonwealth Banks, is ☾open daily 9am-5pm, and has many items of interest including animated robots, and the original gallows.

The Museum, *234 Macquarie Street*, includes a village square with 14 shop exhibitions. It is ☾open daily 9am-5pm.

Dubbo Regional Art Gallery in *Darling Street, ☎6881 4342*, has changing exhibitions every four to six weeks, and you can book in advance for tours by trained guides. The Gallery is ☾open Mon, Wed, Thurs, Fri 11am-4.30pm, Sat-Sun 10am-noon, 1-4pm.

Western Plains Zoo, *Obley Road (6km south of the city), ☎6882 5888*, is Dubbo's main tourist attraction, and entry is ☾daily 9am-4pm, but visitors are welcome to remain until 5pm. The Zoo, opened in 1977, is a sister zoo to Sydney's Taronga Park. It is administered by the Zoological Parks Board of New South Wales, and is Australia's only official open range zoo. Its 300ha (741 acres) of open bushland and landscaped exhibits are home to more than 2000 animals. Visitors can hire a bike or mini moke, or fitness fanatics can walk. There are several picnic areas en route, as well as free gas barbecue facilities, or you can lunch at the licensed bistro, open noon-2pm, or grab a bite to eat from the fast food outlet.

The Dubbo Military Museum, *Newell Highway, ☎6884 5550*, has a whole range of WW2 military equipment in an open air setting. The museum is ☾open daily 10am-4.30pm.

Yarrabar Pottery and Gallery, *Peakhill Road, ☎6884 2455*, has a potter in action, and can make functional and decorative pottery to your requirements. The Gallery is ☾open daily 9am-5pm.

Facilities

Golf, lawn bowls, tennis, fishing, sauna, cinema, swimming pool, ice skating rink, ten pin bowling, slot car racing and horse racing. Paddle boats, canoeing and water skiing on the Macquarie River.

On the second Sunday of the month, Markets are held in the Showground, 10am-1pm, and hundreds of stall holders sell everything from plants and toys to furniture.

Festivals

The **Orana Country Music Festival** is usually held during the Easter period. The Dubbo Agricultural Show is held in May. There are events held every month in Dubbo, and the Visitor Information Centre has all the details.

Outlying Attractions
Peak Hill

Located 71km (44 miles) south-west of Dubbo, on *Roose Road, Peak Hill*, is the site of an open cut gold mine, ☎6869 1733. It consists of two holes of enormous depth. When you view the mine from the lookouts, it is hard to realise that these holes were originally gouged out by hand. The walls of the holes reflect an array of colours, due to the presence of iron, calcium, magnesium and other trace elements. To get to the lookouts, turn right at the Ex-Services Club and follow the signs.
Peak Hill Visitor Information is at *105 Caswell St*, ☎6869 1981.

Parkes

Parkes is 121km (75 miles) south-west of Dubbo, and is the major centre of the Lachlan Valley, servicing the towns of

Peak Hill, Alectown, Bogan Gate, Trundle and Tullamore.

Parkes has a town population of 10,250, and Parkes Visitor Information Centre is on the *Newell Highway*, ☎6862 4365 or email ✉tourism@parkes.nsw.go v.au They are ⊙open 9am-5pm Mon-Fri, 10am-4pm Sat-Sun.

The main attraction in the area is the **Radio Telescope.** The Visitors Centre is ⊙open daily 8.30am-4.15pm, ☎6861 1776, and you shouldn't miss the audio-visual show entitled "The Invisible Universe", which is screened daily from 8.30am, with the last show at 3.30pm. There is a moderate admission fee.

For those who love statistics: The radiotelescope is neither a tracking station for Earth-orbiting satellites, nor a communications station. It's for astronomy. It was built in a very quiet radio interference zone, near a large service town, close to Divisional headquarters in Sydney, and in a location with a low recorded average wind speed. The telescope was opened on October 31, 1961. The dish and drive mechanism weigh about 1,000 tones. The dish is 64m (210 ft) in diameter and 0.4ha (1 acre) in area. There are about 20 full-time staff, not all astronomers. Only 4 live on site, the rest live in and around Parkes. When the dish is pointing vertical to the zenith, the astronomers are not observing. The telescope is normally operational 24 hours a day, seven days a week.

Other attractions in Parkes include: **Henry Parkes Historical Museum,** *316 Clarinda Street,* ☎622 815; **Motor Museum** - *Craft Corner, cnr Bogan and Dalton Streets;* **BHP Gold Mine,** 6km

south-west of Parkes; **Pioneer Park**, a collection of agricultural machinery and road transport; **Bushman's Hill Development,** the restoration of the Bushman's gold mine adjacent to the Visitor Centre; and **Mugincoble**, a Wheat Terminal with inspections arranged by the Tourist Centre.

Forbes

35km (22 miles) south-west of Parkes on the *Newell Highway*, is Forbes, which has many well attended parks and gardens and historic buildings. **Forbes Railway Arts and Tourist Centre**, *Union St*, can be contacted on ☎6852 4155.

Forbes is Ben Hall country. The famous bushranger was part of the notorious Gardiner Gang who carried out a gold escort robbery at nearby Eugowra. He met his death in a hail of bullets at the age of 28 and is buried in the Forbes Cemetery. **The Forbes Museum,** in an old Music Hall which once formed part of the Osborn Hotel, houses an interesting collection of relics of the bushrangers, and outside of Forbes a plaque marks the spot where Ben Hall was killed.

Other interesting graves in the old cemetery are those of Kate Foster, sister of Ned Kelly, and Rebecca Shield, grand-niece of Captain Cook.

The **Lachlan Vintage Village**, ☎6852 2655, is one kilometre from Forbes on the Newell Highway, and visitors can relive the past of an old gold town with exhibits dating from 1860 to 1900. Many of the early buildings and commercial businesses of the area have been reconstructed in a central part of the 81ha (200 acres) village to provide the visitor with a view of a country town from yesteryear. The complex also contains: the **Lachlan Diggings,** built on the site of the Forbes goldfield, where you can try your luck panning for gold in the creek; the Farming Museum, an 1860s farm complete with equipment, animals and the historic 'Nelungaloo' homestead with original furniture; **Ben Hall's Cottage;** the home of the famous Australian poet, Henry Lawson; and the Trigalana Woolshed, the entry building which houses the Blackridge Restaurant and a souvenir shop.

Forbes also has three wineries, two of which have their own distilleries. For inspections and cellar door sales enquire at the Tourist Centre.

Wellington

Situated on the Mitchell Highway, 50km (31 miles) south-east of Dubbo, Wellington is famous for the **Wellington Caves**, 8km (5 miles) south of the town. There are tours of the caves every hour 9am-4pm, except 1pm, ☎*6845 1733*, and accommodation is available in nearby Caves Caravan Park, ☎*6845 2970*.

The Wellington Visitor Information Centre is at *Cameron Park,* ☎*6845 1733*, and they have information on attractions in the town, which include a clock museum, a winery, and arts and crafts galleries. You can email them at ✉wellvic@australis.aunz.com and they are ☉open 9am-5pm daily except Christmas Day.

The **Burrendong Dam** is 32km (20 miles) upstream from Wellington, and there you can waterski, sail, swim, fish, or relax in the sun. Burrendong's arboretum covers an area of nearly 160ha (395 acres), set aside for the cultivation and preservation of plant life native to Australia. Mookerawa, another section of the Burrendong State Recreation Park, and Burrendong offer great facilities for visitors who love to camp.

Gilgandra

The town of Gilgandra is on the *Newell Highway*, 66km (41 miles) north of Dubbo, on the western side of the Warrumbungles. It was known originally as the town of windmills, and is home to one of the country's best privately owned observatories. The Gilgandra Visitor Information Centre is on the *Newell Highway,* ☎*6847 2045* email ✉gilinfo@tpg.com.au It is ☉open 9am-5pm daily, closed Christmas Day. Drop in here for information on the attractions in the town, and available accommodation.

Coonabarabran

Situated 95km (59 miles) north-east of Gilgandra, Coonabarabran Shire has a population of around 7000. The town name means 'Inquisitive Person' and the Visitors Centre is on the *Newell Highway* at the southern end of town, ☎*6842 144*, email ✉coonavic@lisp.com.au, ☉open daily 9am-5pm. They have enough information to satisfy any inquisitive person on accommodation and attractions, which include **Miniland and Museum**, and **Crystal Kingdom**.

The main attraction, however, is the **Anglo-Australian Observatory,** in Siding Spring, whose visitor's gallery allows visitors to view some of the workings of this immense piece of equipment. On the site there is also a fascinating permanent exhibition, 'Exploring the Universe', which should not be missed. **The Observatory** is 28km (17 miles) west of the town, and is ☉open daily 9am-4pm, ☎*6842 6291*.

35km (22 miles) from town is the **Warrumbungle National Park**, covering 21,004ha (51,880 acres) and containing magnificent scenery and prolific fauna and flora. The Park has spires and domes that are remnants of violent volcanic activity some 13 million years ago, and they are a spectacular sight. Food is not available in the park, and pets are prohibited. For further information ☎*1300 361 967* or visit ▇www.npws.nsw.gov.au

Between the Warrumbungle Mountains and the Namoi River is the **Pilliga Forest and Nature Reserve,** a vast flat area covering approximately 5400 sq km (2084 sq miles) of natural wild forest and scrublands known as the Pilliga Scrub.

The town of Baradine is the heart of the Pilliga, and there you can visit the **Baradine Forest Centre,** *Lachlan Street,* ☎*6843 1607*, and find out details of the many forest drives, and the location of the numerous sandstone caves.

Broken Hill

Population 21,000
Broken Hill lies in the Barrier Ranges in outback New South Wales, near the South Australian border, making it's area code 08. It is a long way from anywhere - 1170km (727 miles) from Sydney; 882km (548 miles) from Melbourne; 510km (317 miles) from Adelaide.

Climate

The city is 304m (997 ft) above sea level, and has an average rainfall of 235mm (9.25 ins) which is spread fairly evenly throughout the year with the greatest fall usually in June. As a rule the temperature only climbs above 38C (100F) eight or nine time a year. Maximum summer temperatures are generally in the low 30s (around 85F), but this causes little discomfort due to the low humidity. The nights are cold throughout the year. The winter months of May, June and July can be quite cold during the day as well.

Characteristics

Broken Hill is first and foremost a mining town, and in earlier days the dust problem appeared insurmountable, but due to a regeneration scheme started in 1930s, this problem has been largely overcome, at least as far as local storms are concerned. It has one of the richest silver and lead deposits in the world. Recently its popularity in the tourist market has grown.

Visitor Information

The Broken Hill Visitor Information Centre is on the corner of *Blende and Bromide Streets*, ☎*(08) 8087 6077*, email ✉tourist@pcpro.net .au. It is ⏲open 8.30am - 5pm daily.

How to Get There
By Bus

Pioneer have a Sydney/Adelaide service via Broken Hill.
Greyhound have a service from/to Melbourne.
Stateliner have a service from Adelaide.

By Rail

The **Indian Pacific** (Sydney/Perth) and **The Alice** (Sydney/Alice Springs) stop at Broken Hill.

↘ Let's Stay Here

Here is a selection of budget accommodation with prices which should be used as a guide only. The telephone area code is 08.

Sturt Motel, *153 Rakow Street,* ☎*8087 3558.* 19 units, swimming pool - ✪*$55-60.*

The Tourist Lodge YHA, *100 Argent St,* ☎*8088 2086,* ▣*www.yha.com* Located only metres away from the Visitor Information Centre, bus terminal and the shops. The pubs and cafes are not far either. Warm atmosphere. Facilities includes a kitchen, laundry, TV lounge, swimming pool and a barbecue area. Bike hire and parking available. *Dorms from* ✪*$18; BC MC VA*

Caravan Parks
Broken Hill City Caravan Park, *Rakow Street,* ☎*8087 3841.* (Pets allowed in a restricted area) 173 sites, barbecue, heated pool - *powered sites* ✪*$18 for two, on-site vans $32 for two.*

Lake View Broken Hill Caravan Park, *1 Mann Street,* ☎*8088 2250.* (Pets allowed under strict control) 137 sites, pool - *powered sites* ✪*$20 for two, on-site vans $30 for two.*

Let's Eat

Broken Hill has plenty of restaurants, cafes, clubs and hotels serving meals. Here are some you might like to try.

Betina's, *271 Kaolin St,* ☎*8088 2999.*

Oceania Chinese Restaurant, *423 Argent Street,* ☎*8087 3695.*

Pagoda Chinese Restaurant, *357 Cobalt Street,* ☎*8087 3679.*

Silver City Workingmen's Club, *402 Argent Street,* ☎*8087 5337.*

The Haven Restaurant, *577 Argent St,* ☎*8088 2888.*

Points of Interest

Broken Hill has two Tourist Drives - the Silver Arrow tour 1 and 2, and maps are available from the Tourist Centre.

Walking Tours depart from the Information Centre ⏲Mon-Fri and Sun at 10am, and are of approximately one and half hour's duration.

The Sundown Nature Trail, situated in the rocky Sundown Hills on the northern edge of the city Common, winds through the countryside for 2.8km (2 miles) and affords an opportunity to examine the sparse vegetation up close. It takes about one and a half hours, and is at its best just before sunset or just after sunrise.

Interesting and informative inspections of the surface workings of **North Mine** are conducted every afternoon Mon-Fri, and the Information Centre has details. NB solid footwear must be worn.

Underground tours are available ⏲Mon-Fri 10.30am and Sat 2pm, ☎*8088 1604,* but children under 8 are not admitted. **The Daydream Mine,** ☎*8088*

5682, near Silverton, 45 minutes away, also has underground tours with no age limit.

For tours of the **Royal Flying Doctor Base**, enquire on ☎*8080 1777*. The School of the Air is open weekdays, and bookings for this are handled by the Information Centre.

At the **Whites Mineral Art and Mining Museum**, *1 Allendale Street* ☎*8087 2878*, you can see life size replicas of current and old-time mining procedures.

The **Railway Mineral and Train Museum**, *Blende Street*, ☎*8088 4660*, has a large display of old railway machinery.

Broken Hill has more than twenty-one Art Galleries open for public viewing. Here are a few names and addresses:

The **Broken Hill City Art Gallery**, *cnr Chloride and Blende Streets*, ☎*8088 5491*, ☉open Mon-Sat 9am-4pm, with guided tours Tues-Sat at 11.30am.

Pro Hart Gallery, ☎*8087 2441*, *108 Wyman Street*, ☉open Mon-Sat 9.30am-5pm.

Hoppy Hopgood Gallery, *589 Fisher Street*, ☉open daily from 9am.

Facilities
Car Hire
Avis, ☎8087 7532; Budget, ☎8087 9151; and Hertz, ☎8087 2719.

Taxi services
Yellow Radio Cabs, ☎13 1008.

There are two laundromats, 3 Council run libraries, 3 swimming pools (one heated), golf, horse riding, lawn bowls, indoor cricket, squash and tennis.

The Royal Automobile Association of South Australia has an office at *261 Argent Street*, ☎*8088 4999*.

Outlying Attractions
Menindee
Situated 110km (68 miles) south-east of Broken Hill, there is a series of natural lakes stretching 50km (31 miles) north and 35km (22 miles) south of the town of Menindee, and areas have been developed for caravan parks, weekend cottages, speedboats, water skiing, sailing, safe swimming and good fishing.

The **Kinchega National Park**, on the western bank of the Darling River adjacent to Menindee, is a significant example of one of the major landscape categories of the arid and semi-arid regions of New South Wales.

The Menindee Regional Tourist Association is in the *Railway Station, Maiden St*, ☎*8091 4274*.

Silverton
On a sealed road 25km (16 miles) north-west of Broken Hill, is Silverton, once a thriving community of over 3000, but now a ghost town where many films have been shot, e.g. A Town Like Alice, Mad Max II and Razorback, and several commercials and documentaries.

The **Sturt National Park** begins just north of Tibooburra, which is 337km (209 miles) north of Broken Hill, and reaches to the spot where the New South Wales, Queensland and South Australian borders meet. At the three-state corner the dingo fence can be seen. It is part of the 'longest fence in the world'.

White Cliffs
The well-known opal field and township of White Cliffs is 295km (183 miles) north-east of Broken Hill. There you can try your luck at fossicking, see the superb opalised Plesiosaur skeleton, and the dugouts where many of the residents live. Facilities include a hotel, motel, general store and cafe. Fossicker's Licences are available from the Visitor Information Centre in *Karara Road*, ☎*8091 6611*.

New South Wales – North-West
Tamworth
Population 37,000
Tamworth is situated at the junction of the New England and Oxley Highways, on the banks of the Peel River. It is 411km (255 miles) from Sydney; 1152km (715 miles) from Melbourne; 1,446km (898 miles) from Adelaide; 589km (366 miles) from Brisbane.

Climate
Average temperatures: January max 30C (88F) - min 17C (63F); July max 16C (61F) - min 4C (39F). The town is 389 metres (1276 ft) above sea level and has an average rainfall of 650mm (25in). Occasional snow falls in winter on the hilltops around Nundle (60km [37miles]) to the south.

Characteristics
As well as being famous as the Australasian Country Music Capital, Tamworth was also the first city in the country to install electric street lighting. The city is in the heart of the biggest gemstone fossicking region of NSW, and is surrounded by picturesque countryside.

How to Get There
By Rail
An air conditioned Countrylink service operates daily to Tam-worth from Sydney. The Countrylink connects in Tamworth with a fleet of luxury coaches which travel over a large area of north-west NSW.

By Bus
Tamworth is on the main Brisbane/Sydney, Brisbane/Melbourne and Brisbane/Adelaide routes which are covered daily by **Greyhound Pioneer** and **McCafferty's**.

Visitor Information
The Tamworth Visitor Information Centre is on the corner of Peel and Murray Streets, ☎6755 4300 or email ✉tourism@tamworth.nsw.gov.au Their opening hours are ☼8.30am-4.30pm Mon-Fri, 9am-5pm weekends.

⤴ Let's Stay Here
Make sure you ask for a room away from the highway as trucks travelling at night can destroy your sleep. Here is a selection of budget accommodation which should be used as a guide only. The telephone area code is 02.

Roydon's Motel,
Cnr New England Highway and Church Street, ☎6765 7355. 12 units, basic facilities - ✪$55-60.

Southgate Inn,
cnr. Kathleen and Kent Streets, ☎6765 7999. 6 rooms (private facilities), unlicensed restaurant - *from* ✪$60.

Tamworth Hotel,
Marius Street, ☎6766 2923. 1 - ✪$40.

Tamworth YHA,
169 Marius St, ☎6761 2600, ▣www.yha.com Located in the centre of town and close to train station and foodstores. Bus depot is about a km away. Facilities includes kitchen, laundry, TV lounge, internet access and barbecue area. *Dorms from $22; double/twin $46*

Caravan Parks
City Lights Caravan Park,
New England Highway, ☎6765 7664. (Pets allowed on application) 102 sites, pool, playground, barbecue - *powered sites* ✪$16-25 *for two, on-site vans $30-45 for two.*

Austin Caravan Park,
581 Armidale Road, ☎6766 2380. (Pets allowed on application) 104 sites, barbecue, pool, good facilities - *powered sites* ✪$19 *for two, cabins $35-75 for two.*

Let's Eat
There are licensed clubs which provide lunch and dinner, and have activities and live entertainment for guests. Visitors are always welcome. There are a number of fully licensed restaurants mainly associated with the major hotels, and many fast food outlets such as **McDonald's** and the local cafes.

83 Restaurant, *199 Marius St,* ☎6766 2383.

Bangkok Thai Restaurant, *North-*gate Shopping Centre Shop, 18 Peel St, ☎6761 3098.

Deepka Indian Restaurant, *23 Brisbane St,* ☎6766 1771.

Empress Chinese Restaurant, *455a Peel St,* ☎6766 1616.
Valentino's Italian Restaurant, *2 Byrnes Ave,* ☎6766 4246.

Points of Interest
The Department of Lands has created a Heritage Walk and a Nature Walk in Tamworth. Maps of both walks are available from the Visitor Information Centre in *Kable Avenue.*

The **Powerstation Museum** in *Peel Street* celebrates Tamworth's centenary as Australia's first city with electric street lighting, and features working steam-powered electricity-generating equipment.

Calala Cottage in *Denison Street* was constructed in 1875 as the home of Tamworth's first Mayor, and today forms part of the local Historical Society complex.

Munro's Mill in *Peel Street* opened in 1863. Built from handmade bricks and hand-forged nails, it was the first commercial flour mill in New England. Today, it is an antique shop.

The Country Collection, ☎6765 2688, on the New England Highway offers an interesting combination of attractions including the Rock, Gem and Mineral Collection, a wax museum filled with legends of country music, and Britten's Boutique Brewery which produces a series of Tamworth ales. Endeavour Drive, at the top of Brisbane Street, takes you to Oxley Park, a peaceful sanctuary for kangaroos and other native wildlife, with full amenities, picnic and barbecue facilities.

Bicentennial Park, in *Kable Avenue,* is a peaceful 'people's place' of parkland, pathways, fountains, pergolas, restaurant and a central pool. The pool is ringed by granite etched with depictions of the district's history and wildlife.

Tamworth City Gallery, ☎*6755 4459,* in *Marius Street* has a silver collection on permanent display. It also houses travelling exhibitions and is the site for the National Fibre Exhibition.

Festivals

The **Australasian Country Music Festival** is held over ten days each January. The festival normally has over 600 concerts and events.

The **Tamworth Arts in Action Festival** is held biennially in October. It includes concerts, displays of homecrafts, opera and live theatre.

Facilities

Excellent sporting facilities are available in Tamworth for just about every type of sport from tenpin bowling to clay target shooting. At Lake Keepit you can water ski, canoe, fish, sail and bushwalk. There are also facilities for gliding (Keepit Soaring Club). The hilltop countryside around Tamworth is best appreciated on horseback. Four Wheel Drive enthusiasts will find the back roads around Manilla, Hall's Creek and Bendemeer challenging.

Outlying Attractions
Manilla

On the Namoi River, it is known for **Dutton's Meadery** in Barraba Street, where you can taste their

honey-based alcoholic drink, which is reputedly mans' oldest liquor.

Kootingal
Pyramid Planetarium on the New England Highway features a working model of the solar system.

Moonbi
Braecroft Cottage Gallery, Braefarm Road is the home of the ceramic artist Fred Hillier and his range of ceramic figurines and Australian bush buildings.

Nundle
If you want to try your luck fossicking then try around this historic village especially in the '**Hills of Gold**' area, after visiting Hanging Rock, and asking one of the locals for advice. The **Nundle Historical Museum** is in *Jenkins Street,* ☎*6769 3292.*

Armidale
Population 25,000
Armidale is situated in the New England Tablelands, part of the Great Dividing Range which stretches from around Newcastle to the Queensland Border. The city is surrounded by National Parks - Oxley Wild Rivers National Park, New England National Park, Cathedral Rock National Park and Beautiful Gorge Country. Distance from Sydney 563km (35 miles), Melbourne 1268km (788 miles), Brisbane 464km (288 miles), Adelaide 1636km (1017 miles).

Climate
Average temperatures: January max 26C (79F) - min 14C (57F); June max 14C (57F) - min 2C (36F). Average annual rainfall is 795mm (31 ins). Situated 1000m

(3281 ft) above sea level. Armidale has definite seasons, and occasional snowfalls in winter.

Characteristics
The principal town of the area, it is an education centre with over 8 high schools and other institutions, and it is the site of New England University. The surrounding district produces fine merino wool, wheat and fruit.

How to Get There
By Bus
Border Coaches, Bus Australia, Trans City and McCaffertys have services to Armidale from Sydney and Brisbane.

By Rail
There is a daily Countrylink service from Sydney to Tamworth, with a connecting coach to Armidale.

Visitor Information
Armidale Visitor Information Centre is at 82 Marsh Street, ☎*6772 4655* or email ✉armvisit@ northnet.com.au ⏱opening hours are 9am-5pm Mon to Fri, 9am-4pm Sat, 10am-4pm Sun. It is closed on public holidays.

↩ Let's Stay Here
Here is a selection with prices which should be used as a guide only. The telephone area code is (02).

Armidale Rose Villa Motel, *New England Highway,* ☎*6772 3872.* 10 units, undercover parking, barbecue - ✪*$50-75.*

Armidale Acres Motel, *New England Highway,*

☎6771 1281. 11 units (some with private facilities), pool, tennis, barbecue - ✪$55-60.

Pembroke Tourist and Leisure Park YHA,

39 Waterfall Way, 6772 6470 or 1800 355 578, 🖳www.yha.com Situated in a semi-rural area on the way to New England National Park, New England Uni and the city centre. Nearest foodstore is about a km away. Built in well-equipped bunkhouse within a caravan park. Facilities includes a kitchen, laundry, recreation room with TV, open fireplace, entertainment area, swimming pool and a barbecue area. Kiosk and internet access on site. There is bike hire. Parking available. *Dorms from ✪$20; double/twin from $45; BC MC VA EFTPOS*

Caravan Parks
Pembroke Tourist and Leisure Park, *39 Waterfall Way,* ☎6772 6470. (Pets allowed on leash) pool, barbecue, tennis, excellent facilities - *powered sites* ✪$20-25 *for two, on-site vans* $30-40 *for two.*

Highlander Van Village,
76 Glen Innes Road, ☎6772 4768. (Dogs allowed on leash) pool, barbecue, playground - *powered sites* ✪$16-18 *for two, on-site vans* $35 *for two.*

Let's Eat
As usual there are many places to eat in the main street, and the licensed clubs welcome visitors. Armidale Cattleman's Motor Inn, 31 Marsh Street, ☎6772 7788, has an a la carte menu.

Lizebeth's, *208 Dangar St,* ☎6772 9800.

Mandarin Restaurant, *213 Beardy St,* ☎6772 6535.

Ming Court Restaurant, *11 Beardy St,* ☎6772 9363.

Minio's Restaurant, *201a Brown St (Cnr Markham St),* ☎6771 4555.

Moore Park Motor Inn, *New England Highway,* ☎6772 2358, also has a licensed restaurant and cocktail bar which is open seven days.

Squires Cottage Restaurant, *86 Barney St,* ☎6772 8511

Points of Interest
Central Park is attractive in all seasons, and contains a tourist directory, rotunda, a memorial fountain and picnic facilities. There is a sign posted Tourist Drive which takes in the main attractions.

University of New England, *off Queen Elizabeth Drive, 5km north of town, west of centre,* ☎6773 3333, has 5 faculties and is ☼open for inspection daily 9am-5pm. Booloominbah, an historic house, is the Administrative Centre. It also has a deer and kangaroo park.

The Folk Museum, *Cnr Rusden and Faulkner Streets,* ☎6770 3536, is classified by the National Trust and has displays of early transport, lighting, handicrafts, and more, ☼open daily 1-4pm.

The New England Regional Art Museum, *Kentucky Street,* ☎6772 5255, houses the famous Hinton, Armidale City and Coventry Collections, ☼open

Mon-Sat 10am-5pm, Sun 1-5pm. Other museums include the **CB Newling Campus Educational Museum** in Kentucky Street, the **Museum of Printery**, also in Kentucky Street, and the **Museum of Antiquities** in *Queen Elizabeath* and *Madgwick Drive.*

The Berry Best Cafe and Bakehouse on the *New England Highway* towards the airport, is the largest hydroponic berry farm in Australia, ☎6772 5974. They specialise in pies and strudels, and are ☼open daily 8.30am-6pm.

From **Apex Lookout** you can obtain a view of the whole city.

St Mary's Roman Catholic Cathedral, *Dangar Street* near Central Park, is built in Gothic Revival style and has a fine spire, marble sanctuary and Flemish bondwork, ☼open 7am-6pm daily. Nearby is St Peter's Anglican Cathedral (cnr Dangar and Rusden Streets), which has an Ecclesiastical Museum with exhibits relating not only to the church itself, but also to Armidale in general.

Festivals
Woolexpo is held annual in March, and the **Arts Festival**, lasting about a week, is held biennially in October.

Facilities
Lawn bowls, trout fishing, golf, squash, swimming pool and tennis.

Outlying Attractions
Dangar's Falls
The Falls and Lagoon, 22km (14 miles) south of Armidale, feature a large rock pool and many species of birds. **Dumaresq Dam**, 8km from town, has a boat

ramp (only non-powered boats permitted) and swimming.

Ebor Falls

These are 74km (46 miles) to the east, and it is a delightful picnic spot. The falls are divided into two with a total drop of 115m (377 ft).

Hillgrove

An old ghost town about 27km (17 miles) east of Armidale, Hillgrove has been carefully restored to serve as an uncanny reminder of its vibrant and colourful past.

Wollomombi Falls

The highest falls in Australia, Wollomombi Falls have a drop of 460m (1509 ft).

For rockhounds and gem fossickers: The area has numerous little pockets which contain sapphires, zircons, topaz, diamonds, gold, silver, tin, jelly beans, quartz, smokey quartz, grass stone, agate, rhodorite, tourmaline, petrified wood, and almost anything else you can think of. Inverell, to the north-west, is one of the more popular fossicking towns.

Lightning Ridge

Population 6,000 (est.)
Lightning Ridge is situated 770km (478 miles) north-west of Sydney and about 60km (37 miles) from the Queensland border.

Climate

The area has long hot summers and short cold winters, with summer temperatures dropping as much as 20C (68F) degrees at night.

Characteristics

An old fashioned, carefree, 'tomorrow will do if it can't be done today' atmosphere, which is treasured and preserved by local residents as a valuable way of life. The only place in the world where a wet pudding can be seen (the operation which is used to separate opal nobbies from the clay in which they are found). This area is world famous for its black and blue opals and that is why it has merited inclusion in this guide. It attracts many tourists.

How to Get There
By Rail and Coach

Trains and buses run from Sydney via Dubbo every day.

Visitor Information

The Lightning Ridge Visitor Information Centre is in *Fred Reece Way*, ☎*6829 0565*. At *51 Morilla Street* you will find the Opal Cave Tourist Centre, ☎*6829 0333*.

↵ Let's Stay Here

The standard of accommodation is comfortable. Prices included here are for a double room per night, which should be used as a guide only. The telephone area code is 02.

Wallangulla Motel, *cnr Morilla and Agate Streets*, ☎*6829 0542*. 42 units, basic facilities - *from* ✪*$55*.

Caravan Parks
Crocodile Caravan and Camping Park, *Morilla St*, ☎*6829 0437*. (Pets allowed on a leash) 30 sites, barbecue, pool - *powered sites* ✪*$14 for two, cabins $45-55 for two.*

Lightning Ridge Caravan Park, *Harlequin Street*, ☎*6829 0532*. (Pets allowed on leash) 84 sites, barbecue, basic facilities - *powered sites* ✪*$14 for two, on-site vans $35 for two.*

Lightning Ridge Motel Hotel, *Onyx Street*, ☎*6829 0304*. (Pets allowed on a leash) 47 sites, licensed restaurant, barbecue, pool - *powered sites* ✪*$11 for two, cabins $40-50.*

Let's Eat

Take-aways or eat-in:

Diggers Rest Bistro and Takeaway, *Opal St*, ☎*6829 2410*.

Miners Mate, *Lot 4 Opal St*, ☎*6829 2725* - Chinese and Thai, open 7 days, licensed.

Nobby's Restaurant, *Onyx St*, ☎*6829 0611*.

Wong's Restaurant, *14 Opal St*, ☎*6829 2330*.

Points of Interest

Visitors can explore the mining fields and fossick for opal. At the **Big Opal Bazaar**, *3 Mile Road*, you can see opals being cut, and at **Spectrum Mines**, *Bald Hill Road*, ☎*6829 0581*, there is a daily film show and an underground display.

At the **Bush Museum**, *Hatters Flat*, ☎*6829 0016*, there is memorabilia from the early mining days. At the **Drive-in Mine**, *13 Gem Street*, old and new techniques used in mining for opals are displayed and the **Walk-in Mine**, *1 Bald Hill Field*, has underground tours.

Other attractions include **Kangaroo Hill Wildlife Park**,

☎6829 0155, the **Bottle House Mining Museum,** ☎6829 0618, the **Bird of Paradise Art Gallery,** ☎6829 0538, and the **Lightning Ridge Bore Baths** in *Pandora Street,* ☎6829 0429.

Festivals

The **Great Goat Race** is held during Easter and the **Opal Festival** during the NSW September school holidays.

Facilities

The town has artesian baths, a children's park with a BMX track, a drive-in theatre, horse riding facilities, tennis courts, bowling club, golf course and a pistol club.

Outlying Attractions
Walgett

This town is near the junction of the Namoi and Barwon rivers and a little over 100km (62 miles) from Lightning Ridge. It is surrounded by pastoral properties stretching far in each direction. Irrigation has opened up large new areas to cotton, sorghum, maize and other crops. There is good fishing in the area.

Bourke

A town with its own folklore, Bourke is approximately 300km (186 miles) south-west of Lightning Ridge, 946km (588 miles) south-west of Brisbane, and 781km (485 miles) north-west of Sydney. It has been included in this section as it is even further from anywhere else. Its population varies but is generally in excess of 3,000 people.

The town is 110m (361 ft) above sea level and has an annual rainfall of 325mm (13 ins). The area produces wool and beef, and in recent years cotton and other

irrigated crops have been grown. A cotton gin operates in the area.

Bourke is situated on the upper banks of the Darling River, and its Post Office still flies the pennant indicating it is a port, from the days when boats would travel up and down the Darling transporting goods and produce. Now the wharves are broken up and hang in mid-air, a symbol of another era, whilst over the years the river has silted up making such transport impossible.

The town is considered to be the last before the vast empty centre. Just about everyone uses the expression "out the back of Bourke" when they want to describe the loneliness and emptiness of the centre of Australia.

The Bourke Visitor Information Centre is in *Anson Street,* ☎6872 2280 or email ✉tourinfo@lisp. com.au ☉opening hours are daily 9am-5pm.

⮌ Let's Stay Here
Bourke YHA - Gidgee Guesthouse,
17 Oxley St, ☎6870 1017, 🖳 *www.yha.com.au.* An old 'London Bank' building circa 1888 with an accommoda-tion wing attached. One of Bourke's finest buildings. A very warm atmosphere. Walk-ing distance to the nearest shop. The wing surrounds a shady courtyard, gardens, a fountain and the barbecue area. Other facilities includes a kitchen, laundry, lounge rooms, TV rom and an in-ternet access. Bike hire and parking available. *Dorms from ✪$18; double/twin from $26pp; BC MC VA EFTPOS*

South Syndey
Southern Highlands
Population 50,000
The Southern Highlands are south of Sydney, and the district includes, amongst others, the towns of Bowral, Mittagong, Moss Vale, Berrima, Bundanoon, Robertson and Kangaroo Valley.

Climate
Average temperatures: January max 25C (77F) - min 18C (64F); July max 10C (50F) - min -2C (28F). Average annual rainfall varies from 760mm (30 ins) in the north and west to 1140mm (45 ins) at Moss Vale and 1950mm (77 ins) at Robertson.

Characteristics
The rich, the famous and the powerful have long valued the Highlands as a rural retreat. The Governor of New South Wales used the Highlands as a 'holiday home' as early as 1868 when the Earl of Belmore rented Throsby Park. Later Hillview at Sutton Forest became a permanent vice-regal country residence, thus sealing the popularity of the area with the well-to-do citizens of Sydney. Many fine homes of the period remain. More recently, the Highlands have become a centre for artists and craft-workers, who find inspiration for their work in the quiet of the country and the beauty of their surroundings.

How to Get There
By Bus
All the major interstate bus companies stop in the Southern Highlands on their Sydney/ Canberra/Melbourne routes. There are regular bus services between Moss Vale and Canberra,

and a daily service between Moss Vale and Nowra.

By Rail
There are daily services from Sydney and Canberra.

Visitor Information
The Southern Highlands Visitor Information Centre is at *62 -70 Main Street, Mittagong,* ☎*4871 2888.* You can email them at wingtour@wsc.nsw.gov.au The ⏱opening hours are 8am-5:30pm daily. There is a comprehensive website at ▪www.southernhighlands.com.au

Points of Interest
Mittagong
The area was one of the first settled by Europeans when the government allowed settlement south of the Cowpastures (now Camden). In 1821, William Chalker, principal overseer of government stock at the Cowpastures, was granted 200 acres of land on the Old South Road as a reward for service, and although he died before the grant was surveyed, his widow took up the grant, and his descendants still live in the area. In fact, in 1988 the family erected a cairn on the Old South Road to mark the site of the original grant, and from there you can get a good view of Mittagong and the surrounding countryside.

Many gracious sandstone buildings were constructed in the town in the 1860s, not only public buildings, but small cottages, and many of these can be found in the side streets between the Hume Highway and Lake Alexandra.

The town has many specialty craft outlets, that display and sell the works of both local and outside artists, including such items as tapestry, stained glass, woodwork, pottery and weaving.

In and around Mittagong there are several easily accessible walking tracks, including one to the old **Box Vale Mine**. There are also a number of trails around Mittagong's **Lake Alexandra**, which was built by damming drainage water from the town, and attracts a wide variety of domestic and wild birdlife. The Visitor Information Centre in Winifred West Park has full details of all the walks available.

The Southern Highlands Visitor Information Centre is in *Main Street.*

⤳ Let's Stay Here
Mittagong Motel,
7 Old Hume Highway, ☎*4871 1277.* 28 units, unlicensed restaurant - ❂*$55-90.*

Mittagong Caravan Park,
Hume Highway, ☎*4871 1574.* 71 sites, basic facilities - powered sites ❂*$18 for two,* on-site vans *$35 for two.*

Let's Eat
Following are some restaurants you might like to try in the various towns.

1890 Restaurant and Cafe, *84 Hume Highway,* ☎*4871 1871* - licensed, French Continental a la carte - ⏱open Mon-Sat 6-9.30pm, Fri-Sun noon-2.30pm.

B C's Italian Restaurante, *79 Hume Hwy,* ☎*4872 1777.*

The Blue Cockerel Bistro, 95 Hume Hwy, ☎4872 1677.

Lesters Restaurant of Mittagong, *16 Bowral Road,* ☎*4871 2696*
- licensed, Italian - ⏱open Wed-Mon 5pm-10pm, plus Sun noon-2.30pm.

Lion Rampant, *Cnr Victoria Street and Hume Highway,* ☎*4872 2980* - Bistro - ⏱open Wed-Sun 6-8.30pm, counter lunches noon-2pm.

Mittagong Chinese Restaurant, *91 Hume Hwy,* ☎*4871 1704.*

Thonburi Thai Restaurant, *Beaumont Gardens Shp 1/ Bowral Rd,* ☎*4872 1511.*

Mount Gibraltar
The mount (863m - 2831 ft), known locally as The Gib, is the highest point between the Illawarra Coast and the Great Dividing Range beyond the Wollondilly River. It rises 240m (787 ft) above Mittagong to the north, and 180m (591 ft) above Bowral on its southern flank. From the summit, on clear days, there are views to the Sydney area (north), the Blue Mountains (north and north-west), the Cuckbundoon Range (south-west) and to Mt Keira above Wollongong.

There are fire trails and foot tracks for dedicated bushwalkers. The Visitor Information Offices have details of all the lookouts, and maps of the various tracks.

Bowral
Bowral was originally part of a property granted to the explorer John Oxley, and in 1859, 200 acres of his estate were subdivided by members of his family to coincide with the news of the coming of the railway. The village was first known as Wingecarribee (now the name of

the Shire), then Burradoo, and finally in 1867, Bowral. The town was the site of the first store in the district, but development was slow until the opening of the railway. From 1870 onwards, the village grew rapidly, and by 1890 was considered a fashionable resort where Sydneysiders could retreat from the heat of summer.

Now, with a population of 10,000, the town is a blend of historic buildings, quaint old residential cottages and commercial premises. There is a uniformity to the architecture, and a large number of mature deciduous trees form a backdrop for magnificent public and private gardens.

Bendooley Street is subject to a Heritage Commission protection order, to prevent it from being altered. The Berrima District Historical Society has compiled an historical tour of Bowral, beginning at the Corbett Gardens, one block east of the main street, and visiting twelve attractions. The Information Centre has details.

The Bradman Museum, ☎4862 1247, is in St Jude Street, overlooking the Bradman Oval, and opposite his former home (52 Shepherd Street, which is a private residence), ⊕open daily 10am-4pm. It was on the Oval that Bradman played his first game of cricket when he was twelve, and where, in 1925, he scored a sparkling 234 for Bowral against the Wingello team that included bowler Bill O'Reilly.

The Museum has an incredible array of cricket-related material, ranging from an oak bat of the 1750s through to Allan Border's helmet used during the 1989 Ashes series. But, naturally,

anything to do with the late Sir Donald (1908-2001) takes pride of place, and he has donated many objects, including the bat he used at Headingley in 1934 to score his second highest Test innings of 304. Admission is ⊙$7.50 adults. A website containing everything you want to know about The Don is: ▇www.bradman.org.au

For cricket fans, there is also **The Bradman Walk,** a self-guided tour through Bowral visiting some of the sites associated with the great cricketer. It begins at the Museum and Oval, and includes the school, St Simon and St Jude's Church, the Empire Cinema, his workplace in Bong Bong Street and two houses where he once lived.

Let's Eat

Following are some restaurants you might like to try in the various towns.

House of Lowe, 236 Bong Bong Street, ☎4861 2308 - licensed, Chinese and seafood - ⊕open daily for dinner from 5pm, and for lunch Wed-Sun noon-2pm.

Jack Style Thai Restaurant, Boolwey and Station Street, ☎4862 1905.

Prego Trattoria Pizzeria, 412 Bong Bong Street, ☎4862 5009.

Da Giacomo Cafe Restaurant, 275 Bong Bong Street, ☎4862 2996.

Station Street Restaurant, 48 Station Street, ☎4861 7171.

Toshis Japanese Restaurant, Bong Bong Street, ☎4861 4274. Shanghai Restaurant, 265 Bong Bong Street, ☎4861 1774.

Moss Vale

The town of Moss Vale stands on part of the original grant made to the district's first European settler, Charles Throsby, who played an important part in the exploration of New South Wales, opening up not only the Southern Highlands, but also the South Coast, Goulburn and Canberra regions. His nephew, also named Charles, came to live in the district and established Throsby Park as a well respected grazing property.

Throsby Park was inhabited by the family until 1990, and although originally a colonial Georgian home, it was added to in later periods, evident in the architecture, furnishings, decoration and garden. The site is open by arrangement and guided yours are available, contact The National Parks and Wildlife Service ☎4887 7270 for information and bookings. The is a small entry fee for park usage, with all proceeds going to the restoration and maintenance of Throsby Park.

Scenic attractions in the area include **Belmore** and **Fitzroy Falls,** and **Morton National Park,** with its 55km (34 miles) of river frontages and virgin bushland.

Moss Vale Village Park, *Willow Drive*, ☎ *4868 1099*. (Pets allowed under supervision) 114 sites, excellent facilities - *powered sites* ☻$15 *for two, on-site vans* $35 *for two.*

Let's Eat
Following are some restaurants you might like to try in the various towns.

Argyle St Bistro, *Argyle Street*, ☎ *4868 1599*.

Cedar's Lebanese Restaurant, *490 -494 Argyle Street*, ☎ *4869 4600*.

Chow's Hong Kong Restaurant, *443 Argyle Street*, ☎ *4868 2208* - licensed, Chinese - open daily for lunch 11.30am-2.30pm, dinner Sun-Wed 5-9.30pm, Thurs 5-10.30pm, Fri-Sat 5-11pm.

Peking Restaurant, *Moss Vale Mall*, ☎ *4868 2366*.

Sattahip Thai Restaurant, *Shop 2/ 249 Argyle Street*, ☎ *4869 1891*.

Seafood Affair, *515 Argyle Street*, ☎ *4868 1726* - open Mon-Sat for dinner, Tues-Sat for lunch.

Fitzroy Falls
The falls are within 100m of the car park and visitor information centre in Morton National Park, one of the largest National Parks in New South Wales, covering an area of over 154,000ha (380,380 acres). The Falls cascade 82m (269 ft) to the valley below, and there are two scenic walking tracks, one on each side of the escarpment, that provide spectacular views from a series

of lookouts along the way. Each track is approximately 3km in length, taking 1-2 hours walking. The visitor information centre has details of these, and of other attractions through the park.

Berrima
Situated 14km (9 miles) south of Mittagong on the Hume Highway, Berrima is considered the best remaining example of a small Australian town of the 1830s. The town was founded in 1829 by Sir Thomas Mitchell, the Surveyor-General of New South Wales, and in its heyday was an affluent community with a population of over 500. Many of the original buildings have been restored, and former hotels now trade as craft shops, galleries and restaurants.

The walking 2.5km tour of Berrima begins at the **Berrima District Historical Museum and Information Centre**, and visits the following: **Berrima House**, built in 1835, and once host to bushranger Ben Hall; **Berrima Bridge Nursery**, formerly a private girls' school; **Brian McMahon's Pub**, 1840; **The Coach and Horses Inn**, 1835, now a private home; **The Market Place Park; Victoria Inn**, 1834; **The Barn Gallery; The Large Oak Tree**, planted by Sir Henry Parkes in 1890; **Post Office**, 1836; **Surveyor General Inn**, 1835, the oldest continuously licensed inn in Australia still trading within its original walls; **Superintendent's House**, built in the 1880s as the **Governor's House for the Gaol; Berrima Gaol; Deputy Superintendent's House; Bulls Head Fountain; Lambie's Well**, 1840; **Court House**, 1833; **Sandstone Cottages** in *Argyle Street*; **Presbyterian Church;**

Bellview House; Ardleigh; Harper's Mansion, 1834; **Old Well; Colonial Inn; The Berrima Gallery;** the **Old Bakery; Holy Trinity Church; Magistrate's House; The White Horse Inn;** and **St Francis Xavier Catholic Church**, 1849.

There are also a few other walks that take visitors further afield, and the Information Centre has details.

Let's Eat
Following are some restaurants you might like to try in the various towns.

Journeyman Bistro, *Old Hume Highway*, ☎ *4877 1911* - licensed, specialise in flare-grill - open 7 days for lunch and dinner.

Old Breens Restaurant, *Hume Hwy*, ☎ *4877 1977*.

Victoria Inn, *Jellore Street*, ☎ *4877 1475* - licensed, gourmet a la carte - open for dinner Wed-Sat, lunch Sun.

Robertson
The town was named in honour of John Robertson who was responsible for the Land Act of 1861 under which land was thrown open for selection before survey. The **Robertson Nature Reserve**, located 300m south of the township, is easily accessible and is an important conservation area, containing about 5ha (12 acres) of the Yarrawa Brush vegetation which, prior to European settlement, covered about 2500ha (6175 acres) around what is now Robertson township. Up until the 1950s, farmers in the area were still clearing the native timber, and the

casual visitor must wonder what made them persevere against such overwhelming odds.

Today the Robertson area is one of the most beautiful to be found anywhere, with its rolling red soil country and rugged bushland

Let's Stay Here

Robertson Country Motel, *Illawarra Highway,* ☎ *4885 1444.* 6 units, basic facilities - ✪$*60-85.*

Let's Eat

Ranelagh House, *Illawarra Highway,* ☎ *4885* 1111 - BYO, country style cooking - open 7 days for lunch and dinner (except when house closed for conferences).

Bundanoon

The town of Bundanoon has been a holiday spot for decades, but still manages to retain a quiet village atmosphere. It is a bushwalker's paradise, with walks going to **Glow Worm Glen, Fern Glen, Fairy Bower Falls,** and **the Amphitheatre,** amongst other places. The Southern Highlands Visitor Information Centre has all the details on durations of walks, and fitness required.

In April, Bundanoon goes Scottish in more than name alone, with the popular annual **"Brigadoon" Festival.** The entertainment is as you'd expect, the day filled with the unmistakable tune of bagpipes, traditional dancing and a host of highland games.

Let's Stay Here

Bundanoon YHA, *Railway Ave, 4883* 6010, ▪ *www.yha.com* Gateway to Morton National Park. 1km to bus stop and railway station. Great hospi-

tality you can almost expect breakfast hampers. Big verandahs and a barbecue area, large lounge room with log fire in winter, laundry, kitchen, communal bathrooms, 5 acres of grounds. Middle of nowhere but you can be connected. Parking available. *Dorms from* ✪$*20; double twin from $48; BC MC VA EFTPOS.*

Morton National Park, *Church Street,* ☎ *4887 7270.* (No pets allowed) - no power, advance site reservations only - ✪$*10-18 for two.*

Let's Eat

Bundanoon Chinese Restaurant, *21 Railway Avenue,* ☎ *4883 6368.*

Highlander Restaurant, *Anzac Parade,* ☎ *4883 6242* - licensed, a la carte with German influence - open Wed-Sun from 6.30pm, Sun noon-2pm.

Tree Tops Guest House, *101 Railway Parade,* ☎ *4883* 6372 - BYO, International and Indian cuisine - open for dinner Fri-Sat.

Kangaroo Valley

Kangaroo Valley is situated on a plateau between the Highlands and the coast, and is easily accessible. The Kangaroo River winds through the valley, and is crossed by the Hampden Suspension Bridge, built in 1898 of castellated stone by convict labour. The bridge is named after Viscount Hampden, Governor of New South Wales at that time. The river under the bridge is popular for swimming and canoeing. Barbecue and toilet facilities are provided.

Adjacent to the bridge is the

Pioneer Settlement Museum, with a fully furnished old farm homestead, a dairy, and a machinery shed, set in picnic grounds with barbecue facilities. The museum is open daily 9am-5pm.

Historic Barrengarry Store and Post Office is found 1km north of the Suspension Bridge. They were established in 1880 and retain the old-world charm of a pioneer general store that sells almost everything.

The Kangaroo Valley village has many coffee shops, craft shops and specialty stores, while the river offers many spots for picnicking, swimming, bushwalking and canoeing.

Bendeela Pondage and **Pumping Station** is 7km (4 miles) west of the Main Road, on Bendeela Road. Here water is pumped 127 (417 ft) vertically to a reservoir above Fitzroy Falls. A picnic area, barbecues and toilets are provided.

Kangaroo Valley can also be reached easily from Nowra.

Let's Stay Here

Kanagroo Valley Glenmack Caravan Park, *Main Road,* ☎ *4465 1372.* (No pets allowed) 108 sites, barbecue, tennis, mini-golf - *powered sites* ✪$*18-20 for two, cabins from $50.*

Kangaroo Valley Tourist Park, *Moss Vale Road,* ☎ *4465 1310.* (No dogs allowed) 60 sites, canoeing, playground, barbecue - *powered sites* ✪$*17 for two, cabins from $45.*

Let's Eat

Restaurant Deville, *Moss Vale*

Road, ☎4465 1314 - licensed, char grill, blackboard menu - open Wed-Sun 10am-3pm, Fri-Sat from 7pm.

Festivals

January - **Bowral Horse Show.**
February - **Mittagong Dahlia Festival and Fun Run. Kangaroo Valley Show.**
March - **Robertson Show. Moss Vale Show.**
Easter - **Berrima Art Society Exhibition. Musica Viva (biennial).**
April - **Brigadoon Day, Bundanoon.**
August - **Bowral Horse Show.**
September - **Tulip Time Festival,** Bowral. **Bowral Fun Run.**
October - **Tulip Time Festival,** Bowral. **Berrima District Art Society Exhibition.**
December - **Moss Vale Summer Gymkhana.**

Facilities

The towns have a wide range of facilities for all types of sporting activities, and the Visitor Information Centres have all the details.

New South Wales – South-West
Goulburn

Population 22,500
Goulburn, 638m (2093 ft) above sea level, is 197km (122 miles) south-west of Sydney and 94km (58 miles) north-east of Canberra.

Climate

Average temperatures: January max 26C (79F) - min 12C (54F); June max 12C (54F) - min 0.5C (32.5F). Average annual rainfall: 671mm (26 ins).

Characteristics

Goulburn is Australia's oldest inland city dating back to the earliest days of the colony. Many of the buildings in the town have beautiful cast iron lace work. Wheat was grown in the locality as early as the 1820s, and today primary industry is still important. Goulburn is also an administrative centre for several State Government Departments. It was the last town of the British Empire to become a city by virtue of the Royal Letters Patent in 1863. Goulburn is home to 'Rambo' the 14m (46 ft) high ram at the Big Merino complex.

How to Get There
By Bus

Most of the major coaches stop at Goulburn on the Sydney/Melbourne and Sydney/Canberra/Melbourne routes.

Visitor Information

The Goulburn Visitor Information Centre, 201 Sloane Street, ☎4823 4492, is ⊙open 9am-5pm every day except Christmas Day. The website is 🖥www.igoulburn.com and you can email ✉visitor@goulburn.nsw.gov.au

⤳ Let's Stay Here

Places to stay in Goulburn are excellent and varied. Here are some budget accommodation prices which should be used as a guide only. The telephone area code is 02.

Alpine Heritage Motel, *248 Sloane Street,* ☎4821 2930. 45 units, unlicensed restaurant - *from ✪$45.*

Hillview Motel, *2 Cowper*

Street, ☎4821 3130. 20 units, basic facilities - ✪$45-50.

Nomads Tattersalls Hotel, *76 Auburn St,* ☎4821 3088, 🖥www.nomadsworld.com
Located near the Goulburn rail and coach terminals, just at the south end of the main street where all shops and tourist activities are within walking distance. Accommodation is situated above a pub which is not much to look at, but is actually nice. Just renovated. Kept clean and well maintaned. Facilities includes your basic kitchen, laundry, TV lounge and internet access. There is also a bar and bistro, TAB and gaming room and a beer garden downstairs with pool tables, jukebox, darts. Parking available. *Dorms ✪$20; double/twin $45; triple $50*

Caravan Parks

Governors Hill Carapark, *77 Sydney Road,* ☎1800 227 373. (No dogs) 60 sites, good facilities, barbecue - *powered sites ✪$19-21 for two, on-site vans $35 for two.*

Goulburn South Caravan Park, Hume Street, ☎4821 3233. (Pets allowed under supervision) 112 sites, basic facilities - *powered sites ✪$17 for two, on-site vans $40-60 for two.*

Let's Eat

Goulburn has restaurants, coffee bars, family style cafes and licensed clubs, so whatever your budget you will find something to suit. Here are a few you might like to try:

Billabong Station Restaurant, *Cnr Hume Hwy and Lansdowne Street,* ☎ *4822 8014.*

Blue Plate Restaurant, *Lagoon St,* ☎ *4821 5666.*

Goulburn Italian Pizza Restaurant, *147 Auburn Street,* ☎ *4821 5998.*

Hung Win Chinese Restaurant, *277 Auburn Street,* ☎ *4821 8933.*
Khun Lek Thai Restaurant, *150 Auburn Street,* ☎ *4821 2025.*

Riley's Restaurant, *148 Sloane Street,* ☎ *4822 747.*

McDonalds has two locations, one in North Goulburn on the corner of the Hume Highway and Common Street, the other in South Goulburn on the Old Hume Highway.

Points of Interest

A walking tour of Historic Goulburn and a walking tour of the Wollondilly River are available to the traveller - brochures may be obtained from the Goulburn Visitors Centre.

Some of the historic buildings are open to the public, including the **Court House, St Clair, St Saviours Cathedral** and **Riversdale.**

Other attractions include the **Big Merino Complex,** on the corner of the *Hume Highway* and *Lansdowne Street,* ☎ *4822 8013,* which has a craft centre, educational area, lookout and restaurant.

The Goulburn Yurtworks, ☎ *4821 5931,* is the only producer of Yurts in Australia (yurts are roundhouses based on Mongolian tents).

The Rocky Hill War Memorial dominates the town and is Goulburn's landmark.

The **Black Stag Deer Park,** Gorman Road, ☎ *4821 4386,* has fallow red deer as well as Australian wildlife.

The **Goulburn Rail Heritage Centre,** in Braidwood Road, features many pieces of industrial steam machinery, and is open the first weekend of every month.

The **Goulburn Regional Art Gallery** is in the Civic Centre, on the corner of *Bourke* and *Church Streets,* ☎ *4823 4443.*

Gulsons Craft Village, located at the historic Gulsons brickworks, *Common Street,* features many quality craft shops.

More information on these and other attractions may be obtained from the Goulburn and District Visitors Guide - available from the Goulburn Visitors Centre.

Festivals

The **Lilac City Festival** is held during the October long weekend.

The **Argyle County Fair** is held in November each year.

Carnivale, which is part of the NSW Government sponsored festival, is held in September each year.

Goulburn also stages an annual show and rodeo.

Facilities

There are many sporting facilities available in Goulburn, including squash courts, tennis courts, indoor cricket and sports centre, ten pin bowling centre, swimming pool and water slide. Lawn bowls, golf, darts, and fishing are also catered for. Contact the Visitor Information Centre for all the details.

Outlying Attractions
The Bungonia State Recreation Area

Situated approximately 35km (22 miles) south-east of Goulburn, the Bungonia is the largest State Recreation Area in New South Wales. Bushwalking, caving, climbing, canoeing, and spectacular lookouts are all available there.

Wombeyan Caves

The caves are 77km (48 miles) north-east of Goulburn, and there are five cave tours. Many pleasant hours may also be spent strolling through the beautiful bushland reserve surrounding the caves. The road to the caves is very winding, so it is best to have the attitude that this excursion is a full day, and take your time. The Wombeyan Caves Visitors Centre and Caravan Park can be contacted on ☎ *4843 5976.*

Snowy Mountains

The Snowy Mountains are in the south-east corner of New South Wales, and the highest peak is **Mt Kosciusko,** 2230m (7316 ft). The mountains are home to the ski fields of New South Wales, and they conjure up visions of fashionable skiers hurtling down ski slopes before sipping their apres-ski drinks, but that is only one facet of the Mountains. One of Australia's engineering marvels is also to be found here, the **Snowy Mountains Hydro Electric Scheme,** which captures the water from the melting snow destined for the coast, and redirects it through mountain channels to the interior.

The mountains are a carpet of wildflowers in summer and there are numerous trails for bushwalkers. The many lakes and rivers are an aquatic paradise for those wishing to get away from it all. **Lake Jindabyne** (three times the size of Sydney Harbour) is ablaze with sailboard and catamaran sails, and the lakes and rivers abound with trout.

Cooma

Population 8,500
Cooma is where the Snowy Mountains begin, and is near the New South Wales-Victorian Border. Distance from Canberra 114km (71 miles); from Sydney 420km (261 miles); from Thredbo 97km (60 miles); from Charlotte Pass 105km (65 miles); from Perisher 98km (61 miles); from Adaminiby 52km (32 miles); from Mt Selwyn 99km (62 miles).

Climate
Cooma is 810m (2657 ft) above sea level. Average temperatures: January max 26C (79F) - min 11C (52F); July max 9C (48F) - min 1C (30F). Annual rainfall 450mm (17 ins).

Characteristics
If you are travelling to the snow by train or air, Cooma will be your port of call. It is a pleasant town and offers transport to Jindabyne and the snowfields.

How to Get There
By Bus
Greyhound Pioneer have services from Sydney and Canberra.
Snowliner Coaches, ☎*6452 1584*, provide services from Bega and Canberra.

By Rail
There is a train service from Sydney via Canberra daily, with connections to Melbourne from Goulburn.

Visitor Information
The Cooma Visitor Information Centre, 119 Sharpe Street, ☎*6450 1742*, is ⏰open 9am-5pm daily. Email them at ✉cvc@snowy. net.au or visit the website, 🖥www. snowymountains.com.au

↪ Let's Stay Here
Cooma has motels, hostels and caravan parks. Here is a selection with prices which should be used as a guide only. The telephone area code is 02.

Alpine Country Guest House, *32 Massie Street,* ☎*6452 1414.* 13 rooms (private facilities), unlicensed restaurant - ⭕*$30-60.*

Cooma Bunkhouse Backpackers, *28 Soho St,* ☎*6452 2983,* 🖥*www.backpackers.com.au* Located in the centre of Cooma within walking distance to buses, shops and restaurants. This backpackers is family operated with a relaxed atmposhere. The units are all self-contained in a tranquil garden setting. *Dorms $20; double $35pp*

Hawaii Motel, *192 Sharp Street,* ☎*6452 1211.* 23 units, unlicensed restaurant - ⭕*$50-60.*

Caravan Parks
Snowtels Caravan and Camping Park, *Snowy Mountains Highway,* ☎*6452 1828.* (Pets allowed under supervision and by arrangement) 134 sites, good facilities, tennis,

ski hire - *powered sites* ⭕*$20 for two, cabins from* $40, *on-site vans* $35-55 *for two.*

Let's Eat
Many of the motels have licensed and BYO restaurants, and the licensed clubs offer good family meals. There are several takeaway food outlets.

Bahn Thai Noodle Restaurant, *178 Sharp Street,* ☎*6452 4277.*

Cooma Truckstop Restaurant, *1 Polo Flat Road,* ☎*6452 5550.*

Grand Court Chinese Restaurant, *Snowstop Village, Sharp Street,* ☎*6452 4525.*

McDonald's is in *Sharp Street.*

Points of Interest
Tourist Drive markers signpost an easy drive through and around Cooma, taking in the town's many points of interest. The first marker is at Centennial Park near the Visitors' Centre, and from there it goes past **Cooma Creek, Lions Lookout, the Murrumbidgee Water Filtration Plant, Snowy Mountains Authority Information Centre, the Snowy Memorial, Festival Pool, Nannygoat Hill, Cooma Cenotaph, Cooma Prison, Lambie Street, Raglan Gallery, Mt Gladstone, Alpenthaler Park, Southern Cloud Park, Christ Church, the Lookout, Polo Falt,** and back to the Centre.

The **Snowy Mountains Hydro Electric Authority Information Centre,** *Monaro Highway,* ☎*1800 623 776,* ⏰open Mon-Fri 8am-4.30pm, Sat 8am-noon, has displays and models of the Snowy Mountains Scheme, and a film show, Mon-Fri at 11am and 3pm.

Visit ■www.snowyhydro.com.au for further details.

Snowy Mountain Scheme Tours to Adaminaby, Old Adaminaby, Providence Portal, Kiandra, Cabramurra, and Tumut underground Power Station, can be organised through the information centre.

For those who are energetic, there is the **Lambie Town Walk,** which passes through residential and natural areas of scenic and historic interest in Cooma. One part of the walk is through the town area (5km) and the bushland section is also 5km, and takes approximately 2.5 hours.

Llama World, *Snowy Mountains Highway,* 19km (12 miles) from Cooma, has llamas and alpacas, a tractor ride through their paddocks, rides in llama-drawn sulkies, and the Inca Gallery, which sells souvenirs, South American and llama products including yarn, fleece and made-up garments. ☉open Fri-Mon (weather permitting), ☎6452 4593.

Festivals
Man from Snowy River Marathon in October each year.

Facilities
Bowling club, golf course, horse riding, swimming pool (heated), snooker, squash, tennis courts, gliding, ski hire shops, car hire depots and taxis.

Outlying Attractions
Adaminaby
The town of Adaminaby is 51km (32 miles) from Cooma, and is the home of The World's Largest Trout. The town was moved to its present site in 1956-57 to allow for the filling of Lake Eucumbene. Facilities include boating, fishing,

sailing, snow skiing, tennis and water skiing.

Yarrangobilly Caves
The caves are just before the site of Yarrangobilly, and 6.5km (4 miles) off the Snowy Mountains Highway. They were carved out of the limestone by the Yarrangobilly River around 440 million years ago, and are a strange landscape of rugged bluffs and disappearing streams. Beyond the half light of the cave entrance is an underworld of unrivalled beauty.

The self-guiding **Glory Hole Cave** is ☉open daily, 10am-4pm. Guided inspections of either the North Glory, Jersey or Jillabenan Caves are conducted at 1pm each non-holiday week day. Additional tours are scheduled during weekends and school holidays. There are plenty of walking tracks in the area, and the Yarrangobilly Caves Visitor Information Centre, ☎6454 9597, has brochures and information, and is ☉open 7 days a week, 9am-4.30pm, 8.30am to 5.30pm in the peak season. Yarrangobilly is a day use area only, and camping is available at Yarrangobilly Site or Three Mile Dam.

Jindabyne
Population 1800
Situated 40km (25 miles) from Cooma, Jindabyne is the closest centre to the ski fields. Many people choose to stay in the town and drive to the fields each day. In summer time, Lake Jindabyne is the attraction for staying here.

Visitor Information
The Snowy Region Visitor Information Centre is in Kosciuszko Road, ☎6450 5600. Their ☉opening hours are 8am-6pm in the winter

holidays and Easter, 8.30am-5pm the rest of the year. They can be contacted by email at ✉srvc@ npws.nsw.gov.au or you might like to visit the website at ■www.kos .com.au for a preliminary look.

⤷ Let's Stay Here
Here is a selection of budget accommodation available, with prices that should be used as a guide only. Never go to Jindabyne in the winter thinking you will be able to pick up accommodation without a booking, it is far too cold to sleep in the bus station. The telephone area code is 02.

Snowy Mountains BP VIP, *7-8 Gippsland St,* ☎6456 1500 or 1800 333 468, ■ *www.snowy backpackers.com* Located in the heart of Jindabyne, minutes from the Kosciuszko National Park, and a short walk to the shores of Lake Jindabyne. Clean and well maintained. It has your basic kitchen, laundry, TV lounge room and internet access. There is also the rare massage and therapy, and ask about the discount vouchers. On site is a cafe on the ground floor, perfect for that hot chocolate. Being on the Snowy Mountains, this hostel also rents out ski and snowboards. *Dorms ✪$30; double $45pp*

Yowi Lodge, *6-7 Gippsland Street,* ☎562 547 - 14 units, unlicensed restaurant, swimming pool, spa, sauna - *B&B from ✪$60.*

Caravan Park
Snowline Caravan Park, *cnr Kosciusko Road and Alpine*

Way, ☎6456 2099. (No pets allowed) 178 sites, excellent facilties, sauna, spa, cafe, barbecue, tennis - *powered sites ◐$20-25 for two, cabins $40-205 for two.*

Jindabyne Holiday Park, *Kosciusko Road, ☎6456 2249.* 200 sites, basic facilities - *powered sites ◐$20-26 for two, cabins $55-130 for two, on-site vans $40-90 for two.*

Let's Eat

It is well known that cold weather makes everyone hungry, so there is no shortage of eating places in this neck of the woods. Here is a selection.

Bacco Italian Restaurant, *Nuggets Crossing, Shop 10, Kosciuszko Road, ☎6456 1420.*

Brumby Bar and Bistro, *Kosciusko Road, ☎6456 2526.*

Chit Thai Restaurant, *Snowline Caravn Park, cnr Kosciusko Rd and Alpine Way), ☎6456 2052.*

Gringo's Mexican Restaurant, *Aspen Chalet, Kosciusko Road, ☎6457 2229.*

Il Lago Restaurant, *Nuggetts Crossing Shopping Centre, Shop 19a, Kosciusko Road, ☎6456 1171.*

Pom's Balcony Bistro, *upper level Petamin Plaza (Town Centre), ☎6456 2144* - fully licensed, steak and seafood, open daily 6pm-31m.

Restaurant 14, *Town Centre, Shop 14, Kosciuszko Road, ☎6457 2660.*

Ski and Equipment Hire

Ampol Jindabyne, Kosciusko Road, ☎6456 1177; BP Lakeside, Kosciusko Road, ☎6456 1959; Arlberg Ski Centre, Jindabyne Road, Berridale, ☎6456 3177; Jindabyne Sports Store, Shop 12, Town Centre, ☎6456 2216; Snowy Mountains Sports, Petamin Plaza, ☎6456 2530; Thredbo Sports, Nuggetts Crossing, &6459 4119; Wilderness Sports, Nuggets Crossing, &6456 2966.

Ski Fields

Mt Selwyn (1614m - 5295 ft) The lowest field, Mt Selwyn is very popular with families and school groups. There is no accommodation at Mt Selwyn.

Ski lifts: 1 Double Chair, 4 T-Bars, 2 Pomas, 1 Platter and 4 Beginner Ropes and 1 Toboggan Lift. Ski slopes: beginners 40%, intermediates 48%, advanced 12%.

Facilities/services: ticket office, ski school, ski hire, information centre, ski patrol, ski and souvenir shop, licensed cafeteria, resort booking centre.

Prices: half day ◐$35 adult, $20 child; full day $46 adult, $23 child; lift and lesson package $68 adult $45 child.
Information:
🖳www.selwynsnow .com.au.
✉snowinfo@selwynsnow .com.au
or ☎64549 488.

Perisher Blue

Includes Perisher/Smiggins (2034m - 6673 ft), Mt Blue Cow (1980m - 6496 ft) and Guthega (1932m - 6339 ft) - an extensive 1250 hectares of skifields.

Facilities/services: ticket office, ski school, ski hire, information centre, resort booking centre, ski patrol, childminding, ski shops, Skitube train station, oversnow transport to lodges, bars, bistros, restaurants, coffee shops, takeaway food outlets (including on-slope), banks, post office, newsagents, chemist, supermarket, bottle shop, photographic services, medical services, souvenirs, lockers, ski-storage.

Transport: Skitube Trains depart frequently as required in peak times during winter. Below snowline on Alpine Way, so no chains required.

Bullock's Flat Terminal (Alpine Way) - free car parking for 3,000 cars and 250 buses. Ticket office for combined Perisher Blue and Skitube tickets. Ski hire, information centre, National Parks and Wildlife Service sales and information, souvenir and ski accessories shop, takeaway food outlet.

Perisher Valley Terminal: ticket office for Perisher/Smiggins and Mt Blue Cow plus train tickets. Ski minding and locker service, coffee shop, licensed bistro, ski equipment and accessories, children's clothing shop, gift shop, takeaway snack bar, full Medical Centre and Police Office, oversnow transport to Perisher Valley lodges.

Prices: check current prices at the time of your visit on the updated website.

Information and prices: 🖳www. perisherblue.com.au, ☎1300 655 822.

Thredbo (2037m - 6683 ft)

⤴ Let's Stay Here
Thredbo YHA,
8 Jack Adams Pathway, 6457 6376, ◻www.yha.com.au Luxury purpose-built lodge in the heart of Thredbo Village. Fantastic view of the ski fields and mountains. Foodstore is close. Facilities includes kitchen, laundry, internet access, lounge room and a barbecue area. *Dorms from ✪$21; twin from $48; BC MC VA EFTPOS*

Ski lifts: 4 Double Chairs, 6 Quad Chairs, 2 Triple Chairs, 22 T Bars, 4 J Bars, 11 others, 3 Ski carpet, Skitube
Ski slopes: beginners 22%, intermediates 60%, advanced 18%.

Ski lifts: 2 high-speed quad detachable chairlifts, 1 beginner quad chairlift, 3 double chair-lifts, 7 T-bars, 2 rope tows.
Ski slopes: beginners 16%, intermediates 67%, advanced 17%.

Facilities/services: ticket office, ski school, ski hire, information huts, resort booking centre, ski patrol, ski shops, bars, bistros, restaurants (including on-slope), coffee shop, takeaway food outlets (including on-slope), bank, post office, newsagent, chemist, supermarket, bottle shop, photographic services, medical services, souvenirs, overnight ski storage.
Prices: full day ✪$75 adult, $41 child; lift and lesson $100 adult, $67 child; group lessons $40. Check current prices at the time of your visit.
Information: ◻www.thredbo.com.au, ☎6459 4100.

Charlotte Pass
The ski lifts are virtually on the front doorstep.

Ski lifts: 1 triple chairlift, 1 T-bar, 2 poma lifts, 1 rope tow.

Transport: Charlotte Pass is the most isolated resort with access by oversnow transport (snowcats) from Perisher Valley. The journey takes about 35 minutes. If travelling by car, you have to park at the Skitube Terminal at Bullocks Flat and travel on the tube to Perisher. The snowcat part of the trip costs ✪$28 adults each way.

Prices: full day ✪$75 adult; half day $60 adult. Check current prices at the time of your visit.

Information: ◻www.charlottepass.com.au, ☎1800 026 369.

Inland South
Wagga Wagga
Population 57,000
The city of Wagga Wagga is situated on the banks of the Murrumbidgee River, 459km (285 miles) south-west of Sydney.

Climate
Average temperatures: January max 35C (95F) - min 18C (64F); July max 14C (57F) - min 5C (41F). Average annual rainfall: 669mm (26 ins).

Characteristics
The area was first settled by the largest Aboriginal tribe in New South Wales - the Wiradjuri. It is from their language that the city gets its name, Wagga (Wahga or Wahgam) means 'crow' and the repetition of the word expresses the plural.

In 1829, the land was explored by Captain Charles Sturt while he was on his famous expedition discovering the Murrumbidgee and Murray River systems. Settlement followed and Wagga Wagga was proclaimed a town in 1849. It became a city in 1948, and is the largest provincial city in New South Wales.

How to Get There
By Bus
Greyhound Pioneer have services daily from/to Sydney, Adelaide and Canberra.

By Rail
The Sydney-Melbourne and Melbourne-Sydney **Countrylink** stops at Wagga Wagga, daily.

Visitor Information
The Visitors Information Centre is in Tarcutta Street ☎6926 9621. They have a website at ◻www.tourismwaggawagga.com.au and you can email them at ✉visitors@wagga.nsw.gov.au
The centre is ☉open daily 9am-5pm.

⤴ Let's Stay Here
Wagga Wagga has plenty of motels and caravan parks for a town its size. Here are some selection with prices for a double room per night, which should be used as a guide only. The telephone area code is 02.

Allonville Motel, *Sturt Highway, Gumly Gumly,* ☎6922 7269 - 29 units, licensed restaurant, swimming pool, BBQ - ✪$51.

Palm and Pawn Motor Inn, *Hampden Avenue,* ☎6921

Perisher

Sunrise in the Southern Highlands

Wagga Wagga

6688. 25 units, licensed restaurant, tennis, barbecue - ✪$60.

Caravan Parks

Horseshoe Motor Village, 23 Horseshoe Road, ☎6921 6033. (Pets allowed by arrangement) 44 sites, good facilities, pool - powered sites ✪$15 for two, cabins $45-50 for two.

Easts Van Park Riverview, 93 Hammond Avenue, ☎6921 4287. (No pets allowed)100 sites, good facilities - powered sites ✪$20 for two, on-site vans $45 for two.

Airport Caravan Park, Sturt Highway, Forest Hill, ☎6922 7271. (Pets allowed under control)14 sites, basic facilities, barbecue, playground - powered sites ✪$14 for two.

Let's Eat

As with any city of its size, Wagga Wagga has a good selection of restaurants and takeaway food outlets. Here are some you might like to try.

Barter's Restaurant, 143 Fitzmaurice Street, ☎6921 1922 licensed, traditional and nouvelle cuisine, seven nights a week.
Capers Restaurant, Morgan Street, ☎6921 6444.

Golden Season Family Restaurant, 31 Forsyth Street, ☎6921 1177.

Indian Tavern Tandoori Restaurant, 176 Baylis Street, ☎6921 3121.

La Porchetta Pizza Restaurant, 161 Baylis Street, ☎6921 5122.

Locksley Steak House, 137 Peter Street, ☎6921 4886 - licensed, also serves seafood, chicken, etc.. - open Wed-Fri noon-2pm, Tues-Sat 6pm-midnight.

Montezumas Mexican Restaurant, 85 Bayliss Street, ☎6921 4428 - licensed - open Wed-Fri noon-2pm, Tues-Sun from 6pm.
Olivers, 8 Day Street, ☎6921 3646.

The Rivergum Restaurant, Sturt Highway, ☎6922 7256.

McDonalds and **Pizza Hut** are in Edward Street, and **KFC** is on the corner of Edward and Baylis Streets, and in Fitzmaurice Street.

Points of Interest

The Visitor Information Centre has maps of three historic walks through the city which were put together by the National Trust.

Amongst other places these walks highlight many of the historic buildings which date from 1865, including houses, churches, old gas works, police station, **Lands Department, Court House, Post Office** and the **ANZ Bank**.

In 1999 an impressive new Civic Centre was opened. It contains the regional art gallery, the **Museum of the Riverina** and the national art glass gallery. The city is proud of its civic centrepiece, and it is worth stopping in to have a look.

The **Wagga Wagga Regional Art Gallery,** on the corner of Bayliss and Morrow Streets, has changing exhibitions of international, national and regional art. It is ☺open Mon, Wed-Sat 11am-5pm, Sun 2-5pm,

☎6926 9610.

The **Wagga Wagga and District Historical Museum** in Willan's Hill, ☎6925 2934, is open weekends, public holidays and school holidays, and ☺Tues-Wed from 2pm.

Wagga Wagga is the Garden City of the South, and the many parks and gardens range from the formal **Shakespearian Garden** to **Apex Park** located on the shores of Lake Albert.

The **Botanic Gardens, 6923 5499, are set in 8.9ha (22** acres) on Willans Hill, and have many garden displays such as the Tree Chapel, with trees and shrubs of biblical significance, a rough-hewn cross and altar, complete with pews, which is a popular spot for weddings. Also in the Gardens are the Camellia, Cactus, Succulent and Shakespearian Gardens, and an Outdoor Entertainment Centre and Music Bowl which can accommodate a symphony orchestra and has seating for 3,000 people. A model railway runs through the gardens and features a station and booking office. The train operates on the 1st and 3rd Sundays of the month.

Wagga Wagga City Library is in Gurwood Street, and is the headquarters of a regional library. The service caters for 89,000 people in seven council areas - Coolamon, Cootamundra, Gundagai, Lockhart, Temora and Tumut. It is ☺open Mon-Fri 9am-8pm, Sat 9am-noon.

Sunday Markets are held from 8am-noon in Woolworth's Car Park.

Visitors are welcome to drive through the grounds of the **Charles Sturt University** - Riverina, and visit the College

Winery, in Boorooma Street, North Wagga, which is ☉open Mon-Fri 10am-4pm, Sat 11am-4pm, for wine tastings and sales.

Aurora Clydesdale Stud and **Pioneer Farm,** *Cameron's Road,* 9km past Collingullie, towards Narrandera, has antique machinery, a pioneer's hut and Clydesdales in action. There is also a large collection of birds and animals, ☎*6928 2215* for information and times.

Murray Cod Hatcheries and Fauna Park on the *Sturt Highway,* ☎*6922 7360,* is home to Big Murray, a 52kg (115 lb) Murray Cod, who measures 1.37m (4.5 ft). The park also has Crab Eating Macaquehs (monkeys) from South East Asia, native snakes, camels, wombats, koalas, kangaroos, native fish and many native birds. There is a gift shop selling pottery, paintings and souvenirs, and a snack bar. Barbecues and playground equipment are set in the picnic area, and the complex is ☉open daily 8.30am-5.30pm.

Kapooka Military Camp invites visitors to view the parades held each Monday at 11am. The camp is the base for the Army's 1st Recruit Training Battalion. The Kapooka Band performs during the parades, and holds a series of Music at Midday concerts in Wagga Wagga city. You can join a Green Arrow Tour of the base by reporting to the guard room at the main entrance. The camp is 10km (6 miles) west of Wagga on the Olympic Way.

Festivals

The **Gumi Festival** is held on the last Saturday in February each year. Gumi is pidgin for 'rubber', and the Gumi Race consists of

hundreds of craft made from inner tubes floating down the 11km course on the Murrumbidgee River.

The **Wagga Wagga Agricultural Show** is held over the long weekend in October (the first Monday in October sets the dates of the long weekend).

Facilities

Lawn bowls, croquet, fishing, golf, greyhound racing, horse racing, trotting, sailing, water skiing, sailing, swimming, boating and tennis. The city has 4 licensed Clubs with dining facilities and poker machines.

Outlying Attractions
Lockhart

Proceed south from Wagga Wagga along the Olympic Way to **The Rock**, then turn left. Lockhart is 42km (26 miles) further on. The Rock (the town), originally named Kingston, is located 6km east of craggy outcrops which rise more than 360m (1181 ft) above the surrounding districts. The peak of the **Rock Hill Nature Reserve** is the only place in Australia where the Senecio wildflower is found. The Yerong Nature Trail within the Reserve takes about 3 hours to complete, and is worth the effort. The 3km track is gentle on the lower slopes, but fairly steep at the higher levels.

Lockhart has a well shaded caravan park, a motel and licensed Ex-Services, golf and bowling clubs. The centre of the town is an outstanding example of a turn-of-the-century streetscape, and has been classified by the National Trust. Also classified is the Old Urangeline Woolshed, which originally had 100 shearing stands. It is built from local timber

with a shingle roof, and although on private property, is open for inspection by arrangement. Contact the Visitor Information Centre in Wagga Wagga, ☎*6926 9621,* for details.

The **Pioneer Memorial Gates,** is an unusual structure set at the entrance of the Lockhart Showground. The 22 'wool bales' are branded with the stencils of original homesteads. **The Lockhart Museum,** in *45 Urana Street,* ☎*6920 5674,* contains many fine memories of the district's pioneering past. Approximately 16km (10 miles) north of Lockhart is Galore Hill Recreation Reserve. The reserve comprises 510ha (1260 acres) of natural bushland, and Galore Hill rises to a height of 215m (705 ft) above the surrounding countryside.

Coolamon Shire

The shire includes the townships of Coolamon, Ardlethan, Ganmain, Beckom, Grong Grong, Matong and Marrar, and is the agricultural centre of the Riverina.

Ganmain, situated between Junee and Narrandera, is the centre of the chaff industry of Australia, and the residents, with the aid of the Shire Council, have constructed a building in Pioneer Park, Ford Street, to give the impression of a haystack. From the viewing area you can see a workable binder, a mural of a hay scene, photographs and history of hay in the district, and a video giving an insight into the hay industry.

Coolamon is 39km (24 miles) north-west of Wagga Wagga, and has many old world antique shops. The **Coolamon Golf Club,** ☎*6927 3178,* welcomes visitors to play a round on the sand green course, and visit their Chinese restaurant.

Junee

The town of Junee is built to an unusual plan with the railway running down the middle of the central business district. The railway has been important to the town as is shown by the impressive railway station, built in 1883.

Monte Cristo, a homestead in traditional Georgian design, is ☺open daily 10am-4pm, and is a museum of Victorian furniture and antiques.

Temora

Temora, a centre of Harness Racing (Paleface Adios, the famous pacer, and winner of the Inter Dominion, was born here), was established after the 1880 gold rush when the famous Mother Shipton nugget weighing 258 ounces was found. The decline of gold saw the town become a major wheat growing district.

Most of the mining areas have disappeared, though several, including the Mother Shipton mine, are located off Moroney's Lane.

The Temora Rural Museum, ☎6977 1291, is ☺open daily 2-5pm, and is a .8ha (2 acres) complex with agricultural machinery, antique tractors and engines, a pioneer cottage with lifestyles of yesterday, and a rock and mineral display.

The Temora Visitor Information Centre is at *294 -296 Hoskins Street,* ☎6977 1511.

Cootamundra

The town of Cootamundra, with a population of 6,600, is the home of the Cootamundra Wattle (Acacia Baileyana) and the birthplace of the late Sir Donald Bradman, Australia's famous cricketer. The cottage where he was born is privately owned but may be viewed from the street (89 Adams Street).

The focal point of the township is the **Bicentennial Post Office Plaza,** which incorporates the historical post office building and clock tower, and the old Peppercorn tree.

Pioneer Park, on the southern outskirts of Cootamundra, off the Olympic Way, commands extensive views of the town and district.

Bethungra Rail Spiral is 23km (14 miles) south-west of Cootamundra, and is a unique engineering feat. The rail line spirals around Bethungra Hill, crossing itself and the south line while traversing some of the deepest rail cuttings in Australia.

The Cootamundra Visitor Information Centre, Hovell Street, ☎6942 4212.

Gundagai

The famous **Dog on the Tucker Box** is, as every Australian knows, 5 miles (8km) from (north of) Gundagai, on the western side of the *Hume Highway.* Opposite the memorial to Mateship between man and dog, are copper representations of the Dog, and Dad, Dave, Mum and Mabel at Snake Gully, the characters of Steele Rudd.

The Gundagai Visitor Information Centre, *294 Sheridan Street,* ☎69 44 1341, is ☺open daily Mon-Fri 8am-5pm, Sat-Sun 9am-5pm. You can contact them by email at ✉ztc1@gundagaishir e.nsw.gov.au. The Centre houses the **Rusconi Marble Masterpiece,** a cathedral in miniature containing 20,948 pieces of NSW marble, built by Mr Frank Rusconi in his spare time over a period of 28 years. The Centre also has a gemstone collection, flood inundation maps and flood scenes of Gundagai.

The walking tour, devised by the Tourist Centre, takes in: the **Dr Gabriel Gallery;** the **Court House** built in 1859, where Moonlight the Bushranger was tried; the **Gundagai Historic Museum;** the **Old Flour Mill** constructed in 1849; and the two bridges, **Railway Bridge,** 1901, and **Prince Alfred Bridge,** 1866, the longest timber viaduct in Australia.

The Tourist Centre also has details of the Mount Parnassus Walking Tour, and can arrange coach tours and canoe tours of the Murrumbidgee and Tumut Rivers.

On the *Hume Highway* is the Tucker Box Tourist Centre, ☎6944 1450, which serves as an alternative information source.

⤵ Let's Stay Here

Blue Heeler Guesthouse, *Sheridan St, 6944 2286* If you're looking for cheap accommodation in the centre of town, then this is it. Don't expect much though. Imagine comboy movies with deserted old hotels and you'll get the feel of it. Expect basic facilities. *Dorms $15*

Tumut

In 1824, Explorers Hume and Hovell crossed the Tumut River slightly south of the site of present day Tumut. The local natives called the area Doomat or Tumott, which meant "quiet resting place by the river".

In the early days, Tumut was squatter country, and was populated mainly by unfriendly Aboriginals. The town grew slowly, and by 1856 had one school, several slab and bark buildings, and three hotels. By 1870, the number of hotels had grown to 18. Dairy farming was the main industry then, but today, timber is big business, particularly softwood like Pinus Radiata, with 52,520ha (130,000 acres) being grown within 25km (16 miles) of Tumut.

Tumut is now a town of around 6,500 people, and the **Festival of the Falling Leaf** is held there every year in April-May. There are street parades, band recitals, Plaza Night and a Family Fun Day at the Sports Club.

Tumut is 128km (80 miles) west of Canberra, about midway between Sydney and Melbourne, and is the gateway to the giant Snowy Mountains Scheme. The town is surrounded very picturesque countryside, and the rivers and mountain streams within easy access are stocked with trout.

There are regular air and rail services to Tumut, the road access is very good, and the climate averages between 35C (95F) in summer to a low of 5C (41F). The Visitor Information Centre is at the Old Butter Factory, *5 Adelong Road*, ☎ *(02) 6947 7025*.

The **Yarrangobilly Caves,** which are covered in the Snowy Mountains section, are 77km (48 miles) south of Tumut.

Griffith

Located 196km north west of Wagga Wagga, Griffith is worth considering for a day trip or overnight stay. It is part of the Riverina district, its soil made rich and fertile by the irrigation scheme bringing water all the way from the Snowy Mountains. Wine, fruits, vegetables, rice, and poultry products are grown and cultivated here.

There are a number of interesting attractions, including the extensive **Pioneer Park Museum,** the **Regional Art Gallery, Catania Fruit Farm,** and the natural wonders of **Lake Wyangan** and **Cocoparra National Park.**

Griffith Visitor Information Centre, *cnr Banna* and *Jondaryan Avenues*, ☎ *6962 4145* or ☎ *1800 681 141*. You can email them at ✉griffithvc@griffith.nsw.gov.au

⤷ Let's Stay Here
Griffith International Hostel, *112 Binya St,* ☎ *6964 4236* 🖥 *www.griffithinternational.com.au* Situated only minutes walk from the buzz of town. Rooms have heating and air-conditioning. Facilities includes a fully equipped large kitchen, laundry, TV and video facilities and a barbecue area. There is also an inside and outside sport and recreational areas. Very secure complex. Off-street parking. *Dorms from ✪$19*

Albury-Wodonga
Population 95,000
The twin cities of Albury-Wodonga sit astride the magnificent Murray River, touching the edges of the Upper Murray, North-East Victoria, the Riverina, the South-West Slopes of NSW and the Murray Valley.

Distance from Sydney 592km (368 miles), from Canberra 195km (121 miles), and from Melbourne 300km (186 miles).

Climate
Average temperatures: January max 32C (90F) - min 15C (55F); June max 14C (57F) - min 2C (36F). Average annual rainfall: 796mm (31 ins) - wettest month August. Elevation - 195m (640 ft) above sea level.

Characteristics
Hume and Hovell carved their names in trees beside the Murray in 1824 and Hovell's still stands today. In 1836, Robert Brown arrived and constructed a punt to cross the river, built an inn, and the settlement was born. In 1974 Albury-Wodonga was designated the national growth centre.

How to Get There
By Bus
Greyhound Pioneer travel to/from Melbourne, Sydney, Canberra and Brisbane.

By Rail
Albury-Wodonga is three hours by train from Melbourne on the Sydney/Melbourne route.

Visitor Information
Tourist Albury Wodonga Gateway Information Centre, is in *Lincoln Causeway*, ☎ *6041 3875*, freecall ☎ *1300 796 222*.

⤷ Let's Stay Here
The twin towns have 50 quality hotels and motels and 7 caravan parks. Here is a selection of budget accommodation with prices that should be used as a guide only. The telephone area code is 02.

Albury Backpackers,
452 David St, ☎ *6041 1822,*
🖥 *www.alburybackpackers.c*
om Located conveniently on
the bus and train routes. A
small and friendly hostel just
renovated. Really great atmosphere. Amenities includes a
kitchen, laundry, a small TV
lounge and a really fast internet access. There are also
great BBQ nights. The staff
organises canoe trips on the
Murray River. Farm jobs arranged for those wanting to
make a buck. There's also airport pickup service. Bike hire
and parking available. *Dorms*
✪*$17; double/twin $19pp*

Albury Motor Village YHA,
372 Wagga Road, Lav-
ington, ☎ *6040 2999,*
🖥 *www.yha.com* Fairly modern and a quiet place which is
purpose built, 250 metres to
the nearest foodstore. Facilities includes basic kitchen,
laundry, TV lounges, internet,
swimming pool, lounge room
and barbecue area. Parking
available.
Dorm from ✪*$18.50; double/*
twin from $22.50; BC MC VA
EFTPOS

Sodens Australia Hotel/
Motel, *cnr David and Wilson*
Street, ☎ *6021 2400.* 50 units,
licensed restaurant, barbecue
- ✪*$40-45.*

Caravan Parks
Trek-31 Tourist Park,
cnr Wagga Road and Cather-
ine Crescent, ☎ *6025 4051.*
-excellent facilities, pool, barbecue - *powered sites* ✪*$19-*
22 for two, cabins from $45
for two.

Albury Central Tourist Park,
North Street, ☎ *6021 8420.*
(Pets allowed under control)
127 sites, barbecue, tennis,
playground, pool - *powered*
sites ✪*$16 for two, cabins*
$45-55 for two.

Let's Eat
Albury-Wodonga offers a diverse
range of cuisine styles from fine
dining to fast service takeaway.
Here are a few you might like
to try.

Beefeater's Bistro, *324 Wodonga*
Place, ☎ *6041 1711.*

Gourmet Inn Restaurant, *473b*
Dean Street, ☎ *6021 4321.*

Il Sogno Restaurant, *639 Dean*
Street, ☎ *6023 4585* - proclaim
themselves 'The Flavour of Italy'.

Indian Tandoori Restaurant,
449a Dean Street, ☎ *6041 4705.*

Thai Grand Palace Restaurant,
592 Kiewa Street, ☎ *6041 1238.*

One Six Eight, *1081 Mate Street,*
☎ *6025 9816* - Chinese cuisine.

Puti Vegetarian Restaurant,
1083 Mate Street, ☎ *6025 0086*
- takeaway available.

Santino's Licensed Family
Bistro, *14 City Walk, Dean Street,*
☎ *6041 1997* - caters for all seven
days and nights.

Points of Interest
The most famous attraction is,
of course, the **Murray River,**
which starts as a tiny stream fed
by melting snow high on the
Australians Alps, near the NSW-
Victorian border. Slowed by Lake
Hume, the river's twists and turns

divide the two cities of Albury
and Wodonga. It then flows on to
enter the Southern Ocean through
Lake Alexandrina in South
Australia, 2500km (1553 miles)
from its source. The total Murray
system, including the Darling and
Murrumbidgee rivers and their
tributaries, drains a seventh of the
total area of Australia. The Murray
supplies 49% of SA's domestic
and industrial requirements, and
almost all the water for irrigation.

The first industry of the area
was established by Robert Brown
in 1838, when he built a rough
punt at the **Crossing Place,**
followed by an accommodation
house for travellers. This
established a tradition for the
district, and Albury-Wodonga
today has more 'accommodation
houses' than any other Australian
country centre.

Albury-Wodonga's river
queen, the **PS Cumberoona,** was
modelled on a former steamer
of the same name that chugged
up and down the Murray in the
heyday of the paddlesteamer
trade, and was the flagship of
the Albury Steam Navigation Co.
The new paddlesteamer operates
daily from October through to
May, depending on water flow and
water level, which depends on the
release of irrigation water from
Lake Hume.

Other attractions are: **Kinross**
Woolshed, which hosts bush
dances and jazz nights; **Frog**
Hollow, complete with a maze,
minature golf and Mr F. Frog;
Hume Weir Trout Farm, the
largest trout farm in the area; and
the restored **Cobb and Co** coaches
that provide an alternative method
of transport.

15km (9 miles) north of Albury
is the original **Ettamogah Pub.**

As their ad says, "the Ettamogah Mob needed a good excuse to work up a thirst...so we built a town around our Pub", and the end result is a complex which will keep every member of the family occupied for hours. For the kids, there is the **Comedy Cop Shop** (police station), dodgem cars, and a lock up if they misbehave. For the parents, there's a pottery and a bladesmith's, a souvenir shop selling only Aussie made, and the Winery with good quality wine at cellar door prices. For all, there is good Aussie tucker at the pub, and at the Ettamogah Cafe, or you might prefer Coopers Courtyard Restaurant next to the Winery. **The Pub**, ☎*6026 2366*, is ☉open daily 9am-midnight, and the Winery is open Mon-Fri 9am-5pm, Sat 10am-5pm, Sun 9am-4pm.

At **Albury Pottery**, *Lincoln Causeway, Wodonga,* ☎*6041 6835*, you can take a self-guiding tour and watch the potters at work - ☉open daily. If it's culture you seek, the **Albury Regional Art Centre,** *546 Dean Street, Albury,* the **Museum**, *66 South Street, Wodonga,* the **Pioneer Museum** in *Urana Street, Jindera,* and the **Albury Botanical Gardens** will get you off to a good start.

Albury's licensed Clubs provide meals, entertainment and, of course, poker machines. Thousands of people from Victoria travel to Albury to try and win the big one at the "pokies".

For aquatic sport, head for **Lake Hume**, only 12km (7 miles) upstream from town. It has 320km (199 miles) of shoreline, and is ideal for sailing, swimming, water skiing, canoeing, windsurfing, pedal boating and fishing. If you intend to fish, make sure you have both a NSW and Victorian

Fishing Licence. The Wyamah ferry links NSW with Victoria, and is operated by friendly folk. At **Dora Dora** there is a 130-year-old hotel which is more like an entertainment centre than a pub.

There is a lovely **Riverbank Walk** at Albury (Travel Centre has leaflets). The 7.5km (5 miles) marked trails from Nail Can Hill go along the river, over Monument Hill and past old gold diggings.

A visit to the **Flying Fruit Fly Circus** is a must - for booking and details, ☎*6021 7044*.

Festivals

Winery Walkabout is held over the long weekend in June, and the **Golden Horseshoe Festival** is held at Easter.

Facilities

The area has 14 licensed lawn bowls clubs. Canoes can be hired, and water skiing tuition is available on Lake Hume. Regular horse racing meetings are held in Albury/Wodonga. Other facilities include golf, tennis, fishing (cod, perch and trout) and swimming (pool and river).

Outlying Attractions
Howlong

A typical Murray River township, Howlong is 26km (16 miles) west of Albury on the Riverina Highway. The town's river frontages are ideal for walking, horseriding and photography, and the river offers boating, fishing and swimming. The town gets its name, which means 'the beginning of the plain', from the Howlong run, a property of 20,000ha (49,400 acres) that fronts the river.

Corowa

Corowa is 56km (35 miles) west of Albury, and its wide main street extends to the Murray River's banks. The Visitor Information Centre is in *Sanger Street,* ☎*6033 3221*, and they have information on accommodation, and the many buildings of historical and architectural interest. They are ☉open 9am-5pm daily and can be emailed at ✉corowa.tourinfo@albury.net.au. Additional information is available on the internet at 🖥www.corowa. nsw.gov.au

Corowa is known as the birthplace of Australian federation. When Victoria broke away from NSW in 1835 to become a separate colony, it caused the constant irritation dealing with customs officers stationed at every crossing place along the Murray River. The citizens of Corowa and Wahgunyah on the other side of the river, were particularly affected, and the first Border Federation League was established in Corowa in January, 1893. The historic conference of the various border leagues was held in July of that year, and together they continued to agitate until the referendum of 1898, when the decision in favour of federation was carried.

Anyone interested in Australian history should visit **Corowa's Federation Museum** in *Queen Street,* ☎*6033 1568*.

Mulwala

The town of Mulwala is 40km (25 miles) west of Corowa, and is renowned for its year-round mild climate. Nearby **Lake Mulwala** offers swimming, sailing and cruising.

Mulwala is often linked with Yarrawonga, on the other side

of the river, and the Visitor Information is there on the corner of *Irvine* and *Blemore Streets*, ☎*5744 1989* or ☎*1800 062 260*. There is a website at 🖥www.yarrawongamulwalainfo.com and their email address is 📧ymt@cnl.com.au

Jindera

Only about 20km (12 miles) north-west of Albury, Jindera has a **Pioneer Museum** that is rated a world-class attraction. It is housed in an old store and home that belonged to the pioneering Wagner family, and the store is stocked with authentic goods of the 19th century. The Museum is ☉open daily 10am-4.30pm, ☎*6026 3622*.

The Jindera district was settled in the 1860s by German migrants, the township was gazetted in 1869, and a century later a cairn was erected to honour these pioneering families.

Culcairn

Culcairn is 53km (33 miles) north of Albury-Wodonga, in the heart of 'Morgan' country. Other towns in the area are Henty, Walla, Jindera, Gerogery, Cookardinia, Morven and Walbundrie.

Bushranger Dan Morgan began his criminal career at Round Hill at Culcairn in June, 1864. Events surrounding the incident can be read at a site overlooking Round Hill, about 3km east on the Holbrook Road.

A life-sized effigy of Dan Morgan is displayed in the **Billabong Art and Crafts Centre's** 'Mad Dog Morgan' art cellar. The effigy was made for the movie of the same name, filmed in the district in 1975, and the first Australian film to win an award at the Cannes Film Festival.

Holbrook

The Visitor Information Office is in the **Woolpack Inn Museum**, ☎*60 36 2131*, email 📧woolpack@dragnet.com.au, ☉open daily 9.30am-4.30pm. Behind the museum is an enclosed area with a vast array of horse-drawn vehicles and farming equipment. The museum also has a section devoted to the exploits of Cdr Norman Holbrook, after whom the town was named. In December, 1914, British submarine commander Lt Norman Holbrook guided a B11 submarine below a minefield to torpedo an enemy Turkish battleship, the Messudiya. The submarine was immediately attacked by destroyers and on-shore forts, and during the trip back through the minefields Holbrook and his crew were forced to stay submerged for nine hours, an incredible feat for a 1914 submarine.

At this time the town was called Germanton, but the wave of anti-German feelings caused by World War I had the citizens searching for a new name. The news of the extraordinary bravery exhibited by the British submarine crew ended their search, and the town became Holbrook.

Holbrook is midway between Sydney and Melbourne on the Hume Highway, and still provides a resting point for travellers, as it did in its early days as a staging post. Ten Mile Creek park divides the town, providing restful, attractive areas merging into a flora and fauna reserve.

⤵ Let's Stay Here
Glenfalloch,
Off Hume Highway, Holbrook,
☎*6036 7203*, 🖥*www.yha.com*

A sheep and cattle property 9km. 50 km south of Tarcutta, 18 km north of Holbrook in NSW. Amenities includes self-catering kitchen, log fires, barbecue and a swimming pool. *Dorms ✪$16.50*

Having travelled all over NSW we now return to the south of Sydney and head down the coast.

Wollongong
Population 258,000
Wollongong is situated on the coast of New South Wales, 80km (50 miles) from Sydney, and 238km (148 miles) from Canberra.

Climate
Average temperatures: January max 26C (79F) - min 18C (64F); July max 17C (63F) - min 9C (48F). Average annual rainfall: 1275mm (50 ins).

Characteristics
Wollongong is the nineth largest city in Australia, and the gateway to the Illawarra and Southern Highlands region. To its north, cosy mining villages dot the coastline against a dramatic backdrop of green escarpment. Here the Illawarra coastal plain is narrowest, at times reduced to nothing, as rocky sea cliffs reach right to the pounding waves.

In the seaside village of Thirroul, D.H. Lawrence wrote *Kangaroo*, and from Stanwell Park, aviator Lawrence Hargraves tested his kites.

How to Get There
By Rail
Electric trains run regularly between Sydney's Central Station

and Wollongong, connecting with on-going services to Port Kembla and south to Bomaderry on Nowra's northern outskirts, ☎ 13 2232.

By Bus

Greyhound Pioneer, ☎ 13 2030, and McCaffertys, ☎ 13 1499, stop at Wollongong daily on their Sydney/Melbourne via the Princes Highway services.

Visitor Information

The Wollongong Visitor Information Centre, 93 Crown Street (corner of Kembla Street), ☎ 4277 5545 or ☎ 1800 240 737 (free call), is ⊕open seven days a week 9am-5pm Mon-Fri, 9am-4pm Sat and 10am-4pm Sun. They can be emailed at ✉ tourism@wolongong .nsw.gov.au and the website to explore is ☐ www.wollongong.nsw. gov.au

↘ Let's Stay Here

The Illawarra coast boasts a comprehensive range of accommodation from caravan parks on many of the beaches and lakesides, quality motels and hostels. Here is a selection with prices that should be used as a guide only. The telephone area code is 02.

Beach Park Motor Inn, *10 Pleasant Avenue, North Wollongong,* ☎ 4226 1577. 16 units, barbecue - ✪$60-170.

Crown Hotel Wollongong YHA,
309-311, ☐ *www.yha.com.au Crown St,* ☎ 4229 7444, Located at the heart of the city, only a walk away from train station, shops, cafes and pubs. Beach-

es are not too far either along with entertainment complexes. Built within an art deco, heritage listed Australian pub built in 1927. Facilities includes a fully equipped kitchen, laundry, internet access and common rooms with TV lounge. There's also a licensed restaurant in pub on site. *Dorms from ✪$20; single from $55; double/twin from $32pp; MC VA EFTPOS*

Keiraleigh House,
60 Kembla St, ☎ 4228 6765, ☐ www.*tourismwollongong.c om/hotels/hotelDetails.asp?h otelNo=63*
Accommodation in a in a big old heritage house with a friendly atmosphere. Located in central Wollongong, close to beach, shops, transport, restaurants and nightlife. Facilities includes communal kitchen, laundry, TV room and barbecue area. *Dorms ✪$18; single $30; double $50*

Caravan Parks

Corrimal Beach Tourist Park, *Lake Parade, Corrimal,* ☎ 4285 5688. 397 sites, barbecue - *unpowered sites ✪$15-25 for two, cabins $60-165 for two.*

Windang Beach Tourist Park, *Fern Street,* ☎ 4297 3166. (No pets) 259 sites, barbecue - *unpowered sites ✪$15-25, cabins from $60, bungalows from $40.*

Bulli Beach Tourist Park, *1 Farrell Road,* ☎ 4285 5677. (No pets allowed), 269 sites - *powered sites ✪$20-25 for two, cabins $60-165 for two.*

Let's Eat

Wollongong's cosmopolitan community offers you a wide choice of superb restaurants, snack bars and coffee lounges. Here are some you might like to try.

Amigos, *116 Keira Street,* ☎ 4229 8181. Mexican selection.

Bangkok Orchid Thai, *Shop 1, 119 Corrimal Street,* ☎ 4229 6620.

Beach House Seafood Restaurant, *16 Cliff Road,* ☎ 4228 5410.

Branches, *Blackbutt Motel, Shellharbour Road, Shellharbour,* ☎ 4297 1323. Italian and seafood.

Charcoal Tavern, *18 Regent Street,* ☎ 4229 7298. Modern Australian dining, seafood and steaks.

Fuji Yama Tepan Restaurant, *35 Flinders Street,* ☎ 4226 2609, specialise in Japanese barbecues.

King's, *26 Flinders Street, North Wollongong,* ☎ 4228 6976. Chinese cuisine.
Mammas Pizza Roma, *56 Crown Street,* ☎ 4229 9166.

Nam, *4 Kenny Street,* ☎ 4228 3646. Vietnamese and Chinese food.

Tandoori Village Indian Restaurant, *Shop 2, 120 Corrimal Street,* ☎ 4225 7876.

During business hours a good place to eat is the Food Court, lower level of the **Gateway** on the Mall shopping complex, *Cnr*

Paragluiding at Taree

Lookout near Tamworth

Burelli and Keira Streets. They have tables in the centre and you can choose from Chinese, Italian, Austrian, Mexican, crepes, chicken, pies, kebabs, hamburgers, and so on.

McDonald's have outlets at 115 Corrimal Street and Wollongong *Crown Central, Shop 97, 200 Crown Street.* There are branches in all other Wollongong localities as well.

Pizza Hut have outlets in localities surrrounding Wollongong. You will find them on the corner of the Priness Highway and *McGrath Street, Fairy Meadow, 32 Princes Highway, Dapto* and on the corner of King Street and Kemblawarra Place in Warrawong.

KFC can be found at cnr Princes Highway and *McGrath Street, Fairy Meadow; 74 Princes Highway, Unanderra; cnr Kemblawarra Road* and *King Street, Warrawong; 136 Princes Highway, Dapto;* and *Holm Place, Shellharbour Square.*

Entertainment

For movie goers, Wollongong has two cinema complexes:
Regent Theatre, *197 Keira Street,* ☎*4228 9238.*
Town Cinemas, *Burelli Street,* ☎*4228 4888.*

The **Illawarra Performing Arts Centre,** *Burelli Street,* ☎*4226 3366,* has live theatre and musical presentations.

Points of Interest

Most historic buildings can be visited on a walking tour commencing at **Flagstaff Hill** (parking available). The sights visited are:
Wollongong Head Lighthouse; Breakwater Lighthouse; Belmore Basin; Drill Hall; Throsby's

stockman's hut monument; Market Square; Illawarra Historical Museum; Congregational Church; Wollongong Courthouse; St Michael's Provisional Cathedral; Wollongong Uniting Church; The Town Hall; Wollongong East Post Office; Visitor Information office; St Francis Xavier's Provisional Catholic Cathedral; and **Andrew Lysaght Park.**

Mount Kembla Historic Village, 7km (4 miles) from Wollongong was the site of the 1902 mining disaster, but it is full of art and craft centres today.

Wollongong Botanic Garden, in Keiraville, is a pleasant spot for picnics and quiet walks, and offers many areas of interest - Sir Joseph Banks Plant Houses, where plants from the wet tropics, deserts and temperate regions are displayed; The Rose Garden; Woodland Garden; Flowering Trees and Shrub Garden; Succulent Plants from South Africa and Central America; Australian Plant Habitats; and The Herb Garden. The Garden is ☉open daily 7am-4.45pm Mon-Fri and 10am-4.45pm Sat-Sun. During winter the gardens close at 6.45pm.

The Wollongong City Art Gallery, *85 Burelli Street,* ☎*4228 7500,* has a fine collection of modern and traditional paintings, with changing exhibitions. It is ☉open Tue-Fri 10am-5pm, Sat-Sun noon-4pm.

Magnificent views of the coastline can be obtained from **Mount Kembla Lookout, Sublime Point** and **Bulli Lookout,** all of which are only about 15 to 20 minutes' drive from the centre of town.

Kelly's Falls, 2km off the

Princes Highway at Stanwell Tops, has a picnic area and easy walking tracks to the falls. Flannel flowers are abundant in spring and early summer.

Nearby is **Symbio Wildlife Gardens,** *7 Lawrence Hargrave Drive,* ☎*4294 1088,* which has native and exotic animals, free barbecues, swimming and wading pools and lunchtime demonstrations of activities from milking a cow to handling reptiles. The gardens are ☉open daily from 9.30am, and they advertise that feeding time is 'all the time'. To get to these attractions, take the old Princes Highway from Wollongong, not the F6.

While you are in the area, drive north for half an hour to **Bald Hill Lookout,** where there is a memorial to Lawrence Hargraves, and if the wind is favourable you will see many brightly coloured hang-gliders floating by.

Stanwell Park is in the valley below, and you can call in and browse through Articles Fine Arts Gallery, *111 Lawrence Hargrave Drive,* ☎*4294 2491,* and have a Devonshire tea on the outdoor terrace. The hang-gliders land in the park next to the sea.

South of Wollongong is **Lake Illawarra,** renowned for fishing and prawning, and often ablaze with colourful sailing boats and sail boards. The lake is actually a lagoon covering an area of 35 sq km (14 sq miles), with its entrance at the foreshore suburb of Windang.

The **Illawarra Escarpment State Recreation Area** has many fine walking trails through the rainforest, ☎*9585 6444* for details.

Australia's largest steel mill is

located around the foreshores of **Port Kembla Harbour.** The harbour sees millions of tons of coal exported each year from the surrounding mines, as well as steel from the steelworks. Wollongong has two bicycle tracks. The one to the north starts at North Beach and goes to Corrimal, 14km (9 miles) away. The southern one starts near the Windang bridge and skirts the shores of Lake Illawarra.

Festivals

The **Festival of Wollongong** is held each year in November.

Facilities

Ten-pin bowling, catamaran and sailboard hire (Lake Illawarra and Belmore Basin), tennis, squash, horse riding (Otford Valley Farm, ☎ *4294 2442*), golf, joy flights (Albion Park Aerodrome), fishing, leisure centre with heated pools (Beaton Park, ☎ *4229 6004*), horse racing (Kembla Grange, ☎ *4261 7211*), greyhound racing (Bulli, ☎ *4267 1467* and Dapto, ☎ *4261 2449*), harness racing (Bulli, ☎ *4267 4224*) and indoor cricket (Albion Park Rail, ☎ *4256 6138* and Unanderra, ☎ *4271 6685*). Deep sea charter boats leave from Belmore Basin. Roller skating is available at Dapto, ☎ *4261 6333*.

Outlying Attractions
Shellharbour

The town of Shellharbour is around twenty minutes' drive south of Wollongong on the coastal road. There are caravan and camping areas, modern motels, one of the state's largest licensed clubs, an attractive corner pub in the old area, golf, bowls, great restaurants and

beautiful beaches.

It has also given its name to the suburban sprawl that has developed inland to **Albion Park** and north to **Primbie**. The location is listed on the **Heritage Commission Register,** and is regarded as one of the two most important archaeological sites on the NSW coast.

Bass Point is a popular diving area, as part of its waters form a marine reserve. There is an airport at nearby **Albion Park,** and joy flights are offered. Nearby is the turnoff to **Jamberoo Recreation Park**, where you can play mini golf, go bobsledding, grass ski, or take the chairlift to the mountain top. There is also a maze, a licensed family restaurant, children's play area and a barbecue hut.

For more information contact the Shellharbour Visitor Information Centre, ☎ *4221 6169.* They are located in Lamerton House, *Lamerton Crescent,* and are ☺open 8.30am-4.40pm Mon-Fri, closed weekends and public holidays.

They can be emailed at ✉tourism@shellharbour.nsw .gov.au and the web address is ▣www.shellharbour.nsw.gov.au

Kiama

Kiama is a seaside town 36km (22 miles) south of Wollongong. **The Blowhole** is the main attraction. It's floodlit until 9.30pm.

On foot, visit the burial site of one of the members of the **First Fleet,** and then walk around the showground that overlooks Storm Bay's jagged rocks, to the town's popular Surf Beach. You can picnic in the adjoining park, or continue through the town centre

taking in the historic grand old homes and commercial buildings on the way.

The Terraces, a row of historic timber cottages, are now gift and specialty stores, and a good place to pick up a bargain. Most of the stores are ☺open daily 10am-5pm.

The Family History Centre, *7 Railway Parade,* ☎ *4233 1122,* has comprehensive in-house microform and data inventory to enable people to trace their family trees. The Centre is ☺open daily 9.30am-4.30pm.

The **Quarry Leisure Centre**, *Havilah Place,* ☎ *4232 1877,* has a 25m heated swimming pool, a wading pool, sauna, spa, aerobics, and facilities for indoor sports.

Minnamurra Falls. The Falls are 15km (9 miles) west of Kiama, in a dense subtropical rainforest, and plunge some 50m (164 ft) into a deep gorge. There is a delightful walk from the parking area through the rainforest to the Falls, and the round trip takes about an hour.

Barren Grounds Nature Reserve. The Reserve is 25km (16 miles) west of Kiama on the Jamberoo Mountain Road, and affords magnificent views from the lookout. There is a unique hanging swamp and bird observatory, and picnic and barbecue facilities.

The Kiama Visitors Centre is on *Blowhole Point Road,* ☎ *4232 3322* or ☎ *1300 654 262* (free call). ☺open 9am-5pm daily. They have information on accommodation available, and all the places of interest. You can check the area out on the web at ▣www.kiama. com.au and email them for more information at ✉kiamatourism@ ozemail.com.au

⤙ Let's Stay Here
Kiama Backpackers Hostel,
31 Bong Bong St, ☎ *4233 1881.* Located near the train station. The beds have linen. A small backpackers with the basic facilities that includes a small kitchen, TV lounge and internet access. *Dorm $20.*

Gerrigong and Geroa
South of Kiama are the towns of Gerrigong and Geroa which boast holiday facilities, camping grounds, golf courses and the beautiful **Seven Mile Beach.**

Berry
Called the Town of Trees, Berry more than lives up to its name, and is 16km (10 miles) north of Nowra. The town has a population of around 2500, with shopping facilities, motel and hotel accommodation, restaurants, and many antique and craft shops.

The **Berry Historical Museum,** *Queen Street,* is ⊕open Sat 11am-2pm, Sun 11am-3pm and public holidays 11am-2pm, ☎ *4464 1551,* and they can point out the other buildings in the town classified by the National Trust, such as the Court House and National Bank.

Berry Country Fair, featuring local crafts and second- hand goods, is held at Apex Park, cnr Princes Highway and Prince Alfred Street, on the first Sunday of the month.

Local information can be obtained from Pottering Around, on the corner of *Queen* and *Alexandra Streets,* ☎ *4464 2177.*

New South Wales – South
Nowra
Population 24,000
Nowra is situated on the banks of the Shoalhaven River, on the south coast of New South Wales.

Climate
Average temperatures: January max 26C (79F) - min 18C (64F); July max 17C (63F) - min 9C (48F). Average annual rainfall: 1275mm (50 ins).

Characteristics
Nowra is the hub of the City of Shoalhaven, which has a population of around 83,000. The city area stretches from Berry to Durras North, and has 109 ocean, bay and lakeside beaches, lush rolling pastures, craggy mountain haunts and bush trails.

The town has produced two Melbourne Cup winners - Archer and Arwon.

How to Get There
By Rail
Bomaderry is the terminus of the **South Coast Railway**, and there are train services daily from and to Sydney, ☎ *13 2232.*
Pioneer Motor Service operates a daily bus service which connects with the train, ☎ *13 3410.*

By Bus
Greyhound Pioneer, ☎ *13 2030,* have daily services from Sydney/ Melbourne/Sydney which stops at Nowra.

Visitor Information
The Shoalhaven Visitor Information Centre, *cnr Princess Highway* and *Pleasant Way,* ☎ *4421 0778* or ☎ *1800 024*

261, is ⊕open 9am-4.30pm daily. Their internet details are ▣www.shoalhaven.nsw.gov.au for Visitor Information and ✉bev erlyc@shoalhaven.nsw.gov.au for email contact.

⤙ Let's Stay Here
Here is a selection of available accommodation with prices that should be used as a guide only. The telephone area code is 02.

Nowra Backpackers,
1a Scenic Drive, ☎ *4422 8006,* ▣ *www.nowrabackpackers.co m* Located close to banks of Shoalhaven River. This 1920s house is beautifully designed by Walter Burley Griffin, who designed Canberra. A very warm atmosphere. All beds come with linen, soap and towels. Facilities includes a large kitchen, a common room and a fireplace, games room with pool tables, TV with cable and outside is a barbecue area. *Dorms from* ✪*$25; single* (breakfast included)

Riverhaven Motel,
Scenic Drive, ☎ *4421 2044.* 22 units, licensed restaurant, indoor heated pool, barbecue - ✪*$60-75.*

Caravan Parks
Shoalhaven Caravan Village, *Terara Road,* ☎ *4423 0770.* (Pets allowed under control) - *powered sites* ✪*$17 for two, cabins $30-70 for two.*

Rest Point Caravan Park, *Browns Road,* ☎ *4421 6856.* (No pets allowed) 80 sites, playground, barbecue - *pow-*

ered sites ◐*$20-24, cabins $55-100.*

Let's Eat

Nowra has a wide selection of restaurants, coffee shops, and four licensed clubs. Many of the motels also have restaurants. Some of the choices are:
Boatshed, *Wharf Road,* ☎*4421 2419.*

Captain's Table, *202 Kinghorne Street,* ☎*4421 0555.*

Leong's Chinese Restaurant, *83 North Street,* ☎*4421 2131.*

Nowra Palace, *54 Berry Street,* ☎*4421 4902.* Malaysian and Chinese selection.

Nowra Steak House, *16 Kinghorne Street,* ☎*4423 4193.*

Riverhaven, *Riverhaven Motel, 1 Scenic Drive,* ☎*4421 2044.*

Shoreline, Parkhaven Motel, *cnr Kinghorn and Douglas Streets,* ☎*4421 5444.*

Trevi Fountain, *223 Kinghorne Road,* ☎*4423 0285.* Italian cuisine.

Theodore's Brasserie, *116 Kinghorne Street,* ☎*4421 0300.*

McDonald's is on the corner of *Cambawarra Road, Bomaderry, and the Princes Highway and Browns Road, South Nowra,* ☎*4421 1099.* **KFC** is in *Lot 22, Princes Highway, South Nowra.* **Pizza Hut** is on the corner of *McLean Street and the Princes Highway in Nowra,* ☎*4421 4199.*

Points of Interest

Cruises of the Shoalhaven River are available from **Shoalhaven River Tours,** *49 Greenwell Point Road, Greenwell Point,* ☎*4447 1978.*

The old Shoalhaven River bridge was erected in 1881. To cope with the heavy volume of traffic across the River, a second bridge was erected in 1980. In **Moorhouse Park,** *Bridge Road,* there is an old flood rescue boat from Terara.

Nowra Olympic Pool and **Nowra Waterways** are in *Scenic Drive* and are open from September to Easter, ☎*4421 2093.*

The Showground, in West Street, is the venue for the two-day agricultural show held in February each year. In the Showground there is the Council Youth Centre, and the Memorial gates, which were built to commemorate servicemen who died in action in the two World Wars.

At the western end of the Showground is **Hanging Rock,** a precariously positioned formation with views across the River and Nowra Golf Course.

Ben's Walk is a walking track which follows the river bank from the track head near Shoalhaven River Bridge to Nowra Creek, which is spanned by a suspension bridge.

On the corner of West and Worrigee Streets, is **Meroogal,** an historic house built by Robert Taylor-Thorburn in 1886. It is now owned by the Historic Houses Trust of New South Wales, and is ◐open Sat 1pm-5pm and Sun 10am-5pm. For further information, ☎*4421 8150.*

Shoalhaven Historical Museum, *cnr Kinghorn and Plunkett Streets,* is ◐open Sat-Sun 1-4pm, and on Mon, Wed and Fri during school holidays

1pm-4pm, ☎*4421 2021.*

Werninck Craft Cottage, *102 Plunkett Street,* is ◐open Mon-Fri 9.30am-3.30pm, Sat-Sun 10am-4pm, ☎*4423 2419.*

Situated on the corner of Kinghorn and Kalandar Streets is a **Sea Venom Jet**, which has been donated by HMAS Albatross. A short history of the aircraft and type of service is on a plaque at the site.

HMAS Albatross

Travel south from Nowra along the Princes Highway to the Kalandar Street intersection, turn right at the traffic lights and follow the signs.

The Royal Australian Naval Air Station, HMAS Albatross, 9km (6 miles) south-west of Nowra, is the home of the Fleet Air Arm. The fixed-wing section at the base was disbanded, due to the lack of an aircraft carrier, and the station now has helicopters. Educational tours can be arranged, ☎*4421 1211* for more information.

The **Naval Aviation Museum** at the Air Station has the finest collection of historic military aircraft in Australia, and a good collection of engines, aviation equipment, models, uniforms and memorabilia. Picnic, barbecue and toilet facilities are provided, and it is ◐open daily 10am-4pm, ☎*4421 1920.*

Near the base is the **Nowra Hill Lookout,** with panoramic views of the Shoalhaven and Jervis Bay area. There is a pleasant stroll from there along **Commodore's Walk** to the **Harry Sawkins Memorial Lookout**.

Festivals

February - **Nowra Agricultural Show.** November - **The Shoalhaven Spring Festival.**

Facilities

Lawn bowls, canoeing, fishing, golf, sailing, scenic drives, squash, swimming, tennis, water skiing, 4WD escapes and bushwalking tours. Check with the information centre.

Boats can be hired from the following outlets:

Aquatique, *125 Junction Street,* ☎*4421 8159* - canoes, scuba and diving gear, surf and wave skis. Shoalhaven Caravan Village, *Terrara Road,* ☎*4423 0770* - canoes.

Shoalhaven Heads

The township of Shoalhaven Heads is at the southern end of Seven Mile Beach, about 13km (8 miles) east of Bomaderry. It is a popular holiday spot near **Seven Mile Beach National Park.** The town offers a bowling club, fishing facilities and a swimming pool. You can hire bicycles at Shoalhaven Heads Hardware Store, ☎*4448 7707.*

Nearby is **Coolangatta Estate Historic Village Resort**, 1*335 Bolong Road,* ☎*4448 7131,* the site of the first settlement in the Shoalhaven district. The complex comprises buildings erected by the district's founder, Alexander Berry, that have been restored as motel units. There is also a 9-hole golf course, a winery, and picnic areas and barbecues.

The **Coolangatta Craft Centre,** *1180 Bolong Road,* is housed in the original school house, established in 1861. It is ⏲open Wed-Mon 9am-5pm, and daily during school holidays, ☎4448 7205.

Cambewarra Mountain Lookout. The lookout is on Tourist Road, Beamont, north of Bomaderry, and offers panoramic views of the Shoalhaven River

Valley and the coastline. Picnic, barbecue and toilet facilities are provided. There is also a kiosk which is ⏲open Fri-Wed 9am-5pm and daily during the Christmas school holidays, ☎*4465 1321.*

Bomaderry/North Nowra

The town of Bomaderry is really a northern suburb of Nowra, separated from it by the river. It has a large shopping centre, Narang Road Supergrass Tennis Centre, Shoal-haven Sporting Complex, and a Basketball Stadium. Bomaderry Railway Station is the terminus of the South Coast Railway Line, ☎*4423 6416.*

Bomaderry Creek Walk is a track that follows Bomaderry Creek from below the Ten Pin Bowling Centre in Narang Street. Walkers have a choice between a three hour walk and a one hour walk, and picnic and barbecue facilities are available at the track head.

Nowra Golf Club is situated under bush-covered escarpment, near the river in North Nowra, Greys Beach. The clubhouse has first class facilities, and the scenic 18-hole course offers a challenge. Visitors are welcome, ☎*4421 3900* (pro-shop ☎*4421 2249*).

The **Grotto Walk,** west of the golf course, is an easy walk following the River, and beginning off Yurunga Drive.

From **Rockhill Lookout,** off McMahons Road, you can get a spectacular view of the river.

Nowra Wildlife Park is set in 6ha (16 acres) off Rockhill Road, North Nowra, overlooking the river. You can walk amongst the animals, and have your photo taken with the resident koalas.

The park has a well appointed picnic and barbecue area, a kiosk and a camping area, and is ⏲open daily 8am-5pm, ☎*4421 3949.* Admission is ◐$6 adults.

Huskisson

The town of Huskisson, on the shores of Jervis Bay, is 24km (15 miles) south-east of Nowra, and has a shopping centre, a modern RSL club and bowling clubs. It is a real holiday spot, and during the Christmas holiday period a movie theatre and carnival operate in the town. The sands of Jervis Bay are renowned as the whitest in the world, and each Easter Huskisson hosts the White Sands Carnival.

The Lady Denman Heritage Complex in Dent Street is worth a visit. The Lady Denman is an old Sydney ferry which was originally built at Huskisson, and saw many years of service on Sydney Harbour. After she retired she was sailed back to Huskisson, placed in the park at the Heritage Complex, and now contains the **Museum of Jervis Bay, Science and The Sea.** The park is ⏲open daily 9am-5pm, and the museum is ⏲open Tues-Fri 1-5pm, Sat-Sun and school holidays 10am-5pm. Nearby is Lady Timbery's Aboriginal Arts and Crafts Centre, ☎*4441 5999.*

Jervis Bay Territory

This area is part of the Australian Capital Territory, and is 35km (22 miles) from Nowra. It contains the **Royal Australian Naval College, HMAS Cresswell, the Jervis Bay Nature Reserve** and **Botanic Gardens Annex.** The ruined lighthouse overlooking the ocean is quite interesting. It was built in the wrong place and proved to be a navigational hazard luring boats to their doom on the rocky coastline. The navy was requested to shell it!

At **Jervis Bay Village** you will find a public telephone, police station, supermarket, general store and petrol station. The Administrative Office of Jervis Bay Territory is situated in the grounds of the village, ☎ *4442 1217*.

Booderee National Park is managed by Jervis Bay Administration, and there is a Visitors Centre on the left near the entrance, ☎ *4443 0977*. In keeping with the protection of the environment, spear guns, handspears, dogs and other domestic animals are not permitted in the reserve, and fires can only be lit in defined barbecue areas. For enquiries about camping in the park, call into the Visitor Centre, which is ☉open 8.30am-5pm in the Christmas-Easter period, and 9am-4pm during the off-peak season. Entry into the park is ✪$5 per car weekly.

Green Patch is a camping and picnic area within the National Park, and has a sheltered beach, toilets, hot showers, wood barbecues and picnic tables. There is prolific birdlife, many interesting bush walks, and a camping ground that allows a maximum of three weeks' stay.

Murrays Beach, Summer Cloud Bay and **Cave Beach** are other popular spots within the Reserve.

HMAS Cresswell was established as an officer training college in 1915, and visits to the grounds of the college are permitted on a limited basis (20 minutes on weekends and most public holidays), ☎ *4429 7985* for details.

In the college is the **Royal Australian Naval College Historical Collection,** with a display of artefacts specifically related to the college and the Jervis Bay area, and Peter Webber's collection of model sailing ships. It is ☉open on the last Sunday of each month, or by appointment, ☎ *4429 7845*.

The **Jervis Bay Annex** to the **Australian National Botanic Gardens** is 2km along the Cave Beach Road, and has a large variety of native plants collected from all parts of Australia. Facilities include nature walks, toilets and picnic area, but no barbecues are permitted. The annex is ☉open Mon-Fri 8am-4pm, and the first Sunday of the month 10am-5pm. Hours may be extended during public and school holidays, ☎ *4442 1122*.

Milton

Milton is 7km (4 miles) north of Ulladulla, and 61km (38 miles) south of Nowra. It was established in 1860, has many historic buildings, and in the **Mick Ryan Park** there is a giant fig tree that is estimated to be over 110 years old.

A flea market, featuring local crafts and second-hand goods, is held at the **Settlement Courtyard** on the first Saturday of the month.

Over the long weekend in October every year Milton celebrates the **Milton Settlers' Fair,** which consists of markets, art and craft exhi-bitions, music and dancing.

Ulladulla

Ulladulla is 68km (42 miles) south of Nowra, on the Princes Highway, and there is much to see around the harbour and wharf. Trawlers of the fishing fleet are

anchored in the harbour behind the safety of the breakwater. Each Easter Sunday, the traditional **Blessing of the Fleet Ceremony** is conducted on the harbour breakwater. This is a religious custom which has been practised by the Italian fishermen for many generations. Each year this ceremony has become quite a celebration which is worth seeing. Trawlers are decorated for the event and there is a carnival atmosphere.

The Royal Volunteer Coastal Patrol maintains full sea search and rescue facilities at Ulladulla, for the area from Jervis Bay to Batemans Bay. Radio cover is provided on 2182KHz, 2524KHz and VHF Channel 16 during weekends and holidays periods, and at any other time of day or night by arrangement. However, a continuous watch is maintained 7 days a week on 27880KHz. Pleasure craft owners are urged to lodge sailing plans with the Coastal Patrol Ulladulla either by telephone, ☎ *4455 3403*, or by radio, to ensure they have an adequate radio cover while at sea, and then to advise the base of their safe arrival at their destination.

Pedal boats can be hired on the beach surrounding the harbour during holiday periods.

On **Wardens Head,** the southern point of Ulladulla Harbour, is the lighthouse, and from there you can get an uninterrupted view of the coast. A track leads from the lighthouse to the beach where there is good fishing and surfing.

South Pacific Heathland Reserve stretches from *Dowling Street* to *Pitman Avenue*, and features the Chris Humphries

Nature Walk covering 12ha (30 acres).

Funland, *93 Princes Highway,* ☎ *4455 3053,* is one of the largest indoor fun parks in New South Wales. There are three floors of attractions, including dodgems, the 'sizzler' thrill ride, controlla boats, air hockey, slot cars, kiddy rides, and more. ⏲open daily from 10am, closes 10pm Sat and school holidays, 5pm Sun-Fri.

The Ulladulla Visitors Centre, Civic Centre, *Princes Highway,* ☎ *4455 1269,* is ⏲open Mon-Fri 10am-5pm, Sat-Sun 9am-5pm, and should be your first port of call. There is no shortage of accommodation or restaurants in the town, and the Visitor Centre has all the details.

Just north is the Mollymook Beach and golf course.

⤳ Let's Stay Here
South Coast BP VIP,
63 Princess Hwy, ☎ *4454 0500,* 🖥 *www.southcoastba ckpackers.com* Located just 5 minutes walk to beaches. Close to shops, cafes, restaurants, clubs and entertainment and the Aboriginal Cultural walking trails and National Parks. All rooms include free bed linen and bath towels. The facilities that you'll find here are a fully equipped kitchen, laundry, TV lounge, internet access, sun rooms and deck, and an outdoor area at the back with barbecue and some hammocks. There is also a free pick up service from the bus station. What you'll also find are free beach towels, surf and body boards, free fishing gear, bike hire and helmets. Parking available. *Dorms* ✪*$20; twin $42; double $45;*

Batemans Bay
Population 15,600
Batemans Bay is situated on the Clyde River Estuary, at the foot of Clyde Mountain, 306 km (190 miles) south of Sydney.

Climate
Average temperatures: January max 23C (73F) - min 16C (61F); July max 16C (61F) - min 6C (43F). The average annual rainfall: 916mm (36 in). The hours of sunshine per day are 7 in summer and 6 in autumn, winter and spring.

Characteristics
Batemans Bay is a weekend and holiday retreat for people from Canberra. The beaches of the area are clear and clean with superb fishing. It has all the facilities of a beach resort but it is all very understated. It is the only place where the commercial fishing trawlers are permitted to sell their catch direct to the public. The general atmosphere is very friendly; strangers smile and say hello in the street.

How to Get There
By Air
Rex, ☎ *13 1713,* fly to Moruya and Merimbula from Sydney, Melbourne, Brisbane and Adelaide, with at least two flights daily.

By Bus
Priors Scenic Express operates between Sydney and the Eurobodalla Coast, with a focus on the sightseeing opportunities of the trip, ☎ *1800 816 234.*

Murrays offer daily services from Canberra, ☎ *132 251.*
V-Line have a combined road/rail service between Melbourne and Batemans Bay, ☎ *132 232.*

By Rail
The trains from Sydney, ☎ *13 2232,* terminate at Bombaderry, on the northern side of the Shoalhaven River, so you will have to organise an alternative form of transport to complete the trip south, be it a hire car or one of the coach services listed above.

Visitor Information
The Eurobodalla Visitor Information Centre, *cnr Princes Highway* and *Beach Road, Batemans Bay,* ☎ *4472 6900* or ☎ *1800 802 528,* is ⏲open daily 9am-5pm (closed Christmas Day). Email them at ✉info@naturecoast-tourism. com.au or visit their website at 🖥www.naturecoast-tourism. com.au

Accommodation
Batemans Bay, as with most towns on the south coast of New South Wales, is well endowed with a variety of accommodation. Although motels and holiday units dominate, you can usually rent out cottages in the area at reasonable prices, outside of school holiday periods. Contact Estate Agents in the area or the local Visitor Centre.

Prices vary considerably depending on the standard of accommodation and the season. Here we have a selection, with prices which should be used as a guide only. The telephone area code is 02.

⤳ Let's Stay Here
Batemans Bay Shady Willows YHA,
Corner Old Princess Hwy and South St, ☎ *4472 4972,* 🖥 *www.yha.com* Situated

within a camping/caravan park with plenty of shade and surrounded by garden. About a km away from the nearest foodstore but a walk away from pubs and cinemas. Facilities includes a kitchen, laundry, TV lounge room, internet access, swimming pool, an outside deck and a barbecue area. Free pick up available. Bike hire and parking available. *Dorms from ❂$21; single from $28; double/ twin from $23pp; BC MC VA EFTPOS*

Beach Road Backpackers Hostel,
92 Beach Rd, ☎4472 3644
Located nicely just across the sea and from the marina, about a km from town. This hostel used to be a simple house that was converted. All rooms comes with linen, duvets and towels. The amenities here is a kitchen, laundry, TV lounge and an outdoor area with a barbecue. The manager organises trips to Pebbly Beach.
Dorm ❂$23; double $48

Hanging Rock Golf Club Family,
Beach Road, ☎4472 4466. 27 units, playground, barbecue, swimming pool - ❂$55-60.

Caravan Parks
Coachhouse Marina Resort, Beach Road, ☎4472 4392. (No dogs allowed) - *powered sites ❂$25-35 for two, on-site vans from $40 for two.*

Shady Willows Tourist Park,
Old Princes Highway, ☎4472 4972. (Dogs may be permitted on application) - *powered sites ❂$15-25 for two, on-site vans from $35 for two, cabins from $40.*

Shady Willows Youth Hostel,(part of the Caravan Park) *corner of Old Princes Highway and South Street,* ☎4472 4972. Pool, TV, lounge room, bicycles, 1 km from nearest foodstore, internet, on site parking, iron, laundry. 11 rooms, 38 beds, 2(6),1(2), 3(4) + caravans *$24, $60 for family room. BC,MC,V.*

Let's Eat
The area boasts fine restaurants with particularly good fish dishes. Most of the larger motels have licensed restaurants which can be recommended. There are also a good number of **Clubs** - Bowling (☎4472 4502), Golf (☎4472 4967), **Returned Servicemen** (☎4472 4847) - that also contain restaurants. Here are some additional venues.

Pinky's Pizza, *3 Clyde Street,* ☎4472 3073.

Raymond's, *19 Clyde Street,* ☎4472 5700. Chinese cuisine, open daily.

Vietnamese, Thai and Malaysian, *Shop 7, Bay Plaza Centre, Orient Street,* ☎4472 7274.

McDonalds is on the corner of Hill and Vesper Streets and **KFC** is on the *Princes Highway.*

Points of Interest
The population increases to 100,000 during the peak holiday season (from about mid December to early February).

Batemans Bay has 16 golden beaches, with some sheltered calm waters. **McKenzie's Beach** is a small beach that has consistent small to medium waves, with the best area at **Malua Bay**, south of the Surf Club. To the north, there are several good beaches including **South Durras** near Wasp Head, and **Depot, Pebbly** and **Merry** beaches accessible through **Murramarang National Park.**

The **Clyde River**, which is quite a spectacular waterway, is navigable for 51km (32 miles) from Batemans Bay up into the hills. Regular cruises are available up to Nelligen, which boasts a number of historically significant buildings.

The **MV Merinda** offers a great time out on the Clyde River (☎4472 4052), or you can hire a boat in the town for your own 'explore and see', combined with a little fishing.

The area is well known for its fishing. **Durras Lake,** to the north of Batemans Bay, has flathead, whiting and bream, and various points and bays between there and North Head offer other good spots. Up from the town near the oyster beds and the mangrove flats on the **Clyde River,** many people catch whiting, mulloway and bream. There is also quite a deal of fishing from the bank around the town. To the south, Malua Bay and Pretty Point are perhaps the most popular spots.

There are many National Parks and forests in the region, and maps are available from the Visitors Centre. The nearest one to Batemans Bay is **Murramarang**, which lies between South Durras and North Head. Access is via the Princes Highway and Durras Road, and there are six well-defined walks beginning from the road.

> Walks from the town include:
> 1. Beach walk from Clyde River to Cullendulla Creek - about 3 km (2 miles) long around the coast. Easy, okay for kids.
> 2. Guerilla Bay to the lighthouse - 1.5km (1 mile).
> 3. Along the Princes Highway to the Round Hill Fire Tower.

There are many other coastal walks recommended by the Visitors Centre.

The **Birdland Animal Park** at *55 Beach Road* is ⏲open 9.30am-4pm daily. It includes 'Wombat World', snake demonstrations, an animal nursery, a koala exhibit, and a scale model train. Admission is ✪$8 adults, ☎4472 5364.

The **Historical Society Museum** is in the old court house, *cnr Beach Road* and *Orient Street*, and is ⏲open Thu-Sat 1pm-4pm, ☎4472 8993.

The **Mogo Goldfields**, on the Tomakin Road near Mogo Village 15km (9 miles) from town, are ⏲open weekend and school holidays, 10am-4pm. There is a guided tour of the old underground gold mine. You can camp here with all the amenities, ☎4471 7381. The Village is open most of the time and depicts a bygone era. It is well-known for its art and craft shops.

Festivals
The **Neptune Festival** is held each November.

Facilities
Boat, catamaran and sailboard hire, golf, tennis, lawn bowls and ten-pin bowling are all provided for in the area.

Outlying Attractions
Burrill Lake
Situated 5km (3 miles) south of Ulladulla, Burrill Lake is crossed by the Princes Highway at its eastern arm, but the main expanse reaches inland almost to the township of Milton. The inlet and beach are to the east of the Highway, and if you take the road to Dolphin Point and follow Seaside Parade you will come to the picnic area, rock platforms and popular fishing spots. Accommodation is available in caravan parks, motels and holiday units close to the lake and beach.

Burrill Lake offers boating, sailing, lake and beach fishing, surfing, swimming, windsurfing and prawning in season. Boats can be hired, and there are three launching ramps. A boat hire service, ☎4454 0951 operates from the reserve on the foreshores in Moore Street.

At **Bungalow Park**, you can feed the lorikeets, which arrive at 8am and 3pm (during daylight saving 9am and 4pm), or play mini-golf on a course which is a replica of the Mollymook Hilltop Golf Course. There are also boats available for hire, ☎4455 1621.

Moruya
The town of Moruya is 27km (17 miles) south of Batemans Bay on the Princes Highway. It has some fine old buildings, including the **Wesleyan Church** built in 1864 with local granite. The airport, which caters for the area, is on the north headland of the river entrance. South Moruya has a fine surf beach.

Accommodation is not plentiful in the area, since Batemans Bay to the north and Narooma in the south provide such facilities. If you are planning to stay here, however, there are a limited number of motels, lodges, guesthouses and B&Bs to choose from. Most are along the Princes Highway, so keep an eye out as you drive through.

The area has excellent fishing in the **Deua River** with its mangrove swamps, and along the various coastal headlands. Surfing is great from Moruya Heads to Congo, North Head, Broulee South, North Broulee, Pink Rocks (off the north face of Broulee Island - experienced riders only, 6m waves) and Mossy Point near the mouth of the Tomago River.

Behind Moruya, along the Araluen Road, is the 81,158 ha (200,460 acres) **Deua National Park** which extends up the coastal ranges to Batemans Bay. You can try hiking - good luck and be sure to let the ranger know your plans.

Moruya has an **Historical Museum** in *85 Campbell Street*, ⏲open Mon and Fri 11am-3pm and on Saturdays 11am-1pm (during peak Christmas and Easter seasons it open daily). Admission is ✪$2 adults.

Each Saturday from 9am the **Moruya Country Markets** are held in Shore Street, and the Congo Crafts Gallery, ☎4474 2931, is ⏲open Wed-Mon 11am-5pm during school holidays, but it's best to phone beforehand.

Kiora House, along the Araluen Road, is a National Trust classified building that offers quaint old world charm. There is no public access to this building, but its recollections of colonial heritage can be admired from the street.

Moruya boasts a speedway, and a horse racing complex together with golf courses, tennis and bowling clubs.

Bodalla

24km (15 miles) south along the Princes Highway is the town of Bodalla, made famous by Bega cheese which uses it as a brand name. The **All Saints Church** is one of several photogenic buildings in this attractive little town. Just before Bodalla is the turnoff to Tuross Head, where you can hire boats for fishing and boating on the lake of the same name.

Narooma

This town is 44km (27 miles) south of Moruya, on the estuary of the **Wagonga River.** It is another popular fishing resort with excellent beaches for surfing (Mystery Bay, Handkerchief Beach, Narooma Main Beach, Bar Beach, Dalmeny Point, Potato Point, Blackfellows Point and Tuross Head). It has a narrow channel that leads to a small harbour. As with the other towns on the south coast, it offers excellent bushwalks and is very much a family holiday area.

Montague Island, 8km (5 miles) offshore, is a flora and fauna reserve, and the area around there is well known for its game fishing. The island is the halfway point in the Sydney to Hobart Yacht Race.

Contact the Narooma Visitors Centre, Princes Highway, ⊕open every day except Christmas Day 9am-5pm, ☎4476 2881 or ☎1800 802 528, with any queries, or to assist in booking accommodation, restaurants or tours. Alternatively, you can email them at: ✉eurovcn@acr.net.au or visit the website at 🖥www.nat urecoast-tourism.com.au

⤴ Let's Stay Here

Narooma Blue YHA,
8 Princes Highway, Narooma,
☎*4476 4440,* 🖥*www.yha.com*
This is a good seaside hostel which has an nice location, near the water just at the northern end of town. Close to the foodstore and bus depot. Just newly renovated and is housed in several small buildings. Most accommodation is in the units to the rear of the main building. The main building (the house at the front) has common areas including an Internet cafe. Other facilities includes kitchen, laundry, TV room and barbecue area. Canoes and bikes available for hire. Parking on site. *Dorm bed from ◉\$21; double room \$22.50pp BC MC VA* (prices includes breakfast)

Central Tilba

21km (13 miles) south is Central Tilba, which neighbors Tilba Tilba. Both of these tiny settlements are in the shadow of an ancient volcano, **Mount Dromedary.** Situated in rather pleasant hilly country at the base of Mt Dromedary, Central Tilba has become a tourist spot with art and craft shops, an old wooden general store, a cobblers cottage, a pub, and a quaint restaurant with displays of the traditional crafts. A pleasant day excursion from Narooma.

Bega

The town of Bega is 170km (106 miles) south of Batemans Bay, and 80km (50 miles) south of Narooma. It is the commercial centre of the district with a population above 4000. The district is famous for its dairy industry and cheeses.

The **Bega Cheese Heritage Centre** on the northern side of the *Bega River, Lagoon Street,* ☎*6491 7777*, is ⊕open for inspection and tasting daily 9am-5pm.

The **Bega Family Museum**, cnr Auckland and Bega Streets, is ⊕open Mon-Fri 10.30am-4pm, Sat 10am-12pm, ☎*6492 1453*.

Brogo Valley's Rotolactor is 23km (14 miles) north of Bega on Baldwin Road, Brogo, and is ⊕open to the public Mon and Wed 2-5pm, with milking at 3pm, ☎*6493 8330*.

The **Grevillea Estate** winery and vineyards is on the Buckajo Road, ☎*6492 3006*.

Mumbulla Falls Picnic Area, 20km (12 miles) north of Bega off the Princes Highway along a gravel road, is a very pleasant spot for picnics and a swim. Because of the gravel road, only try it in dry weather.

The largest farm in the Bega Valley is **Kameruka Estate** which is classified by the National Trust. The homestead is set in extensive gardens, with its own church and clock-tower. It is ⊕open daily, ☎*6492 0509*.

Candelo Village, situated 20km (12 miles) south-west, still retains its old world charm with galleries and restaurants. It is a pleasant place for afternoon tea after a short drive.

Mimosa Rocks National Park, sprawls across its 17km coastal stretch north of Tathra and east of Mt George Mountain. It is a perfect site for a picnic, and for enjoying the natural wonders of landscape and wildlife. Camping areas are also available, and it is best to discuss plans and ideas with the Visitor Information Centre.

Starfish and coral in Jervis Bay

Secluded Beach in Jervis Bay

Ulladulah Beach

The Sapphire Coast Visitor Information Centre, *Office 2, 163 Auckland Street, Bega*, ☎*6492 3313* or ☎*1800 663 012*, tends to be the arrival and departure point for coaches, and is the place to obtain assistance for accommodation and suggestions on where to dine. If you have internet access, or are planning your holiday from home, contact them at ✉info@ sapphirecoast.com.au, or visit the web page at 💻www.sapphirecoast. com.au

Tathra

Tathra is a quiet seaside village 18km (11 miles) east of Bega, with a beautiful beach and great fishing spots. Tathra offers the best of both worlds: beautiful beaches with ocean activities as well as the opportunity to explore the wildlife of nearby **Mimosa** and **Bournda National Parks.** There is a campground at **Bournda National Park** with very basic facilities for ✪$10-15 a night for two, ☎*6495 4130*. Tathra Tourist Centre on Tathra Wharf, Wharf Road, ☎*6494 4062,* is the best place to find out what you wish to know. The local people are very friendly and helpful.

Merimbula

This flourishing resort town on **Lake Merimbula** is 26km (16 miles) south of Bega. Merimbula is an activity-based centre, with surfing on Main Beach, Short Point and Tura Beach, sailboarding and water skiing on Lake Merimbula, golf at the 27-hole Pambula-Merimbula golf course, lawn bowls at the ubiquitous bowling clubs and a variety of other activities - tennis, canoeing, horseriding and

cycling. It has an RSL club with 'pokies' and live entertainment.

The **Magic Mountain Family Recreation Park**, with its water slides, mini Grand Prix race track and mountain toboggan slide, is just north of the town on *Coast Drive,* ☎*6495 2299.* The park ⏲opens at 10am and admission is ✪$22 adults.

The area also boasts an **Aquarium** (*Lake Street,* ☎*6495 4446),* **Yellow Pinch Wildlife Park** (Princes Highway, ☎*6494 9225),* **Milingandi Leisure Farm** (☎6495 6125) and a **Museum** in Main Street.

The Visitor Information Centre is on Beach Street, ☎6495 1129, ⏲open Mon-Fri 9am-5pm, Sat-Sun 9am-1pm. This is the place to get all the information on available accommodation, of which there is plenty.

Eden

Eden is situated some 61km (38 miles) south of Bega, on Twofold Bay. A former whaling station, it is now a deep water fishing port, and the fishing and timber industries are of utmost importance to the survival of the town.

The town's **Killer Whale Museum**, *94 Imlay Street,* ☎*6496 2094*, gives an overview of Eden's history, and houses the skeleton of 'Old Tom' a legendary whale from the area. Also featured is the **Seaman's Memorial Wal**l, commemorating those lost at sea. The museum has limited opening times daily.

The **Ben Boyd National Park** flanks Twofold Bay to the north, with its famous Red Cliffs, and borders historic Boyd's Tower to the south. You can camp in the park, and at East Boyd Bay the Forestry Commission runs the Edrom Lodge for students.

For more information on accommodation and things to do, contact the Eden Visitor Information Office, Princes Highway (at the round-about), ☎*6496 1953*. It is ⏲open Mon-Fri 10am-4pm, Sat-Sun 10am-noon.

Wonboyn Lake

The locals are proud of Wonboyn Lake, some 30km (19 miles) south of Eden, and surrounded by **Ben Boyd National Park** and **Nadgee Nature Reserve.** In addition to the stunning scenery of Ben Boyd and Nadgee, Wonboyn has a reputation for the finest lake fishing on the Sapphire Coast.

Australian Capital Territory

Canberra

Population 320,000
Canberra, in the Australian Capital Territory, is situated in the southern tablelands of New South Wales, 100km (62 miles) from the coast. It is 300km (186 miles) from Sydney, 654km (406 miles) from Melbourne, 1654km (1028 miles) from Brisbane, and 1201km (746 miles) from Adelaide.

Climate
Average temperatures: January max 28C (82F) - min 13C (55F); July max 11C (52F) - min -1C (30F). Average annual rainfall is 650mm (25 ins).

Characteristics
Canberra, Australia's national capital was founded in 1913. From its inception it has been developed as a garden city and is unique in that it was planned from the outset. In 1912, an American, Walter Burley Griffin, won first prize in a world-wide competition to design the new capital.

Since 1915, thousands of trees have been planted annually and the variation in the shades and colours of the leaves during spring and autumn leave a lasting impression. Over half of the city is parkland and open space dotted with picnic areas.

The Commonwealth Parliament did not sit in Canberra until 1927, when the provisional Parliament House was opened. The new Parliament House was completed in 1988, the Bicentennial Year.

How to Get There
By Air
Qantas, ☎ *13 1313*, **Virgin Blue** 13 6789 service Canberra with

their domestic lines, but you can check the availability of other regional flights with your agent.

By Bus

All the major coach companies have daily services from/to Sydney and Melbourne, and less frequent services from/to Adelaide, Brisbane, Wollongong, Cooma, Yass, Batemans Bay and Orange.

By Rail

Countrylink, ☎ 13 2232, has train services Sydney-Canberra three times a day.

From Melbourne there is no direct rail service to Canberra, but there are a few alternatives: train to Yass, then coach; train to Wodonga, then coach; train to Bairnsdale, then coach, ☎ 13 6196 or ☎ 13 1368.

By Car

From Sydney and Melbourne, via the Hume Highway. The trip takes just over 3 hours from Sydney and about 8 hours on a good run from Melbourne. To get around Canberra easily, you really need a car.

Visitor Information

The Canberra Visitor Information Centre can be found at *330 Northbourne Avenue* in Dickson, and it is ⏰Open 9am-5pm Mon-Fri and 8.30am-5pm on the weekend and public holidays.

Contact them on ☎ *(02) 6205 0044* or ☎ *1800 100 660*, or by email at ✉canberravisitorcentre @msn.com.au. You can browse through their web page at 💻www. canberratourism.com.au Another web site worth exploring is 💻canberra.citysearch.com.au

Canberra also has a Hire-A-Guide service which operates seven days a week, and can be contacted on ☎ *6288 7894* or visited at 4 Reveley Crescent, Stirling. The guides are available to individuals or coach parties.

↙ Let's Stay Here

The Tourist Centres have full details of accommodation in the city and suburbs, including apartments, cabins, on campus, hostels and farm stays.

Prices given here for hostels should be used as a guide only. The telephone area code is 02.

Canberra City Backpackers,

7 Akuna Street, ☎ *6257 3999,* 💻*www.canberrabackpackers.net.au* Voted Best Backpacker In Canberra 2002/03. Centrally located in the city and only minutes away from everything. Three floors of accommodation with each floor having it's own lounge room. Fantastic atmosphere. All rooms have lockers and key card access and very secured. Air conditioned. The facilities includes a kitchen, laundry, common rooms, TV rooms, indoor pool, the rare gym and internet access. There is an on site cafe and bar. Bike hire available. **Highly Recommended.** *Dorms from ✪$22; single $55; double $40pp; twin $35pp;*

Canberra City YHA Hostel,

191 Dryandra St, O'Connor, ☎*6248 9155,* 💻 *www.yha.com .au* Received a Canberra Tourism Award in 2001. Housed in 2 large buildings in a bush setting 3.5 kilometres from city centre, (about a 10 min bus ride). Located 1 km to nearest food store in a quiet suburb. Facilities includes large kitchens, laundry and iron, TV room, internet access and a barbecue area. There's also a nice balcony. There are many free attractions, just ask at the reception. Courtesy shuttle bus available. Take advantage of the bike hire to see the sites. On site parking available.
Dorms from ✪$19; double /twin from $55 BC MC VA EFTPOS

City Walk Hostel,

2 Mort Street, ☎*6257 0124,* 💻 *www.citywalkhotel.com.au* This is a budget hotel in the middle of town. It is above O'Malleys Pub in a great location just next to the bus depot. All with private facilities, kitchen, laundry, common room, mountain bike hire, lockers, linen supplied and internet. Cafe downstairs with a pub and an on site restaurant. *Dorm ✪$45 ($24 for two; double $60 (without bathroom)*

Girvan YHA Hostel,

36 Greys Lane, Girvan, ☎*4997 6639,* 💻*www.yha.com.au* This is your basic let-us-get-away-from-everything accommodation in the middle of nowhere. Nevertheless, it's nice and simple in a beautiful bush setting which used to be a school. Closest store is at Bulahdelah. No linen provided in rooms. Watch out for the pit toilets. Very basic facilities plus a barbecue area. Parking available. *Dorm ✪$13.50*

Canberra

Kingston, Canberra

Accommodation

1. Canberra City Backpackers
2. City Walk Hotel
3. Kingston Hotel
4. Victor Lodge

Kingston Hotel,
*73 Canberra Ave,
Kingston,* ☎*6295 0123*
Basic accommodation. The
only facility is a shared
kitchen. Situated above a pub
in a suburbian location close
to the train station. *Dorm from
✪$16.50 + $5.50 for extra
linen.*

Victor Lodge,
*29 Dawes Street, King-
ston,* ☎*6295 7777,*
🖳 *www.victorlodge.com.au*
Around 7 kms from the city
centre. Located in between
the Parliament House and
the train station at a quiet
residential area. 300m
to Kinsgton shops and
restaurants just at the back of
the hostel. Kept clean and the
rooms are non-smoking and
are fanned. Facilities includes
a fully equipped kitchen,
laundry, TV room with
cable, internet access and
a nice garden outside with
a barbecue area. Bike hire
available plus free maps. Free
pick-up and drop off service.
Off-street parking. *Dorm
✪$23 ; single $49; double/
twin $32.50pp;* (breakfast
included)

University Colleges have
accommodation available
out of term. The one
advantage here is that they
solely provide single room
accommdation. If you prefer
university halls of residence
you may prefer to stay here.
Fenner Hall is not on campus
but on the main thoroughfare
into the city. You may prefer to
stay there.

**ANU Student
Accommodation,**
*Bruce, Burton and Garran
Halls, Daley Road,* ☎*6267
4700, bandg.anu.edu.au*
ANU 2 kms from the city
centre. There are shared
bathrooms, communal
cooking facilities, meals
available, laundry facilities,
irons and tea/coffee making
facilities. *Dorms from ✪$50*

Others of a similar style are
Burgman Hall, ☎*6267 5222*
during the breaks at April,
July and September. *Bed and
Breakfast $55.*

**Caravan Parks
Canberra Motor Village,**
Kunzea Street, O'Connor,
☎*6247 5466.* (No pets
allowed), licensed restaurant,
barbecue, tennis, pool - *powered sites ✪$20 for two, cab-
ins $64-126 for two.*

**Canberra South Motor
Park,** *Canberra Avenue,
Symonston,* ☎*6280 6176.*
(No pets allowed), licensed
restaurant - *powered sites
✪$17-18 for two, cabins $45-
75 for two.*

**Canberra Carotel Caravan
Park,** *Federal Highway,
Watson,* ☎*6241 1377.* (No
pets allowed) - *powered sites
✪$12 for two, on-site vans
$33 for two.*

Let's Eat
Canberra's eateries cater for
all tastes and pockets, and the
Tourist Centres have complete
lists. Here are some budget food
places you may wish to try:

Ardeche, *cnr City Walk and
Ainslie Avenue, Canberra City,*
☎*6230 4800.*

Brindabella, *1 Binara Street,
Canberra City,* ☎*6274 5506.*

**Canberra Vietnamese
Restaurant,** *21 East Row,
Canberra City,* ☎*6247 4840.*

Great Wall, *113-119 Marcus
Clarke Street, Canberra City,*
☎*6247 5423.* Chinese food with
yum cha lunches and a take-away
option.

Lemon Grass, *71 London Circuit,
Canberra City,* ☎*6247 2279.*
Traditional Thai.

Rincon Latino, *5 Garema Place,
Canberra City,* ☎*6247 0840.*

Shogun, *70 Bunda Street,
Gareema Centre, Gareema Place,
Canberra City,* ☎*6248 8888.*
Traditional Japanese cooking with
sashimi and sushi.

Taj Mahal, *39 Northbourne
Avenue (upstairs), Canberra City,*
☎*6247 6528.* Indian dining.

Tasuke, *122 Alinga Street,
Canberra City,* ☎*6257 9711.*
Japanese selections.

Tu Tu Tango, *124 Bunda Street,
Canberra City,* ☎*6257 7288.*
Cafe and bar, woodfire pizzas a
specialty.

Zydeco, *173 City Walk, Canberra
City,* ☎*6248 8709.*

If you can't make up your mind
what you fancy to eat, take a trip
to **Glebe Park** in *Coranderrk
Street, Canberra City.* There

you will find eight food outlets - patisserie, hamburgers, refreshments bar, continental, Asian, Italian, carvery, seafood and bottle shop. The complex is open seven days, ☎*0412 626 7252*.

As in other cities, the Clubs offer good value for money, and welcome visitors. Some examples are:

Ainslie Function Centre in the **Ainslie Football Club**, *52 Wakefield Avenue, Ainslie,* ☎*6248 8422*, serves a Grand Seafood Buffet on Thursdays, but their extensive steak, seafood and salad menu should suffice on other days.

Canberra Workers Club Bistro, *cnr University Avenue and Childers Street, Canberra City,* ☎*248 0399,* have a budget-priced bistro.

The Canberra Club, *45 West Row, Canberra City,* ☎*6248 9000,* has French cuisine in their restaurant.

The Canberra Labor Club, Chandler Street, Belconnen, has an upmarket bistro at downmarket prices, ☎6251 5522.

KFC outlets are at *Shop B07, Bunda Street, Canberra City; Bengendore Street, Queanbeyan;* and *151 Canberra Avenue, Fyshwick.* **McDonald's** are found at the corner of *Badham Street and Dickson Place, Dickson; 20-24 Wanniassa Street, Queanbeyan; cnr Namatjira Drive done MacNalley Street, Weston.* **Pizza Hut** is in *Woolley Street, Dickson and the Kippax Centre, Holt,* ☎*13 1166* for delivery.

Something different
Belconnen Fresh Food Market, *Lathlain St,* ☎*6251 1680,* ⏲open 8.00am-6pm Wed-Sun with over 20 speciality shops from the organic to the prosaic. **Fyshwick Fresh Food Market** at the other end of town, *Cnr Canberra Ave and Mildura St,* ☎*6295 0606* open 8.00am-5.30pm Thurs-Sun.

Silo Bakery, *36 Giles St, Kingston,* ☎*6260 6060* selling excellent cheeses and pasteries.

Local Transport
Bus
Canberra has a public bus service, operated by Action Buses. The buses are large and orange and not easy to miss. The territory is divided into three zones, North, Central and South, and you will have to check your starting point against your destination to determine if you need a 'one zone' or 'all zone' ticket. The flat fares for adults are ♻$2 one zone and $4 all zone, but keep in mind that Faresaver tickets are available for extended use of this service.

Ticket agents can be found right across the area, and for more detailed information contact Action on ☎*13 17 10* or for timetable information, either ☎*6207 761*1 or visit the website at ▣www.action. act.gov.au

Bicycle
Otherwise you can hire a bicycle at the Youth Hostel, *Dryandra Street, O'Connor,* ☎*6248 9155;* or Mr Spokes, near the Acton Ferry, *Barrine Drive,* ☎*6257 1188*.

Car Rental
Avis, *17 Londsdale Street, Braddon,* ☎6249 6088; Thrifty ☎*1300 367 227*, Europcar ☎*1300131390* and Hertz ☎*13 30 39*. Using a car is a good idea in Canberra.

Organised Tour
Round About Tours, ☎*6262 8389;* Canberra Region Tours, ☎*6247 7281*; Grand Touring Coach Charter, ☎*6299 1600.*

Points of Interest
Canberra has five sign-posted Tourist Drives which take in most of the sights. Each begins at the **City Hill Lookout**, and three concentrate on the central area of Canberra, while the others take in the popular stops on the city outskirts and beyond. The Visitor Centre will give you detailed information on these Drives.

Three popular tourist attractions in Canberra are **Parliament House**, the **War Memorial** and the **National Library**.

Parliament House
Parliament House, in keeping with Walter Burley Griffin's original plan, is the central landmark of Canberra. The building took eight years to complete, and was opened in 1988. While some might not be taken with the 81m (266 ft) stainless steel flagpole that dominates the city, all have to agree that the interior of the building is magnificent. There are imposing marble columns and stairs, extravagant halls, outstanding collections of paintings, sculptures, photographs and ceramics and well-worked timber masonry. Two halls are open to the public. In the Great Hall hangs one of the largest tapestries in the world, based on a painting by Australian artist, Arthur Boyd, that has to be seen to be believed.

Public galleries overlook the **House of Representatives Chamber** at the eastern side of the building, and the **Senate Chamber** to the west. The colours of the decor in both chambers reflect the natural green and red tones in native Australian flora. Visitors are welcome to view the Chambers between ☉9am-5pm, and at all times when Parliament is sitting, even in the early hours of the morning. Guides are at key areas throughout the public areas of the building, and are happy to answer questions. There are also free guided tours available every 30 minutes. Facilities for visitors include a theatrette, an exhibition area, a post office, and on the first floor there is a cafeteria. The bookshop in the Foyer has many publications on Parliament and Parliament House, and a wide range of souvenirs. Pedestrian access is through the northern entrance, the side which overlooks the lake. Access to the underground carpark, which incidentally has room for 2000 vehicles, is via the ramps running off *Commonwealth Avenue* and *Kings Avenue*. Details on sitting hours of either of the Houses are available at the information desk in the foyer, or ☎6277 7111.

The **National Library,** *Parkes Place*, is on the southern shores of Lake Burley Griffin. It has over 6 million books, periodicals and newspapers, thousands of paintings, maps, films, photographs, music scores, oral histories, and treasures. Exhibitions are held throughout the year, and tours of the Library are available on weekdays. The Library is ☉Open every day except Good Friday and Christmas Day, and hours for the reading rooms, licensed bistro, shop and exhibition areas vary. For further information, ☎6262 1111.

Australian War Memorial, *Limestone Avenue, Campbell,* commemorates the Australians who gave their lives for their country. The stylised Byzantine building houses a collection of relics, paintings, models, displays and records from all theatres of war. Exhibitions cover the history of Australians at war from Gallipoli to Vietnam. There is a free carpark and picnic areas, a licensed kiosk, and a shop selling a comprehensive range of military books, prints, posters and model kits and souvenirs. The memorial is ☉Open daily 9am-4.45pm, ☎6243 4211.

The National Gallery opened in 1982 and houses the national art collection. Eleven galleries provide more than 7000 square metres (8372 sq yds) of exhibition space spread over three levels. Sculpture is displayed in the garden. Regular lectures, film screenings and guided tours are available, and there are frequent special exhibitions, including some from overseas. Facilities include a shop, restaurant and snack bar. ☉Open daily 10am-5pm, ☎6240 6502.

The **High Court of Australia**, *Parkes Place, Parkes*, is on the lake shore parallel to the Library. The building features extensive public areas, and is linked to the National Gallery by a pedestrian bridge. The three elegant courtrooms are open to the public. The court contains many interesting national murals and ceremonial plaques, and has a licensed cafeteria. ☉Open daily 10am-4pm. If you are in the mood for a meal, the Sufficient Grounds restaurant (☎6270 6820) can be found here - surely one of the most inventive theme names around!

Questacon, The National Science and Technology Centre, is located on the shores of Lake Burley Griffin, between the High Court and the Library. The Centre has over one hundred 'hands-on' exhibits, and visitors of all ages are entertained, intrigued and reassured about the science in our lives. Here you can experience an earthquake, operate a hovercraft, observe an active bee hive, and view a gallery of optical illusions, among other things. There is a cafe and science shop, and all are ☉Open daily 10am-5pm, ☎6270 2800.

Seventy countries have diplomatic representation in Canberra, and most of their Embassies are in the suburbs of Yarralumla, Forrest and Red Hill. Two have special exhibitions open to visitors: Papua New Guinea, *39-41 Forster Crescent,* ☎6273 3322 and Indonesia, *8 Darwin Avenue,* ☎6252 8600. Some embassies are open for public inspection on occasions during the year, and the Visitor Information Centre has the details, as well as a brochure on all the embassies, and their addresses. Some of the embassies are built in their traditional style, including India, Thailand, Indonesia and China, and perhaps this explains the cattle that graze on the lawns of the New Zealand High Commission.

Government House, *Dunrossil Drive, Yarralumla,* the official residence of the Governor General, is not open for inspection, but there is a good view of the building from a lookout on Lady Denman Drive, south of Scrivener Dam.

The Prime Minister's Lodge is on the corner of Adelaide Avenue and National Circuit, Deakin, but it is not open to the public either.

Weston Park, Yarralumla, on the shores of the Lake, has picnic areas and gas barbecues. Features include a miniature railway, a mouse house and a maze. The maze takes about 15 minutes to negotiate and is suitable for all ages. ☼Open weekends and public and school holidays 11am-6pm. Miniature train rides are available 10.30am-5pm, ☎6282 2714.

Lake Burley Griffin is named after Canberra's designer, American architect Walter Burley Griffin. The lake was formed in 1963 by the construction of Scrivener Dam to hold back the waters of the Molonglo River. Over 400ha (988 acres) of parkland has been developed around the 35km (22 miles) foreshore, with numerous picnic areas and sailing boat launchings (power boats are prohibited). Swimming spots can be found at Black Mountain Peninsula, Yarralumla Bay and Springbank Island. Boat hire and cruises are available at Acton Terminal in West Basin, take Barrine Drive off Commonwealth Avenue.

The relatively inaccessible wetlands in **East Basin**, between Jerrabomberra Creek and the Molonglo River, provide a sanctuary for a variety of bird life.

Although they appear tranquil, Canberra's lakes can be dangerous for small craft as wind gusts can attain a velocity of 25 knots. Weather bulletins issued by the media include wind forecasts, and boating enthusiasts should also heed orange spherical signals raised by water police, which indicate sailing conditions. The temperature of the water surface falls to 6.5C (44F) in winter, and obviously it is even colder below the surface, so this can also be a hazard.

The **Captain Cook Memorial Water Jet,** powered by two 560Kw motors, spurts a column of water 140m (459 ft) above central Lake Burley Griffin near Regatta Point. The jet and lakeshore Terrestrial Globe were built to mark the bicentenary of Captain Cook's discovery of eastern Australia in 1970. ☼Operating times are 10am-noon and 2pm-4pm, subject to weather conditions.

The **National Capital Exhibition** is at Regatta Point in Commonwealth Park, ☎6257 1068. There are audio-visual presentations, photographs and displays explaining the history and development of the Nation's capital. Regatta Point provides an excellent vantage point of Lake Burley Griffin, and from the observation area and terrace restaurant there are views of the Captain Cook Water Jet, the Lake's Central Basin, and the Parliamentary Triangle. The Planning Exhibition is ☼Open daily 9am-5pm, and there is a gift and book shop.

St John's Church and Schoolhouse, Constitution Avenue, Reid, were built in the 1840s, and are Canberra's oldest surviving buildings. The schoolhouse features relics of Canberra's early history, ☎6248 8399. St John's is still an active parish.

Blundells Cottage is on Wendouree Drive, off Constitution Avenue, Parkes, and has a museum display of family life from the nineteenth century. The cottage was built about 1860 by Robert Campbell, and was part of his Duntroon Estate. The first long-term occupants were William and Mary Ginn, and their daughter, Gertrude, was the first child born in the cottage. Mr Ginn was the head ploughman on the Duntroon Estate. The farm house was occupied for 100 years until Mrs Oldfield, the final occupant, passed away on September 8, 1958. The cottage is ☼Open Tue-Sun 10am-4pm, ☎6273 2667.

The Carillon, on Aspen Island, Lake Burley Griffin, Wendouree Drive, Parkes, is a three-column belltower, a gift from the British Government to mark Canberra's 50th jubilee. There are free 45 minute recitals in the afternoon daily, ☎6257 1068. The HMAS Canberra Memorial is nearby.

Royal Military College, Dun-troon, is Australia's first military college and was founded in 1911. Tours of the grounds are available at limited times, ☎6265 9537 for details.

Civic Square is the civic heart of Canberra. Canberra Theatre Centre is at the head of the square and the famous old merry-go-round is in nearby Petrie Plaza. The statue of **Ethos** is in the foreground, flanked by government offices.

The **National Philatelic Exhibition**, Alinga Street, on the first floor of the GPO building, ☎6209 1680, has a gallery featuring Australia's largest and most valuable collection of stamps, including sheets of

Australian stamps issued from Federation to the present.

The new, high-tech **National Museum of Australia** is on the *Acton Peninsula*, ☎*6208 5000*. It houses a vast and impressive collection in five permanent exhibitions and other temporary displays. Themes include First Australian's, Tangled Destinies, Nation and Eternity. An emphasis is placed on the unique people of Australia – historically and in the contemporary era. A visit to the museum is an interactive and immersive experience. There's plenty to see and do, with a range of engaging multimedia that means you'll probably come away learning something new. Plan to spend at least three hours exploring. A restaurant, cafe and shop are part of the complex. ☺Open 9am-5pm daily. Admission is free.

Scrivener Dam lookout is off Lady Denman Drive. Nearby is the **National Aquarium and Wildlife Park**, ☎*6287 1211*, with exhibitions of aquatic life, furry fauna and colourful birds. There is a walk-through oceanarium with sharks, rays, Barrier Reef fish, crocodiles, turtles and barracuda, though obviously not all in together. The complex also has a theatrette showing continuous films, a reasonably-priced Brasserie, seating 240 indoors and 300 outdoors, and a gift shop, all set in 5ha (12 acres) of landscaped grounds. It is ☺Open daily 10am-5.30pm and admission is ✪$12 adults.

The Royal Australian Mint, *Denison Street, Deakin*, is responsible for the production of Australia's circulating and collector coinage. The Mint

also manufactures medals and medallions, and supplies coinage for several overseas nations. There is a display of past and present Australian coins and old minting equipment, and the Coin Shop offers a wide range of collector's coins and associated products. Ample parking is available, and the grounds are perfect for a picnic. The Mint is ☺Open Mon-Fri 9am-4pm, Sat-Sun 10am-3pm, ☎*1300 652 020* or ☎*6202 6800*.

St Christopher's Catholic Cathedral, *55 Manuka Street, near Manuka Park*, ☎*6295 9555*, has a Byzantine flavour to it.

The **Free Serbian Orthodox Church**, *32 National Circuit, Forrest*, has vivid murals covering the walls and ceiling, the work of the late Karl Matzek, who painted them at the age of 87. The Church is not open to visitors on Sunday mornings, ☎*6295 1344*.

The **Telstra Tower** is on the summit of *Black Mountain*, ☎*6248 1911*, and from its lookout platforms, kiosk and restaurants, there are panoramic views of the whole region. **Black Mountain Drive**, the road to the Tower, runs off Clunies Ross Street, near the Botanic Gardens. Telstra Tower is ☺Open daily 9am-10pm, adults ✪$4, concession $2. The kiosk and coffee shop provide refreshments and light meals, but for something special, the revolving restaurant in the Tower offers international cuisine for lunch and dinner seven days a week, ☎6248 6162.

Australian National Botanic Gardens, also off *Clunies Ross Street, Black Mountain*, are devoted to growing Australian native plants and have over 6000 species. Special

features include the Rainforest Gully, Eucalypt lawn and the Rockery. The Visitor Centre has displays and leaflets on walks around the gardens, and there is a kiosk and bookshop. ☺Open daily, 9am-5pm, ☎6250 9540.

All Saints Anglican Church, *1 Bonney Street, Ainslie*, was for 80 years the mortuary railway station at Rookwood Cemetery, Sydney. It was re-erected here stone by stone as the Parish Church of Ainslie, and is ☺Open daily, with tour guides on duty, ☎6248 7420.

The Australian Institute of Sport, *Leverrier Crescent, Bruce*, was the training ground of many athletes who took part in the 2000 Olympic Games in Sydney. It has become a popular tourist destination, particularly in recent years. Some tours are led by the athletes themselves, and take the visitor through the modern facilities and sporting memorabilia, as well as provide an insight into gruelling training programs. Admission is ✪$10 adults, $5 children and $24 for families, ☎6214 1444.

Stromlo Observatory, *Cotter Road, Weston Creek* was destroyed by bushfires in early 2003 and is to be rebuilt. So no sightseeing here.

- Duntroon. Embassy inspections. October - **Octoberfest.** November - **Spring Show.**

Facilities

Special, clearly marked cycleways have been provided in Canberra to separate cyclists from other traffic. A map of the metropolitan cycleways is available from the Canberra Visitors Centre. Cycles can be hired for an hour or a day around the lake (see under Local Transport).

Windsurfers, catamarans and other sailing craft can also be hired (Lake Burley Griffin Boat Hire, Acton, ☎6249 6861).

The Visitor Information Centre has details of these and other sporting facilities, ☎1800 100 660.

Outlying Attractions
Gold Creek Road

The *Gold Creek Road*, a tranquil rustic setting embracing the historic **Ginninderra Village**, is only ten minutes' drive from Canberra City, following the Barton Highway. There are several interesting places to visit in the area.

Cockington Green, *11 Gold Creek Road, Nicholls,* is Canberra's piece of Great Britain, and has accurate one-twelfth scale model buildings spread in acres of colourful fairytale-like gardens. Other facilities include an outdoor kiosk, gas barbecues and picnic areas. ⊙Open daily, 9.30am-5pm. Admission is adults ✪$12.

Gems Gallery, is opposite *Cockington Green,* ☎6230 2740. The display in this museum is the largest presentation of Australian opals, and there is also a priceless collection of Aboriginal artefacts, some pieces being over 70 thousand years old. The cafeteria is open for meals daily, and there is an opal and souvenir shop. ⊙Open daily 9.30am-4.30pm.

Gold Creek Cultural Centre, *O'Hanlon Place,* has locally made crafts, Australian souvenirs, hand painted clothing, unique garden pots and other accessories from a variety of shops. ⊙Open daily 10am-5pm, ☎6241 8811.

Nearby is the **Ginninderra Gallery,** with paintings, pottery, wood-turnings, glassware and leather works, all with an Australian theme. ⊙Open daily 10am-5pm, ☎6230 2922.

National Dinosaur Museum, on the corner of the *Barton Highway, Gungahlin,* ☎6230 2655. The museum houses more than 300 exhibits, including full-scale skeletal replicas and astonishing prehistoric facts. It is ⊙Open daily 10am-5pm and admission is ✪$10 adults.

George Harcourt Inn is an 'old English' pub, where you can dine outdoors, or in winter, inside before the open log fire. ⊙Open daily from 11am for lunch, and closes at midnight Thu-Sat, an hour earlier during the rest of the week. For further information, ☎6230 2484.

Canberra Walk-in Aviary, *Federation Square, Gungahlin,* ☎6230 2044. Hundreds of bird finches can be viewed in this unique environment. ⊙Open daily 10am-4pm. Admission prices are ✪$6 adult.

Bywong
Historic Bywong Mining

Town is 33km (21 miles) north of Canberra, off the *Federal Highway, Millyn Road, Gearys Gap.* It is a gold mining village with areas classified by the Heritage Council. Guided tours of the village are available. ⊙Open daily 10am-4pm, ☎6236 9183.

Ginninderra Gorge and Falls

The Falls are in *Parkwood Road,* the continuation of Southern Cross Drive, West Belconnen (NSW). There are spectacular views of Ginninderra Gorge and the Falls, scenic nature trails, canoeing, picnic facilities and camping. ⊙Open daily 10am-5pm.

Cotter Dam

The source of Canberra's original water supply and first major construction work is located 22km (14 miles) west of the city, on *Cotter Road.* It is a very popular spot for picnics, camping and swimming in the river. There are playgrounds, a kiosk, shop, and licensed restaurant. ⊙Open daily.

Tidbinbilla Space Centre

Situated 40km (25 miles) south of Canberra, off *Paddys River Road,* still in the ACT, the space

Telstra Tower

Stained Glass, War Memorial

War Memorial

tracking station is one of three such facilities located around the world to provide complete 24-hour tracking coverage. The other two are in the United States and Spain. ⏱Open 9am-5pm, ☎6201 7838.

Tidbinbilla Nature Reserve

The Reserve is a wilderness area with marked trails and free-range wildlife enclosures, containing red and grey kangaroos, wallaroos, emus and water birds, and the occasional koala. The walking trails in the area are graded from easy to difficult, and you can walk 70m or 7km. The Reserve is off Paddys River Road and opens every day, except Christmas Day and days of total fire ban. At the Visitor Information Centre there are displays, audio visual presentations, literature and helpful staff who will answer your enquiries, ☎6205 1233. The Reserve is ⏱Open 9am-6pm daily, with extended hours in season, and are charged at ✪$9 per day for entry.

Corin Forest Recreation Area and Ski Facility

Corin Forest is off Tidbinbilla Road, Smokers Gap, a 30 to 40 minute drive from the city. It is home to Australia's longest bobsled/alpine slide (800m - 875 yds), which winds down through mountain forests, achieving a speed of up to 75km/h (47mph). During June through September, providing there is sufficient snow, there is skiing, ski hire and ski school, and snow tobogganing. ⏱Open every weekend 10am-5pm, and all school and public holidays. There is also a licensed restaurant. For further information, ☎6247 2250.

Lanyon Historic Homestead

In *Tharwa Drive*, off *Monaro Highway, Tharwa*. The Homestead is classified by the National Trust, and is set in landscaped gardens and parklands on the banks of Murrumbidgee River. In the early days it assumed the proportions of a self-contained village. There is a coffee shop, gift shop, and the **Sidney Nolan Art Gallery** is close by. ⏱Open Tues-Sun 10am-4pm, with 1 hour tours available, ☎6237 5136. ✪$6 adults.

Cuppacumbalong Craft Centre

Another historic property in *Naas Road, Tharwa*, featuring three cottages, nine out-buildings and a private cemetery. There are craft galleries, studios, a restaurant, and picnic and barbecue areas near the river. ⏱Open Wed-Sun and public holidays 11am-5pm, ☎6236 5116.

Queanbeyan

Although Queanbeyan is in New South Wales, it is virtually a suburb of Canberra, with a population of around 25,700. The town has plenty of accommodation, and generally the prices are lower than in Canberra. Many people find it worthwhile to stay in Queanbeyan, and drive the 12km (7 miles) into the city to commence their sightseeing. The Queanbeyan Visitor Information Centre, 1 *Farrer Place* (cnr Lowe Street), ☎(02) 6298 0241 or ☎1800 026 192, is ⏱Open Mon-Fri 8.30am-5pm, Sat 9am-1.00pm. The office has details of all accommodation, and also of tourist drives they have mapped for you to visit the interesting sights. You can

email them at ✉tourist@qcc. nsw.gov.au, or go to the web page at 🖥www.queanbeyan.nsw.gov.au

In **Farrer Place** there is a memorial commemorating the valuable work carried by the Father of the Wheat Industry, William James Farrer, and also the **Queanbeyan and District Historic Museum**. The museum is housed in the former police sergeant's residence, built in 1877, and has relics of early local families and items from pioneering days. There are also two rooms furnished in the style of the late 1890s. It is ⏱Open Sat-Sun 2-4pm, ☎6297 1978.

The Millhouse Gallery, *6 Trinculo Place*, was built in 1883 and restored and reopened in 1983. It is a unique building with rooms housing rare books, antique furniture and arts and crafts. The Gallery is ⏱Open Wed-Sun 10am-2pm, ☎6297 8181.

Lookouts in the area include **Bungendore Hill**, 4km east of the city, and Jerrabomberra, 5km west.

Googong Dam was built south of the town to supply water to Queanbeyan, and to supplement supplies to Canberra. The area is ⏱Open 8am-5pm and it is a good idea to drop into the Visitor Centre by the entrance for maps and recreational ideas, ☎6207 2779. Activities include canoeing, sailing, fishing and walking. Points of interest include **London Bridge Homestead,** a woolshed and shearer's quarters. The turnoff to the dam is about 10km along the Cooma Road.

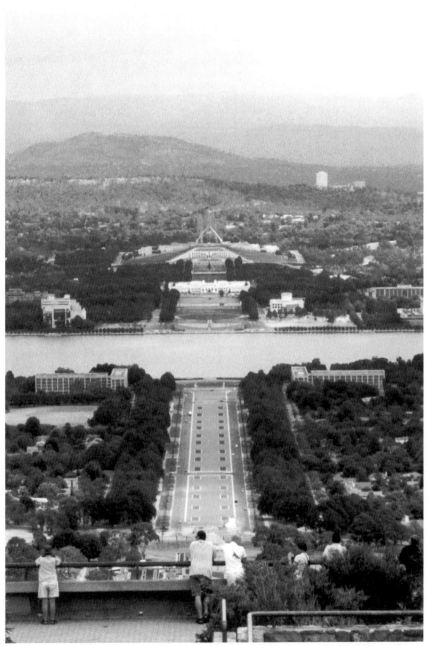

Canberra from viewing platform

Queensland

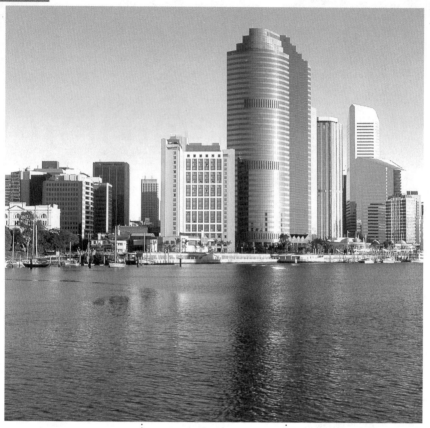

Brisbane

Population 1,637,000
Brisbane, the capital city of
Queensland, is situated on the
banks of the Brisbane River,
32km (20 miles) upstream from
Moreton Bay.
\

Climate
Average temperatures: January
max 30C (86F) - min 19C (66F);
July max 18C (64F) - min 6C
(43F). Average annual rainfall
- 1148mm (45 ins).

Characteristics
Brisbane, the capital of the
Sunshine State, is a major
international and interstate
gateway to an exciting hub of
tourism in the Pacific.

The sub-tropical city enjoys
an easy-going, relaxed lifestyle,
and offers the visitor a great
introduction to the holiday resort
destinations of the Gold Coast,
and the less developed Sunshine
Coast.

Just 20 minutes from the city
centre you can see (and hold)
koalas in their natural habitat at
Lone Park Koala Sanctuary or
watch sheep shearing at the Australian Woolshed. Brisbane Forest
Park, with its abundant fauna and
flora, not to mention rainforest, is
right on the doorstep. So too are
the islands of Moreton Bay - all
300 of them.

In the last decade, Brisbane has
turned to the river. Developments
like Southbank and The Riverside
Centre, famous for its popular
Sunday craft markets, Waterfront

Place, have changed the look of the city. A sightseeing cruise on the paddlewheeler, River Queen, is a highlight of any visit to the city.

How to Get There
By Air
As you would expect of a capital city, the Brisbane Airport is well-serviced.

International flights arrive direct from New Zealand, Asia and Pacific, Britain and Europe. North America is linked via Sydney and Auckland.

The domestic carrier **Qantas**, ☎ *13 1313* has direct flights from/to Australian capital cities and selected major regional towns. At present, **Virgin Blue**, ☎ *13 6789*, operates from eastern state capital cities only.

By Bus
Greyhound Pioneer, ☎ *13 2030*, and **McCaffertys**, ☎ *13 1499*, have the following return services: Brisbane/Sydney, Brisbane/Cairns with connections to Darwin and Alice Springs, and Brisbane/Melbourne.

By Rail
Queensland Rail, ☎ *13 2232*, operates a Traveltrain service that links destinations around the state. **Citytrains**, ☎ *131 230* run north from Brisbane to the Sunshine Coast and south to the Gold Coast. The **Queenslander** and **Sunlander** are two additional services connecting Brisbane to areas as far north as Cairns. The Capricornian links the capital city with Rockhampton.

From Sydney, **Countrylink XPT** trains run directly to Brisbane daily. Alternatively, you can take the XPT to Murwillumbah and change to a connecting coach to complete the journey.

From Melbourne, you must take a **Countrylink** train to Sydney and then change trains for the next leg of the trip.

Visitor Information
The Brisbane Visitor Information Centre is situated in the *Queen Street Mall*, ☎ *(07) 3006 6290*. It is ⊕open Mon-Fri 9am-5pm, Sat 9am-4pm, Sun 10am-4pm. Their email address is ✉enquiries@brisbane tourism.com.au and the website to visit is 🖥www.brisbanetourism.com.au

The Queensland Travel Centre, *30 Makerston Street*, ☎ *13 8833*, is ⊕open Mon-Fri 8.30am-5pm, Sat 9am-1pm. They can be emailed at ✉queensland@qttc.com.au or visited at the website 🖥www.tq.com. au

Tourism Queensland, *Level 36, Riverside Centre, 123 Eagle Street*, ☎ *(07) 3406 5400*, is ⊕open Mon-Fri 9am-5pm.

Two other internet addresses worth visiting are the Brisbane section of 🖥www.queensland-holidays .com.au or the local council website at 🖥www.brisbane.qld.gov.au

For Backpacker Budget Beaters, contact the Brisbane Visitor Information Centre. They offer a number of activities with reduced prices, such as ✪$10 return ferry to nearby North Stradbroke Island, where you can go bushwalking and dolphin spotting.

The newspaper, the **Courier-Mail** publishes a travel section every Friday, which details drives, picnic and camping spots.

Emergency telephone numbers:

Police, Fire Department, Ambulance - ☎ *000*; **Doctor - Travellers Medical Service** - ☎ *3211 3611*; **Police Station** - ☎ *3364 6464*.

The **Royal Automobile Club of Queensland** has a breakdown service, ☎ *131 111*.

Banks are ⊕open 9.30am-4pm Mon-Thu, and until 5pm on Fri. Major banks are represented by branches in the city centre, chiefly on *Queen* and *Adelaide Streets*.

The **Australian Foreign Affairs Department** is in the *Commonwealth Centre, 295 Ann Street*, ☎ *3225 0122*.

⤳ Let's Stay Here
Brisbane has a large range of accommodations. As with any large city, staying in the suburbs is often less expensive than in the city itself, and the Visitor Information Centres has a list of what is available.

Here we have a selection of budget accommodation with prices that should be used as a guide only. The telephone area code is 07.

Aussie Way Backpackers, *34 Cricket St, Petrie Terrace*, ☎ *3369 0711 or 1800 242 997*, 🖥 *www.backpacke rs.com.au* Situated behind Transit Centre and the food halls at Caxton St. You'll find it in a quiet residential street, in a small old colonial house. Newly renovated and good homely feel to it. All rooms have airconditioning and fans. Facilities includes a fully equipped kitchen, laundry, common room, TV lounge, internet access, a nice swimming pool and a barbecue

Brisbane

Accommodation

1. Aussie Way Backpackers
2. Banana Bender Backpackers
3. Brisbane Backpackers Resort
4. Brisbane City YHA
5. City Backpackers
6. Palace Backpackers
7. Roma Street Backpackers Travellers Hostel
8. Tinbilly Travellers
9. Yellow Submarine

Botanic Gardens

Parliament House and Annexe

Queensland University of Technology

Maritime Museum

Vulture Street

SOUTH BRISBANE

Southbank Parkland

Old Conservatorium of Music

Performing Arts Complex

Brisbane Convention and Exhibition Centre

Plaza

Musgrave Park

WEST END

State Library

Art Gallery

Museum

South Brisbane

River

Brisbane

Victoria Bridge

Captain Cook Bridge

William Street

Alice Street

Margaret Street

Mary Street

Charlotte Street

Elizabeth Street

Albert Street

George Street

Queen Street

Quay

Grey Street

Melbourne Street

Cordelia Street

Merivale Street

Russell Street

Browning Street

O'Connell Street

Montague Rd

Hope Street

Vulture Street

Colchester Street

Ernest St

Grenier St

Stanley Street

River

NORTH

0   200   400 metres

m Jolly Bridge

area. There is also a balcony that overlooks the street. Airport Shuttle and parking available. *Dorms ○$24; single $36; double/twin $50*

Balmoral House,

33 Amelia St, Fortitude Valley, ☎3252 1397, 💻www.que enslandholidays.com.au/ brisbane/508167/index.cfm Located not far from the city centre and close to the shops of Fortitude Valley. Two storey cavity brick building set in an industrial area but rebuilt and upgraded to true classic 1930's style restoration. Features a fully equipped kitchen, internet access, TV lounge and a yard outside. Airport shuttle bus available. *Dorms ○$16; double $38*

Banana Bender Backpackers,

118 Petrie Terrace, Petrie Terrace, , ☎3367 1157 or 1800 241157, 💻www.bananabenders.com All rooms are fanned. Facilities includes a fully equipped kitchen,TV room, internet access, pool table and a barbecue area. There is also a bar on site, a tropical garden and a number of balconies. Enquire about the 'Job Club' for those looking for employment. During the hot seasons, there is also free entry to the local pool. An airport shuttle service is also available. *Dorms from ○$21; double/twin $50*

Brisbane Backpackers Resort,

110 Vulture St, West End, , ☎3844 9956 or 1800 626 452 Situated at the South of

Brisbane close to cafes and restaurants, but a fair walk to the city centre which isn't too too far. Southbank beach is also close by. Large hostel with rooms having their own en suite bathrooms, TV and fridge and some open into a balcony. Features a basic kitchen which has limited equipments. There's also laundry facilities, swimming pool and sauna and a tennis court. On site bar and restaurant with pool tables and large screen TV and offer cheap meals. Parking available. *Dorms from ○$17; double/twin from $48*

Brisbane City YHA,

392 Upper Roma Street, ☎3236 1004, Located in the heart of Brisbane, Brisbane City YHA is modern, boutique-style accomodation hostel. All the rooms are air conditioned, and there are kitchen and laundry facilities available for guests. There are personal lockers, secure luggage storage, internet access and a reading room. Brisbane City also has its own restaurant, where you can indulge in their cuisine. *Adult ○$19-23, double/twin $24-$26 ($34 ensuite)*

City Backpackers,

380 Upper Roma Street , ☎3211 3221, or 1800 062 572, 💻www.citybackp ackers.com With fantastic river and city views, City Backpackers offers free pickup from Brisbane Transit Centre, state of the art security monitoring, onsite party pub and job assistance. There are

kitchen and laundry facilities, a TV common room with cable, a rooftop swimming pool and private rooftop sundeck and security deposits. Linen is provided and the friendly staff are available 24 hours a day. *Dorm ○$16; single $40; double/twin$48*

Globetrekkers,

35 Balfour St, New Farm, ☎3358 1251, 💻www.globetrekkers.net Smallest backpackers' hostel in a 100 year old house in Brisbane. Located not far from the shops of Brunswick St and the cliffs above the Brisbane River. Conveniently close to everything else too. Get the ferry ino town. Serene and homely atmosphere. Rooms have polished wooden floors,fans and furnished. All womens dorm available with en suite and verandahs. Features a small kitchen, laundry, small library, TV lounge room and internet access. There's also a nice swimming pool outside. Free pickup and delivery from the Brisbane Bus Transit Center available plus parking. *Dorms ○$19; single $35; double/twin $44 (from $40 with ensuite)*

Homestead,

57 Annie St, New Farm, ☎3358 3538 Located close to the New Farm Village shops. Well known to working backpackers. Includes your basic kitchen, TV lounge, pool table and an internet access. Parking available. *Dorms ○$16; single $35; double/twin $42*

Moreton Bay Lodge

45 Cambridge Pde, Manly, ☎ *3396 3020,* ▤ *www.mo retonbaylodge.com.au/#* Ideally located in the heart of harbourside Manly on the coast, near cafes, bars and restaurants and the supermarket. Ferries to the islands of Moreton Bay is also close by. This is a renovated 100 year old building that has loads of character and a lively atmosphere. Features kitchen, laundry, TV lounge. The harbour view from the balcony is spectacular. There is also bike hire from the information centre. Free rail and airport pickup and parking availale. **Recommended**. *Dorms* ✪ *$19; double/twin from $45*

Palace Backpackers,

Cnr Ann Street and Edward Street, ☎ *3211 2433 or 1800 676 340,* ▤ *www.palacebac kpackers.com.au* Located at the heart of Brisbane, Palace Backpackers offers free luggage storage, free courtesy bus, free linen and free use of the barbecue. Each room has a lockable cupboard, mirror and hooks for clothing. Some rooms have direct balcony access while others have direct roof access. There are kitchen and laundry facilities, internet access, wheelchair access available, TV room with cable TV and state of the art fire detection system. *Dorms from* ✪ *$21; single $36; double $48; twin $26*

Prince Consort Hotel

230 Wickham Street, Fortitude Valley, ☎ *3257 2252 or 1800 225 005,* ▤ *www.nomadsworld.com* Located in the hub of Brisbane's nightlife, Prince Consort Hotel is a historic Queenslander style hostel. It boasts free drinks, linen and tea and coffee and has 24 hour internet access, laundry and kitchen facilities and a full entertainment system. Prince Consort Hotel also has an on site bottle shop and games room and an inhouse English pub and restuarant. *Dorms from* ✪ *$15.50; single $48; double/twin $48 (double with A/C $52); triple $22pp*

Reef O,

14-20 Constance St, Fortitude Valley, ☎ *1800 173 336* Located close the shops and food halls in Fortitude Valley and a fair walk to the city centre. Newly renovated and freshly painted. Features a small kitchen, laundry, TV lounge room and an internet access. There is also an on site bar and restaurant that serves cheap all-you-can-eat meals. Great value for your money. *Dorms from* ✪ *$10; double $40*

Somwhere to Stay

Cnr Brighton Road and Franklin Street, West End, ☎ *3846 2858 or 1800 812 398,* ▤ *www.somewheretostay.com .au* This delightful, family-run business boasts an old style Queenslander house with a beautiful garden and saltwater pool with shaded deck. Most of the rooms have an ensuite, fridge and TV and linen is supplied. Located at the top of a hill, Somewhere To Stay has fantastic views of Brisbane city and when night falls, the hostel is lit up by fairylights. There is a BBQ, kitchen facilities, internet access, job assistance and a tour desk. You can simply relax on one of the reclining chairs, or explore the city via the free hourly bus that will take you there. **Recommended**. *Dorms* ✪ *$18; private room from $19.50-25*

Tinbilly Travellers,

462 George St. ☎ *1800 446 646,* ▤ *www.nomads world.com* Located centrally, directly opposite Roma Street Transit Centre and blocks away from the Queen Street Mall. This is a newly built backpackers hostel with immaculate facilities. All rooms have en suite and are airconditioned. Features a kitchen, laundry, TV lounge room and internet access. The ground floor has on site bar and restaurant plus a tour booking office. **Recommended**. *Dorms from* ✪ *$20; double/twin $37pp; deluxe king bed $42pp*

Yellow Submarine,

66 Quay St, Petrie Terrace, ☎ *3211 3424,* ▤ *www.bpf.com.au/yellow_ submarine.htm* Three story historic house with a nautical theme and brightly painted. Just 15 minutes walk from Transit Centre. Set in tropical gardens with a swimming pool, covered outdoor area and BBQ's. There's also a small fully equipped kitchen, laundry, TV lounge, common rooms with pool tables and internet access. Very friendly, helpful staff offer work assistance and tour advice. Airport bus comes to the door with free pick-up. It'd be advisable to book ahead especially during peak season. **Recommended.** *Dorms from* ✪*$20; double/twin $48*

Caravan Parks
Colonial Village Motel, *351 Beams Road, Taigum,* ☎*3865 0000.* Licensed restaurant, tennis, pool - *powered sites* ✪*$20 for two, cabins $55-65 for two.*

Sheldon Motel and Caravan Park, *27 Holmead Road, Eight Mile Plains,* ☎*3341 6166.* Pool, barbecue - *powered sites* ✪*$16 for two, cabins $55 for two.*

Gateway Village, *200 School Road, Rochedale,* ☎*3341 6333.* 148 sites, barbecue, pool, playground, recreation room - *powered sites* ✪*$24 for two, villas $85-100 for two.*

Durack Gardens Caravan Park, *758 Blunder Road, Durack,* ☎*3372 7300.* Tennis, pool, barbecue - *powered sites* ✪*$17 for two, on-site vans $25 for two, cabins $45 for two.*

Local Transport
Bus
Bus routes and timetables can be downloaded from the 🖥www. transinfo.qld.gov.au webpage, or you can phone ☎*13 12 30* (interstate callers: ☎*07 3215 500).*

As a basic guide, the **CityCircle** bus (333) is blue and white, and travels around the centre of the city frequently. The white and yellow Citybuses service the city

and suburbs, with many stops in between. Buses with blue and yellow stripes are the Cityxpress buses, which have express routes every half hour from designated stops. Buses to most suburbs leave from the city terminal. Day Rover tickets are available for ✪$8, entitling you to unlimited trips on all public buses, ferries and **City Cats.** Fare saver cards are also available. Buses to the Redcliffe Peninsula operate daily from outside the Transit Centre.

The City Sights tour is designed to familiarise visitors with the city so that they have an idea about what's on offer and can decide for themselves the places where they would prefer to spend some time. The tour costs ✪$20 and includes unlimited travel on buses and **CityCats** on the same day. Phone ☎*13 12 30* for more details.

Train
The new **Airtrain** now operates from Brisane Airport to the Gold Coast, stopping at Brisbane Central and Roma stations. For information, ring Transinfo ☎*13 12 30,* interstate ☎*3215 5000,* or visit the website at www.transinfo.qld.gov.au

A suburban train service operates regularly throughout the city. The main city centre stations are Roma Street at the Brisbane Transit Centre, Central (next to the Sheraton Hotel on *Turbot Street*), and Brunswick Street Station in Fortitude Valley. For information, visit the same website listed above or call Transinfo on ☎*13 12 30.*

Ferry
Regular commuter services operate daily on the Brisbane River. For details and **City Cat**

and **City Ferry** timetables, explore the website mentioned above or phone ☎*13 12 30.*

Taxi
Taxis may be hailed in the street, engaged at taxi stands, or at the front of the big city hotels, or you can book by phone. Two companies are: **Yellow Cabs,** ☎*13 1924* and **Black and White Cabs,** ☎*13 1008.*

Car
Car hire companies are:

Avis, ☎13 6333; Budget Rent A Car, ☎13 2727; Thrifty Car Rental, ☎3252 5994; Abel Rent A Car, ☎13 14 29; Hertz, ☎13 30 39.

There are many parking stations in and around the city, and the Visitor Information Centre has a full list.

Let's Eat
City centre restaurants, riverside bistros and off-the-beaten-track food halls provide a host of different menus from around the globe.

Queensland's famous mudcrabs are always a favourite with locals and visitors alike, as are the not-so-famous Moreton Bay Bugs, which are a cross between a lobster and a crab. Tropical fruits also feature prominently on most menus.

The Tourist Bureau has a full list of restaurants, both in the city and in the suburbs, but here are some you might like to try.

Big Fortune, *Shop 8, Merthyr Road, New Farm,* ☎*3358 6633.* Chinese restaurant also serving laksas and noodles. It is BYO and open for lunch and dinner 7 days.

Brisbane

Captain Cook Bridge, Brisbane

Blu Poles, *6a, 110 Macquarie Street, Teneriffe,* ☎*3257 2880.* Licensed restaurant offering an interesting and unusual menu, such as corn-fed duck livers. Lunch Wednesday to Sunday and dinner every day except Sunday.

Captains Cove, *44 Ferry Street, Kangaroo Point,* ☎*3891 6644.* River views, interesting menu, breakfast daily, dinner Monday to Saturday.

Cha Cha Char Grill, *Eagle Street Pier,* ☎*3211 9944.* Licensed restaurant, open for lunch and dinner, serving beef in all its forms for steak-lovers.

Fujiyama, *cnr Ann and Duncan Streets, Fortitude Valley,* ☎*3252 3275.* Traditional Japanese.

George's On Wickam, *256 Wickam Street, Fortitude Valley,* ☎*3854 1198.* Thai and Filipino cuisine.

Gertie's, *699 Brunswick Street, Fortitude Valley,* ☎*3358 5088.* Licensed restaurant set in an area with a European atmosphere. Modern flavours are the focus.

Govinda's, *99 Elizabeth Street,* ☎*3210 0255.* Vegetarian fare. Green Papaya, 898 Stanley Street, East Brisbane, ☎3217 3599. Vietnamese menu.

King Ahirim, *88 Vulture Street, West End,* ☎*3846 1678.* Lebanese selections.

Mirch Masala, *95 Turbot Street,* ☎*3220 0377.* Indian food.

Pancakes at the Manor, *18 Charlotte Street,* ☎*3221 6433.*
Enjoyable family dining, inexpensive meals of a good quality. Licensed and open 24 hours.

Romeo's, *216 Petrie Terrace,* ☎*3367 0955.* Award-winning traditional Italian restaurant with a Venetian emphasis. The interesting menu includes pastas, meats and seafood.

Rosie's Tavern, *235 Edward Street, City,* ☎*3229 4916.* International cuisine, moderate prices, open for lunch and dinner Mon-Sat.

Summit, *Sir Samuel Griffith Drive, Mt Coot-tha,* ☎*3369 9922.* Claims the best views over Brisbane, from the Mt Coottha Lookout. Licensed, Modern Australian cuisine. Open for lunch and dinner, brunch on Sundays. The Kuta Cafe and Kuta Gift Shop are nearby. Open daily.

Vroom, *Shop 1, cnr James and Doggett Streets, Fortitude Valley,* ☎*3257 4455.* This original Italian cafe is perfect for a light snack or meal.

Wang Dynasty, *Ground Level, Riverside, South Bank,* ☎*3844 8318.* Most Asian styles are represented, including Chinese, Thai, Japanese and Singaporean, but there are a couple of surprises, like crocodile and kangaroo. It is open for lunch and dinner seven days, and has views of the river and parklands nearby.

Also, keep in mind **Cafe 21** at the Treasury Casino for a cheap breakfast. You can get yourself a hot-and-hearty meal for less than ten dollars, which may be all you
can scrape out of your pocket after an unlucky night in the gaming rooms next door.

McDonalds have branches in *Queen, Albert (2), Ann, Eagle, Edward and Roma Streets,* as well as many outlets further afield. **KFC** is in *Roma, Albert and Eagle Streets,* and adjoining areas. **Pizza Hut** is on the corner of *Queen Street Mall and Albert Street,* ☎*3221 0199.*

Entertainment
Cinemas
Myer Centre Cinemas, *cnr Albert and Elizabeth Streets, City,* ☎*3221 4199.*

Village Twin Cinema, *701 Brunswick Street, New Farm,* ☎*3358 2021.*

Hoyts Regent Entertainment Centre, *167 Queen Street, City,* ☎*3229 5544.*

Hoyts - Southbank Cinemas, *Grey Street, South Bank,* ☎*3844 4222.*

Dendy Cinemas, *346 George Street,* ☎*3211 3244.*

IMAX, *cnr Ernest and Grey Streets,* ☎*3844 4222.*

Theatres
Arts Theatre, *210 Petrie Terrace, City,* ☎*3369 2344.*

Brisbane Entertainment Centre, *Melaleuca Drive, Boondall,* ☎*3265 8111.*

Festival Hall, *65 Charlotte Street, City,* ☎*3229 4250.*

Cremorne Theatre, *at the Performing Arts Complex,* ☎*13 62 46.*

Princess Theatre, *8 Annerley Road, Woolloongabba,* ☎*3891 3800.*

Queensland Cultural Centre, *South Bank,* ☎*3840 7100.*

Metro Arts Theatre, *109 Edward*

Street, ☎ *221 1527.*

Queensland Theatre Company, *Stanley Street, South Brisbane,* ☎ *3840 7000.*

Opera Queensland, *114 Grey Street, South Bank,* ☎ *3875 3030.*

Programmes for the above can be found in the entertainment pages of the daily newspapers, **The Courier-Mail** and **The Sun.**

Shopping

Whether you're after a souvenir, a gift for someone special, or just feel like shopping for yourself, Brisbane's malls, markets and arcades offer a cornucopia of good buys. There are nine city centre shopping arcades housing national department stores, specialty stores, Australiana and all sorts of welcome refreshment stops.

Shopping hours are:
City - ☺Mon-Thurs 9am-5.30pm, Fri 9am-9pm, Sat 9am-5pm, Sun 10.30am-4pm.
Suburbs - ☺Mon-Fri 8.30am-5.30pm, Sat 8.30am-4.30pm, Thurs 8.30am-9pm.

City Shopping

If you feel that a shopping tour might best overcome your unfamiliarity with the city's commercial centres, **The Brisbane Shopping Spree Company**, *2 Sheppard Street,* ☎ *3289 3367,* offer a service that stops at bargain factory and warehouse outlets in the Brisbane area. They have included a buffet lunch at the Mt Coottha lookout.

Queen Street Mall. This colourful, lavish, modern and entertaining pedestrian mall contains more than 500 specialty shops, and is the premier shopping venue in Brisbane city. The department stores on the mall

are David Jones and Myer, and there are a number of banks, fast cash services, buskers, flower sellers, and plenty of chances for alfresco eating. The mall stretches between *George and Edward Street*s.

Wintergarden on the Mall. A three-storey complex housing a number of specialty shops, a food fair and five levels of parking. The emphasis here is on fashion. It extends from *Queen Street* to *Elizabeth Street* under the **Hilton Hotel.**

Myer Centre. The vast Myer Centre joins *Queen, Elizabeth and Albert Streets*, and has been designed to reflect the Victorian age. It has six shopping levels with 200 stores, and houses the national department store, Myer, as well as numerous specialty shops, restaurants, delicatessens and cinemas.

Rowes Arcade. The arcade is a mixture of old and new, with the restored cedar panelling of the *Edward Street* end and the contemporary *Adelaide Street* entrance, though it seems to have fallen on hard times in recent years. Two shopping levels contain up-market boutiques and designer wear outlets, and a very good coffee shop. The arcade runs towards Post Office Square.

Post Office Square. Located opposite Anzac Square, and joining *Adelaide and Queen Streets* with an entrance to Rowes Arcade, Post Office Square has specialty shops, bookshops, coffee shops, delicatessens and a restaurant. Underground parking is available.

Riverside Centre. Situated on *Eagle Street*, in the centre of Brisbane's financial district, Riverside is set back from the Brisbane River and has up-market restau-

rants and designer boutiques.

Brisbane Arcade. This turn-of-the-century, heritage-listed arcade is full of up-market clothing and gift shops. It runs from Queen Street Mall to *Adelaide Street.*

T and G Arcade. Halfway up Queen Street Mall is the T and G Arcade, whose shops specialise in designer fashions, shoes and accessories, jewellery, fine silver, ceramics, glassware and antiques.

Other Shopping Centres in the City

Chopstix. Located in the heart of Brisbane's Chinatown, Fortitude Valley, this food and retail emporium is for lovers of the Orient, with specialty shops, kitchens and restaurants.

Paddington. Only 3km from the city centre, Latrobe and Given Terraces are home to a collection of restored colonial buildings housing boutiques, cottage crafts centres, galleries, Australiana specialists and restaurants.

Savoir Faire. An up-market shopping and eating experience on *Park Road, Milton*, ten minutes from the city centre. The shopping area features boutiques, open air restaurants, coffee shops and underground parking.

Suburban Shopping

Out of town there is even more shopping, with eight major everything-under-one-roof shopping centres, each featuring large department stores and a variety of specialty shops. The Brisbane City Council operated **'Great Circle Line'** is the easiest way of getting to these centres.

Markets

Riverside Markets, *Riverside Centre, Eagle Street, City, 3833*

2400 - ☉open every Sunday 8.15am-3pm.
"McWhirters" Marketplace, *cnr Wickham and Brunswick Streets, City -* ☉*open daily.* Southbank Markets, Friday nights, Saturday and Sunday.

Points of Interest

The city centre is best seen on a walking tour, and the **Brisbane Transit Centre**, slightly to the northwest of your city, or your hotel are good places to start. It was opened in mid-1986 and is an integrated coach and railway terminal in Roma Street. The train service from Sydney comes right to the city centre at Roma Street Station, from where all the long distance country trains leave. The suburban electric trains also leave from here, as well as interstate, intrastate and local buses. There are also long and short term car parks, taxi ranks, a hotel, commercial offices, shops and a Visitor Information office (**☎***3236 2020*). Queensland has an electric train service from Brisbane through Gladstone, Rockhampton, and inland to its central **Queensland Coal Fields**.

The newly opened **Roma Street** parklands have been built on the site of the old railway yards. You can enjoy several self-guided walks past the lake, over bridges, through palm forests and formal gardens.

It is a leisurely stroll from the Transit Centre, of some 15 minutes, to **King George Square** and **City Hall**. This imposing building is a combined cultural and community centre. An excellent view of the city can be obtained from the clock tower, but try to avoid being up there at noon, as it gets very noisy. Also facing the square is the **Albert**

Street Uniting Church, dwarfed by the high rise office blocks around it. The church is in the Gothic revival style in red brick and white sandstone, and was opened in 1889.

Around the corner in *Ann Street* is the **Ann Street Presbyterian Church** which was opened in 1872. Continue along *Ann Street* and you will come to **Anzac Park and the Flame of Remembrance,** opposite Central Station. Walk down the stairs and through the park, across *Adelaide Street,* through the **Post Office Square** shopping complex, and you will come to the **GPO in Queen Street**, **☎***3405 1202*. There is a **Postal Museum** on the first floor which is ☉open Tues-Thurs 10am-3pm, and Mon-Fri during school holidays. Beyond the Post Office you come to St Stephen's Catholic Cathedral set in grounds on *Elizabeth St*. Mass at 8am, 10: 30am and 5:30pm on Sunday.

Walking west along **Queen Street Mall.** At the end you come to the former **Treasury** building (now facilitating the Casino) near Victoria Bridge. It is built around a central courtyard in Italian Renaissance style. Turn left into *William Street*, and head south for just over one hundred metres. On your right you will see the **Commissariat Stores,** now the site of the Royal Historical Society. This building is one of only two that were built for the initial settlement and still stand today. Continue along *William Street* until you reach the French Renaissance style **Parliament House**, whose ceremonial frontage overlooks the **Botanic Gardens**. After all that walking, the gardens will provide a spot for rest and recuperation, as well as a view of the **Captain**

Cook and Story bridges. Or you can continue your walk over the newly-built **Goodwill Bridge** to **Southbank Parklands** and the **Maritime Museum.**

Other attractions:
The **Old Windmill Observatory**, was built as a windmill in 1829 by convict labour. It is the other legacy of the first settlement on Wyndham Terrace.

The **Queensland Sciencentre,** *110 George Street,* **☎***3220 0166,* takes visitors through the weird world of science.

Queensland Art Gallery and **Queensland Museum,** are on Southbank. Head south, and there's the **Queensland Cultural Centre.** The 1988 World Expo, held on the south bank of the Brisbane River, saw the completion of the **Queensland Cultural Centre.** The Centre houses the Performing Arts Complex, and the annexed Art Gallery, Library and Museum. The **Art Gallery**, **☎***3840 7303*, has an extensive collection of Australian art from colonial times to the present. The **Performing Arts Complex**, **☎***3840 7444*, is ☉open daily 10am-5pm, and until 8pm on Wednesday. **The Museum** takes the visitor from the prehistoric age of dinosaurs up to Australia's colonial history, and is open daily, **☎***3840 7555*.

The **South Bank Parklands** have restaurants, cinemas, parklands, markets, subtropical gardens, lagoons, park areas, sightseeing attractions and Australia's only inland city beach (**Breaka Beach**), sprawl over 16 hectares. **Queensland Maritime Museum**, has on display a number of impressive vessels from varying eras. **☎***3844 5361*.

Gold Coast

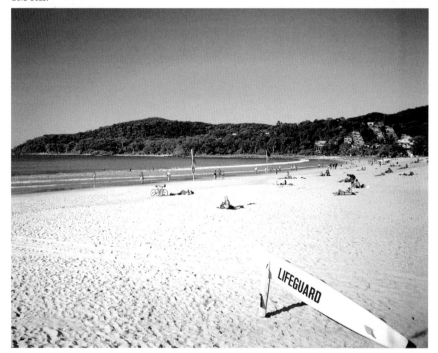

Sunshine Coast

Brisbane River is spanned by five bridges, all of which have a unique architectural style and are worth seeing - the **Story Bridge, the Captain Cook Bridge, the Victoria Bridge, the William Jolly Bridge** and **the Goodwill Bridge**.

Gateway Bridge, links the city with the Gold Coast and the Sunshine Coast.

Kookaburra River Queen. One of Brisbane's most popular attractions, on a paddlewheeler with great views of the city and its bridges. Phone ☎3221 1300 for bookings and departure times.

City Cat Cruises takes you along the 19km length of the Brisbane River in 2 hours. Information can be acquired and tickets purchased from the Council Customer Service outlets, lower ground level of the Brisbane Administration Centre, *69 Ann Street*, or TC Beirne Centre, *Brunswick Street Mall,* or at Embarkation Point on Eagle Pier.

Suburban Attractions
The Southern Cross, Sir Charles Kingsford Smith's plane, is preserved in a glass-walled building off Airport Drive at Brisbane Airport. Admission is free and the display is open daily.

New Farm Park has almost 12,000 rose bushes and a Jacaranda and Poinciana avenue. Like the Botanic Gardens, it is situated on the riverbank, and although it can be reached by bus, a more scenic way to visit is by the City Cat Ferry. For ferry times, contact Transinfo, ☎*13 12 30.*

The **Mt Coottha Botanic Gardens** are only ten minutes' drive from the city, and have a large collection of Australian native plants, tropical plants, an arid-zone area and tropical plant display dome, ⊙open daily 8am-5.30pm. **The Sir Thomas Brisbane Planetarium** in the gardens is the largest in Australia. There is also a Japanese Garden, a Fragrant Plants and Herb Garden, and Australian rainforest. The picnic area at the top of Mt Coottha is a popular stop for a panoramic view of the city, day or night.

Lone Pine Koala Sanctuary, *Jesmond Road, Fig Tree Pocket,* ☎*3278 1366*, shouldn't be missed. It is situated on the banks of the river, and is best reached by boat - the Mirimar Boat Cruise departs from North Quay daily at 10am, ☎*3221 0300*. The Sanctuary is Australia's oldest, and also has a variety of native animals, reptiles and birds. It is ⊙open daily 7.30am-4.45pm, and admission is ❍$14 adults.

Temple of the Holy Triad, *cnr Park and Higgs Streets, Breakfast Creek,* is an historic Chinese Temple built in 1885, ☎*3262 5588*. The pillars of the building were set crookedly as a reminder to all that nothing in life is perfect.

Miegunya, *31 Jordan Terrace, Bowen Hills,* was built in 1884, and is a good example of colonial architecture. It is dedicated to the pioneering women of Queensland.

Newstead House in Newstead Park, *Breakfast Creek Road, Newstead,* ☎*3216 1846* or ☎*1800 061 846*, is Brisbane's oldest surviving residence. It is on the banks of the river near its junction with Breakfast Creek, and is ⊙open Mon-Fri 10am-4pm, Sun 2-5pm.

The **Queensland University** at *St Lucia*, ☎*3365 1111*, is almost completely surrounded by the river, and has spacious parklands and sandstone buildings which are joined by sheltered walkways called The Cloisters. They are decorated with carvings of other universities' coats of arms, sculptures and grotesque faces and animals. Worth a visit if you are into varsity ambience and style.

Alma Park Zoo, *Alma Road, Dakabin,* ☎*3204 656*, features Australian and exotic fauna, tropical gardens, picnic and barbecue facilities. There are regular feeding times for a variety of animals. It is ⊙open daily 9am-5pm. Admission is ❍$20 adults. The zoo is located 28km (17 miles) north of Brisbane and takes about half an hour to reach.

Licoriceland, *21 Jijaws Street, Sumner Park,* ☎*3376 6945*, is Queensland's only licorice factory. It is ⊙open 9.30am-3.30pm Mon-Fri, except in January when it is closed to visitors. Tours are available, and there is also a sweet shop selling samples.

The **Australian Woolshed,** *148 Samford Road, Ferny Hills,* ☎*3872 1100*, is a wonderful experience for people who don't have time to visit the great Aussie Outback. You can see seven different breeds of sheep, watch one being shorn, and then see the fleece spun into yarn. Once you've had a taste of Australia's rural backbone, you might like to expand your activities. Native animals are on display, waterslides are open at selected times for ❍$5 an hour, and a nine-hole round of mini golf is available for ❍$4. Every Saturday night there is a Woolshed dance which includes dinner. The Woolshed is about 20 minutes drive from the city centre and admission prices are ✪$18 adults. A Park Package ticket is available, which includes a variety of these activites for ✪$20.

The Boondall Wetlands are a protected area maintained by Brisbane City Council, consisting of woodlands, tidal flats and swamp areas, north of Brisbane on the rim of Moreton Bay. The region can be explored on foot, bike or canoe, and birdwatching and explanation of Aboriginal culture are features. The Boondall Wetlands Visitor Centre has further details, ☎3865 5187.

Tours

Bus tours operate daily from Brisbane, taking in the very best of the city sights and venturing further afield to beautiful beaches and natural bushland. Following are some examples.
Brisbane Tours and Detours, ☎3830 4455:

Koalas and Brisbane Parklands Tours, ◷2.15pm-4.15pm, ✪$50 adults;
Highlights of the City, ◷9.15am-1.15pm, ✪$40 adults;
Brisbane Moonlight Tour, ◷6.45pm-8.45pm, ✪$40 adults;
Australian Day Tours, Level 3, Transit Centre, Roma Street, ☎3236 4155 or ☎1300 363 436 (free call):
Sights and South Bank, ◷9.30am-1.30pm, ✪$40 adults.
Brisbane Ghost Tours, ☎3344 7264: A historical tour with a difference!
Mr Day Tours, Aminya Close, My Nebo, ☎3289 8364:
Gray Line Tours, Level 3, Transit Centre, Roma Street, ☎3236 9444:
Rob's Rainforest Explorer Day Tours, 44 Felix Street, Lutwyche, ☎0409 49 6607:
Glasshouse Mountains and Kon-dalilla Falls, ◷8am-6pm,

✪$55 adults;
LamingtonSpringbrook National Parks, ◷8am-6pm, ✪$55 adults;
Mt Glorious and Samford Valley Tour, ◷8am-6pm, ✪$55 adults.
See More Scenic Tours, 4 Mallee Street, Marsden, ☎3805 5588:
Sunrover Expeditions, 1 Eversleigh Road, Redcliffe, ☎3203 4241:

Regular tours to Dreamworld, Sea World, Movie World, Wet'n'Wild, Gold Coast, Noosa and Sunshine Coast, Moreton Bay, Tamborine Mountains, Toowoomba and Darling Downs are also conducted.

Festivals

The **Valley Fiesta** held at Chinatown and Brunswick Street Malls is a multicultural music and arts festival held in July.
The Royal National Show (The Ekka) is held in the Brisbane Exhibitions Grounds, Fortitude Valley, over ten days in August.
The **Spring Hill Fair** is held in Water Street in September.
Brisbane River Festival is held from August to September.

Facilities

The Gabba is Brisbane's main cricket venue for International and interstate matches, and it is in *Stanley Street, Woolloongabba*, across the river to the south of the city centre, ☎3891 5464.

The main football ovals are: Rugby League - Suncorp Stadium, *Castlemaine Street, Milton*, ☎3876 6511; Rugby Union - *Ballymore, Clyde Road, Herston*, ☎3352 8120; Australian Rules - The Gabba. There are also games of all three codes played at suburban grounds on the weekends in winter.

Baseball is also played at Suncorp Stadium, and

for Basketball, the Brisbane Entertainment Centre, Melaleuca Drive, Boondall, is the home of the Brisbane Bullets.

For names and addresses of other sporting facilities, it is best to consult the Yellow Pages telephone directory.

Outlying Attractions
Moreton Bay and Island

The bayside suburbs of **Wynnum, Lota, Manly, Wellington Point** and **Cleveland** are great places for boating, and North Stradbroke and Moreton Islands are really worth a visit. They provide the opportunity for an island holiday without travelling far from Brisbane.

Moreton is the second largest sand island in the world (after Fraser Island), and much of it is National Park. There are unspoiled beaches, abundant birdlife, and the sand dunes are magnificent. In the centre, amongst the sand dunes where there is practically no vegetation, you can imagine that a camel train might arrive at any moment. **Mount Tempest** is one of the highest coastal sand dunes in the world. The **Wild Dolphin** resort at Tangalooma, the site of the old whaling station, offers standard and deluxe motel and cabin accommodation and a restaurant. Prices start from ✪$90 per person twin share in the peak season.

For those who prefer a simpler holiday, camping areas are found at **Accommodation Moreton Island,** *The Strand Bulwer,* ☎3408 3798. Facilities include water, toilets and showers. Moreton Island Visitor Information Services, located at The Strand Bulwer, can provide further details, ☎3408 2661.

Access to Moreton Island is by launch or air. **The Tangalooma Flyer** leaves Holt Street in Brisbane, with a courtesy coach transfer from the Transit Centre in *Roma Street* at 9am daily. The launch transfers cost ✪$33 return for adults. Air transfers are from Brisbane Airport to Moreton Island, a trip lasting about 15 minutes. Enquire about your preferred transfer method when booking your accommodation or by contacting the Visitor Information Centre.

North Stradbroke Island

North Stradbroke Island is larger and has more varied scenery than Moreton Island. There are mangrove swamps, lakes, bushland and great surfing beaches.

Vehicular ferries operate from Cleveland and Redland Bay.

The Stradbroke Island Visitor Information Centre is at the end of *Middle Street, Cleveland,* ☎3821 3821. Stradbroke Island Tourism is in *Junner Street, Dunwich,* ☎3409 9555 or email ✉redlands tourism @redlands.net.au

⤻ Let's Stay Here
Stradbroke Island Guesthouse,
1 Eastcoast Rd, Point Look-out, ☎3409 8888, *www.stradb rokeislandscuba.com.au* Situated about 3km from central Point lookout, just right on the beach. All rooms are fanned. This hostel is well known to divers. Clean and well maintained. Features a fully equipped kitchen, a TV room, internet access, games room with pool tables and ping pong, and there's also

a nice courtyard. *Dorms* ✪*$22; double/twin $50*

Straddie Hostel,
76 Mooloomba Rd, Point Lookout, ☎3409 8679 Located on the surfside of the island. Quaint but boast of a good atmosphere. Accommodation is in four self-contained units, with en suite bathrooms and a kitchen. Downstairs you'll find the common room with the TV. *Dorms* ✪*$17; double/twin $40*

Beenleigh

If you are heading south to the Gold Coast from Brisbane, take time out to visit the **Beenleigh Tavern** at *124 Distillery Road,* ☎3287 4777. It is ⏰open Mon-Fri 10.30am-10pm, Sat 11am until late, Sun 11am-6pm. For a moderate fee, tours are conducted between limited hours daily and include a tasting of Beenleigh rum (after all, that is why you came here).

Gold Coast
Population 438,473
The Gold Coast, Australia's most famous tourist destination, is situated in south-east Queensland.

Climate
Average Temperatures: January max 28C (82F) - min 20C (68F); July max 21C (70F) - min 9C (48F). Average annual rainfall: 1724mm (68 ins); driest months July-September.

Characteristics
The Gold Coast region is made up of the Gold Coast City, Albert and Beaudesert Shires. It covers

4254 sq km (1642 sq miles) and stretches 42km (26 miles) along south-east Queensland's world-famous, sun-drenched coastline and 100km (62 miles) inland into the Gold Coast Hinterland (see separate listing). The district has rolling surf, golden beaches, rainforest areas, non-stop entertainment, and millions of visitors every year.

How to Get There
By Air
Qantas, ☎13 1313 services the Gold Coast frequently.

The closest airport is at Coolangatta, and there is no problem arranging coach transfers to your hotel anywhere in the Gold Coast area. The following regional services are available:

Coolangatta Airport Transfers, ☎5588 8747;
Airporter, ☎5588 8777;
SkyTrans, ☎3236 1000;
Sunbus, ☎5588 8740.
Coach Service to and from Brisbane City, ☎13 12 30;

By Coach
Greyhound Pioneer, ☎13 2030, and **McCaffertys,** ☎13 1499, stop at the Gold Coast on their Sydney/Brisbane routes. Greyhound Pioneer has a Brisbane/Gold Coast service, and McCaffertys has a Gold Coast/Toowoomba service.

By Rail
From Sydney, a train to Murwillumbah then a bus to the Gold Coast, ☎13 2232.

Visitor Information
There is a Visitors Centre at Cavill Mall, *Surfers Paradise,* ☎(07) 5538 4419, ⏰open 8am-4pm

Mon-Fri and 8am-3pm Sat. You will also find the head office of the Gold Coast Tourism Bureau in Surfers Paradise on *Level 2, Ferny Avenue,* ☎*5592 2699*. They have a web site at ▪www.goldcoast tourism.com.au and an email address at ✉info@gctb.com.au

If you require a money exchange facility, Kings Currency Services, *Shop G21 Shopping Plaza, Elkhorn Ave, Surfers Paradise,* ☎*5526 9599*, places no charges on cash and is ◔open 7 days, 8.30am-10pm.

🠦 Let's Stay Here

Accommodation is not a problem on the Gold Coast. The motels, apartments, guest houses and camping grounds are more dense here than any-where else in Australia. As a result of this, there is really no need to book in advance, ex-cept in school holidays. Many airlines, bus compa-nies, tour operators, travel bureaux and even the railways offer package holidays, which are very good value. The tel-ephone area code is 07.

Local Transport
Shuttle

There is an efficient and economical public transport system. **Gold Coast Tourist Shuttle Bus Service**, ☎*1300 655 655* provides unlimited travel day or night for the one price. It travels from one end of the coastal strip to the other. 1 day pass: adult ◔$14. Theme park transfers also available. Or you can rent a Pedicab, a moped (**Moped Hire**, *cnr Hamilton Ave and Gold Coast Hwy, Surfers Paradise,* ☎*5592*

4087) or a bicycle. At the other end of the scale, you can splurge and hire a stretch limousine.

For full information on all these options, contact the Visitor Information Centres, or browse the Yellow Pages telephone directory.

Combined Rail, Bus and Ferry South East Explorer, ☎*13 12 30*. All day travel on participating services, Explorer ticket 1 - ◔$10, Explorer ticket 2 - ◔$16, Explorer ticket 3 - ◔$24.

Bus
Surfside Bus Timetables. For information on routes phone and ☎*13 12 30*.

Coach
The following services are available:

> Gold Coast Get Around, 1300 361 966; Theme Park Transfers, 1800 426 224; Coach Charter, 55 888 780.

Let's Eat
The Gold Coast is said to have the largest collection of restaurants per square kilometre in Australia, and indeed there are more than 500 different restaurants on the coastal strip. You can eat and drink riverside, seaside, inside or outside. Almost every national cuisine is represented, and you can choose from licensed or BYO. The only problem is making up your mind which restaurant is going to get your patronage, and this is taken care of by phoning the Restaurant Infoline, ☎*916 699*, for information and bookings. Here is a taste of the wide selection, from low to lavish prices:

Cav's Steakhouse, *30 Frank St, Labrador,* ☎*5532 2954*. Licensed, steak, seafood, pasta and salad.

Grumpy's Wharf, *Mariners Cove, 60-70 Seaworld Drive, The Spit, Main Beach,* ☎*5532 2900*. Seafood, lunch Fri-Sun, dinner 7 days.

Hard Rock Cafe, *cnr Cavill Ave and Gold Coast Hwy, Surfers Paradise,* ☎*5539 9377*. Restaurant open 7 days 12pm-late.

Holy Mackeral, *174 Marine Pde, Labrador,* ☎*0* Seafood, licensed, open 7 days, lunch and dinner.

Imperial Palace, *cnr Elkhorn Ave and Gold Coast Hwy, Surfers Paradise,* ☎*5538 9544,* Chinese restaurant, open 7 days.

Mango's, *Tiki Village, Cavill Avenue, Surfers Paradise,* ☎*5531 6177*. Modern international cuisine with an emphasis on seafood, open 7 nights, dinner.

Mariners Cove, *Sea World Drive, Main Beach,* ☎*5531 3030*. Licensed or BYO.

Mikado, *cnr Elkhorn Ave and Gold Coast Hwy, Surfers Paradise,* ☎*5538 2788*. Japanese cuisine including traditional sushi and teppanyaki dishes, open 7 days.

Montezuma's, *Aloha Building, 8 Trickett Street, Surfers Paradise,* ☎*5538 4748*. Mexican, licensed.

Pancakes in Paradise, *cnr Gold Coast Hwy and Clifford St,* ☎*5592 0330*. Licensed, open 7 days, lunch and dinner.

Rusty Pelican, *cnr Orchid Ave and Elkhorn Ave, Surfers Paradise,* ☎5570 3073. Lunch 11.30am-10.30pm, licensed until midnight, open 7 days.

Seashells Restaurant, at the *Novotel Beachcomber, 18 Hanlan St, Surfers Paradise,* ☎5570 1000. International seafood buffet.

The Aztec, Victoria Square, *Broadbeach Mall,* ☎5538 8477. Mexican cuisine, licensed, open 7 days, lunch and dinner.

Times Cafe Restaurant, *cnr Elkhorn Ave and Gold Coast Hwy, Surfers Paradise,* ☎5538 3211. Steak, seafood and pasta, open 7 days. Breakfast, lunch and dinner

McDonalds is on the corner of *Cavill Mall and The Esplanade.* **Pizza Hut** is in *Raptis Plaza, Cavill Avenue,* ☎13 11 66. There is an abundance of fast food eateries in the area, and the selection will guarantee that you are not left wanting.

Entertainment

For after-dinner entertainment, you can choose between cabarets, discos, live bands, top international performers, sophisticated night clubs, poker machine palaces, and the world famous **Jupiter's Casino**. Or you can opt for something completely different - the bizarre **Dracula's Cabaret** restaurant.

Shopping

The Gold Coast is like one massive shopping centre, and in fact Surfers Paradise is known to some as 'Shoppers Paradise'. There are dozens of shopping centres, of every shape and size,

and it is rumoured that some people never actually see the beach. To help you find your way through this consumers' paradise, the following list can be used as a guide:

On the Broadwater Spit is the stylish **Marina Mirage**, which offers good shopping, an aviary, and several food outlets including a 50s rock 'n' roll cafe with its own FJ Holden.

Sanctuary Cove, 20 minutes' drive north of Surfers, has the **Marine Shopping Village,** ☎5577 6011, with over 80 specialty shops and its own brewery offering Bavarian style beer - Island Lager.

Australia Fair, *Marine Parade, Southport,* ☎5532 8811. Over 230 specialty stores, ☼open 7 days.

Pacific Fair Shopping Centre, *Hooker Blvd, Broadbeach,* ☎5539 8766. Queensland's largest shopping centre with over 260 specialty stores and 12 cinemas, ☼open 7 days.

Mariora Australia, *3290 Gold Coast Highway, Surfers Paradise,* ☎5538 9899. Opal retailer.

DFS Galleria, *cnr Cavill Ave and Gold Coast Highway, Surfers Paradise,* ☎5570 9401. Duty free and tax free, ☼open 7 days 8.30am-10pm

Nerang Disposals, *6 Spencer Rd, Nerang,* ☎5596 4434. Camping and outdoor store.

Carrara Markets, *Nerang-Broadbeach Rd,* along the road west of Pacific Fair. 500 stalls, open all day every Saturday and Sunday.

Fashion Factory Outlet, *4107 Ferry Rd, Southport,* ☎5531 1837. Ladies' fashion and lingerie, men's and children's fashion, swimwear, ☼open 7 days

9am-5pm.

Marina Mirage, *Sea World Drive, Main Beach,* ☎5577 0088. ☼open 7 days 10am-6pm.

Paradise Centre, *Cavill Ave, Surfers Paradise,* ☎5592 0155. Over 120 shops, ☼open 7 days.

Robina Town Centre, off *Robina Pkwy, Robina,* ☎5575 0480. More than 200 specialty shops and 6 cinemas.

Raptis Plaza, *Cavill Mall and The Esplanade, Surfers Paradise,* ☎5592 2123. Home to a full-size replica of Michelangelo's David, which stands in the Food Court. Open 7 days 10am-late.

The Oasis, *Victoria Ave, Broadbeach,* ☎5592 3900. Over 100 specialty stores, direct link to Jupiters Casino via monorail.

Runaway Bay Shopping Village, *Lae Drive, Runaway Bay,* ☎5537 2566. Over 100 specialty stores, Boardwalk Foodcourt, water views, ☼open 7 days.

Sportsmans Warehouse, *32 Strathaird Rd, Bundall,* ☎5531 6511. Australia's largest sporting warehouse, free bus from Surfers Paradise, ☼open 7 days.

Niecon Plaza, *Broadbeach Central Mall, Victoria Ave, Broadbeach,* ☎5531 6659. Licensed bar, al fresco cafes.

Points of Interest

The main attractions are, of course, the beaches - and there are plenty of them, all offering clean, golden sand, and sparkling surf. But the Gold Coast has much more to offer, with special attractions in every town.

Southport

Situated across the Broadwater from The Spit, Southport was the first settlement in the Gold Coast, having been established in 1875. It is now the business and commercial centre for the region, along with neighbouring Labrador, Biggera Waters and Runaway Bay.

Inland from Southport, on the Pacific Highway, is the **Wet'n'Wild Water World**, ☎*5573 2255*, with a giant fresh water wild wavepool that has one metre surf and its own lifeguards. The park also has Wild Billy the surfing kangaroo, white water twisters, and a breathtaking toboggan drop. The latest addition is the Super 8 Aqua Racer. The water park is ⊘open daily from 10am. Adults ✪$31.

Further north along the Pacific Highway brings you to **Koala Town**, where you can cuddle a koala and see the many animals that lived on Old MacDonald's Farm. Also featured are sheep shearing and horse shoeing demonstrations.

Continuing north, you come to **Dreamworld**, *Dreamworld Parkway*, ☎*5588 1111*. It comprises 100ha (247 acres) of landscaped gardens and Australian bushland featuring nine wonderful worlds of fantasy, including 16 rides, seven live shows, a tiger exhibit, and the Imax Theatre with a six-storey high screen that creates an experience of light and sound which makes the viewer feel part of the film. The new **Giant Drop** and **Tower of Terror** are the fastest and tallest rides in the world. Dreamworld is ⊘open every day, and is an experience that should not be missed. Adults ✪$52, .

Almost opposite Dreamworld is **Warner Bros Movie World**, ☎*5573 8485*, which is based on the world-famous Hollywood Movie set. Terrific theme rides

such as Lethal Weapon and Batman Adventure lead the attractions. Movie World has movie-making facilities, which are used for actual productions. Entry costs adults ✪$52. The live shows are a must-see.

Further north is the **Le Mans Kart Racing Complex**, *Pacific Highway, Pimpana Tourist Area,* ☎*55 46 6 566*. There is a 700m circuit with fast karts and timed laps. No licence is necessary, but age restrictions do apply for safety reasons. The complex is ⊘open 7 days 10am-5pm. ✪$28 for 7 laps, $33 for 10 laps. Not far away, for those who are fascinated by (maybe obsessed with) the amber liquid, the **Carlton Brewhouse**, *cnr Mulles Rd and Pacific Highway, Yatala,* ☎*3826 5858*, offers 45min brewery tours at 10am, 12pm and 2pm - adults ✪$8.

⤴ Let's Stay Here

Southport
Broadwater Tourist Park, *Gold Coast Tourist Highway, Southport,* ☎*5581 7733*. 307 sites - *powered sites* ✪*$30-35*

Southport Tourist Park, *6 Frank Street, Gold Coast Highway, Southport,* ☎*5531 2281*. 55 sites, *powered sites* ✪*$20-30; cabins from $45; caravans from $35.*

Surfers Paradise

The heart of the Gold Coast, Surfers Paradise is the ultimate tourist resort, and its malls and avenues are crammed with a multitude of places to eat, drink, shop, see and be seen. Condominiums abound, rising skyward one after another amid

lush vegetation and island upon island reclaimed from the sea. It has been described as 'a pristine Miami Beach'.

For entertainment there are performances by international stars, spectacular revues, cabaret shows, top restaurants, intimate bars, discos, and dinner cruises departing from the Nerang River on the western side of Surfers. There are several different cruises, from a two- hour 'scones and cream' tour, to a tropical luncheon feast, a night shipboard cabaret, a twilight trip, or a raging disco. For family fun, right in the centre of town is Grundy's Paradise Centre, with over 300 different activities in the one complex, ranging from games of skill to the latest electronic arcade machines.

In **Raptis Plaza**, Cavill Mall, there is the only **Odditorium** in the southern hemisphere, which in true **Believe It Or Not!** tradition has six-legged calves, bearded women, Siamese twins and many more exhibits. The museum is ⊘open 7 days 9am-11pm, ☎*5592 0040*. Entry fees: adults ✪$12, concession $8.

The Centre, the Gold Coast's entertainment and arts complex, is on Chevron Island, and has all types of theatrical performances from opera to pantomime. There is also an Art Gallery which has changing exhibitions.

For a cool change to the typically humid climate, **Frozen World**, *cnr Ocean Avenue and Gold Coast Highway*, ☎*5570 3922*, offers mini-golf on ice, exhibitions of ice sculptures and carvers, a snow and ice playground, and a kids' club. Warm jackets are supplied for those who forgot to pack for snowy conditions on the

Gold Coast. Adults ✪$17 and concession $12.

To the north of Surfers is Main Beach, fast becoming the 'best address' on the Coast, and nearby is the Broadwater, which offers still water swimming as an alternative to the open surf.

On Broadwater Spit is Australia's famous marine theme park, **Sea World**, ☎*5588 2205*, which has the country's first monorail, the **Three Loop Corkscrew**, and **Free Fall Water Slide**, performing dolphins, killerwhales, sea lions, water skiing shows, and lots more. The most recent attraction is a 3D Pirate adventure. Sea World is ☻open every day from 10am, and you are advised to get there early if you want to see and do everything available. Adults ✪$52.

Another attraction on the Spit is **Fishermans Wharf**, which has a swimming pool, children's playground, and live band performances on the weekend.

�厶 Let's Stay Here

Surfers Paradise Aquarius,
44 Queen St, Southport, ☎*5527 1300 or 1800 229 955,* ▆*www.aquariusba ckpack.com.au* This is a nice backpackers hostel located close to the centre of Southport and the Australia Fair shopping centre. Surfers Paradise is about 5km away to the south. Features new facilities including a fully equipped kitchen, laundry, and some nice sofas in the TV lounge room. Outside there's a bar and barbecue area, swimming pool and spa, plus on site bar with a pool table.

A shuttle bus service will gladly take you to Surfers Paradise. *Dorms ✪$20; double/twin $45* (price includes breakfast)

Backpackers In Paradise,
40 Peninsula Drive, Surfers Paradise, ☎*5538 4344* This fabulous piece of paradise boasts a 50 metre pool, a theatre room, bar/cafe on location, and pool tables. There is a great common room for relaxing and sharing meals with friends and the hostel is extremely close to town. Should you run out of supplies, there is a convienent store right next door and there is always something arrange for the guests every night, except Mondays. *Dorms ✪$17-$20; double/twin from $50*

British Arms Youth Hostel,
Mariners Cove, 70 Seaworld Drive, Main Beach, ☎*5571 1776, www.britisharms.com.au* 3 minutes from Seaworld. Dorms single sex, 1 family room, all have their own ensuite, cheaper foodstores in Surfers about 2 km into town. British pub across the road serves cheap meals. Bus 2 and 9 stop at the hostel. Facilities includes iron and ironing board, laundry, kitchen, communal bathrooms, TV room, lounge room. Restaurant on site. Parking available. *Dorms from ✪$21; double/twin fom $50 BC MC VA EFTPOS*

Cheers Backpackers,
8 Pine Ave, ☎*5531 6539 or 1800 636 539* This is

the partiest of party hostels that you'll find in town.The partying usually starts in their on site bar with pool tables and foosball. Other facilties includes their TV lounge with a DVD player, there's a swimming pool outside plus a barbecue area. Big plus on the free internet access and of course the normal kitchen and common rooms. The hostel also organises loads of activities including club and pub crawls. **Recommended.** *Dorms ✪$18; double/twin $46*

Couple O Days,
18 Peninsula Dr, ☎*5592 4200* Just your friendly hostel with a homely atmosphere. Your normal facilities of a kitchen, TV lounge room and a swimming pool outside witha barbecue area. There's also free internet access. *Dorms ✪$20; twin $40*

Islander Backpackers Resort,
6 Beach Rd, ☎*5538 8000,* Smack bang in the middle of Gold Coast, situated next door to the bus station. This is the closest backpackers resort to everything you need such as the beach, restaurants, nightlife and shops.This is a very large backpackers place housed within a hotel. All room have en suite bathrooms plus their own TV, fridge and the rooms lookout unto a balcony. The great thing about it is that they have free shareware of the hotel facilites next door including their swimming pool, sauna and spa, their tennis and squash courts and the bar and restaurant. Also features

a kicthen, laundry, and games room with loads of entertainment including a pool table, pinball, video games and air hockey. Airport pick up, bicycle hire and parking available. *Dorms ✪$18; double/twin $50*

Gold Coast International Backpackers Resort ,
28 Hamilton Ave, Surfers Paradise 4217 ☎5592 5888, ▣*www.nomadsworld.com* Formerly known as Mardi Gras Backpackers located not too far from most attractions and

Surfers Paradise

Accommodation

1. Backpackers in Paradise
2. Couple O Days
3. Gold Coast International Backpackers Resort
4. Islander Backpackers Resort
5. Sleeping Inn Surfers
6. Surfers Paradise Backpackers Resort

the city centre. All rooms have ensuites and TV, fridge and a balcony. Kept clean and well maitained. New three storey building very near the beach. Staff desk are really helpful. TV in every room. Closest food store is nearby. Facilities includes kitchen, laundry, iron, internet access, TV room with cable and a barbecue area. Bar and restaurant on site. There's also the ever-rare gym. Free use of boogie boards, pool, games room. On site parking. *Dorms from $18; doubles/ twins $30pp BC MC VA*

Main Beach Tourist Park,
Main Beach Parade, Gold Coast, ☎*5581 7722.* (No pets allowed) 170 sites, playground, pool - *powered sites ✪$20-23, self-contained sites $25-29.*

Sleeping Inn Surfers
26 Peninsula Dr, ☎5592 4455 or 1800 817 832, ▣*www.sleepinginn.com.au* All new apartment style hostel located just minutes from most attractions and the transit centre. Quite nice and modern. Accommodation is in self-contained units, including 3 dorms. There's a small kitchen, common area and a bathroom in each. Other facilities within the grounds are a fully equipped kitchen, laundry, TV and video lounge's, games room, pool table, internet, tropical salt water swimming pool and spa, discounted tours and water sports. *Dorms ✪$20; single $50 ($60 with en suite); double/twin $50 ($60 with en suite); triple $25pp*

Surfers Paradise Backpackers Resort,
2837 Gold Coast Highway, ☎*5592 4677 or 1800 282 800,* ▣*www.surfersparadiseb ackpackers.com.au* Situated at the south end of of town, very close to the beach. Fully equipped self contained units with TV/video, kitchen and bathroom. Rooms have ceiling fans. Other features are a kitchen, laundry, TV room (incl cable), internet access, safe deposit, luggage storage, common rooms, a swimming pool, barbecue area, small gym, games room, tennis court and a bar. Free use of boogie boards and volleyball. Courtesy bus and parking available. *Dorms ✪$22; double/twin $26pp; triple $26pp*

Surf n Sun Beachside Backpackers,
3323 Gold Coast Highway, ☎*5592 2363,* ▣*www.surfnsu n-goldcoast.com* All rooms have ensuites and TV. Facilities includes kitchen, laundry, luggage storage and internet access. There are also common rooms, TV Room, pool, barbecue area, games room and safe deposits. Staff here are very helpful and there's also a courtesy bus services. Parking available. *Dorms from ✪$22*

Trekkers,
22 White St, Southport, ☎*5591 5616* Situated close to the heart of Southport, north to Surfers Paradise. One of the original backpackers in the state. Small yet friendly. All rooms have en suite, bed

lamps, wardrobes and are fanned and one room has a bathtub. Watch out for the waterbed in the twin and double rooms plus each has a TVs. Other facilities includes a fully equipped kitchen, laundry, TV lounge, pool table, common room with a piano, internet access and a swimming pool and barbecue area. There are also theme nights and a free use of boogie boards and surf boards. A Shuttle bus service, bike hire and parking available. **Recommended.** *Dorms* ✪*$22; double/twin $52*

Broadbeach

The town is internationally famous as the site of **Jupiter's Casino**, and the Gold Coast's first world-class hotel, the $185 million Hotel Conrad. A monorail links the casino with the Oasis-On -Broadbeach Shopping Resort and the Pan Pacific Hotel.

⤺ Let's Stay Here
Montego,
2671 Gold Coast Highway, ☎*5539 9956.* 24 units, salt water pool - ✪*$55-135.*

Portobello Beachside,
2607 Gold Coast Highway, ☎*5538 7355.* 46 units, heated pool, spa, secure parking - *from* ✪*$60*

Burleigh Heads

Burleigh is the half-way point between Coolangatta and Surfers, and hosts one of the greatest week long surfing events in Australia, held in March each year.

The town has a more relaxed atmosphere than Coolangatta or Surfers, and many people

choose to stay here, and visit the other two when they want to get into the action. If you are into bushwalking, there is a 3km graded track that meanders among the habitat of koalas and bandicoots in the **Burleigh Heads National Park.**

The Gold Coast Highway then continues past the surfing beaches of Miami, Nobby's and Mermaid to Broadbeach.

⤺ Let's Stay Here
Burleigh Beach Tourist Park,
Goodwin Terrace, Burleigh Heads, ☎*5581 7755.* Pool adjacent to park, centralised location close to all facilities, 200m from Burleigh Beach, *powered sites* ✪*$20-25 for two.*

Casino Motel,
1761 Gold Coast Highway, ☎*5535 7133.* Natural setting adjacent to Burleigh National Park. 250m from Burleigh Point, 300m from Burleigh central shops, 15km from Sea World, 35km from Movie World. 12 units, swimming pool, barbecue - *from* ✪*$45-110.*

Elite Motel,
1935 Gold Coast Highway, ☎*5535 2920.* 8 units, barbecue - ✪*$35-80.*

Currumbin

Situated about 6km (4 miles) north of Coolangatta, past the settlements of Kirra, Bilinga and Tugun, Currumbin is home to the world-famous **Currumbin Wildlife Sanctuary,** *Gold Coast Highway, Currumbin,* ☎*5534 1266,* a 20ha (50 acres) wildlife reserve with the the world's largest

collection of Australian native fauna. The Sanctuary is visited every morning and afternoon by thousands of brightly coloured wild Rainbow Lorikeets, which don't need much encouragement to eat out of your hand, or sit on your head, and seem to love having their photographs taken. Also at the Sanctuary, which is ⏱open daily 8am-5pm, are waterfalls, rainforest pools, and 250 individual species of birdlife, including the glossy black cockatoo. Entry fees: adults ✪$18. North of Currumbin are Pacific and Palm Beaches.

Outlying Areas:
⤺ Let's Stay Here
Billinga Beach Resort,
281 Golden Four Drive, Billinga Beach, ☎*5534 1241.* 23 units, 3 divided rooms, pool, undercover parking - ✪*$60.*

Camden Colonial Motor Inn,
2371 Gold Coast Highway, Mermaid Beach, ☎*5575 1066.* 15 units, undercover parking, spa, salt water pool - *from* ✪*$60.*

El Rancho,
2125 Gold Coast Highway, Miami, ☎*5572 3655.* 8 units, 1 suite, barbecue, pool, spa, playground - *from* ✪*$35.*

Limassol,
109 Frank Street, Labrador, ☎*5591 6766.* 14 units, salt water pool - *from* ✪*$50.*

Caravan Parks
Miami Caravan Park,
2200 Gold Coast Highway, Miami, ☎*5572 7533.* Kiosk, barbecue, no pets allowed, 200 sites - *powered sites* ✪*$16-19.*

Ocean Beach Tourist Park Miami,
2 Hythe Street, Miami, ☎*5581 7711.* Shared facilities, barbecue. 81 sites. ✪*$18-22, 58 powered sites $20-25.*

Runaway Bay Caravan Park,
20 Bayview Street, Runaway Bay, ☎*5537 1636.* 83 powered sites ✪*$19-21.*

Festivals

January - **The Magic Millions Horse Race Meeting**. The **Daikyo Palm Meadows Golf Cup.**
July - **Gold Coast International Marathon and Half-Marathon**.
August - **The Jupiter's Yacht Classic** between Sydney and the Gold Coast.
November - The **Queensland Open Golf.**

Sports and Facilities

The Gold Coast has all the facilities you could think of. You can play tennis, squash, golf, ten-pin bowling, lawn bowls or croquet, and go rollerskating or horseriding.

You can fish, swim, waterski, sailboard, sail, and more. There are also facilities for horse racing, greyhound racing, hot-air ballooning, mountain trekking, parasailing and many health and fitness centres.

Putt and Games, *cnr Crescent Ave and Gold Coast Hwy, Mermaid Beach,* ☎*5575 3381.* ☼open 7 days.

Tours and Cruises

If you have the time and desire to become intimate with the Gold Coast environment, the following selection of tours and cruises should cover all the aspects.

Tall Ship Sailing Cruises, Wharf D12 Marina Mirage, ☎5532 2444. Four different cruises, ship sails ☼9am daily.
Amphibious Aquabus Canal Cruises, Aquabus Safaris, 7A Orchid Ave, Surfers Paradise, ☎5539 0222, combined bus tour and canal cruise, bookings recommended, departs frequently throughout the day, 7 days, adults ✪$28.
Gold Coast Kayaking, ☎5527 5785. Offers morning tour or afternoon kayak snorkle tour, ☼9am-9pm, 7 days.
Aries Tours, 16 Barnett Pl, Ernest, ☎5594 9933. Focus on eco-tourism, choices include a Southern Skytour (☼5.30pm-10.30pm nightly), a Kingfisher Hinterland Tour (☼8am-2pm daily) and a Night Safari Tour (☼5.30pm-10.30pm nightly).
Tweed Endevour Cruises, Tweed River Cruise Terminal, River Terrace, Tweed Heads, ☎5536 8800. Offers 4hr rainforest and river cruise or 1.5hr river and lake cruise, lunch included, bookings essential.
Island Queen Showboat Cruises, Marina Mirage, Main Beach, ☎5571 0219. A number of cruises with various destinations, lengths and themes, prices on application.
Whale Watch, Moreton Island, ☎5591 5599. Luxury coach transfers, meals provided on cruise.
Day Tours, ☎3236 4165. Various coach tours.

Outlying Attractions
The Hinterland

Away from the coastal plain of the Gold Coast, the terrain climbs steadily but steeply up over 1000m (3281 ft) into some of Australia's richest highlands, passing through rolling rural landscapes along the way. The Hinterland is easily accessible by a number of roads, and offers spectacular views and walking trails into rainforests.

One of the most popular lookouts is called '**The Best of All**' and is reached from Lyrebird Ridge Road. Good views can be also be obtained from **Purlingbrook Falls**, which cascade about 190m (623 ft) to the rocks belosw. You can walk to the base of the cliff and follow a track that leads behind the falls.

In the **Numinbah Valley**, just within the Queensland border, is the **Natural Arch** in the **Natural Arch National Park.** Here there are several walks through rainforest, one of which leads to the stone archway through which a waterfall plummets to a rock pool below. There is also a **Glow Worm Cave** for walkers to discover.

Lamington National Park, 45km (28 miles) from the Coast, near the state border, is the largest preserved natural stand of sub-tropical rainforest in Australia, and the park has 160km (100miles) of graded walking tracks leading to many of its highlights, including **Mount Merino, Echo Point, Coomera Gorge, Picnic Rock,** and the **Aboriginal Cooking Caves.** In all, the park has more than 500 waterfalls, and majestic blackbutt, bloodwood, and giant cedar trees.

Mount Tamborine is a plateau on the McPherson Ranges, 35km (22miles) west of the Gold Coast, and comprises seven small National Parks totalling 375ha (926 acres) of rainforest in which there are 15,000 year old Macrozamia palms, said to be the oldest living things in the world.

St Bernards historic hotel, one of the mountain's oldest establishments, is famous for its smorgasbord lunches and beautiful gardens, and there are many other guest houses and restaurants in the area.

Other popular spots in the Hinterland are **Rosin's Lookout**, which overlooks the Numinbah Valley, and **Mount Warning**, off the *Nerang Beechmont Road*. Mount Warning is the first point in Australia to be struck by the rays of the morning sun.

Coolangatta and Tweed Heads

The twin towns of Coolangatta and Tweed Heads are the southern gateway to the Gold Coast, and occupy opposite headlands of the Tweed River, with Tweed Heads in New South Wales, and Coolangatta in Queensland.

A popular attraction in the Tweed Heads area is **Tropical Fruit World**, ☎*6677 7222*. It is a tropical fruit plantation with 50 types of tropical and jungle fruit, overlooking the Tweed River, and is an ideal place for a picnic. Safaris, fruit tasting, boat cruises and live shows are on offer. There is also a cafe. Tropical Fruit World is ⊕open daily 10am-5pm, ✪*$25 adults*.

Close to Coolangatta is the lighthouse at **Point Danger**.

Both towns have holiday resort centres, shopping, restaurants and tour facilities, and opportunities for all water sports on the river and the beaches.

There is a Visitor Information Centre in Shop 14B, **Beachhouse Plaza**, *Coolangatta Place, cnr Griffith and Warner Streets, Coolangatta*, ☎*5536 7765*.

For more information on Tweed Heads, contact the Visitor Information Centre at *4 Wharf Street*, ☎*(07) 5536 4244* or ☎*1800 674 414*, ⊕open

9am-5pm Mon-Fri, 9am-12pm Saturday. You can email them at ✉info@tactic.nsw.gov.au or visit the web page at 🖥www.tactic. nsw.gov.au

➘ Let's Stay Here

Coolangatta/Kirra Beach YHA,
230 Coolangatta Rd, Bilinga, ☎*5536 7544, www.yha.com.au* Situated about 3km north of town and close to the airport. The bus stop to Surfers paradise is just across the road. Feature a fully equipped kitchen, laundry, TV lounge, games room which has a pool table, ping pong and a piano, and there's a swimming pool and barbecue area outside. They hold BBQ nights. On site is an internet kiosk and shop. A courtesy bus will take you to Kirra and Duranbah. Bike hire and parking also available. *Dorms* ✪*$20; double/twin $44 BC MC VA EFTPOS* (price includes breakfast)

Sunset Strip Budget Resort, *199 Boundary St,* ☎*5599 5517,* 🖥*www.sunsetstrip.co m.au* Located just opposite Tweed River, the shopping centre and only 200m to Twin Towns RSL club.Two types of budget accommodation, guesthouse/backpackers and self contained holiday flats. Rooms are fanned. No dorms offered. You won't find the backpacker atmosphere here. Facilities includes a big kitchen, laundry, commn room with a pool table, swimming pool and a nice sundeck. parking available. *Single $35; double/twin/triple $27.50pp*

Toowoomba
Population 89, 928
Toowoomba is situated at the top of the Great Dividing Range, 130km (81 miles) inland from Brisbane, and has an altitude of 606m (2000 ft). It is the commercial centre of the rich pastoral area of the Darling Downs.

Climate
Toowoomba has a temperate climate and therefore is less humid than on the coast, with frosts in winter and rare light snowfalls on the highest points of 'the Range'. Average temperatures: January max 27C (81F) - min 17C (63F); July max 16C (61F) - min 4C (39F).

Characteristics
A garden city which was first settled in 1849. Originally the area was thought to be too swampy for a town, and the first settlement in the area was at Drayton, now a suburb of Toowoomba. But water was scarce at Drayton, and the town of Toowoomba was born. Many German immigrants settled around the town in the 1860s, successfully farming the fertile land. The soil on the Darling Downs is rich, deep and black. It is extremely fertile, but a quagmire after heavy rain, and forms deep cracks in dry weather. Toowoomba is often called 'The Garden City'.

How to Get There
By Bus
McCaffertys have a Brisbane/ Sydney service via Toowoomba, and also a Brisbane/Roma service which stops at Toowoomba. **Skenners** stop at Toowoomba on their Brisbane/Charleville service, and also on their Brisbane/Longreach Service.

By Rail

There is a daily service from Brisbane. Quite a few people get off the train at Helidon and take the **McCaffertys** bus to Toowoomba because it is faster than travelling the whole way by rail. A combined rail/bus ticket is available.

The **Westlander** stops at Toowoomba on its twice weekly run to Roma and Charleville.

Visitor Information

There are two Toowoomba Visitor Information Centres. One is in *86 James Street*, ☎ *(07) 4639 3797*, the other is in *476 Ruthven Street*, ☎ *(07) 4638 7555*. They share the email address ✉infocentre@ toowoomba.qld.gov.au and have a website at ⬛www.toowoomba. qld.gov.au

There is also the Toowoomba and Golden West Regional Tourist Association, located at *4 Little Street*, ☎ *(07) 4632 1988* or ✉tgwrta@iqnetl ink.com.au.

Or you can contact the Toowoomba Local Tourist Association, on ☎ *(07) 4635 4056*.

⤳ Let's Stay Here

Toowoomba has its fair share of motels, hostels and caravan parks. Here is a selection, with prices that should be used as a guide only. The telephone area code is 07.

Downsview Lodge,

cnr Handley and Rub Streets, ☎ *4630 1460* Located close to the university. Rooms have communal bathrooms, dining room, laundry coin operated, iron, lounge rooms, cable TV/DVD/Video and swimming pool. *Single* ✪ *$45;* (Breakfast/lunch/dinner)

Also outside of term time you could try one of the colleges on the campus of the **University of Southern Queensland**. **McGregor College** has 60 bedrooms with own bathrooms and a further 134 bedrooms where every two bedrooms share one bathroom. **Concannon College** has 102 bedrooms where every two bedrooms share one bathroom. **Steele Rudd College** has 132 bedrooms where the private common bathroom facilities in blocks are shared between either 10 or 15 students. ☎ *4631 2650, www.usq.edu.au*

Caravan Parks

Garden City Caravan Park, *34 Eiser Street*, ☎ *4635 1747*. (No pets) - *powered sites* ✪*$19 for two, on-site vans $31 for two*.

Glenfield Motor Lodge Caravan Park, *cnr Ruthven and Stenner Streets*, ☎ *4635 4466*. (No pets) - *powered sites* ✪*$18 for two*.

Toowoomba Motor Village Caravan Park, *821 Ruthven Street*, ☎ *4635 8186*. (No pets) - *powered sites* ✪*$18 for two, on-site vans $29 for two, park cabin section $42-55, cabin section $40*.

Let's Eat

Toowoomba has a good selection of restaurants, bistros, coffee shops and takeaway outlets. It even has four **McDonald's** - one at *277 Margaret Street*, another at *827 Ruthven Street*, a third on the *corner of Bridge and McGregor Streets*, and the fourth in the

Grand Central Shopping Centre on *Dent Street*. Following is a selection of food halls you might like to investigate.

Banjo's Steakhouse, *cnr Ruthven and Hanna Street*, ☎ *4636 1033* - licensed, steak/seafood.

Da Vinci's, *22 Hill Street*, ☎ *4638 4606* - licensed and BYO, Italian.

Dee's Vintage Thai Restaurant, *515 Ruthven Street*, ☎ *(07) 4632 5125*.

Gaby's Restaurant, *210 Herries Street*, ☎ *4632 7382* - licensed, International.

Mexican Cantina Grill, *164 Margaret Street*, ☎ *4638 1888* - BYO, Mexican.

Railway's Heritage Restaurant, *Station Street*, ☎ *(07) 4631 3223*.

Westlake, *127 Anzac Avenue*, ☎ *4634 7188* - licensed, Chinese/ seafood.

Points of Interest

Toowoomba has beautiful tree-lined streets with many parks and beautiful private gardens. The city has an active cultural and artistic life. It looks its best in September for the **Carnival of Flowers**. People come from all over the State to look at the gardens entered in the competitions. There are several categories, eg new private garden, good neighbours, factory garden, etc. The whole of the town seems to take pride in their gardens. Toowoomba's chosen the violet as its floral emblem as this small, fragrant flower flourishes here.

The view from **Picnic Point Lookout** is panoramic. On one

side you have the city, and on the other side, the Lockyer Valley with Table Top and Sugar Loaf Mountains in the foreground. The range stretches off into the distance to the south. West of the city is the distinctive **Gowrie Mountain** and the **Kings-thorpe Hills**.

The scenic **Prince Henry Drive** starts and finishes at the eastern end of *Bridge Street* and follows the cliff top around a small spur of the Great Dividing Range. It is a one-way traffic thoroughfare from which there are breathtaking views. It goes through the suburb of Prince Henry Heights, and past **Redwood Park Fauna Sanctuary**.

For a view of the city lights at night, try *Ruthven Street* which becomes Crows Nest Road, to the top of **Mount Kynoch**, the site of the city reservoir. There is a 360 degree view of the town and the districts of Crows Nest, Ravensbourne, Lockyer and Gowrie Mountain.

Queen's Park and the **Botanic Gardens** cover more than 28ha (70 acres), and provide an attractive display all year round. **Laurel Bank Park** has a scented garden for blind visitors.

Toowoomba has some fine old buildings including the post office, court house, the White Horse Hotel, and Gabbinar and Clifford House, both built in the 1860s, as well as the more humble Tawa, a home built soon after allotments were first handed out in 1849.

The old centre of Drayton, now a suburb of Toowoomba, has not been completely lost to development. The **Royal Bull's Head Inn**, the earliest hotel on the Downs, has been restored by the National Trust. The 1850s building incorporates part of the original hostelry. **St Matthew's Church** was built in 1887, and contains records dating back to 1850 from an earlier building. It has a splendid hammer beam roof, and the knocker on the vestry door originally graced the Bull's Head where the settlement's first services were held.

Smithfield, a stately homestead built at the end of the last century, is now a restaurant. There is also a memorial to author Arthur Hoey Davis (Steele Rudd) who made Dad and Dave famous. Davis was raised at Emu Creek, 20km (12 miles) from Drayton, where he was born in 1868.

The **Toowoomba Regional Art Gallery,** adjacent to the City Hall, ☎ *4688 6652*, has an interesting collection of paintings and antiques - ⏰open 11am-3pm Mon, Wed and Fri.

The **Lionel Lindsay Art Gallery,** *27-37 Jellicoe Street,* ☎ *4688 6693*, has a collection of works by great Australian artists, authors and poets. It is ⏰open Tuesdays, Wednesdays and Thursdays 11am-3pm and Sundays 1pm-4pm.

The **Cobb and Co Museum**, *27 Lindsay Street,* ☎ *4639 1971*, has a unique display of horse-drawn vehicles, and is ⏰open Mon-Fri 10am-4pm, Sat-Sun 1-4pm. Admission is ✪$2 for adults.

Festivals

The **Carnival of Flowers** is held each year in September, and the **Garden Fest** in April.

Facilities

Toowoomba has all the facilities you would expect of a town with such a large population - golf, tennis, squash, horse racing, lawn bowls, ten-pin bowling, croquet, swimming pools, cinemas, theatres, and so on.

Outlying Attractions

The **Darling Downs** is Queensland's main wheat growing area. Neat homesteads speckle the land, and a pattern of fields stretches over the horizon. There are not only wheat fields, but other grains are grown, as well as sunflowers, other oil seeds, and cotton. Dairy and beef cattle graze on the hills, and sheep further west. No visit to Toowoomba would be complete without a drive through the surrounding countryside.

Cooby Creek Dam

The source of Toowoomba's water supply is also a popular picnic spot. Travel along the Crows Nest Road, turn left 17km (11 miles) from the post office, and the dam is a further 17km (11 miles).

Oakey

Half an hour's drive north-west of Toowoomba, on the *Warrego Highway*. The **Museum of Australian Army Flying**, ☎ *4691 7666,* has one of the best displays of aviation memorabilia in the world. In several hangars and an outdoors area are the aircraft, which range from a fully restored replica Box Kite, and the first aeroplane in service, as well as Bristols, Cessnas, Bells, Austers and more. Admission is ✪$5 adult.

Jondaryan Woolshed Museum, on the Warrego Highway just past Oakey, is the oldest and largest continuously used shearing shed in Queensland. The woolshed is ⏰open daily 8.30am-5pm, and guided tours are available.

There are lots of working displays and machinery, and colonial style lunches with damper and billy tea are available. For more information phone ☎4692 2229.

Dalby

Known as the Hub of the Downs, Dalby is 83km (52 miles) from Toowoomba, on the Warrego Highway, and is home to one of Queensland's principle agricultural colleges.

An oasis in the middle of town is the **Thomas Jack Memorial Park**, facing the Warrego Highway. The park consists of more than 3ha (7 acres) of lawns, gardens and shrubberies, with a children's playground, shelters, barbecue facilities, a lily pond and a large area suitable for social cricket. The Visitor Information centre is located in the north-eastern corner of the park.

In Black Street is the **Pioneer Park Museum**, ☎4662 4760, which is open seven days a week for visitors to catch a glimpse of the rural past, ⊙Mon-Fri 10am-3pm, Sat-Sun 10am-4pm. There is a small admission charge, and craft items are for sale.

The Dalby Visitor Information Centre can be contacted on ☎(07) 4662 1066 and are located in Thomas Jack Park, on the corner of Drayton and Condamine Streets. You can email them at ✉dalbychamber@dalby.qld.gov.au or visit ▤www. dalbytown.com.au on the web.

↳ Let's Stay Here
Commercial Hotel,
Cunningham Street, ☎4662 3211 Mary Benny does a great job. It is nothing flash but many reps stay here.

Communal facilities, 6 single rooms. *Bed and breakfast* ❍*$27.50, dinner, bed and brekafast $37.50, bed only on weekends(no meals) $21.00.*

Dalby Hotel/Motel,
Cunningham Street, ☎4662 3422 ❍*$35 per night 2 star.*

Bunya Mountains National Park

The Park is 60km (37 miles) north-east of Dalby and covers 11,700ha (28,900 acres). The Bunya Mountains form an isolated section of the Great Dividing Range, rising abruptly from the surrounding countryside to an average elevation of 975m (3199 ft) reaching 1100m (3609 ft) at Mount Mowbullan and Kiangarow.

The district has considerable historic ṣignificance. Once, Aborigines visited the mountains regularly for six-week tribal ceremonies of hunting, feasting, mock fighting and corroborees. These visits coincided with heavy croppings of Bunya Pine cones, usually every three years. The vegetation of the park comprises 13 types, but can be broadly grouped into rainforest, eucalypt forest and grasslands. More than 200 plant species have been identified. The Bunya Pine, with its characteristic dome-shaped top, rises in stately elegance above the other vegetation. It is unique in its abundance in the area.

The graded walking track system throughout the park provides the bushwalker with an opportunity to discover all types and varieties of vegetation for themselves. They will also come across water falls, and plenty of

animal life, including the Bunya Mountains ringtail possum, found only on the mountain.

There are two camping areas - Burton's Well and Dandanbah. Burton's Well provides toilets, water and picnic facilities. Dandanbah has camping and unit facilities as well as a kiosk and restaurant. For more information contact Rosella's Restaurant in the park, ☎4668 3131.

Miles

Continuing along the *Warrego Highway* from Dalby to Roma, brings you to Chinchilla and further on, Miles.

Miles is well known for the **Miles Historical Village and Museum** in *Murilla Street,* ☎4627 1492. The village is open daily 8am-5pm. Another touch of history in the town is **Possum Park**, ☎4627 1651, where ammunition bunkers were built underground during World War II. Now the bunkers are used as visitor accommodation.

At Chinchilla, the **Chinchilla Historical Museum**, ☎4662 7014, has a vast collection of steam-powered traction engines. Chinchilla is one of the largest petrified wood areas of the world. The wood is from the Jurassic Age, about 140-180 million years ago. Fossicking can be done on the Hurse family's property, **Eddington Stud**, at a small cost per bucket. Locals Fred and Merle Newman, who live at 95 Boyd Street, Chinchilla, have a collection of rocks and petrified wood, and a large workroom where the cutting and polishing are done.

The Chinchilla Visitor Information Centre is in *Chinchilla Street,* ☎(07) 4668 9564.

Rollercoaster at Warner Brothers World

Jetski

Wet 'n' Wild Water World

ScubaDiving off the Sunshine Coast

At Boongara, 8km east of Chinchilla, the **Cactoblastis Hall** is a memorial to a small insect imported from South America in the 1920s to eat out a plant that had become the curse of the west, the prickly pear.

Roma

Gas was discovered in Roma, over 400km (248 miles) north-west of Toowoomba, at the beginning of the century during a water-drilling procedure on Hospital Hill. Eight years later, Roma suffered the first petroliferous gas well fire, which took more than a month to extinguish.

The maiden oil well in Roma was discovered in 1927 but soon dried out, though more oil was discovered. Roma is also the biggest and best inland store cattle market, and has had the biggest sale yarding in Australia. It is a flourishing town of 6,500 people. Crops in the district include wheat, sorghum, oats and sunflowers, and a number of fruit crops are also produced, from stone fruit to citrus. Festival time in Roma is Easter, with street parades, goat races, more traditional horse races, dancing, open-air concerts and rodeos.

One person who spent a lot of time in Roma, mostly in the courthouse, was Henry Readford, who was the initiator of Australia's most famous cattle theft. Along with a handful of others, he stole several hundred cattle from Bowen Downs in central Queensland and drove them on a mammoth trek to Blanchewater in northern South Australia. This man's real life story is almost as amazing as the that of the book loosely based on it - *Robbery Under Arms*. Readford, or Captain

Starlight, appeared in Roma Court on at least four occasions and was let off each time. When he was tried in Toowoomba, the result was different and he was sentenced to eight months in prison with hard labour.

The Roma and District Visitor Information Centre is at *2 Riggers Rd*, ☎ *1800 222 399*

North of Brisbane
Sunshine Coast
Population 120,000

The Sunshine Coast stretches from Caloundra, 90km (56 miles) north of Brisbane, to Double Island Point in the north. It boasts 55km (34 miles) of white sandy beaches and rocky headlands.

Climate

Average Temperatures: January max 29C (84F) - min 20C (66F); July max 21C (70F) - min 7C (45F). Average annual rainfall -1776mm (70 ins). Driest months June-September. A lot of the summer rain falls in evening storms after hot sunny days.

Characteristics

The Sunshine Coast is rather like the Gold Coast was in the 1960s, but it has a friendlier, laid-back air with less razzamatazz. The beaches and surf compare favourably with the Gold Coast, and there are fewer high rise buildings that cast shadows on the beaches in the afternoons.

The high rocky headlands and areas of natural bushland divide the resorts, and afford the holiday maker the opportunity to walk along shady paths in the heat of the afternoon, or drop a fishing line into the shallow waters of the rivers and savour the peace

and quiet.

There are still secluded beaches which can only be reached by narrow sandy paths meandering through sand dunes, and the mouths of the rivers are ideal places to fish, canoe, row or sail.

The Noosa River, which is navigable to near its headwaters at Tin Can Bay, is home to thousands of birds. The river flows through several lakes on its way to the sea, and many houseboats are to be found along its reaches. There is plenty to entertain, and the area boasts of excellent restaurants.

How to Get There
By Air

The major airport for the region is the Sunshine Coast Airport, centrally located at Mudjimba, and equipped for jet aircraft.

Qantas, ☎ *13 1313* and **Virgin Blue** *13 6789* flies directly from Sydney and Melbourne, with connections from other capital cities.

By Bus

Suncoast Pacific, ☎ *5443 1011*, and **McCafferty's**, ☎ *13 1499*, operate routes that service the Sunshine Coast frequently.

By Rail

Queensland Rail, ☎ *13 2232*, electric trains service the area from Brisbane to the main Sunshine Coast station at Nambour.

Visitor Information

Tourism Sunshine Coast Ltd, *The Wharf, Parkyn Parade, Mooloolaba*, ☎ *(07) 5477 7311*. The web site is: ■www.sunzine.net/suncoast/tsc/index.html and the email address is ✉tourism@sunzine.net

Maroochy Tourism and Travel, *Sixth Avenue, Maroochydore*, ☎ *(07) 5479 1566,* have an email facility at ✉admin@maroochytourism .com and a web page at 🖥www. maroochytourism.com

Caloundra City Information Centre, *7 Caloundra Road, Caloundra,* ☎ *(07) 5491 9233.* Their web address is 🖥www.caloundra.qld.gov .au and the email address is ✉c.stewart@ caloundra.qld.gov.au

Tourism Noosa Information Centre, *Hastings Street Roundabout, Noosa Heads,* ☎ *(07) 5447 4988.* The web site is 🖥www.tourism noosa.com.au and you can email them here at ✉info@tourismnoosa .com.au

There is another outlet in the area: Noosa Junction Visitor Information Centre, *Shop 5 The Oasis Centre, 20 Sunshine Beach Road, Noosa Heads,* ☎ *(07) 5447 3755.*

✍ Let's Stay Here

A good variety of accommo-dation, ranging from caravan parks, motels, hotels, guest houses, self-contained units and five-star resorts are avail-able throughout the coast from Noosa to Caloundra. For a copy of the Sunshine Coast Accommodation Guide, ☎ *(07) 5477 7311.*

You'll find a selection of budget accommodation under some listed towns. This should be used as a guide only. The telephone area code is 07.

Let's Eat

The Sunshine Coast is a gourmet's delight. Dozens of restaurants feature fresh local seafood complemented by delicious sun-ripened tropical fruit such as avocados, pineapples and pawpaws. Beach and river fronts are dotted with picnic tables where visitors can enjoy takeaway or picnic food. Here is an idea of what is available in each district.

Local Transport

Sunshine Coast Coaches operate daily bus services from Caloundra to Nambour, and Noosa District Bus Lines operate a daily service from Nambour to Noosa.

Points of Interest

Visitors to the area will quickly discover why it is one of Australia's premier tourist destinations. With golden beaches, scenic hinterland, lush rainforest, breathtaking mountains views, crystal-clear lakes and waterways, the Sunshine Coast has it all. For most visitors, the main attractions are sun, surf and sand.

The beaches stretch from Caloundra in the south to **Double Island Point** in the north, taking in popular holiday spots like **Mooloolaba, Maroochydore, Coolum and Noosa.**

Everyone, though, soon discovers that the hinterland also has much to offer, with its patchwork of tropical fruit farms, rainforests, State Forests and National Parks. It is the perfect complement to the coastal resorts. You can enjoy a bushwalk, while away the hours in one of the many arts and crafts galleries, sit down to a Devonshire tea, or take in the spectacular panoramic views.

Caloundra
Population 72,400
Caloundra City, at the southern entrance to the Sunshine Coast, is an attractive and affordable holiday destination. Located just an hour north of Brisbane by four-lane highway, it is the perfect place to shake the nine-to-five blues. Apart from 30km (19 miles) of beaches, Caloundra has a special attraction which makes it the envy of other coastal resorts - the Pumicestone Passage. It is a haven for a wide variety of water sports, is famed for its fishing and harbours as well as two of the safest swimming beaches on the Sunshine Coast - **Bulcock Beach** and **Golden Beach**.

✍ Let's Stay Here

Altons Palm Breeze, *105 Bulcock Street,* ☎*5491 5566.* 19 units, 1 suite, swim-ming pool, barbecue. - *from* ✪*$55.*

Caloundra Beach Backpackers, *84 Omrah Ave,* ☎*5499 7655* Located only minutes away from the beach and the Sunland Shopping Centre. Quite new and purpose built with brand new furniture. Fa-cilities includes 2 small fully equipped kitchen, laundry, 2 TV rooms and a barbecue area. parking available. Free pick up service. *Dorms* ✪*$17; double $48; twin $40*

Caloundra Motel, *30 Bowman Road,* ☎*5491 1411.* 14 units, swimming pool, barbecue, undercover parking - ✪*$55-65.*

Caravan Parks
Hibiscus and Tripcony Caravan Park, *Bowman Road,* ☎*5491 1564.* (No pets allowed) - *powered sites*

$20-26 for two, on-site vans $35-60, cabins $40-60 for two.

Danmira Tourist Park, *1 Onslow Street, Golden Beach,* ☎*5492 1731.* 70 sites, barbecue, pool - *powered sites* ✪*$20-25 for two, units $55-95 for two, cabins $40-85 for two.*

Dicky Beach Family Holiday Park, *Beerburrum Street, Dicky Beach,* ☎*5491 3342.* 124 sites, tennis, swimming pool - *powered sites* ✪*$18-30 for two, cabins $45-65 for two.*

Let's Eat
Bamboo Garden, *95 Bulcock Street,* ☎*5491 2768.*

Blue Orchid Thai Restaurant, *22 Bulcock Street,* ☎*5491 9433.*

Brunos Taverna Italian Ristorante, *725 Nicklin Way,* ☎*5493 1806.*

Chinese Holiday Restaurant, *106 Bulcock Street,* ☎*5491 6066.*

Flower Lounge Indian Restaurant, *Shop 4 The Strand, Bulcock Street,* ☎*5499 7677.*

You will find **McDonalds** on the corner of *Erang Street and Nicklan Way* and on the corner of *Fourth Avenue and Bowman Road.* **KFC** is at *73b Bowman Road.* **Pizza Hut** is at *69 Bowman Road,* ☎*5491 5100.*

Maroochy
Population 120,000
Mooloolaba, Alexandra Headland and Maroochydore are the main coastal townships of the Maroochy Shire.

Mooloolaba Beach, with **Point Cartwright** on the southern side and the Mooloolaba Harbour wall, is a protected beach which is popular with families and windsurfers. Mooloolaba is home to a large fishing fleet, and fresh fish can be purchased daily from the Mooloolaba Fisheries Co-operative.

Alexandra Headland is renowned for its great surf. In summer, board riders flock to the tiny cove every day.
Underwater World at the Mooloolaba Wharf is an enjoyable experience. The moving acrylic tunnel allows glass-housed sharks, stingrays, and fish to swim over and around the visitors.

Maroochydore, at the mouth of the Maroochy River, is a thriving tourist and business centre. It has a fine surfing beach, and the river is a favourite spot for watersports and fishing alike.

Travelling north along the coast the major townships are **Coolum Beach, Peregian Beach, Marcus Beach, Sunshine Beach** and, **finally, Noosa Heads.**

⤵ Let's Stay Here
Blue Waters,
64 Sixth Avenue, ☎*5443 6700.* 20 units, swimming pool, undercover parking - *from* ✪*$60.*

Coolum Beach Budget Accommodation,
Crn David Low Way and Ann St, ☎*5471 6666, www.coolum.com.au/budget/*
Coolum Beach is between Noosa nad Maroochydore. The hostel is situated very close to the shops, the beach and the National Park. Kept clean and well maintained. This is for the peace lovers and note the no alcohol rule. The great facilities includes a fully equipped kitchen, pool table and a swimming pool and a barbecue area at the back. *Dorms* ✪*$22; double $45*

Cotton Tree Beach House,
15 The Esplanade, ☎*5443 1755, www.cottontreebackpack ers.com* Close to the shops and warm beaches, a small hostel with facilities that includes TV lounge, internet access, pool table, a small kitchen and barbecue area. Free use of surf and boogie boards, kayaks and surf skis. *Dorm bed* ✪*$21 ($19 YHA); double/twin $46 ($42 YHA); single $38 ($35 YHA)*

Longboarders Lodge,
10 Memorial Ave, Cotton Tree, ☎*5443 2981* This great hostel is situated in a quiet location that is close to everything. It prides itself by being flexible and able to cater for the individual. The appartments are large, well maintained and comfortable with ensuites, a kitchenette and TVs. There are laundry facilities and a clothesline provided, a tour desk to fill your days with activity and free board hire, so you can crest those waves. There's a barabecue area at the back. You can also learn how to surf, sail, scuba dive or fly a trapeze. Linen is supplied, carpark in the vicinity and luggage storage. *Dorms* ✪*$18; double/twin $45*

Maroochydore

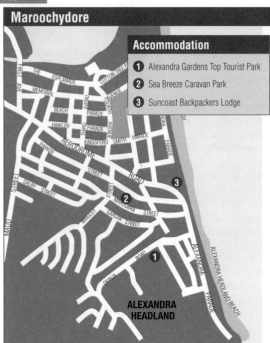

Accommodation

1. Alexandra Gardens Top Tourist Park
2. Sea Breeze Caravan Park
3. Suncoast Backpackers Lodge

ALEXANDRA HEADLAND

Maroochy River, *361 Bradman Avenue*, ☎ *5443 3142*. 8 units, swimming pool - *from* ✪*$55*.

Maroochy River Bungalows, *46 David Low Way*, ☎ *5448 4911 www.maroochyriver bungalow.com.au* Simple waterfront holiday accommodation with its own private river beach and boat ramp. Facilities are lounge and kitchen, double bed, fans in each cabin, balcony plus on street parking. *Cabins* ✪*$55*

Maroochydore YHA Backpackers,
24 Schirrmann Dr, ☎ *5443 3151 or fax 5479 3156*,
www.yhabackpackers.com Situated in the heart of the Sunshine Coast, this hostel

is set in the luscious tropical landscaped gardens. A minute walk to the Maroochy River and a park adjacent to the hostel. Facilities includes a swimming pool, pools and games room, TV lounge, barbecue area, self catering kitchen, kiosk, laundry and off-street parking. Free ice-cream every night except Sundays. Offers $10 tours to the Glasshouse Mountains, Blackall Ranges and National Parks. *Dorm* ✪*$18; double/ twin $21; single $30. BC MC VA EFPTOS*

Mooloolaba Beach Backpackers,
75 Brisbane Rd, Mooloolaba, ☎ *5444 3399 or 1800 210 120* Situated close to most attractions in this happening town.

Quite nice and boast of really good facilities. Accomodation has new furnishings. Each floor has their own kitchennette. Other facilities includes a TV lounge, internet access, ping pong table, a swimming pool and barbecue area in the back. On site cafe is where the common room is. *Dorms from* ✪*$21; double from $52*

Suncoast Backpackers Lodge,
50 Parker St, ☎ *5443 7544* Facilities includes TV lounge, kitchen, outdoor area with a pool table and barbecue. Free use of boogie boards and surfboards. Plenty of fast food places nearby and beaches close by. *Dorm bed* ✪*$19 ($18 VIP/YHA), double $40 ($38 VIP/YHA)*.

Caravan Parks
Alexandra Gardens Top Tourist Park, *Okinja Road*, ☎ *5443 2356*. (No pets allowed) All cabins with fans and selected few with A/C. Facilities includes games room, heated pools , playgrounds and on site shop. 200 metres from the beach. *Non-powered sites* ✪*$21; powered sites $22 for two; cabins $45 no unsuite for two ($56 unsuite)*.

Maroochy Palms Holiday Village, *319 Bradman Avenue*, ☎ *5443 8611*. (No pets allowed) - *powered sites* ✪*$26 for two*.

Maroochy River Cabin Village and Caravan Park,
Diura Street, ☎ *5443 3033*. (Pets on application) - *powered sites* ✪*$19-21 for two, on-site vans $40-55*

Sea Breeze Caravan Park, *Cnr Melrose Pde and Sixth Ave,* ☎ *1800 461 167, www. maroochydorepark.ql d.gov.au* 120 site, 3 cabins. Right on the beach, shops and take away outlets adjacent to the park. (No dogs allowed) *Non-powered sites ✪$18; powered sites $21.*

Let's Eat

Azzurro Ristorante Italiano, *93 Aerodrome Road,* ☎ *5443 3500.*

Gauchos Mexican Restaurant, *Kingsford-Smith Parade,* ☎ *5443 8877.*

Indian Hathi Restaurant, *37 Aerodrome Road,* ☎ *5443 5411.*

Jimmys Place, *Shop 4, Broadmeadow Road,* ☎ *5479 2241.*

Sun See Chinese Restaurant, *Shop 1, 50 Aerodrome Road,* ☎ *5443 2636.* BYO, wide range of cuisines with an oriental emphasis. Open 5pm-9pm every day.

Som Tam Thai Restaurant, *cnr Fifth Avenue and Aerodrome Road,* ☎ *5479 1700.* BYO (wine only), open 5pm-10pm 7 days and 12pm-2.30pm Fri-Sun, closed Public Holidays.

McDonalds has two locations in Maroochydore: *14-18 Aerodrome Road and in Sunshine Plaza.*

Pizza Hut is on the corner of *Horton Parade and First Avenue.*

Noosa
Population 38,000
Noosa Heads, with its northerly facing beach, is protected from the prevailing south-easterly winds. Noosa has a cosmopolitan atmosphere, coupled with the natural beauty of the area. The headland is a National Park and there are several walks meandering through it to the various attractions, including **Boiling Pot, Hell's Gates** and **Paradise Cave.**

Noosa's boutiques and restaurants in **Hastings Street** are first class, and there is no shortage of entertainment.

There are coloured sands at **Teewah** can be reached at low tide. Tours are available from Noosaville or Tewantin. Upstream from Tewantin, the Noosa River meanders through lakes which are surrounded by wetlands with prolific bird life. This area is the **Cooloola National Park.** In the 1870s, huge log rafts were guided down the river to Tewantin, where they were sorted before continuing their way to Brisbane. Five lakes are linked in a waterway network stretching for almost 80km (50 miles). **Lake Cootharaba** has a special area for learner water skiers, and many visitors spend holidays on houseboats wandering through the river system.

Inland is **Nambour,** the most southern of Queensland's sugar towns, where the old cane trolleys ramble across the main street to the **Moreton Central Sugar Mill.** Pineapple and other tropical fruit plantations are also found around the district.

At the **Sunshine Plantation,** 6km south of Nambour, you can see the **Big Pineapple,** *Nambour Connection Road, Woombye,* and take a tour of the plantation by train. It is ☉open daily 9am-5pm, ☎ *5442 1333*

Bli Bli has a **Fairytale Castle,** *David Low Way,* ☎ *5448 5373,* a replica 11th century Norman Castle with moat, portcullis and drawbridge. Inside, fairytales are depicted in elaborate dioramas. Popular with children, the castle is ☉open daily 9am-5pm.

Nostalgia Town, *596 David Low Way,* ☎ *5448 7155,* is another attraction, just north of Bli Bli at Pacific Paradise. Call in and have a laugh at the past.

Big Cow Antique Centre, ☎ *5446 8477,* home of the **Big Cow,** is 6km north of Nambour on the Bruce Highway, and milking demonstrations and feeding of nursery animals are some of the highlights.

Another 3km north at Yandina is **Gingertown,** *Pioneers Road,* ☎ *5446 8455,* the largest ginger processing factory in the southern hemisphere. The ginger processed here is grown in rich red soil between the Blackall Range and the coast.

On **Tanawha Forest Glen Tourist Drive,** visitors can visit three attractions: **Super Bee's Honey Factory** near the Buderim turnoff, ☎ *5445 3544,* has collecting demonstrations and is ☉open daily 9am-5pm. Admission is free.

At the **Forest Glen Deer Sanctuary and Wildlife Park,** ☎ *5445 1274,* free-roaming deer can be fed from your car. Koalas, kangaroos and emus can also be seen. It is ☉open 9am-5pm, daily.

The **Moonshine Valley Winery,** *Bruce Highway,* ☎ *5445 1198,* specialises in fruit wines. Free tastings are held daily.

About and hour away from Noosa in between Brisbane is the **Australia Zoo.** Come and meet the famous crocodile hunter himself, Stever Irwin. All of the 750 animals kept here

Noosa

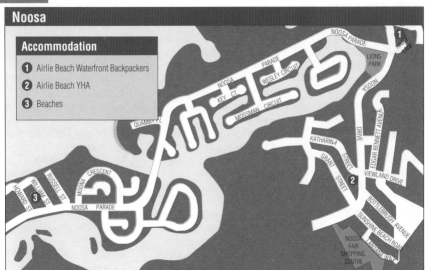

Accommodation

1. Airlie Beach Waterfront Backpackers
2. Airlie Beach YHA
3. Beaches

were caught by him and his dad. ⏰Open daily from 8:30am-4pm. Adults 🔾 $23, concessions $19.

🔾 Let's Stay Here

Gagaju Bush Camp,
118 Johns Rd, ☎*5474 3522* 🖥*www.travoholic.com/ gagaju/* Bush setting with unique bush bunkhouses and nightly camp fires, TV room and 70 plus videos, full kitchen, internet access, bushwalking, fishing rods, table tennis, volleyball, canoe adventures, gym and free tea and coffee. *Camping own tent* 🔾 *$11 ($12 first night); camping our tent $14 ($15 first night)*

Halse Lodge Guesthouse YHA,
2 Halse Lane, Noosa Heads, ☎*1800 242 567 or 5447 3377* 🖥*www.halselodge.com.au* An 1880's restored National Trust and Heritage listed Historic Building. Close to the beach, shops, cafes bars and

nightclubs. Noosa's National Park is also only minutes away. 26 rooms. Facilities includes kitchen, TV lounge, barbecue area, secured lockers, games room, surfboards, bodyboards, internet access, parking and bikes for hire. **Recommended.** *Dorm* 🔾*$23; double/twin $55; single $55 BC MC VA EFTPOS*

Koala Beach Resort VIP,
44 Noosa Dr, ☎*1800 357 457 or 5447 3355* Noosa's well known party hostel, it boasts of an excellent bar with live music on Wednesdays. Set among lush tropical greens, facilities include ensuite bathrooms, laundry, kitchen, internet access, beach volleyball court and swimming pool. Situated near Noosa Fair shopping centre and the shops on the Sunshine Beach Rd. *Dorm* 🔾*$20; double/twin $45*

Noosa Backpackers Resort,
13 William St, Noosaville, ☎*5449 8151 or 1800 626 673,* 🖥*www.noosabackpa ckers.com* A pleasant hostel with gorgeous beach surround, located about 15mins walk to the nearest shops. Clean and well maintained. Facilities include kitchen, laundry, games room, internet access and a swimming pool. There's also an an on site bar and cafe found at the entrance. Free use of surf and boogie boards and kayaks available. *Dorm* 🔾*$20; double $45-55 (prices includes breakfast)*

Noosa North Shore Retreat,
Maximilian Rd, Noosa North Shore ☎*5447 1225* 🖥*www.noosaretreat.com.au* This hostel has a serene bush setting in the north of Noosa. Get there by ferry. Dorms and self contained cabins. Facilities includes swimming pool, bar, bistro, pokies and complex general store. It even

has a pond with ducks and geeses. Watch out for the chance to see native wildlife like kangaroos just in the surrounding areas. Live music mostly on Saturday nights and regular transfer into Noosa free for guests. *Dorms* ✪*$15-20; double $50*

Caravan Parks
Noosa River Caravan Park-Munna Point, *Russell St, Noosaville,* ☎*5449 7050.* 135 sites. There are showers and laundry facilities. (No pets allowed) *Powered sites from $20; unpowered from $16;*

Let's Eat
Emerald House Chinese Restaurant, *11 Sunshine Beach,* ☎*5447 3356.*

Indian Empire, *Shop 4 Noosa Wharf, Quambi Place, Noosa Sound,* ☎*5474 5655.*

Michels, *1 Hastings Street,* ☎*5447 3880.*

Pommies, *Quamby Place, Noosa Wharf Shopping Centre,* ☎*5474 8600.*

Roma Pizza Restaurant, *Sunshine Beach Road,* ☎*5447 3602.* Offers prawns, pizza, pasta and steak. Open 5pm-10pm.

KFC is in 5 *Sunshine Beach Road.* **Pizza Hut** is on the *corner of Lake Weyba Drive and Weyba Road,* ☎*5449 7711.*

Outlying Attractions
Gympie
Gympie is a large township situated about halfway between Maryborough and Maroochydore on the Bruce Highway. Like many towns in the north of Queensland it was once known for its abundance of gold, after its discovery by James Nash. The town sprung up during a rush in 1868 and it didn't take more than a few months for 25,000 hopeful prospectors to cram the fields nearby.

Gympie's attractions are mainly historic, including **The Gold and Mining Museum,** the **Woodworks Forestry** and **Timber Museum** and a number of buildings reminiscent of the town's colonial heritage.

There are two places you can contact for further information: the Gympie Visitor Information Centre, *Bruce Highway, Lake Alford,* ☎*(07) 5482 2847* or the Coloola Regional Development Bureau, *224 Mary Street, Gympie,* ☎*(07) 5482 5444.*

Blackall Range
The Blackall Range, on Brisbane's Sunshine Coast, is a world apart, with its art and craft galleries, Devonshire teas, comfortable pubs, green fields, hedgerows, and a feeling of Olde England. From high vantage points between **Mapleton** and **Maleny,** the small farms and cane fields of the coastal plain stretch out to join the blue Pacific, and south from Maleny are the dramatic **Glass House Mountains**. Throughout the Blackall Ranges are national and forestry parks, offering superb walks through tropical rainforest, picnic spots beside waterfalls, and rock pools for swimming.

The website to visit is 🖳www. sunshinecoast.com/ blackallranges .html

Maryborough
Including Hervey Bay and Fraser Island
Population 73,000
Maryborough is 255km (158 miles) north of Brisbane, on the Mary River.

Characteristics
Maryborough is known as Heritage City due to its magnificent homes and public buildings.

Situated on a curve of the broad Mary River, close to 150 years of history can be found in the city. The Mary River was discovered by Andrew Petrie in 1842, and not long after a member of his party returned to establish sheep farming near Tiaro. However by March 1843, the venture had failed due to disease in the sheep and attacks by natives. In June, 1847, George Furber settled in one of the deserted outstations on the south bank and built a wharf, store and shanty. The schooner Sisters arrived in December to load wool from the stations and Maryborough became a wool port.

How to Get There
By Air
Qantas, ☎*131313,* have daily fights to/from Brisbane.

By Bus
McCafferty's, ☎*13 1499,* **Greyhound Pioneer,** ☎*13 2030,* and **Suncoast Pacific,** ☎*5443 1011,* stop at Maryborough on their Brisbane-Cairns routes. **Wide Bay Transit,** ☎*4121 3719.*

By Train
QR CityTrain operates to Maryborough. www.citytrain.com.au. ☎*13 12 30.*

Visitor Information

The Fraser Coast - South Burnett Regional Tourism Board Ltd. is located at *388-396 Kent Street, Maryborough*, ☎*(07) 4122 3444*. The web address is ▣www.frasercoast.org and the email address is ✉info@frasercoast.org The Maryborough Visitor Information Centre is at *30 Ferry Street, Maryborough*, ☎*4121 4111*.

You will find the Hervey Bay Tourist and Information Centre at *353 The Esplanade*, ☎*4124 4050*. There is also an Information Centre at *63 Old Maryborough Road, Pialba*, ☎*4124 9609*.

If you wish to make bookings, the following two outlets will be able to assist you:

The Whale Booking Office, *419 The Eplanade*, ☎*4125 3399*, and Hervey Bay Accommodation Centre, *139 Boat Harbour Drive, Hervey Bay*, ☎*4124 2424*.

Points of Interest
Maryborough

The site of the original Maryborough township illustrated the real environs and features of early settlements in the then colony of New South Wales. Of particular relevance is the scale of the early settle-ment, with the landing, the inns, the sawpits, the water supply, trades and industries, and even the burial ground - all within walking distance.

In the town there are two marked Walking Routes to see the attractions. For Route Number 1, start at the Information Centre and follow the Red Marker posts. Walk Number 2 branches from near the site of **George Furber's Inn** and returns past **Baddow House**.

Baddow House, *366 Queen Street*, ☎*4123 1883*, is one of Maryborough's most historic homes, and is fully furnished with authentic period furniture. It has exhibits of colonial and museum pieces, and is ⊙open daily 10am-4pm. Devonshire teas and souvenirs are available.

There are **Pioneer Graves** at the northern-most extremity of the Original Maryborough township, in *Aldridge Street, Baddow*. The harshness and difficulties of frontier life ensured that the early township experienced loss of life, but death from natural causes or old age was virtually unknown.

Queens Park, *Sussex Street*, was established more than a century ago, and many of its huge trees were planted as experiments by the Acclimatization Society. Features of the park are the fernery, waterfall and lily pond, lace-trimmed band rotunda built in 1890, and the 13cm gauge model railway built by the Model Engineers and Live Steamers Association. On the last Sunday of the month the Association meets in Queens Park to relive the steam age.

Ululah Lagoon, *Lions Drive*, was originally the water supply in the early days of settlement. The lagoon is now a wildlife sanctuary where tame black swans, ducks and waterfowl can be hand fed. The lagoon is surrounded by tree-studded parkland with picnic tables and barbecues.

Bottlebrush Crafts (Maitlia Potters), *320 Albert Street*, ☎*4122 2533*, have sales and promotion of local crafts, regular exhibits and workshops. ⊙open Mon-Fri 10am-3pm, Sat 10am-1pm.

Caltex Mountain View Roadhouse, *Bruce Highway, Bauple*, ☎*4129 2267*, has an extensive range of rocks, minerals, gems and fossils, including thundereggs and petrified woods.

Macadamia Plantation, *cnr Bruce Highway and Owany-illa Boundary Road*, south of Maryborough, has brought the world of macadamia nuts to the public. Stage one of the complex, the processing and retail plant, is a major tourist attraction. Guided tours of the plantation aboard the **Nutty Choo Choo**, with running commentary, are very popular. There is also a shop selling unusual souvenirs, a kiosk with light refreshments, and barbecue lunches are available. ⊙open daily 9am-5pm.

The **MV Duches**s has hourly cruises on the Mary River on Wed, Thurs and Sun afternoons. Her low profile design enables her to travel unrestricted up river under all the bridges, passing past and present sites of early industry and architecture, an island bat colony and much more. There is informative and humorous commentary. For more information contact the Maryborough Visitor Information Centre, ☎*4121 4111*.

↘ Let's Stay Here

There are a number of budget accommodation available in the South Burnett Region. This is just a selection with prices which should be used as a guide only. The telephone area code is 07.

Maryborough City, *138 Ferry Street*, ☎*4121 2568*. 17 units, licensed restaurant (closed Sun), swimming pool, barbecue - ✪*$60*.

Royal Centre Point, *326 Kent*

Street, ☎4121 2241. 18 units, licensed restaurant - *from* **❍$55.**

Caravan Parks
Wallace Units and Caravan Park, 22 Ferry Street, ☎4121 3970. Pool, barbecue - *powered sites* **❍$14** *for two, units $50 for two, cabins $30 for two.*

Huntsville Caravan Park, 23 Gympie Road, ☎4121 4075. (Pets allowed on application) - *powered sites* **❍$16** *for two, on-site vans $25 for two, cabins $30 for two.*

Maryborough Caravan Park, 209 Gympie Road, ☎4121 6379. 50 sites, barbecue, pool - *powered sites* **❍$14** *for two, cabins,* **❍$40** *for two.*

Country Stopover Caravan Park, Bruce Highway, ☎4121 2764. (Pets allowed on application) - *powered sites* **❍$17** *for two, on-site vans $25 for two.*

Let's Eat
If you are having trouble deciding where to eat, here is a list of restaurants in the Maryborough area, with numbers and locations, from which you might like to make a choice. The telephone area code is 07.

Casino Royale, 338 Kent Street, ☎4121 6225.

China Dragon Restaurant, in the Central Hotel, 171 Adelaide Street, ☎4123 1399.

Colony Room Restaurant, cnr Ferry and Albert Streets, ☎4121 2366.

Lucky Chinese Restaurant, 302 Kent Street, ☎4121 3645.

Muddy Water Cafe, 71 Wharf Street, ☎4121 5011.

Red Roo Hotel, 100 Adelaide Street, ☎4121 3586.

The Gardenia, 193 Adelaide Street, ☎4121 4967.

McDonalds is on the corner of Quarry Road and the Bruce Highway, as well as on the corner of Alice and Ferry Streets. **KFC** is on the corner of Walker and Ferry Streets. Pizza Hut is on the corner of Alice and Ferry Streets, ☎13 1166.

Hervey Bay
Situated 34km (21 miles) east of Maryborough, Hervey Bay is one of Australia's best value holiday destinations. It has a climate similar to that of Hawaii, and virtually year-round swimming in a safe and sheltered environment.

The Bay offers a variety of charter boats for fishing trips. These vary in length from a couple of hours out on the water to day/night trips. Most trips are out to the deep waters off **Sandy Cape, Breaksea Spit, Rooney's** and the gutters around **Fraser Island**. Reef fish which abound in the Bay's waters include Coral Bream, Blackall, Snapper, Coral Trout and Cod. A few companies specialising in cruises are:

Lady Elliot Island Reef Resort Day Tours, 1800 072 200 for reservations.
Splash Safaris, 6 Inman Street, Point Vernon, 0500 555 580.
Stefanie Yacht Charters, 7 Burum Street, Hervey Bay, 4125 4200.

Hervey Bay now has international recognition as one of the best vantage points for studying the Humpback Whale. From early August to mid-October, these gentle giants stop in at Hervey Bay on their return south to Antarctica. They frolic in the warm waters of the Bay, almost oblivious to the people watching eagerly from the safety of tour boats.

Some of the companies operating whale watch tours are:

Islander Whale Watch Cruises, Buccaneer Avenue, 4125 3399.
Mimi Macpherson's Whale Watch Expeditions, 449 The Esplanade, Torquay, 4125 1700 or 1800 683 368.
Spirit of Hervey Bay Whale Watch Cruises, 864 Boat Harbour Drive, Urangan, 4125 5131.
Whalesong Cruises, Torquay, Whale Watch and Dolphin Cruises, 4125 6222.

For further details on tours and cruises, contact the Hervey Bay Tourist and Visitors Centre, 353 The Esplanade, ☎ 4124 4050.

The **Whale Festival**, held in August, is a weekend full of activities to officially launch the whale watching season. Features include an aquatic carnival, illuminated procession of boats, the Princess of Whales competition, and the World Smiling Championships.

Hervey Bay Nature World, Maryborough Road, Pialba, on the main highway at the entrance to Hervey Bay, is an Australian theme park set in 15ha (37 acres) of bushland. Calling the place home are kangaroos, wallabies, wombats, emu, deer, buffalo, waterbirds and a large number of crocodiles. The crocodiles feed daily in summer and twice weekly in winter. Feeding time is 11.30am. Lorikeets feed daily between 3-4pm. There are free paddle boat rides, playground, barbecue and picnic areas, and toilets for the disabled. ⊕open daily 9am-5pm. You can phone them on ☎4124 1733.

Dayman Point features sweeping views of Great Sandy Strait, picnic facilities and two memorials: one to Z Force and their vessel The Krait; the other to Captain Matthew Flinders, who landed nearby on August 6, 1799, and Lt Joseph Dayman, RN who passed in the schooner *Asp* after making the first passage through Fraser Island (now Great Sandy) Strait in 1847.

↩ Let's Stay Here

The accommodation for the Bay is in the towns of Torquay, Urangan, Pialba and Scarness.

Beaches Backpackers,
195 Torquay Terrace, Scarness, ☎*4124 1322 or 1800 655 501,* ▉*www.beaches.com.au* If you want a nice and bright accommodation? Then you can't miss

these yellow and blue cabins from this backpacker place. Their quality varies from cabin to cabin though. Has a bar, swimming pool, kitchen and TV lounge and barbecue area. Good place. *Dorms from* ✪*$17; double $45.*

Colonial Log Cabins YHA,
820 Boat Harbour Drive, Urangan, ☎*4125 3161 or 1800818280,* ▉*www.coloniallogcabins.com/* Situated towards the harbour, a fair way from anything. This secluded complex is actually quite large with 15 separate buildings. Cabins are all different from each other and most are self contained units with their own TVs and fridges. Other facilities includes a kitchen, laundry, internet access, a swimming pool and spa. The common areas are really good and features an on site bar and restaurant plus pool tables. There is also a basketball and tennis court out in the courtyards. *Self contained cabins* ✪*$18pp; single $18; double/twin $22pp ($27pp with en suite)*

Fraser Escape Backpackers,
21 Denman Camp Rd, Scarness, ☎*4128 1484 or 1800 646 711.* This used to be a caravan park, turned into a backpackers. Accomodation varies from small cabins to basic caravans. You're really after the value for money here more than anything. *Dorms from* ✪*$9-15; double $35*

Frasier Roving,
412 The Esplanade, Torquay. ☎*4125 6386 or 1800 989 811,* ▉*www.fraserroving.com.au* This used to be a hospital located on the Esplanade. Rooms are really big and spacious. There's a swimming pool and spa, big kitchen, internet access, a TV lounge with comfy sofas and barbecue area. *Dorm* ✪*$15-45.* (prices includes breakfast)

Friendly Hostel,
182 Torquay Rd, Scarness. ☎*4124 4107 or 1800 244 107.* This small hostel has self conatined units with a nice, quiet shared deck area and barbecue. The views from the back area is quite nice.

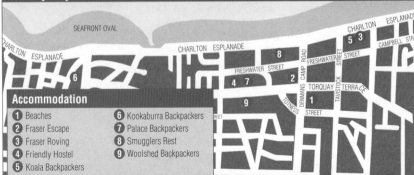

Hervey Bay

Accommodation

1. Beaches
2. Fraser Escape
3. Fraser Roving
4. Friendly Hostel
5. Koala Backpackers
6. Kookaburra Backpackers
7. Palace Backpackers
8. Smugglers Rest
9. Woolshed Backpackers

Kept clean and well maintained. *Dorms ○$19-44.*

Koala Backpackers,
408 The Esplanade, Scarness. ☎*4125 3601 or 1800 354 535,* 💻*www.koalabackpacke rs.com* You'll find accommodaation here in either self contained units or in dorms. Facilities includes kitchen, laundry, TV room, swimming pool and bar. Has restaurant that serves cheap meals. *Dorms from ○$18; double $45*

Kookaburra Backpackers,
264 Charles St. ☎*1800 111 442,* 💻*www.kookaburraback packers.com* Another hostel that used to be a hospital in the 1920s changed into a backpackers. Set in a nice old building with a great atmosphere. Some dorms have their own en suite. Features a laundry, common room with comfy couches and big screen TV, internet access, pool tables and a barbecue area. There's also an on site beer garden. Bus shuttle and car park available. *Dorms ○$18; doubles $40* (prices includes breakfast and dinner)

Palace Backpackers,
184 Torquay Rd, Scarness, ☎*1800 063 168.* A pretty good hostel with self contained units. Kept clean and well maintained. Common area with pool table, TV room and a swimming pool. *Dorms from ○$18; double/twin $40.*

Woolshed Backpackers,
181 Torquay Rd, Scarness. ☎*4124 0677.* A pretty good

backpackers with a nice bush setting. Has a real outback feel to it. Kept clean and well maintained. Basic but good quality facilities including your kitchen, TV lounge and common rooms. *Dorms ○$17; double $40.*

Caravan Parks
Anchorage Caravan Park,
Boat Harbour Drive, Urangan, ☎*4128 9286.* Pool, barbecue - *powered sites ○$16-19 for two, on-site vans $35-40 for two.*

Harbour View Caravan Park,
Jetty Road, Boat Harbour, Urangan, ☎*4128 9374.* 80 sites, pool - *powered sites ○$16-18 for two, on-site vans $30 for two.*

Happy Wanderer Village Caravan Park, *105 Truro Street, Torquay,* ☎*4125 1103.* 92 sites, pool, spa - *powered sites ○$21 for two, on-site vans $30 for two, cabins $45-55 for two.*

Magnolia Caravan Park,
cnr Boat Harbour Drive and Taylor Street, Pialba, ☎*4128 1700.* 53 sites, pool, barbecue - *powered sites ○$14 for two, on-site vans $30 for two.*

Pialba Beachfront Tourist Park, *Esplanade, Pialba,* ☎*4128 1399.* Powered sites ○*$18-22 for two.*

Scarness Beachfront
The Hervey Bay Youth Hostel is at *Boat Harbour Drive,* ☎*4125 1844.* 29 rooms. ○*$18pp twin share.*

Shelly Beach Caravan Park,
61 Ocean Street, Torquay, ☎*4125 1105.* (No dogs allowed) - *powered sites ○$17 for two, on-site vans $25-30 for two, cabins $40-45 for two.*

The Palms Caravan Park,
cnr Roberts and Truro Streets, Torquay, ☎*4125 1704.* Pool, barbecue - *powered sites ○$17 for two, on-site vans $25-35.*

Torquay Beachfront Tourist Park, *Esplanade, beach front-age,* ☎*4125 1578.* (No dogs) - *powered sites ○$18-22 for two.*

Tourist Park,
Esplanade, Scarness, ☎*4128 1274.* (No dogs allowed) 160 sites - *powered sites ○$14 for two.*

Windmill Caravan Park,
17 Elizabeth Street, Urangan, ☎*4128 9267.* 60 sites, barbecue, pool - *powered sites $18-20 for two, on-site vans $30-40 for two.*

Let's Eat
Bay Central Chinese Kitchen,
Boat Harbour Drive, Hervey Bay, ☎*4124 1200.*

China Palace, *38 Torquay Road, Pialba,* ☎*4124 8808.*

Curried Away, *174 Boat Harbour Drive, Pialba,* ☎*4124 1577.*

Don Camillo Ristorante Italiano,
486 Esplanade, Hervey Bay, ☎*4125 5466.*

Fryer Tucks, Urangan Plaza, *564 Esplanade, Urangan,* ☎*4125 5933.*

Hervey Bay Chinese Restaurant, *Shop A, 3 Fraser Street, Torquay,* ☎ *4125 6906.*

Marty's on the Beach, *344 Esplanade, Scarness,* ☎ *4128 1233.*

Raphaels, *564 Esplanade, Urangan,* ☎ *4125 2183.*

Thai Diamond, *355 Esplanade, Scarness,* ☎ *4124 4855.*

The Deck, *Hervey Bay Marina, Buccaneer Avenue, Hervey Bay,* ☎ *4125 1155.*

KFC is on the corner of T*orquay Road and Taylor Street* in Hervey Bay. **Pizza Hut** is in *Lot 2 Boat Harbour Drive, Pialba,* ☎ *13 1166.*

Fraser Island

Fraser Island is the largest sand island in the world, a fishing paradise, and one of the world's last wilderness areas. It is 11km (7 miles) from Hervey Bay, and is composed almost entirely of siliceous sands which extend to more than 600m (1968 ft) below sea level. The only rock outcrops on the east coast are at **Indian Head, Middle Rock and Waddy Point.** On the west coast there is a small outcrop of hard rock at **Bun Bun Rocks.**

The island has an area of 184,000ha (454,480 acres), is 123km (76 miles) long, and has an average width of 14km (9 miles), ranging to 22km (14 miles) at its widest part. Dune heights reach to 240m (787 ft).

Most of the island is crown land, national park or State forest reserve. Five main tourist centres - at Eurong, Happy Valley, Orchard Beach, Cathedral Beach and Dilli Village - cater for

those who like home comforts. If you prefer a real wilderness experience, you can camp in a secluded spot and explore the island by forest tracks, which are suitable for 4WD only.

All visitors to the island are required to have permits. The fee charged is used to provide facilities for visitors and to provide effective protection for the unique island environment. Permit costs are: ✪$34 per vehicle prior to arrival, ✪$45 per vehicle on the island. They are available from Department of Environment and Heritage, Rainbow Beach, ☎ *(07) 5486 3160* or in Brisbane, ☎ *(07) 3227 7111.*

Fraser Island can be reached by sea and air. Cruises and vehicular barges operate from Hervey Bay, Mary River Heads and Rainbow Beach. Charter flights and tours are also available.

There are over 40 freshwater lakes on the island. As well as the perched dune lakes, there are window lakes, formed when the shifting sand falls below the level of the island's dome-shaped water table. Remarkable is **Lake Wabby**, an easy walk from the ocean beach. It is the deepest of the island's lakes, and contains the greatest variety of fish, but it is dying, slowly being strangled by a sandblow that encroaches four metres each year.

Up to 72 different colours have been recorded in the sands on the island. The most famous area of coloured sand cliffs is **The Cathedrals** on the eastern side of the island midway between **Happy Valley** and **Orchid Beach**.

The island has hundreds of kilometres of white sand beaches, its own wreck (the Maheno, which beached during a cyclone

50 years ago) and countless freshwater streams.

Dingoes are also found on the island, not as pets or in cages, but living freely. It is generally accepted that if you leave them alone, they will leave you alone, but it is requested that you do not feed them. They find their own food, and do well without handouts.

This hostel is just an extension of the Rainbow beach Hotel/Pub. The rooms surrounds the swimming pool which also has a barbecue area plus hammocks are about. Also features a kitchen, laundry, an open-air lounge with a huge screen TV and there's also internet access. There's also an on site restaurant. Body and surf board and bike hire available. *Dorms* ✪*$15; double $45*

Fraser's on Rainbow Beach
18 spectrum St, Rainbow Beach, ☎*5486 8885 or 1800 100 170* Accommodation here is set out like motel accommodation, with rooms having their own en suite bathrooms and TVs. Quite a good place to stay at, with their huge commercial kitchen, laundry, common areas, lounge and big screen TV, internet access and a swimming pool with a barbecue area. There's also an on site bar with a pool table. **Recommended.** *Dorms* ✪*$22; double/twin with ensuite $30pp*

Rainbow Beach Backpackers,
66 Rainbow Beach Rd, Rainbow Beach, ☎*5486 32888* Quite a quaint backpackers that's kept clean and well maintained. Features a kitchen, TV lounge room, internet and barbecue area and ping pong. Air conditioned. *Dorm* ✪*$18; double $44*

The Rocks YHA Backpackers Resort,
Spectrum St, ☎*5486 3711 or 1800 646 867,*

www.yha.com.au You'll find good accommodation and great facilities with this tropical covered purpose built, resort style hostel. All rooms have en suite bathrooms. Facilities includes a small kitchen, laundry, internet access, TV lounge room, swimming pool and a barbecue area. There's also a nice on site bar and bistro that serves cheap meals. Parking available. *Dorms from* ✪*$18; double/twin $19pp BC MC VA EFTPOS*

Outlying Attractions Burrum Heads, Toogoom, Howard, Torbanlea
Burrum Heads and Toogoom are two small coastal resorts located at the mouth of the Burrum River, both popular for their good fishing and relaxed atmosphere. In the winter months especially, fishermen come from miles around to catch whiting.

Burrum Heads is growing rapidly and is well serviced with shops. In September the area is vibrant with colourful wildflowers. Toogoom has plenty of good picnic spots, and over ninety species of birds have been identified in the area. Both of these resorts have caravan parks and holiday homes.

The Burrum River crosses the highway between Howard and Torbanlea. It is a picturesque waterway for boating, fishing and crabbing, and has a caravan park on its banks. Most houses in these two townships are the cool high-set timber Queenslander homes. Howard has all the facilities of an up-and-coming small town.

Approximately 20km north

of Maryborough on the Bruce Highway, there is an exit for Burrum Heads.

Bundaberg
Population 56,000
Bundaberg is situated on the Burnett River, 378km (235 miles) north of Brisbane. Strictly speaking, it is not part of the Great Barrier Reef and in fact sits on the southern side of the designated boundary. If you are travelling along the coast in either direction, there are a number of factors which may encourage you to stop here.

Climate
Average temperatures: Jan max 30C (86F) - min 21C (70F); July max 21C (70F) - min 11C (52F). Average annual rainfall: 1149mm (45 ins); heaviest rainfall falls December-March.

Characteristics
The Bundaberg district grows approximately one-fifth of Australia's sugar crop, and in recent years has become a virtual salad bowl, growing large supplies of tomatoes, avocados, pineapples, beans and more. And, of course, the Famous Aussie Spirit, **Bundaberg Rum**, is produced here in this Sugar City.

How to Get There
By Air
Qantas Link ☎*13 1313* operate several flights daily to/from Cairns, Brisbane, Rockhampton, and Gladstone.

By Bus
McCafferty's and Greyhound Pioneer, ☎*13 2030* or ☎*13 1499,* stop at Bundaberg on their Brisbane/Cairns route.
Premiere, ☎*13 3410* also

stops at Bundaberg on their Brisbane/Cairns route.

Oz Experience, *1300 300 028,* stops at Bundaberg on their Brisbane/Airlie Beach route.

By Rail
Bundaberg is on the main Brisbane/Cairns line. The **Queensland TILT, Sunlander, Queenslander and Spirit of Capricorn** all stop at Bundaberg, ☎ 13 2235.

Visitor Information
Bundaberg District Tourism and Development Board is at the Hinkler Glider Museum, *271 Bourbong Street,* next to the Base Hospital, ☎ *4152 2333.* ⊕opening hours are Mon-Fri 8.30am-5pm, Sat-Sun 9am-5pm.

↪ Let's Stay Here
There are over 30 motels in Bundaberg as well as hotels, caravan parks and backpacker

accommodation. Here is a selection, with prices which should be used as a guide only. The telephone area code is 07.

City
Bourbong Street Motel,
265 Bourbong Street, ☎4151 3089. 17 units - ✪*$55.*

Bundaberg Backpackers Lodge,
2 Crofton St, ☎ *4152 2080* Located just in front of the bus depot. Well maintained and very clean. Rooms are all air conditioned and the only ones you'll find in Bundaberg. There's a communal kitchen, TV room and also internet access. Security is also pretty good with everyone having their own locker. There's a nice balcony that overlooks the street. Note that this is an alcohol free zone. *Dorm* ✪*$20*

Central Hotel,
18 Targo St, ☎ *4151 2400* Check-in is located in a pub in the centre of town, but the accommodation is somewhere else. Caters for travellers on working holidays. Your average facilities. Free sausage sizzle on Saturdays. *Dorm* ✪*$20*

City Centre Backpackers,
216 Bourbng St, ☎ *4151 3501* Located close to the train station just at the main street. Caters largely to travellers on working holidays. Facilities includes a large kitchen, TV room and a nice eating area outside. Everyone's nice and friendly and the staff runs weekend trips to the beach. Note that this is an alcohol free zone. *Dorm* ✪*$19; double $40;*

Federal Backpackers,
221 Bourbong St, ☎ *4153 3711.* Situated near the train station on the main street. Also close to the pool and shops. Located above a pub in a historical building. There are tropical verandahs and a beer garden. Another one that caters for travellers on a working holiday. Just your basic facilities. *Dorm* ✪*$23*

Lyelta Lodge and Motel, *8 Maryborough Street,* ☎ *4151 3344.* 20 rooms, undercover parking available. *Dorms* ✪*$35-40.*

Nomads Workers and Divers Hostel,
64 Barolin St, 4151 6097 Located on a residential area about a km from town. Built

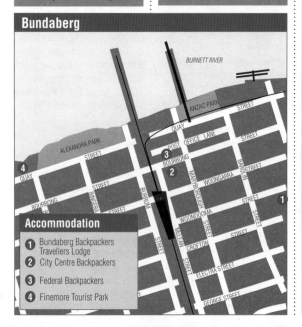

Bundaberg

BURNETT RIVER

ANZAC PARK

QUAY STREET

POST OFFICE LANE STREET

ALEXANDORA PARK

STREET

QUAY

BOURBONG

PINGERRA STREET

BOURBONG

MARYBOROUGH STREET

WOONGARRA STREET

BURRUM

WOONDOOMA STREET

MCLEAN STREET

CROFTON STREET

ELECTRA STREET

GEORGE STREET

BAROLIN STREET

STREET

Accommodation
1. Bundaberg Backpackers Travellers Lodge
2. City Centre Backpackers
3. Federal Backpackers
4. Finemore Tourist Park

within an old Queenslander-style house. The facilities you'll find are your normal kitchen, games room with pool tables, table tennis and foosball, internet access and a nice common area outside with a barbecue. There's also a swimming pool. *Dorms* ✪*$19; double/twin $36*

Sunray Backpackers, *12 Queen St,* ☎*41524573* Located close to shops. Rooms have ensuite bathrooms. Your normal facilities, with kitchen, laundry and swimming pool. Parking available. *Dorms* ✪*$25.*

Caravan Parks
Absolute Ocean Front Tourist Park, *117 Woongarra Scenic Drive, Bargara,* ☎*4159 2436.* 42 sites, barbecue, kiosk, spa, pool - *powered sites* ✪*$14 for two, on-site vans $30-38 for two, cabins $40-47 for two.*

Bargara Beach Caravan Park, *Nielson Park, The Esplanade, Bargara,* ☎*4159 2228.* (Pets on application) 300 sites, barbecue, playground, 2 tennis courts, kiosk - *powered sites* ✪*$16 for two, on-site vans $28 for two, cabins $38-46 for two.*

Bargara Beach Motor Inn, *7 Bauer Street, Bargara,* ☎*4159 2395.* 6 units, barbecue, undercover parking - ✪*$55.*

Cane Village Holiday Park, *Twyford Street,* ☎*4155 1022.* 84 sites, playground, barbecue, pool - *powered sites* ✪*$17-16 for two, cabins $35-38 for two.*

Finemore Tourist Park, *33 Quay Street,* ☎*4151 3663.* (No pets) 66 sites, barbecue, pool - *powered sites* ✪*$14 for two, cabins $38 for two.*

Oakwood Caravan Park, *Gin Gin Road,* ☎*4159 9332.* 86 sites, pool, barbecue, kiosk - *powered sites* ✪*$15 for two, on-site vans $25-30 for two, cabins $40-45 for two.*

Let's Eat
Bundaberg has an abundance of licensed and BYO restaurants, licensed clubs and hotels, and plenty of coffee lounges, takeaways and snack bars. If you wish, get in touch with the Visitor Information Centre, ☎*4152 2333,* for a list of culinary establishments and local advice on the best places to dine. If you're not in an adventurous mood, the major fast-food chains have branches in Bundaberg.

Mexican Border, *27 Elliots Head Road,* ☎*4152 1675.* Licensed, Mexican dishes.

New China Dragon Restaurant, *32 Targo Street,* ☎*4151 1955.* Seafood cuisine, BYO. Open 5am-9pm seven days and 11am-2.30pm Mon-Fri, closed Public Holidays.

Numero Uno, *167a Bourbong Street,* ☎*4151 3666.*

Oriental Pearl Chinese Restaurant, *69 Takalvan Street,* ☎*4152 8655.*

Rendezvous, *220 Bourbong Street,* ☎*4153 1747.* Licensed, open 24 hours.

The Strand, *55 Woongarra Street,* ☎*4151 2099.* Curry a speciality on Sunday nights. Open 8am-midnight every day except Public Holidays (closed).

Zulus, *61 Targo Street,* ☎*4152 4691.*

You will find **KFC** at *263 Bourbong Street,* **McDonalds** on the *corner of Woongarra and Targo Streets* and **Pizza Hut** on the *corner of Bourbong and Branyon Streets,* ☎*13 6611.*

Local Transport
There are regular bus services to North Bundaberg, South Bundaberg, Norville, West Bundaberg, Sugarland Shoppingtown, Bargara and Burnett Heads, Elliott Heads, South Kolan/Bingera, Kepnock, Moore Park and Gin Gin - contact the Visitor Information Centre for details and timetables.

Points of Interest
A trip to the reef aboard the **MV Lady Musgrave** takes just over two hours from Bundaberg. The office is located in *Shop 1 Moffat Street, Bundaberg Port Marina,* ☎*4159 4519* or ☎*4152 9011.*

Lady Musgrave Island, 49km (30 miles) from the coast, is a truly unspoiled, uninhabited coral atoll where you can stroll through the pisonia and casuarina trees and view the nesting seabirds. The launch trip includes morning and afternoon tea, smorgasbord luncheon, snorkelling gear and glass-bottomed boat rides. A fun day is assured. (See separate listing.)

Bundaberg has several memorials to its most famous son, Herbert John Louis Hinkler (Bert Hinkler) - locally he was known as 'Hustling Hinkler'. He was the first aviator to fly solo from England to Australia, in 1928. **Hinkler House**, *Mt Perry Road*, was transported brick by brick from Southampton, England, to Bundaberg in 1983, by a team of dedicated workers. Hinkler designed the house and lived in it from 1926-1933. It is now an aviation museum ☼open daily 10am- 4pm, ☎*4152 0222*.

There are memorials to Hinkler in **Buss Park** beside the Civic Centre, at the southern end of the traffic bridge, and on the **Hummock**, 10km east of the city. **The Hinkler Glider Museum** contains a replica of Hinkler's glider which he successfully flew 35m from the sand dunes of Mon Repos Beach in 1912. The historical museum is in the same complex and contains a fascinating collection of domestic items and farm equipment. **The Botanical Gardens** and steam railway are also in the **Hinkler Rose Garden Tourist Complex**, along with the Hinkler Rose Garden Restaurant, ☎*4153 1477*.

Bundaberg Rum Distillery, *Whitred Street*, ☎*4150 8686*, has five conducted tours every weekday, which run for approximately one hour. You can see the rum being processed from raw sugar through to the bottled product - the 'Famous Aussie Spirit', although you will not get to sample the end product for free!

Schmeiders Cooperage and Craft Centre, *5 Alexandra Street, East Bundaberg*, ☎*4151 8233* or ☎*1800 222 440*, sells small handcrafted American Oak Casks. You can see the coopers at work making these casks in their workshops. Also in the Craft Centre are potters, a blacksmith,

woodturner, artists and many more. There is a cafe as well, where you can grab a bite to eat.

Alexandra Park Zoo, is on the banks of the Burnett River, west of the main railway line. It is ☼open Mon-Fri 6.30am-3.30pm and admission is free.

The House of Dolls, *Douglas Road*, ☎*4159 7252*, has a wonderful display of dressed dolls, in national and period costumes, and a display of the Royal Wedding.

Boyd's Antiquatorium, *295 Bourbong Street*, ☎*4152 2576*, has a collection of classic racing motorcycles, vintage cars, early cameras, farm machinery, a coin collection, and a great musical instrument display. The display is directed at all ages.

Take a stroll through the fragrant **Pennyroyal Herb Farm** which is a delightful place to visit. The display gardens are set in native Australian bush.

Avocado Grove, *Douglas Road*, ☎*4159 7367*, has something for everyone. Exotic and sociable peacocks roam the grounds whilst many native birds live happily in aviaries amid the lush, sub-tropical gardens.

What caused those strange craters just north of Bundaberg? The **Mystery Craters** are said to be 25 million years old, and their origin remains unexplained. The fascinating area has a garden setting, observation tower, kiosk, rocks, souvenirs, currency display and playground. The area, in *Lines Road, South Kolan*, is ☼open 8am-5pm. The admission fee is ♻$5 adults, ☎*4157 7291*.

For an unusual treat, stop and buy some tropical fruit wine at Bundaberg's unique **Winery** at *78 Mt Perry Road*, ☎*4151*

5993. Owners, Carole and John Gianduzzo, will explain the merits of the various wines. Another unusual facet is the large range of soft drinks now produced on the premises. It is ☼open Mon-Sat 9am-5.30pm and 9am-midday on Sundays. Admission is free.

Bargara Beach is the aquatic playground for the sun and sea aficionados of Bundaberg. Just a 15 minute drive from Bundaberg, it offers safe surfing at Neilson Park. A very modern shopping centre known as **'Bargara Centrepoint'** caters for everyone's needs. The town is serviced by a modern hotel/motel, motel and unit accommodation, caravan parks, TAB, convenience store, takeaway food outlets and fine restaurants. **Kelly's Beach** has a natural still-water tidal swimming pool and is a patrolled beach.

Mon Repos Beach, with magnificent sand dunes, is the largest and most accessible mainland turtle rookery in Australia. It is an environmental park and contains a magnificent Kanaka stone wall. It was the site of Bert Hinkler's first flights. The conservation park ☼opens from 7pm onwards between November and March, and the Information Centre is open 8am-4pm March-October. Admission is ♻$5 for adults.

Burnett Heads, with **Oaks Beach**, is 18km (11 miles) from Bundaberg at the mouth of the Burnett River and has ample shops, a hotel and a couple of caravan parks. The lighthouse is located next to the hall and was taken out of service in 1972. **Moore Park**, 21km (13 miles) north of Bundaberg, is an excellent seaside beach with 16km (10 miles) of firm sandy

Bundaberg Cane Train

Shipwreak, Fraser island

Marlborough

shores. Lifesavers patrol this beach throughout the surfing season. There is a motel and a caravan park.

The Town of 1770 (and Agnes Water to the south of Round Hill) was visited by Queensland's first tourist, Captain James Cook, in the Endeavour in May 1770. The small town takes its name from this event. Day trips to Lady Musgrave Island depart from the Town of 1770, and a bus pick-up operates from Bundaberg.

Outlying Attractions
Eidsvold
Situated on the Burnett Highway 250km (155 miles) west of Bundaberg, via Gayndah, Eidsvold was established as a gold mining town in 1888 and is now a major producer of beef cattle. The town's past can be seen in the slab homestead 'Knockbreak' which is part of the Eidsvold Historical Museum. Eidsvold has a unique museum housing the George Schaffer bottle, rock and gemstone collection - a display of unusual items gathered over one man's lifetime. The Eidsvold Motel and General Store, 51 Moreton Street, can provide you with Visitor Information. ☎(07) 4165 1209.

Mundubbera
Mundubbera is situated on the banks of the Burnett River, 35km south-east of Eidsvold on the Burnett Highway. The River passes through the small sub-tropical valley of the Central Burnett. One-third of Queensland's citrus is produced here and the area is surrounded by orchards, and has the Enormous Ellendale (Big Mandarin). The Golden Mile Orchard has an extensive packing facility. The Auburn Falls National Park is 35km (22 miles) west, and has beautiful rock pools and formations. Visitor Information can be obtained from the Big Mandarin complex in Durong Road, ☎(07) 4165 4549.

Gayndah
Found 166km (103 miles) south-west of Bundaberg on the Burnett Highway, Gayndah is Queensland's oldest town, and was in the running with Ipswich and Brisbane for the title of State capital.

In the 1840s Gayndah was originally settled as sheep country, and it wasn't until 1892 that William Seeney planted the first orchard, for which Gayndah is now famous. Even if you weren't aware of it before, you could hardly miss the Big Orange complex.

The Golden Orange Hotel-Motel, Maltby Place, is the supplier of regional information for tourists, ☎(07) 4161 1107.

Biggenden
Craggy, blue mountain ranges are the backdrop for Biggenden, 100km (62 miles) south-west of Bundaberg. Along with agricultural pursuits - beef, grain crops, dairying, citrus, piggeries, peanuts and timber - the area is rich in minerals.

Established in the goldrush of 1889, attractions include the historic Chowey Bridge, the old Mt Shamrock Gold Mine, the operational open-cut magnetite mine, the Coalstoun Lakes, Mt Walsh National Park and Mt Woowoonga Forest Reserve.

You will find Visitor Information at the Biggenden Shire Council, Edward Street, ☎(07) 4127 1177.

Childers
Located 50km (31 miles) south of Bundaberg, Childers has rich red soil, and is famous for its avenue of leopard trees, colonial buildings, the Olde Butcher Shoppe and the Hall of Memories. It is on the Bruce Highway. There was an infamous fire at a backpackers place here several years ago. Visitors Information Centre for accommodation.

Less than half an hour's drive away is Woodgate Beach and Woodgate National Park, which has many boardwalks allowing access to the swampy areas. There is also a special bird-watching shed. The beach is popular and stretches for about 16km (10 miles).

Rockhampton
Population 65,000
Gateway to the Capricorn Coast, Rockhampton is 660km (410 miles) north of Brisbane, on the Tropic of Capricorn. The city is situated on the Fitzroy River about 16km (10 miles) from the coast.

Climate
Average temperatures: January max 31C (88F) - min 22C (72F); July max 23C (73F) - min 9C (48F). Most rain falls between December and March - approximately 500mm (17 in).

Characteristics
'Rocky' is the heart of the beef cattle country. The main breeds are Santa Gertrudis, Hereford, Braford, Brahman, Africander and Zebu. Rockhampton also has two flour mills which process wheat from the Central Highlands around Emerald. Ever since Queensland became a separate state, there have been people politicising for the

establishment of a separate North Queensland state.

How to Get There
By Air
Qantas Link - Impulse Airlines, ☎ *13 1313*, fly to/from Bundaberg, Gladstone, Mackay, Maryborough, Townsville and Cairns, Great Keppel Island and Toowoomba.

Check with your travel agent at the time of your trip.

By Bus
Greyhound Pioneer, ☎ *13 2030*, and **McCaffertys**, ☎ *13 1499*, stop at Rockhampton on their Brisbane/North Queensland route.

McCaffertys have a daily service to/from Longreach. Greyhound also have a Rockhampton to Longreach service departing 3 times weekly.

By Rail
Queensland Tilt Trains, ☎*13 2235*, including The **Spirit of Capricorn**, service Rockhampton fairly frequently, with either day or overnight travel. The **Sunlander** and the **Queenslander** both leave Brisbane in the early morning and stop at Rockhampton.

Visitor Information
Capricorn Tourism, is at 'The Spire' in *Gladstone Road*, ☎*4927 2055*, adjacent to the Tropic of Capricorn Spire. It is ☺open 7 days a week.

The email address is ✉captour@rocknet.net.au and the website is ▉www.capricorncoast.com.au

You will find the Rockhampton Visitor Information Centre in Quay Street, ☎4922 5339.

⤵ Let's Stay Here
Rockhampton has no shortage of motels, and there are plenty of older style hotels near the city centre. There is also no shortage of camping grounds. Below we have given a selection with prices which should be used as a guide only. The telephone area code is 07.

Denham Lodge,
62 Denham St, ☎*4922 4424* Quiet and has basic facilities for the more private type. Common kitchen and a barbecue area in the back. No dorms. *Single ✪$20; twin $35* (prices includes continental breakfast)

Downtown Backpackers - Oxford Hotel,
Corner Denham and East Sts, ☎*4922 1837* Located above a pub in the centre on the town. Facilities includes a common room with TV, kitchen and internet access. *Dorm ✪$16.50; double/twin $33*

Leichardt Hotel Rockhampton,
cnr Bolsover and Denham Streets, ☎*4927 6733*. 60 rooms, 8 suites, licensed restaurant and bistro - *from ✪$55*

Rockhampton Youth Hostel YHA,
60 MacFarlane St, North Rockhampton, ☎*4927 5288*, ▉*www.yha.com.au* Fully equiped self-catering kitchen, internet, barbecue area, laundry, dining and lounge rooms with TV. Dining area decorated in '50s rock 'n' roll items including a juke box. Olympic cabins air conditioned, used on the Sydney Olympics. Parking available. Located in North Rockhampton in a quiet area five minutes drive to town. *Members dorm ✪$19 ($22.50 non members); double/twin $44 ($49 non members)*

Caravan Parks
Capricorn Caves,
30 Olsen Rd, The Caves, ☎*4934 2883* (No pets allowed) 20 sites. Lodgings for groups are available and cabins are going to be added soon. (enquire about them) Facilities are mainly swimming pool, barbecue area, playground with ping pong tables etc. Well known for their cave tours. *Powered sites ✪$18;*

Gracemere Caravan Park,
Old Capricorn Highway, ☎*4933 1310*. 100 sites, barbecue, pool - *powered sites ✪$13*.

Ramblers Motor Village,
Bruce Highway, North Rockhampton, (opposite Shopping Fair), ☎*4928 2084*. (No pets) 60 sites, playground, pool - *powered sites ✪$19 for two, units $55-60 for two, cabins $40-50 for two*.

Riverside Tourist Park Rockhampton,
Reaney Street, North Rockhampton, ☎*4922 3779*. (No pets allowed) 150 sites - *powered sites ✪$16 for two*.

Rockhampton Village Van Park and Motel, *810 Yaamba Rd, North Rockhampton*, ☎*4936 1037* (Pets allowed) Next to the Parkhurst tavern.

18 sites. All cabins are air-conditioned, and the motel style ones are fully contained. Swimming pool and barbecue area. *Powered sites for two ✪$17; camping $12; tourists and motel cabins for single $47 ($53 for two)*

Southside Holiday Village, *Lower Dawson Road,* ☎4927 3013. 200 sites, heated pool, tennis (half court) - *powered sites ✪$21 for two, on-site vans $30-40 for two, cabins $50-55 for two.*
Tropical Wanderer Resort, *394 Yaamba Road,* ☎4926 3822. (No pets) 150 sites, licensed restaurants, barbecue, tennis (half court), pool - *powered sites ✪$22 for two, cabins $55-65 for two.*

Let's Eat
Most of the hotels serve casual counter meals, and the steaks in Rocky are particularly large, as this is the heart of the cattle country. The hotels, and several motels, also have licensed restaurants. A wide assortment of cuisine is available, from Chinese to seafood. Here are some names and numbers of establishments in the area:

Cactus Jacks Restaurant, *243 Musgrave Street, North Rockhampton,* ☎4922 2062.

Dragon Gallery, *295 Richardson Road, North Rockhampton,* ☎4928 3399. Traditional Chinese cuisine.

Friends Bistro, *159 East Street, Rockhampton,* ☎4922 2689.

Hogs Breath Cafe, *Aquatic Place,* *North Rockhampton,* ☎4926 3646.* Hamburgers and steaks.

Hong Kong Seafood Restaurant, *98a Denham Street, Rockhampton,* ☎4927 7144.

Jans Restaurant, *Pilbeam Theatre, Victoria Parade, Rockhampton,* ☎4922 3060.

Le Bistro on Quay, *194 Quay Street, Rockhampton,* ☎4922 2019.

Pacinos, *cnr Fitzroy and George Streets, Rockhampton,* ☎4922 5833. Italian fare.

Thai Tanee Restaurant, *cnr Bolsover and William Streets, Rockhampton,* ☎4922 1255.

Wah Hah, *70 Denham Street, Rockhampton,* ☎4927 1659. Chinese selections.

There are two **McDonalds** branches, one on the *Bruce Highway* in North Rockhampton and the other on the *corner of George and Fitzroy Streets, Rockhampton.* **KFC** also has two outlets, one at the *corner of George and Arthur Streets, Rockhampton,* and the other on the *corner of Linnet Street and Queen Elizabeth Drive, North Rockhampton.* **Pizza Hut** is on the *corner of High Street and Bruce Highway, North Rockhampton,* and on the *corner of Denham Street and Bruce Highway in Rockhampton,* ☎13 1166.

Entertainment
Rockhampton has a three cinema complex in **Shopping Fair,** *North Rockhampton,* ☎4926 6977, and indoor and outdoor concert venues.

There are three nightclubs in the city:
Strutters, *cnr East and Williams Streets,* ☎4922 2882.
The Party Shack, *cnr William and Alma Streets,* ☎4927 2005.
William Street Nite Club, *4 William Street,* ☎4927 1144.

The **Pilbeam Theatre** in *Victoria Parade* attracts regular performances by national and international artists, ☎4927 4111.

For details of current entertainment programs at hotels, clubs, and so on, ask at the Visitor Information Centre.

Shopping
Rockhampton has never been described as a shopping capital, but the **Shopping Fair,** *Yaaamba Road, North Rockhampton,* ☎4928 9166, was refurbished a few years ago and should cater to your basic needs. It has a departent store, two supermarkets, over 100 specialty shops, a food court, and a licensed restaurant.
The **City Heart Mall**, in *Bolsover Street*, has local art and craft markets on Saturdays, ☎4936 8481.

Points of Interest
Rockhampton was first settled in the 1850s by Charles and William Archer. Today, historic **Quay Street** contains over 20 buildings which have been classified by the National Trust.

The city is the commercial and administrative centre of central Queensland. Its wide streets are lined with trees and solid buildings, indicating a prosperity dating back to the early days. The **Australian Estate Co Ltd** offices were built in 1861, and the **Customs House** in 1901. It has a handsome copper dome and a striking semi-circular portico. Queens Wharf is all that remains of the quays of the port that was very busy until silt caused the demise of the river trade. **St Joseph's Cathedral**, *cnr Murray and William Streets* and **St Paul's Anglican Cathedral** are both built in Gothic Style from local sandstone. **The Royal Arcade** was built in 1889 as a theatre with a special feature - the roof could be opened on hot nights.

The Botanic Gardens in *Spencer Street*, ☎ *4922 4347,* are reputed to be one of the finest tropical gardens in Australia. Spreading over 4ha (10 acres), these gardens contain many native and exotic trees, ferns and shrubs, as well as a large walk-in aviary, orchid and fern house and a small Australian Zoo, which includes its own Koala Park. As part of a sister city agreement with Ibusuki City in Japan, separate Japanese Gardens were created in 1982. There are also paddle boat rides available on the lagoon. The gardens are ☺open 6am-6pm daily and admission is free.

The Pilbeam Theatre, ☎ *4927 4111* and **Art Gallery**, ☎ *4936 8248*, in Victoria Parade, form the cultural centre of Rocky. The Art Gallery has an extensive collection of Australian paintings, pottery and sculpture. The Pilbeam Theatre attracts regular performances by national and international stars.

St Aubin's Village, on Canoona Road beside the airport, consists of one of Rockhampton's oldest houses, and a number of gift shops specialising in cottage industries. It is ☺open 9am-6pm Mon-Sat and on Sundays 9am-2pm. Admission is free.

Callaghan Park Racecourse, ☎ *4927 1300*, is Queensland's premier provincial racetrack. Thursday night has greyhound racing, Saturday evening has harness racing, and on Saturday afternoon it's the gallopers' turn.

Fitzroy River Ski Gardens, near the Barrage bridge, beside the boat launching facilities, has picnic facilities, a children's playground and electric barbecues.

Old Glenmore Homestead, ☎ *4936 1033*, through the Parkhurst Industrial Estate in the north of the city, is a 130-year-old complex consisting of a log cabin, slab cottage and an adobe house. Old Glenmore holds Queensland's first Historic Inn Licence, so visitors can sample some of the State's best fermented beverages in this pleasant old world setting. Bush dances and home-style cooking are also features. It is ☺open only on Sundays between 11am and 3pm. Admission is ✪$7 for adults. Groups are allowed by appointment.

Cammoo Caves, ☎ *4934 2774*, and **Olsen's Capricorn Caverns**, ☎ *4934 2883*, approximately 23km (14miles) north of Rockhampton, are two cave systems which are open to the public. Cave coral, fossils and gigantic tree roots can be inspected in these dry, limestone caves. Cammoo Caves are ☺open daily 8.30am-4.30pm and have conducted tours. Entry fees are adults ✪$8. Olsen's, about 2km east of Cammoo, is privately owned, and 3 hour half-day tours into these caves cost ✪$33 adults, departing from your accommodation in Rock-hampton around 9am.

The Dreamtime Cultural Centre, ☎ *4936 1655,* is a large Aboriginal Cultural Centre, and is on the *Bruce Highway* opposite the turn-off to Yeppoon. The centre is ☺open daily 10am-5.15pm, with guided tours between 11am and 4pm (2 hours duration). Refreshments are available (eating bush tucker is not compulsory). Adults are charged ✪$13.

Rockhampton Heritage Village is in *Boundary Road, Parkhurst*, ☎ *4936 1026*. Attractions include a blacksmith's shop, wheel wrighting, dairy, fully furnished slab cottage, pioneering tools, vintage cars, horse-drawn vehicles, Hall of Clocks and a kiosk. Tours are conducted daily, and there are working demonstrations on the last Sunday of each month. It is ☺open daily 10am-4pm and admission is ✪$12 adults.

Koorana Crocodile Farm is in *Koowonga Road*, off *Emu Park Road*. This is a breeding farm, not a protective reserve, so don't be surprised when you find crocodile kebabs on the menu, and crocodile skin shoes and purses for sale in the gift shop. The Crocodile Farm is ☺open daily and costs adults ✪$15 and $12 per person for groups.

Sport

Rockhampton has all the usual facilities you would expect of a town of its size. The beach is 45km to the Capricorn Coast.

Diving

Capricorn Reef Diving, *189 Musgrave Street, North Rockhampton*, ☎ *4922 7720*, offer 5-day open water certificate PADI course. Classes are taken in Rockhampton, followed by 4 dives on the Keppel Island Group.

Tours

Rothery's Coaches, *13 Power Street, North Rockhampton,* ☎*4922 4320,* offer tours of the city and to the Capricorn Coast, Koorana Crocodile Farm, Cooberrie Park, The Caves and the Dreamtime Culture Centre. Duncan's Off Road 4WD Tours are in *Kent Street, Rockhampton,* ☎*0418 986 050* (mobile).

Outlying Attractions Capricorn Coast

The Capricorn Coast stretches some 48km (30 miles) from Yeppoon and the Byfield area in the north to Keppel Sands in the south. The area enjoys a similar climate to that of Hawaii. The main area of the Capricorn Coast begins at the town of Joskeleigh in the south and reaches north to the forests and national parks of Byfield. The primary town on the coast is Yeppoon, and the main city is Rockhampton, 41km inland. Rockhampton airport is the departure point for flights to the nearby islands of the Reef.

If you are swimming in the tropical waters of the Capricorn Coast, remember that deadly box jellyfish can be present in the sea anywhere north of the Tropic of Capricorn in the summer months.

The web page to visit online is ■www.capricorncoast.co m.au Email for the Capricorn Coast Tourist Organisation is ✉capcoast@ cqnet.com.au

Yeppoon

A modern town with a population of approximately 12,000, Yeppoon nestles beside pineapple-covered hills on the shores of Keppel Bay.

Palms and pines line the main street, and shady trees continue to line the road to Rockhampton. There is a 4m difference between high and low tide, so trawlers, yachts and dinghies are left high and dry.

Yeppoon is the main town on the Capricorn Coast and is one of the largest and fastest growing coastal communities in Queensland. It is a popular holiday spot, offering access to more than 40km of safe beaches.

Cooberrie Park, 15km (9 miles) north of Yeppoon on Woodbury Road, is a bird and animal sanctuary with barbecue and picnic facilities. If you want to pat a kangaroo, this is the place to do it. They also have koalas and other native animals wandering freely through the parkland. It is ☻open daily 9am-4.30pm and costs adults ✪$12 ☎*4939 7590*.

Byfield State Forest Parks are 17km (10 miles) north of Cooberrie Park, and are popular picnic areas. They include Stoney Creek, Water-park Creek and Red Rock Forest Parks.

Nob Creek Pottery, ☎*4935 1161*, established in 1979, is located in the tropical Byfield Forest, and has gained a reputation as a quality cottage industry.

Wreck Point at Cooee Bay provides a spectacular view overlooking the Keppel group of islands. It is situated on the southern outskirts of Yeppoon.

Rosslyn Bay Boat Harbour is the base for a large fishing fleet, charter boats, cruise boats and catamarans. Cruises available include coral viewing, boom netting and, weather permitting, a visit to Middle Island Underwater Observatory.

Emu Park, 19km (12 miles) south of Yeppoon and linked by the Capricorn Coast Scenic Highway, has an unusual memorial to Captain Cook - a singing ship. The mast, sail and rigging contain hollow pipes, and the ship 'sings' when the wind blows. This picturesque town is worth the short and scenic drive for a visit.

The Capricorn Coast Tourist Organisation has an office at the roundabout as you drive into town (you can't miss it!) and it is ☻open daily 9am-5pm, ☎*4939 4888*.

Facilities includes a kitchen, common room with a pool table and a piano and a swimming pool along with the barbecue area. Parking available. *Dorms ✪$18; double/twin $38*

Great Keppel Island

The island is a very popular tourist destination. Fringed by 17km (10 miles) of white, sandy beaches and offshore coral reefs, it provides an ideal setting for holiday makers and day trippers alike. **The Keppel Island group of 30 islands is situated 55km from Rockhampton, and 15km east of Rosslyn Bay on the Capricorn Coast**. Great Keppel is the only island in the group to have been developed, and this is because of its permanent water supply as well as its size (14 sq km). There are ample opportunities for fishing, cruising, boom netting, windsurfing and bushwalking.

Some islands in the group are national parks - **North Keppel, Miall, Middle, Halfway, Humpy** and **Peak** - where camping is permitted, but numbers are limited. All drinking water has to be taken to these islands, but some have water for washing, and some have toilets, but it is best to get full information from either the Naturally Queensland Information Centre in Brisbane, ☎3227 8187.

Although not situated on the Reef, Great Keppel is the gateway to the Outer Reef and North West Island, the largest coral cay in the Great Barrier Reef. It is a major breeding ground for Green Turtles, White Capped Noddy Terns, Wedge Tailed Shearwaters and Olive Head Sea Snakes.

Day trips to Great Keppel Island are available from **Keppel**

Tourist Services, ☎*4933 6744* or ☎*1800 356 744* (free call). The trip lasts 8 hours and includes a cruise transfer from Rosslyn Bay, snorkelling and boom netting, buffet lunch and free time. The day trip costs ✪$80 adults.

The **Middle Island Underwater Observatory** is a popular attraction. It is surrounded by natural coral, and the area teems with marine life of every type imaginable. A sunken wreck nearby also provides a haven for fish, sea snakes, turtles and a school of huge cod. The Underwater Observatory is ☉open daily 8am-5pm, if weather conditions are favourable, and admission charges are ✪$10 adults.

A glance at a map will show that the Great Barrier Reef is a long way from the mainland at this point, but there is some good diving closer to Great Keppel Island. **Bald Rock** and **Man and Wife Rocks** are popular diving venues, and between the southern end of Halfway Island and Middle Island Reef there is some good coral. If the weather is calm there is good diving at **Parker's Bombora,** off the south-eastern tip of Great Keppel. It begins in water about 20m deep and is encircled by sea ferns, sponges, coral and hundreds of fish. The outer islands of the Keppel group, particularly Barren Island, have deeper and clearer water than Great Keppel, so larger species of sea life are encountered, like turtles and manta rays. All diving gear can be hired from the accommodation outlets on Great Keppel.

If you would like online details of the Great Keppel Island Resort, the web site

is ▇www.mpx.com.au/adventures/gk/keppel.htm

↵ Let's Stay Here

Great Keppel Island Holiday Village,
☎*4939 8655 or 1800 180 235* A nice and friendly hostel that would offer to take you on boat trips, snorkelling and canoeing. *Dorms ✪ $24; double from $50*

YHA Backpackers Village, Yeppoon, ☎*4927 5288, www.yha.com.au* These are self contained units with en suite set in a tropical garden safari style. Facilities includes your kitchen, laundry, TV lounge room, internet access and barbecue area. There is also an on site bar, bistro and kiosk where meals are available. Canoe hire available. **Recommended.** *Dorms from ✪$17.60; double/twin from $20pp (from $30-35 with en suite) BC MC VA EFTPOS*

Heron Island

The island is about 72km east of Gladstone, roughly 100km from Rockhampton, and has an area of 19ha. It is a true coral cay that sits on the Tropic of Capricorn, surrounded by 24 sq km of reef. It is possible to walk around the island in less than half an hour, and there is usually an organised beach and reef walk every day. Heron's eastern end has a track system that leads through dense pisonia forest and open grassy shrubland, with information posts along the way. In the summer months be sure to stay on the track, or you could destroy one of the many shearwater burrows that honeycomb the island.

Unfortunately, due to its distance from the mainland, Heron Island is one of the most expensive islands to visit. Access is by helicopter for around $270 adults one-way or a choppy 2-hour catamaran trip for around $85.

At other islands on the Reef it is sometimes necessary to travel 70 or 80 km for scuba diving and snorkelling, but at Heron the Reef is at the very foot of the white sandy beaches. One of the most spectacular diving sites is the well-known **Heron Bommie**, a head of hard coral rising more than 18m from the seabed that is home to all kinds of fish and marine life. All equipment can be hired from the resort's dive shop.

Heron hosts a week-long **Dive Festival** in November each year, when divers from all over the world gather to swap knowledge and experience. There are those who think that this island rates highly among the world's premier dive locations, and given that there are twenty unique sites nearby, they are probably right.

The Resort can be phoned direct on ☎ *132 469*. There is a website at ▣www.heronisland.com and email at ✉visitors@greatbarrierreef.aus.net

Lady Musgrave Island

Lady Musgrave Island is part of the Capricorn Bunker Group, and is about 100km north-east of Bundaberg. It is a true coral cay, approximately 18ha in area, and rests on the edge of a huge coral lagoon that measures some eight kilometres in circumference and covers an area of around 1192ha. The lagoon is one of very few on the Reef that ships can enter, making the island very popular

with the yachting fraternity. Lady Musgrave is a National and Marine Park, and an unspoilt section of the Great Barrier Reef.

The island is reputedly one of the finest dive sites on the Great Barrier Reef, and is home to around 1200 species of fish and 350 varieties of coral. The lagoon is reasonably shallow, allowing longer dives to be undertaken.

MV Lady Musgrave always has qualified diving instructors on board for the inexperienced, but they can also head certified divers in the best direction to get the most out of their trip.

If you wish to stay on Lady Musgrave Island you must camp. There are staff on-site, toilets and walking trails, and that is it. You have to first obtain a camping permit from the QNP and WS or Naturally Queensland, ☎*3227 8187*, and fees are ✪$3.50pp per night.

Lady Elliot Island

The most southerly of the islands of the Great Barrier Reef, Lady Elliot has an area of 0.42 sq km and has been nicknamed Queensland's "Shipwreck Island". This name is not unwarranted, as the wrecks of many ships can be seen littered around the island's shores. The first was probably in 1851, the Bolton Abbey cargo ship, and the latest was the Tenggara II which hit the reef in April, 1989. The island is also popular with bird watchers as 57 species are known to flock here, with more than 200,000 birds nesting here during the summer. Sea turtles also nest on Lady Elliot.

It only takes about an hour to walk around the entire island, and it is one of the least commercialised.

There are ten excellent diving sites that include **Lighthouse Bommie, Coral Gardens, Moiri and Shark Pool**. Visibility ranges from 80 to 25 to 50 metres. This island is also paradise for those who like exploring shipwrecks. All equipment can be hired from the resort for around $60, and open water courses are available. Shore dives cost ✪$30, boat dives $45 and night dives $60.

Contact the resort on ☎*3348 8522* or ☎*1800 072 200* (free call). You can visit the web page at ▣www.ladyelliot.com.au or send an email to ✉info@ladyelliot.com.au

Away from the Coast
Mt Hay Gemstone Tourist Park

It is 40km (25 miles) west of Rockhampton on the Capricorn Highway, Wycarbah. There you can fossick for 120 million-year-old **Thundereggs**. When the eggs are cut in the gemstone factory on the premises, beautiful agate patterns are exposed. Facilities here also include a swimming pool, craft and gift shop, barbecue facilities and powered caravan sites (✪$14 per night for two people), ☎*4934 7183*.

Mount Morgan

The historic township of Mount Morgan is 40km (25 miles) south of Rockhampton, and here you can tour through a 100-year-old mining town that is the real thing, not a reconstruction. Mt Morgan was listed as a Heritage Town by the Australian Heritage Commission in 1980, and by the National Trust of Queensland in 1981. **The Museum** on *Morgan Street*, ☎*4938 4122*, traces the history of the fabulously rich mine. Inspections of the mine are conducted by **Mt Morgan Mine Tours**, *38 Central Street,* ☎ *4938 1081.*

Whilst in town, you can call into the **Golden Nugget Hotel** on the *Central Street,* for a cool ale.

Capricorn Highlands

The highlands stretch from Carnarvon to Clermont (Gregory Highway) and from Blackwater to Jericho (Capricorn Highway). The region is one of the most diverse and productive areas in the country. Coal, sapphires, cattle, sheep, wheat, sunflower, sorghum and cotton are but a few of the riches produced from around here. The Emerald Irrigation Scheme, along with the Fairbairn Dam, has increased rural productivity tenfold in the heart of the Highlands.

A visit to this area can be a rewarding experience. The **Carnarvon Gorge** offers a breathtaking view of scenery, lush vegetation and Aboriginal art.

The town of Springsure has the famous **Virgin Rock**, and from Emerald, the hub of the Central Highlands, you can join a conducted tour of the **Gregory Coal Mine**, ☎ *4982 8200.*

Travelling through Capella brings you to the township of Clermont, which was almost completely destroyed by a flood in 1916, and was moved to its present location with the aid of a huge steam engine. The engine has been preserved as a memorial in the centre of the town.

A National Park at Blackdown Tablelands offers camping facilities and good views.

After crossing the Drummond Range, the country opens out into Queensland's vast grazing

lands, and towns like **Alpha** and **Jericho** are becoming increasingly popular stopovers for people visiting this outback area. It has become even more so since the opening in 1988 of the **Stockman's Hall of Fame**, ☎ *4658 2166,* on the *Landsborough Highway* in **Longreach**.

The Central Queensland gemfields are a popular tourist spot in the Capricorn Region, and visitors come for a chance to 'stub their toe on a sapphire'. Towns such as Anakie, Sapphire, Rubyvale and the Willows Gemfields must be experienced to be fully appreciated. In Rubyvale you can visit a walk-in mine, called **Bobby Dazzler**, which has guided tours and is ☺open daily. It is in *Main Street,* ☎ *4985 4170.*

Central Highlands Tourism Queensland can be contacted on ☎ *4982 4942* or emailed at ✉chtour@maxspeed.net.au You will find plenty of useful information at ▤members.tripo d.com/central highlands/

Gladstone

Located 107km south of Rockhampton, Gladstone is a bustling port centre, one of the busiest and largest in the country. From its modest beginnings in 1847 as a small penal colony with a population below 200, it has grown to become home to more than 42,000 people. Heron Island is only 73km off the coast of Gladstone.

The **Gladstone Art Gallery and Museum**, is in *Goondoon Street* and ☺opens 10am-5pm on weekdays and 10am-4pm on weekends. The building itself is a unique mix of architectural designs, and complements the collection of Australian art and

local memorabilia contained within. Admission is free.

The **Tondoon Botanic Gardens** cover 83ha and are considered the best of their type among Queensland's regional centres. The landscape is made up of lakes and forest and the fauna includes colourful birds and turtles. Access is between ☺9am and 6pm in the summer months, and half an hour earlier (morning and evening) during winter. The Gardens can be entered through *Glenlyon Road.*

Just off the coast of Gladstone are the outlying Curtis and Quoin Islands.

Monto, 203km (126 miles) south west of Bundaberg, is the largest town of the North Burnett and the service centre for the surrounding dairy industry.

24km (15 miles) north-east is **Cania Gorge**, with its spectacular sandstone formations and crystal pools. Walk-ways and boardwalks extend well into the gorge. 8km further on is the massive Cania Dam, where there are attractive picnic areas. Gold was discovered at Cania in 1891, and some flecks can be panned from the streams even today.

The Gladstone Area Promotion and Development Bureau is at *Ferry Terminal, Gladstone Marina, Bryan Jordan Drive,* ☎ *4972 4000,* and they will be able to assist you with enquiries. They have an online address at ▤www. gladstoneregion. com and email at ✉gapdl@ gladstoneregion.org.au

Mackay

Population 75,000
Mackay is a coastal city, on the banks of the Pioneer River, 975km (606 miles) north of Brisbane.

Climate

Average temperatures: January max 31C (88F) - min 22C (72F); July max 23C (73F) - min 10C (50F). Average annual rainfall - 1672mm (66 ins), with over 1000mm (39 ins) falling January-March. The driest months are June-November.

Characteristics

Mackay is surrounded by miles and miles of sugarcane fields, which give the city its title of Sugar Capital of Australia. The district produces about one-third of Australia's total sugar crop, which is exported through the Port of Mackay.

Tram tracks meander through the fields, for the miniature engines that transport the cane to one of the seven sugar mills in the district. In some places the fields are torched between June and December, just before harvesting, and the night skies turn red with the reflections from the fires. These days this method is more frequently replaced by 'green harvesting', which involves cutting rather than burning. See under Points of Interest for details of a sugar farm tour.

North-east of Mackay, just off the coast from Shute Harbour, is the Whitsunday Group of Islands containing some of the most popular of the resort islands of the Great Barrier Reef. Although these islands are not coral cays, the scenery is similar to those featuring in your dreams of lazing on a palm-fringed beach on a tropical island.

The beautiful Eungella National Park, 84km inland from Mackay, has graded tracks leading through rainforest to waterfalls and cool pools (see separate listing).

How to Get There

By Air

The **Qantas** regional airlines of **Airlink** and **Sunstate** service Mackay, ☎ *131 313*. Brisbane, Townsville, Rockhampton.

By Bus

McCaffertys and Greyhound Pioneer, ☎ *13 2030*, ☎ *13 1499*, also operates a Brisbane/Mackay service which takes the inland route from Rockhampton.

By Rail

Queensland Rail Travel Trains operate **The Sunlander, The Queenslander** and **The Spirit of Tropics** from Brisbane throughout the week, contact ☎ *13 2235*. The number for the Mackay Railway Station is ☎ *4952 7418*.

Visitor Information

Mackay Tourism and Development Bureau Ltd is in 'The Mill', *320 Nebo Road*, ☎ *4952 2677*, and they are ⏲open Mon-Fri 9am-5pm, Sat-Sun 9am-4pm. Their email is ✉mtdb@mackay.net.au

⤻ Let's Stay Here

Mackay has a wide range of accommodation, from international resort hotels and motels, to caravan parks and camping grounds. Here is a selection of budget accommodation with prices which should be used as a guide only. The telephone area code is 07.

Bona Vista Motel,
Cnr Malcomson Street and Norris Road, ☎ *4942 2211*. 18 units, licensed restaurant, swimming pool, barbecue. Rooms have air conditioning and TV. *Rooms* ✪*$45-55.*

Boomerang,
307 South Nebo Road,

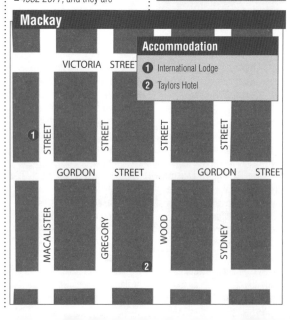

Mackay

Accommodation
1. International Lodge
2. Taylors Hotel

VICTORIA STREET

GORDON STREET   GORDON STREET

STREET   STREET   STREET   STREET

MACALISTER   GREGORY   WOOD   SYDNEY

☎*4952 1755.* 23 units, unlicensed restaurant, playground, pool and parking available. Rooms are air conditioned. Close to the race track. *Rooms ✪$45-49.*

Hi Way Units,
215 Nebo Road, cnr Webberley Street, ☎*4952 1800.* 7 units, undercover parking, barbecue, swimming pool and laundry. Rooms have fans and air condition. *Rooms ✪$50-55.*

International Lodge,
40 MacAlister Street, ☎*4951 1022.* Located at the city centre, close to th bus terminal. Tea and coffee facility, TV, fans and air conditioning in the rooms. *Dorms ✪$48-56*

Taylors Hotel,
Cnr Wood and Alfred Streets, ☎*4957 2500.* A block away from the main town. Lodgings is above the pub which has a licensed restaurant and gaming room. Mainly caters for men only and only single room available. Room are basic with fans and fridge. *Dorms ✪$25*

Caravan Parks
Alligator Creek Store and Caravan Park, *Hay Point Rd,* ☎4956 4100 (Pets allowed) 22 sites. Barbecue area and swimming pool. On site store. Close to the river and beaches. *Non-powered site ✪$10 for one person, $12 for two; powered sites $15; on-site vans $22 upwards.*

Andergrove Caravan Park, *Beaconsfield Road, Andergrove,* ☎*4942 4922.* (Pets allowed on application) 160 sites, barbecue, playground, pool - *powered sites ✪$18 for two, on-site vans $35 for two, cabins $45 for two.*

Mackay Harbour Caravan Park, *Harbour Rd,* ☎*4955 1496* (Pets negotiable) 40 sites, 19 rooms. Close to the harbour and about 6km to the city. Swimming pool and barbecue area and there will be a general kitchen soon. All rooms have their own kitchen and are all air conditioned. *Non-powered sites for two ✪$10; powered sites for two $12; single rooms $15; double $20*

Tropical Caravan Park Melanesian Village, *Bruce Highway,* ☎*4952 1211.* (Pets allowed on application) 170 sites, barbecue, playground, kiosk, pool - *powered sites ✪$19 for two, on-site vans $28 for two, villas $55-60 for two, units $45 for two.*

Let's Eat
Most of the motels have licensed restaurants, and many hotels serve inexpensive counter meals. Here are a few restaurants that you might like to try:

Pippi's Italian Restaurant, *cnr Palmer and Grendon Streets,* ☎*4951 1376.* BYO, Italian and Mediterranean, open Tues-Sat from 5.30pm.

The Beachhouse Seafood Restaurant, *2 Ocean Avenue, Slade Point,* ☎*4955 4733.* Metres from the water's edge. Generous platters and Live Mud Crab Tank. Open for dinner seven nights, lunch Thursday, Friday and Sunday.

Toong Tong Thai Restaurant, *10 Sydney Street,* ☎*4957 8051.* Dinner 7 days from 5.30pm, lunch Mon-Fri 11.30am-2.30pm.

McDonald's is at the corner of *Hicks Road and the Bruce Highway,* ☎*4942 3999.* **Pizza Hut** has a free delivery service ⏰Mon-Thurs 4-11pm, Fri-Sun noon-11pm, ☎*4957 2481.*

Local Transport
Car Hire
The following companies operate in the area.

Avis, Mackay Airport, ☎4951 1266.
AAA Rental-U-Drive, 6 Endevour Street, ☎4957 5606.
Budget Rent-A-Car, 19B Juliet Street, ☎4951 1400
Thrifty Car Rental, 3 Mangrove Road, ☎4957 3677.
Mackay Economy Rentals, 139 Sydney Street, ☎4953 1616.
Hertz Rentals, Mackay Airport, ☎4951 4685.
Network Rentals, 196 Victoria Street, ☎4953 1022
Cut Rate Rentals, 105 Alfred Street, ☎4953 1616

Public Transport
Buses service the Mackay area on weekdays only, not on public holidays, ☎4957 8416 for timetable information from Mackay City Buses.

Taxis
Taxi Transit, *Victoria Street,* ☎*4951 4990.*
Mackay Taxis, *Victoria Street,* ☎*13 1008.*

Entertainment

If you fancy seeing a movie, head for the cinema complex in *Gordon Street*, ☎*4957 3515*.

For some live entertainment contact the Mackay **Entertainment Centre,** also in *Gordon Street*, ☎*4957 1757* or ☎*1800 646 574*, to find out about current shows.

The **Conservatorium of Music**, *418 Shakespeare Street*, has regular classical and jazz concerts, often featuring overseas artists, ☎*4957 3727*.

For night owls, there are a few night clubs where you can dance to the wee small hours:

Whitz End, *The Whitsunday Hotel, 176 Victoria Street*, ☎*4957 2811*.

The Blue Moose Nightclub, *144 Victoria Street*, ☎*4951 2611*. ⊙open Wed-Sun nights.

The Balcony, *144 Victoria Street*, ☎*4957 2241*.

Katie O'Reilly's Irish Bar and Restaurant, *38 Sydney Street*, ☎*4953 3522*.

The Saloon Bar, *99 Victoria Street*, ☎*4957 7220*.

If you are in town on a Thursday night you might like to go to the greyhound racing at the **Mackay Showground** in *Milton Street*, ☎*4951 1680*.

Shopping

Centrepoint Shopping Centre, ☎*4957 2229*, is in *Victoria Street*, in the heart of the city, where you will also find some good street shopping.

Caneland Shoppingtown, ☎*4951 3311*, is in *Mangrove Road*.

Mt Pleasant Shopping Centre, *Phillip Street, North Mackay*, is more convenient for those staying to the north of the city.

Weekend markets are held as follows:

The Foundry Markets on Harbour Road - ⊙Thursday, Sat-Sun 8am-4pm.
Mackay Showground Markets in Milton Road - hSat 8am-1pm.
Victoria Street Markets - ⊙Sun 8.30am-12.30pm.
First Sunday of every month Paxtons Markets, River Street ⊙9am-1pm.

Points of Interest

John Mackay discovered the Pioneer River Valley in 1860, but he named the river the Mackay. He returned with stock and registered "Greenmount" the first pastoral run in the district in 1862. Others followed and the settlement was named Mackay in his honour. The river's name, however, had to be changed to Pioneer because there was already a Mackay River.

It was only a few years before sugar became the main industry, pioneered by the efforts of John Spiller, T. Henry Fitzgerald and John Ewen Davidson. Nowadays Mackay Harbour is home to the world's largest bulk sugar terminal.

The port for Mackay was originally on the river, but because of the enormous tides (around 6.5m), a new port was built on the coast.

Tourism Mackay have put together a **City Walking Tour** that visits the historic buildings, including the **Police Station** (1885), **Court House, Commonwealth Bank** (1880), **Town Hall** (1912), **Holy Trinity Church, Masonic Temple, National Bank, Mercury Building, Pioneer Shire Chambers, Post Office and Customs House** (1901).

The closest beach to the city is **Harbour Beach**, on the southern side of the outer harbour wall.

It has a children's playground, toilets and shady picnic areas, and is patrolled during summer by the Mackay Surf Club.

Queen's Park Orchid House, *cnr Gordon and Goldsmith Streets*, has an excellent display of native and foreign orchids.

Illawong Fauna Sanctuary, at Illawong Beach, 4km from Mackay centre, is a beachfront family recreation area amid tropical landscaping. There are kangaroos roaming free, a swimming pool, trampoline, video games and full catering facilities, as well as crocodiles (not roaming free). Feeding times are ⊙9am, 11.30am and 3.30pm. For further information, ☎*4959 1777*. The sanctuary is ⊙open 9am-6pm daily, and until 10pm on Friday night.

You can get a good panoramic view of the city and the countryside from the **Mt Oscar Lookout** in *Norris Road, North Mackay*.

Tours of the **Racecourse Sugar Mill**, *Peak Downs Highway*, are conducted during the crushing season, from June to November, ☎*4953 8276* for more information.

Polstone Sugar Farm Tours, *Masotti's Road, Homebush*, adjacent to Orchid Way, conduct a 2 hour tour covering the history, equipment and process of growing and preparing sugar cane for the mill. Costs, including refreshments, are ✪$15 adults, ☎*4959 7298*.

North of Mackay are several popular beach resorts. **Blacks Beach** is approximately 6km in length, and is probably the best beach in the area for swimming and fishing. **Bucasia** and **Eimeo** beaches are in the semi-rural area, about a 10 minute drive north of Mackay, and are long sandy beaches that are safe for swimming and have good play areas for kids. They also offer good views of the countryside and off-shore islands.

⚓ Beaches

Illawong (Far Beach) and **Iluka** (Town Beach) offer views of Flat and Round Top Islands and Dalrymple Bay/Hay Point coal loading terminal.

Harbour Beach has a surf lifesaving patrol, toilets, adventure playground and picnic area.

Lamberts Beach has a lookout that provides island views.

Blacks Beach is a long secluded beach with picnic facilities.

Dolphin Heads has accommodation available.

Eimeo Beach has a small picnic area next to an avenue of century old mango trees.

Sunset Beach has a shaded foreshore picnic area.

Bucasia Beach has a summer swimming enclosure, picnic area and views to Dolphin Heads and islands.

Shoal Point Beach has a picnic area, toilets and lookout. The Esplanade offers views of islands, Cape Hillsborough and Hibiscus Coast, and there is a causeway to Little Green Island.

South of Mackay

Twenty-five kilometres south of Mackay, at Hay Point, is the **Dalrymple Bay Coal Terminal Complex,** the largest coal export facility in the southern hemisphere. The wharves stretch 3.8km out to sea, and coal trains up to 2km long arrive at the port daily. The Port Administration Building has recorded information and a

viewing platform, ☎4943 8444.

The Big Prawn is at *Lot 1, Grasstree Beach Road, Grasstree Beach,* and is the only commercial hatchery in Australia that is open to the public.

The sugar town of Sarina is 37km south of Mackay. It has a population of around 9,000, some picturesque scenery, and some excellent beaches. (See also separate listing.)

Cape Palmerston National Park is 80km south of Mackay and has 4WD only access. It offers long sandy beaches, palm forests, fresh-water lagoons and large stands of melaleuca. Attractions include **Ince Bay** to the north, **Temple Island** and the volcanic plug of **Mt Funnel.** There is camping, but facilities are very basic.

↪ Let's Stay Here

La Solana, *15 Pacific Drive, Blacks Beach,* ☎4954 9544. 12 units, barbecue, playground, cooking facilities, swimming pool, half-court tennis - *from* ◎*$55.*

Tropic Heart Units, *64 Waverley Street, Bucasia,* ☎4954 6965. 7 units, barbecue, undercover parking, cooking facilities, swimming pool - *from* ◎*$44.*

⚓ Beaches

Campwin Beach, 8.5km from Sarina, is home to a rich fishing and prawning industry. Boat launching and mooring facilities are available and there is easy access to nearby islands.

Armstrong Beach is 9.5km from Sarina and has a picnic and camping, and an orchid nursery that is open by appointment only.

Sarina Beach, 13km from Sarina, has a picnic area, store, boat ramp, and a surf lifesaving patrol. Coral Lookout is at the southern end of the beach.

Grasstree Beach, 13km from Sarina, has a picnic area and boat ramp in a wide sheltered bay.

Salonika Beach, 24km from Sarina, is a quiet sandy beach with an inland lagoon teeming with birdlife.

Halftide Beach, 28km from Sarina, is home to the Tug Boat Harbour that services Hay Point Coal Terminal.

North of Mackay
Cape Hillsborough National Park, 45km (28 miles) north-east of Mackay, covers 830ha and features a variety of vegetation, elevated lookouts and peaceful beaches. It is not unusual to see a couple of kangaroos lazing on the beach undisturbed by humans doing the same thing.

Cathu State Forest is 70km (44 miles) north of Mackay. Drive along the *Bruce Highway* to 3km north of Yalboroo, turn left and continue for 12km (8 miles) along the gravel road to the Forestry Office. Within the forest is the **Jaxut State Forest Park** which has shaded picnic areas with friendly kangaroos, camping facilities and toilets.

Midge Point is reached by turning right off the *Bruce Highway* at Bloomsbury, and travelling 18km through the Condor Hill to the village of Midgetown. Named after a small survey vessel, the Midge, in the early 1920s, this area has been 'discovered' by developers, and has become a tourist destination.

🏖 Beaches

Roughly 25km north of Mackay, turn right onto *Seaforth Road* then travel 20km to the Hibiscus Coast. This includes the beach-side settlements of Seaforth, Halliday Bay, Ball Bay and Cape Hillsborough. These beaches are all nesting sites for green and flatback turtles who lay their eggs during the three month period from October each year. The baby turtles hatch between late January and early April.

Halliday Bay has a sandy beach swimming enclosure, ac-commodation and a restaurant. It is reached from *Cape Hillsbor-ough Road*.

Seaforth is 48km north-east of Mackay, and offers camping and picnic facilities overlooking the beach.

Belmunda Bay is reached by turning right about 5km along the *Cape Hillsborough Road*. The bay has secluded beaches with several fishing shacks. After rain has fallen, the nearby freshwater lakes are visited by crowds of water birds, including the brolga.

Festivals

The **Sugartime Festival** is held in the first week in September each year.

Sports
Swimming

The **Memorial Swimming Pool**, *Milton Street,* is near Caneland Shopping Centre. It is ⏰open Tues, Thurs and Fri 5am-8.45pm, Wed, Sat and Sun 5am-6pm (closed June and early July).

Whitsunday Waterworld, *Harbour Road, Mackay,* ☎4955 6466, is a complex with waterslides, mini golf, pinball, video machines and kiosk. It

is ⏰open Sat-Sun and school holidays 10am-10pm.

Indoor Sports

BG's Sports Centre on the *Bruce Highway* south of the City Gates, is one of the largest indoor recreational and fitness centres in Australia. It offers tenpin bowling, roller skating, squash and many other sports, ☎4952 1509. It is ⏰open daily 9am-midnight.

Diving

The **Diver Training Centre**, ☎4955 4228, has a dive shop by the sea next to the departure point for Roylen Cruises, where you can hire snorkel and scuba gear. They also have 5-day dive courses.

Barnes Reefdiving, *153 Victoria Street,* ☎4951 1472, offer diving trips to the Great Barrier Reef on Mon, Wed and Fri; Reef and Wreck Dive Trips on Tues; and Island Dive Trips on Thurs.

Mackay Diving, *1 Mangrove Road,* ☎4951 1640, also offer gear hire and diving lessons.

Tours and Cruises
Natural North Discovery Tours, *11 Rafelo Drive, Farleigh,* ☎4952 2677 or ☎4959 8360.

The **Great Barrier Reef** can be reached from Mackay by sea and air. **Credlin Reef**, one of the 2100 reefs that make up this coral colony, is only 2 to 3 hours from Mackay Harbour by high speed catamaran. There is a shaded pontoon, underwater viewing area and a seasub that make for excel-lent snorkelling, scuba diving and coral viewing.

Bushy Atoll, a half-hour sea-plane flight from Mackay airport, is the only quay on the entire Reef to have an enclosed lagoon.

Elizabeth E II Coral Cruises,

102 Goldsmith Street, Mackay, ☎4957 4281, offer trips from two to 21 days aboard their specially built monohull dive and fishing boat, Elizabeth E II. The boat is stabilised and has the latest navigation aids, as well as 240v throughout and a 110v charging system.

Mackay Adventure Cruises, *320 Nebo Road,* ☎4952 2677. High-speed catamaran transport to the Credlin Reef pontoon for coral viewing.

Whitsunday Dreamer, ☎4946 6611. Snorkelling and fishing. Stopovers to Daydream Island, Long Island and Sun Lovers coral reef.

Roylen Cruises, *Harbour Road,* ☎4955 3066, have daily cruises to Brampton Island; Sat, Sun and Wed cruises to Lindeman and Hamilton Islands; Mon, Wed and Fri cruises to Credlin Reef; and 5-day luxury cruises through the Whitsunday Islands and to the Great Barrier Reef, all departing from the outer harbour. The 5-day cruise departs every ⏰Monday 1pm and returns Friday 4pm.

Outlying Attractions
Sarina

The town of Sarina is 37km (23 miles) south of Mackay, and 296km (185 miles) north of Rockhampton, on the Bruce Highway. It is yet another sugar town in the area, cradled by rainforest and the **Conners Range** mountains. 13km (8 miles) to the north east is a charming little village by the sea, Sarina Beach. Fishing and snorkelling is popular in the tropical islands and reefs close to the mainland.

Broad Street, the main street of the town, is indeed broad with a median strip in the centre offering tables, park benches and public amenities, and best of all, shade.

There are plenty of sandy beaches and offshore islands to entice you to swim, jog, fish or go boating.

The **Dalrymple Bay Coal Exporting Facilities** at H*ay Point,* ☎ *4943 8444,* are the largest of their type in the Southern Hemisphere.

Helpful local information is provided by the Sarina Tourist Art and Craft Centre, *Lot 3 Bruce Highway,* ☎ *4956 2251.*

Eungella National Park

This stunning National Park is 84km (52 miles) inland from Mackay, and the bitumen road leading to it follows the Pioneer River and its tributaries up the valley past Finch Hatton, and through Eungella township at the top of the range. **Finch Hatton Gorge** has attractive mountain-fed waterfalls, a natural swimming pool, plus good walking tracks.

The **Broken River** area provides shady pools for swimming, and well marked bush walking tracks are a feature of the Park. If you are lucky you may see a platypus near the bridge.

At the top of the range at Eungella, the fully licensed **Historic Eungella Chalet Mountain Lodge,** ☎ *4958 4509,* has 12 rooms, a playground and pool - *from* ❂$50

A permit is required to camp in any of the local National Parks, and this can be obtained from the Ranger at Seaforth, ☎ *4959 0410,* the Ranger at Eungella, ☎ *4958 4552,* or from the **Queensland National Parks and Wildlife Service,** c*nr Wood and River Street, Mackay,* ☎ *4951 8788.* Typically, it costs ❂$3.50 per

person per night to camp.

For information on all National Parks, the organisations to contact for information are the Environmental Protection Agency, ☎ *3224 5641,* or the Queensland National Parks and Wildlife Service, ☎ *3227 8187* (Naturally Queensland). Connect online to ▆www.env. qld.gov.au

Cape Hillsborough

Located 47km (29 miles) north of Mackay, the Cape Hillsborough National Park provides a beachfront picnic area with barbecue facilities. The park is relatively small (830ha - 2050 acres), but it is typical of the best of North Queensland, with rainforests, beaches and abundant wildlife. Walking tracks take you to billabongs, great lookouts and unusual volcanic formations. The fishing in the park is excellent.

Halliday Bay

Situated north of Mackay, near the town of Seaforth, Halliday Bay is noted for its white sandy beach and safe swimming enclosure. The bay adjoins **McBride's Point National Park,** and has a shop and boat hire facilities. The Bay is named after Captain Halliday, whose century-old stone cottage is still standing.

Whitsunday Coast
Proserpine

Proserpine, 127km (80 miles) north of Mackay, is mainly a sugar cane town. It serves as the centre of the Whitsunday region, in administrative terms, but most visitors by-pass its scenic charm on their way to the more seductive coastline. The town has full facilities and a good range of accommodation. You may wish to

stay close to the Bruce Highway on a northward/southward journey, but if you plan to be in the Whitsundays area for any significant length of time, and are not planning to stay on an island resort, the coastal settlements of Airlie Beach and Shute Harbour have all the good views. West of the town is Lake Proserpine, where waterskiing is a popular sport.

The Whitsunday Information Centre on the *Bruce Highway* is in *Proserpine,* ☎ *4945 3711.*

Shute Harbour

Shute Harbour is the focal point for departure of many tourist vessels cruising to the Whitsunday Islands. Not only is it the second busiest passenger port in Australia, it boasts the second largest bareboat industry in the world (a bareboat is a boat hired without a crew).

Shute Harbour is mostly a gateway for cruises out to the islands, and is one of the smaller satellite areas for Proserpine, as well as being superceded by Airlie Beach as an accommodation centre. Nevertheless, there are a couple of places to stay here. Use the contact details for Whitsunday Tourism.

Airlie Beach

Airlie Beach, the main resort town on the Whitsunday coast, has a relaxed atmosphere, and is 8km (5 miles) from Shute Harbour, 24km (15 miles) from Proserpine. The town borders the 20,000ha Conway National Park, and is the mainland centre for the Whitsundays. Airlie Beach is a picturesque village and offers a lot to the holiday-maker on its own account, but when you add the close proximity of the Reef islands, it is not hard to figure out why some people choose to stay at Airlie and take day trips to the islands. It is a haven for young backpackers, which makes for interesting nightlife.

The **Barefoot Bushman's Wildlife Park,** Lot 2, Shute Harbour Road, Cannonvale, ☎4946 1480, has a terrific array of Australian wildlife with shows throughout the day. There are pythons, brown snakes, lizards, frogs, ducks, pelicans, owls, kookaburras, possums, wombats, fruit bats, native birds, doves, emus, dingoes and crocodiles, to name a few. Highlights include the Snake Show, where the world's deadliest snakes are put on display, and the Crocodile Feeding, where you can see these huge reptiles snapping up their lunch. The Wildlife Park is ☉open 9am-4pm every day and admission is ✪$18 adults.

The Airlie Visitor Information Centre is at *277 Shute Harbour Road, Airlie Beach,* ☎*4946 6665,* and can be emailed at the address ✉*abtic@whitsunday.net.au*

↘ Let's Stay Here
Airlie Beach YHA,
394 Shutue Harbour Rd,
☎*4946 6312 or 1800 247 251,* ▉*www.yha.com.au*
Located within minutes away from town and not far from the beach. All rooms have en suite.This quiet hostel also features your normal big kitchen and dining, laundry, TV lounge, internet access and a swimming pool. Parking available. *Dorms from* ✪*$19; double/twin $47 BC MC VA EFTPOS*

Airlie Waterfront Backpackers,
6 The Esplanade, ☎*4948 1300 or 1800 089 000,* *www.airliebackpackers.com.au/* Centrally located and not far from the Coach

Terminal. This is a nice and quiet hostel and all rooms are fully air conditioned. Your usual facilities of kitchen and dining plus TV lounge room. The views from the balcoy of the beach is great. **Recommended.** *Dorms from* ✪*$20; double/twin $55*

Backpackers by the Bay,
12 Hermitage Dr, ☎*4946 7267 or 1800 646 994,* ▉*www.backpackersbythebay.com* This small seaside resort is situated not far away from town. You'll find good facilities in this hostel. Some rooms are air conditioned. features a kitchen, laundry, TV lounge. common room and pool table. There's also access to the internet, swimming pool and barbecue area plus great views. *Dorms* ✪*$20; double $48*

Beaches,
356-362 Shute Harbour Rd,
☎*4946 6244 or 1800 636 630,*

Airlie Beach

Accommodation
1. Airlie Beach Waterfront Backpackers
2. Airlie Beach YHA
3. Beaches
4. Club 13 Begley St
5. Club Whitsunday Backpackers Hostel
6. Koala
7. Magnums

🖥 www.beaches.com.au
Located opposite the lagoon at the heart of town. Accommodation is in self-contained units. Dorms are air conditioned and either come with or without en suite. Double room have their own TVs and fridge. Facilities includes a communal kitchen, laundry, TV lounge, a swimming pool and barbecue area. There is also an on site internet cafe, bar and restaurant. *Dorms ✪$20; double from $45*

**Bush Village
Backpackers Resort,**
*2 St Martins Rd, Cannonvale,
☎4946 6177 or 1800 809 256*
Situated in Cannonvale, not far from Airlie Beach. Self contained units with their own en suite bathroom, TV and fridge. Features a kitchen, TV lounge, internet access, pool table, a swimming pool and spa. *Dorms from ✪$20; double/twin from $45 (price includes breakfast)*

Club 13 Begley St,
1313 Begley St, ☎4946 6312 or 1800 247 251, 🖥 *www.whit sundaybackpackers.com.au*
This used to be an apartment complex turned into a backpackers place. Accommodation is still split into 6 apartments each having their own kitchen and laundry facilities. Also features a swimming pool and a spa. The balcony also boasts nice views the of town. *Dorms ✪$20; double/twin from $50 (cheaper when you stay longer)*

Koala,
Shute Harbour Rd, ☎4946

6001 or 1800 800 421,
www.koala-backpackers.com
Set amongst tropical gardens situated in the very heart of Airlie Beach, just opposite the beach and swimming lagoon. You'll find basic Melanesian style accommodation in self contained units with en suite bathrooms, TV, fridge and a kitchenette. Also features a communal kitchen, laundry, internet access, ping pong table, a nice big swimming pool, barbecue area and a volley ball court outside. On site bar available. Also offers a free courtesy bus pick up. *Dorms from ✪$22; double/twin $30pp*

Magnums,
Shute Harbour Rd, ☎4946 6266 or 1800 624 634
This party hostel is located at the heart of Airlie Beach. Accommodation varies here from top rooms to the basic ones set in cabins among tropical gardens. Just your basic facilities including a kitchen, laundry, TV lounge and some common rooms. There's the on site bar and nightclub though, that rages on 'til the wee hours of the morning. *Dorms from ✪$15; double/twin $42*

Reef 0,
*147 Shute Harbour Rd,
☎4946 6137 or 1800 800 795,* 🖥 *www.reeforesort.com*
Situated in Cannonvale, just outside of Airlie Beach. Quite a good resort-like backpackers set in tropical gardens with some real value for money accommodation. Self contained units with en

suite. Also features a kitchen, laundry, a swimming pool and barbecue area. On site bar and restaurant is a must, plus a store and internet cafe. There is a shuttle bus service that comes often. *Dorms from ✪$12; double $55 (price includes breakfast)*

Whitsundays
The Islands
The Whitsundays consist of 74 islands from the Cumberland and Northumberland Island groups, and they form the largest offshore island chain on Australia's east coast. The islands are the remains of a mountain range that was drowned when sea levels rose at the end of the last ice age. Most of them have National Park status, and all are situated in the marine park. The islands were named by Captain Cook when he sailed through the passage on Whitsunday, 1770. Some like to point out that it was not actually Whitsunday, since the good old captain neglected to take into account the fact that he had crossed the international date line, and so was a day out. However, because he made so few nautical and mathematical errors on his journey, Captain Cook is usually forgiven his Whitsunday oversight. Later, when European settlement began on several of the islands, there were some violent confrontations with the resident Aborigines which tarnish the history of this idyllic place.

The Whitsunday Visitors and Convention Bureau, ☎4946 6673, is found on the corner of *Shute Harbour and Mandalay Roads,* one kilometre from Airlie. They can be emailed at the web address tw@whitsundayinformation. com.au and the website can be seen at ■www.whitsundayinf ormation.com.au Alternatively, there is a website at ■www. whitsunday.net.au

The Whitsunday Information Centre is on the *Bruce Highway in Proserpine*, ☎ *4945 3711.*

There are basic camping facilities on Hook, North Molle, Whitsunday, Henning, Border, Haslewood, Shaw, Thomas and Repulse Islands. These consist of toilets and picnic tables, with a ranger patrolling. Costs are ✪$3.50 per person per night. All permits can be obtained over the phone by calling the Naturally Queensland Information Centre in Brisbane on ☎ *3227 8197* or emailing them at ✉nqic@env.qld. gov.au For more information on camping in the region, contact any QNP and WS branch.

Whitsunday Island

Although Whitsunday is the largest of the island in the Whitsunday Group, it does not have a resort. But it does have **Whitehaven Beach**, the longest and best beach in the whole group, and the destination of many cruises. There is good snorkelling off the southern end of the beach. There are several camping sites on the island.

Lindeman Island

The island has 20km (12 miles) of walking tracks that lead through 500ha (1235 acres) of National Park. There are seven secluded beaches, and at dusk from the top of **Mt Oldfield**, you can see the sun set over islands that stretch to the horizon in every direction. Lindeman has an area of 8 sq km, most of which is national

park, and was named after George Lindeman, whose job in the Royal Navy was to chart safe passages through the Whitsunday Islands. Lindeman has six beaches and 20km of walking trails. Its highest point is Mt Oldfield, 210m. There is a resident Park Ranger who will advise and even accompany walkers.

There is not much here for scuba divers, but the Resort arranges diving trips out to the Reef. Snorkelling trips to Hardy Lagoon take place several days a week.

Contact the resort directly or follow the links to Lindeman Island at the Club Med website: ■www. clubmed.com.au

South Molle Island

The island covers 405ha (1000 acres) and is 4km long and 2.4km wide. It is situated in the heart of Whitsunday Passage, and offers fishing, golf, tennis, water skiing, coral viewing, scuba diving, parasailing and bushwalking. **South Molle** has an area of 4 sq km, and is the largest of the Molle group. It is close to Mid Molle, and in fact you can walk from South Molle to Mid Molle at any time. Another island that is very close is **Daydream.** The oldest of the resorts in the Whitsunday Group, South Molle is mostly national park and offers some good, if short, walks. The highest point is **Mt Jeffreys** (198m), and from it there are great views of the surrounding islands. **Balancing Rock** and **Spion Kop** also allow you to take in breathtaking vistas. The first European settler was Henry George Lamond, who moved in with his wife and children in 1927 and stayed for ten years. There is a memorial to his son, Hal, on top

of **Lamond Hill**.

South Molle is very much a family resort, there is even a pre-school nursery as well as activities for school-age children.

There is a Resort Dive Shop that offers short courses for beginners, and organises trips out to various parts of the reef. The resort can be contacted on ☎ *4946 9433*. The web site is ■www.southmolleisland.com.au with an email service at ✉info@ southmolleisland.com.au

Long Island

The island is directly off the coast of Shute Harbour, and adjoins the Whitsunday Passage. It is deliberately underdeveloped, and the untamed tropical rainforest and protected **Palm Bay Lagoon** make for a very informal holiday. There are 13km (8 miles) of well graded bushwalking tracks, and a variety of beaches for swimming and fishing. Long Island is separated from the mainland by a channel that is only 500m wide, making it the closest resort island to the Queensland coast. It has an area of 12 sq km, but is about 11km long, so it is apparent that it is extremely narrow, only about 1.5km at its widest.

Long Island has 20km of bush walks through the National Park, and there are some nice sandy beaches on its western side, but at **Happy Valley** the tidal variations cause the water to be so far from the beach that it is easier to swim in the pool. The box jellyfish makes its appearance in the vicinity from March to November. The beaches on the eastern side tend to be rocky and usually windy, but the dredging that has been undertaken at **Palm Bay** makes it ideal for swimming, and for mooring yachts.

The **Club Crocodile Resort** can be contacted on ☎ *4946 9233*, and for a preliminary look at what the island has to offer, follow the links to Long Island at ▣www.club crocodile.com.au

Hayman Island

The island is a resort offering a balance between luxury living and natural beauty. Curving around the sandy shoreline of the blue lagoon on the south-western side of the island, Hayman looks out toward **Langford Reef** and an island called **Bali Hai**. All sports, both on land and water, are catered for at the resort.

Hayman Island has an area of 4 sq km, and is the most northerly of the Whitsunday resort islands. Its resort is one of the most luxurious on the **Great Barrier Reef**, and it was once considered to be one of the top ten resorts in the world. There are several bushwalks on Hayman, including an 8km circuit and walks to **Blue Pearl Bay or Dolphin Point**. It is also possible to walk to nearby **Arkhurst Island** at low tide.

Hayman is closer to the outer Reef than other resort islands, and Hayman has a full-time dive boat to cater to every diver's desires. Thirty kilometres north-east of Hayman are the Hardy and Black Reefs.

Hamilton Island

Hamilton has an area of 6 sq km, and is home to the largest resort in the South Pacific with its own jet airport.

The resort is actually a small town with shops, restaurants and a 135-berth marina. There are a few walking tracks on the unde-veloped parts of the island, and

the main one leads up to **Passage Peak** (230m) the highest point on the island. To get around the island, you can rent a golf buggy and drive yourself. Hamilton even has island bus tours that operate daily. There is a **Fauna Park** at the northern end of the island, with native animals, crocodiles and performing cockatoos. 4WD safari tours, go-karts and skirmish are further activities.

Hook Island

Hook Island has an area of 53 sq km, some great beaches and some of the best diving sites in the Whitsundays, but it has one of the smallest resorts. The focus here is on the budget market, with a choice between camping sites, beachfront cabins and backpacker dorms. Hook Island has two long, narrow bays on its southern end - Macona Inlet and Nara Inlet. **Macona** has a National Park camping site, and **Nara** has caves with Aboriginal wall paintings. There is a variety of wildlife on the island, but one that can prove quite pesky is the large goanna. These have been known to chew through canvas to get to campers' stores.

The island is home to an underwater observatory that has an abundance of colourful corals and marine life. Though with so many trips available to the Outer Reef and the modern semi-submersible craft that tour operators use, you have to wonder why anyone would want to visit an underwater observatory. Still, it is popular with many visitors.

The northern end of Hook Island has some good diving and snorkelling sites - **Pinnacle Point, Manta Ray Bay, Butterfly Bay** and **Alcyonaria Point.** The

resort can organise reef trips.

The **Wilderness Resort** can answer any further enquiries, ☎ *4946 9380*. There is a website ▣www.hookislandresort.co m.au and an email address ▣enquiries@hookis .com

Daydream Island

Daydream is a small island with an area of just 17ha. It is a little over 1km long and no more than a couple of hundred metres at its widest point, but it has one of the largest resorts. Originally known as West Molle, the island is the closest resort island to Shute Harbour. It was first settled in the 1880s by graziers, but the first resort was opened by Paddy Murray, who had purchased the island in 1933 and changed its name to Daydream after his boat.

Sunlover's Beach, at the north-eastern end of the island, behind the resort, has a 50m strip of sand and some good coral offshore for snorkellers. The Whitsunday tidal range does not affect Daydream as much as the other islands. The Resort dive shop offers courses, and day cruises to Hardy Reef, about 50km offshore.

Contact the resort on ☎ *4948 8488* or ☎ *1800 075 040* (reservations). The official web page is found at ▣www.daydream.net.au

Brampton Island

Brampton is not strictly in the Whitsunday region. It is part of the Cumberland Group of Islands about 32km north-east of Mackay, at the entrance to the Whitsunday Passage. The island is a National Park, with an area of 4.6 sq km, and has unspoilt bush, lush tropical foliage, swaying coconut palms and many stunning and secluded beaches. It is connected to **Carlisle Island** and to **Pelican Island** by sand bars that can be crossed at low tide.

A mountainous island with lush forests, nature trails, kangaroos and emus, Brampton also has seven sandy beaches and is surrounded by coral reefs. The walk around the island is about 7km, takes around three hours, and is best done in a clockwise direction. There is a walk up to the island's highest point, **Brampton Peak,** beginning near the resort golf course and the round trip takes about two hours. Both walks offer great views. The island is a 45 minute cruise from the Great Barrier Reef, but you can see underwater coral gardens and myriads of tropical fish off **Brampton's East Beach.**

There is nothing at Brampton itself to excite divers, but cruises from Mackay to Credlin Reef aboard the **Spirit of Roylen**, ☎*4955 3066*, call in at Brampton to pick up and set down. Credlin Reef is in the Hydrographers Passage area, and there is a permanent pontoon over the reef, an underwater observatory and a semi-submersible. Resort diving courses are conducted on board the Spirit of Roylen in transit to Credlin Reef, or at the Resort by special arrangements.

The contact number for the resort is ☎*4951 4097*, and the website is ▤www.bramptonislandresort.com

Townsville
Population 140,000
Townsville is situated on the eastern coast of Australia, 1443km (897 miles) north of Brisbane.

Climate
Average temperature: January max 31C (88F) - min 24C (75F) and high humidity; July max 25C (77F) - min 15C (59F). Average annual rainfall is 1194mm (47 ins) - wettest months January-March, with an average of 873mm (34 ins).

Characteristics
The second largest city in Queensland and main commercial centre of northern Queensland, Townsville sprawls along the shores of Cleveland Bay and around the foot of Castle Hill. It offers not only easy access to the attractions of the Magnetic North and the Great Barrier Reef, but also all of the facilities of a major city.

Careful zoning has ensured that the city retains much of its original architecture and character. A walk around town will show you what makes North Queensland so different. Old wooden, highset houses stand everywhere, built to allow cooling breezes under the house and to provide a refuge during the heat of the day. In the gardens, mango, paw paw and banana trees seem exotic to the visitor, but are the normal homegrown product of the Townsville backyard.

Townsville is also a busy port that services Mt Isa, southern cities and south-east Asia. It has two metal refineries and other industrial enterprises.

How to Get There
By Air
Qantas, MacAir and **Sunstate Airlines**, ☎*13 1313*, www.qantas.com.au - have flights to/from Brisbane, Cairns, Mount Isa, Hamilton Island, Mackay and Sydney.

Virgin Blue, ☎*13 6789*, ▤www.virginblue.com.au Have flights to Townsville from Brisbane everyday.

Alliance, ☎*1300 130 092*, www.allianceairlines.com.au, flies to Townsville from Brisbane twice on Mondays and Fridays and once every other day. No flights on Sunday.

By Coach
McCaffertys and Greyhound Pioneer, ☎*13 1499* or *13 2030*, both stop at Townsville on their Brisbane-Cairns services. **Premiere,** *13 3410*, both stop at Townsville on their Brisbane-Cairns services once a day.

By Rail
The Queenslander, **the TILT** and the **Sunlander** services connect Townsville to both Brisbane and Cairns four times weekly, ☎*13 2235*. Sleeping berths and motor rail facilities are available.

Visitor Information
The Townsville Enterprise Tourism Bureau is in *Enterprise House, 6 The Strand,* ☎*4771 3061*. There is also a Visitors Information Centre in *Flinders Mall,* ☎*4721 3660*, ⏲open 9am-5pm Mon-Fri and 9am-1pm Sat-Sun.

⤵ **Let's Stay Here**
Townsville has over 30 motels, hotels, guest houses, hostels and half a dozen camping grounds. Here is a selection of budget accommodation with prices for a double room per night, which should be used as a guide only. The telephone area code is 07.

Adobi,
86 Abbott Street, ☎*4778 2533
or 4778 2745.* 12 units, pool
- ✪*$50.*

**Adventure
Backpackers Resort,**
*79 Palmer St, South Towns-
ville,* ☎*4721 1522.*
Nice rooms and great facilities
including a large fully-
equiped kitchen, a number of
TV lounges, internet access,
barbecue on every floor
and plenty of parking. All
rooms have fridges and air
conditioning. Minutes away
from the Maritime Museum.
Dorm bed ✪*$20 ($18 VIP/
YHA); single room $32 ($29
VIP/YHA); double room $42
($38 VIP/YHA).*

Civic Guesthouse,
262 Walker St, ☎*4771 5381.*
▇*www.backpackersinn.com
.au* Small hostel with clean
rooms ranging from dorms
to twin and double rooms.
Games room, TV lounge and
basic kitchen. Air conditioning available and fans in all
rooms. Close to the movies
and job centres. Centre of town
right next to Diving Dreams.
Free BBQ on Fridays. *Single
rooms from* ✪*$39 (with fans)
+ $4 A/C; shared 4 bed dorms
$19 (with fans); shared 6 bed
dorms $20 (A/c); double twins
$42-60.* (mention website
when booking and get $2 off
your first night)

**Globetrotters
Harbourside Inn,**
*45 Palmer St, South Towns-
ville,* ☎*4771 3242.* Good
dorm rooms. Facilities in this
hostel are kitchen, barbecue

and swimming pool. Close
to Transit Centre. *Dorm beds
* ✪*$20; single room $42-50;
double room $47; triple room
$57-60.*

Reef Lodge,
4 Wickham St, ☎*4721 1112.
www.reeflodge.com.au* At the
centre of the city, very close
to the Transit Centre, 2 minute
walk from the Magnetic
Island ferry terminal, Flinders
Mall and Reef HQ. Nicely
renovated, most rooms have
air-conditioning, fans and
fridges, and have a nice
barbecue area. Laundry facility also available. Most credit
cards accepted. *Dorm bed
* ✪*$15-17; double/twin $38.*

**Southbank Village
Backpackers,**
*35 Plume St, South Towns-
ville,* ☎*4771 5849* Offers
simple accommodation for
a low price. Swimming pool
and barbecue area. *Dorms
* ✪*$10; single room $12;
double room $30; twin $24.*

**Townsville Transit Centre
Backpackers YHA,**
*Corner Plume and Palmer
St, South Townsville.* ☎*4721
2322 or 1800 628 836.*
▇*www.tcbackpacker.com.
au* First class facilities and
location at a budget price.
Situated at the Transit Centre.
In the middle of all city, surrounded by cafes, restaurants,
pubs, mseums and galleries.
Facilities includes kitchen,
TV lounge, barbecue area,
internet access, laundry,
disabled facilities and
parking. *Dorms* ✪*$17 YHA
members, $38 single rooms,*

*$40-48 twin/double. BC MC
VA EFTPOS*

Caravan Parks
Coonambelah Caravan Park,
547 Ingham Road, ☎*4774
5205.* (Pets on application) 75
sites - *powered sites* ✪*$17
for two, on-site vans $35-40
for two, cabins $40-50 for
two.*

**Town and Country Caravan
Park,** *16 Kings Road,* ☎*4772
1487.* (No pets allowed) 72
sites, pool, barbecue, playground - *powered sites* ✪*$18
for two, on-site vans $35 for
two, cabins $55 for two.*

Woodlands Holiday Village,
548 Bruce Highway, ☎*4751
6955* ▇*www.qparks.asn.au/
TVE.html* 76 ensuite sites.
Barbecue area, childrens
playground, recreation room,
kiosk and luxury villas with
bathroom, fans colour TV
and kitchen. (No pets) *$27
for ensuite caravans; $22 for
non-powered sites; $24 for
powered sites.*

Let's Eat
Townsville has many hotels
serving counter lunches and
takeaways, and some good restaurants. The international hotels
have at least one restaurant, and
the staff where you are staying
can probably recommend a
restaurant on the basis of price
or cuisine. Following is a broad
sample for all tastes and budgets.

Hogs Breath Cafe, *247 Flinders
Street,* ☎*4771 5747.* Open for
lunch 11.30am-2.30pm and
dinner 5.30pm-2.30am every day.

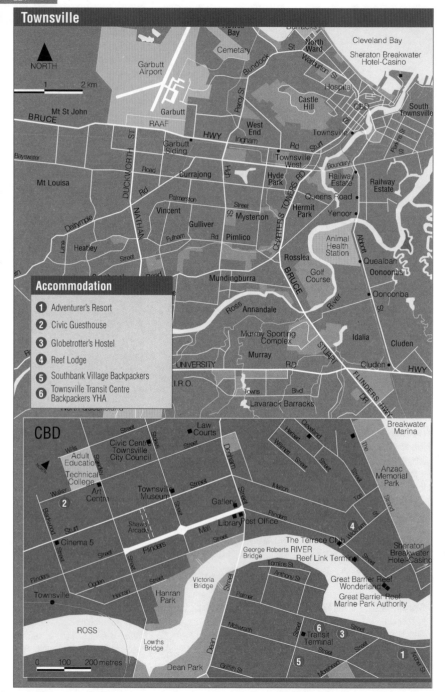

Townsville

NORTH

1   2 km

Accommodation

1 Adventurer's Resort

2 Civic Guesthouse

3 Globetrotter's Hostel

4 Reef Lodge

5 Southbank Village Backpackers

6 Townsville Transit Centre
Backpackers YHA

CBD

0   100   200 metres

Hong Kong Restaurant, *455 Flinders Street, West Townsville,* ☎*4771 5818.* A-la-carte menu with home-style cooking a specialty. Open 5pm-8pm Mon-Sat and for lunch Mon-Fri, closed Sunday and Public Holidays.

Scirocco Cafe Bar and Grill, *61 Palmer Street,* ☎*4724 4508.* Mediterranean and Asian cuisine, alfresco dining. ⏱Open Tues-Sat 6pm-midnight, and for lunch from midday-2pm, 10am-4pm on Sunday, closed Monday and Public Holidays.

Taiping Chinese Restaurant, *350 Sturt Street,* ☎*4772 3619.* A-la-carte, yum cha and buffet selections. Open midday-2pm and 5.30-midnight 7 days, closed Public Holidays.

Wayne and Adeles Garden of Eating, *11 Allen Street, South Townsville,* ☎*4772 2984.* Open 6.30-11pm Mon, Wed-Sat and Public Holidays, Sun 11am-3pm, closed Tuesday.

McDonalds is on the corner of *Flinders Mall and Denham Street.* **KFC** is in the *Nathan Plaza Stockland Shopping Centre.* **Pizza Hut** is at *260 Ross River Road* and on the *corner of Charters Towers and Bayswater Roads,* ☎*13 1166.*

Entertainment

First and foremost in this category would have to be the:
Sheraton Townsville Hotel and Casino, *Sir Leslie Theiss Drive,* ☎*4722 2333.* It was North Queensland's first licensed casino. Here you can try blackjack, the Sheraton wheels, two-up, roulette, keno, mini-dice, craps and mini baccarat. They

also have video games and Sky Channel. To get the tourists in they offer a free courtesy bus service to most hotels and motels. The casino is ⏱open from noon to the early hours of the morning.

Townsville Civic Theatre is in *41 Boundary Street, South Townsville,* ☎*4727 9013* or ☎*4727 9797* (box office), and can seat 1066 people. It offers culturally diverse programs.

The Entertainment and Convention Centre, ☎*4771 4000,* on *Entertainment Drive,* is primarily for indoor sport, such as basketball, but if a big-name performer or band hits town, this is where the concert will be.

Fisherman's Wharf in O*gden Street* has live entertainment seven nights a week, a restaurant, coffee shop and a bar.

If you are in the mood for dancing, head for Flinders Street where there is a night club, **Bullwinkles,** ☎*4771 5647.* For a pub night out try the Great **Northern Hotel** in *496 Flinders Street,* ☎*4771 6191.*

Shopping

Flinders Street Mall has several boutiques and specialty shops and Northtown on the Mall, ☎*4772 1566,* but the big shopping centres are out of town.

At Aitkenville, 20 minutes from the city centre is **Stockland,** *310 Ross River Road,* ☎*4779 6033,* which has David Jones department stores as well as specialty shops. Nearby is **K-Mart Plaza,** *Nathan Street,* ☎*4779 9277,* which has food shops and, of course, K-Mart.

The suburb of Pimlico has **Castletown,** *35 Kings Road,* ☎*4772 1699,* which has a variety of chain stores, including Target.

The suburb of Kirwan has **The Willows,** *Thuringowa Drive,* ☎*4773 6333.*

North Queensland's largest arts and crafts market is held in Flinders Mall every ⏱Sunday 9am-1pm. Called **Cotters Market** it has pottery, jewellery, paintings, leadlighting, leatherwork, wood-work, crocheting and knitwear, original handicrafts, wooden toys, hats, homemade goodies, plants and preserves, islander crafts, timber, fishing lures, homemade chocolates, Devonshire teas, orchids, souvenirs, and seasonal fruit and vegies.

Points of Interest

Castle Hill (286m - 938 ft) offers a panoramic view of Townsville. It is topped by an octagonal restaurant which commands a 260 degree view of the town and the bay. Nearby **Mount Stuart** is also an excellent vantage point.

Flinders Mall is virtually the heart of the city. It is a landscaped pedestrian mall with a relaxed atmosphere.

The **Perc Tucker Regional Gallery** is in the mall, ☎*4727 9011,* and it houses an extensive collection of national and regional art in an impressive building that was originally a bank. It is ⏱open Mon-Thurs 10am-5pm, Fri 10-6pm, Sat-Sun 10am-2pm, and admission is free. Nearby **St Joseph's Cathedral** in *Fryer Street, North Ward,* ☎*4772 1973,* is a reflection of the architecture of the past.

The Strand, Townsville's sea promenade, has many parks including the **Sister Kenny Park,** and the **Anzac Memorial Park** with its Centenary Fountains, waterfall and bougainvillea gardens. Also along The Strand is the **Tobruk**

Mt Isa Rodeo

Whale Watching at Hervey Bay

Snorkelling on a reef tour, Townsville

Memorial Swimming Pool.

Queen's Gardens next to Queen's Park, encompasses Kissing Point and Jezzine Army Barracks. An all-tide rock swimming pool, a restaurant and a kiosk are also in the gardens.

The Town Common Environmental Park is a flora and fauna sanctuary where visitors may see some rare water fowl, including the primitive magpie goose. In the winter months, at the height of the dry season, as many as 3000 brolgas, along with up to 180 other species of bird, flock to the Common's salt-marsh lagoons and waterholes. The brolga is famous for its courting ritual, and the park provides visitors with an excellent opportunity to see this dance at close quarters. The park is ☺open daily 6.30am-6.30pm and barbecue facilities are available.

Great Barrier Reef Wonderland in *Flinders Street East,* is one of the most popular attractions in Townsville. It features the **Great Barrier Reef Aquarium,** ☎*4750 0891* - the world's largest living coral reef aquarium. Conceived and operated by the Great Barrier Reef Marine Park Authority, the aquarium includes a huge main tank containing a living coral reef, a smaller tank displaying sharks and other reef predators and an extensive area containing numerous display tanks, educational exhibits, a theatrette and a large touch-tank. You actually walk beneath the water through a transparent tunnel surrounded by hundreds of coral reef animals. Admission costs are ✪$16 for adults. This very popular attraction is ☺open 9am-5pm.

Wonderland also houses: the operational headquarters of the Great Barrier Reef Marine Park Authority, the federal government agency responsible for safeguarding the Great Barrier Reef Marine Park (Reef HQ); a licensed restaurant featuring tropical cuisine; a shop with a variety of souvenirs and educational material; a post office; and an information centre with all you need to know about national parks, marine national parks, camping permits and locations, walking trails, and wildlife.

An **Imax Theatre,** ☎*4721 1481* is close to the aquarium, at *86 Flinders Street.* The theatre is dome-shaped and uses a special type of projection so that the image is projected above and around the audience - a fascinating experience. The theatre seats 200 people, including facilities for the handicapped.

The Museum of Tropical Queensland, *78-102 Flinders Street,* ☎*4726 0600,* has recently undergone a complete transformation. The former museum has been expanded and modernised into a new and improved complex, opened in June 2000. It has an extensive array of exhibits, from the life-cycle of the world's largest moth to various Aboriginal crafts, and is worth a visit.

From the Wonderland ferry terminal there are cruises leaving for **Magnetic Island** and the Great Barrier Reef throughout the day. And while you are waiting to pick up your cruise, or the next show at the theatre, you can spend some time in the specialty shops in the complex.

Pangola Park, *Spring Creek,*

☎*4782 9252,* between Giru and Woodstock, is about 40 minutes' drive from Townsville. It has ideal swimming spots and adjoins a National Park with mountain streams and waterfalls. There is good bushwalking, picnic areas, barbecues, caravan and camping sites, a licensed kiosk, fishing spots, minibikes, and conducted horse and pony rides on weekends and public holidays. The park is ☺open daily and an admission fee is charged. Camping and powered sites are available.

South of Townsville, in fact much closer to the town of Ayr, the wreck of the **Yongala** lies off **Cape Bowling Green**. A coastal steamer, she was bound for Cairns when a cyclone struck on March 14, 1911, and she went down with all hands - 121 people including officers and crew. The wreck was discovered in 1958, but has only been dived regularly since the 1980s.

Diving the Yongala is rated as one of the best wreck-dive experiences in the world.

The wreck is 110m long, and supports a system of hard and soft corals and many different marine animals including pelagics, stingrays, gropers, turtles and sea snakes. She lies in 30m of water with her funnel only 15m below the surface. The Yongala is protected by the Historic Shipwreck Act as a memorial to all who went down with her, so nothing may be taken from the ship. This is a temptation as there are dinner plates, knives, forks, and some evidence of human remains, but where they are they must stay. See the Diving section under Sport for operators who will take divers to the wreck.

Festivals

Pacific Festival is held each September/October, and lasts for 10 days.

The Visitor Information Centre will advise on all current events at the time of your trip.

Sport
Swimming

There are three salt water mesh swimming enclosures, one at Rowes Bay, one at Pallarenda, and one next to the rock pool in Queen's Gardens. They provide safe sea swimming free from sharks, sea-stingers and other marine hazards.

Diving

Diving courses are not cheap, and you should expect to pay at least ✪$400 for a comprehensive open water instruction program. If you are already a qualified diver, the cost for a guided dive is considerably less, and depends on the location and duration of the dive. Following are a few examples of companies operating in the area.

Mike Ball Dive Expeditions, 252 Walker Street, ☎4772 3022 - internationally acclaimed 5 star PADI dive centre providing PADI instruction from entry level to Dive career programs - expeditions to Yongala wreck and Coral Sea, also Cod Hole - ☉open Mon-Fri 8.45am-5pm, Sat 8.45am-noon.
The Dive Bell, 16 Dean Street, South Townsville, ☎4721 1155 - sport diving and dive shop - commercial diving school - diving trips to Yongala wreck and the reef - ☉open Mon-Fri 8.30am-5pm, Sat 9am-noon.
Pro-Dive Townsville, Great Barrier Reef Wonderland, Flinders Street, ☎4721 1760. PADI scuba diving

school - 5 star Gold dive shop - charter boats, hire equipment, learn to dive - Yongala wreck dives (up to 3 days) - ☉open daily 9am-5pm.

Skydiving

Coral Sea Skydivers, *Shop 3, 14 Plume Street, Townsville,* ☎*4772 4889.* Tandem and accelerated free fall dives for beginners and experienced jumpers - souvenir videos, photos and certificates - Tandem Dives: 8,000 feet starts at ✪$245; 12,000 feet $350 - Accelerated Free Fall Course: $500 - Complete Free Fall Course, including training and 12 jumps: $2400.

Tours

Detours, *Shop 5, Great Barrier Reef Wonderland Complex,* ☎*4721 5977,* offer the following trips:
Billabong Sanctuary - wildlife sanctuary - 4 hours - ✪$38 adult (includes entrance fee) - 10am daily.
Tropical City Tour - more than 9 points of interest visited - 2 hours - ✪$26 adult, - 11am weekdays.
Night Tour - Castle Hill, Casino, Entertainment Centre - 1 hour - ✪$20 adults, - 6pm-7pm Mon-Thu May-Oct.

Raging Thunder, *52 Fearnlet Street, Cairns,* ☎*4030 7990.* Although based in Cairns, this company has a 5-day tour that departs Townsville and takes in the best of the Tropical North. The highlight of day one is 5 hours of Tully River rafting then transfer to Cairns. Day two comprises a 5 hour reef cruise. Day three begins with a Hot Air Balloon flight above the Atherton Tablelands, a visit to Kuranda Markets, then a return trip to Cairns on the

Skyrail. Day four is an exploration of Cape Tribulation and Daintree, including a Crocodile Cruise on the river. On day five you are taken to Fitzroy Island to relax or take the optional tour, then return later to Cairns.

The cost of the tour is ✪$520 per person, but you must arrange your own accommodation for the duration of the tour.

Cruises
Coral Princess Cruises,
Breakwater Terminal, Sir Leslie Thiess Drive, ☎4721 1673 or ☎1800 079 545 (free call), offer these trips:

Magnetic Island Ferry, *Ross Street, South Townsville,* ☎*4772 5422,* offer:
Cruise to Magnetic Island - open return ticket, free pick up from accommodation - bus and mokes available - ✪$16 adult.
Magnetic Island Cruise/Bus - open duration, pick up from accommo-dation, cruise and bus tour of island with commentary, exploring and swimming - ✪$28 adult.
Cruise/Moke Hire - return ferry fare with moke hire on the island - includes insurance and island map - ✪$32 per person.

Outlying Attractions
Fitzroy Island

Fitzroy has an area of 4 sq km, and is situated 26km south-east of Cairns. It is only 6km from the mainland and was named by Captain Cook after the Duke of Grafton, a politician of the time. In 1819 Phillip King reported that Welcome Bay, where the resort is, was a good anchorage for passing ships because of its fresh water and supplies of timber.

Fitzroy Island is not a great

place for swimming as the beaches tend to be corally rather than sandy, although **Nudey Beach** has some sand. There are a few walking trails - the round trip to the lighthouse; a short rainforest walk to the **Secret Garden**; and the walk to Nudey Beach. Canoes and catamarans are available for use, and sailing is popular. There is good diving water right off-shore, and the Reef is not far away. The resort dive shop hires out all gear for snorkelling and diving, runs courses, and provides daily trips to Moore Reef.

Contact the **Fitzroy Island Resort** on ☎4051 9588 or ☎1800 079 080 (toll free) or visit the website at 🖳www.fitzroyislandresort.com.au

Mission Beach

At Mission Beach, about halfway between Townsville and Cairns, a chain of mountains runs down to the sea, and surrounds the small coastal settlements. Offshore lie the **North and South Barnard, Dunk** and **Bedarra Islands**, and beyond them, the **Great Barrier Reef**. Mission Beach is set on a stretch of 14km of coastline that includes **Garners Beach, Bingil Bay, Narragon Beach, Clump Point** and **Wongaling Beach.** There is a daily water taxi service from Mission Beach to nearby Dunk Island, and many visitors choose to stay on the mainland and visit the islands, rather than pay resort prices. The town is named after the Aboriginal Mission that was set up in 1912 at South Mission Beach, but the first settlers were the Cutten brothers who landed to the north at Bingil Bay in 1882 and founded a farming dynasty. They introduced

pineapple growing to this part of Queensland and founded tea and coffee plantations. In 1918 the 'cyclone of the century' levelled the settlements and farms in the district. Nowadays the main industries are banana and sugar-cane growing, and tourism.

Four villages comprise the Mission Beach area: **South Mission Beach, Bingil Bay, Wongaling Beach** and **Mission Beach**. The region's attractions include 14km of pristine beaches, **Dunk Island**, the offshore Reef, rainforests, and rafting on the **Tully River**.

The main activities in Mission Beach involve water sports and reef viewing, so if you wish to view land-based attractions, you will have to travel a little further afield. Here are a few suggestions, and the Visitor Centre can provide you with detailed directions to each.

The **Australian Insect Farm,** *Davis Road, Gurradunga,* ☎4063 3860, offers regular tours daily Tues-Sun, adults ✪$10.

Paronella Park, *Japoonvale Road, Mena Creek,* ☎4065 3225, comprises historic rainforest gardens. It is ⏰open 9am-5pm and costs adults ✪$14.

The **Australian Sugar Industry Museum,** *Bruce Highway, Mourilyan,* ☎4063 2656, has a wealth of memorabilia from old harvesters to historical photographs.

Johnstone River Crocodile Farm, *Flying Fish Point Road, Innisfail,* ☎4061 1121, facilitates crocodile breeding and displays wildlife. It is ⏰open 7 days 8.30am-4.30pm, adults ✪$15.

In addition, trips can be taken to these popular environmental destinations: **Tully Gorge, Hinchinbrook Island, Murray**

Falls and the **Atherton Tablelands.**

The Mission Beach Visitor Information Centre, *Porter Promenade,* ☎4068 7066, can be found 100 metres from the post office. The Centre has a wealth of information on every part of the area. They can be contacted by email at ✉visitors@znet.net.au

Tully

With a population of around 3000, Tully is set at the foot of Mt Tyson, and is the centre of a large sugar cane and banana growing region. The **Tully River** rapids provide some very fine whitewater rafting and canoeing, and there is plenty of fishing for enthusiasts.

It should be noted that Tully has the highest annual rainfall in Australia (along with Innisfail) of around 3700mm. There is a definite Wet Season which begins in December and peaks in March. During this period it can rain every day, and sometimes all day. People intending to spend their holiday on either Dunk or Bedarra Islands should keep this in mind, since the paradise appeal of tropical islands is somewhat diminished when the rain just doesn't stop.

The **Kareeya State Forest** is accessible via a spectacular drive up the Tully River gorge.

The Tully Information Centre, is on the *Bruce Highway in Tully,* ☎4068 2288.

Cardwell

Cardwell is a fishing village situated between the mountains and the sea. It is in the middle of a natural wonderland, with world heritage rainforests, waterfalls, swimming holes, wilderness tracks, white-water rafting, canoeing, crabbing, fishing and prawning. The **Cardwell lookout** offers panoramic coastal views and there are very scenic drives to **Murray Falls, Blencoe Falls, the Edmund Kennedy National Park, Dalrymple's Gap Track** and **Cardwell Forest.**

Cardwell is also the gateway to **Hinchinbrook Island**, the world's largest Island National Park.

Edmund Kennedy National Park, nestles into the coastline about 4km north of the township. Its features a range from mangrove swamps to open woodland to pristine rainforest. There is a 3km walking track, with wooden boards and bridges for an easy stroll, which serves as the best and safest way to view the region.

Nearby natural wonders include **Tully Gorge** and **Dalrymple's Gap,** as well as the **Falls: Murray, Blencoe** and **Wallaman** (Australia's highest single-drop falls at 305m).

For Visitor Information, contact the Development Bureau of Hinchinbrook and Cardwell Shires, *77 Townsville Road, Ingham,* ☎ *4776 5381.*

Dunk Island

Dunk Island, across the bay from Mission Beach, is mostly National Park land, but there is one luxury resort. The island is shaped by rolling hills and deep valleys. It is home to the famous **Ulysses** butterfly. Dunk Island is also part of the Family group of islands, and its Aboriginal name is Coonanglebah which means "isle of peace and plenty". Captain Cook named it Dunk after Lord Montague Dunk, the Earl of Sandwich, who was the First Lord of the Admiralty at the time. It is the largest island in the group and is sometimes called the Father of the Family Group (Bedarra is the Mother). The island's area is 10 sq km, but 7.3 sq km is national park. The Wet Season, when it is best not to visit, lasts from December to the end of March.

Dunk is very much a family resort and it has some good high tide beaches, but at low tide they are too shallow and have a lot of weeds. The island doesn't seem to have a significant problem with box jellyfish, but it is wise to keep an eye out during the November-March period.

There are 13km of walking tracks, and the 10km walk around the island rates among the best of any on the Barrier Reef islands.

Bruce Arthur's Artists' Colony is situated just beyond the Resort garden. The colony's longest term resident is former Olympic wrestler Bruce Arthur, who produces large and beautiful tapestries. He and his cohorts lease the land, and have an open house ☉10am-1pm between Thursday and Sunday (small entry fee) when they chat about the island and their projects, and present their work for sale.

The **Great Barrier Reef** is an hour away by Quickcat, the high-speed catamaran, and there are four reefs to dive: **Beaver, Farquharson, Yamacutta** and **Potter**. They have some of the best coral and marine life on the Reef, and feature feeding stations, coral walls, caves, caverns and gardens. Trips to **Beaver Reef** include glass bottom boat, semi-submersible rides, lunch and onboard dive instruction.

Contact the Dunk Island Resort directly on ☎ *4068 8199*, visit the website at 🖳www.dunkislandresort. com or email an information request at ✉visitors@greatbarrier reef.aus.net

Bedarra Island

Part of the Family Group of Islands, Bedarra lies about 6km south of Dunk Island and about 5km offshore. It is privately-owned and is shown on marine charts as Richards Island. Bedarra has an area of one square kilometre, and is a rainforest with natural springs and plenty of water. It has some very good sandy beaches. Note that it has a very definite Wet Season from December to the end of March, when it can rain every day and sometimes all day. There is a walking track from Bedarra Bay to the resort, which is in fact the only walking track.

Activities which are not included in the resort tariff are: Great Barrier Reef trips, boutique/shop, float plains, game fishing charters, hair salon (available on Dunk Island), private boat charters, sailing charters.

The **Bedarra Island Resort** can be contacted on, ☎ *4068 8233*. There is a web page at 🖳www.bedarra island-australia.com with an email address at ✉visitors@greatbarrier reef.aus.net

Hinchinbrook Island

Hinchinbrook is the world's largest island national park, with over 45,000ha (393 sq km) of tropical rainforests, mountains, gorges, valleys, waterfalls and sandy beaches. It is one of the most beautiful tropical islands in the world and offers some of the best bushwalking in Australia. A magnificent jagged mountain range drops to warm seas and coral reefs, dominating the skyline. The rainforests offer spectacular views.

The island is separated from the mainland by Hinchinbrook Channel, a narrow mangrove-fringed strip of water that is very deep. From further out at sea, the channel cannot be seen, and in fact, when Captain Cook sailed past he did not record the presence of an island.

The best walk on any of the Great Barrier Reef islands is the three to four day walk along the eastern side of Hinchinbrook, but it is strongly recommended that information be obtained from the National Parks and Wildlife Service in Cardwell (near the jetty), ☎4066 8601, before setting out. They can advise you on facilities on the island, give tips for climbing the mountains and protecting your supplies from the local wildlife, and issue permits for camping.

Remember that marine stingers may be around in the October-May period, and that crocodiles may be found in channel waters and estuaries.

Apart from the resort, the island has limited camping at ❂$3.50 per person per night (permit required, ☎4066 8601). Macushla Camping Area - patrols, picnic tables, shelter shed, toilets, fires prohibited. Walking tracks, ocean swimming beaches, fishing spots, rainforest areas. **Goold Island** - patrols, picnic tables, shelter shed, toilets, fires prohibited. Fishing and swimming.

For further information, contact the Development Bureau of Hinchinbrook and Cardwell Shires, *77 Townsville Road, Ingham, ☎4776 5381.*

Alternatively, call the Island Resort on ☎*4066 8585.* Updated information is provided at ▣www.hinchinbrookresort.com.au

Orpheus Island

This island is mostly national park, but has a secluded resort at one end. Orpheus Island is encircled by wide beaches and a warm shallow sea. A fringe reef possesses a rich variety of marine life and provides excellent diving.

Orpheus Island has an area of 14 sq km and is the second largest in the Palm Island group. There are ten main islands in the group, but eight of them are Aboriginal reservations and permission must be obtained to visit. Orpheus is National Park while Pelorus, the other island not part of the reserve, is Crown Land.

The island is 80km north of Townsville and roughly 20km off Lucinda Point near Ingham. It was named in 1887, after the HMS Orpheus - the largest warship in Australia, which sank off New Zealand in 1863 with the loss of 188 lives. **Orpheus is long and narrow and its fringing reef is probably the best of all the resort islands.** It is heavily wooded and is home to a large population of wild goats. The goats were introduced many years ago as food for people who might be shipwrecked on the island, but they have obviously not been needed and have multiplied to the point where they are causing some problems.

There are a few beaches on the island, although some, such as **Hazard Bay** and **Pioneer Bay,** are only suitable for swimming at high tide. When the tide is out they become wading pools.

Mangrove Bay and **Yankee Bay** are good places to swim at low tide. Good reefs are found off **Pelorus Island** to the north and **Fantome Island** to the south. The Resort dive shop offers local dives and diving courses, but remember that these activities are not included in the Resort tariff. There are many opportunities for bush walking and rainforest study, and snorkelling, as always, remains popular.

As far as bushwalks are concerned, there is a shortage of them on this island. One traverses up to **Fig Tree Hill**, and the other winds from **Hazard Bay** through a forest to **Picnic Bay.**

The zoning for most of the water around Orpheus is **Marine National Park B**, although part of the south-west coast is zoned 'A'. So limited line fishing is allowed in the 'A' part, but collecting shells or coral is strictly forbidden.

Camp sites are found at **Pioneer Bay** and **Yankee Bay.** They are patrolled, and have picnic tables, toilets and drinking water. For further information and booking, get in touch with the **Rainforest and Reef Centre**, *Bruce Highway, Cardwell,* ☎*4066 8601,* or call Naturally Queensland on ☎*3227 8187.* Campers cannot buy meals at the Resort, and fires are not permitted on the island, so if you are intending to camp bring all your provisions, including water and a fuel stove.

Magnetic Island

Magnetic lies 8km across Cleveland Bay from Townsville, fifteen minutes by catamaran. It is roughly triangular in shape and has an area of 52 sq km. With 16 beaches, plenty of reasonably-priced places to stay, and an ideal climate, this is one of the most popular islands on the Reef. The island's first visitor was Captain Cook in 1770, and he declared it Magnetic Island, believing that it had interfered with his compass. The island now has a permanent population of more than 2200 people, and draws millions of holiday-makers.

It is one of the largest islands on the Great Barrier Reef, and 70 percent of it is National Park. A high spine of mountains covered by forests of eucalypts and wattles, and strewn with granite boulders, runs across the island. Below the peaks lie sheltered white beaches, rocky coves and coral reefs.

More than 22km (14 miles) of walking tracks lead over and around hills to secluded coves and quiet bays. The four small settlements of **Picnic Bay, Nelly Bay, Arcadia** and **Horseshoe Bay** offer a plentiful range of services for the visitor. You will also find an aquarium and a koala sanctuary.

Box jellyfish are present around Magnetic between October and April, so during this time it is wise to swim only in the netted areas at Picnic Bay and Alma Bay. The north coast of Magnetic is zoned Marine Park B, so fishing is not permitted. There are quite a few good diving locations on the island's southern and eastern shores.

For details about other attractions on the island, contact either the Magnetic Island Visitor Information Bureau and Central Booking Office, *26 The Grove, Nelly Bay,* ☎*4778 5596,* or the Magnetic Island Holiday and Information Centre in Picnic Bay Mall, ☎*4778 5155.* They can

advise on your tour bookings, accommodation, vehicle hire, travel arrangements and the best way to climb Mt Cook (497m).

Home Hill and Ayr

The twin towns of Home Hill and Ayr are 90km (56 miles) south of Townsville on the Bruce Highway, and sit either side of the delta of the Burdekin River, slightly inland from the coast. The Burdekin is the main waterway of the Magnetic North, and its catchment area includes the mountains to the north and the goldfields to the west.

The **Ayr Nature Display,** *119 Wilmington Street, Ayr,* ☎*4783 2189,* has stunning displays ranging from reptiles to butterflies, birds to insects and fossils to shells. Admission is ✪$3 adults, and the Nature display is ⊙open 8am-5pm daily.

The river and its tributaries offer some of the best freshwater fishing for barramundi, grunter and bream in Australia, while the river delta and **Alva Beach** tempt the salt water fisherman with whiting, flathead and salmon. The **Burdekin River** is also the hub of other river-based activities from water skiing to picnicking.

The wreck of the **SS Yongala** lies 20km (12 miles) out to sea and is a fine diving site.

Cape Upstart National Park, some 70km (43 miles) from town, is an imposing granite headland rising from the sea.

The Burdekin Visitor Information Centre is in Plantation Park, on the *Bruce Highway, Ayr,* ☎*4783 5988.*

Charters Towers

The Outback is just on the other side of the mountains. If you wish

to divert from your coastal holiday for a while, the old gold rush town of Charters Towers can be reached 135km (84 miles) south-west of Townsville on the Flinders Highway. Now a town of 10,000 people, Charter Towers was once home to more than twice this number.

Three itinerant prospectors discovered gold in 1871, and between then and 1911, some seven million ounces of gold were taken from the region. The memories may be growing dim, but the town looks much the same as it did a century ago. Historic buildings line the streets and remnants of the gold mining era dot the surrounding countryside. In recent years a few small scale operations recommenced, and some gold was extracted from the area.

The **Venus Gold Battery,** in *Milchester Road,* contains a restored gold crushing mill which operated for a century. It is ⊙open from 9am-5pm daily with guided tours available. Admission prices are ✪$4 adults.

The **Zara Clark Museum and Military Display** is at *36 Mosman Street.* The aim of the complex is to enshrine the history of Charters Towers, particularly the nostalgia of its gold rush era. There is a range of memorabilia, and some interesting period photographs. It is ⊙open from 10am-3pm daily and costs adults ✪$4.

Ravenswood is about 60km east of Charters Towers. It is also a heritage town and another centre of the gold rush. Although it once had no fewer than 55 pubs, it now has a population of less than one hundred. The town seems largely untouched by time.

Burdekin Falls Dam is a large

catchment area that now provides the once dry cities of the coast with a plentiful water supply. Nearby, Burdekin Dam Holiday Park Motel, ☎4770 3178, offers accommodation and activities for patrons, ✪$45-55 for two.

For more information contact the Charters Towers Dalrymple Visitor Information Centre, *74 Mosman Street, Charters Towers,* ☎4752 0314. You can email them at ✉tourinfocentre@httech.com.au

The Hinterland

The Hinterland is to the north, sweeping towards the Gulf. Volcanoes once peppered the area, and the vast underground Undara Lava Tubes have become a notable attraction. The trip from Charters Towers to Undara covers a distance of about 380km (238 miles). Undara Lava Lodge offers several different tours of the Undara Experience, starting from ✪$33 adults for two hours, ☎1800 990 992 for reservations.

There is a website at ▣www. undara-experience.com.au, which you can check out beforehand to see if you think the attraction is worth the long drive.

Bowen

Situated just north of the Whitsunday Islands, Bowen is a town where the ocean laps the edges of the main street. It is 210km (130 miles) south of Townsville on the Bruce Highway, and has one of the best climates in Australia. The surrounding coast is indented with innumerable small headlands and quiet coral beaches. Inland, the Don River Plain is a fruit growing region.

The **Bowen Historical Society Museum**, *22 Gordon Street,*

☎4786 2035. In it you will find shipwreck relics, information on early pioneers and indigenous artefacts. It is ⏰open 10.30am-4pm Mon-Fri and 10.30am-12pm Sunday and costs ✪$3 adults.

Bowen's stunning coastline encapsulates its attraction for visitors. Of particular note are idyllic **Horseshoe Bay** and **Murray Bay**. **Queens Beach** is also a popular haven.

In the southern area of Bowen, swimming, fishing, diving and snorkelling are year-round activities, and for those who prefer to stay on terra firma, there is fossiking for sapphires, amethysts, crystals and opalised woods.

The Bowen Visitor Information Centre is on the *Bruce Highway, Bowen,* ☎4786 4222.

Cairns
Population 135,000

The Far North Queensland region extends from Cardwell in the south to the Torres Strait in the north, and west across the Gulf of Carpentaria to the Northern Territory border, an area of 377,796 sq km (145,829 sq miles) which is almost twice the size of the state of Victoria. Cairns, its major city and service, administration, distribution and manufacturing centre, has recorded the second highest percentage of population growth of any Australian city since 1979. In fact, it was named Australia's most livable regional centre back in 1995.

Climate

Average temperature: January max 32C (90F) - min 24C (75F); July max 25C (77F) - min 16C (61F). The humidity is high in summer, and the best time to visit is from May to October.

Characteristics

Cairns, in the heart of the tropical wonderland, is an international tourist mecca. It is a modern, colourful city situated on the shores of a natural harbour, Trinity Inlet, with a magnificent backdrop of rugged mountains covered with thick tropical rainforest.

The major glamour activity in Cairns is Big Game Fishing, and numerous fish over 450kg (992 lb) are caught each year. The game fishing season starts in early September and continues through to late November, however light game can be caught all year round.

As well as being a major city for tourism, Cairns is an important centre for the export of sugar and the agricultural products of the Atherton Tablelands.

The city was named after William Wellington Cairns, the third Governor of Queensland.

How to Get There
By Air

Qantas, ☎13 1313 have frequent daily flights to Cairns from the major southern ports of Brisbane, Sydney and Melbourne.

Sunstate and **National Jet Airlines**, **Qantas Air Link** ☎13 1313, operate daily flights to/from Cairns, Darwin, Gove, Horn Island, Weipa, Ayers Rock, Alice Springs, Townsville and Hamilton Island.

Cairns International Airport accepts many international airlines including **Qantas, Thai International, Air Nuigini, Australian Airlines, Air New Zealand** and **Japan Airlines.**

Cairns' Domestic and International airports, ☎4052 9703, are approximately 6km from the centre of the city. Regular coach services depart from the domestic terminals for the city and the northern beaches, and there is also an inter-terminal coach service.

By Rail

The Queenslander and **The Sunlander** operate regular services from Brisbane to Cairns. Both services provide sleeping berths, sitting cars, dining and club cars, and a lounge car. The Brisbane to Cairns trip takes about 32 hours on these fast and luxurious trains. For more information, ☎ 132 235.

By Bus

Greyhound Pioneer, ☎ 13 2030, and **McCafferty's**, ☎ 13 1499, operate regular daily express coach services from major southern cities.

Visitor Information

The Visitors Information Centre is on the *Cairns Esplanade* (near the pier complex). ◷open 7 days, 9.30am-5.30pm.

For information relating to all areas in North Queensland, contact Tourism Tropical North Queensland on ☎ 4051 3588 or at ✉ttnq@tnq.org.au. If you wish, visit the website at 🖳www.tnq.org.au

The Great Barrier Reef Visitors Bureau has developed a web site encompassing the entire region, with detailed and up-to-date information on accommodation, sightseeing, tours and more for every major locality. The address is 🖳www.greatbarrierreef.aus.net with email at ✉visitors@greatbarrierreef.aus .net

⤳ Let's Stay Here

The Cairns area has over 40 motels, as well as hotels, guest houses, holiday apartments and over 20 caravan parks. Prices vary considerably depending on the standard of accommodation and the season. Here we have a selection of budget accommodation with prices which should be used as a guide only. The telephone area code is 07.

Adobe,

191 Sheridan Street, ☎*4051 5511.* 15 units, offering cable TV, tea and coffee facilities in room and laundry. There's also a salt watered pool and off-street parking. Split air-conditioning and ceiling fans in rooms. *Rooms ✪$55 for single; $60 for two.*

Assylum Cairns,

149 Grafton St, ☎*4031 1474,* 🖳*www.asylumbackpackers.com* Formerly known as Tracks Hostel, has new added facilities and has a different atmosphere. Facilities includes a swimming pool, games room, cable TV, free 15min internet access, laundry, barbecue area and fenced and off-street car park. Board games, guitars and musical keyboards available at reception upon request. Free pick-ups and drop offs at airport and bus terminus. Mad pub parties every Monday. *Dorm ✪$15; single $25; double $34-38*

Bel-Air by the Sea,

155-157 The Esplanade, ☎*4031 4790 or 1800 649 517,* 🖳*www.cairns.net.au/ ✉haka/index.html* Located on

the waterfront of the Cairns Esplanade walking distance from the centre of Cairns. Offers air-conditioned and fan rooms, a refreshing pool and spa, kitchens, pool tables and spacious recreation and barbecue areas, including free cable TV. Will pick you up from anywhere in the Cairns area, just ring our freecall number. *Dorm ✪$15-18; double/twin $34-38*

Bellview,

85-87 The Esplanade, ☎*4031 4377* All dorm rooms have ensuite, fridge, fan and air-conditioning. Facilities have TV lounge, laundry, kitchen and swimming pool. Quiet hostel. *Dorm ✪$14-20; double from $49; twin $42-45*

The Big Backyard,

34 Martyn St, ☎*4031 3133 or 1800 025 070* Well maintained hostel. This hostel consists of three newly renovated Queenslanders all having their own kitchen and bathroom. Rooms are either fanned or air-conditioned. Other facilities includes a cable TV lounge, free internet access, swimming pool, laundry and a beach volleyball court. Recommended. *Dorm room ✪$15-18; double twin $30-36* (prices include a voucher for free dinner at the Woolshed)

Billabong Central Backpackers,

69 Spence St, ☎*4051 6949 or 1800 280 180* Located in the city centre near Cairns Central, it offers basic accommodation. There's a kitchen, TV lounge outside, barbecue

Cairns

Accommodation

1 Balcony City Backpackers
2 Bellview, The
3 Billabong Central Backpackers
4 Cairns International Hostel
5 Caravella's 77
6 Central City Backpackers
7 Global Palace
8 Hostel 89
9 Jimmy's
10 Leo's Retreat
11 Rosie's Backpackers
12 Shenannigans
13 YHA Cairns Central
14 YHA on the Esplanade

Charters Towers

Cape York Swa,p

Cairns

Cairns Casino (below)

area, a swimming pool and a pool table. *Dorms ✪$17; double/twin $38*

Bohemia Resort,

231 Mcleod St, ☎1800 155 353, 💻www.bohemiaresort. com.au Located just five minutes from the city, this resort looks fantastic and is in excellent and new condition. All rooms have air-conditioners with balconies and vanities. Facilities includes an an outdoor area with large luxury swimming pool, bar and pool tables and full self-serve kitchen and laundry. There's also an air-conditioned TV lounge room and a barbecue area. Free pickups and free courtesy bus. **Recommended.** *Dorms ✪$20; double/twin $52 without ensuite* (prices includes breakfast)

Cairns Beach House,

239 Sheridan St, ☎4041 4116, 💻www.cairnsbeachhou se.com.au Most rooms have ensuite bathroom. Facilities include internet access, basic kitchen, a bar area with swimming pool, laundry and a big parking area. Cheap meals are offered at the big Beer and Garden Sports Bar and are open to the public. Offers free bus transfers. *Dorm ✪$18; double/twin $40 ($50 with en suite batroom)*

Cairns Girls Hostel,

147 Lake St, ☎4051 2016, 💻www.cairnsgirlshostel.c om.au Home to travelling women from all over the world located in Cairns City Centre. Each room is equipped with fans, wardrobes, bedside

tables and writing desks and consist mainly of single beds. Facilities includes internet access, laundry, TV lounges and kitchens. Voted "Cairns best Hostel" for under $15 per day. *Dorm from ✪$13 (from 16 years)/$16; single $20; twin $36*

Cairns International Hostel,

67 The Esplanade, 4031 1545 Being in the centre of town makes this an excellent location. Facilities includes a games area, TV lounge, kitchen and internet access. The rooftop sundeck give great view of the sea and the Esplanade. *Dorm ✪$19; double $48; twin $46.*

Calypso Inn,

5-9 Diggers St, ☎4031 0910 or 1800 815 628, 💻www.caly psobackpackers.com.au Probably one of the funkiest looking Inn in town. Accommodation is in five seperate houses with their own kitchen facilities and airconditioning. There is also a licenced bar and an-all-you-can-eat buffet, broadband internet, large pool, beautiful tropical gardens and guest laundry. Offers free courtesy bus to and from city, airport, and bus station. **Recommended.** *Dorm ✪$21 ($20 VIP); double/twin $23 ($22 VIP)*

Captain Cook Backpackers Hostel,

204 Sheridan St, ☎4051 6811 or 1800 243 512, 💻www.backpacker- cairns.com Fun in the Sun tropical resort setting with 2 inviting swimming pools with

beach/water volleyball and half tennis courts. All dorms offer en-suites, balconies, and in-room safe's for added security of your valuables. Not all rooms have air-conditioning, en-suite bathrooms, fridge, tea and coffee facilities, private phones, and cable television, plus daily serviced. There's also laundry, internet lounge, fax and photocopying services plus wake-up calls. Also offers free transfers on arrival and shuttle bus operates a regular free service into the city centre of Cairns for your convenience. *Dorms from ✪$17; singles from $25; double from $40*

Caravella's 77,

77 The Esplanade, ☎4051 2159 or 1800 112 159, 💻www.caravella.com.au Located on the esplanade with only a short walk to the city. Air conditioned with share facilities, some with private bathroom, fridge and sink in room. There's also a large swimming pool, barbecue, pool table and table tennis, TV and video lounge, internet access and laundry facilities. Has a party atmosphere. *Dorm ✪$19; double/twin $40; single $30.*

Dreamtime Hostel,

4 Terminus St, ☎4031 6753, 💻www.dreamtimetravel.com. au/dt Located just a mintues walk from Cairns Central and the train station. Facilities includes swimming pool and spa, tropical garden barbecue, well equipped kitchen and laundry. Offers discounted tours and free pick up/drop off from the city and the airport. **Recommended.** *Dorms ✪$18; double/twin $40*

Gecko's,
187 Bunda St, ☎ *4031 1344 or 1800 011 344,* ▇ *www.g eckosbackpackers.com.au* Dorms are nice and big with single beds and no bunks. Not all rooms are air-conditioned, but every other room has fans. Features a nice kitchen, internet access, a barbecue area and swimming pool. **Recomended.** *Dorm ✪$19; single $28; double/ twin $40-45*

Global Palace,
City Place, ☎ *4031 7921 or 1800 819 024* Facilities includes 2 common areas, two laundries, and a fabulous kitchen. One common room is open-aired common room with pool table and balcony looking over the street, whilst the other situates itself on the top floor with table tennis, another pool table and big screen TV. On the rooftop is also the swimming pool and a sundeck. Only some air-conditioned dorms. **Highly recommended.** *Dorm ✪$23; double $52; twin $50* (price includes dinner at PJ O'Briens)

Gone Walkabout,
274 Draper St, ☎ *4051 6160 or 1800 045 161,* ▇ *www.gonewalkabout.com* Conveniently located 5 minutes away from the main shopping area and railway station in Cairns and 10 minutes from the center of the city. Facilities includes

2 kitchens, free car parking, barbecue area, laundry, swimming pool and on-site internet access. With comfy beds and free air conditioning in all rooms. they also offer free pick up from bus station. **Recomended.** *Dorm ✪$18 ; single $28; double 38;*

Inn The City,
141 Lake St, ☎ *4031 1326* Newly furnished and renovated. Saltwatered pool, barbecue area and volleyball court. Some rooms are air conditioned with TV and fridge. Located just behind A1 car Rentals in the centre of Cairns. *Dorm ✪$21 ($18 downstairs, no aircon or fridge); double $48 ($42 if you're staying for a week;* (with free dinner and breakfast)

Inn The Tropics,
141 Sheridan St, ☎ *4031 1088 or 1800 807 055* Accommodation just 5 minutes away from Cairns. Facilities includes kitchen, TV lounge and laundry. Good outdoor area for barbecue including a swimming pool. *Dorm ✪$18; single $33; double/twin $44; family (2 adults - 2 kids) $55*

International Hostel Dorm,
67 The Esplanade, ☎ *4031 1545* VIP member. Right in the heart of Cairns, the International is situated opposite the waterfront recreational area of the city with cool sea breezes and mountain views. They will happily design itineraries for you. There are ceiling fans in every room and all bedrooms

are air conditioned. Facilities includes kitchen, laundry, shaded garden area, roof top sun deck and internet access. Salt water lagoon is also close by for swimming. They have a courtesy bus with free airport picks up. *Dorm ✪$21; single $30; twin $48; double with A/C $50;* (free meal with each night's stay)

Jimmy's Backpackers,
83 The Esplanade, ☎ *4031 4411* Right at the heart of the city centre just on The Esplanade. All rooms have coin-operated air conditioning and ensuite bathrooms for male and female dorms. Facilities includes laundry, a number of kitchens, swimming pool and barbecue area. *Dorms ✪$22; single $40; double $48*

Leo's Retreat,
100 Sheridan St, ☎ *4051 1264 or 1800 080 809,* ▇ *www.backpackeraustralia .com.* Three buildings, one air-conditioned and the rest are fan cooled, with great big balconies. Facilties includes internet access, kitchen with lockers and a backyard area with a swimming pool. BBQ is also offered every Thursday. *Dorms ✪$18; single $29; double $49;* (prices includes breakfast)

Pete's Backpackers Resort,
242-248 Grafton St, ☎ *4031 6938 or 1800 122 123,* ▇ *www.petescairns.com.au* Just newly furnished, the rooms are set in old Queenslander houses. The huge outdoor area has big cable screen TV, hammocks are

everywhere, a vollerball court and a swimming pool. *Dorm ✪$18; twin $40; double $45;* (free dinner every night)

Ryans Rest,

18 Terminus St, ☎4051 4734 Located in the quiet residential street close to the train station and the shopping centre at Cairns Central. Old Queenslander building wonderfully renovated is more secluded, quiet and private than most hostels in the city. Offers a laundry facility and swimming pool. **Recomended.** *Dorm ✪$20; double $45;*

Serpent Nomads Hostel and Bar,

341 Lake St, ☎4040 7777 or 1800 737 736 ▣*www.serpenthostel.com or* ▣*www.nomadsworld.com* Brand new purpose built resort hotel one block to The Esplanade. Air-conditioned rooms. Facilities includes several TV rooms, internet access, pool tables, laundry, huge tropical pool and beach volleyball court. With lush garden settings, they also have Serpent Bar and Cafe on the premises. Also offers a free shuttle bus from the airport and hotspots around town. **Recomended.** *Members dorm ✪$20; single $52; double $52;*

Shenannigans,

Corner Spence and Sheridan Sts, ☎4051 2490, ▣*www. shenannigans.com.au* Located in the centre of the city above a pub. Offers basic accommodation with a nice balcony. *Dorm ✪$16; single $30; double/twin $38* (Meals are often included

if you opt to stay for 3 nights or more)

Travellers Oasis,

8 Scott St, ☎4052 1377 ▣*www.travoasis.com.au* Set in a relaxed atmosphere and a luscious tropical garden with some rooms air-conditioned. Facilities include swimming pool, outdoor seating, barbecue, and internet access. Very quiet hostel with no TVs. **Recomended.** *Dorms ✪$20; single $30; double $44;*

✤Tropic Days,

26-28 Bunting St, ☎4041 1521, ▣*www.tropicdays.com. au* Set in an old Queenslander building. Just renovated with facilities including a nice reading room, TV and video lounge, kitchen, laundry, internet access. They also have bike hires. On the outside is a swimming pool, barbecue area and some hammocks. Located about 20 minutes walk from the city centre with courtesy bus that can take you there. **Recomended.** *Dorm ✪$20; double/twim $45; camping $11* (price includes free dinner at the Woolshed)

Up Top Down Under,

164-170 Spence St, ☎4051 3636 Not much in appearance outside on the streets. Inside offers nicer feel, with kitchen, a number of TV lounges, pool table, internet access, barbecue area and a nice swimming pool. *Dorm ✪$18; single $32; double/ twin $40;*

Utopia Cairns Backpackers Resort,

702 Bruce Highway, Woree, ☎1800 354 599 ▣*www.nomadsworld.com* A former motel built around a courtyard with swimming pool, palm trees and sun lounges. All shared rooms are catered with fridges, telephone, ensuite bathrooms and air conditioning. Facilities also includes pool table, table tennis, barbecue and internat access. There is also a licensed bar and cafe. Located far from the city but a courtesy bus will gladly drive you there every hour. Offers free BBQ every Friday. *Members dorm ✪$19; single $44; double/twin $44;*

YHA Cairns Central, *20-24 McLeod St, ☎4051 0772,* ▣*www.yha.com.au*

More like a motel than a hostel. Landscaped swimming pool and cark park are located at the courtyard. Not all rooms are air-conditioned. Facilities also includes TV lounge, cheap internet access and kitchen. Minutes away from the train station and Cairns Central shopping centre. Winner of the 2001 Tropical North Queensland Tourism Award. ✪*$21 per person twin share. Members dorm ✪$20; double/twin $25 BC MC VA EFTPOS*

YHA on The Esplanade, *93 The Esplanade, ☎4031 1919,* ▣*www.yha.som.au* Located at the heart of The Esplanade of Cairns, overlooking the Coral Sea. Multi-share rooms are air-conditioned, whilst

ensuites and other room are fan cooled. Basic facilities including kitchen, laundry, cable TV and private courtyard. *Members dorm ✪$20; double/twin $22 BC MC VA EFPTOS*

Caravan Parks

Cairns Coconut Caravan Resort, *cnr Bruce Highway and Anderson Road*, ☎*4054 6644*. (No pets) 279 sites, recreation room, barbecue, playground, cafe, transfers, tennis, pool, mini golf, basketball - *powered sites ✪$28 for two, cabins $50-85 for two, units $80-95 for two.*

First City Caravilla Caravan Park, *Little Street*, ☎*4054 1403*. (No pets) 100 sites, barbecue, playground, kiosk, mini golf, pool - *powered sites ✪$22 for two, cabins $50-75 for two.*

Cairns Villa and Leisure Park, *28 Pease Street, Manunda*, ☎*4053 7133*. (No pets) 163 sites, recreation room, lounge, barbecue, playground, shop, pool - *powered sites ✪$17-25 for two, units from $55 for two, cabins from $50 for two.*

Crystal Cascades Holiday Park, *Intake Road, Redlynch*, ☎*4039 1036*. 92 sites, recreation room, barbecue area, salt water pool, spa - *powered sites ✪$21 for two;*

Local Transport

There are public transport services to all Cairns city areas, suburbs and beaches. Timetables and routes are available at hotels and bus depots.

Cairns City Airporter, ☎*4031 3555*, have an airport/city/airport service, and bookings are essential for trips to the airport. They also have vehicles available for charter.

Coral Coaches, ☎*4031 7577*, have daily services between: Cairns, Hartley Creek, Port Douglas, Mossman, Daintree, Cape Tribulation, Bloomfield, Cooktown - Inland and Coast Road. They also have airport transfers to/from: Northern Beaches, Port Douglas, Mossman and Cape Tribulation.

Whitecar Coaches, ☎*4051 9533*, service the Atherton Tabelands and Chillagoe.

Car Hire

Avis, *135 Lake Street*, ☎*4051 5911*, **and** Cairns International Airport, ☎*4035 9100*.
All Car Rentals, *30 Grafton Street*, ☎*4031 6322*.
Cairns Tropical Rent-A-Car, *141 Lake Street, Cairns*, ☎*4031 3995*.
Hertz, *436 Sheridan Street, Cairns*, ☎*4053 6701*.
Mini Car Rentals, *150 Sheridan Street, Cairns*, ☎*4051 6288*.
Peter's Economy Rent-A-Car, *36 Water Street, Cairns*, %*4051 4106*.
Cairns Leisure Wheels, *314 Sheridan Street, Cairns*, ☎*4051 8988*.
National Car Rental, *135 Abbott Street, Cairns*, ☎*1800 350 536*.
Honeycombs Cars and 4WD's, *303-307 Mulgrave Road, Cairns*, ☎*4051 9211*.

Entertainment

Cairns has nightclubs, discos, karaoke bars, theatre restaurants, live theatre and cinemas. There are street musicians and all types of performing artists in and around the shopping areas, taverns and bars:

Club International and **My Karaoke Bar**, *40 Lake Street*, ☎*4052 1480*.
Sports Bar, *33 Spence Street*, ☎*4041 2533*.
The Beach Nite Club, *78 Abbott Street*, ☎*4031 3944*.
The Cat House Night Club, *78 Abbott Street*, ☎*4051 6322*.

Because the weather is quite warm at night there are always lots of people to be found along the Esplanade, eating at pavement tables, or picnicking on the lawns.

Cairns also has a couple of clubs who welcome visitors and offer free temporary membership for those who live more than 40km from the club.

Brothers Leagues Club (Cairns), *99 Anderson Street, Manunda*, ☎*4053 1053*.
The Yacht Club, *4 The Esplanade (between Hilton Hotel and Great Adventures)*, ☎*4031 2750*.

Shopping

There are plenty of shopping opportunities in Cairns. The large hotels have boutiques offering imported fashion items and jewellery, and then there is **The Pier Marketplace**, ☎*4051 7244*, in *Pierpoint Road*. The Pier is a landmark in Cairns. The building contains the Radisson Plaza Hotel and a specialty retail leisure centre.

It has separate theme walkways, the most glamorous of which is the Governor's Way, where Cairns' best fashion stores and boutiques are found. The main entrance leads to Trader's Row, which has a colonial air and some appealing shops that are not the usual 'high fashion'.

The **Mud Markets** are held on Saturday and Sunday in the main amphitheatre of the specialty retail centre, and local artisans and artists set up stalls selling all sorts of interesting objects from handcrafts to glassware. Live entertainers roam around the markets, creating a really festive atmosphere.

The **Pier Marketplace** is ☺open daily 9am-9pm, but most of the shops in the city centre are open Mon-Thurs 8.30am-8pm, Fri 8.30am-9pm, Sat 8.30am-5.30pm, Sun 3-8pm. Those in the suburbs have shorter hours with night shopping on one night only.

Let's Eat

Cairns has some of the best eating places in Queensland. Most of the international standard hotels and motels have at least one restaurant as well as a bistro, or the like. There is also a good selection of restaurants, some of which can be found along the Cairns Esplanade, where you can enjoy both the meal and views of the natural harbour inlet. Here is a selection of restaurants in the area:

Aphrodisias Restaurant, *82 Sheridan Street*, ☎4051 5871.

Brothers Leagues Club (Cairns), *99 Anderson Street Cairns*, ☎4053 1053. Betting and gambling facilities. Open 9am-11pm daily except on Public Holidays.

Golden Sun Inn, *313 Kamerunga Road, Freshwater*, ☎4055 1177. Chinese cuisine, BYO and licensed. Open 5pm-10pm every day except Tuesday and Public Holidays.

Jango Jango Club Restaurant, *Level 1 Palm Court, 34 Lake Street*, ☎4031 2411. Asian influenced fare and karaoke. Open 6pm-2am daily.

Red Ochre Grill, *43 Shields St*, ☎4051 0100. Modern Australian cuisine with seafood and outdoor dining facilities. Open 10am-11pm Mon-Sat, 3pm-11pm Sunday and Public Holidays.

Tandoori Oven, *62 Shields Street*, ☎4031 0043. Open 6.30pm-10.30pm daily, closed Sunday and Public Holidays.

Thai Pan Restaurant, *43-45 Grafton Street*, ☎4052 1708. Licensed and BYO, take-away and free home delivery available. Open 6pm-8pm every day.

The Sorrento, *70 Grafton Street*, ☎4051 7841. Italian cuisine, pizza, seafood and steak.

McDonalds is in both the Cairns *Central Shopping Centre* and on the *Esplande*. **KFC** is at *Shop 5, 71-75 The Esplanade* and at the *corner of Mulgrave and Florence Streets*. **Pizza Hut** is on the *corner of Aurnullar Street and Mulgrave Road*, ☎13 1166.

Points of Interest

There are no sandy beaches in Cairns itself, only mudflats, but prolific birdlife gathers here. Palms line many streets, with parks and gardens displaying a riot of colour from bougainvillaea, hibiscus, poinciana and other tropical blooms. The old part of town is to be found around *Wharf Street* and *The Esplanade*. The National Trust has put out a walking tour brochure about this part of town.

The Esplanade is 5km (3 miles) long and runs along the side of the bay. This park-like area is a very pleasant place to relax in the cooler part of the day.

The **Flecker Botanic Gardens**, *Collins Avenue, Edge Hill*, are ☺open daily and feature graded walking tracks through natural rainforest to Mount Whitfield. From here there are excellent views of the city and coastline.

The **Centenary Lakes**, *Greenslopes Street, Cairns North*, are an extension of Flecker Botanic Gardens and were created to mark the city's centenary in 1976. There are two lakes - one fresh water, the other salt. Bird life abounds and barbecue facilities have been provided. **Mount Mooroobool** (610m - 2000 ft) in the background is the city's highest peak.

The Pier Marketplace hosts live entertainment daily, and is the departure point for most reef cruises and fishing boat charters. Sit on the verandah for a quick snack or a delicious meal from one of the many food outlets, while checking out the magnificent views over Trinity Inlet.

The Royal Flying Doctor Base, *1 Junction Street, Edge Hill*, ☎4053 5687, has fully guided tours, film shows, and displays of the history and present operations of this legendary service. ☺open seven days.

Sugarworld Waterslides, *Mill Road, Edmonton*, ☎4055 5477, is 14km south of Cairns City centre, and has tropical horticulture, a licensed restaurant, tours, rides and waterslides.

The Reef Hotel Casino, *35-41 Wharf Street*, ☎4030 8888, offers what all casinos offer: a glitzy way to part with your money.

The **Cairns Convention Centre**, *cnr Wharf and Sheridan Streets*, ☎ *4042 4200*, may have a function on at the time of your visit.

Festivals

The festival season begins with the **Mareeba Rodeo** in early July and then onto the **Cairns Show** for three days of entertainment. The **Cairns Amateur Horserace Meeting** is held in September, and the week-long **Fun in the Sun Festival** is in October.

Sports

All types of water sports are catered for, as well as the usual sporting activities.

Diving

The following companies in Cairns offer diving trips and lessons.

Pro Dive, 116 Spence Street, ☎4031 5255. 5 day learn to dive courses are held 4 times weekly. 3 day/2 night liveaboard cruises 4 times weekly - PADI 5-Star facility.
Deep Sea Divers Den, Wharf Street, ☎4031 5622. Dive and snorkel trips, dive courses (beginner to instructor level), diving/fishing charters on the Outer Barrier Reef.
Taka 2 Dive Adventures, 131 Lake Street, ☎4051 8722. Offer dives in Cod Hole, Ribbon Reefs, Coral Sea - liveaboard, departs bi-weekly.
Great Diving Adventures Cairns, Wharf Street, 4051 4444. PADI open water dive courses available on tropical Fitzroy Island, including accommodation, meals, transfers and certification - other great dive locations include Norman Reef and Michaelmas Cay, both on the Outer Barrier Reef.

Tours

Cairns is a staging place for tours to the Great Barrier Reef, the Islands, the Atherton Tablelands, the Barron Gorge, Cooktown and Cape Tribulation. Here are a few.

The **Cairns Explorer** bus leaves from Lake Street Transit Mall every hour 9am-4pm Mon-Sat. It visits Wescourt shopping, Earlville shopping, Freshwater swimming hole, Freshwater Connection, Mangrove Boardwalk, Botanical Gardens, Flying Doctor and Centenary Lakes. For bookings and enquiries, ☎ *4033 5344*.

Tropic Wings Luxury Coach Tours, *278 Hartley Street*, ☎ *4035 3555*. Specialise in day tours around Cairns and The Tropical North - Atherton Tablelands, Port Douglas and Daintree, Cape Tribulation, Chillagoe, 3 day Outback and Gulf.

Down Under Tours, *Cairns*, ☎ *4035 5566*. Offer tours to Kuranda, Daintree/Port Douglas, The Tablelands, Cairns and Orchid Valley, Weatherby Station (outback).

Australian Pacific Tours, *278 Hartley Street, Cairns*, ☎ *4041 9419* or ☎ *1300 655 965* (reservations). They have an extensive range of half and full days tours, as well as extended tours from 2 to 12 days.

Wilderness Challenge, *15 Tranguna Street, Trinity Beach*, ☎ *4055 6504*. 4WD adventure safaris from 1 to 14 days or charters - travel to Cape York, Hinchinbrook, Cooktown, Daintree, Kakadu, Lava Tubes, and more.

Billy Tea Bush Safaris, *94 Upper Richardson Street, Whitfield*, ☎ *4032 0077*. 1 day to 14 day safaris available to Cape

York, Alice Springs, Ayers Rock, and more.

Oz Tours Safaris, *Captain Cook Highway, Smithfield*, ☎ *4055 9535*. 7, 9, 10 and 12 day overland/air or 16 day all overland Cape York safaris. Both camping and accommodated options available - also Cairns-Cape York-Thursday Island.

Barrier Reef Cybertours, *Shop 9, 7 Shields Street*, ☎ *4041 0666*.
Cairns Eco-Tours, *85 Lake Street*, ☎ *4031 0334*.
Cairns Harley Tours, ☎ *0417 45 4962* (mobile).

Cruises

Sunlover Cruises, cnr Tingara and Aumuller Streets, ☎4050 1333. Luxurious travel aboard Super-Cats to Moore or Arlington Reef - most innovative reef pontoons afloat, underwater theatre and marine touch tanks, free guided snorkelling tours, delicious buffet lunch - free semi-sub (Moore Reef), Supa Viewer (Arlington Reef), and glass bottom boat rides - all levels of diving catered for - optional helicopter and sea plane joyflights (Moore Reef only) - free guided rainforest walk on Fitzroy Island.
Ocean Spirit Cruises, 33 Lake Street, Cairns, ☎4031 2920. Daily departures aboard the Ocean Spirit I or Ocean Spirit II sailing vessels, to either Michaelmas or Upolu Cay - delicious tropical seafood buffet available.
Big Cat, Pier Marketplace, ☎4051 0444. Has cruises that depart daily from The Pier at 9am and travel to Green Island - snorkelling, glass bottom boat tours, lunch served on board, submersible reef coral viewer, guided snorkel tours - return Cairns 5pm - from J$70 adults.
Captain Cook Cruises, Trinity Wharf, ☎4031 4433. Offer 3, 4 and 7 day Reef Escape cruises every week - cruise to

Hinchinbrook and Dunk Islands, or Cooktown and Lizard Island. Coral Princess Barrier Reef and Island Cruises, Shop 5, 149 Spence Street, ☎4031 1041. Sails between Cairns and Townsville, calling at island resorts and uninhabited islands for beachcombing, swimming and a tropical barbecue.

Clipper Sailaway Cruises, 287 Draper Street, Cairns, ☎4052 8300. Sail on SV Atlantic Clipper - a 140' sailing ship catering for 34 passengers - cruises from Cairns to Lizard Island, Great Barrier Reef, Cape York.

Seahorse Sail and Dive, B16 Marlin Marina, ☎4041 1919. Snorkelling, diving, lunch included.

Auspray Seafaris, 125 Aumuller Street, 4035 3931.

Sport n Game Fishing Charters, 23 Bolton Street, 4053 1828.

Barrier Reef Luxury Cruises, Marlin Marina, 4051 3555.

Blue Whaler Charters, Marlin Marina, 4051 141**4.**

Outlying Attractions
Cape York

This remote mainland spur is Australia's northernmost tip, 2753km north of Brisbane. Like an outstretched finger the peninsula points towards the south coast of Papua New Guinea, just over 100km away on the other side of the Torres Strait. The **Jardine National Park** hugs the eastern portion of the Peninsula about 50km south of the Cape.

From Cairns, the most direct route is by **4WD only** via the *Peninsula Development Road* which cuts through the eastern side of the peninsula to Cape York. The journey is 861km on the direct route and 1062km if you weave through the National Parks. Road conditions vary with each Wet season, so it is

essential that you check current road integrity with the Visitor Information Centre in Cairns, ☎4031 4355, or visit the relevant web pages listed in the Visitor Information chapter.

Crocodile farming at the **Edward River Crocodile Farm**, ☎4060 4177; pearl farming; black boar hunting; barramundi fishing, ☎4031 3988; and **Aboriginal Corroborees at Bamaga Mission**, are just a few of the unique attractions Cape York has to offer.

Several cruises sailing to Cape York and the Torres Strait are available, and this is probably the best way to visit this remote region if you are not the rugged, adventurous type.

For a preliminary look, the web pages to explore are ▇www.tnq.org.au and ▇www.visitcapeyork.com Additional information can be obtained from the Cooktown Tourism Association, ☎4069 6100 or ☎1800 001 770. Their email address is ✉info@cooktownau.com

Lizard Island

With an international reputation as the place for big game fishing, Lizard Island is 97km (60 miles) north-east of Cooktown and is basically a 1000ha National Park boasting pristine natural beauty. It has an area of 21 sq km, and is the most northerly of the Barrier Reef resort islands. It is 240km from Cairns, but close to the outer Barrier Reef, and has 23 beaches that are good for swimming and snorkelling, and a superb coral lagoon.

Captain Cook and Dr Joseph Banks landed on Lizard Island, after they had repaired the Endeavour at what is now Cooktown. They named it after the many large

lizards they found there.

Lizard has over 1000ha of National Park, and some good walks. The climb to the top of Cook's Look is the most popular, and is well signposted, and from the Resort it is a short walk to the ruins of the Watson's house. The waters around the island are home to coral reefs and countless tropical fish, including the renowned Black Marlin. From August to November it attracts fishermen worldwide.

The Island is very remote and exclusive, with access only via a scenic air one-hour flight from Cairns Airport. You can make arrangements when booking accommodation.

There are no regular ferry or boat services to Lizard Island, but it is included as a destination in some of the cruises run by **Captain Cook Cruises**, ☎4031 4433.

Camping is also available at **Watson's Bay,** by application and with a permit. Facilities include toilets, drinking water, barbecues and picnic tables. Contact the National Parks and Wildlife Service in Cairns, ☎4052 3096, for more information.

Some believe that Lizard Island has the best diving along the Great Barrier Reef, and in fact it is surrounded by excellent coral reefs.

The **Ribbon Reefs** lie only a 20 minute boat ride from the island. These are comprised of a string of ten coral ramparts that support an immense undersea world of living coral and sea animals, and the most spectacular underwater scenery. All the Ribbon Reefs are great, but following are a few highlights:

The **Code Hole** is world

renowned and very popular. It is at the northern tip of Reef No. 10, and divers can hand feed giant Potato Cod, some over 2.5m in length.

Pixie Pinnacle is a coral bommie on the southern end of Reef No. 10. Here divers will find species of pelagic fish, black coral, and a host of tropical fish.

Dynamite Pass is a narrow area of water just north of Ribbon Reef No. 10. the depths range is from 4m to 40m below the surface, but visibility is about 30m and there is plenty to see.

Detached Reefs are located in the Coral Sea half-way between Cooktown and Cape York. Both reefs extend from a metre or so under the surface to the seabed some 500m below. This is sheer wall diving at its best with visibility extending more than 40m. Expect to see giant sponges, sea whips, Angelfish, Clownfish, Manta Rays, sharks and varieties of coral.

You can explore the website at ▆www.lizardislandresort.com

Cooktown

Cooktown is 246km north of Cairns. Its close proximity to Aboriginal culture, diverse wildlife, rainforests, unique land formations and extensive surrounding savannah, means that it can be described as the geographical intersection of Reef and Outback. The town is clustered on the banks of the scenic **Endeavour River.**

Cooktown is etched in history, drawn from the early days of its Aboriginal inhabitants, to Captain Cook's forced landing, to gold rush times and the adventures of subsequent pioneers and explorers.

Apart from the picturesque surrounds, it is worth exploring the historical buildings in Cooktown, including the old **Post Office, Westpac Bank** and **the Sovereign Hotel.** The **James Cook Historical Museum** is in *Helen Street,* ☎*4069 5386.* **Cook's Monument, The Cannon, Grassy Hill** and **the Chinese Graveyard** are additonal points of interest.

Cooktown Tours, ☎*4069 5125,* will take you by coach on a two-hour guided historical tour of the city for ◑$18 adults, departing at 9am.

The Cooktown Tourism Association can be contacted on ☎*4069 6100* or ☎*1800 001 770.* They have a website at ▆www.cooktownau. com and their email address is ✉info@cooktownau.com

Daintree and Cape Tribulation

25km (16 miles) north of Mossman and about 146km (92 miles) south of Cooktown lies the township of Daintree, nestled in the heart of the Daintree River catchment basin, surrounded entirely by the rainforest-clad **McDowall Ranges**. The **Daintree National Park** lies to the west and Cape Tribulation National Park to the east; both have flourished largely unspoilt for millions of years. A World Heritage listing now ensures the continued preservation of this 17,000ha region.

Cape Tribulation, where the rainforest meets the reef, is an increasingly popular tourist area for both camping and day visits. Crystal clear creeks and forests festooned with creepers and vines, palm trees, orchids, butterflies and cassowaries,

are part of the Cape Tribulation experience in one of the country's finest rainforest areas.

There are several resorts, hostels and camping grounds. The atmosphere is relaxed and 'alternative' in this tropical rainforest retreat. It is a very popular haven for backpackers.

The township has art and craft centres, and the **Daintree Timber Museum and Gallery**, *12 Stewart Drive,* ☎*4098 6166.* The real attraction, however, is the National Park itself.

Given the majestic quality of the natural environment, the emphasis here is on eco-touring. Several cruises operate on the Daintree River offering passengers a leisurely tour observing the beauty of the river and rainforest, and enjoying morning or afternoon tea.

The Daintree Visitor Information Centre is in *5 Stewart Street,* ☎*4098 6120.* The Great Barrier Reef website has a section on Daintree at ▆www. greatbarrierreef.aus.net as does Tourism Tropical North Queensland at ▆www.tnq.org.au The famous "bouncing stones" are just north of **Thornton's Beach.**

Mossman

171km south of Cooktown and only 20km (12 miles) north of Port Douglas, Mossman is in the heart of the Mossman Valley. It is a sugar town surrounded by green mountains (highest is **Mt Demi**, 1159m-3802 ft) and fields of sugar cane. Mossman is fast becoming well-known as a centre for exotic tropical fruit growing, and a number of farms conduct tours and offer their products for sale.

The business centre of the Douglas Shire, Mossman has wide tree-lined streets, colourful gardens and a large sugar mill. Guided tours of the **Mossman Sugar Mill**, *Mill Site*, ☎ *4098 1400,* are conducted during the cane crushing season (June to December).

A few minutes' drive from the township, a sealed road leads to the **Mossman Gorge** in Daintree National Park. This is a wilderness area of 56,000ha (138,320 acres), with crystal clear running streams, waterfalls, walking tracks through towering rainforest, barbecue picnic sites and a unique suspension bridge over a steep ravine.

Port Douglas

The 83km (52 miles) drive north from Cairns to Port Douglas covers some of the most spectacular coastal strips and beaches in Australia. The Captain Cook Highway is wedged between towering, lush forest-covered mountains and the Coral Sea. Situated 6km east of the highway, Port Douglas is one of the closest towns to the Great Barrier Reef. It has all the charm of a fishing port tastefully combined with modern tourism facilities. This place draws visitors like a magnet, but as long as you plan ahead there is little chance of you finding yourself without a bed in Port Douglas.

The township was settled in 1877 as the main port for the Palmer River goldfields, and today it is a popular departure point for professional and amateur fishermen, for trips to the outer reef and islands, and for scuba diving and aquatic sports.

Flagstaff Hill offers a great view over **Four Mile Beach.**

The **Rainforest Habitat** in *Port Douglas Road,* ☎ *4099 3235,* has over 300m of elevated walkways with thousands of butterflies, native birds, crocodiles, koalas and wallabies set among waterways and shaded tropical gardens. They have over 1,000 animals representing more than 140 species. Breakfast With the Birds and The Koala Spot are two popular attractions. The Habitat is ☉open daily from 8am-5.30pm, with admission prices at ✪$18 adults.

Ben Cropp's Shipwreck Treasure Trove Museum, is located on *Ben Cropp's Wharf,* ☎ *4099 5488,* and houses nautical exhibits of historical significance, including Spanish galleons, a century-and-a- half-old wreck and a lost loot. It is ☉open daily 9am-5pm and admission is ✪$6 adults.

The **Bally Hooley Steam Express** travels through Mossman and its countryside to the sugar mill. For more details, contact the Information Centre in *Grant Street,* ☎ *4099 5051.*

The Port Douglas Visitor Information Centre is in *23 Macrossan Street,* ☎ *4099 5599.* The relevant website is ▤www.portdouglas.com and there is an email service at ✉reserv@greatbarrierreef.aus.net

↪ **Let's Stay Here**

Dougies Backpackers,
111 Davidson St, ☎ *4099 6200,* ▤ *www.dougies.com.au*
Set in tropical gardens in a resort type accommodation. All rooms are all air conditioned. TVs and fridges are in the double rooms. Excellent facilities includes a fully equipped kitchen, an outdoor TV lounge, a games room with some pool tables and a swimming pool. There's also an on site bar with another pool table and foosball. **Recommended.** *Dorms ✪$21; double $30pp; camping from $10*

Parrotfish Lodge,
37-39 Warner St, 4099 5011 or 1800 995 011, www.parrotfishlodge.com
Excellent accommodation with really high standards. This is a new purpose built hostel. Dorms have ex-Olympic Village bunks, en suite bathrooms and are all air conditioned. The great facilities includes a kitchen, internet access, pool tables and a swiiming pool with heaps of deck chairs. **Recommended.** *Dorms from ✪$20; double $37.50pp*

Port O'Call YHA Lodge
7 Craven Close, ☎ *40995422 or 1800 892 800,*
▤*www.portocall.com.au*
Another high class hostel with lots of new facilities. Located 5 minutes from the beach and not far from town. Kept clean and well maintained. There's dorms with en suite and air conditioning and then you'll find some doubles with motel type accommodation with TV and fridge. You'll also find a bunkhouse with large dorms. Features a kitchen, laundry, internet access and a swimming pool. There's also an on site bar and bistro. Meals available. Bike hire and parking available. **Recommended.** *Dorms from ✪$20; double/twin $35pp BC MC VA EFTPOS*

Green Island

The island has an area of 15ha and is 27km north-east of Cairns. It is a true coral cay surrounded by coral reefs. Incidentally, this island was also named by Captain Cook, after his chief astronomer.

The island grew out of debris washed from its surrounding platform of coral, and is gradually being pushed north-west by prevailing currents. The waters abound with sea life, and the beach is quite beautiful. It only takes about 20 minutes to walk around the island, passing tropical vegetation, casuarinas and pandanus. Green Island is very popular with day trippers.

Green Island's Underwater Observatory is well known. From 5m below the surface, the ever-changing panorama of marine life can be seen through portholes.

Marineland Melanesia, ☎4051 4032, has been the island's main attraction for many years. It is an underwater observatory which also features Cassius, the largest salt water crocodile in captivity. It has interesting displays of Melanesian tribal art, and a collection of early Coral Sea sailing relics. Interest in the observatory draws many people out to Green Island for the day. There are shows at 10.30am and 1.45pm, daily. Marineland Melanesia is ☺open 9.30am-4.30pm every day and costs adults ☯$8.

For information on Green Island, either contact the Green Island Resort directly, ☎4031 3300, visit the web page at 🖳www.green islandresort.com.au or email them at ✉res@greenisla ndresort.com.au

Marlin Coast - Northern Beaches

The Marlin Coast area extends from Machans Beach, at the mouth of the Barron River 13km (8 miles) north of Cairns to **Ellis Beach**, passing by **Holloways Beach, Yorkeys Knob, Clifton Beach, Palm Cove and Kewarra Beach**. **Trinity Beach** and Clifton Beach are popular holiday destinations, and Palm Cove and Kewarra Beach have international resorts. All beaches have picnic areas and regular bus services to and from Cairns. Palm Cove and Ellis Beach are regularly patrolled in the summer season by the local Life Saving Club members. Water-sporters can hire catamarans, windsurfers and surf skis at most of the major beaches in the area. Countless cruises to the coral creefs are also available, and the Visitor Information Centre can advise.

Two attractions are located on the magnificent *Cook Highway*, both of which are popular with tourists and locals alike. 40km north of Cairns is **Hartley's Creek Crocodile Farm**, ☎4055 3576, where admission rates are ☯$16 for adults. **Wild World,** ☎4055 3669 at Palm Cove along the same stretch of road 20 minutes north of Cairns, is a wildlife sanctuary with a hands-on approach. It is ☺open daily 8.30am-5pm and costs ☯$22for adults. Trinity Beach and Yorkeys Knob have their own web sites: 🖳www.trinitybeach.com, email at ✉info@trinitybeach.com and 🖳www.yorkeysknob.com, email at ✉hmbr@internetnorth.com.au

For other information on the Marlin Coast, use the same contact details as those listed under Visitor Information for Cairns.

The Atherton Tablelands

Inland from Cairns are the **fertile Mareeba, Atherton** and **Evelyn Tablelands**, rising in three gigantic steps from the coastal plains. Jungle-fringed volcanic crater lakes, waterfalls and fertile farmlands, coupled with the only temperate climate in the Australian tropics, lure many visitors to the Tablelands each year. Views from the lookouts on the **Kuranda, Gillies, Rex** and **Palmerston Highways** are spectacular.

Kuranda, a tiny mountain hamlet in the rainforest, is the first stop-off stage on the Tableland journey. The town can be reached by train from Cairns (☎4032 3964) and the ride passes waterfalls and stunning views to the coast before ending at picturesque **Kuranda Station.** Kuranda has many attractions including **Pamagirri Dancers,** an Aboriginal theatre presenting daily shows based on Dreamtime legends; **Australian Butterfly Sanctuary**, the largest butterfly farm in the world, listed in the Guinness Book of Records; and the **Kuranda Wildlife Noctarium**, which provides a close-up look at the rarely seen nocturnal inhabitants of the rainforests, and guided walks into the jungle. The town's main street is lined with galleries, shops and restaurants. The terraced **Kuranda Markets**, at *5 Therwine Street,* are considered the best in the north, ☎4093 8772.

The Mareeba/Dimbulah district, approximately 66 km (41 miles) west of Cairns, is the largest tobacco growing area in Australia.

Atherton, with its red volcanic soil, is the central town of the Atherton Tablelands. Maize silos dominate the skyline.

Malanda is situated in the heart of tropical Australia's only viable dairying district. The Malanda milk factory boasts the longest milk run in the world, which extends as far as Darwin in the Northern Territory.

Millaa Millaa is the waterfall capital of the Tablelands, taking in the **Millaa Millaa, Zillie** and **Elinjaa Falls.**

The Millstream Falls, south of Ravenshoe, when in flood are the widest waterfalls in Australia.

Herberton is the north's historic mining town, and tin is still produced in the area.

Irvinebank situated near Herberton, is steeped in history. Its tin crushing plant has been in operation since 1890, and it has other historic buildings.

Ravenshoe is situated on the western side of the Evelyn Tablelands, and is the gateway to the back country and gemfields of the north. It is a major timber town providing some of Australia's most beautiful woods. Close by you will find **Koombooloomba Dam** and **Tully Falls,** with many walking tracks to **Eyrie Lookout**.

Some of the individual Tableland attractions include **Tinaroo Dam, the Crater National Park**, the twin crater lakes of **Eacham** and **Barrine**, the **Curtin Fig Tree** and **Herberton Tin Fields**. Further north of the Evelyn Tablelands is the **Chillagoe Caves National Park,** which is accessible by road and air charter from Cairns Airport, ☎ *4052 9703*.

The Tropical Tableland Promotion Bureau has an outlet at the Old Post Office Gallery Information Centre, *Herberton Road, Atherton,* ☎ *4091 4222*.

They have a terrific website at ◼www.athertontableland.com and can be emailed at ✉info@ athertontableland.com

Mount Isa
Population 22,000
Mount Isa is situated on the Leichhardt River in the Selwyn Range, which is the only relief in the north-western flatness. It is 198km (123 miles) from the Northern Territory border, 917km (570 miles) from Townsville, and 1854km (1152 miles) from Brisbane.

Climate
Mount Isa has two distinct seasons - The Wet and The Dry. The Wet lasts from December to March, but the rainfall is not as heavy as further north, averaging 250mm (10 ins) for the four months, compared with the Burketown (about 340km - 211 miles north) average of 700mm (28 ins) for the same period. Average temperatures: January max 37C (99F) - min 24C (75F); July max 24C (75F) - min 10C (50F).

Characteristics
The Isa, as the locals call it, is a modern mining town with over 100 clubs and 70 sporting associations. Because of its isolation, the people of Mt Isa have endeavoured to make life as pleasant as possible, and like other outback towns, it exudes a 'tougher' atmosphere than the coastal cities. This is probably caused by the harshness of the surrounding countryside.
Mount Isa is listed in the Guinness Book of Records as 'The Largest City in the World in Area', and with an area of 40,977km2

(15,817 sq miles), the record will stand for a long time.

How to Get There
By Rail
There is a twice weekly service from/to Townsville, and the **Inlander** takes 21 hours for the journey

Visitor Information
The Riversleigh Fossil Centre and Mount Isa Visitor Information is at *19 Marian Street,* ☎ *(07) 4749 1555*. The website is ◼www. mountisa.qld.gov.au and you can email them at ✉isatourism @mountisa.qld.gov.au

Features baby bath, laundry facilities, swimming pool, kiosk and playground. *Powered sites ✪$18; unpowered sites $11.*

Copper City Caravan Park, *185 West Street,* ☎*4743 4676.* (Pets allowed on application) - *powered sites ✪$18 for two, on-site vans $39 for two.*

Riverside Tourist Caravan Park, *195 West Street,* ☎*4743 3904.* (No dogs allowed) - powered sites ✪$18 for two, park cabins $30.50 for two.

Sunset Caravan Park, *14 Sunset Drive,* ☎*4743 7668.* (Pets on application) - *powered sites ✪$18 for two, on-site vans $35 for two.*

Let's Eat

The Clubs welcome visitors, and most of the pubs serve counter meals. Several of the motels have licensed restaurants, and there are restaurants and takeaway outlets in the centre of town. Below are a few options.

Abyssinia Cafe Restaurant, *103 Marianne Street,* ☎*4749 0655.*

Mystros Restaurant, *26 Miles Street,* ☎*4749 0388.*

Red Lantern Chinese Restaurant, *1 Simpson Street,* ☎*4743 4070.*

Points of Interest

The focal point of the town is the mine and the stacks. The lead smelter stack is 266m (873 ft) high, and can be seen for miles around. **Mount Isa Mines** employs one in five of the city's population, and most other people in the city are dependent on the mine. **Mount Isa Mines Limited** is Queensland's largest single industrial enterprise, and its richest.

Mount Isa dates back only to 1923, when the prospector John Campbell Miles found an ore outcrop, which is now marked by an obelisk. His ashes are buried beneath a memorial clock in *Marian Street,* opposite the Post Office. It was Australia's first company town, and an example of early company housing, a tent house, is on display in *Fourth Avenue,* and is a far cry from the company house of today. **The Tent House** is open from April - September, and the Tourist Centre can advise of the hours.

John Middlin Mining Centre is in *Church Street,* ☎*4749 1558,* and has exhibits of mining methods, historical photographs, rock specimens, examples of ore, film of mining and smelting operations, all contained in an historic building with garden surroundings. It is ⊕open daily 9am-4pm.

Surface tours of the Isa Mines show take you through mine shafts, workshops, mills, smelters and past those huse stacks that dominate the skyline, giving you an insight into some of the processes of the industry and the equipment used. Costs are ✪$18 adults, ☎*4749 1555.*

Underground tours depart early and mid morning Monday to Friday. They are designed to be a hands-on approach to learning about and experiencing life in the mines, covering ladder climbing, encountering and dealing with the dangers of working underground and navigating tricky surfaces. Age and health restrictions apply, ☎*4749 1555.* The cost is ✪$60 per person.

Frank Aston Underground Museum, in *Shackleton Street,* has displays of early homestead equipment, plus a simulated Aboriginal encampment depicting tribal customs of the district. The museum was built by mining into the hill beneath one of the city's early reservoir tanks, which is now part of the museum. It is ⊕open daily 9am-4pm, ☎*4749 1558.*

The Royal Flying Doctor Service Base, at *11 Barkly Highway,* has a display and film of the Service's history to the present day. ⊕open Mon-Fri 9am-5pm, ☎*4743 2800.*

School of the Air, in the RFDS Base complex, *11 Barkly Highway,* gives visitors an insight into radio and telephone use that augments correspondence education for primary school children of the Outback. Tours are organised at 9am and 10am on weekdays.

The City Lookout in *Hilary Street,* offers a 360 degree panoramic view of the city and mine area, and is worth a second visit at sunset or later, when the lights of the mine are a spectacle in themselves. The lookout has a global signpost, with distances to cities all over the world, further proof that Mount Isa is a long way from everywhere.

Lake Moondarra, 15.5km (10 miles) north of the city off the *Barkly Highway,* is a sanctuary and Mount Isa's regular water storage. There are barbecue facilities, children's play area, safe swimming, canoeing, sailing, water-skiing and a kiosk.

Riversleigh Fossils Display, *West Street,* ☎*4749 1555,* has amazing fossil discoveries of

World Heritage listing significance, including new mammal species, bats and huge snakes, and make sure you see '**Big Bird**'. Some of the specimens date back 30 million years. ⏱opening Times are Mon-Fri 8.30am-4.30pm, Sat-Sun 9am-2pm. Entry is free, but there is an admission charge of ✪$9 adult for the Interpretive Displays. This award-winning attraction should not be missed.

Kalkadoon Tribal Centre and Cultural Keeping Place, *Marian Street* (next to the Visitor Information Centre), has artefacts of the fierce fighting tribe indigenous to this area. It is ⏱open to visitors Mon-Fri 9am-5pm, and there is a charge of ✪$2 for adults.

The **Civic Centre** in *West Street*, is Mount Isa's pride and joy, and a showcase for local and visiting performances, presentations and conferences.

Ray Donaldson Memorial Lookout and Walking Track, at the top end of *Pamela Street* on the far eastern side of the city, follows the ridge of spinifex hills as far as the Overlander Hotel, and offers some great views.

The Visitor Information Centre has information on several tours in and around Mount Isa, including heritage tours (✪$26), tours to Aboriginal rock art sites ($55), scenic flights to the Gulf ($405) and horseback trail rides ($45).

Facilities

Mount Isa has very good sporting facilities: boating, lawn bowls, golf, sailing, swimming, tennis, water skiing. Gem fossicking is very popular in the area.

Outlying Attractions
Camooweal

Situated 188km (117 miles) west of Mount Isa, Camooweal is only a few kilometres from the Northern Territory border. It is a supply town for large cattle stations in the vast outback border area. During the 1880s, it was an important stop on the great cattle droves, and today the road trains, which transport the cattle to the coast, still stop at Camooweal.

An interesting attraction here is the **Camooweal Caves National Park**, featuring an extensive system of caverns and caves with some vertical shafts up to 75 metres deep. Only people with caving experience should enter. Check road conditions before visiting, and it is recommended that you make the trip during the winter. Camping is available in the National Park with a permit obtainable from the Ranger Station in Mt Isa, ☎4743 2055.

Lawn Hill National Park

Also known as Boodjamulla, this fertile National Park has a spectacular gorge, scenic sandstone ranges, thriving vegetation and freshwater springs. The main activities are conoeing and walking. A number of rewarding walking trails, from 2-7km in distance, are outlined on a detailed pamphlet by Queensland Parks and Wildlife, available from the Visitor Centre in Mt Isa. To book camp sites, ☎4748 5572.

Mary Kathleen

The now deserted town of Mary Kathleen is 60km (37 miles) east of Mount Isa. It was established in the 1950s to mine the then largest known deposit of uranium in Australia. The mine was closed in 1963, reopened in 1976 and modernised, then finally closed again in 1982.

Cloncurry

Locally known as 'The Curry', Cloncurry is 124km (77 miles) east of Mount Isa. The surrounding hills hide many old ghost towns, and ruins of early copper mines. The area was a big copper producer until Mount Isa was developed. Maps of the ghost towns are available from the **Court House** for those who wish to explore, or to try their hand at gem fossicking. Most of these areas are only accessible by 4WD vehicles. Gold is also found in small amounts around the area.

It was here in 1928 that the Flying Doctor Service had its beginnings, and a Cloister of Plaques has been erected to commemorate its pioneers on the site where the first pedal wireless call for help was received.

The **Mary Kathleen Memorial Park** is situated at the eastern end of the town. The park contains a museum housing one of the best rock collections in Australia, as well as memorabilia of Mary Kathleen, and explorer Robert O'Hara Burke's water bottle. The park is ⏱open daily 8am-5pm.

Beside the highway where it crosses the Corella River, 43km (27 miles) west of Cloncurry, is a cairn commemorating the ill-fated Burke and Wills expedition to cross the continent from south to north in 1860-61. At nearby

Lake Corella there are picnic and barbecue facilities. The lake was formed to supply the former mining town of Mary Kathleen.

The highest official shade temperature, 53.1C (127.58F), was recorded in Cloncurry in 1889.

Cloncurry's Merry Muster is a weekend event preceding Mount Isa's **Rodeo** in August.

A popular swimming hole, about 9m (30 ft) deep with practically no shallows, is found at Mount Frosty, which can easily be reached in dry weather. An old limestone mine is nearby and the area is ideal for gem fossicking. On the Burke Development Road, 378km (235 miles) north of Cloncurry, is **Normanton**, the main centre for the Carpentaria Shire. The town was established in 1868, and has a population around 930. It is situated on the Norman River, 50km (31 miles) from the coast as the crow flies, and was once an important port. The wharf has long since rotted away, and the cattle are now transported to the eastern seaboard by cattle trains. Here is found the only rail line not linked to the main system in Queensland, and once a week there is a service between Glenore and Croydon, a distance of 132km (82 miles).

The Cloncurry Information Centre can be contacted on ☎ *4742 1251*.

Karumba

Karumba, on the mouth of the Norman river, is 74km (46 miles) from Normanton by road, and is the centre of the $10 million prawning industry in the southern part of the Gulf of Carpenatria. The trawlers bring the prawns to Karumba, and there they are snap frozen and air freighted to the southern states and overseas.

For more information, contact the Karumba News and Trevel Centre, located in, *63 Yappar Street*, on ☎ *4745 9187* or visit ▣ www.gulf-savannah.com.au

Winton

Situated 343km (213 miles) south-east of Cloncurry on the Landsborough Highway, Winton was the birthplace of QANTAS. **The Queensland and Northern Territory Air Service** had its first registered office in Winton in 1920, but moved to Longreach, 180km (112 miles) south-east.

Winton is synonymous with sheep, and there is a cairn on Winton's town common commemorating the Great Shearers' Strike of 1891-4. In nearby Elderslie Street is **Herb Young's wagon**, the last horse drawn wagon to bring wool to Winton's railhead. Road trains now bring cattle from the Channel Country and the Northern Territory to the railway.

Banjo Paterson wrote "Waltzing Matilda" at **Dagworth Station** in the Winton area in 1895, and a statue of a swagman has been erected in commemoration near the swimming pool. In Elderslie Street is the **Waltzing Matilda Centre**, ☎ *4657 1466*, a large complex housing the Station Store, the Billabong Complex, the Home of the Legend exhibition, the Qantilda Museum, the Outback Regional Art Gallery, and the Coolibah Country Kitchen Restaurant. Contact the Centre for further information on the town.

Other attractions in town include the National Trust classified **Corfield and Fitzmaurice Store, the Royal Theate, Arno's Wall** and **Opal Walk.**

At **Castle Hill,** west of Winton, is Australia's hottest artesian bore, at 78.95C (174F).

Dinosaur footprints can be viewed from a suspended walkway at **Lark Quarry**, 5km off the Winton Jundah Road, 105km (65 miles) south of Winton.

Northern Territory

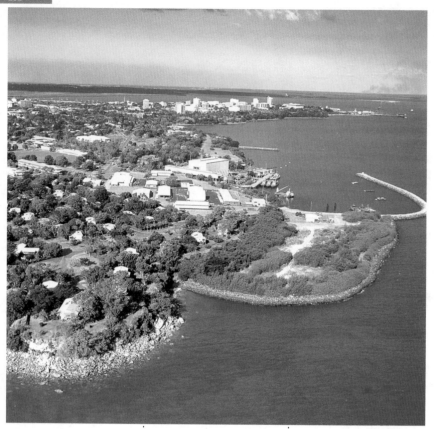

Darwin

Population 68,378

Darwin, the capital of the Northern Territory and Australia's most northerly city, is situated on the tropical north coast by the Arafura Sea. Darwin is actually closer to South East Asia than to some Australian capitals. For example, Denpasar in Indonesia is 1900km (1181 miles) from Darwin, while Sydney is 3200km (1988 miles) away.

Climate

Average temperatures: January max 32C (90F) - min 25C(77F); July max 30C (86F) - min 19C (66F). The average annual rainfall is 1525mm (60 in), and mostly falls between November and April.

Characteristics

Through the decades, Darwin town gained a reputation as a frontier of prawn trawlers, buffalo-catchers, croc shooters and wild waterfront bars. It was the boozing capital of a thirsty nation. Records show the first European explorers arrived in 1623 aboard the Dutch ship, Arnhem. In the early 1820s,

the British began establishing military outposts in northern Australia, hoping to establish a stronger claim to the region than their Dutch and French rivals. Darwin Harbour was discovered in 1839 by the first officer of the HMS Beagle, and was named in honour of Charles Darwin, who had sailed on an earlier expedition on the ship. It was a strategic outpost for the British during World War II, and suffered tremendous damage during 64 air raids, with the loss of 243 lives. The Tiwi people on Bathurst Island, who were the first to see the Japanese bombers, perform a corroboree that tells the story. On December 24, 1974, Darwin was struck by one of the greatest natural disasters in Australian history, Cyclone Tracy, which left only about 500 of the city's then 8000 homes habitable. Today Darwin is considered a relaxed tropical city with a relatively young population numbering above 70,000.

How to Get There
By Air
Darwin Airport caters for international and domestic flights. International services include **Qantas, Royal Brunei, Garuda, Singapore** and **Merpati**. Frequent interstate services to all capital cities and many major centres are provided by Qantas. The airport is approximately 8km (5 miles) from the city centre.

The **Darwin Airport Bus Service** departs regularly for the city from the airport, and services all city accommodation. There is a taxi rank at the airport, and the trip takes about 10 minutes. **Darwin Radio Taxis**, ☎ *13 1008*, has a direct telephone link for airport bookings. Taxis can be multi-hired and mini-bus taxis are available on request.

By Sea
International cruise ships call at Darwin throughout the year, and cargo ships, naval vessels and private cruising yachts also use the port.

By Rail
The Ghan now travels from Adelaide to Darwin departing Sunday and Thursday, and takes 2 days. Cost ✪*$440 one way seat only, $1390 one way sleeper. Contact Tourism Top End ☎(08) 8936 2499* or *132 147*.

By Bus
Greyhound Pioneer have services to Darwin from Adelaide via Alice Springs; Brisbane via Mt Isa; and Perth via the Kimberleys.

Visitor Information
The Northern Territory Visitors Centre is on the first floor, *38 Mitchell Street,* ☎*(08) 8936 2499* or email ✉info@northernterritory.com

The Northern Territory Tourist Commission has its head office in Darwin at *43 Mitchell Street,* ☎*(08) 8999 3900.*

Both can organise accommodation, tour bookings, foreign exchange, luggage storage, airport shuttle bus tickets and Visitor Information.

Brochures are available on exploring the National Parks of the Northern Territory, 4WD travel, Aboriginal tours, fishing, boating, and many other interests.

A couple of websites to visit are ▣www.tourismtopend.com.au and ▣www.ntholidays.com.au

⤵ Let's Stay Here
Accommodation in Darwin can be found to suit all price ranges and preferences. Backpackers and youth hostellers are well catered for in the city centre as well as number of caravan parks. Here is a selection which should be used as a guide only. The telephone area code is 08.

Banyan View Lodge,
119 Mitchell St, ☎*8981 8644,* ▣www.*banyanviewlodge.com.au* Winner of two Brolga Awards for Budget Accommodation in 1998 and 2001. Operated by YWCA (Young Women's Christian

Association). Close to the CBD and the Mitchell Street Tourist Precinct. Quite large in size and has a dormsitory feel to it, being quiet and provides privacy. Only with a few dorms, the rest are twins, double and single rooms. Facilties includes spas, laundry and kitchen. Free fridge and coffee and tea in rooms. Secured parking available. **(All profits generated from the Lodge are used by the YWCA of Darwin to provide services to homeless and disadvantaged youth, women and families in the local community) *Dorms* ✪*$18; single $38 ($43 with air conditioning); double/twin $48 ($53 with air conditioning)*

The Cavenagh,
12 Cavenagh St, ☎*8941 6383* ▣www.*thecavenagh.com* Located at the heart of the city, it's only a stone's throw away from the bustling Smith Street Mall, State Square and the city's main shopping centre and the nightcub hub. Newly renovated. All rooms have en suite and air conditioning. Fridge and TV are provided with the double rooms. Facilties includes a large central swimming pool and a bar. They also offer free transfers to and fro the airport. **Recommended.** *Dorms* ✪*$23; double $46; single $58 (group rates are also available)*

Chillis Backpackers,
69A Mitchell St, ☎*8941 9722 or 1800 351 313,* ▣www.*chillis.com.au* VIP member. Situated right at

Darwin

Frances Bay

Stokes Hill Wharf

Fishermans Wharf

Flinders Dr

Drive

Charles Street
Anna St
Mary St
Melers St
Gott erburg St
Henry St
Margaret St

Stuart Highway

Beach Rd
Dinah Beach Rd
Queen St
King St

Harvey St
Mary St
Peel St

Ramirez Rd
Hill Cres
Gardens Rd

Darwin Botanical Gardens

Gardens

Mindil Beach Reserve

Diamond Beach Casino

Livers Avenue
Maria St
Chin Quan Rd

Gardens Park Golf Course

Houston St
Smith St

Woods St
Cavenagh St

Mitchell St
Daly St

Knuckey St
Bennett St
Litchfield St

Post Office
Austin La
Smith St
Searcy St

Civic Centre
War Memorial
Marye St
Frances St
Herbert St
Esplanade
Knuckey St
Edmunds St

Mall
West La

Whitfield St
Lindsay St
Esplanade

Bicentennial Park

Coach Terminal
Lyons Cottage Museum

Arts Centre
Esplanade

Overland Telegraph Memorial

Mitchinson St
Huberts Ave

Iron Ore Wharf
Fort Hill

Harbour
Port

Mitchell St
Barossa St
Carba St

Allen Ave
Malabar St
Larrakeyah St

Kahlin Ave
Kahlin Oval

Myilly Point Park
Myilly Point

Cullen Bay Marina

Larrakeyah Military Area

Fanny Bay

Emery Point

Metres

0   500

Accommodation

1. Banyan View Lodge
2. The Cavenagh
3. Chillis Backpackers
4. Darwin International YHA
5. Elke's Backpackers
6. Frogshollow Backpackers
7. Gecko Lodge
8. Globetrotters Lodge
9. Melaleuca Lodge
10. Wilderness Lodge

the heart of the Tourist Precinct of Darwin. Exceptional facilities and all are nice and clean. Facilities includes internet access, secured lockers, spa, sundeck, barbecue area, kitchen and an open-air dining area overlooking Mitchell St. All rooms are either fan-cooled or air conditioned. They also offer airport pick-up. Parking is available. **Recommended.** *Dorms ✪$21 ($20 YHA); twin/double $48 ($53 with showers)* (prices includes breakfast)

Darwin International YHA,
69 Mitchell St, ☎8981 3995, ▤*www.yha.com.au* Very good feel YHA and located just in the heart of the city. Large in size with over 300 beds, all air conditioned with security lockers and wash basins. New facilities and exceptionally clean and tidy. Other facilties includes internet access, on site shop, laundry, TV lounge room, pool table and fully equipped open-air kitchen. There is also a large swimming pool and a sundeck at the rooftop which is a must in Darwin. Bikes are able to be hired from the front desk. Parking is also available. Winner of the 1989 Northern Territory Brogla Tourism Award. **Highly recommended**. *Dorms members ✪$20 ($23.50 non-members); double $50 ($53.50 for non-members) BC MC VA EFPTOS*

Elke's Backpackers,
112 Mitchell St, ☎8981 8399 ▤*www.elkesbackpackers.co m.au* Laid back in nature and

surrounded by lush gardens and swimming pool. Just a moments stroll from the lodge picturesque esplanade and the famous Darwin sunsets and ocean views. Facilities includes internet access, laundry, several kitchens and TV lounge. The staff will gladly help you book tours. They also offer a free drop off/pick-up service to the bus station. *Dorms ✪$22; single/twin $53 ; double $56* (special internet rates apply if you go to their website)

Frogshollow Backpackers,
27 Lindsay St, ☎8941 or 1800 068 686, ▤*www.frogs-hollow.com.au* Facilties includes a tropical garden set swimming pool, two spas, small kitchen, laundry, internet access, games room, open air dining and common room with TV and video, and a barbecue area. There are also large tropical verandas off their rooms. Regular Aussie BBQ's $5 (all you can eat). Located just across Frogs Hollow Park and Art Centre close to the city centre. You can rent a push bike from the premises. They also offer free airport shuttle transfer to hostel (with min 2 nights stay) and they can pick you up at the bus terminal. There is off street parking. *Dorms ✪$21; double/twin/single $50; double/twin/family en suite $60* (prices includes continental breakfast)

Gecko Lodge,
146 Mitchell St, ☎8981 5569 or 1800 811 250 ▤*www.geckolodge.com.au*

This hostel lies on the northern end of Mitchell St. Facilties includes a swimming pool, spa, internet access, kitchen, laundry and an open-air TV lounge. There are also weekly barbecues and evening meal deals. There are some accommodation in the annex with some basic lodging. Bus pick-ups are 24 hour and they even provide you with free town maps. Bike hire is available. Also, they offer a new 'Backpacker Car Rental' which could be convenient for your travels. *Dorms ✪$20; single/double $55* (prices includes breakfasts including homemade pancakes)

Globetrotters Lodge,
97 Mitchell St, ☎8981 5385, ▤*www.globetrotters.com.au* Built around a nice swimming pool, this lodge used to be a motel leaving the atmosphere and comfort less than what you'd usually expect in other hostels. Other facilities includes a kitchen and bar that has cable TV showing European sports. All rooms have en suite bathrooms. *Dorms ✪$22 ($20 YHA/VIP); single $60 ($56 YHA/VIP); double $58 (YHA/VIP)*

Mandorah Beach Hotel,
Mandorah, ☎8978 5044 Located right on the beach. Fantastic value accommodation with a lovely beachfront settings across the harbour from Darwin. All rooms have fantastic views, with basic but spacious accommodation. Dorms have enuite bathrooms. Facilities includes a swimming pool, beach vol-

leyball and a gaming area with pool table, video games and pinball machines. Also has a licensed restaurant with a 24-hour bar. The hostel is best reached by ferry from Cullen bay. Tickets cost $16 return. Very relaxing place. **Recommended.** Dorms ✪$14.

Melaleuca Lodge,
50 Mitchell St, ☎8936 1096 or 1800 623 543, ▨www.sout hernlodges.com.au
Large hostel with 250 beds. Most dorms are small, but the double rooms comes with a fridge, TV and fans. Facilities includes a number of kitchens, swimming pool and a barbecue area with outdoor pool tables. Parking is also available. Dorms ✪$20; single/double $58

Wilderness Lodge,
88 Mitchell St, ☎8941 2161 or 1800 068 686, ▨www.wildlodge.com.au Located at the quieter northern end of Mitchell Street, a about a five minute walk to Smith St Mall. Small in size but laid back in atmosphere. All rooms have air conditioning. This hostel features a nice swimming pool, internet access, laundry, barbecue facilities and a kitchen. Bike hire is also available. Also offered are free pick ups from airports and bus terminals and they give you free town maps. **Reccomended.** Dorms ✪$18; single/double $50; (prices includes breakfast)

Caravan Parks
Coolalinga Caravan Park,
Stuart Highway, Howard Springs, ☎8983 1026. (Dogs allowed on leash) 101 sites, good facilities, swimming pool - powered sites ✪$18 for two, cabins $60 for two.

Palms Village Resort, 907 Stuart Highway, Berrimah, ☎8935 0888. (Pets allowed by arrangement) 400 sites, excellent facilities, barbecue, pool - powered sites ✪$24 for two.

Shady Glen Caravan Park,
cnr Stuart Highway and Farrell Crescent, Winnellie, ☎8984 3330. (No pets allowed) 280 sites, swimming pool - powered sites ✪$22 for two, on-site vans $50 for two.

Howard Springs Caravan Park, 170 Whitewood Road, Howard Springs, ☎8983 1169. (No pets allowed) 170 sites, swimming pool - powered sites ✪$20 for two.

Mary River National Park
Bark Hut Inn, Arnhem Highway, Annborroo, ☎8978 8988 Offers clean accommodation in pre-fabricated units. Swimming pool, laundry, a bar with TV, barbecue area and a shop within the premises are the facilities offered. Camp ground toilet and showers. Parking is also available. Bunk beds and singles ✪$45; double/twin $60

Mary River YHA,
Arnhem Highway (3km before Annaborroo), ☎8978 8877, ▨www.maryriverpark.com.au Formerly a buffalo hunting ground, located within the Mary River Park Lodge and is opposite the Mary River National Park. Set on 500 acres of land featuring hiking trails, a billabong and natural wildlife like crocodiles. Air conditioning, fans and towels are available at an extra charge. Facilities includes an internet access, on site shop, swimming pool, spas, volleyball area, a barbecue area with decks and a nice dining area. There is also a licensed bar and restaurant. Parking available. Members dorms/double ✪$25 ($12 group booking of 10 with YHA card) BC MC VA EFTPOS

Local Transport
Bus
The **Darwin Bus Service,** ☎8924 5463, has a city terminus in Harry Chan Avenue, and from there services the city area as well as the suburbs of Casuarina and Palmerston. ☺Buses run every day except Sunday, and there are extended services during special events and festivals. The Tour Tub, an open air bus, has a set route around the city, inner suburbs and most tourist attractions. ☺The bus runs on the hour, and day tickets can be purchased allowing you to stop anywhere and reboard when another bus comes, ☎8981 5233.

Taxi
Darwin taxis operate around the clock and can be found at taxi ranks, hotels and transport terminals, or you can hail them in the street. The city rank is outside Woolworths in Knuckey Street, and there are also ranks in the suburbs. Following are a few

numbers for taxi services ☎8981 3777, ☎8981 2222, ☎13 1008, ☎8947 3333.

Car

Most of the major car rental companies have offices in Darwin, and they require a current driver's licence and a deposit. Most also offer 4WD vehicles.

Avis, ☎8981 9922; Budget Campervans, ☎8981 0148; Budget Rent A Car, ☎13 2727; Hertz Rent A Car NT, ☎1800 891 112; Territory Thrifty Car Rental, ☎8924 0000.

The Automobile Association of the Northern Territory has an office in Darwin at 81 Smith Street, ☎8981 3837, and reciprocal membership is offered to members of affiliated international and interstate auto clubs. AANT has emergency road service and carries a comprehensive list of road maps. Leaded, unleaded, LPG and diesel are available at almost all filling stations. Most stations are ⊕open 7am-6pm, while a few are open 24 hours-a-day.

Ferries

The **MV Darwin Duchess** leaves Stokes Hill Wharf on weekdays for cruises to Mandorah. For timetables and bookings contact Mondaorah Ferry Service, ☎8978 5015.

Let's Eat

Darwin is a melting pot of people and cultures, so it is not surprising that this is reflected in the restaurants of the city. Whether you want Creole, Italian, Thai, Greek, French, Chinese, Mexican, Indian or Malaysian, you will not be disappointed. Or, you can be

adventurous and go for kangaroo, buffalo, crocodile or camel, maybe for the first time. Whatever your fancy, the Visitor Information Centre has a complete list of eateries. Here are a few names and addresses:

Alchemy Restaurant, 130 Smith Street, ☎8941 2126.

Castaways BBQ Restaurant, cnr The Esplanade and Peel Street, ☎8941 0755.

Charlie's, cnr Knuckey Street and Austin Lane, ☎8981 3298

Guiseppe's Italian Restaurant, 64 Smith Street, ☎8941 3110.

Hanuman Thai Restaurant, 28 Mitchell Street, ☎8941 3500.

La Chaumiere Restaurant, 13 Shepherd Street, ☎8981 2879.

Magic Wok Restaurant, 48 Cavenagh Street, ☎8981 3332.

Passage To India Restaurant, 50 Smith Street, ☎8981 4340.

Rooftop Restaurant, 3 Buffalo Court, ☎8981 5333.

Sakura Japanese Restaurant, Unit 1/52, Marina Boulevard, ☎8981 4949.

Swiss Cafe and Restaurant, 60 Smith Street, ☎8981 5079.

Waterhole Restaurant, cnr Knuckey St and Smith Street, ☎8944 9120.

Entertainment

In Darwin it is illegal to consume alcohol in a public place within

two kilometres of a licensed premises without a permit. That covers just about everywhere in the city. However, a few foreshore places are exempt, and the Visitor Information Centre can advise. There is no doubt that Darwin is the beer drinking capital of Australia, after all the Darwin stubby holds 2 litres (3.5 pints)! But there are rules and regulations regarding the selling and imbibing of alcohol, and they are as follows: As a general rule, hotels trade ⊕between 10am to 10pm Mon-Fri, with extended weekend hours. Nightclubs are ⊕open until 6am, but some do not open till 10pm. Roadhouses can operate 24 hours, depending on their licence. The trading hours for takeaway alcohol are ⊕10am-10pm Mon-Fri and Sun. Trading hours for Saturday and public holidays are 9am-10pm.

The legal age for drinking in a licensed establishment is 18 years. In-house hotel guests can usually order liquor 24 hours a day. The **MGM Grand Darwin Hotel and Casino**, on Gilruth Avenue, ☎8943 8888, is the city's top entertainment venue. Apart from keno, roulette and every game of chance you can think of, there are European and Asian restaurants, bars, and a disco from 11pm-6am on Friday and Saturday nights.

Galleries

For a small city, Darwin has a large selection of galleries and shops catering for the collector of arts and crafts. Featured are works from both prominent local and interstate artists, and styles range from contemporary art to traditional Aboriginal. The Visitor Information Centre has a complete list, but here is one you should inspect.

Raintree Aboriginal Art Gallery, *14 Knuckey Street,* ☎*8981 2732,* which is also the only outlet for the Raintree Collection of fashion day wear and casual mix and match.

Shopping

Darwin has all the shops, stores and facilities a city should have for residents and tourists alike. Shops trade ⊙seven days a week, 9am-5pm, with late trading to 9pm on Thursday and Friday. Many items are for sale that are typical of the Northern Territory, such as handcrafted leather goods, local fashion items, and the bushmen's famous Akubra hats. There is also a wide selection of Aboriginal arts and crafts, including bark paintings, carvings, fish nets and hooks, didgeridoos and hand-painted fabrics such as those made by the Tiwi people on Melville Island, as well as the works of many very talented local artists, potters and weavers. The **Smith Street Mall** is the main shopping area, and there are shopping centres at Casuarina and Palmerston. The large hotels, of course, have the usual range of boutiques and souvenir shops.

Markets

The **Big Flea Market,** Darwin's oldest market, is held ⊙every Sunday, 8am-2pm, at Rapid Creek Shopping Centre on *Tower Road.*

The **Parap Market** is held ⊙every Saturday, 8am-2pm, and many people visit in search of breakfast or brunch. There are fresh fruit drinks and ices, plus stalls offering South-East Asian soups and satays. There are also second-hand books and knick-knacks.

At **Banyan Junction**, next to the Transit Centre in Mitchell Street, an international food market is held every day from 6pm, against a backdrop of Melbourne trams.

⊙Every Friday 5pm-10pm during the Dry season, the **Palmerston Night Market** is held in Goyder Square. There are arts and crafts stalls, a wide choice of culinary delights and local musicians. Buses ⊙depart Darwin terminal (route 8) at 5.15pm and return 8.30 or 9.40pm. Buses leave Casuarina (route 9) at 5.30pm, return times as above.

Mindil Beach Sunset Market is held ⊙each Thursday from about 5pm-10pm, May to October. It offers a variety of taste treats from such lands as Indonesia, Laos, Sri Lanka, Thailand, The Philippines, South America, as well as some fair dinkum Aussie tucker. There are also arts and crafts stalls.

Points of Interest

A stroll around the city will take you to most of the important historical sites.

The **Tree of Knowledge**, behind the Civic Centre on *Harry Chan Avenue*, has been a locally-famous landmark through the town's history. It is a banyan tree (Ficus virens), a species revered by Buddhists worldwide as the 'tree of knowledge' under which Buddha gained enlightenment.

Christchurch Cathedral was built in 1975 using some of the ruins of the original cathedral which was devastated by Cyclone Tracy.

Brown's Mart, cnr *Harry Chan Avenue* and *Smith Street,* ☎*8981 5522,* was intended as a mining exchange when it was built in the 1882. It has served many

purposes through the years, despite the roof being blown off by two cyclones. In recent years, the exposed roof framing was extended to increase its lateral stability, and the building was converted to a community theatre.

The **Old Town Hall** is in *Smith Street*, and when it was erected in 1883 during a mining boom, it created, along with Brown's Mart and Christchurch, a streetscape of stone. In World War II it was used for naval administration, and after that was an art gallery. Now, the ruined walls make a dramatic backdrop for outdoor theatre.

The **Old Courthouse and Police Station**, cnr *Smith Street* and *The Esplanade*, was built in 1884 for the South Australian government, in early South Australian style. Cornerstones connected the courthouse to the police station with a cellblock in the back. The navy used these buildings from World War II until Cyclone Tracy. The interior was then reconstructed, while retaining the facade, and the building now houses the offices of the Administrator of the Northern Territory.

Government House has been known as *The Residency* and also as *The House of Seven Gables*, and is an 1883 replacement in stone of a timber structure built 13 years earlier, which suffered a white ant attack. Verandahs with louvres, providing the main living area, encircle the building. The gardens and gables certainly give it a colonial look.

Hotel Darwin, in *The Esplanade*, is one of Darwin's oldest hotel sites. The original pub, *The Palmerston*, was proud of its 'accommodation suitable for ladies' when it opened in

1883. It was severely damaged by Cyclone Tracy and forced to close for 18 months. A convention and function centre was added to the rebuilt hotel in 1983. It is now the Carlton Hotel Darwin.

One of the few buildings left standing after Cylcone Tracy is the **St Mary Star of the Sea**, *90 Smith St*, ☎ *8981 2863*. It's open high ceilings and unique architecture make it quite a landmark.

Admiralty House, *The Esplanade*, is one of the few tropical-style houses still surviving from the 1920s, and is now used as an arts and crafts gallery and tearooms.

Lyons Cottage, *cnr Knuckey Street and The Esplanade*, was built in 1924-25 to house the manager of the British Australia Telegraph Company (BAT). The Georgian Revival-style bungalow was later occupied by one-time Darwin mayor John Lyons. Among its innovations is a separate kitchen in the rear, linked to the residence by a covered walkway for protection against the tropical climate. The house is now the **BAT Museum**, and admission is free, ☎ *8981 1750*. It is ☼open daily 10am-4.30pm.

Victoria Hotel (*The Vic*), ☎ *8981 4011*, in the centre of the Mall, has survived everything thrown at it, including bombs and a cyclone. When it was built in 1894, it was called the *North Australian Hotel*, and has since undergone a name change and four major reconstructions, although always maintaining its architectural integrity.

The **Star Village**, opposite *The Vic*, is a shopping arcade, built before the war and housed one of Darwin's early cinemas. The

original entrance and projection bridge is still the modern day entrance.

The **Commercial Bank**, *cnr The Mall and Bennett Street*, retains the colonnade from the original 1893 'Stone Bank'. The bank was so nicknamed because the Commercial Bank of Australia had chosen to build in local stone to counter the Tin Bank erected by a nearby competitor.

The **Chinese Temple**, in *Wood Street*, was heavily hit by the cyclone, which left only the floor, masonry block for the altars and the stone lions, all of which are incorporated in the current temple, built in steel and concrete. The simple yet elegant curved roof is new, and the entire 1978 structure received approval from Singapore-based religious leaders. The temple is ☼open Mon-Fri 8am-4pm, Sat-Sun 8am 3pm.

The National Trust headquarters are housed in Myilly Point Heritage Precinct, at *2 Khalin Avenue*, on the outskirts of the city centre. It is composed of four pre-World War II houses, built originally for high-ranking government employees. The Trust has an information centre and a gift shop, and is ☼open Mon-Fri 8.30am-4.30pm, ☎ *8981 2848*.

The Botanic Gardens, in *Gardens Road* off *Gilruth Avenue*, were first planted by Dr Maurice Holtze more than a century ago. They have the Southern Hemisphere's largest array of tropical palms, an orchid farm, nursery, rainforest, waterfall and wetlands flora, as well as an amphitheatre where there are often live concerts. Admission is free and the gardens are ☼open Mon-Fri 7.30am-5pm, Sat-Sun 8.30am-5pm.

Aquascene, *28 Doctors Gully Road* at the end of *The Esplanade*, ☎ *8981 7837*, has become Darwin's most popular attraction. Every day, at high tide, hundreds of fish come in from the sea to be fed, and you can be there to serve them. ☼opening times depend on the tides, so it is best to enquire at your hotel reception, or ring Aquascene direct. Prices are ⊙$5.50 adult.

The Museum and Art Gallery of the Northern Territory, in *Conacher Street, Fannie Bay*, ☎ *8999 8211*, features galleries of Aboriginal Man and of Oceania, full of art, artifacts, maps, photos, flora and fauna - including the legendary Sweetheart, a huge crocodile which used to terrorise trolling fishermen. The museum is also a research and scientific institute, categorising new species of plants and animals each year. In the Art Gallery, there are works by Lloyd Rees, Sidney Nolan, Clifton Pugh, Russell Drysdale, Donald Friend and Arthur Streeton, among others. It is ☼open Mon-Fri 9am-5pm, Sat-Sun 10am-5pm and admission is free.

Wishart Siding, built before the end of the19th century, with sun control and ventilation devices, is a typical building for the area. Timber framed with corrugated galvanised iron.

The **Australian Aviation Heritage Centre**, on the *Stuart Highway, Winnellie*, is ☼open daily 9am-5pm, ☎ *8947 2145*. Its major exhibit is a B52 bomber on permanent loan from the US Air Force, one of only two displayed outside the USA. Also of interest is the wreckage of a Zero Fighter shot down on February 19, 1942, during the first air raid on Darwin. There are many other exhibits from

World War II, as well as displays documenting the history of aviation in the Northern Territory. Admission is ✪$11 adult.

The **East Point Military Museum**, at *East Point Reserve*, has many exhibits, including a 15 minute movie with actual footage of the 1942 bombing of Darwin. It is ⏰open daily 9.30am-4.30pm, ☎8981 9702.

Fannie Bay Gaol Museum, on **East Point Road**, ☎8999 8290, is ⏰open daily 10am-4.30pm, and admission is free. The gaol closed in 1979 after 84 years of service, and opened as a museum in 1983. The gaol was emptied in 1942, after Japan bombed Darwin, and again in 1974, after Cyclone Tracy damaged the complex. Fourteen men were hanged in the gaol, the last two in 1952.

Indo Pacific Marine in **Lambell Terrace, Larrakeyah**, ☎8981 1294, is not really a museum, but rather a marine display. It features living coral reef eco-systems which have been isolated from the sea, and is one of four such exhibitions in the world. It is ⏰open 10am-5pm daily, and as it takes at least an hour to see everything, the management closes the doors one hour before closing time. Price of admission is ✪$16.40 adult.

Crocodylus Park, in *McMillans Road, Berrimah*, ☎8922 4500, is Darwin's newest attraction. It features crocodiles, of course, as well as other interesting wildlife, including lions and tigers. The park is ⏰open 9am-5pm daily, and prices are ✪$19.50 adult.

Festivals

The Northern Territory is renowned for its bizarre festivals and carnivals. One of the oddest is the **Beer Can Regatta** in which vessels made almost completely of beer cans race on Darwin Harbour in August. One of the major Aboriginal festivals is the **Barunga Festival** held over the long weekend in June. Aborigines from all over the Territory gather at Barunga, 80km (50 miles) south-east of Katherine, for four days of traditional events such as dancing, fire lighting, and boomerang and spear throwing contests. The **Darwin Cup Carnival** in July/August is held over six weeks of fashion, food, frivolity, and yes, there is also a horse race.

Facilities

Cycling - pushbikes, tandems and mountain bikes are available. For information, contact the Darwin Amateur Cycling Club, ☎8953 4360.
Football - Australian Rules and Rugby Union are popular, with some support for Rugby League. Both indoor and outdoor soccer are played.
Swimming - it is inadvisable to swim in the ocean between October and May due to the presence of the box jellyfish. During this time the locals tend to use the inland waterways such as Berry Springs and Howard Springs, or municipal pools in Darwin, Casuarina, Nightcliff, and Palmerston. Swimmers should check carefully for any signs warning of crocodiles.
Ten pin bowling - Darwin Ten Pin Bowling, 8985 4416.
Squash - courts can be found at a number of locations including the Darwin Squash and Aerobics Centre, ☎8948 4889; Howard Springs Squash Courts, ☎8983 2907.
Tennis - contact the Darwin Tennis Centre, ☎8985 2844, or Tennis Association, ☎8981 2181. Night tennis is popular.

Outlying Attractions

South of Darwin
Palmerston

Palmerston is a new town, 20km (12 miles) south of Darwin, which was designed to become a self-sufficient city. The present population is around 20,000, and four suburbs have been developed. The town has many tourist attractions, and foremost among them is **Marlow Lagoon**, noted for its year-round swimming, playground, barbecue and other facilities. The town also has a nine-hole golf course and a sport and leisure centre with an olympic-sized pool and a gymnasium.

Howard Springs

Situated 34km (21 miles) south of Darwin, on and around the Stuart Highway, Howard Springs is the centre for **Howard Springs Nature Park**. The Park has the closest and most attractive public fresh water swimming pool to Darwin. Next to the Park is the Territory's only duck and goose hunting reserve. There is also a road leading off nearby to the Gunn Point fishing paradise. Shooters need a permit, and there is an official shooting season, so enquiries should be made at a police station, or a branch of the Parks and Wildlife Commission, ☎8983 1001. Hunters and fishermen should also be aware that this is saltwater crocodile country, and they love fish and birds.

Noonamah

The town of Noonamah is 40km (25 miles) south of Darwin on the *Stuart Highway*, and its main attraction, the **Crocodile Farm**, is 2km before the town itself. The Farm is the first and largest in Australia and has more than 7000 residents, including giant crocs, baby crocs, pygmy crocs, an albino croc and American alligators. The reptiles are bred here for their skin and meat. The Farm is ☉open daily 9am-4pm, and feeding time is 2pm daily, with an extra feeding on Sunday at 11am. Entry is ◑$10 adult. ☎8988 1450.

Berry Springs

Territory Wildlife Park is 10km (6 miles) west of the *Stuart Highway* turnoff, which is 48km (30 miles) south of Darwin. The park is a world-class wildlife sanctuary set in more than 400ha (988 acres) of bushland, and exhibits native and feral animals of the North Territory. It is designed on an open range plan, without bars or cages. The park is ☉open daily 8.30am-6pm, with last visitors admitted at 4pm. Fees are ◑$18 for adults, ☎8988 7200.

Next door to the wildlife park is the **Berry Springs Nature Park**. The springs create natural swimming pools fringed with rainforest. They are ☉open year-round, 8.30am-6.30pm, although they are temporarily closed after very heavy rains. There are grassed picnic grounds and barbecue facilities, ☎8988 6310.

Batchelor

Batchelor is 13km (8 miles) west of the Stuart Highway, from the turnoff 87km (53 miles) south of Darwin. It was established as a town for miners working the **Rum Jungle Uranium Mine** in 1954. The mine closed in 1963 as the remaining ore was uneconomic to treat. The treatment plant closed in 1971 when the stockpiled ore

had been processed. The site, which has been rehabilitated, can be visited, but only on tours organised by **Batchelor Caravillage**, *Rum Jungle Road*, ☎8976 0166.

Batchelor also has some relics from World War II, when it was the site of an air base, bombed by the Japanese in 1942. Its main function now, though, is as the gateway to **Litchfield Park**, one of the Territory's newest parks.

Litchfield National Park

The 65,700ha (162,279 acres) park features permanent water and changing terrain that makes it one of the better bush walking areas in the Top End. There are monsoonal rainforests, hot springs, the Tabletop range escarpment with its imposing sandstone outcrops, spring fed creeks, huge groves of cycads and historic tin mines. For the more adventurous there is the **Lost City**. This limestone rock formation appears to be a huge petrified city of castles, statues, people and animals. It is quite a find, hiding deep in the Park, and is only accessible by 4WD, horseback or to the hardy bushwalker. The rest of the area is accessible by conventional and 4WD vehicles, and is a photographer's delight. Camping facilities are available. Before venturing into the Park it is advisable to obtain a map of the area from any of the businesses in Batchelor, and to call Road Report, ☎1800 246 199, for up to date information on the Park's road conditions, and the Parks and Wildlife Commission, ☎8976 0282, for further information on the park.

Adelaide River

The town of Adelaide River is 110km (68 miles) south of Darwin on the Stuart Highway. It is situated on a river of the same name, and was a major military centre during World War II. Attractions include the **War Cemetery, Snake Creek Arsenal** and **Robin Falls.** The pub is worth a visit, and the owners also offer some good value tours of the local region, ☎8976 7047.

East of Darwin
Humpty Doo

Humpty Doo is situated on the Arnhem Highway, 11km (7 miles) east of the Stuart Highway, and 45km (28 miles) from Darwin. A very large crocodile on the roadside, complete with boxing gloves, tells you that you are entering 'croc country', which is a good thing to keep in mind. The town is mainly a service centre for the rural belt, and has basic facilities and services. It was the site of the Humpty Doo Rice Growing Project, which began in 1956 using water stored in the nearby **Fogg Dam**, but was abandoned in the early 1960s.

Attractions in the town include: **Graeme Gow's Reptile World**, a display of some of the most deadly reptiles in the world. It is ☉open daily 8.30am-5pm, ☎8988 1661; **the Humpty Doo Hotel**, ☎8988 1372, which hosts the annual **Darwin Stubby Drinking Competition** in July; and the **Adelaide River Queen**, a flat-bottomed river boat that departs Adelaide River Bridge for cruises along the river, ☎8988 8144. There are regular departures for the two and a half hour cruises along a stretch of river which is home to about 60 crocs and prolific bird and animal life. The croc feeding sessions enable visitors to see the speed and power of these reptiles as they actually jump out of the water to catch the food.

Kakadu National Park

Kakadu National Park is a natural wonderland - 20,000sq km (7,720 sq miles) of magnificent sights, sounds and experiences. It has a World Heritage listing, and is owned by the Aborigines under the Gagudju Association. Kakadu begins about 250km (155 miles) east of Darwin on the Arnhem Highway, and is made up of three regions: the almost inaccessible Arnhem plateau; the rolling lowlands; and the flood plains. There are 120 known rock galleries of Aboriginal art along the escarpment, with those at **Obiri Rock and Nourlangi Rock** being the most easily accessible. It is extremely important to remember that the galleries are very old and they are still important and significant to the Aboriginal people today. PLEASE KEEP TO THE MARKED PATHWAYS, AND DO NOT TOUCH ANY PAINTED SURFACE. Although almost one-third of Kakadu is bare rock, the rest is lush lowlands which support 960 identified species of plants. There is also an incredible variety of animal life, with 51 species of native mammals. Other creatures include crocodiles and frill-necked lizards. A cruise on the **Yellow Waters Billabong** or **South Alligator River** offers one of the best opportunities to see the water flowers and wildlife. There are excellent bushwalks throughout the park, and drives into the bush lead to spectacular

sights such as **Twin Falls** and **Jim Jim Falls**. Probably the best way to see Kakadu is with a tour operator who knows all the history and can show you the special and unique places, and many are available in Darwin. If you decide to travel on your own, you should call into the Bowali Visitor Information Centre near *Jabiru*, ☎8938 1120, for advice, brochures and to pay your ✪$16.25 park fee. There is also a Tourist Centre in Tasman Plaza, *Jabiru*, ☎8979 2548.

↵ Let's Stay Here

Gagudju Lodge YHA, *Cooinda, off Kakadu Highway*, ☎8979 0145 💻www.gagudju-dreaming.com Situated just on the Yellow Water Billabong, in Kakadu National Park. Part resort complex with pricey lodging and caravan and camping areas. With prefabricated units facing a nice shady veranda. Kitchen area has fridge and two barbecues. Other facilities includes laundry, on premises gift shop, internet access, and swimming pool. Bikes are hireable. Tours of scenic flights and guided fishing trips are offered at the desk and also offers foreign exchange. A licensed bar and restaurant is within the lodge including a petrol station. Parking available. *Members dorms ✪$27 ($30.50 non-members); double $60 BC MC JCB VA EFTPOS*

Kakadu Ubirr Hostel, *Oenpelli Rd, Ubirr, East Alligator, Kakadu National Park*, ☎8979 2232 Set in a natural bushland, this

hostel is situated just next to the beautiful Ubirr Rock, and is minutes away from the many attractions of the Kakadu National Park. Basic accommodation. Facilities includes an above ground swimming pool, barbecue area, kitchen, laundry and the Border Shop is just right across the premises. Ask about the bike and canoe hire at the desk. Parking available. *Dorms ✪$25 ($22 YHA); single/double $25 ($22 YHA); BC MC VA EFTPOS*

Arnhem Land

Arnhem Land is the area east of Kakadu National Park, and is traditionally inhabited by the Aborigines. A restricted number of tours take visitors through tropical bush abundant with wildlife and on to the coastal dunes from which the seascapes are truly magnificent. A permit is required for entry into this area, and can be obtained from the Tiwi Lands Council, Highway House, *Bishop Street, Stuart Park*, ☎8981 4898. The rock galleries of Aboriginal Art in Arnhem Land are generally regarded as even more impressive than those in Kakadu, but they can only by visited whilst on an organised tour.

North of Darwin

Bathurst and Melville Islands

The islands are 80km (50 miles) off the coast of Darwin, and are owned by the Tiwi Aborigines. Until recently, the islands had received almost no visitors from the mainland for thousands of years, but there are now day and half-day tours to Bathurst Island, or you can stay overnight at Putjimirra camp on Melville Island. The tours are offered by Tiwi Tours, ☎ *8924 1115*.

Cobourg Peninsula/Victoria Settlement

The peninsula north-east of Darwin is in Arnhem Land, and was where a brave but futile attempt was made to first settle the area. The ruins of the **Victoria Settlement** at Port Essington can still be seen, but a permit is required. In the early1990s an environmentally sensitive wilderness habitat called **Seven Spirit Wilderness**, opened on the Cobourg Peninsula, ☎ *8979 0277*.

Tennant Creek

Population 3,500
Tennant Creek is on the Stuart Highway, 24km (15 miles) south of the junction of the Barkly Highway. It is 507km (314 miles) north of Alice Springs, and 675km (419 miles) south of Katherine.

Climate

As with most outback towns, Tennant Creek has two seasons, the Wet (November-March) and the Dry (April-October). Average temperatures: Dry Season max 35C (95F) - min 10C (50F); Wet Season max 43C (109F) - min 26C (79F).

Characteristics

The country of the Warumungu People centres on Jurnkurakurr, the focus of many dreaming tracks and a place of spiritual significance for several tribes. In 1860, John McDouall Stuart passed by the same spot, and named the creek there Tennant Creek, after John Tennant of Port Lincoln, South Australia. In 1872, an Overland Telegraph

Line repeater station was built at Tennant Creek.

From hard beginnings, the town has steadily developed. Townsfolk worked hard to get facilities that people 'down south' took for granted. In the last 50 years, people from all over the world have settled at Tennant, and today it is a multi-cultural and harmonious township, where everyone is encouraged to participate fully in community affairs.

Tennant Creek has grown from a small and dusty outback settlement, to a busy community and a vital part of the Northern Territory.

How to Get There
By Bus

Greyhound Pioneer stop at Tennant Creek on their Darwin/Alice Springs routes.

Visitor Information

Tennant Creek Visitor Information Centre, *Battery Hill, Peko Road*, can be contacted on ☎ *(08) 8962 3388* or emailed at ~info@tennant creektourism.com.au. The website is 🖥www.tennantcreektourism. com.au

↪ Let's Stay Here

Here is a selection of available accommodation, with prices that should be used as a guide only. The telephone area code is 08.

Safari Backpackers YHA,
12 Davidson St, ☎ *8962 2207,*
🖥www.*yha.com.au* Located just at the centre of town. Just your basic accommodation. Facilities includes air conditioned rooms, TV lounge, tour information,

laundry, kitchen and off street parking. *Members dorms* ➌*$14 ($16 non-members); double/twin $36 ($38 non-members) BC MC VA EFTPOS*

Tourist Rest Hostel,
Corner Windly and Leichardt Sts, ☎ *8962 2719,* 🖥www.*touristrest.com.au* Small and offers basic accommodation. Airconditioning and fans in all rooms. Facilities includes swimming pool, barbecue area, kitchen and two TV rooms. Play Stations are available for hire. Free courtesy bus pickup. Secure Off street parking. *Dorms* ➌*$18; single/ double $40*

Caravan Parks
Banka Banka Station,
Camping Grounds, Stuart Highway, ☎ *8964 4511* Located 100 km north of Tennant Creek. Clean amenities, toilets, bathroom and hot showers. Other facilities includes a camp kitchen and barbecue area with fridge. There's also an on site kiosk. *Camping* ➌*$5pp*

Outback Caravan Park, *Peko Road,* ☎ *8962 2459.* (No dogs allowed) 150 sites, spa, pool, barbecue, good facilities - powered sites ➌*$20 for two, on-site vans $50 for two.*

Tennant Creek Caravan *Park, 208 Paterson Street,* ☎ *8962 2325.* (Pets allowed on leash) 90 sites, barbecue, pool - *unpowered sites* ➌*$18 for two, cabins from $40 for two.*

Let's Eat
Fernanda's Restaurant, 1 *Noble Street,* ☎ *8962 3999.*

Tennant Creek Chinese Restaurant, *63 Patterson Street*, ☎ *8962 3347.*

Points of Interest

Near the Visitor Information Centre, there is a **Celebrity Walk,** where famous people who have passed through the town have left behind prints of their hands and feet.

From **Anzac Hill,** in *Davidson Street,* there is a good view over the town, and on the top there is a **War Memorial,** and seats.

The **Church of Christ The King**, in *Windley Street,* was built at Pine Creek in 1904, and trucked to Tennant in 1936 to serve the growing town. Major restoration work was done in 1986, and the church is classified as an Historic Building by the National Trust.

The National Trust Museum building was constructed by the army in 1942, then used as the Outpatients Clinic until taken over by the National Trust in 1978. Items of interest include: the old gaolhouse; reconstruction of a miner's camp; archive collection; and early photographs. The Museum is ⊙open during the Dry season from 4-6pm daily, and during the Wet Season by appointment only, ☎ *8962 4257.*

The Old Australian Inland Mission was built in 1934, and is the oldest building constructed here. It is a good example of the early corrugated iron buildings, most of which have not stood the test of time. The Mission is next to the Uniting Church in *Paterson Street.*

The **Aboriginal Mural,** in *Paterson Street,* was a community project, and it encompasses Aboriginal mythology and contemporary life. Many local Aboriginal artists participated in its planning and painting.

The **Civic Centre** and **Public Library** are in *Peko Road.* The Civic Centre has a gem collection and an art display, as well as the Council Chambers, and is ⊙open Mon-Fri 9am-4.15pm. The Library houses the Tennant Creek Collection, written material about the region, and is ⊙open Mon-Fri 10am-4.15pm, Sat 9am-12.15pm.

The Government Stamp Battery is further along *Peko Road.* Number 3 Battery is the last of the Government batteries still operating in the Territory. It is used to crush and treat free milling or easily freed gold ores. Interesting things to see include an operating 10 head 575.6kg stamper, various displays of historic artifacts, and the former battery site and buildings. Guided tours are available, and the Visitor Information Centre can advise on times and costs.

Continuing along *Peko Road* you come to **One Tank Hill,** Tennant's main lookout point. There are plaques set into a semi-circular wall that provide distance and direction markers for 11 significant sites.

Nobles Nob, on *Peko Road* 16km (10 miles) east of the town, was the richest gold mine in Australia. It was discovered in 1933, and produced $64,975,256.00 worth of ore by the time it closed in 1985. It was an underground mine, but the crown pillar collapsed in 1967, and the mine was converted to a huge open cut. The pit is 283m (930ft) long, 146m (480 ft) wide, and 82m (270 ft) deep. Work continues at Nobles Nob with gold from the White Devil Mine being processed there. There is a tourist lookout, from which visitors can see the crushing and mill buildings, and tailings dam, as well as good views of the eastern region.

Mary Ann Dam is 3km (2 miles) north of Tennant Creek, and was built in 1980 as a recreation lake. It provides excellent swimming and boating (non-power boats only), and has covered picnic tables and seats, barbecues, boat ramp, toilets, showers and playground equipment. There is also plenty of bushwalking available in the Honeymoon Ranges, and a bike track connects the dam to the town for people with that form of transport. Camping is not allowed at the dam.

The **Old Telegraph Station**, 10km (6 miles) north of town, was completed in 1876 as part of a network stretching from Adelaide to Darwin. Only 4 of the original 11 buildings still remain, and they are the oldest in the Territory. They were used by linesmen and telegraph station operators until the transfer of communications to the **Tennant Creek Post Office** in 1937. Between then and 1986, the area was leased to various pastoralists, but it now forms part of a conservation area and is being restored as a museum. The old buildings in their pastoral setting provide an insight into the lives of early pioneers.

There are two interesting isolated graves to the west of the station. The northernmost one is that of **Tom Nugent**, who established Banka Banka Station, and who had apparently in his younger days been a member of the Ragged Thirteen, a gang of cattle duffers (rustlers) who roamed the Territory at the turn of the century. Another member of the Ragged Thirteen was Harry Redwood, who built **Brunette Downs**, and was immortalised in Boldrewood's novel Robbery Under Arms as Captain Starlight. The other grave is not his, though, it belongs to Archibald Cameron, an OTS linesman who died around 1918.

The **Devils Pebbles** are an interesting granite rock formation scattered over a large area. To see them drive 11km (7 miles) north of Tennant Creek on the *Stuart Highway*, then turn left on a dirt road for a further 6km (4 miles). The best time to visit is at sunset when the rocks seem to come alive as the sun's rays strike them. The area is inhabited by various wildlife species including rock wallabies. There are barbecue facilities.

Festivals

May - **Goldrush Festival** with street pageants, gold nugget finds, bogout competitions, music and more.
October - **Desert Harmony Festival**, a week of arts activities. There are theatre productions, bands, cabaret, arts and crafts displays, fashion parades, Aboriginal dancing and cultural displays.

Facilities
Olympic swimming pool, golf course, lawn bowls, squash, tennis and fossicking.

Car Hire: Budget Rent A Car, ☎8962 2402; Herz Rent A Car, ☎8962 2459; Rocky's Taxi Service, ☎8962 252**2**.

Outlying Attractions
South of Tennant Creek
Devils Marbles
Located 108km (67 miles) south

of Tennant Creek on *Stuart Highway*, the Marbles are huge rounded boulders, incredibly balanced on each other. Some of the boulders seem to have been cleanly sliced in half, but in fact, their shape comes from millions of years of erosion. Sizes of the boulders vary from half a metre to six metres, and some weight thousands of tons. Aboriginal people say that these formations are the fossilized eggs of the Rainbow Serpent, and the site is sacred to them.

Facilities include wood barbecues, picnic area and basic toilet facilities. Camping is allowed, but there is no water.

Devils Marbles Tours operate out of Tennant Creek and can be contacted on ☎*8962 2718* or by email ✉info@devilsmarbles.com.au

Wauchope
Wauchope, which incidentally is pronounced 'walk up' is 113km (70 miles) south of Tennant Creek on the *Stuart Highway*.

The settlement is actually a pub, offering accommodation, fuel, food, ice and souvenirs, etc. It is good base for exploring the Chinese diggings in the **Murchison Ranges**. Each July visitors come from miles around to attend the 'Wauchope versus the World' cricket match!

Wycliffe Well
A well stocked store and recently modernised pre-war roadhouse, Wycliffe Well is 136km (84 miles) south of Tennant Creek. The Well was worked by a lady called Doreen Crookes in the 1920s. She married a man named Bill and founded the well-known property, **Mt Doreen Station**, in Central Australia. She then became

interested in heritage and founded the NT National Trust.

There is a licensed restaurant, shop, motel units, swimming pool (guests only), takeaway food and Visitor Information. Shaded picnic and barbecue areas are available.

Barrow Creek
The tiny township of Barrow Creek, population 12, is 224km (139 miles) south of Tennant Creek. It consists of the historic **Barrow Creek Telegraph Station**, and the oldest roadhouse on **'The Track', 'The Barrow'**.

The Telegraph Station was built in 1872, and is preserved as a memorial to Johns Franks, a linesman, and James Stapleton, the station master, who were killed in a surprise attack by Kaytej tribesmen in 1874. It is open to the public. The Barrow is the ultimate in outback pubs, in that it is exactly as those portrayed in movies of the outback, with real outback characters as patrons. The pub in itself is worth the long drive, and offers accommodation, a bar, dining room, shop, swimming pool (guests only), 6-hole golf course, showers for travellers, takeaway food, ice and fuel, ☎*8956 9753*.

North of Tennant Creek
Three Ways
Situated at the junction of the *Stuart* and *Barkly Highways*, 25km (16 miles) north of Tennant Creek, Three Ways is the major intersection in the heart of scrub country. There is a roadhouse, and a motel, Visitor Information, licensed restaurant, swimming pool (guests only), takeaway food, souvenirs, fuel, and usually, lots

Magnetic Termite Mounds

Nitmiluk National Park

Devils Marbles

of people. The roadtrains pull in here, and hitchhikers wait here for a lift in one of the three possible directions.

Nearby is a large stone cairn commemorating the Reverend John Flynn.

Attack Creek Historical Reserve

The reserve is 70km (43 miles) north of Tennant Creek, and there is a monument to **John McDouall Stuart**, whose first attempt at crossing the continent from the south ended here in 1894 when the party was attacked by Aborigines. An inscribed plaque tells the story.

Churchill's Head is 10km (6 miles) further north, and is a rocky outcrop on the *Old Stuart Highway*, whose shape closely resembles the head of the British statesman. During the war some American soldiers stuck a log in the 'mouth' of the rock to act as a cigar.

Camping in the area is allowed, and there are picnic tables and wood barbecues.

Renner Springs

Renner Springs, 94km (58 miles) north of Tennant Creek, is a wayside inn that is completely surrounded by the **Helen Springs Cattle Station.** The roadhouse offers accommodation, and good homestyle food, ☎*8964 4505.* The building is an old army hut, and it has a small museum of historical objects.

Nearby, at **Lubra's Lookout**, there is a marker peg for the change from arid to sub-tropical zone.

Elliott

The town of Elliott is 187km (116 miles) north of Tennant

Creek, and approximately half way between Alice Springs and Darwin. It has a population of around 600, and is the second largest settlement in the Barkly. The town had its origins in World War II when it was a staging camp for troops on the move between Darwin and Alice Springs, and it is named after Captain Elliot from Adelaide, the officer in charge of the wartime camp.

There is a hotel/motel, and camping areas, and the hotel has a licensed dining room, ☎*8969 206.*

North of Elliot, and 3km (2 miles) west of the *Stuart Highway*, is the old droving township of **Newcastle Waters**. The small town is situated at the intersection of the Murranji and Barkly stock routes and near the intermittent waters of Newcastle Creek. If features historic buildings, and a **Drovers' Memorial Park**. During the Bicentennial year 1988, the Last Great Cattle Drive began here.

Uluru (Ayers Rock) and Kata Tjuta (The Olgas)

Uluru National Park is 465km (289 miles) south-west of Alice Springs, and has an area of 1325 square km (511 sq miles), measuring 72km (45 miles) east-west and 16.5km (10 miles) north-south.

The **Yulara Resort**, which can accommodate well over 5,000 people a day in the various establishments, is 20km (12 miles) from Ayers Rock.

Climate

Average temperatures: January max 37C (99F) - min 22C (72F);

July max 19C (66F) - min 5C (41F). Average annual rainfall - 200-250mm (8-10 ins).

Characteristics

The National Park is Australia's first Aboriginal Park, and has the Territory's greatest attraction, Ayers Rock. The Mutitjulu Community are permanent residents in the Park, and 'Uluru' is the Aboriginal name for Ayers Rock.

Uluru is one of the world's greatest monoliths and undergoes amazing colour changes at sunrise and sunset.

The Olgas, 32km (20 miles) to the west, consist of a series of large domes whose colouring and shape are impressive. The Aboriginal name for the Olgas is 'Kata Tjuta' (sometimes written as one word).

How to Get There
By Bus

Greyhound Pioneer have daily services to Yulara.

Visitor Information

National Park Visitors Centre is in *Yulara Drive, Yulara*, ☎*(08) 8957 7377,* and is ☺open daily 8.30am-5pm.

The Information Centre can be contacted on ☎*(08) 8957 7888 or 1300 134 044.*

The Uluru-Kata Tjuta Cultural Centre, Uluru-Kata Tjuta National Park, Yulara, ☎*(08) 8956 3138,* has displays with a wealth of information on Aboriginal culture, wildlife, landscape and geology of Ayers Rock and the Olgas. It is ☺open 8am-5pm.

There is a Ranger Station at Uluru, with toilets, a kiosk, and information on tours and walks around Uluru and Kata Tjuta. The websites to explore are www.centralaustraliantourism.com or www.voyages.com.au

Points of Interest

There is an entrance fee to the National Park of ✪$16.25 per adult, which is valid for 3 consecutive days. If this seems a bit steep, it may help to know that the funds go straight back into the maintenance of the park, and to helping the traditional Anangu owners in their community.

Uluru (Ayers Rock)

The first European to climb Uluru was Englishman William Christie Gosse, and it had taken him about three months to reach the Rock, travelling from Alice Springs with a camel train. The year before, the Rock had been sighted by Ernest Giles, but he never actually reached it, being forced to turn back to Alice Springs because of the salty marshes of Lake Amadeus, 50km (31miles) north of Ayers Rock.

Gosse named the Rock after Sir Henry Ayers, then Chief Secretary and later Premier of South Australia. Giles had previously named the Olgas after Queen Olga of Wurtemberg in Germany.

The first plane landed at the Rock in 1930, piloted by journalist Errol Coote, a member of the support party which accompanied Lasseter in an unsuccessful attempt to locate a reef of gold in the south-west corner of the Northern Territory. The same year, the first rough track was carved by pastoralist Sid Stanes of Erldunda Station, to Ayers Rock from the Station.

In the early 1940s the first graded road linked the Alice and the Rock, but it was usually impassable after heavy rains.

At this time, Ayers Rock and the Olgas formed part of the **Petermann Aboriginal Reserve**, which covered almost 45,000 sq km (17,370 sq miles) of the south-western part of the Territory. In 1958, both rock formations and about 1325 sq km (511 sq miles) were excised from the reserve to become the **Uluru** (Ayers Rock/Mt Olga) **National Park**. The first ranger, Bill Harney, was appointed the same year on a part-time basis, only spending the winter at the Rock.

It was around this time that Alice Springs resident Len Tuit established a base camp to the west of the Ayers Rock climb and started the first tourist operations. The first official record of visitor numbers showed that in 1958, 2296 people made the arduous twelve hour journey from the Alice to gaze in wonder at the giant monolith. The next year leases were granted to two tour companies for the operation of a hotel, four motels, a store, and a service station and fuel depot at the airstrip.

Improvements were made to the road from Alice Springs during the 1960s, and the number of visitors in 1968 was 23,000.

It had been decided in 1965 that there was a need for a resort such as Yulara, but establishing a virtual town in an isolated area with extreme temperatures and no power, water or sewerage was a monumental task. There were many feasibility surveys carried out by both private and government authorities, and finally the **Yulara Resort** was completed in 1984, one year after the Alice Springs-Ayers Rock road became an all-weather sealed highway.

Now to 'The Rock' itself. The maximum height above ground is 348m (1142 ft); the area is 3.33 sq km (1.28 sq miles); the circumference is 9.4km (5.8 miles); and the height above sea level is 862.5m (2829.7 ft).

Many visitors want to climb Uluru. The traditional owners advise against it – not only because of spiritual beliefs, as is widely thought, but also because of the dangers involved. Far fewer people make the climb now than a decade ago. It is not as easy at it looks, and those with high blood pressure, asthma, angina, fear of heights, or vertigo, should not even contemplate it. There are plaques near the designated climbing spot, dedicated to people who have died trying. For the fit and healthy, the climb up and back takes about two hours, and there is a hand chain to aid climbers on the way up, and steady them on the way down. It is much steeper than it looks. Remember to take plenty of water, and a few oranges. If you want to experience at least part of the climb, many people manage to get to 'Chicken Rock', where the chain begins, without much trouble. For those who would prefer to stay at ground level, the **Australian National Parks and Wildlife Service** have some interesting guided walks, which are free. They either leave from the Ranger Station, or from the Climb Car Park, and hbegin about 9.30am. For information, times, and bookings ☎8956 2299.

One walk is around the caves at the base of the Rock with their ancient Aboriginal paintings, and another, with an Aboriginal guide, introduces visitors to the 'bush tucker' which abounds in

Kata Tjula

Uluru (Ayers Rock)

the seemingly barren landscape. Both tours include talks on the history and geology of the area, the Aboriginal perception of Uluru, and the flora and fauna.

Then there is the round-the-rock walk, which is on flat land all the way, and takes about 3 to 4 hours. All you need are strong shoes, a sun hat, plenty of cool drinks, and a nice added touch is a picnic hamper from one of the hotels at Yulara. The track is well marked, and passes caves with Aboriginal paintings, little Ayers Rock (known to the Aboriginal people as Taputji), and the beautiful Maggie Springs. When you are walking around the Ayers Rock area you will see signs denoting Aboriginal sacred sites, which are off-limits to visitors. These signs must be obeyed, and that will in no way effect your enjoyment of the walk.

If you want to take the almost obligatory photograph of the Rock at sunset, you'll have no trouble finding the best spot to take it from, just follow the crowds.

Kata Tjuta (The Olgas)

The 36 domes of Kata Tjuta, together with Uluru and the lesser-known flat-topped monolith called Mount Conner, are all that is left of a mountain chain formed some 600 million years ago. There is no doubt that Uluru is the most famous of the trio, but many visitors judge Kata Tjuta to be more spectacular, and like the Rock, they also change colours at sunrise and sunset.

The **Mount Olga Gorge** walk is fine for all the family for the first part, then the trail enters a narrow track and becomes more difficult. The Mount Olga Lookout walk is about 3km long, and takes about 90 minutes there and back. It is suitable for all, but only those with some experience should continue along the top of the dome and down to the car park.

The **Valley of the Winds** walk follows the creek around the base of the dome to the lookout and takes about 2 hours. It is best to check with the Ranger Station at Uluru about details of the walks, and make sure you have plenty of water.

The only facilities at Kata Tjuta are walking trails, car parking areas, and pit toilets.

Yulara

The completion of Yulara (which is an Aboriginal word meaning 'howling' as dingoes do) in late 1984 meant that not only could around 5000 people a day be accommodated near Uluru, but also that the fragile and endangered ecology of the sand-dune lands immediately surrounding the Rock could be restored and protected from further damage.

Prior to the development of Yulara, a collection of old and sub-standard motels and camping areas had grown haphazardly in the shadow of the Rock, and vehicles and visitors had gradually caused damage to the flora. This prevented the sand-dunes from drifting, and caused the animal life to retreat to safer and more peaceful areas.

Uluru was a national park which had been included in a world network organised by UNESCO, and it was obvious that a far-reaching plan was needed to protect the park, and provide better facilities for a growing number of visitors. When you first see the national park, with its red sand-dunes reaching up to 13m, it appears that there could not be much in the way of flora and fauna, but this is not the case. It is home to more than 566 species of flora, approximately 24 species of native mammals, several species of introduced Feral animals (including rabbit, fox, cat, house mouse, camel and dog), around 72 reptiles, and a number of amphibians and aquatic crustaceans. Approximately 161 species of birds have been sighted in the park, many of them being migratory. It was decided to construct Yulara outside the park boundaries, about 20km (12 miles) from Uluru and 30km (19 miles) from Kata Tjuta. This site was selected for a number of reasons - its acceptability to the Aboriginal people who have inhabited Central Australia for around 10,000 years; its proximity to underground water sources; and the views of Uluru and Kata Tjuta which could be afforded visitors. The old accommodation places were closed down and the landscape returned to its natural state. Yulara was designed by Australian architect Philip Cox, and caused quite a sensation when the artist's impressions were first released in 1981.

The reality is no less sensational, with the many characteristic 'sails', used to create shade, making up the main feature. In the complex are shopping, entertainment, information, convention centres and accommodation from five-star downwards.

Separated from the main resort complex by sand-dunes are the campgrounds, staff accommodation, a school, police station, fire station, service station and essential service operations.

Yulara has a resident community of around 3000 people, and is the fourth largest population centre in the Northern Territory when fully booked.

⬐ Let's Stay Here
Outback Pioneer Lodge YHA,
Ayers Rock Resort, ☎*8957 7888 or 1300 139 889,*
🖳*www.yha.com.au*
Offers clean and basic accommodation but very pricey. Facilities includes swimming pool, kitchen and internet access. There is also a restaurant with free live entertainment, a kiosk, foreign exchange and car rental hire on site. They also have a free resort shuttle that picks up and takes you to the airport. Parking available. *Members dorms* ✪*$37 ($40 non members) - 4 share, $29 ($32 non members) - 20 share BC MC JCB VA DC EFPTOS*

Tours
There are many National Park and Resort Tours available, and the Visitors' Centre at Yulara has all the details. There are trips to the major attractions of Central Australia, camel rides, cattle station visits, scenic flights, cultural tours, dinner and champagne tours, and more.

A selection of operators to contact are Austour ☎1800 335 009, Australian Pacific Touring ☎1800 891 121, Anangu Tours ☎8956 2123, Frontier Camel Tours ☎8956 2444, Uluru Experience ☎1800 803 174, VIP ☎1800 806 142 and Sahara Outback Tours ☎1800 806 240.

Katherine
Population 10,500
Katherine is situated on the Stuart Highway, 317km (197 miles) south of Darwin and 1182km (734 miles) north of Alice Springs.

Characteristics
Katherine is the heart of the real Outback, and is attracting an increasing number of visitors. In fact, tourism is Katherine's biggest industry, although it also has a rich horticultural and agricultural centre. The RAAF base at Tindal provides jobs for a number of local residents as well as accommodating some 700 personnel and their families. A dairy industry has been established locally, as well as chicken farms, quarries and the manufacture of building products.

The town is also a base for a growing number of gold and other mines, an educational and medical centre, and a major regional base for Commonwealth and Territory Government Departments.

Attractions in the area include places of historic interest, birds and wildlife in their natural surroundings, caves and gorges, Aboriginal lore and art, and for the adventurers, magnificent waterfalls, canyons and billabongs that are still unspoiled.

How to Get There
By Bus
Greyhound, Pioneer and **Bus Australia** have daily services from Darwin and Alice Springs.

Visitor Information
The Katherine Regional Tourist Association can be contacted on ☎*(08) 8972 2650* or by email at ~krta@nt-tech.com.au

The Katherine Visitor Information Centre can be found on the Stuart Highway (cnr Lindsay Street), ☎*(08) 8972 2650.*

⬐ Let's Stay Here
Here is a selection of available budget accommodation, with prices that should be used as a guide only. The telephone area code is 08.

Coco's Didj Backpackers,
21 First St, ☎*8971 2889* Small 16 bed hostel that offers just your basic accommodation and kitchen. Plenty of musical instruments. Very popular with artists, musicians, cyclist and Japanese backpackers touring Australia by motorcycle. On site shop that sell Aboriginal art and didgeridoos. *Dorms* ✪*$16; double $40*

Kookaburra Backpackers,
Corner Lindsay and Third Sts, ☎*8971 0257 or 1800 808 211* 🖳*www.kookaburraback packers.com.au* The nearest hostel to shopping and the Transit centre. Self-contained units with en suite bathroom and a small kitchen, fans and air condition. Other facilities includes laundry, swimming pool, barbecue area and an outdoor TV lounge. They offer a number of free stuff like 20 mins internet if your accommodation is pre-booked, bus transfers and maps, games, hats and sunscreen. Bike hire is available. Very helpful with organising canoe trips to the Katherine Gorge. Pre-book and you get 20 minutes free internet access. Off street parking. *Dorms*

❋$19; double/twin $59 (prices includes breakfast)

Palm Court Backpackers YHA,
Corner Gilles and Thrid Sts,
☎8972 2722 or 1800 626 722
Located within walking distance from the shops and has a good atmosphere. All rooms have fans, whilst 20 of the rooms have air conditioning, fridge and en suite bathrooms. Facilities includes TV lounge, kitchen, swimming pool, barbecue area, laundry and internet access. Offers free pick-up services. Plenty of parking available. *Members Dorms* ❋$17; single/double with en suite $48 BC MC VA EFTPOS (prices includes a pancake breakfast)

Victoria Lodge,
21 Victoria Highway, ☎8972 3464 or 1800 808 875 ▣www.viclodge.citysearch.com.au
Self-contained, clean and have en suite bathroom, small kitchen with a living room and TV. Other features are a swimming pool, shady barbecue area and laundry facilities. Parking available. *Dorms* ❋$17; single $40; double/twin $55

Caravan Parks
Katherine Low Level Caravan Park, *Shadforth Road,* ☎8972 3962. (Pets allowed at owner's discretion) 163 sites, excellent facilities, licensed restaurant, spa, pool, barbecue - *powered sites* ❋$21 for two, no on-site vans.

Manbulloo Homestead,
Victoria Hwy, ☎8972 1559

36 sites. Located just on the Banks Katherine River, on a rural block, 15 minutes drive away from town. Facilities includes a TV room and barbecue area. *Powered sites* ❋$10pp; non powered site $8pp; Hotel rooms with air conditioning $40 single, $45 double; self contained cabins double $35pp, $50 single; backpacker rooms with fans without linen from $13-20; with air condition and linen from $18-25

Nitmiluk (Katherine) Gorge Caravan Park, *Nitmiluk Gorge National Park,* ☎8972 1253 (No pets allowed) 100 sites, licensed restaurant - *powered sites* ❋$20 for two, no on-site vans.

Riverview Caravan Park,
440 Victoria Highway, ☎8972 1011. (No pets allowed) 116 sites, spa, barbecue, pool - *powered sites* ❋$19 for two, cabins $65-80 for two.

Shady Lane Tourist Park,
1828 Gorge Rd, ☎8971 0491 (No pets allowed) Facilities includes laundry facilities, kitchen, swimming pool, barbecue area and an on site kiosk. There's also canoe hire. *Powered sites* ❋$22; unpowered site $19;

Let's Eat
As mentioned above, most of the motels have licensed or unlicensed restaurants. A couple of other you might like to try are:

Annies Family Restaurant,
Hendry Road, ☎8972 3637.

Regent Court Restaurant, *25 Warburton St,* ☎8971 1555.

Points of Interest
Katherine Historical Museum,
Gorge Rd opposite Katherine Hospital, is housed in the old airport terminal, and has many exhibits of Katherine's colourful past including the Gypsy Moth flown by Dr Clyde Fenton in 1934. The museum is managed by the Katherine Historical Society, and you can buy souvenirs and books on the history of the town. ⏰opening hours are Mon-Fri 10am-4pm, Sat 10am-2pm, Sun 2-5pm, ☎8972 3945.

Knott's Crossing, 5km (3 miles) from Katherine via *Gorge Road* (turn off just past the hospital) is the original river crossing for the young settlement of Katherine. It was made famous by Mrs Aeneas Gunn's book *We of the Never Never,* and is a pleasant picnic and swimming spot.

The **Railway Station Museum,** *Railway Terrace,* is the National Trust headquarters. The present township grew around the railway after the railbridge was built in 1926. It provided a vital link to Darwin and the southern capitals for the small town. The museum has interesting displays of railway memorabilia, information on the historic sites of Katherine, and has maps, books and other items of interest for sale. It is open Mon-Fri 11am-1pm.

Katherine School of the Air, *Gorge Street,* ☎8972 1833, has ⏰guided tours Mon-Fri at 11am, except during school and public holidays.

Hot Springs are found 3km (2 miles) along *Victoria Highway,* on the banks of the Katherine River. It is a popular swimming spot, with a caravan park and motel adjacent, and a youth hostel nearby.

Katherine Low Level Nature Park, 5km (3 miles) from Katherine via the *Victoria Highway,* is open shady parkland on the banks of the Katherine River with easy access for swimming and fishing. The river here flows over the weir into a series of shallow rapids. Between November and March, visitors should check the river level on the bridge markers before entering the water. The current can be very strong and dangerous after rain. Facilities include picnic and barbecue areas, but camping is not allowed. There is a privately owned caravan and camping ground nearby.

Springvale Homestead, 8km (5 miles) from Katherine via *Zimin Drive* and *Shadforth Road,* ☎ *8972 1355,* was the destination on one of the Territory's most epic droving treks. Alfred Giles, well known explorer and pastoralist of the time took 19 months to drive stock from Adelaide. The original homestead is the oldest extant in the Territory. It is shaded by huge Indian raintrees planted by Giles' wife, one for each of her children. The privately operated tourist park runs free tours daily - hApril to October 10.30am and 2pm; November to March 2pm.

Facilities

A wide range of sports are played in the area. Weekly competitions may be in progress when you visit. Check in the local newspapers for fixtures.

Tours

There are many tours available from Katherine, some to the Gorge, others further afield. The Visitor Centre has details of current prices and times of all tours, and here are some you might like to enquire about.

Barramundi Fish Feeding, Territory Manor, Mataranka, ☎8975 4516.
Borroloola Scenic River Cruises, McArthur River Caravan Park, ☎8975 8734.
Brolga Tours (Roper River cruises), Mataranka Homestead, ☎8975 4544.
Crocodile Spotting Cruise Katherine River, Travel North, ☎8971 9999.
Cutta Cutta Caves, Travel North, ☎8971 9999.
Fishing Safaris, Rod and Rifle, ☎8972 1020.
Kakadu Camping Safari ex Katherine, Travel North, ☎8971 9999.
Kakadu Scenic Flights ex Katherine, Kakadu Air, ☎8979 2411.
Katherine Day Tours, Travel North, ☎8971 9999.
Katherine Extended Tours, Travel North, ☎8971 9999.
Katherine Gorge Cruises, Travel North, ☎8971 9999.
Katherine Gorge Scenic Flights ex Katherine, Travel North, ☎8971 9999.
Mataranka Day Tours ex Katherine, Travel North, ☎8971 9999.

Outlying Attractions
Nitmiluk Katherine Gorge National Park

The main entrance to the park is 32km (20 miles) from Katherine on a sealed road. A second park entrance leads to Edith Falls, north-west of the Gorge.

The 180,000ha (444,600 acres) National Park was created to preserve one of the Northern Territory's greatest natural wonders. Over millions of years, torrential summer rains in Arnhem Land during the west season, have caused the waters of the Katherine River to cut thirteen spectacular serpentine gorges. During the dry season, the gorges are placid and calm, but in the wet season they can change into turbulent floodwaters with whirlpools and waves over 2m high.

Cut into ancient rock, the canyon walls climb steeply above cool blue water, and there is abundant bird, fish and animal life, including the fresh water crocodile. The rocks also have excellent examples of ancient Aboriginal art. Privately operated guided boat tours are available to the fifth gorge, or it is possible to hire canoes. A boat tour in the gorges is a highlight of any trip to the Northern Territory, and even if you have seen photographs or films of the scenery, you are still not prepared for the outstanding beauty nor the atmosphere that prevails. Facilities in the Park include a Visitor Centre, picnic and barbecue areas, toilets and a public boat ramp, where boats up to 4m with motors up to 10hp may be launched. No cats or dogs are permitted in the privately owned caravan and camping ground, and dogs are only permitted in the National Park on controlled leads.

There are over 100km (62 miles) of marked walking tracks maintained for easy access to interesting features in the Park. If you intend to do the longer hikes, you must notify the Park Rangers first, and all walkers should collect a guide pamphlet available from the Visitor Centre.

It also should be noted that when taking one of the boat tours, there is some walking involved between gorges. Between the first and second - approximately 500m of well formed pathway and rocks; between second and third - approximately 20m of unformed pathway and rocks; between third and fourth - approximately 1km of unformed pathway, rocks and some climbing; between fourth and fifth - approximately 600m of unformed pathway, rocks and some climbing. The distances vary for canoeists. It is strongly recommended that you wear comfortable, flat, walking shoes.

Cutta Cutta Caves Nature Park

Situated 27km (17 miles) south of Katherine on the *Stuart Highway*, the caves were formed millions of years ago, and are still developing today. They are about 15m (49 ft) below the earth's surface, and spread for almost a kilometre. The landscape surrounding the caves is unique and provides a short and interesting walk. Ranger guided tours are available ☉daily April to October, usually on the hour, ☎*8972 1940*. Entrance underground is available only at these times.

Local tour operators in Katherine also have tours available to the caves.

Edith Falls Nature Park

The second entrance to Katherine Gorge National Park is 74km (46 miles) north of Katherine, via the *Stuart Highway*, and a sealed access road that turns off 47km (29 miles) from the town.

Edith Falls is a series of waterfalls on the edge of the Arnhem Land escarpment. The main waterfall runs all year into a huge natural billabong surrounded by pandanus palms. There are walking tracks,

swimming, barbecue and picnic areas, and a camping ground with simple amenities.

Mataranka

Mataranka is 110km (68 miles) south of Katherine on the *Stuart Highway*, in the heart of Never-Never country. The **Mataranka Pool Nature Park** was dedicated as a reserve in 1967 to ensure the preservation of the thermal spring in its environs. The pool is a constant 34C (93F) and flows at an amazing 22.5 million litres (4,949,406 gallons) each day. A swim in the pool is an experience that should not be missed. The surrounding rainforest survives from an earlier age, and feeds from the thermal spring's deep source. Combined with the thermal pool, it creates a very welcome oasis that is a popular spot for visitors.

Mataranka Homestead was established in 1916 by Dr Gilruth, the Administrator of the Northern Territory as an experimental cattle station. It has since become a major tourist resort, and among its attractions is the **Elsey Homestead Replica**, a faithful copy of the original hand-hewn timber homestead, which contains many interesting displays, and is open to the public.

Elsey Station was established in 1881 and the lease encompassed Mataranka, then known as *Bitter Springs*. Aeneas Gunn was appointed manager of the Station in 1901, and assumed the position in 1902. The following year he contracted malaria and died. His wife, Jeannie, managed the station for a short time, then returned to Melbourne and wrote her story *We of the Never Never*. The

Homestead Replica was used for the set of the film of the book.

Near the homestead are Aboriginal gunyahs, constructed by the 'Duck Creek' people. A free homestead tour is conducted daily ☉May-October, departing from the kiosk at the Mataranka Homestead Tourist Resort, ☎*8975 4544*.

The **Elsey Cemetery,** containing the graves of the Station pioneers, including Aeneas Gunn, Muluka, and Henry Peckham (Fizzer) the mailman is 8km (5 miles) east of the Stuart Highway, 13km (8 miles) south of the town.

↩ **Let's Stay Here**
Mataranka Homestead, *Homestead Rd, Mataranka,* ☎*8975 4544* Located just about 9km from town, just right next to Esley National Park and metres away from the thermal springs. Offers basic accommodation in a homestead that was established in 1916. Offers mainly two bed dorms. Facilities includes laundry and kitchen. There is also a licensed bar, restaurant and shop on the premises. *Dorms ✪$17; double $36*

Larrimah

Gateway to the tropics, Larrimah is 72km (45 miles) south of Mataranka. The township originated in World War II when over 3,000 servicemen were based in and around Larrimah, then the largest army base in Australia. The **Gorrie airstrip** and railsiding still remain, but are no longer in use. One of the pubs was originally an officers' mess. Larrimah Green Tourist Complex on the *Stuart*

Highway, ☎8975 9937, have live Johnson River crocodiles on display.

Daly Waters

The small township of Daly Waters is 72km (45 miles) south of Larrimah on the *Stuart Highway*, and is home to the oldest pub in the Territory - the **Daly Waters Pub**, ☎8975 9927. The pub is virtually an institution, and you really can't say you have seen the Territory if you haven't spent some time in the bar.

Victoria River

On the *Victoria Highway*, 190km (118 miles) west of Katherine, is the township of Victoria River. The river itself was discovered in 1839 by Lt John Lort Stokes aboard the British Navy sloop Beagle. The town now has a privately owned motel and camping ground servicing the nearby **Gregory National Park**.

Pine Creek

Pine Creek is situated 92km (57 miles) north of Katherine on the *Stuart Highway*. It was the scene of extensive mining in the 1880s, and is now experiencing a renewal of interest with the reopening of mining activities. In fact, it now hosts one of the biggest gold mines in the Territory. The population of the town is around 600, and there are numerous historical buildings still standing, including the **Old Playford Club Hotel**, the **Repeater Station**, **the Bakery** and the **Railway Siding Complex**. Private tour operators conduct tours of the surrounding area. For more information contact the **Pine Creek Hotel** on ☎8976 1288.

Umbrawarra Gorge Nature Park

The Park is 122km (76 miles) from Katherine, and 22km (13 miles) south-west of Pine Creek. The gorge is very rugged, but has pools quite close to the car park. There is a camping ground, picnic facilities, wood barbecues and toilets.

Alice Springs

Population 28,000
Alice Springs is situated in the geographic centre of the Australian continent, 23km (14 miles) south of the Tropic of Capricorn, and at the foot of the picturesque MacDonnell Ranges.

Climate

Average temperatures: January max 36C (97F) - min 21C (70F); July max 20C (68F) - min 4C (39F). In summer the temperatures can reach up to 42C (107F), but the humidity is always low. The town is 610m (2001 ft) above sea level.

Characteristics

The Northern Territory's most famous, and second largest town, The Alice is a place to visit in its own right, but equally, it is a good base from which to explore the wonders of The Centre. The spectacular MacDonnell Ranges stretch for 150km (93 miles) to both the east and west of Alice Springs, and contain many beautiful and unusual chasms and gorges.

How to Get There
By Air

Alice Springs is 15km (9 miles) south of the airport. There is an Airport Shuttle Service which meets every incoming and outgoing flight, and picks up and drops off from all city accommodation places. **Virgin Blue**, ☎13 67 89 and **Qantas Link**, ☎13 13 13 flies to Alice Springs on a regular basis.

By Bus

Coach companies which travel Australia wide and have depots in Alice Springs are **Greyhound Pioneer and McCaffertys.**

By Rail

The Ghan travels from Sydney and Melbourne to Adelaide and Alice Springs, ☎13 21 47.

Visitor Information

The Central Australian Tourism Industry Association is in *Gregory Terrace*, ☎(08) 8952 5199 or ☎(08) 8952 5800. The regional office of the Northern Territory Tourist Commission is at *67 Stuart Highway North*, ☎(08) 8951 8555.

Additionally, you can phone ☎13 3068 for general information, email ✉nttc@nttc.com.au or visit ▣www.alice.com.au

---

🔖 Let's Stay Here

A wide variety of budget accommodation is available here and the Tourist Centre has a complete list. Here is a selection which should be used as a guide only. The telephone area code is 08.

Alice Lodge,
4 Mueller St, ☎*8953 1975 or 1800 351 925*
▣*www.bpf.com.au/alice_ lodge_backpackers.htm*
Located in the quiet suburban area. The town centre is five minutes walk with

Crocodile Hotel - Jabiru

Tennant Creek Signpost

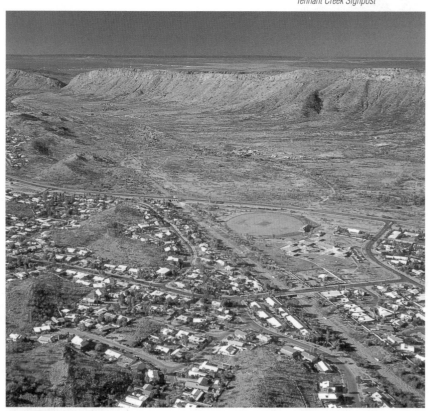

Alics Springs

supermarket/liquor store just two minutes away. Homestyle comfort offering basic accommodation, air conditioned. The double rooms are in caravans. Features a swimming pool, TV room, laundry, internet access and a small kitchen. Bike hire available. Bus and train pickups. *Dorms ✪$20 - 4 share, $18 - 10 share; single $38; double/twin $48* (price includes breakfast)

Annie's Place,
Traeger Ave, ☎8952 1545 Built around a cosy courtyard with a swimming pool and a great atmosphere. All rooms have air conditioning, heating, en suite bathroom and a portable TV. There is also a licensed bar and restaurant which serve good value meals. Internet access in also available. **Recommended.** *Dorms ✪$16; double $55*

Elke's Backpackers Resort,
39 Gap Rd, ☎8952 8134 or 1800 633 354, 🖳www.*elkes.com.au* Located south of town, situated close to all facilities in Alice Springs. Formerly built as a motel. All rooms are self-contained with en suite, TV, bathroom and a small kitchen with free tea, coffee and hot chocolate. The only backpackers place in Alice Springs to offer air conditioning and heating in every room. Very friendly staff. Facilities includes a swimming pool, volleyball court, bicycle and scooter hire. They also offer a shuttle service around town. Free pick ups and drop

offs to the airport, train or bus station. Parking available. *Dorms ✪$12-18 ; double/twin $45-50; triples $50-56* (prices includes breakfast)

Melanka Lodge Backpackers,
94 Todd St, ☎8952 1322 or 1800 815 066, 🖳www.*melanka.com.au* Located on the edge of the city centre, the largest hostel in town and boasts of about 500 rooms. Not the greatest in facilities, but there's a lot

of them. Facilities includes two swimming pool, beach volleyball court, bike hire, laundry, internet access, small kitchen and TV lounge. There is also a pizza bar and grill, a licensed restaurant and a bar with nightly entertainment on the premises which serves good value meals. Quite popular with tourists which livens the place a little. Offers airport pick-up and railway and bus transfers. Ample

Alice Springs

Accommodation
❶ Annie's Place
❷ Elke's Backpacker Resort
❸ Melanka Lodge Backpackers
❹ Pioneer YHA Hostel
❺ Toddy's

off-street parking. *Dorms ✪$17; single $48 ; double $50*

Ossie's Hostel,
Corner Lindsay Ave and Warburton St, ☎*1800 628 211* ▰www.ossies.com.au Located north-west of town. A nice and quaint hostel which is kept clean and tidy. Features a swimming pool and barbecue area outside, and internet and a pool table inside the lounge. *Dorms ✪$16; single/double $40*

Pioneer YHA Hostel,
Corner Leichardt and Parsons Sts, ☎*8952 8855* ▰www.yha.com.au Winner of the 2000 Northern Territory Brogle Tourism Award. Built around the walls of a heritage-classified outdoor movie theatre. Best located hostel in town. Close to the shops, cafes and pubs. Facilities includes a TV lounge, kitchen, laundry, internet, swimming pool, barbecue and a nice recreational area outside. Bikes are hireable. They also organise tours and travel packages. *Members dorms 8 share ✪$19 ($22.50 non-members); dorms 4 share $22 ($25.50 non-members) BC MC JCB VA EFTPOS*

Toddy's,
41 Gap Rd, ☎*8952 1322 or 1800 027 027* Located at the south of the town centre. A well equipped hostel with an open-air bar, barbecue area and a feel good atmosphere. They also serve and all-you-can-eat barbecue every night for ✪$8.50 that starts from

7pm and there is a licensed bar on the premises. Features a swimming pool, kitchen, TV lounge and pool tables. Bikes are hireable. Off street parking available. *Dorms from ✪$14 ($18 with en suite bathroom) ; double/twin $46 ($59 for Motel styled rooms with en suite bathrooms)* (prices includes free breakfast)

Caravan Parks
Alice Springs Heritage Caravan Park, *Lot 8483 Ragonesi Rd,* ☎*8952 3135* (Pet's allowed on leash) 72 sites. Includes laundry facilities and barbecue area. There's also an on site shop. *Powered site ✪$24; unpowered $18; on site van from $41*

Gap View Hotel, *115 Gap Rd,* ☎*8952 3069* About 150 camping sites. Located about a kilometre from the shops and very close to the Gap. Has your normal amenities, bathrooms and laundry. Other facilities includes a gazebo like barbecue area, little kitchenette, two pools, spa and a tennis court. At the hotel is also a bottle shop and a bar and kitchen. *Camping and non powered sites from ✪$10pp*

G'Day Mate Tourist Park, *Palm Circuit,* ☎*8952 9589.* (No dogs allowed) 86 sites, excellent facilities, pool - *powered sites ✪$20-22 for two, on-site vans $50-55 for two, from cabins $55 for two.*

Heavitree Gap Outback Lodge, *Palm Cct,* ☎*8950*

4444 (No pets allowed) 190 sites. Includes laundry facilities, swimming pool, barbecue area, on site shop and petrol station. Meal available. *Powered sites ✪$18.40; unpowered site $16.40*

Jim Cotterill's Wayside Inn, *South Stuart Hwy,* ☎*8956 0808.* Twenty four sites and camping grounds. Amenities includes showers and bathrooms and swimming pools for a price. On site is also a bar, kiosk, restaurant and fuel stop. *Powered sites ✪$17; camping $7; cabins $15*

MacDonnell Range Holiday Park, *Palm Place,* ☎*8952 6111.* (No pets allowed) 273 sites, excellent facilities, barbecue, pool playground - *powered sites ✪$23 for two, cabins from $55 for two.*

Stuart Caravan Park, *Larapinta Drive,* ☎*8952 2547.* (No dogs allowed)150 sites, barbecue, pool - *powered sites ✪$21 for two, cabins from $50 for two.*

Tilmouth Well, *PMB 3, Tanami Hwy (via Alice Springs),* ☎*8956 8777* Located about 187 kilometers out of Alice Springs. Your normal amenities plus a barbecue area, swimming pool, golf course and a conference room with a TV and some games. There is also an on site restaurant, bar and an art gallery showing Aboriginal art. *Camping ✪$7pp; additional $7 for* *powered and non powered sites pp; cabins single $50; double $32.50pp*

Wintersun Cabin and Caravan Park, *Stuart Highway*, ☎ *8952 4080*. (No pets allowed) 105 sites, pool - *powered sites* ✪ *$20 for two, cabins $45-90 for two.*

Camping

There are quite a few over-night camping sites in the Centre. For information and pamphlets contact the Parks and Wildlife Commission of the Northern Territory, South Stuart Highway, ☎8951 8211.

The sites are: **Henbury Meteorite Craters, Kings Canyon, Chambers Pillar, Trephina Gorge, Ellery Creek Big Hole, Ormiston Gorge, Finke Gorge, Corroboree Rock, N'Dhala Gorge, Ruby Gap, Serpentine Gorge, Redbank Nature Park and Rainbow Valley.**
Camping in the Centre is not your ordinary overnight campout, and several precautions have to be taken as regards water, petrol, tyres, clothing, and the risks of fire. The Commission can advise on all these aspects, and their advice should not be ignored.

Local Transport

All major car rental companies are represented in Alice, and there are plenty of taxis.

Bicycles can be hired from Melanka Lodge, ☎ *8952 2233*, and mopeds from Shell Todd, cnr Todd Mall and Wills Terrace, ☎ *8952 2279*.

The Alice Wanderer operates on an hourly circuit visiting the major attractions, and is an explorer-type service. For bookings and enquiries ☎ *8952 2111*.

Let's Eat

As with accommodation, Alice has a wide variety of eating places, ranging from takeaways and coffee shops along Todd Mall and in the Yeperenye Shopping Complex on Hartley Street.

Bojangles Saloon and Restaurant, *80 Todd Street*, ☎ *8952 2873*.

Golden Inn Chinese Restaurant, *9 Undoolya Road*, ☎ *8952 6910* - licensed, Cantonese, Szechuan, Malaysian - ⏱open Mon-Fri noon-2pm, 5-10.30pm, Sat-Sun 5-10.30pm.

Keller's, *Diplomat Hotel, Shop 1, Gregory Terrace*, ☎ *8952 3188* - Swiss and Indian cuisine - take away available.

La Casalinga, *105 Gregory Terrace*, ☎ *8952 4508* - licensed, Italian and pizza bar - ⏱open seven days, restaurant 6-10pm, pizza bar 5pm-1am.

The Overlanders Steakhouse, *72 Hartley Street*, ☎ *8952 2159* - licensed, Australian food including buffalo, camel and kangaroo steaks - ⏱open seven nights from 6pm, and weekdays for lunch.

The Palms Restaurant at Alice Springs Pacific Resort, *34 Stott Terrace*, ☎ *8951 4545* - licensed, a la carte menu, ⏱open nightly from 6.30pm.

KFC, Red Rooster, Hungry Jacks, Long John Silvers have all found their way to the Alice, and counter lunches can be obtained at the

Stuart Arms Bistro in Todd Mall.

Entertainment

The famous **Ted Egan Outback Show**, with tall tales and outback songs, is presented ⏱Tues, Thurs, Sat and Sun at 8pm at the Chateau Hornsby Winery, *Petrick Road*. Bookings are essential, ☎ *8952 9952*. Ted is almost an Alice Springs legend, and his show is top entertainment. If you notice that many people are singing along with him, it is because they are part of coach tours that have been listening to tapes of his songs all the way to the Alice. Dinner is available from 6pm.

Lasseters Hotel Casino, *93 Barrett Drive*, ☎ *8950 7777*, has poker machines and keno from 1pm and gaming tables from 7pm, and is ⏱open till very late. Dress regulations apply - no cords or jeans for men or women, and men must wear dress shoes.

Rio's Nitespot, at the Casino, has a disco from 9.30pm on Thurs-Sat. **Simpsons Gap Bar** in the Sheraton Hotel has live entertainment from 8.30pm, Mon-Sat.

Heavitree Gap Tavern, at the Heavitree Gap Tourist Resort, *off Ross Highway*, ☎ *8950 4413,* has a disco Fri-Sat 9pm-2am, and live entertainment from 4pm Sun.

Alice Springs Gapview Resort, *115 Gap Road*, ☎ *8952 6611*, has a disco ⏱Wed-Sun 9.30pm-2am.

Araluen Arts Centre, *Larapinta Drive*, ☎ *8951 1120*, has live theatre and films, and on the first Saturday of every month there is a cabaret in the Bistro.

Points of Interest

Your first stop should be **Anzac Hill** which offers a good view of the town and the surrounding ranges. Sunset and sunrise are the best times for photographers, as the hills glow with colour. You can walk up via the Lions walk, opposite the Catholic Church on Wills Terrace.

Adelaide House Museum, *Todd Mall*, was built by the Australian Inland Mission 1920-1926 as the first Alice Springs Hospital, and was designed by Rev John Flynn. It is ☉open to the public Mon-Fri 10am-4pm, Sat 10am-noon (closed December to February). Admission is ✪$3.30 adult.

Flynn Memorial Church, *Todd Mall*, was built in memory of the late Reverend John Flynn, founder of the Royal Flying Doctor Service and Australian Inland Missions.

Museum of Central Australia is in the Alice Springs Cultural Precinct on Larapinta Drive. Displays include the Fine Art and Natural History of this arid region. ☉open daily 9am-5pm, ☎8951 1122. Admission is ✪$7 adult and $4 concession for the Cultural Precinct, which includes the Aviation Museum.

The **Central Australian Aviation Museum** is housed in the Connellan Hangar on Alice Springs' original airport in Memorial Drive. It is ☉open Mon-Fri 9am-4pm, Sat-Sun 10am-2pm, ☎8951 1122.

The **Old Court House**, *cnr Parsons and Hartley Streets*, was built originally as the Administrator's Council Rooms and as the Mining Wardens Court. It can only be viewed from the outside.

The Residency, on the *corner of Parsons and Hartley Streets*, was built in 1926-27 for John Charles Cawood, the first Government Resident in Alice Springs. It is now owned and operated by the Museums and Art Galleries Board of the Northern Territory, and is ☉open daily 9am-5pm, ☎8951 5688. Admission is free.

Old Stuart Town Gaol, *Parsons Street*, was built in 1907-8, and is the oldest building remaining in the Alice Springs town area. The Gaol is ☉open Mon-Fri 10am-12.30pm, Sat 9.30-noon.

Old Hartley Street School was opened at the end of 1929, and the octagonal room was added in 1946. The School is now the office and shop of the National Trust Australia (NT). It is ☉open daily from 10.30am-2.30pm.

The **Panorama Guth**, in *65 Hartley Street,* is a 360 degree painted landscape, and should not be missed. It is ☉open Mon-Sat 9am-5pm, Sun 12-5pm, ☎8952 2013. Admission is ✪$5.50 adult.

Old Tunk's Store, *cnr Hartley Street and Stott Terrace*, was built as a grocery and general store about 1940, and was used as such until 1980. It is now the town office of Hertz NT.

The **Old Government Homes**, further along *Hartley Street*, were designed for senior Government officers in the 1930s.

Royal Flying Doctor Base was funded by the women of South Australia as a centenary memorial to the pioneer women of the State. The late Harry Rolland, a government architect, designed the radio building and operators' quarters. The base is ☉open Mon-Sat 9am-4pm, Sun 1-4pm, ☎8952 1129. Admission is ✪$5.50 adult.

Gnoilya (Wild Dog) Tmerga is a registered sacred site in a chained-off enclosure in the Stuart Transit Plaza. Known as *Wild Dog Rock*, it tells the story of an Aboriginal Legend.

The above attractions, and more, are included in a Heritage Walk that has been organised, and the Tourist Offices have all the details.

The **Telegraph Station**, the original Alice Springs communication post, is 3km north on the Stuart Highway. It features the original building and equipment in an historic reserve, and is a pleasant picnic spot. ☉open daily 8am-5pm, with entry ✪$6 adult.

School of The Air, *Head Street* next to Braitling School, is ☉open for visitors Mon-Fri 1.30-3.30pm. It is closed weekends, public holidays, for school activities and during the Christmas vacation. Admission is ✪$3.50 adult, and it is ☉open Mon-Sat 8.30am-4.30pm, Sun 1.30pm-4.30pm.

Olive Pink Flora Reserve, Tunks Road Golf Course Causeway, has a large variety of native shrubs and trees from a 300km (186 miles) radius of Alice Springs, and an excellent information centre. ☉open daily 10am-4pm, ☎8952 2154.

The **Kookaburra Memorial**, next to the **Aviation Museum** is open during the same hours.

Alice Springs Memorial Cemetery is the final resting place of many pioneers and famous personalities, including Albert Namatjira, Harold Lasseter of the elusive 'Lasseter's Reef', and E.J. Connellan, founder of Connellan Airways, the Territory's first airline.

Diarama Village, on Larapinta Drive, depicts myths and legends of the Australian Aborigines, and also has a good selection of arts and crafts. ☺open daily 10am-5pm, ☎8952 1884.

The **Date Gardens**, *Palm Circuit*, is Australia's first commercial date garden. It is ☺open Mon-Sat 9am-5pm, Sun 10am-4pm, ☎8952 8493.

Frontier Camel Tours, *Ross Highway*, ☎8953 0444, is a camel museum, and offers camel rides. It is ☺open daily 9am-5pm, and is one of the most popular attractions in Alice.

Alice Springs Reptile Centre, *9 Stuart Terrace*, has a large collection of Central Australian reptiles. It is ☺open daily 9am-5pm, ☎8952 8900. Admission is ✪$7 adult, and the centre is ☺open daily 9am-5pm.

Alice Springs Desert Park, Larapinta Drive, ☎8951 8788, showcases a selection of the flora and fauna which are part of the desert landscape. The Nocturnal House is excellent. The award-winning attraction is ☺open 7.30am-6pm daily and admission is ✪$18 adult.

The **Old Timers' Folk Museum**, south on the *Stuart Highway*, has exhibits dating back to the 1890s. It is ☺open daily 2-4pm, ☎8952 2844, with admission prices at ✪$2 adult.

The Ghan Preservation Society, 5km south of Alice in *Norris Bell Avenue*, is ☺open daily, but train rides are only available Wed, Thurs, Fri and Sun, ☎8955 5047. The museum charges admission at ✪$5.50 adult.

Chateau Hornsby, *Petrick Road, off South Stuart Highway*, ☎8955 5133, is 15km (9 miles) from the heart of Alice Springs, and is Central Australia's first and only winery. Tours are available, as are barbecue lunches, and

there is a restaurant. It is ☺open daily 10am-5pm between March and December.

Festivals

The **Bangtail Muster** is held on the first Monday in May, which is a public holiday in the Northern Territory. There is a parade of floats and a sort of Mini-Moomba. It is a great day for the kids.

The **Camel Cup** is held on the second Saturday in May, and is organised by the local Lions Club. This camel race has been held every year since 1971.

The **Food and Wine Festival** is held the day after the Camel Cup on the Lawns of the Verdi Club, *Undoolya Road*, beginning at 11am. There is a great deal of entertainment, with live music throughout the day. **Wynn's Finke Desert Race** - Alice-Finke-Alice, is held over the Queen's Birthday weekend in June. Finke is 240km (149 miles) south of Alice Springs, and the competitors and pit crews camp out in cold temperatures overnight at Finke, then the race recommences next morning for the trip back to Alice.

Alice Springs Rodeo is held in August/September, and cowboys and cowgirls from all over Australia compete for top prize money.

Henley-On-Todd is held in September, and is an incredible event. The ingredients for its success are: a dry river bed, bottomless boats, and plenty of human horse-power. The regatta begins with a parade of the different craft down Todd Mall, then the races start at 9.30am in the Todd River next to the Anzac Oval.

Beerfest is held the day after

Henley-On-Todd at the Verdi Club. It begins at 11.30am, with entertainment throughout the day, 40 different varieties of beer, and lots of food of different nationalities.

Facilities
Lawn bowls, golf, squash, swimming, tennis, indoor cricket and horse racing.

Tours
There are many tour companies in Alice Springs offering tours in and around the town by coach, plane, helicopter, camel or horse. The Tourist Centre has a complete list, and can advise on the best tour to suit your requirements.

Outlying Attractions
The Parks and Wildlife Commission of the Northern Territory offer Ranger guided tours and talks available at the parks around Alice Springs. For information on these very interesting tours contact the Commission, ☎8951 8788, or the Alice Springs Regional Tourist Association.

West of Alice
John Flynn's Grave Historical Reserve
7km (4 miles) west of Alice Springs on *Larapinta Drive*, there is a stone cairn which contains the ashes of Reverend John Flynn, the founder of the Australian Inland Mission, The Royal Flying Doctor Service, the first inland medical centre, and an outback padre patrol system. The cairn is crowned by a large boulder from the Devil's Marbles. The reserve has no facilities.

Simpsons Gap National Park
The Park is located in the West MacDonnell Ranges, 18km (11

Rock hole in the East Macs

Fannie Bay with Pandanus

Florence Falls

Glen Helen Gorge

miles) from Alice Springs, and is one of the largest parks in Central Australia. Access is via Larapinta Drive, then a signposted turnoff into the Park, and is suitable for conventional vehicles. The Park actually commences only 8km (5 miles) from Alice, but the Visitor Centre is a further 10km (6 miles) into the Park, and there is always a Ranger on site. The centre has a display illustrating aspects of the natural history of the area, toilets and a parking area. 5km (3 miles) further into the park there is a developed picnic area. The Park is ⊙open daily 8am-8pm, and is accessible year round, with the cooler months from April to September being the most pleasant. During summer, the high temperatures make bushwalking uncomfortable. The best times to observe the native wildlife are early morning and late afternoon. There are numerous opportunities for bushwalking, and while most walks are not marked, there are natural landmarks that offer adequate guidance.

⌐┐ Let's Stay Here

Glen Resort,
Namitjira Dr, ☎ *8956 7489 or 1800 896 110,* ▣www.melanka.com.au/ melanka_glenhelen/ gh_index.html This large complex offers prices that range from your very expensive down to your average dorms room prices. Backpackers stay in Stockman's Quarters with accommodation in four, six and eight bed dormsitories. Licensed bar and restaurant also on the premises. *Dorms ✪ $20; single/twin/double $55*

Standley Chasm

The Chasm is a steep cleft in the MacDonnell Ranges, and is about 50km (31 miles) west of Alice. The reserve is ⊙open daily 8.30am-4.30pm, and has a kiosk, barbecues and toilets. The entrance fee is minimal, and the Chasm is a photographer's delight when the sun is overhead and lights up the red walls.

Ellery Creek Big Hole Nature Park

93km (58 miles) west of Alice Springs on *Namitjira Drive* is another gorge with high red cliffs and a large waterhole with shady River Red Gums. There are picnic facilities and toilets.

Serpentine Gorge Nature Park

This gorge is 104km (65 miles) to the west, and is narrow and winding with waterholes and bush scenery. The entry road is a bit rough, and there are barbecue and toilet facilities.

Ormiston Gorge and Pound National Park

Pound National Park is the largest park in the Western MacDonnell Ranges, and its most popular feature is **Ormiston Gorge**, the catchment area of the Finke River, thought to be the oldest river in the world. The Gorge has a near-permanent waterhole at its southern end.

Access to the Park is suitable for conventional vehicles, although periods of heavy rainfall can cut the roads due to flooding. Up-to-date information on road conditions are available by phoning Road Reports on ☎ *1800 246 199.*

The park has picnic facilities for day visitors, including gas barbecues and toilets. The small general campground is suitable for tents, campervans and caravans. The other campground caters for large groups and coach tours. Both campgrounds have barbecues, toilets and showers, but all visitors are advised to bring their own drinking water.

There is a Visitor Information Centre in the Park, and they can advise on all the bush walks available.

Glen Helen Gorge Nature Park

Glen Helen Gorge is 133km (83 miles) from Alice Springs, and has been formed by the Finke River cutting through the MacDonnell Ranges. There is a 30m (98 ft) deep waterhole, which the Aborigines believed was the home of the Giant Watersnake. Next door to the Park is the **Glen Helen Homstead**, ☎ *8956 7489,* which offers accommodation, a caravan park and barbecue facilities.

Redbank Nature Park

Redbank Gorge is 30km (19 miles) west of Glen Helen, and there are several very deep and cold pools along its 800m (875 yds) length. As with the other gorges, the scenery is magnificent, and there are picnic facilities.

Hermannsburg

The historic buildings of Hermannsburg are 123km (76 miles) south-west of Alice Springs on *Larapinta Drive.* It was established as a mission by the Lutheran Church, and is now owned by the Aranda People who are restoring the old buildings with the help of the National Trust. The **Kata-anga**

Tearooms are ⊕open daily 9am-1pm, and Aboriginal artefacts are available.

Finke Gorge National Park

The Park covers 46,000ha (113,620 acres), including the famous **Palm Valley**. The Park is best known for its population of the rare palm *Livistona mariae* or *Red Cabbage Palm*. These 3000 or so palms have survived here for at least 10,000 years, and are unique to the area.

The Park is 16km (10 miles) south of Hermannsburg, and 138km (86 miles) from Alice Springs.

⤴ Let's Stay Here

Kings Canyon YHA,
Ernest Giles Rd, Watarka National Park, ☎ *8956 7442 or 1800 817 622,* 🖳*www.voyages.com.au/ desination_KC_accom.cfm* Features a wide variety of accommodation with air conditioned and heated rooms. This YHA offers a lot of facilities. This includes internet, TV, fridge, tea and coffee making facilities, wardrobes or lockers, tables and chairs, kitchen (cooking utensils available for hire at $5 for two people), swimming pool, and barbecue area. Service station with general store, cafe, restaurant and bar are also on site. Bikes are hireable. Parking available. Be warned that this is probably the highest priced dorms you'll see. *Members dorms* ✪*$38 ($43 non members)*; *BC MC JCB VA EFPTOS*

South of Alice
Rainbow Valley Nature Park

The park's main attraction is seen at its best in later afternoon, when the setting sun shines directly onto a stark range of richly-coloured sandstones. There are picnic facilities, and 4WD is recommended. The Park is 101km (63 miles) south of Alice Springs, turning off the *Stuart Highway* at 85km (53 miles).

Henbury Meteorites Conservation Reserve

Located 145km (90 miles) south-west of Alice Springs, the Park can be reached in conventional vehicles, and is accessible year round.

The Reserve contains twelve craters which were formed when a meteor hit the earth's surface at the main crater, 4700 years ago. The meteor disintegrated before impact, and the fragments formed the twelve craters. They are of interest to scientists due to their similarity to the moon's surface.

There is no drinking water in the area, and very little firewood, so visitors should take their own. Facilities include wood barbecues, picnic furniture, a pit toilet and self guiding walking tracks.

Watarrka National Park

This park contains the western end of the George Gill Range, which includes the scenically splendid Kings Canyon, attractive rockholes and areas of lush vegetation. The Canyon features a plateau of rock domes, and sandstone walls rising up 100m, covered with rock carvings formed by the erosive action of wind and water.

The park is about 310km (193 miles) south-west of Alice

Springs, and is accessible by conventional vehicles. Facilities include parking areas, toilets, showers and barbecues. **Wallara Ranch,** near the junction of *Angus Downs* and *Ernest Giles Road*, has accommodation, food and fuel.

Ewaninga Rock Carvings Conservation Reserve

The Reserve is 39km (24 miles) down the *Old South Road* from Alice Springs, and the carvings are thought to predate the Aborigines who reside in the area now, as they have no knowledge of their origin or meaning. There are barbecues, toilets and explanatory signs.

Chambers Pillar Historical Reserve

This impressive sandstone pillar was used as a landmark by early pioneers, and many tales of hardship have been carved in the base. It is 149km (93 miles) south of Alice on the *Old South Road*, and access is by 4WD only.

East of Alice
Emily and Jessie Gap Nature Park

These are two gaps in the Mac-Donnell Ranges, 13km and 18km (8 and 11 miles) respectively, east of Alice Springs. They are very scenic and have great significance to the Aborigines. There are barbecue and toilet facilities.

Corroboree Rock Conservation Reserve

Another scenic pillar of rock which is significant to Aborigines is 48km (30 miles) east of Alice Springs, and has barbecue and toilet facilities.

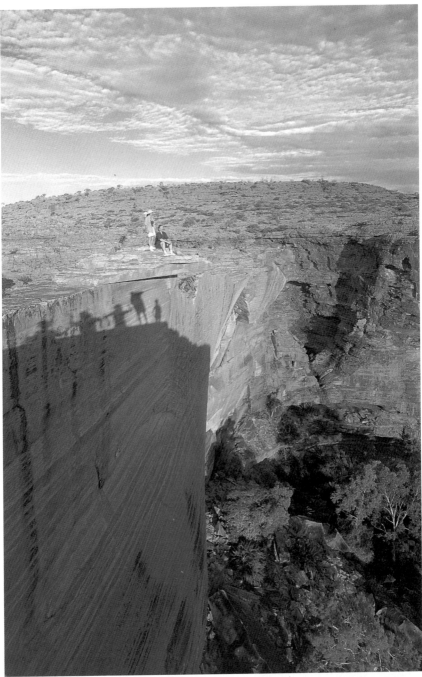

Kings Canyon

Trephina Gorge Nature Park

Situated in the East MacDonnell Ranges, Trephina Gorge Nature Park is noted for its sheer quartzite cliffs and River Red Gum lined watercourses. There are two gorges in the park - **Trephina Gorge**, with its wide views and sandy creek bed, and **John Hayes Rock Hole**, which attracts many animals and birds.

The Park is 85km (53 miles) east of Alice Springs, and is accessible to all vehicles, although the John Hayes Rockhole track is recommended only for vehicles with a high ground clearance, as there are a number of rough crossings.

There are three picnic areas, each with toilet facilities, wood barbecues and picnic benches. Camping areas are located at Trephina Bluff and Trephina Gorge, where water is provided.

Ross River Homestead

Originally the *Love's Creek Station*, this is now a ranch style resort, and is 88km (55 miles) east of Alice, and 15km (9 miles) east of Trephina Gorge. All facilities are available, including fuel.

N'Dhala Gorge Nature Park

Access to this park is 4WD recommended, and it is 98km (61 miles) east of Alice Springs. The scenery is magnificent, and there are ancient Aboriginal rock carvings. The park has barbecue and toilet facilities.

Arltunga Historical Reserve

Alluvial gold was discovered in a dry creek bed downstream from **Paddy's Rockhole** in 1887, and at one time the area supported 3000 people. Mining activity in the area continued for 30 years.

Now you can explore the ruins of a number of stone buildings, some of which have been largely restored.

The Reserve is 110km (68 miles) east of Alice Springs, and can be reached and explored in conventional vehicles. There is a small interpretive visitor display and toilet block near the entrance, and picnic facilities are located at the **Historic Mine Walks** parking area and at the **Great Western Mine** parking area. Toilets and a picnic area are also provided at the Police Station/Kangaroo Well parking area. There are Rangers on duty in the Park. For more information phone ☎ *8956 9661*.

Ruby Gap Nature Park

Access to this park is by 4WD only, and there are no facilities, just beautiful gorges along the Hale River.

Western Australia

Perth

Population 1,400,000
Perth, the Capital City of Western Australia, is situated on the banks of the Swan River in the south-west corner of Australia.

Climate
Perth is the sunniest of all Australian cities, averaging eight hours of sunshine a day. It boasts a superb climate with an average summer day temperature of 30C (86F), which is tempered by the arrival of an afternoon breeze called the **Fremantle Doctor**, and an average night temperature of 17C (63F). The average winter day temperature is a mild 18C (64F), and the night is 9C (48F). February is the hottest month, and July the coldest. The annual rainfall averages 974mm (38 ins). The wettest months are May-August, but half the number of days during this period are sunny and clear. The driest months are November-February, when it seldom rains.

Characteristics
The city of Perth nestles by a kilometre-wide expanse of the Swan River which spreads out like a lake or harbour, edged by expensive suburbs and white sand beaches. It was known as the city of millionaires before the 1,987 Stock Market crash, and still is a place of energetic growth and vigorous youth. It is a well planned city with an efficient freeway system, yet within

walking distance of the city centre is Kings Park, a native bushland with gum trees and wildflowers, commanding magnificent views of the city and the Swan River.

How to Get There
By Air
Perth International Airport, in Baker Road, is serviced by many airlines including **Air New Zealand, British Airways, Cathay Pacific, Malaysian Airlines System, Qantas, Singapore Airlines and Thai Airways International.** For information phone ☎*(08) 9478 8888*, send an email to ✉per@perthairport.net.au or survey the website ▣www.perth airport.com

Domestic flights from other capital cities are by **Qantas** and **Virgin Blue**. The journey from the airport to the central business district takes approximately twenty minutes, and an airport hotel bus service operates between both passenger terminals and hotels and motels.

By Bus
Greyhound Pioneer operate services from/to other State Capitals.

By Rail
The **Indian Pacific** operates between Sydney and Perth.

Visitor Infomation
The Western Australian Tourism Commission operates the Perth Visitor Centre located in Albert Facey House, *cnr Forrest Place* and *Wellington Street*, ☎*1300 361 351*. You can plan many aspects of your holiday using the website at ▣www.westernaustr alia.net and request advice and

further information by email at ✉travel@tourism.wa.gov.au

The headquarters of the **Royal Automobile Club** of Western Australiva are at *228 Adelaide Terrace, Perth*, ☎*9421 4444*. See the website at ▣www.rac.com.au. The RAC of WA service facilities are available to members of the RAC in other States.

There are many tours of Perth and surrounding attractions, operated by companies like **Kings Tours**, ☎*9321 2288*, and **Great Western Tours**, ☎*9490 2455*. The Visitor Centres have brochures and can organise bookings.

⤷ Let's Stay Here
Perth has a range of excellent hostels, motels and other accommodation. As with most cities, accommodation is usually cheaper in the suburbs, and the Visitor Infomation Office has a complete list of accommodation available. Here we have a selection of budget accommdation with prices that should be used as a guide only. The caravan parks we mention are, as is usual, in the suburbs. The telephone area code is 08.

City Centre and Northbridge
12:01,
East, 195 Hay St, ☎*9221 1666 or 1800 001201*, ▣ *www.touch88.com.au/ ✉east1201* Your average hostel with a really cool basement area and pool table. Located somewhat close to the city. Fully air conditioned rooms. Laundry and kitchen with full, modern facilities. Internet access on site. They'll

also help you find work. They meet all the buses, the Indian Pacific and will pick up from the airport (by arrangement). Their internet site has a jukebox that you can listen music in. *Dorm ✪$15; single $38; double $48*

Aberdeen Lodge,
79-81 Aberdeen St, Northbridge ☎*9227 6137* Old looking and worn. There's a pleasant garden at the front though, perfect to relax. Rooms have fans and there's an open fire place. *Dorm ✪$15 ; single $30 ; double/ twin $38*

Adelphi Hotel,
130 Mounts Bay Rd, ☎*9322 4666* An apartment complex with self contained units. Well suited for those working in Perth. All room are en suite bathroom, kitchenette, TV and are fully air conditioned. Downstairs is a bar with pool tables, TV lounge and internet access. *Double ✪$55*

Backpackers International,
110 Aberdeen St, Northbridge ☎*9227 9977* Located at the centre of Northbridge. New reception and common areas. Basic facilities includes a big kitchen, big common room, cable TV and games room. Parking available. *Dorm ✪$11.50; twin $40; double with en suite $50*

Beaty Lodge,
235 Vincent St, West Perth, ☎*9227 1521*, ▣ *www.beattylod ge.com.au* Located a fair half hours away from the city cen-

Perth

Accommodation

1 12:01 East
2 Aberdeen Lodge
3 Backpackers International
4 Billabong Backpackers Resort
5 Britannia International YHA
6 Cheviot Lodge
7 Club Red Backpackers
8 City and Surf Backpackers
9 Coolibah Lodge
10 Exclusive Backpackers
11 Globe Backpackers
12 Governor Robinson's
13 Grand Central Backpackers
14 Hay Street Backpackers
15 Lonestar City Backpackers
16 Mad Cat Backpackers
17 Murray Street Hostel
18 Shiralee Backpackers
19 Spinner's Backpackers
20 Townsend Lodge
21 Underground Backpackers
22 Witch's Hat

METRES
0   300   600

tre opposite the Beatty Park swimming pool and not far from the local shops. A quiet place with facilities which are fairly standard except for the room especially designated for reading. It lacks a kitchen which is somewhat unusual for a hostel, but the cheap cafeteria next door makes up for it. Features a TV room on each floor and a games room. Outside is also a swimming pool in the courtyard. Popular with international students and caters a lot to groups. They serve meals on the premises. You need to leave a deposit for the keys and some other facilities. Note that there is definitely no smoking or drinking allowed on the premises. *Dorm ✪$33; double/twin $46.20; triple $59.40*

Billabong Backpackers Resort,

381 Beaufort St, Northbridge, ☎9328 7720, ▦www.billa bongresort.com.au Voted Four Stars by AAA Tourism for quality accommodation. Quite a modern and big place with exceptional facilities. All rooms have en suite and balconies. Upper levels go up in prices. The extensive facilities includes the ever rare gym, games room with loads of distractions like ping-pong, pool table, foosball, and air hockey. There are several TV rooms and book exchange. Quite popular with international students especially those learning English and other courses next door. *Dorm ✪$18 - 8 share, $19 - 6 share, $20 - 4 share; double/twin $27.50 pp; triple $26 pp;*

Britannia International YHA,

253 William St, Northbridge, ☎9328 6121, ▦www.yha.co m.au Fantastic location being at the heart of the Northbridge district. Only minutes away from Perth central and the bus and train depot. Rooms have secured lockers in them. Minimal facilities though with a fully equipped kitchen, laundry, TV lounge and internet access. There are also lifts and a courtyard with barbecue area. Staff would love to help you with your tours. A shuttle is also available to and from the airport which will drop you off at Northbridge YHA. *Members dorm from ✪$17 ($20.50 non members); single $28.50; double $59 BC MC VA EFTPOS*

Cheviot Lodge,

30 Bulwer St, East Perth, ☎9227 6817, ▦www.chevio tlodge.com Huge old house with basic accommodation. Facilities includes a kitchen, TV lounge with cable and large garden. They also host weekend BBQs. Plenty of parking. *Dorm ✪$12 ; single $30; double/twin $40* (price includes breakfast and internet access)

Club Red Backpackers,

494 Newcastle St, West Perth, ☎9227 9969 or 1800 679 969, ▦www.redbackpackers. com.au Five Stars winner of the Western Australia Tourism Council. Located quite a distance from town, but still within the transit zones. This hostel fits the 'small but good' category. Nice atmosphere. Reputable as a party hostel, and good for those who work.

Fans on all rooms. Facilities includes a laundry, kitchen and there's a bar outside with a pool table. Outside is a cool barbecue area and tables, cable TV, swimming pool. Shop on site. Offers a lot of freebies including first 15 mins free internet on arrival, tea/coffee/ hot chocolate, help and advice with tax file numbers and finding work, maps, night club passes with free drinks and meals and loads of entertainment with guitar nights and karaoke. They also offer free airport/bus/train/metro pick-up. Recommended. *Dorm ✪$18; double/twin $22*

City and Surf Backpackers,

41 Money Street, ☎9227 1234, ▦www.backpacker. com.au/Perth.htm Located not so far from town in a tree filled street. Small with rooms that opens into the courtyard. Facilities includes a kitchen, laundry and TV room. *Dorm ✪$16.50 ; single $38.50 ; double $44*

Coolibah Lodge,

194 Brisbane St, Northbridge, ☎9328 9958, ▦www.cooliba hlodge.com.au Located at the northern end of Northbridge. Bars and cafes are still only about a 10 minute walking distance. They have good facilities including two kitchens, two TV lounges, internet access and a courtyard with barbecue area. Parking available. *Dorm ✪$18; single $36 ; double $50; deluxe room with fridge $53*

Exclusive Backpackers,

158 Adelaide Terrace, ☎9221

9991, ■ *www.exclusivebackpac kers.com* Located further east of town close to the Swan River. Their double rooms have TVs. Facilities includes clean kitchen and dining. They have a balcony that overlooks the street. Parking available. *Dorm* ✪*$17; single $30; double with en suite $48*

Globe Backpackers,

501 Wellington St, ☎ *93214080,* ■ *www.globeb ackpackers.com.au* Quite a large hostel and very good value on the pockets. Rooms have lockers in them. Facilities includes several kitchens, TV lounges and cheap internet access. Parking is also available. *Dorm from* ✪*$18.80; single $35; double $48 (prices includes breakfast)*

Governor Robinsons,

7 Robinson Ave, Northbridge, ☎ *9328 3200,* ■ *www.gov robinsons.com.au* Located on the northern side of Northbridge and built around two colonial character cottages. Quiet and set in a beautiful old building that has hard wood polished floors and stained glass giving it plenty of character. Facilities includes a small fully equipped kitchen, big laundry and some really nice courtyards. They also offer internet access. **Recommended.** *Dorm* ✪*$18 ; double/ twin $50; double with en suite $60*

Grand Central Backpackers,

379 Wellington St, ☎ *9421 1123* Located right at the main shopping area and very close to the train station. Ba-

sic accommodation. Rooms have fans in them. Facilities includes a big commercial kitchen, cable TV and internet access. *Dorm* ✪*$18; single $31; twin $46; double $50*

Hay Street Backpackers,

266 Hay St, ☎ *9221 9880* Quite a good hostel located further east of town. Spacious rooms. Facilities includes a swimming pool and barbecue area outdoors, internet access, TV room, and laundry. Parking available. *Dorm* ✪*$20 ($18 if you stay longer); double $45 ($55 with en suite bathroom)*

Lonestar City Backpackers,

17-21 Palmerston St Northbridge, ☎ *9328 6667 or 1800 247 444* Located a stone's throw away from the city. Fans and fridge in all rooms. Facilities includes kitchen, laundry, TV, ping-pong table and internet access. *Dorm* ✪*$14; double/twin $22*

Mad Cat Backpackers,

55-63 Stirling St, Northbridge, ☎ *9228 4966,* ■ *www.madcatbackpackers.com .au* Located very nicely in town, close to the city and the train station. Quite a good atmosphere built within an old building. Facilities includes a kitchen with a mismatch of old ovens and a fridge, cable TV (also one upstairs for videos) and a games room. There's free rice, tea and coffee. Parking available. *Dorm* ✪*$12 - 11 share, $14 - 4 to 8 share ; single $25 ; double/ twin $40*

Murray Street Hostel,

119 Murray St, ☎ *9325 7627,* ■ *www.murrayst.com* Old but located really nicely within the town district. Quite popular with Asian travellers. Facilities includes a kitchen, laundry, TV lounge and a reading room. Offers some freebies including some tea and coffee, free email (10:00am -10:00pm), Sunday BBQs, and night club passes. *Dorm* ✪*$16.50 ; single/twin $38 ; double $43*

Rainbow Lodge,

133 Sumers St, East Perth, ☎ *9227 1818,* ■ *www.rainb owlodge.com.au* Colourful in nature, located close to East Perth Station. Facilities includes two kitchens, pool table, ping-pong and laundry. There is free internet access (8am-8pm) and coffee and toast. Parking available. *Dorm* ✪*$15; single $30 ; double/twin $24*

Shiralee Backpackers,

107 Brisbane St, Northbridge, ☎ *9227 7448,* ■ *www.shiralee.com.au* Located about a 10 minute walk to the city centre, just north of the city. Close to pubs, cafes and restaurants. Built within an old federation styled house. Features your standard kitchen, laundry, TV lounge and air conditioning. Ask for a parking permit. *Dorm* ✪*$17.50 ; single $35; double/twin $46*

Spinner's Backpackers, *342 Newcastle St, Northbridge,* ☎ *9328 9468,* ■ *www.ic-net.com.au/~spinners*

Located close to Russell Square, northwest of town. A fair distance from town but achievable. The friendliness of the staff enhances their basic facilities. Features a big kitchen, TV lounge with a pool table, internet and barbecue area. Parking available. *Dorm* ☉*$17; double $44*

Townsend Lodge,

240 Adelaide Terrace, ☎*9325 4143,* 🖥*www.tow nsend.wa.edu.au* Located almost south of town. Townsend Lodge caters for a wide variety of needs from temporary students in Perth, to business people that want to save some money on normally expensive accommodation. All the rooms are single which is perfect for those seeking a little more privacy. Facilities includes a laundry, internet access, cable TV and a good games room with pool table, arcade games and even a piano. Very popular with international students which gives it a more institutional atmosphere than your average hostel. *Dorm* ☉*$35*

Underground Backpackers,

268 Newcastle St, Northbridge, ☎*9228 3755 or 1800 033 089,* 🖥*www.undergrou ndbackpackers.com* Located on the northern part of town, only three minutes from the heart of Perth and close to the station. Rooms have air conditioning and heating. Doubles includes luxuries such as a fridge and television as well as a DVD player. Units and dorms have secure lockers in them. Quite a good hostel with facilities including

a big clean kitchen, laundry, TV lounge with home theatre and video library and even a swimming pool. There is also an internet access and a licensed bar with pool table on site. The common areas are located downstairs. Airport Shuttle stops outside. *Dorm from* ☉*$19-22 ; single/ double/twin $58 ($31pp with fridge/TV/DVD)* (complimentary continental breakfast)

Witch's Hat,

148 Palmerston St, Northbridge, ☎*9228 4228 or 1800 818 148,* 🖥*www.witchs-hat.com* One of the few hostel that is tastefully decorated with polished floorboards set in an stunning old building. It's no question why this is one of the best hostels in town. Facilities includes a big kitchen, a lounge with internet access, TV and nice barbecue area outdoors with picnic tables. Parking available. **Recommended.** *Dorm* ☉*$22; three $24 ; double $62; twin $53*

Caravan Parks
Perth Holiday Park, *91 Benara Road, Caversham,* ☎*9279 6700.* (No pets allowed)141 sites, swimming pool, barbecue - *powered sites* ☉*$20-23 for two.*

Perth International Tourist Park, *186 Hale Rd,* ☎*9453 6677.* (No pets allowed) 82 sites, barbecue - *powered sites* ☉*$22-27 for two.*

Coogee Beach Holiday Park, *Coogee Beach Reserve* ☎*9418 1810.* (No dogs allowed) - 186 sites, *powered*

sites ☉*$20 for two, no on-site vans.*

Fremantle Village, *cnr Cockburn and Rollinson Roads,* ☎*9430 4866.* (No pets allowed) - 142 sites, *powered sites* ☉*$22 for two, en-suite sites $27 for two.*

Local Transport
Bus
Buses are operated by **Transperth**: ☎*13 6213,* look up 🖥*www. transperth.wa.gov.au,* or email ✉transperth@transport.wa.gov.a u. The city and its surrounds are divided into 8 zones radiating out from Perth city. A standard fare within Zone 1 costs ☉$1.80 and the journey must be completed within 2 hours of purchase. Fast Cards are available to save travellers money depending on their needs. For comparison, the Multi Rider covers ten journeys within Zone 1 for ☉$15.30, a Day Rider allows unlimited travel for one day for ☉$7.10, and the Maxi Rider offers discounts for a family or group on a return journey.

Free Transit Zone/City Clippers
Within a clearly defined inner City Zone you will be able to travel on all buses free of charge, as part of the Central Area Transit System. The city **CATS** are a modern, efficient bus service with electronic displays at each stop and regular, satellite-updated announcements of when you can expect the next bus to roll by.

The Red CAT ☉leaves every 5 minutes, Mon-Fri, 6.50am-6.20pm, and travels along *Wellington Street, Milligan Street,* and *Emerald Terrace.* It runs in both a clockwise and anti-clockwise direction, and includes *Murray Street, Emerald Terrace*, and *Outram Street* and a shortened circuit on weekends between 10am and 6.15pm (every 45 minutes).

The Blue CAT ⊕leaves every 8 minutes, Mon-Fri, 6.50am-6.20pm, travelling from a terminus in the Barrack St Jetty via *William Street, The Esplanade*, and *Aberdeen Street* to *Northbridge Street*.

A **Fremantle CAT** is also in operation ⊕every 10 minutes Mon-Fri from 7am–7pm.

Subiaco buses 2, 3, 4 and 6 ⊕depart outside Newspaper House alighting Harvest Terrace. For details, ☎*13 6213*.

Train

Suburban trains operate from Perth to the areas of Fremantle, Midland and Armadale. Suburban trains leave from Perth Train Station, *Wellington Street*, interstate trains leave from East Perth Train Station. Westrail Travel Centre is located at East Perth Station. For all information relating to buses, ferries and trains, including time-tables and route maps, see the Transperth website at the address:
🖳*www. transperth.wa.gov.au*

Taxi

Taxis operate all hours and the illuminated sign on the roof tells that they are vacant. All cabs have meters which display the fare, and there is an extra charge for baggage. There are taxi ranks through Perth Central Business District, or they can be ordered by phone. The main taxi operator is **Swan Taxis**, ☎*13 1330*.

Car

A rental car is a convenient way of sightseeing and is relatively inexpensive for a group or family. Daily rate for a late model small car is approximately ❷\$30-35 plus fuel. Here are some names and addresses:

Bayswater Car Rental, 160 Adelaide Terrace, ☎9325 1000; Geddes, 36A Geddes Street, Victoria Park, ☎361 7388; Apex, 400 William Street, Northbridge, ☎9227 9091; Ace Rent A Car, 311 Hay Street, Perth, ☎9221 1333.

Let's Eat

Perth has a reputation for its remarkable variety of BYO and licensed restaurants. The eating places vary from coffee shops and bistros to luxury class restaurants. Whatever your fancy, you have a tempting range of dishes from Europe, Asia, India, Mexico and Lebanon, as well as delicious local seafood and vegetarian dishes. There are also a number of restaurants that offer panoramic views of the city and the Swan River. Fremantle has a large variety of restaurants from side-walk cafes on South Terrace to top class dining. Be sure to try the fresh seafood for which Fremantle is famous. Here are some names and addresses.

El Mambo Citadel Restaurant, *283 William Street,* ☎*9227 5338*.

Gavino Restaurant, *375 Hay St, Subiaco,* ☎*9381 1323*.

Grand Palace Chinese Restaurant, *3rd Floor, 14 The Esplanade,* Perth, ☎*9325 2344* .

Hayashi Japanese Restaurant, *107 Pier St, Perth,* ☎*9325 6009*.
Hilite 33 Restaurant, *Lvl 33/ 44 St Georges Tce,* ☎*9220 8333*.

Mamma Maria's, *Cnr Aberdeen and Lake Sts, Northbridge,* ☎*9227 9828*.

Picnicks Garden Restaurant, *78- 82 Outram St, West Perth,* ☎*9481 6619*.

Royal India Restaurant, *1134 Hay Street, West Perth,* ☎*9324 1368*.

South Sea Chinese Restaurant, *388 Fitzgerald St, North Perth,* ☎*9227 8822*.

The Essex Restaurant, *20 Essex St, Fremantle,* ☎*9335 5725*.

The New Shima Japanese Restaurant, *409 Murray St, Perth,* ☎*9321 1668*.

McDonald's is well represented, with many in the city including *572-576 Hay Street,* ☎*9325 2451;* and one in Fremantle, *Mews Road,* ☎*9430 4308*.

Entertainment

Twenty years ago visitors to WA might have been forgiven for concluding that the state was somewhat lacking when it came to top-class entertainment. However, that view changed dramatically with the construction of the **Perth Concert Hall** and the **Perth Entertainment Centre**, the refurbishing of the famous old **His Majesty's Theatre**, the growth of taverns, restaurants, cinemas and discos, the revitalising of hotels, and the emergence of **Northbridge** as a centre of Perth's night life. And, of course, there is the **Burswood Casino**.

The **Concert Hall** is the home of the **WA Symphony Orchestra**, as well as being a venue for concerts and performances by visiting artists. Perth Entertainment Centre has a seating capacity for 8000 people, and is a venue for circuses, rock bands, musical productions, ballroom dancing championships, classical concerts and ice shows.

His Majesty's Theatre is the residence of the **WA Opera Company**, the **WA Ballet Company** and the **WA Arts Orchestra.** Drama productions are also staged from time to time at several suburban venues and tertiary institution theatres.

The Burswood Resort Casino, *Great Eastern Highway,* ☎ *9362 7777,* is set in 100ha (247 acres) of rolling parklands which include an 18-hole golf course. Burswood overlooks the **Swan River** and dominates the eastern approaches to the city. Apart from the glamour of the casino complex, there's the luxury of a 413 room 5-star hotel, a Las Vegas-style theatre showroom, 20,000 seat indoor stadium called the **Superdome** and a host of recreational facilities. ☉The action in the Casino continues non-stop 24 hours a day, except Christmas, Good Friday and Anzac Day. Covering 6968 sq m (75,000 sq ft) on a single level, Burswood has 111 gaming tables, 540 video gaming machines and a 240 seat Keno lounge.

The city is also served by many cinemas:

Hoyts, City Arcade, *Hay Street Mall,* ☎ *9325 2377.*

Cinecentre 1, 2 and 3, *Murray Street, east of Barrack Street,* ☎ *9325 2844.*

Piccadilly, Piccadilly Arcade, *Hay Street Mall,* ☎ *9322 3577.*

Jaws Cinema, *Hay Street,* ☎ *9225 6144.*

Ace Cinemas, *Adelaide Terrace,* ☎ *9425 5522.*

Programmes and session times will be found in the daily newspapers. There are also a number of suburban cinemas that show first-run movies, and several drive-ins.

Shopping

☉Normal shopping hours in Perth are 8.30am-5.30pm, Mon-Fri, 8.30am-noon Sat, with many shops staying open Thursday evening until 9pm. There are many big shopping centres in the suburbs these days, but Perth city centre has retained its attraction because of the variety of shops. It is the fashion centre of the State, and has particular appeal for the young.

Department Stores

There are two main department stores in Perth -

Aherns is situated between *Murray* and *Hay Streets,* about 50m west of *Barrack Street.*

Myers is between *Wellington* and *Murray Street*s, with one side adjoining *Forrest Place.* Standing on the site where **Boans Department Store** once stood, the new Myer building is architecturally impressive. Overhead walkways are linked to several of Perth's arcades and to the modern Perth Train Station, which in turn is linked to the city's cultural centre.

The Malls

Hay Street, between *William* and *Barrack Streets*, has always been regarded as the very heart of Perth shopping. Before the 1970s, it was probably the most congested section of roadway in WA. Narrow, with parking allowed on both sides of the street, buses, service vehicles and general through-traffic battled for position. That all changed when Hay Street between *William* and *Barrack Streets* was made into a pedestrian mall. Murray Street, between **William** and **Barrack Streets**, was also declared a mall. **Murray Street Mall** flows into **Forrest Place** and the Myer terraces, and is linked to the Hay Street Mall by numerous arcades. The whole effect is to create a pleasant, roomy, traffic-free shopping precinct.

The Arcades

The arcades, while still functioning as 'short cuts' and providing shelter from the rain in winter and the heat in summer, are very attractive. They are often multi-level, twist and turn along their length, interconnect with other arcades and buildings, open out on to small plazas or covered-in areas where shoppers can pause for a breather, go underground, and, in one case, lead on to an overpass that takes shoppers across the busy street below. Shopping arcades are still frequently associated with cinemas, but many of Perth's newest office blocks and luxury hotels have incorporated their own shopping arcades.

London Court

Leading off the Mall, not far from *Barrack Street,* and connecting the Mall with St George's Terrace, is a piece of Olde England known as London Court. Built in Tudor style, carved woodwork, wrought ironwork, hanging signs, paved roadway and medieval towers at each end, help to create the atmosphere.

The clock facing the Hay Street

Mall is an exact replica of the dial of Westminster's Big Ben. Each quarter hour four knights on horseback joust above the clock face in **St George's Terrace**. London Court is a photographer's delight, and is also a drawcard for tourists because of the number of shops catering especially for them.

If you are in the market for a truly Australian souvenir, or work of art, pay a visit to **Creative Native**, *32 King Street, Perth*, ☎*9322 3398*. This gallery offers Aboriginal art, in particular work from the Nyoongah people. Examples of the best artwork are on offer to the discerning collector, ranging from the traditional, carved emu eggs, boomerangs, pottery, jewellery and much more - on to the more contemporary. The gallery has an exclusive artist, Tjyllyungoo, and his work is in great demand.

Points of Interest

The Town Hall, on the corner of *Hay* and *Barrack Streets*, was built by convict labour between 1867 and 1870, in the style of an English Jacobean market hall. It seems that the convicts left their mark on the clock tower of the building, for the windows are shaped like broad arrows. Nearby in Barrack Street, a tablet set into the footpath commemorates the founding of Perth in 1829.

The alignment of *Murray Street* and *Victoria Square* appears on the earliest map of Perth, dated 1833. By the late nineteenth century, many government buildings had been located in *Murray Street* east of *Pier Street*, while buildings of the **Roman Catholic Church** were established in the Victoria Square vicinity. Along *Murray Street* a

large number of these historic buildings remain today, and though built in the late 19th and early 20th centuries, are classified by the National Trust of WA:

The Government Printing Office was originally the site of a home for destitute women, and was acquired for a printing office in 1870.

Government Stores Building was completed in 1911, and was originally occupied by the Treasury Department. Its style was designed to harmonise with other buildings of this period in Murray Street. The nearby **Salvation Army Fortress** was officially opened in 1930.

The Health Department building was completed in 1912, and is believed to be one of the last buildings in Perth to use Donnybrook sandstone for a whole facade.

Young Australia League Building foundation stone was laid by William Morris Hughes, the Prime Minister of Australia, in 1922.

Perth No 1 City Fire Station Building was completed in 1900, and became the headquarters of the Perth City Fire Brigade after it moved from the Town Hall on January 1, 1901.

Kirkman House, constructed in 1909, was used for many years as housing for nurses of the Royal Perth Hospital.

The **Moreton Bay Fig Tree** in front of the house was planted about 1900 and has been placed on the National Trust's Register of Significant Trees.

Royal Perth Hospital Administrative Building was built in 1894.

Colonial Hospital, behind the present Royal Perth Hospital staff

canteen, east of the hospital's administrative building, was constructed with convict labour and was occupied in July 1855.

St Mary's Cathedral stands on the high ground set aside on the first town plan of Perth as **'Church Square'**, known now as Victoria Square. The western part of the Cathedral was built in 1863-5 with bricks made from local clay.

The **Convent of Mercy,** often referred to as the Mother House, was constructed in 1873, and has been used by the Sisters of Mercy ever since.

Convent of Mercy Chapel dates from 1924. The apse contains excellent painted figures copied from a medieval fresco.

Roman Catholic Presbytery, Church Offices and Grounds. The original Bishop's Palace on this site was erected by the Benedictine Brothers in 1859.

Mercedes School House was constructed of limestone during the Gold Rush period in 1895. It was originally used as a convent school house.

Along *St Georges Terrace* is the **Pro-Cathedral of St John the Evangelist** was built between 1844 and 1846 of brick with a shingle roof.

Government House, St George's Terrace, opposite *Pier Street,* is the official residence of the Governor of Western Australia, and was built between 1859 and 1864. It is constructed in a romantic style with Gothic arches and turrets reminiscent of the Tower of London.

Old Court House, in the middle of Supreme Court Gardens, was erected between 1836 and 1837. It is one of the earliest surviving buildings in the city. During the 19th century it served as church, school, immigration depot, supreme court house and store. It stood close to the original river foreshore.

Old Perth Boys' School, on the south side of St George's Terrace, between *Mill and William Streets*, was completed in 1854. It was built of sandstone which was ferried up the Swan River from Rocky Bay by convict labour.

The Cloisters, St George's Terrace, opposite *Mill Street*. Bishop Hale's collegiate school for boys was opened here in 1858. The building has decorative brickwork, and the exterior was renovated in 1871-72. The **Port Macquarie fig tree**, on the east side of the Cloisters, is known to be over 100 years old.

Parliament House is on St George's Terrace not far along from the Cloisters. When Parliament is sitting there are ⏱conducted tours of the House Mon-Fri 10am, 11am, 1pm and 2pm.

Horseshoe Bridge, in *William Street*, between *Wellington* and *Roe Streets*, was built in 1903, replacing a level crossing. Take note of the lamp pillars decorated with swans.

The Police Courts, *Beaufort Street*, between Roe and James Streets, were completed in 1905 by the Public Works Department under the direction of their Chief Architect, J.H. Grainger, father of composer Percy Grainger.

The Art Gallery of Western Australia in the **Perth Cultural Centre**, **James Street Mall**, displays traditional and contemporary paintings, prints, drawings, sculpture and bark paintings. ⏱Open Mon-Sun 10am-5pm, public holidays 10am-5pm, Anzac Day 1-5pm, ☎*9492 6600*.

Aboriginal Art and Craft Gallery is a gallery specialising in the art of Western Australia's Indigineous people. ⏱Open 9-5.30pm daily, it is located on *Fraser Avenue, King's Park*, ☎*9481 7082*.

Alexander Library, *40 James Street*, ☎*9427 3111*, is a reference library and also carries major interstate and overseas newspapers.

The Battye Library of Western Australian History forms part of the library. ⏱Open Mon and Fri 9am-5.30pm, Tues-Thurs 9am-9.45pm, Sat Sun 2-5.30pm, ☎*9427 3111*.

The Old Gaol, in the museum complex in *Francis Street*, is perhaps one of the best examples of colonial architecture in the State. Built in 1856, it served as Perth's original prison until 1888. Many public executions took place in the grounds. Today it has been extensively restored, and in rooms which once housed prisoners, there is an old fashioned dental surgery and pharmacy and many mementoes of Perth's early days.

The Western Australian Museum (entrance in Francis Street) possesses a Marine Gallery containing a 25m blue whale skeleton; an Aboriginal Gallery; a superb collection of veteran and vintage cars; the skeleton of Albert the Dinosaur; and the 11-tonne Mundrabilla meteorite.

The Railway Station, *Wellington Street*, now known as the Perth Train Station, was built between 1893 and 1894, replacing an earlier station built when the railway was opened in 1881. The front of the station has been renovated, and the structure behind extensively remodelled, with walkways connecting it to Myers and the Perth Cultural Centre.

Other museums in and around Perth are:

Army Museum, *cnr Lord and Bulwer Streets, East Perth*, ☎9335 2077

Aviation Museum, *Bull Creek Drive, Bull Creek*, ☎9311 4470 - ⏱open Thurs-Tues 11am-4pm.

World of Energy, *12 Parry Street, Fremantle*, ☎9430 5655 - ⏱open Tues-Thurs 10.30am-4.30pm, Sat-Sun 1-4.30pm.

Fremantle Museum, in *Finnerty Street*, ☎9430 7966, is a branch of the WA Museum. The lime-stone building, constructed in the 1860s as a lunatic asylum, has been described as one of the finest examples of Colonial Gothic architecture in Australia - ⏱open Mon-Thurs 10.30am 5pm, Fri-Sun 1-5pm.

Museum of Childhood, Edith Cowan University, *Bay Road, Claremont* ☎9442 1373 - ⏱open Mon-Fri 10am-3pm, Sun 2-5pm.

Rail Transport Museum, *Railway Parade, Bassendean*, ☎9279 7189 - ⏱open Sun and public holidays 1-5pm, and Wed during school holidays 1-4pm.

Rockingham Museum, *Rocking -ham Road, Rockingham* ☎9592 3455

Telecommunications Museum, *Wireless Hill, off Canning Highway, Melville*, ☎9364 7067 - ⏱open Sat-Sun 2-5pm.

Suburban Attractions

Underwater World, in the *Hillarys Boat Harbour*, Sorrento, has a moving walkway through a tunnel in a large aquarium, and you can come face to face with sharks, rays, octopus and a variety of fish life. There is also a theatre, cafe and bar facilities. ⏱Open daily, 9am-5pm, ☎9447 5888.

The Swan Brewery, *Canning Vale,* offers free guided tours Mon-Wed at 10am, with beer tasting included. There is a gift shop with a range of souvenirs and clothing. Bookings are essential, ☎9350 0650.

The Maze, *Sequola Park, Neaves Road, Bullsbrook,* has not only a maze, but also mini golf, animals and barbecue facilities. Open Wed-Sun and through the school holidays, 9.30am-5pm, ☎9571 1375.

Beatty Park Leisure Centre, *Vincent Street, North Perth,* is open all year with the water heated to 27C (81F) in the winter. ⏱Open daily 5.30am-8pm, ☎9273 6080.

Cottesloe Civic Centre, *109 Broome Street, Cottesloe,* is a Spanish-style mansion with probably the best gardens in Perth. The grounds are open all hours, and the centre by arrangement, ☎9384 1566.

The Old Mill, at the southern end of the Narrows Bridge, was Perth's first flour mill, built in 1835. It has been faithfully restored and contains relics of pioneer days.

Parks and Gardens
Bold Park and **Perry Lakes**, at **Floreat Park,** a short drive from the city, is a large expanse of bushland for enjoyable bushwalks and barbecues. Perry Lakes adds to the scenic beauty. A marvellous view of suburban Perth and the coastline is available from **Reabold Hill**.

Hyde Park has superb lawns and gardens. The huge trees are at their best in autumn, and many species of wildfowl congregate on

an island in the ornamental lake. The **Hyde Park festival** is held annually, and thousands of people come to see the arts and crafts, sample ethnic foods, and see live performances.

Kings Park, overlooks the city and is only five minutes away. It is 404ha (998 acres) of bushland, and the pride of Perth, with its scenic drives, and displays of wildflowers. Attractions include playgrounds, a botanical garden, lookouts, nature trails, bushwalks, a restaurant and barbecue areas.

Lake Monger is a favourite picnic spot with shady trees and green lawns. Many varieties of birdlife are seen here, including black swans and wild ducks.

Queens Gardens, *cnr of Hay* and *Plain Streets,* is a peaceful park with splendid gardens incorporating small lakes and bridges. There is also a statue of Peter Pan which is very popular with the children.

The River Foreshore, between the Causeway (Herrison Island) and the old Swan Brewery building, is within easy reach of the city, and includes the Swan River ferries' jetty and the parks and miniature lakes associated with the beautification of the Narrows Interchange.

Supreme Court Gardens, *cnr Barrack Street* and *St George's Terrace,* include the Stirling Gardens, and are a very popular lunch spot with city workers. The **Perth Music Shell** is in these gardens, and many outdoor concerts are held here during the summer.

Wireless Hill Park, *off Canning Highway, Melville.* The area was originally set aside for the use of OTC. In 1969 it was vested in the City of Melville as an A class

reserve. Rich in native flora, it also has the Telecommunications Museum.

⛱ Beaches
Perth's beaches are within easy reach of the city by Transperth buses (enquiries ☎221 1211), and the service that runs from Fremantle Bus/Train Interchange along the coast to Warwick Bus Station.

🚌 Ocean Beaches
City Beach - bus no 84 from outside Raines Square in Wellington Street terminates at the beach. Return by bus no. 81.
Cottesloe - bus no 72 or 103 from Stand 44 in St George's Terrace.
Leighton - bus no. 103 leaves from Stand 42, on the south side of St George's Terrace, corner William Street.

NorthBeach, Waterman, Mullaloo and **Sorrento** -bus no 81 leaves from the Wellington Bus Station. Transfer to bus no 98 at Selby Street and 424 at Stirling Interchange.
Scarborough - bus no 400 depart from the Wellington Street Bus Station.

River Beaches
Crawley Beach - bus no 24 leaves from St George's Terrace. Como Beach - bus no 33 leaves from St George's Terrace.

🛏 Let's Stay Here
Beaches
Mandarin Gardens, *20-28 Wheat-croft St,* ☎9341 5431, 💻*www.mandarinwa.com* Built much like a motel and nestled in a residential area. Located

minutes walk away from the beach. A little old but is clean. Facilities includes a very basic kitchen, swimming pool and fridge belonging to the museum. *Dorm* ✪*$15; single $25; double/twin $35*

Nomads Indigo Lodge,
256 West Coast Highway, Scaborough, ☎ *9245 3388,* 🖳 *www.indigonet.com.au* Good for those who are looking to stay near the beaches just across the road. Facilities includes basic kitchen, laundry and a small lounge area. It has a nice barbecue area outdoors and an internet cafe on site. They also provide for surfboards, guitars and bike hire. There are free BBQs, organised activities, tour advice and employment information. Parking available. *Dorms* ✪*$22; single $36; twin $51; double $59;*

Oceans Beach Backpackers,
1 Eric St, Cottesloe Beach, ☎ *9384 5111,* 🖳 *www.obh.c om.au/backpackers* Being in the beach front makes this a top choice to stay at for anybody. Located right on the North Cottesloe Beach and close to the train station. New and very clean and built around an atmospheric courtyard. Accommodation is with en suite bathrooms, fridge and lockers and most face the ocean. Facilities includes a fully equipped kitchen and a nice lounge area. Cafe on site downstairs. *Dorm* ✪*$19; single $50; double $59*

Sunset Coast Backpackers,
199 Scarborough Beach Rd, ☎ *9245 1161,* 🖳 *www.backpac*

ker.com.au Located about 10 minutes walk to the beach. Offering basic accommodation with facilities including a kitchen and a barbecue area. They offer free internet access. Parking available. *Dorm* ✪*$16.50; single $38.50; double $44*

Diving
The coast offers very good diving from Yanchep to Fremantle, with many off shore wrecks to explore, and beautiful corals and shells to collect. There is also a wide variety of reef fish, and table fish such as breaksea cod, blue groper, kingfish, and dhufish. There are also plenty of rock lobsters, but they may only be taken in season, and you should enquire at the Visitor Infomation Office, or get in touch with Diving Ventures, *384 South Terrace, Fremantle,* ☎ *9430 5130.*

Festivals
The **Festival of Perth** is held in February/March, and has an extensive programme of music, theatre, dance, film, visual arts and outdoor activities.

The **Perth Cup**, Perth's Premier horse race is held each New Year's Day. **West Week** is held the first week in June to celebrate **Foundation Day**.

The **Perth Royal Show** is an 8 day agricultural affair with exhibitions, animals, entertainment, and is held in September. **The International Festival** is held in Northbridge each December.

Facilities
Cricket is a major sport in Perth, and headquarters is at the WACA Ground, Hay Street East (near the Causeway).

Australian Rules is another sport with a strong following, and the local league has eight teams. The West Coast Eagles and Fremantle Dockers represent WA in the Australian competition.

The Showgrounds at Claremont is the place for speedway, with meetings held on Friday nights in the spring and summer.

WA Water Ski Park, St Alban's Road, Baldivis, has four manmade lakes, with three slalom courses and a jump. Lessons are available.

The city also has many golf clubs, cycling tracks, basketball, tennis and squash facilities.

Outlying Attractions
Fremantle
Fremantle is Western Australia's chief port, and is at the mouth of the Swan River, 19km (12 miles) from Perth. It was founded in 1829 by Captain Charles Howe Fremantle, in a ceremony claiming the entire west coast of New Holland in the name of King George IV. Many of the original buildings still standing were built with convict labour, and parts of the city retain their 19th century atmosphere.

Fremantle can be reached from Perth by bus, train, ferry and taxi. One of the best ways to get acquainted with Fremantle is to take a tram tour. ⏰They leave on the hour, 10am-4pm, from the Town Hall, and travel to Victoria Quay, ☎ *9339 8719*, for more information.

The Town Hall in St John's Square, *cnr Adelaide and William Streets*, is an elegant and gracious building officially opened in 1887 as part of Queen Victoria's Jubilee Celebrations. The Visitor Infomation Office is located here, ☎ *9431 7878*.

The **Western Australian Maritime Museum**, *Cliff Street,* has displays dating from the 1600s to the time of British Settlement. They are re-assembling parts of the 1629 Dutch wreck **Batavia**. ⏰Open 10.30am-5pm daily, ☎ *9431 8444.*

Fremantle Port Authority Building, *1 Cliff Street,* ☎ *9430 4911,* has tours to the Observation Tower ⏰at 9.30am, 10.30am, 11.30am, 1.30pm, 2.30pm and 3.30pm daily.

The **Round House**, *Arthur Head (west end of High Street)* was originally a gaol, and is the State's oldest surviving building, having been built in 1831. From the site there is an excellent view of Fremantle. ⏰Open daily 10am-5pm, ☎ *9430 7351.*

Fremantle Railway Station in *Phillimore Street,* opposite *Market Street,* opened in 1907.

There are many other museums, galleries and craft shops, and of course many leftovers from the America's Cup Challenge. The Tourist Bureau has all the details.

Freemantle

Accommodation

1 Backpackers Inn Freo YHA Hostel
2 Cheviot Marina Backpackers
3 Old Firestation Backpackers
4 Pirates
5 Sundancer Backpackers Resort

↳ Let's Stay Here
Backpackers Inn - Freo YHA,

11 Pakenham St, ☎ 9431 7065, ▣ www.perth.world tourism.com.au/Backpac kersInnFreo/ Once a warehouse converted into a hostel. Located very close to the bus and train station and the Rottnest Ferry. Known for the friendly atmosphere. Basic facilities of kitchen, laundry, TV lounge, internet access, pool tables and a courtyard with a barbecue area. Bike hire is also available. *Members dorm ✪$16; single $35; double $44 BC MC VA EFTPOS*

Cheviot Marina Backpackers,

4 Beach St, 9433 2055 or 1800 255 644, ▣ www.me mbers.tripod.com/cheviot lodge Much better than the Cheviot at East Perth. Located near the inner harbour and the Fremantle Park. The double rooms are almost self contained with a fridge, wardrobe, table and chairs. Facilities includes a big kitchen with a walk-in fridge, dining, games room with pool table and video arcades, internet access and a courtyard. Complimentary tea and coffee. Bar is also on site. Parking available. *Dorm ✪$16; single $30; double/twin $45*

Old Firestation Backpackers,

18 Philimore St, ☎ 9430 5454 or 0419 905 055 or 0419 966 066 or 0419 305 454, ▣ www .firestation.fdns.net Very close to the ferry terminal and the

station. Fantastic atmosphere and very popular with working travellers. Facilities are the big common room with a pool table and a TV lounge. There is also a women's only area with a common room. You can get cheap meals next door at the restaurant. Weekly BBQs. They also offer free internet access. **Recommended.** *Dorm ✪$17; double/ twin $44*

Pirates,

11 Essex St, ☎ 9335 6635 A quaint hostel located right at the heart of town. Facilities includes laundry and a barbecue area in the courtyard. There are pizza and wine nights on Thursday and complimentary tea and coffee. *Dorm ✪$17; single $35; double/twin $45*

Sundancer Backpackers Resort,

80 High St, ☎ 1800 061 144, ▣ www.sundancer-resort.com.au Situated smack at the middle of town, close to the station. Great hostel with loads of atmosphere and good facilities. This includes a fully equipped kitchen and dining, laundry, TV lounge, numerous pool tables and barbecue area and a spa close by. *Dorms from ✪$16-20; single $40; double/twin $50*

Rottnest Island

The name means Rats' Nest, and was given to the island by Dutch mariner, William Vlamingh in 1696, as he thought the small rock wallaby (quokka) inhabitants were rats. Rottnest Island is approximately 11km x 5km (7

miles x 3 miles), and is 19km (12 miles) west of Fremantle, 45 minutes by ferry, 15 minutes by air.

Ferry services operate regular services. **Rottnest Ferry Oceanic Cruises** depart from the end of *Barrack Street, Perth, ☎ 9325 1191*. Another service, **Rottnest Ferry Services**, runs from the Hillary's Marina, north of Perth, and sails to Sorrento, ☎ 9246 1039.

Contrary to most people's thinking, Rottnest is not a deserted island. As well as a wide variety of accommodation, there is a restaurant, school, bakery, laundrette, tennis courts, golf course, and many other signs of habitation. Two places worth noting are, the **Rottnest Museum**, ☎ 9372 7353, and the **Rottnest Rail**, ☎ 9372 9752. Both places reflect the history of the island well, one housing convict and shipwreck relics from the past, the other taking you on a trip to see the island as it is today. The most popular pastime is swimming in the clear water with no worries about sharks or rips. Then there is diving, surfing, boating, water skiing and fishing.

↳ Let's Stay Here
Kingstown Barracks YHA,

Kingstown, ☎ 9372 9780, Located very close to the beaches at your leisure and about 20 minutes away from the ferry terminal. One of the islands most historic buildings and institutional in nature. Quite popular with school groups and the only affordable place to stay on the island. Features a kitchen, TV lounge, internet access and a barbecue area. Meals available. Bike hire on the

premises. Also offers a free shuttle bus service.
Members dorm ✪ *$18.20 ($21 non members); family $43.20 ($50 non members)*
BC MC VA EFTPOS

Rockingham

Situated in Cockburn Sound, one of the safest stretches of water in Australia, Rockingham is 47km (29 miles) south of Perth. The two main islands in the area are **Garden** and **Penguin Islands**. The Tourist Centre is at *43 Kent Street,* ☎ *9592 3464,* and is open daily. **Garden Island** was used as a temporary base by Captain Stirling and the first settlers of the Swan River colony, and it is now the site of the naval base, HMAS Stirling. Visitors are not allowed access by the 4km causeway, but they may visit the island by boat between sunrise and sunset, provided they stay outside the fenced naval area. **Penguin Island** is a part-time home for a colony of dainty fairy penguins, one of only two such colonies in Australia. A flat-bottomed ferry operates between the island and the mainland, and the Tourist Centre has details. Other places of interest are the **Rockingham Museum**, ☎ *9592 3455,* the old **Rockingham Heritage Trail,** ☎ *9592 3464,* and the **Rockingham-Jarrahdale Heritage Trail,** ☎ *9592 3464.*

Mandurah

Mandurah is 74km (46 miles) south of Perth, and can be reached along the Coast Road, or from the South West Highway, either way taking about 50 minutes. The Tourist Bureau is at *5 Pinjarra Road,* ☎ *9535 1155.* They have information on the accommodation available in this holiday town, built around the calm protected waters of the Peel Inlet and Harvey Estuary, one of the largest inland waterways in Australia. The area also has 40km (25 miles) of sandy Indian Ocean beaches, so boating, fishing, surfing and windsurfing fans flock to the region. Attractions include: **Ferry cruises; Bavarian Castle and Adventure Playground; Marapana Deer Park; Hall's Cottage; King Carnival Amusement Park,** the greyhound and horseracing tracks; and one of WA's best restaurants, **Doddi's** at *115 Mandurah Terrace,* ☎ *9581 3735.*

Heading North-East
Swan Valley

The rich, alluvial soil of the valley has attracted many farmers, who have turned their attention to grapes, and the area is noted for its range of high quality wines. The smaller vineyards specialise in ports and dessert wines, however many have been replanting with new varieties to produce lighter table wines, which are winning awards, both locally and overseas. The vignerons welcome visitors to their cellars to sample the wines, and details should be obtained from the Tourist Office in Perth before setting out. Midland is the hub of the Shire of Swan, and for over 100 years it has been a busy railway centre, with all trains inland and to the Eastern States passing through the town. Guildford, at the junction of the Swan and Helena Rivers, has many historic buildings that are excellent examples of early Australian town life. Some are small townhouses, which are not open to the public, other public buildings are open for inspection. They include: **Guildford Court House; Rose and Crown Inn; Guildford Gaol; St Matthew's Church; Wesley Chapel and Manse; All Saints Church; Convict Depot Commissariat; Brockman's House;** and **Kinsella's Hotel.**

Armadale

The town of Armadale is about 30km (19 miles) south-east of Perth on the Albany Highway. Attractions include: **Araluen Park; Canning Dam; Churchman's Brook Dam; Wungong Dam; History House; Elizabethan Village,** an authentic period reconstruction with many fine antiques in the buildings; and **Signal Box Arts and Crafts** (which houses the Bert Tyler Vintage Machinery Museum).

The Armadale Visitor Infomation Centre can be found in *Jull Street,* ☎ *(08) 9497 3543.*

Mundaring

On the Great Eastern Highway, 34km (21 miles) east of Perth, Mundaring is the Gateway to the Foothills. The Mundaring Visitor Infomation Centre is in the Old School, *7225 Great Eastern Highway,* and they will advise on the area's attractions, which include: **Mundaring Weir Gallery Arts and Crafts;** the **Hills Forest Discovery Centre; Mundaring Weir;** the **Bibbulmun Track;** and the **C.Y. O'Connor Museum.**

↘ **Let's Stay Here**
Djaril-Mari,
Mundaring Weir Rd, Mundaring, ☎ *9295 1809* Nestled in between Marri and Jarrah forests in the Mundaring National Park. Located close to the scenic Mundaring Weir (Dam). Kangaroos can be spotted at a

daily basis. A cosy atmosphere with wood fire in winter. Fans in all rooms. Camping is also allowed. Facilities includes a kitchen, TV lounge and a barbecue area. Breakfast and light meals available. Bike hire on the premises. Courtesy bus pick up must be arranged before hand. Parking available. *Members dorm ✪$19 ($22.50 non members); single $33 ; double $44; camping $9.90, Cash or cheque on arrival. Credit card accepted for advance bookings.*

Kalamunda

Located in the hills area, Kalamunda is 26km (16 miles) east of Perth. Places to see are: **Kalamunda History Village Museum, Railway Road; Hills Art Gallery, Railway Road; Stirk Park and Cottage, Kalamunda Road;** and **Lesmurdie Falls, Falls Road, Lesmurdie,** in the **Lesmurdie National Park.** Drop into the Visitor Information Centre at *11 Headingly Road,* ☎ *9293 0299.* They are ⏰open 10am-3pm Fri-Sun only.

South-West
Bunbury

Population 28,000
Bunbury lies at the western end of Leschenault Inlet, 185km (115 miles) south of Perth.

Climate

Average temperatures: January max 28C (82F) - min 18C (64F); July max 17C (63F) - min 8C (46F); number of days a year with temperature over 30C (86F) - 30. Average annual rainfall: 882mm (35 ins); wettest six months - May to October.

Characteristics

Bunbury is the major seaport and administrative centre of the South-West region, and the largest centre in Western Australia outside the metropolitan area. It is an expanding regional centre with a wealth of natural and man-made resources. It is surrounded by much of WA's best agricultural land, and the area is also rich in minerals. Ilmenite, rutile and zircon have been discovered in the sands along the coast, and bauxite is found nearby.

Bunbury, however, is primarily a holiday centre, and each year thousands come here to enjoy their holidays. The city is also used as a base to visit many beauty spots of the South-West.

How to Get There
By Rail

Westrail operates a service from Perth Railway Station daily for Bunbury.

By Bus

South West Coachlines operate a Perth to Bunbury and return service daily.

Visitor Infomation

Tourism Bunbury is in *Carmody Place,* ☎ *(08) 9721 7922.* They are open seven days. Go online to ▇*www.*tourismbunbury.com.au or send them an email at welcome@tourismbunbury.com.au. Alternatively, Tourism South West is located at *61 Victoria Street,* ☎ *(08) 9791 9197.*

↱ Let's Stay Here

As mentioned, Bunbury is a popular holiday resort, so there is plenty of accommodation, but it is always a good idea to book ahead in the holiday season. Here is a selection of budget accommodation with prices which should be used as a guide only. The telephone area code is 08.

Wander Inn YHA, *16 Clifton St,* ☎ *9721 3242,* ▇*www.yha.com.au* Located two hours south of Perth and situated only minutes away from the city. It is also located near some picturesque national parks and some beautiful bays and beaches. Facilities includes a large fully equipped kitchen, laundry, common room, TV lounge, internet access and a great barbecue area. They also provide bike and canoe hire and also fishing and crabbing equipment. Free pick-up from coach and train by arrangement. Parking available. *Members dorm ✪$20 ($23.00 non members); single $32 ($33.50 non members); double/twin $50 ($57 non members); BC MC VA EFTPOS*

Caravan Parks
Riverside Caravan Park, *5 Pratt Road, Eaton,* ☎ *9725 1234.* (No pets allowed) 80 sites - *powered sites ✪$15 - 20 for two, chalet section from $60 for two.*

Waterloo Village Caravan Park, *Lot 9 South Western Hwy,* ☎ *9725 4434.* 70 sites - powered sites ✪$18 for two, on-site vans $40 for two.

Koombana Bay Holiday Resort, *Koombana Drive,* ☎ *9791 3900.* (No pets allowed) 31 sites - *powered* *sites ✪ $15 - 20 for two, chalet $135 for two, cabins $55 for two.*

Let's Eat

There is no shortage of restaurants in all price brackets, and plenty of takeaway food outlets. For a special night out try the restaurant in the **Lord Forest Hotel**, *20 Symmons St,* ☎ *9721 9966.*

China City Garden Restaurant, *47 Victoria St,* ☎ *9721 1711.*

Kokoro Japanese Restaurant, *42B Spencer St,* ☎ *9721 4474.*

Mancini's Cafe Restaurant, *66 Victoria St,* ☎ *9721 9944.*

Points of Interest

The French explorer Nicolas Baudin was the first to sight Leschenault Inlet in 1803, as Commander of the **Geographe**, after which Geographe Bay is named. Baudin named the inlet after his botanist Jean Batiste Leschenault, and the port was first named Port Leschenault. In 1836, seven years after the founding of the Swan River settlement, Governor Sir James Stirling accompanied an expedition in the man-of-war **Sulphur** to explore the Port Leschenault and Busselton regions. Lieut. Henry William St Pierre Bunbury, then in charge of a military detachment in Pinjarra, made the overland trek to meet Governor Stirling in December 1836 at Port Leschenault. For that feat Governor Stirling told the 24-year-old lieutenant that Port Leschenault would be renamed Bunbury in his honour, and records show that he was highly delighted. They also show that he was the first to note the black sand peculiar to the shoreline in the area, recognising the ilmenite and related beach sands which were to develop into a multi-million dollar industry more than a century later.

The only public building surviving from the late 19th century is the **Paisley Centre**, *cnr Arthur* and *Stephen Streets.* It was built in 1894 as a primary school, and its architectural merit lies in the massing of the various parts, the good proportions of the fenestration and the many steeply-pitched gables that give a period character. Local sandstone was used for the window facings.

An earlier school on the same site was notable for a state record - three primary school pupils went on to become State Premiers: Sir John Forrest, Sir Newton Moore and Sir James Mitchell.

The **Rose Hotel**, in *Victoria Street* on the corner of *Wellington Street*, was erected by Samuel Rose in 1865, and rebuilt in 1897. Internally the hotel impresses with items of period furniture and ornaments which reflect the mood of bygone days. The solid stone statue of Henry II which stands in the courtyard was once part of the British Houses of Parliament at Westminster. It was purchased by the management of the hotel and shipped to Australia in 1980.

The **War Memorial** in Anzac Park, *cnr Stirling* and *Parkfield Streets*, opposite the post office, is a fine memorial to World War I armed forces. Alongside is another memorial, to John and Helen Scott, first farmers in the Bunbury District. They began work at Eelup Farm on Sir James Stirling's property in 1838.

Boulter's Heights, Bunbury's most popular lookout is a vantage point for a panoramic view of the city, the port, the north shore and the Leschenault Estuary. The waterfall was constructed in March, 1966, and when in operation, a cascade of water tumbles down the eastern face of the heights. Boulter's Heights is in *Withers Crescent, off Haig Crescent,* and can also be reached on foot from the base of the waterfall at the junction of Stirling and Wittenoom Streets.

Bunbury Regional Art Galleries, *Wittenoom Street,* are in the old Convent of Mercy building, which was opened and blessed in December, 1897. During 1981, the convent complex was purchased by the City Council, as it was no longer being used to house the Sisters of Mercy and their pupils. The Galleries are a multiple use facility, and are available for seminars, meetings, exhibitions, lectures, discussions, etc. They also contain the *City of Bunbury Art Collection*, which numbers 300 works, and has grown from an initial gift of 20 paintings by Claude Hotchin in 1949.

St Patrick's Cathedral, *Parkfield Street, Bunbury,* is situated on the upper level of Bury Hill, and commands a fine view of the inlet, the port and the city. The building was completed in 1921, without the 18.3m (60 ft) steeple which was added 46 years later. The pews and much of the interior of the Cathedral were built of local jarrah.

St Boniface Cathedral, *cnr Parkfield* and *Cross Streets,* was consecrated on October 14, 1962, on land originally purchased in 1916. The most unusual feature of this Anglican Cathedral is the big tower at the east end crowning the sanctuary rather than at the customary west end or in the centre.

Sir John Forrest Monument, *cnr Victoria* and *Stephen Streets,* is in honour of WA's greatest son. Sir John Forrest, Baron Forrest of Bunbury, CMG, KCMG, PC, GCMG, Hon LLD, FRGS, FGS, FLS, Kt of the Order of the Crown of Italy, surveyor, explorer, politician and peer, was born in 1847 at Mill Point at the mouth of the Preston River, 7km from Bunbury. He spent 18 years in State politics, all in executive office, then 18 years in Federal politics, almost half as Cabinet Minister. First MLA for Bunbury, first Premier of WA, five times Federal Treasurer, for a time Forrest was Acting Prime Minister. In 1918, he was created Baron Forrest of Bunbury, the first Australian to be raised to the British peerage. He died that year at sea, aged 71, and is buried in Karrakatta Cemetery. In 1979, Bunbury businessmen commissioned Mark Le Buse to sculpture Forrest's head, now here in St Paul's Place.

Centenary Gardens, *cnr Wittenoom* and *Princep Street,* were built in 1936 to commemorate the town's centenary, and have a shade pavilion dedicated to Lt Bunbury, and a wishing well built by the Apex Club in 1952. Facilities include seating, drinking fountain, toilets and an infant health centre.

Bunbury Lighthouse, *Ocean Drive,* on the ocean side of Casuarina Point, is a striking landmark and one of a fine collection of lighthouses that are part of the state's heritage.

The **Timber Jetty,** *off Henry Street,* was commenced in 1864 and was to be 427m (467 yds) long. In 1957, after several extensions, it reached its ultimate length of 1830m (2001 yds). Due to the development of the inner harbour in the 1970s, the jetty ceased commercial shipping in October, 1982. It is now used for pedestrian traffic and is a popular fishing and crabbing spot.

The **Bunbury Basaltic Rock,** at the northern end of Ocean Beach, is formed from a volcanic lava-flow believed to have occurred 150 million years ago in the cretaceous period. Volcanic activity was quite extensive over the South-West corner for a short period of time. A considerable amount of basalt can still be found west of a line from Bunbury to Windy Harbour, buried beneath sedimentary layers of sand and clay. The basalt rock formation can only be seen in Bunbury and Black Point, south-east of Augusta.

King Cottage Museum, *77 Forrest Avenue,* ☎ *9721 7546,* is a small, well kept cottage dating from 1880, and was opened as a local history museum in 1968. It houses a valuable collection of pioneer material of the area. One of Bunbury's oldest buildings, the cottage was the home of Henry King. Aided by four sons and using home-made bricks, Henry King erected the family dwelling of unique Flemish bond brick design. ☺Open Sat-Sun 2-4pm.

The **Bunbury Recreation Centre,** in Hay Park *off Parade Road,* was officially opened in 1979, and is a large multi recreation centre. The enclosed area allows the presentation of major exhibitions, championships and celebrity presentations. The centre is fully utilised by sporting groups, and is equipped with a heated indoor swimming pool, spa and sauna.

Tourism Bunbury has details of an 11km (7 miles) inland river cruise through scenery abounding with birdlife. ☺The cruise operates from September through May, on Saturday and Sunday.

Other attractions include: wine tasting at the **Geographe Wine Region and Ferguson Valley, Koombana Bay** and the **Old Goldfields Orchard and Cider Factory.**

Festivals

The **Bunbury Racing Carnival** is held in mid-March, with **The Bunbury Cup,** Australia's richest provincial race held on the Thursday of the Racing Round.

Facilities

Squash, tennis, cricket, croquet, bowls, golf, basketball, badminton, archery and bush walking. The Forrest Drive-In and Cinema is on the Bussell Highway, the Little Theatre is in Molloy Street, and information and show times are in the local paper.

Outlying Attractions
Busselton

Located 228km (142 miles) south of Perth, on the Bussell Highway, Busselton lies on the shores of Geographe Bay, where the Vasse River flows into the bay. The Tourist Bureau is at *38 Peel Terrace,* ☎ *(08) 9752 1288.* They have details of the available accommodation, and of the numerous scenic drives in the area.

Attractions in the town include: **The Busselton Jetty,** a long 2km that hosts a small train; **St**

Mary's Church of England, the oldest stone church in the State; **Wonnerup House,** ☉open daily 11am-noon, 1-4.30pm; **Old Butter Factory,** which houses the Historical Society, ☉open Wed-Mon 2-5pm, Fri 9am-11.30am and 2-5pm; **Old School and Teacher's House,** classified by the National Trust; **The Old Courthouse Complex; The Whistle Stop, the old Margaret River railway station,** which closed in 1957, and has been relocated 11km out of Busselton on the Vasse Highway; and **Ludlow Tuart Forest** is a rare rain forest located just outside the town.

⤴ Let's Stay Here

Busselton Backpackers,
14 Peel Terrace, ☎ *9754 2763,*
💻 *www.bsnbpk.com*
Located close to town. Quaint yet friendly hostel built in an old house close to McDonalds. Has a good feel to it along with it's old furniture. Facilities includes a kitchen and a alfresco barbecue area and a big backyard for camping. *Dorm* ✪ *$20; double $40*

Margaret River

The south-west coastal town of Margaret River is 52km (32 miles) south of Busselton on the Bussell Highway. The annual concert at Leeuwin Estate lures the cultural set, while the pounding surf in Prevelly Park challenges competitors in the annual amateur and professional surf competitions. The Tourist Bureau is on the *Bussell Highway* in the town, ☎ *(08) 9757 2147,* and you should visit them for information on accommodation and eateries. They have

Margaret River

Accommodation

1 Inne Town Backpackers

2 Margaret River Lodge

a website at 💻 www.margaretriver wa.com. Send emails to amrta@netserv.net.au
Attractions in the area include: **the Caves** of the south-west - **Mammoth Cave,** 21km (13 miles) south of Margaret River, and **Lake Cave,** 2km further south; **the vineyards** (there are plenty to visit); the **Old Settlement Historical Museum;** the **Berry Farm;** and **Boranup Forest** which showcases some of the State's prettiest karri forest.

⤴ Let's Stay Here

Inne Town Backpackers,
93 Bussell Highway, 9757 3698 or 1800 244 115
Located nicely in town. Quite small in size but good atmosphere. Facilities includes a kitchen, TV lounge with a fireplace and barbecue area with pool table. There is also a balcony. Parking available. *Dorm* ✪ *$19; double $50; triple $60*

Margaret River Lodge YHA,
220 Railway Terrace, ☎ *9757 9532,* 💻 *www.mrlodge.com.au*

This area is well known for it's wine region and this is the biggest hostel in town. Good atmosphere and only 5 minutes away from the centre. Facilities includes a 24 hour fully equipped kitchen, TV lounge, internet access, swimming pool, barbecue area and even a vegetable garden. This hostel also has great sporting facilities including petanque, pool table, volleyball, table tennis, croquet and a huge field to kick balls around. Bike, surf and bodyboard hire can also be arranged. Parking available. *Members dorm* ✪*$18-23; single $39.50; double $26.50pp BC MC VA*

Smiffy's Margaret River Retreat,

343 Bussell Highway, Forrest Grove, ☎ *9757 7419,* ⬛ *www.margaret-river-online.com.au/cape/accom/smiffy/* Located in a quiet rural setting, quite a good distance away from town. Quiet and secluded. Clean and well equipped with dorms quite spacious. They also allow camping on the premises. There is a restaurant on site. Plenty of parking available. *Dorm* ✪*$25; camping $7pp*

Surf Point Resort,

Reidle Dr, Gnaralbup Beach, 9757 1777 or 1800 071 777, ⬛ *www.surfpoint.com.au* Top of the notch place to stay at, it being also a resort. Situated so close to the beach. Very new and clean. Their deluxe doubles and twin rooms are en suite with bathroom, TV and fridge. It features a

well equipped kitchen and a great barbecue area outdoors. There's also laundry, a relaxing TV lounge, internet access and a games room with a pool table and some board games. They hire out boogie boards and bikes too. Staff are very helpful about the local area. Check out their website to get a discount coupon on your stay. **Recommended.** *Dorm* ✪*$23; double $67*

Augusta

Situated 95km (59 miles) south of Busselton, on the Bussell Highway. The Augusta-Margaret River area of the State is commonly known as the South-West Corner, as it is within that anvil shaped protrusion of the land which extends into the Indian Ocean. Renowned as having some of the most picturesque scenery in WA, the district can also boast of spectacular underground attractions - there are many beautiful limestone caves, of which three are open to tourists. Modern lighting is provided and access is easy. Two are mentioned under Margaret River, the other one is The Jewel Cave, 8km from Augusta. Its attractions are the Organ Pipes and the Jewel Casket. It also has the world's largest straw - a stalactite which measures 5.9m (19 ft) in length.

The Augusta Tourist Bureau can be contacted on ☎ *(08) 9758 0166,* and they will advise on accommodation. Other attractions are Cape Leeuwin Lighthouse, Augusta Historical Museum and Hamelin Bay.

↪ **Let's Stay Here**
Baywatch Manor Resort YHA,
88 Blackwood Ave, ☎ *9758*

1290, ⬛ *www.yha.com.au* Top of the notch cheap accommodation and very spacious. Purpose-built two-storey federation-styled manor, overlooking the Blackwood River. Close to the foodstore. Features a kitchen, laundry, barbecue area, open fireplace, internet access, TV lounge and bike hire. Complimentary tea and coffee. Parking available. *Members dorm* ✪*$19-21; double/twin $49 BC MC VA*

Manjimup

Manjimup is 307km (191 miles) south of Perth at the junction of South West and Muirs Highways, right in the heart of the **Karri** and **Jarrah forest**. The town has over 5000 residents, and the Tourist Bureau is on the corner of *Rose* and *Edwards Streets,* ☎ *(08) 9771 1831.* The town has modern shopping facilities and most sports are well catered for, including golf, lawn bowls and five squash courts.

Attractions include: **Manjimup Timber Park;** the **King Jarrah Heritage Trail; Fonty's Pool; Glenoran Pool;** the **Dingup Church;** and the **Perup Ecology Pool.**

Collie

Situated 57km (35 miles) inland from Bunbury, and 203km (126 miles) south of Perth, Collie is important as a coal mining town, and has in fact been WA's only source of coal since the 1890s, and Muja Power Station supplies the State electricity grid. The Tourist Bureau is situated at *156 Throssell Street,* ☎ *(08) 9734 2051.* You can contact them by email at ✉colshire@collie.wa.gov.au or check out the website at ⬛ *www.collie.wa.gov.au*

Pyramid Hill South Roeb

Busselton Jetty

Albany

Cape Naturaliste

Margaret River

Attractions in the town include: **Muja Open Cut/Power Station Tourist Look-out; the Historical and Mining Museum; Steam Locomotion Museum; All Saints Church; Wellington Dam;** and **Collie Scenic Drive.**

Albany

Population 31,000
Albany is situated 406km (252 miles) south of Perth on King George Sound, on the southern coast of Western Australia.

Climate

Albany has a mild Mediterranean climate with an average rainfall of 944mm (37 ins), most of which falls during the winter months. The temperatures, regulated by the ocean, vary from a summer daytime average of 25C (77F) to a winter daytime average of 17C (63F).

Characteristics

The heart of the Rainbow Coast (Great Southern) region of Western Australia, Albany is nestled by the tranquil waters of Princess Royal Harbour. As Albany was the first settlement in the State, it is steeped in history and memories. It sits amidst a relatively unspoilt area of Australia with National Parks, forests, rugged coastline, mountains, wilderness areas and tranquil rivers all within easy reach.

How to Get There
By Bus

Westrail, ☎ *9326 2000,* provides a daily service to Albany via York or Kojonup.

Visitor Infomation

Albany Tourist Bureau, *Old Railway Station, Proudlove Parade,*

☎ *(08) 9841 1088,* is ⊕open seven days a week. Visit the website at ▬*www.albanytourist.com.au* or email them at ✉b@albanytourist. com.au

⤷ Let's Stay Here

A wide variety of accommodation exists in and around Albany including motels, caravan parks, farm stay and backpackers or youth hostels. Information can be obtained from the Tourist Bureau. Here is a selection with prices which should be used as a guide only. ☎The telephone area code is 08.

Albany Backpackers, *Corner Stirling Terrace and*

Spencer St, ☎ *9842 5255* ▬ *www.albanybackpackers.com. au* You won't miss this building with it's colourful murals. Nice and clean and has good fun atmosphere. Your basic facilities plus a huge common room with pool tables. Around are some private areas. The staff are quite good in attending to their guests. Free coffee and cake at nights at 6:30, not to mention the free 15 minute internet access in the mornings. There are also beer vouchers and cheap meals available. Ask about the tours around Albany. Parking on site and off street available. Recommended. *Dorm* ✪*$23 ($46 for four nights special);*

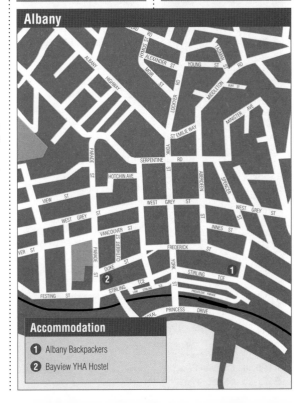

Albany

Accommodation

❶ Albany Backpackers

❷ Bayview YHA Hostel

single $39 (four nights special applies); double/twin $58 (four nights special applies) (prices includes breakfast)

Albany's Cruize-Inn,
122 Middleton Rd, ☎ *9842 .9599* Located at a busy suburban street, a few kilometres out of town. The beach is closer, but not that close. It positions itself as a boutique hostel for the upmarket backpacker. Really good facilities including a fireplace and a pianola. They also hire out fishing rod, bikes and surfboards. The manager offers to pick you up at the bus station. Try driving here and enjoy the scenic view. Facilities includes a kitchen, swimming pool and barbecue area. *Dorm ✪$33; single $60; double/twin $60*

Bayview YHA,
49 Duke St, ☎ *9842 3388,* 💻 *www.yha.com.au* What was originally a old guesthouse is now turned into a hostel. Newly renovated historical building with much space. Facilities includes a large fully equipped kitchen, laundry, wood fire, comfy TV lounge, pool table, internet access and barbecue area. Complimentary tea and coffee. Bike and cheap car hire can be arranged. Parking available. *Members dorm ✪$19 ($ 21.50 non members); organised single $30; double $48 ($51 non members); BC MC VA (prices includes breakfast)*

Caravan Parks
Mt Melville Caravan Park,
22 Wellington Street, ☎ *9841*

4616. (Dogs allowed on bond only) - *powered sites ✪$20-23 for two, on-site vans $44-48 for two.*

Albany Tourist Village,
550 Albany Highway, ☎ *9841 3752.* (No dogs allowed) - *powered sites $17 for two, on-site vans ✪$37-41 for two.*

Middleton Beach Holiday and Caravan Park,
28 Flinders Parade, Middleton Beach, ☎ *9841 3593.* (No pets allowed) - *powered sites ✪$19-23 for two, chalets $75 - 150 for two.*

Let's Eat
Albany has a very good selection of restaurants, offering every type of cuisine, cafes and takeaway outlets, and the Tourist Office has a complete list. Here are some you might like to try:

Al Fornetto Ristorante and Pizzeria, *132 York St,* ☎ *9842 1060.*

Bangkok Rose, *112 York St,* ☎ *9842 2366.*

Dog Rock Restaurant, *Middleton Road,* ☎ *9841 1400* - Licensed, Italian - ☉open Mon-Sat, 5pm drinks, 6.30pm dinner.

Goshu-ya Japanese Restaurant, *1 Mermaid Avenue, Emu Point,* ☎ *9844 1111* - BYO, snacks and seafood - ☉open 10am-late.

Moby Dicks Fish and Chips, *60 South Coast Highway,* ☎ *9841 6142.*

The Curry Pot, *38 Stirling Terrace,* ☎ *9842 9399.*

Kentucky Fried Chicken, *Lockyer Ave,* ☎ *9841 7350.*

Hungry Jacks, *13 Lockyer Ave,* ☎ *9842 1314.*

Points of Interest
The town of Albany lies on a saddle between Mt Melville and Mt Clarence overlooking **Princess Royal Harbour**, one of the greatest landlocked deepwater harbours in the world. It is a pretty town with lovely water vistas at every turn, and many vantage points for breathtaking views and holiday snaps.

Within the main town area there are many historic buildings, including the now refurbished **Town Hall**, built in 1887, the first consecrated Anglican church in WA, and the Western Australian Museum.

The **Western Australian Museum** building was built in the early 1850s, then more rooms were added and it was converted to a house for Government residents in 1873. For eighty years, it was the centre of the town's social activities. For the following twenty years, it had a variety of uses before becoming derelict. It was then rebuilt and converted to its present form. It is located in *Residency Road* and you can contact the museum on ☎ *9841 4844.*

Adjoining the Western Australian Museum is the Brig *Amity* replica and the **Eclipse building**. This building, opened back in 1989, houses the massive $5 million optic from the **Old Eclipse Island Lighthouse** and a **Touch Gallery** full of hands-on exhibits for those more tactile visitors.

The **Old Gaol** is nearby, and

was built in 1851 as the convict hiring depot. In 1872 it became the district gaol, and in the early 1930s, a store house. It then stood empty for many years until 1968, when the Albany Historical Society began its restoration. The museum has an extensive collection of social and historical artefacts.

Patrick Taylor Cottage, in *Duke Street*, was built around 1832, of wattle and daub, and is thought to be the oldest building still standing in Albany. It now contains over 2000 items including period costumes, old clocks, silverware and kitchenware.

A short distance along Middleton Road past the famous **Dog Rock**, is **Old Farm Strawberry Hill.** The Old Farm has enjoyed a colourful history since it was established in 1831 as the Government Farm for the Settlement of Albany. The two-storey home was built in 1836 for the Government Resident Sir Richard Spencer. Restored to its former glory by the National Trust in 1964, it stands serene in the midst of an English garden, hidden from the view of passers-by.

One of the most unusual buildings in Albany is the **Old Post Office** building, located on historic Stirling Terrace. This building was originally used as a customs and bond store, with the middle level being a sorting area and post office. The spiral staircase in the tower is magnificent, and the building now houses restaurants, a weaver and a museum.

An admirable restoration for Albany is to be found on Mount Clarence in **Princess Royal Fortress.** This military establishment was conceived in 1878 and was operational until 1956. After an intensive restoration programme, the fortress now has an important part to play in the region. Within its boundaries are a kiosk and a restaurant with stunning views from timber decking.

For those interested in exploration in the near vicinity, **Torndirrup National Park** will provide much interest. Torndirrup National Park is best known for the **Gap, Natural Bridge, the Blowholes** and **Peak Head**. Panoramic views can be obtained from the **Stoney Hill Heritage Trail,** and **Frenchman Bay Beach** is a lovely sheltered little nook in complete contrast to the coast near the open sea.

Also found in Torndirrup National Park is a museum with a difference. After being part of one of the bloodiest chapters in the history of whaling, Australia's last mainland whaling station, located in Albany, closed in 1978. This whaling station, now known as **Whaleworld,** is a museum of the whaling industry and now plays a most important part in the preservation of the magnificent creatures it once sought to slaughter.

To find out about the history of Albany it would be wise to pick up a copy of The Amity Trail. This brochure gives you a guide to the historic places around Albany.

Facilities

There are good sporting facilities for most sports within the town, in addition to which there are two gyms, a large heated swimming pool with spa, horse riding and two golf courses. On a more cultural level there is an excellent town theatre for movies and stage shows, and art galleries with regular exhibitions. There are many tours available - scenic, adventure, diving and fishing - and river cruises. As Albany is a large regional centre, most needs are catered for. The Tourist Bureau has brochures detailing current events.

Outlying Attractions

The Rainbow Coast area of Western Australia, of which Albany is the heart, stretches from the hamlet of Walpole in the west to Bremer Bay in the east, and from Albany in the south to the towns of Kojonup and Katanning in the north.

A total of seven national parks can be found within the Rainbow Coast and although each has its own special characteristics, they share many common natural attractions.

Walpole/Nornalup National Park

This park covers some 18,000ha (44,460 acres) surrounding the Walpole and Nornalup Inlets at the eastern gateway to the region. It has deep rivers, majestic karri forest, waterfalls, wildflowers and unspoilt coastline. The **Pioneer Cottage,** in *Pioneer Park, Walpole,* was opened in October 1987 and was a joint venture between the Walpole Tourist Bureau and the Department of Conservation and Land Management. The Bureau provided the funds and the department carried out the construction. The cottage follows the basic design of an early pioneer home, but it is not meant to be a replica. It has been provided to commemorate the pioneers of the district who were responsible for opening up the virgin bush areas and laying the foundations of the district as it is today. The Walpole Visitor Infomation Centre is in the *Pioneer Cottage, Walpole, ☎(08) 9840 1111.*

⤷ Let's Stay Here
Tingle All Over YHA,
60 Nockolds St, ☎9840 1041, 🖳www.yha.con.au Located only a few hundred metres from the centre of Walpole on Nockold Street. This place has a homely atmosphere. Facilities includes a large kitchen, laundry, TV lounge and barbecue area. Wood fire in the lounge during the months of winter. There is also a huge chess board and pieces outside perfect for the chess and draughts lover. Complimentary tea and coffee. Taxi tours available from the YHA. Parking available. *Members dorm ✪$19; single $33; double/twin $24pp; BC MC VA*

Walpole Backpackers,
Pier St, ☎9840 1244, 🖳www. walpolebackpackers.com Fantastic atmosphere and the manager is very helpful about what to do and see here. Facilities includes a fully equipped kitchen, common room and a barbecue area. The bathrooms are large. Bike hire is available. *Dorm ✪$20 ; single $32 ; double/twin $48;*

Porongurup National Park
Nestled near Mount Barker, this park is famous for its granite rock formations and luxuriant karri and marri trees. Footpaths lead to several peaks, and other paths and heritage trails cross the ranges.

⤷ Let's Stay Here
Chill Out Backpackers,
79 Hasell St, Mount Barker, ☎9851 2798 Has a very homey feel to it. Quite small and cozy. Built in an A-frame house. Your normal but great facilities plus a spa and a bath. Parking available. **Recommended.** *Dorm ✪$20; single $44 ; double $40*

Porongurup Backpackers,
Porongurup Rd, Porongurup, ☎9853 1110 A nice and small family owned hostel with on site store and tearooms. An ideal spot on the park grounds. Only a number of beds. Holds only a small kitchen, but you can order a two-course meal for just $10. Parking available. *Dorm/double ✪$17*

Stirling Ranges
About 80km (50 miles) north of Albany the rugged peaks of the Stirling Ranges rise abruptly to more than 1000m (3281 ft) above sea level. Stark cliff faces, magnificent views and rare plants ranging from tiny orchids and heathland to flowering gums, are all part of the Stirling Range. Most peaks have paths leading from the parking areas to the top, and offer magnificent views for walkers.

Fitzgerald River National Park
In stark contrast is the Fitzgerald River National Park which covers 270,000ha (666,900 acres) surrounding the inlets of the Gairdner, Fitzgerald and Hamersley Rivers between Bremer Bay and Hopetoun. In this small area of WA can be found nearly 20% of the total number of plant species found in the whole State, includ-

ing 75 that are endemic to this park. The Fitzgerald is the only national park in WA to be gazetted as a World Biosphere Reserve. Public use is varied with a full range from wilderness enjoyment through to coastal fishing at more accessible spots.

Wineries
The mild climate of the Rainbow Coast not only creates an ideal holiday destination, it also lends itself to wines of good quality which are beginning to come to the fore. In the past couple of years recognition has been given to the quality of grapes from this district. Made up mainly of many small vineyards, plantings in Albany, Denmark and Mount Barker all show the splendid purity of varietal fruit that vines achieve in this cool climate region. Now Mount Barker has attracted two large vineyard projects. While the boutique vineyard image won't be lost, the developments will substantiate the Rainbow Coast as a winegrowing region.

The Tourist Bureau has particulars of any winery tours and cellar door sales that are available during your visit.

Denmark
Situated 55km (34 miles) west of Albany on the South Coast Highway, Denmark has a population of around 4000. The Denmark River flows through this charming little town, and the local industries are timber milling, salmon fishing (February to April) and farming - beef cattle, dairying, sheep, pigs and potato growing.

The Tourist Bureau is in *Strickland Street, ☎(08) 9848 2055,* and they will be able to advise on the local attractions, which include: **Wilson Head and Lions Lookout; The Aquarium and Sphinx Rock; Mount Shadford Scenic Drive, William Bay National Park; Wilson Inlet;** and **Parry's Inlet and Beach.**

Ocean Beach, about 8km from Denmark, is one of the finest surfing beaches in the State. The town also has a golf course, bowling greens and tennis courts.

➥ Let's Stay Here
Blue Wren Backpackers, *17 Prince St, ☎ 9848 3300, bluewren.batcave.net* A really good quiet place to stay at. Located at the heart of town. Your usual facilities including a kitchen, laundry, a relaxing lounge area. Parking available. *Dorms ✪$19; twin $48; double $55 with en suite*

Katanning

Situated 170km (106 miles) north of Albany on the Great Southern Highway, Katanning is a bustling and progressive centre, catering for the farming communities. There is excellent accommodation available, and the Visitor Infomation Centre, *54 Austral Terrace, ☎(08) 9821 2634,* has details.

Attractions include the **Old Mill Museum, Kobeelya homestead, Katanning Mosque** and the **Old Winery.**

West Kalgoorlie/Boulder
Population 29,000
Kalgoorlie is situated in semi-desert area, 597 km (371 miles) east of Perth, at the terminus of the Great Eastern Highway.

Climate
Average temperatures: January

max 34C (93F) - min 18C (64F); July max 17C (63F) - min 6C (43F). Average annual rainfall: 263mm (10 ins).

Characteristics
Situated in an area named for gold and riddled with reminders of its presence, Kalgoorlie-Boulder's association with the precious metal stands out. Not for this twin centre the boom, bust and quick extinction into a ghost town, nor any lingering on amongst remnants of former glory. The towns are as busy as ever, and stand next to what was once the richest square mile of gold-bearing earth in the world. And although nearly a century of mining has seen a thousand million dollars worth of gold removed, there is plenty left yet.

Echoes of the boisterous past can still be seen, particularly in Hannan Street, Kalgoorlie, and Burt Street, Boulder.

How to Get There
By Bus
Greyhound Pioneer operate daily services through Kalgoorlie.

By Rail
The Prospector leaves Perth Sun-Fri, and an interstate train leaves five evenings a week.

Visitor Infomation
The Kalgoorlie-Boulder Tourist Centre is at *250 Hannan Street, Kalgoorlie, ☎(08) 9021 1966* or *☎1800 00 1880* (toll free). They are ☺open 8.30am-5pm Mon-Fri and 9am-5pm on weekends. If you have online access, visit ▣*www.kal goorlieandwagoldf ields.com.au* for a preliminary peek or drop them a message at ✉kbtc@emerge.net.au

---

➥ Let's Stay Here
There is quite a range of accommodation to choose from, and the Tourist Offices have a complete list. Here we have a selection, with prices for budget accommodation which should be used as a guide only. The telephone area code is 08.

Golddust Backpackers Hostel, *192 Hay St, ☎ 9091 3737, ▣www.kalgoorliebackpack ers.com* Really good, clean and well maintained hostel. The facilities includes a big kitchen, TV lounge, games room with pool table and arcades games, swimming pool and barbecue area outdoors. They also offer free pick-ups from the airport and bus station. **Recommended.** *Dorms ✪$18; single $30; double $45*

Kalgoorlie Backpackers YHA, *166 Hay St, ☎ 9091 1482 , ▣www.yha.com.au* Situated close to the town centre and the bus and train station. Rooms are clean and air conditioned. Plenty of activities to do around here. Facilities includes kitchen, laundry, TV lounge, and swimming pool. They offer free BBQs. Parking available. *Members dorm ✪$17 ($19 non members); single $27 ($29 non members); double $44 ($48 non members); twin $44 ($50 non members) BC MC VA*

Piccadilly Hotel, *164 Piccadilly Street, ☎ 9021 2109.* 19 rooms (private facilities) *✪$40.*

Caravan Parks

Goldminer Tourist Caravan Park, *Great Eastern Highway,* ☎ *9021 3713.* (No pets allowed) - *powered sites* ✪ *$17 for two, on-site vans $44 for two.*

Prospector Holiday Park, *Lower Hannan Street, Great Eastern Highway,* ☎ *9021 2524.* (No pets allowed) - *powered sites* ✪ *$20-21 for two, cabins from $60 for two.*

Let's Eat

Most of the hotels and motels have restaurants, and there are plenty of takeaway food outlets. Here are a few restaurants you might like to try.

Amalfi, *409 Hannan Street, Kalgoorlie,* ☎ *9021 3088.*

Amy's, *1 MacDonald Street, Kalgoorlie,* ☎ *9021 1749.*

Cornwall Historic Restaurant, *25 Hopkins Street, Boulder,* ☎ *9093 2510.*

Fu-Wah Chinese Restaurant, *Shop 6, Woolworths Plaza, Wilson Street, Kalgoorlie,* ☎ *9021 6242.*

Mangia Bene Italian Restaurant and Takeaway, *Lammington Square, Shop 1 Maritana Street, Kalgoorlie,* ☎ *9021 3553.*

Top End Thai Restaurant, *71 Hannan Street, Kalgoorlie,* ☎ *9021 4286.*

Wah On Restaurant, *110 Burt Street, Boulder,* ☎ *9093 108.*

Points of Interest

In June, 1893, three Irishmen, Patrick Hannan, Tom Flannigan and Daniel Shea, discovered gold near Mt Charlotte. Two other prospectors soon located further large gold deposits three miles to the south - the world famous 'Golden Mile'.

The goldrush this sparked was staggering in size and speed. Men came in thousands from all over the world, ready to live in improvised shacks in a waterless near-desert. Hundreds of mining companies were floated to speculate on the rich reefs, and many of them were fraudulent.

A railway and five civic buildings sprung up in no time, but water seemed to be an insoluble problem, until C.Y. O'Connor devised the Goldfields Water Scheme. This consisted of building a 563km (350 miles) pipeline from a reservoir near Perth, which was a resounding success, but the criticism it received during the construction process caused O'Connor to shoot himself, so he never saw his dream realised.

Gold production reached a peak in 1903, and then declined until the Depression of the 1930s, when world prices increased dramatically.

In 1931, the State's richest nugget was found and named 'The Golden Eagle'. It weighed an incredible 32,177g (1,135 ounces).

The Golden Mile is now managed as a whole for the first time in its history, which should lead to more efficient and longer-lasting exploitation of the gold reserves.

In the late 1890s, the Golden Mile Loop Line was the busiest and best paying in the colony. Over 60 passenger and goods trains passed through Boulder City Station on weekdays, 33 on Saturdays and 27 on Sundays. The locomotives used in those days were N class, and were worked extremely hard. Today the Railway is run by the **Golden Mile Loopline Railway Society Inc,** a voluntary group formed to make sure that the line remains open. Visitors are able to re-live some of the past events of the area while they **'Ride the Rattler'**, travelling over some of the Golden Mile pulled by a Wickham Track Inspection vehicle or Z1153, a jetty shunting locomotive. A full recorded commentary is played so that every feature is explained as you pass.

Regular tours depart from Boulder Railway Station during ☺weekdays and Sundays at 11am, and also on Sundays and public holidays they depart at 1.30pm and 3pm. During school holidays, extra trains run, and further enquiries can be made at the Tourist Bureau, or ☎ *(08) 9021 1966.*

Mining Hall of Fame, *Goldfields Highway,* ☎ *9091 2122,* is one of Australia's most unusual tourist attractions, and provides a unique chance for the whole family to go underground in a real gold mine in safety. It is essential to wear enclosed footwear, and children under 4 are not permitted on underground tours. Children under 16 pay half the adult fee for the tours. You can pan for gold and watch some gold work. The doors ☺open at 9am.

Underground Tours last 1.5 hours, and in the peak season run every half hour, ☺starting at 10.30am, with the last tour at 3pm. In the non-holiday period they run at 10.30am, 1pm and 2.30pm. Gold Room Demonstrations last half an hour, and begin in peak season at 10.30am, 1pm and 3pm, in off peak, 10.30am and 1pm.

Guided Surface Tours last one hour, and begin on completion of the **Gold Room Demonstrations.**

Combined Tours last 3 hours, and in the peak season ⏱commence at 10.30am, 11.30am, 1pm and 1.30pm. The 1.30pm tour is not available in the off-peak season.

Western Australian Museum, Kalgoorlie-Boulder, *17 Hannan Street,* ☎ *9021 8533,* is ⏱open daily 10.30am-4.30pm. The building was formerly the British Arms Hotel, the narrowest hotel in Australia. On display are the developments in the search of gold and aspects of domestic life at the turn of the century.

Mt Charlotte Reservoir holds Kalgoorlie's permanent fresh water supply, which comes by pipeline from the weir at Mundaring in the Darling Range. In January, 1903, Sir John Forrest, explorer and Premier of WA, turned on the water at the Mt Charlotte reservoir, and the town went wild. At the official banquet that night, Sir George Reid said that he had never heard so much talk about water, and seen so little of it consumed. From the lookout at the Reservoir there is a good view of the town.

Paddy Hannan's Statue, in *Hannan Street,* is a replica of the original within the Town Hall. It shows a life-sized Paddy, holding his waterbag.

In a fenced area, near the head of Hannan Street, is a kurrajong tree and a plaque marking the

place where Paddy Hannan first found gold.

Kalgoorlie Town Hall was built in 1908, and has a fine stamped metal ceiling and Victorian style cast seats on the balcony. On the first floor is the Art Collection, ⏱open Mon-Fri 9am-5pm.

The Royal Flying Doctor Base, north of the main city area of Kalgoorlie, has conducted tours ⏱commencing at 2.30pm each weekday. No admission fee is charged, but donations are welcome.

Lord Forrest Olympic Pool and Water Slide is on the corner of MacDonald and Cassidy Streets, and was WA's first Olympic Pool. It was built in 1938, using water from the pipeline. The park nearby has shady trees, a statue of C.Y. O'Connor, and a fountain.

The Boulder Block, back in 1905, was a thriving business centre with 6 hotels which served liquor around the clock to cater for miners on shift work. The area is only 0.5ha (1.2 acres), which makes it hard to imagine.

Boulder Town Hall in *Burt Street,* was built in 1908, and has a distinctive clock tower.

The **Golden Mile Art Exhibition** is in the upstairs gallery at the Boulder Town Hall. It is a permanent exhibition with works by local artists. Visitors are welcome, and arrangements can be made by phoning ☎ *9093 3283.*

The **Cornwall Hotel**, probably the most picturesque in the area, was built in 1898 and is in vintage condition. It photographs well.

The **Goldfields War Museum** is in *Burt Street, Boulder.* It is ⏱open Mon-Fri 10am-4pm.

The **Eastern Goldfields**

Historical Society Museum is in the Boulder City Railway Station. Its ⏱hours of opening are: Mon-Sat 10.30am-12.30pm, Sun 10am-4pm, ☎ *9093 3360.*

Hammond Park, *Lyall Street, Lamington,* is a flora and fauna reserve with a lake, a rustic bridge and a miniature castle made from local stone. There is a grass picnic area with barbecue facilities, and tame emus and kangaroos roam amongst the picnickers. The park is ⏱open daily 9am-5.30pm.

Seven kilometres north of Kalgoorlie is Australia's only legalised *Bush Two-up School,* and business ⏱begins at around 1.30 each afternoon, except on the miners' pay day when the horse races are held in town. For the inexperienced, two-up is a very easy game to learn, and is an easy way to lose money very quickly. We can only suggest that you watch for a while before making a bet, and be careful what you say, as the game has a language of its own and you could find yourself called in as the spinner (person who tosses the coins). By the way, the miners get paid every second Friday - check with the Tourist Centre, ☎ *9021 2180.*

About 18km (11 miles) north-east of Kalgoorlie-Boulder is what is left of the township of **Kanowna.** In 1905 the town had a population of 12,000 with 16 hotels, two breweries and an hourly train service to Kalgoorlie. Now there are tourist markers.

Since you are in gold territory, you might decide to try your luck at fossicking. It's a good idea, but make sure you have a Miner's Right first. You can pick one up at the **Mines Department** on *Brookman Street.*

Goldrush Tours offer a variety of coach tours in the area, including the **Ghost Town Tour,** which ☉departs from the Palace Chambers in *Maritana Street,* every Thursday at 10.45am. For information and bookings phone ☎*(08) 9021 2954* or ☎*1800 620 440* (freecall).

Kurrawang Emu Farm, ☎*9021 2845,* provides you with an opportunity to come face to face with their big birds. It can be found on the *Great Eastern Highway,* 18km west of Kalgoorlie.

Other tours further afield are available, and the Visitor Infomation Centre have all the information, and can make bookings.

Festivals

The **Kalgoorlie Racing Round** is held in September.

The **Community Fair** is held each March in the Cruickshank Sports Arena.

Facilities

There are two golf clubs in the suburb of Hannan; lawn bowls at Kalgoorlie Bowling Club, cnr Maritana and Forrest Streets; swimming and water polo at the Lord Forrest Olympic Pool; motor sports at the 12ha (30 acres) complex near the airport; and gliding, tennis and other sports can be arranged through the Visitor Infomation Centres.

Outlying Attractions
Coolgardie

The town was built to accommodate 15,000 people, and the present population is 1100, so Coolgardie can be regarded as the best-cared-for ghost town in Australia. It is situated 45km

(28 miles) west of Kalgoorlie, on the site of a reef of rich gold, found by Arthur Bayley in 1892, and called 'Bayley's Reward'. By 1900, the town had hotels, smithies, barbers, newspaper offices, stores, and 15,000 people. 'Bayley's Reward' continued to produce gold until 1963, but the town's boom time was really over by 1914 when World War I saw the prospectors volunteer for service.

The **Coolgardie Tourist Bureau and Goldfields Exhibition** is at *62 Bayley Street,* ☎*(08) 9026 6090,* and is open daily. There are a series of historical markers around the township, documenting the history of Coolgardie, with photographs of what each site looked like in times gone by. It is fascinating to compare the photos with what is now in front of you.

Attractions in the town include: **The Goldfields Exhibition** in the same building as the Tourist Bureau, ☉open daily 8am-5pm with daily screenings of the BBC film *Gold Fever.*

The **Railway Station Museum,** in *Woodwood Street,* ☉open daily 8am-5pm ☎*9026 6388.*

Lions' Bicentennial Lookout, 2km from the main street where Bayley's South Headframe is found. **Ben Prior's Open Air Museum** in *Bayley Street,* is dedicated to WA's early explorers and the pioneers of the goldfields.

Bottle and Curio Museum, in the Exhibition Building, ☉open daily 8am-5pm.

Warden Finnerty's Residence, built in 1895 at a cost of 2,800 pounds, and now owned by the National Trust. It is ☉open Mon-Wed, Fri-Sat 1-4pm, Sun 10am-noon, 1-4pm.

The **Old Pioneer Cemetery,** at the end of *Forrest Street* near the oval, has graves dating from 1892 to 1894.

Coolgardie Camel Farm, ☎*9026 6159,* is about 4km west of Coolgardie, and is ☉open daily 9am-5pm, with rides available ranging from around the yard in the farm, to overnight camel treks. Incidentally, the reason that the streets of Coolgardie are so wide is because there had to be room to turn camel trains. You can ask at the farm why they didn't just reverse them.

If all the talk about gold, and people making their fortunes, has sparked a small case of gold fever, you can hire gold detectors and other equipment at the **Railway Lodge,** ☎*9026 6166.* Some people have been lucky! Tours of the area are available, and they include sightseeing, gold panning and detecting, and wildflowers in season. Contact the Tourist Bureau for information and bookings.

Menzies

Named after L.R. Menzies, one of the men who discovered gold in the vicinity in 1894, Menzies is another town that has declined. Within months of gold being found the population was 10,000, within thirteen years it had dropped to 1000, now it is home to 110.

The town is 132km (82 miles) north of Kalgoorlie, and many buildings from its heyday remain, including the town hall and the railway station. The **Menzies State Battery** for processing gold is the most modern in Australia, and visitors are welcome.

Leonora

Situated 237km (147 miles) north of Kalgoorlie, Leonora is a railhead for nearby copper and nickel mines, and the meeting point of the roads radiating north, south and east. It is the administrative town of the North Eastern Goldfields, and the centre of a wool growing area.

Attractions include:

Mt Leonora was first named by the explorer John Forrest in 1869, and rises 100m (328 ft) above the town, so is the best place to get an overall view.

The Sons of Gwalia Goldmine ran continuously for 67 years, and was the largest underground mine outside the Golden Mile. It closed in 1963, and the town of Gwalia died as a result. However, recent technological advances have resulted in lower production costs, and the mine has re-opened, as have some others in the area. A visit is worthwhile, and it is best to allow about half an hour to explore. In the mine office is the **Gwalia Museum,** with artefacts from the early days of mining in the areas. The ghost town of Gwalia is also worth a visit. The town was never officially gazetted, due to its tendency to flood, so it just grew like Topsy, with buildings mostly of galvanised iron. It is hard to imagine now, but the town was once so prosperous that it had the State's first electric tram service.

Situated 69km (43 miles) south-east of Leonora is the township of **Kookynie** which had a population of 1500 in 1905, and now has 10, many of whom work the local hotel, which in itself is worth a visit. There are many old workings and tailings dumps for you to fossick through within a kilometre of the hotel.

Niagara is about 10km (6 miles) from Kookynie, and is another ghost town, with not much to see except for the **Niagara Dam,** built in 1897. The cement for the 250m (820 ft) long wall was carried from Coolgardie by camels!

Laverton

Prospectors from Coolgardie found gold near the present town site in 1896, and soon there was another boom town, apparently a very wild one. It is reported that the only burial resulting from natural causes in the **BurTVille Cemetery,** which is 25km (16 miles) from Laverton, was that of a baby six weeks old. Everyone else died with their boots on.

Laverton is 361km (224 miles) north-east of Kalgoorlie. The town died when the surface gold ran out, but has been revitalised by the Windarra Nickel Project, and it is the support base for the recently reopened **Lancefield Mine.** Attractions include **Billy Goat Hill** which gives panoramic views, **Mt Windarra,** from where there is a good view of the **Windarra Nickel Mine,** and the **Old Laverton Police Station** and **Gaol,** built in 1900.

Ghost towns in the area include **BurTVille, Gladiator, Heffernans** and **Just in Time.** If you wish to explore all the ghost towns in the Goldfields area, you would be wise to invest in a large-scale map from the Mines Department.

Leinster

This town was established in 1977 to service the nickel-mining industry, and is the terminus of a sealed highway north from Kalgoorlie on the way to Wiluna. It is 378km (254 miles) north-west of Kalgoorlie, and Skywest have return flights to Leinster from Perth, ☎ *9037 0749.*

The **Leinster Recreation Association** in *Mansbridge Road,* ☎ *9037 9040,* can answer all your sightseeing and accommodation enquiries.

Attractions include the old towns of **Agnew**, **Lawlers** and **Poison Creek.**

Kambalda

Situated 57km (35 miles) south of Kalgoorlie, Kambalda is a nickel town constructed by the Western Mining Corporation in the 1960s and 1970s. Originally, of course, it was a gold town, the precious metal having been found in 1887 by Percy Larkin, but gold mining ceased around 1907. In 1954, George Cowcill collected some specimens in the area that he thought contained uranium, but analysis proved that it was nickel. In 1962, he and John Morgan submitted the samples to the Western Mining Corporation, who decided to drill several holes, which showed the presence of a massive deposit of nickel sulphides.

The town has approximately 6000 people, and the Kambalda Visitor Infomation is in *cnr Emu Rocks and Marianthus Rd, Kambalda West,* ☎ *(08) 9027 0192,* ◷open Mon-Fri 9am-5pm.

Attractions include: **Red Hill Lookout** in Gordon *Adams Road;* **Lake Lefroy,** a large salt pan that rarely contains water; **Hunts Well,** a remnant of the original gold town; **Lion's Park,** a picnic and barbecue spot with an olympic swimming pool; **John Hill Viewpoint,** which has views over the concentrator, powerhouse, workshops and distant headframes; **King Battery** on Woolibar station where crushed ore was once turned into gold; and **Pioneer Cemetery** where pioneer William Wenzel is buried.

Norseman

Known as Western Australia's 'Eastern Gateway', Norseman is 187km (116 miles) south of Coolgardie, 724km (450 miles) south-east of Perth, and 724km (450 miles) west of the Western Australia/South Australia border. Goldfields Air Services have several flights weekly between Esperance and Kalgoorlie via Norseman, and bus services from all capital cities pass through Norseman.

Gold was discovered in the area in 1892, and many people settled in the town which had grown out of the pastoral activity in the area. Two years later, a horse named 'Norseman' stumbled over a large gold nugget, and the town got its name. The horse's owner later discovered a rich gold reef where his horse had 'turned the first sod'.

In 1905 the population was 3000, and in 1925, 300, and now approximately 900. The **Central Norseman Gold Corporation** still mines one of the earliest finds in the area, which is also the richest quartz reef in Australia. The population of the modern town is 2500.

The Norseman Tourist Bureau is in *Robert Street,* ☎ *(08) 9039 1071,* and ⊙open Mon-Fri 8am-8pm, Sat-Sun 8am-4pm. They can advise on accommodation and sightseeing.

The **Historical and Geological Museum**, run by the Pensioners' League, has among other things, the largest known piece of Skylab,

the US satellite that exploded over Western Australia. **Beacon Hill Lookout,** from where there is a good view of the old mines, the chain of salt lakes, the gypsum hills and the **Jimberlana Dyke,** is reputed to be one of the oldest geological areas in the world.

Lady Miller Area, was one of the area's highest producing gold deposits, but has not been worked since 1950. Many of the mines in the area are accessible by car, and can easily be explored on foot. But it is warned that no attempt should be made to venture underground, as many of the mine shafts are dangerous. Ask the Tourist Bureau for information about all the old mines in the area. **The Salt Lakes** are at their best at sunrise and sunset, and the gypsum crystals which grow in the lakes are worth a close look. Again, care should be·taken to observe all warning signs of mining in progress, and do not drive a vehicle on to the salt lakes. The Tourist Bureau can tell you of the best location for the gypsum crystals.

Dundas Rocks are 22km (14 miles) south of Norseman *off the Coolgardie-Esperance Highway*, and the formations are 550 million years old. There are good picnic areas, and an old ghost town to explore. **Bromus Dam** is an old railway dam on the road to Esperance, about 32km (20 miles) from Norseman, and is a good spot for a picnic and a swim.

The **Lone Grave,** is an enigma on a spit of land on the far edge of Lake Dundas. It belongs to "Stanley Arthur Whitehead, who died April 8th, 1897, aged 7 months", and is the only sign that the area had at one time been inhabited by man. Free tours of

Central Norseman Corporation Gold Mining Operations ⊙leave the Tourist Bureau each weekday morning at 9.30am. They last about two hours, and enquiries should be made at the Tourist Bureau.

If you want to try your luck at fossicking for Moss Agate, Moss Opalite, Chrysophase and Jasper, obtain a permit from the Tourist Bureau. And, don't forget you need a Miner's Right from the Mines Department, if you are going to look for that piece of gold that everyone else has missed

---

↴ Let's Stay Here
Lodge 101,
101 Princep St, ☎ *9039 1541* Remote and located at the centre of town and 2-3 minutes walk from everything. Big family owned hostel with very warm and homely atmosphere. All rooms have fans and electric blankets. Facilities includes a wood fire, kitchen, 2 TV rooms, a barbecue area out the back and car park. *Dorms $19; Single $32; double/twin $50*

Esperance

Situated 369km (229 miles) south of Kalgoorlie on the coast, and 720km (447 miles) south-east of Perth, Esperance is known as 'The Bay of Isles'. Skywest have daily flights from Perth; a Westrail bus connects with the Prospector train from Perth to Kalgoorlie; and there is a Westrail bus service from East Perth three times weekly direct to Esperance.

The town's history began in 1627 when Pieter Nuyts, in command of the Dutch East India Company vessel *Gulde Zeepard*, charted the coast and the Recherche Archipelago, but did not land. The first to do that were men attached to a French scientific mission which was under the command of Admiral D'Entrecasteaux, whose ships sought shelter in a gale. The first ship to enter the bay was L'Esperance, hence the name of the bay. The second ship was the Recherche, hence the name of the Archipelago. The next 50 years saw visits by explorers Flinders and Eyre, and sealers and whalers, who played merry hell with the Aborigines.

In 1863, the Dempster brothers took up the first landholding in the area, and other farmer settlers followed. The discovery of gold at Coolgardie caused Esperance to become the port for the goldfields overnight, and this it remained until the completion of the Perth to Coolgardie rail link.

Now the area is a major farming region with a town population of 11,000, and 13,500 people living in the Shire.

The Esperance Tourist Bureau and Travel Centre is in *Dempster Street,* ☎*(08) 9071 2330,* and is ⊕open Mon-Fri 8.45am-5pm, Sat-Sun 9am-5pm. They have information on the accommodation available, where to fish, the best place to swim, or where to play golf, or any other sport.

Sightseeing attractions include: **Esperance Municipal Museum,** between *Dempster Street* and *the Esplanade,* ⊕open daily 1.30-4.30pm, ☎*9071 1579.* The **Public Library** in *Windich Street* next to the Shire Council, ⊕open Mon 10.30am-6pm, Tues 11am-3pm, Wed-Fri 10.30am-6pm, Sat 9.30am-11.30am.

The Pink Lake, which should

sometimes be called the Purple Lake.

Observatory Point and Lookout, where the two French frigates sheltered from the storm in 1792.

The Dempster Charm Cottage, ☎*9071 1413,* built in 1867, and classified by the National Trust.

National Parks in the area include **Stokes, Cape Le Grand** and **Cape Arid.**

Scenic flights are a perfect way to see magnificent coastal scenery, islands and whales. Contact **Esperance Air Service,** ☎*9071 1467.*

⤳ **Let's Stay Here**

Blue Waters Lodge YHA, *299 Goldfields Rd,* ☎*9071 1040,* 🖥*www.yha.com.au* Located just 20 metres from the sea front with fantastic panoramic view of the bay. Not far from town. Really friendly staff. Facilities includes a kitchen, laundry, TV lounge, internet access a common room with a pool table and barbecue area. Bike hire and parking available. *Members dorm ☯$18; single $30; double $22.50pp BC MC VA*

Esperance Backpackers, *14 Emily St,* ☎*9071 4724* Small and clean hostel at the town centre. Ranging from dorms to self contained units for longer stays. Your basic facilities. *Dorm ☯$20; single $35; double/twin $48*

North From Perth

Geraldton
Population 35,000
Geraldton is located 424km (263

miles) north of Perth on the Brand Highway. It is the gateway to the Abrolhos Islands. The area is known as the Batavia Coast, named after the Batavia which was one of many ships wrecked off the coast.

Climate
Average temperatures: January max 32C (90F) - min 19C (66F); July max 19C (66F) - min 9C (48F). Number of days a year with temperature over 30C (86F) - 76; number of days a year with temperature over 40C (104F) - 8. Average annual rainfall: 475mm (19 ins); wettest six months - April to September.

Characteristics
Geraldton's boundary of safe beaches, its year long surf scene, the wildflowers, scenic attractions and rich historical features, give it a magnetic appeal to those who want a carefree holiday. It is known as Sun City, because it boasts of an average of 8 hours sunshine a day, all year round.

How to Get There
By Air
Skywest have daily flights from/to Perth.

By Bus
The **Westrail** bus departs East Perth Terminal six times weekly, with alternate routes through Moora and Eneabba.
Geraldton is on the **Greyhound Pioneer** Perth/Broome/Darwin route.

Visitor Infomation
The Geraldton Tourist Bureau is situated on the corner of *Chapman Road* and *Bayly Street* at the Bill Sewell Community Recreation

Geraldton

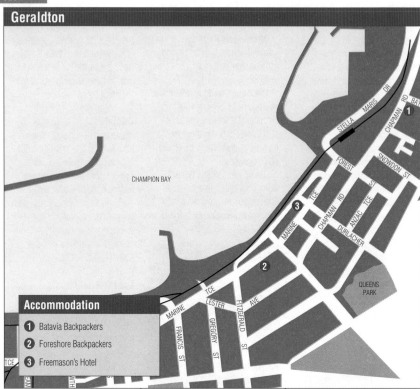

Accommodation

1. Batavia Backpackers
2. Foreshore Backpackers
3. Freemason's Hotel

Complex, ☎(08) 9921 3999. The Bureau is ⊙open Mon-Fri 8am-6pm, Sat-Sun 8am-5pm.

↜ Let's Stay Here

As always with holiday resorts, there is plenty of accommodation available, and bookings should be made ahead. Here is a selection of budget accommodation which should be used as a guide only. The telephone area code is 08.

Batavia Backpackers,
Corner Chapman Rd and Bayly St, ☎9964 3001 Located in a pristine heritage building which used to be the hospital. Provides your basic accommodation and facilities.

There's also an Information Centre on site. Parking available. *Dorm ✪$17; single $23; double $40*

Foreshore Backpackers YHA,
172 Marine Terrace, ☎9921 3275 ▄www.yha.com.au Located in Geraldton's main street making it very close to the shops and malls and all the city hubs. Great views can be seen from the verandah overlooking the beach and the harbour. They say sea lions can be seen from here. Facilities includes kitchen, TV lounge, internet access, laundry and barbecue area. Parking available. *Members dorm*

✪$19 ($16 non members); single $25 ($28 non members); double $40 ($43 non members) BC MC VA

Freemason's Hotel,
79 Marine Terrace, ☎9964 3457 Accommodation is situated above a pub, just at the centre of town. Shared facilities including a microwave, kettle and TV room. Entertainment can be found downstairs during Thursdays to Saturday nights with live music and loud noise. Parking available. *Dorm ✪$20 ($15 for more people)*

Mariner Motel Hotel,
298 Chapman Road, ☎9921 2544. 18 rooms (private fa-

cilities), licensed restaurant, swimming pool ✪$55-60.

Caravan Parks

Batavia Coast Caravan Park, *Lot 3/89 Hall Rd, Waggrakine,* ☎9938 1222. (Pets on application) - *powered sites* ✪$12 *for two , on-site vans $25 for two.*

Separation Point Caravan Park, *Separation Point,* ☎9921 2763. (No dogs allowed) - *powered sites $16 for two, on-site vans* ✪$30-35 *for two.*

Sunset Beach Holiday Park, *Bosley Street* ☎9938 1655. (No pets allowed) - *powered sites* ✪$17 *for two, on-site vans $33 for two.*

Let's Eat

Whatever type of food you fancy, you will find the right place in Geraldton. A stroll down Marine Terrace will take you past plenty of eateries, and then it's only a matter of choosing the one that appeals most. Here are some to consider.

China Moon, 1*98 Marine Terrace,* ☎9923 9924.

Jade House, *57 Marine Terrace,* ☎9*964 1222* - licensed - open Mon-Sat 11.30am-2.30pm, Mon-Sun 5-11pm.

La Famiglia, *1 Fitzgerald Street,* ☎9921 8655.

Lemon Grass, *18 Snowdon Street,* ☎9964 1172.
OK Corral Mexican Restaurant, *185 Marine Terrace,* ☎9964 5424.

Rose, *9 Forrest Street,* ☎9921 5645 -BYO- hopen Tues-Sun 5.30-11pm.

Skeetas Garden Restaurant, *9 George Road,* ☎9964 1619.

Tanti's, *174 Marine Terrace,* ☎9964 2311.

Points of Interest
The **Wishing Well Lookout** in *Brede Street* overlooks the city with its Norfolk pines lining the beach front.

St Francis Xavier Cathedral, *cnr Cathedral Avenue* and *Maitland Street,* was built in stages from 1914 until the opening in 1938. The Byzantine style architecture is one of Monsignor John Hawes' masterpieces.

Bill Sewell Community Complex, *cnr Chapman Road* and *Bayly Street.* Originally this building was the Victoria District Hospital dating from 1887 to 1966, then it was used as a Regional Prison until 1984. The building had major restoration work done, and was re-opened in 1988. The Geraldton Tourist Bureau is situated in this beautiful building and the **Old Gaol Craft Centre** is adjacent.

The **Western Australian Museum Geraldton** occupies two adjoining buildings in Museum Place - the *Maritime Display Building* and *Old Railway Building,* ☎9921 5080. The Maritime Display Building overlooks a long sweep of coast that has witnessed some of the earliest and bloodiest events in Australia's European history. The museum contains finds from Australia's oldest shipwrecks. Three Dutch ships, **Batavia** (1629), **Zuytdorp** (1712) and **Zeewijk** (1727) were wrecked on route to Holland's fabulously wealthy trading empire - present-day Indonesia. Cannon, coins, navigational instruments, pottery and personal gear have been recovered after centuries under the surf. The historic **Old Railway Building** was built for Western Australia's first government railway. Inside, displays depict the region's intriguing variety of plants, animals and minerals. This is interwoven with the absorbing story of man in the region. The museum is ☉open Mon-Sat 10am-5pm, Sun 1-5pm, and admission is free.

The **Lighthouse Keepers Cottage,** *cnr Chapman Road* and *Grenville Drive,* was built in 1870 and was the original lighthouse keeper's residence for the Port of Geraldton. **The Historical Society** is based here, and it is ☉open Thursdays only.

Geraldton Art Gallery is located in the city's original **Town Hall** in *Chapman Road.* The Town Hall was opened in 1907 and renovated in 1984. Admission to the Gallery is free, and it is ☉open Mon-Sat 10am-5pm, Sun 1.30-4.30pm, ☎9921 6811.

The **Point Moore Lighthouse** is rather difficult to overlook, due to its broad red and white stripes. It was built in 1879, and is 35m (115 ft) high and its light is visible for up to 26km (16 miles).

Festivals
The **Sunshine Festival** is held in October each year.

Facilities
Swimming, fishing, yachting, lawn bowls, tennis, cricket, squash, pistol-shooting, go-kart racing, horse racing, golf, roller skating and ten-pin bowling.

Down Brand Highway

Greenough

Situated 25km (16 miles) south of Geraldton on the Brand Highway, Greenough features many examples of early pioneering history dating from the 1850s.

The **Greenough Village** complex looks very much as it did in its heyday. It was restored and is maintained by the National Trust (WA), and features **Pioneer Tea Rooms** and an **Art Gallery**, where works by significant Mid-West artists are displayed and sold. Guided tours through the buildings are highly recommended.

Adjacent to the Village in *Company Road* is the **Hampton Arms Historic Inn** (1861), and next door is the Greenough **Wildlife and Bird Park**, ☎ *9926 1171,* a must for the kids where all kinds of animals can be seen.

Dongara/Port Denison

The Shire of Irwin has three townships: Dongara, Port Denison and Irwin. The townsite of Dongara, 359km (223 miles) north of Perth on the Brand Highway, was surveyed in 1852, and named Dhungarra. It is a little known fact that the Brand Highway is within 2km of beautiful beaches and a rustic, almost forgotten township, that was first settled nearly 150 years ago. For years Dongara and the adjacent townsite of Port Denison have been popular retirement destinations for farmers of the surrounding rural areas. Now tourists and holiday makers are discovering the delights of this historic region. The Dongara Denison Visitor Infomation Centre is in the **Old Police Station Building**, *Waldeck Street, Dongara,* ☎ *(08) 9927*

1404, ◷open Mon-Fri 9am-4pm, Sat 10am-1pm. They are able to advise on available accommodation, and attractions. The town caters for most popular sports - bowls, tennis, yachting, golf, squash, basketball, badminton and gymnastics.

> ↩ **Let's Stay Here**
> **Dongara Backpackers,**
> *32 Waldeck St,* ☎ *9927 1581* Located at the centre of town minutes away from the beach and shops. Accommodation set in three self-contained buildings all with their own kitchen, showers and bathrooms. Other facilities includes laundry, barbecue area out the back and a car park. *Dorms ✪$17.50; single $25; double/twin $40*

Heading Back To Perth

Cervantes

Cervantes is a crayfishing centre, and appeals to anglers because of the wide range of fish which can be caught from the shore, or from a small boat in the local waters. The town is about 245km (152 miles) north of Perth, and the Visitor Infomation is in the Shell Service Station, *cnr Aragon* and *Seville Streets,* ☎ *9652 7041.* Nearby is the **Nambung National Park,** whose main attraction is the **Pinnacles**, an area of sand of varying colours, where there are thousands of limestone pinnacles which range in size from ankle high and pencil thickness to 5m high and 2m thick at the base. Access to the park is difficult and care should be taken to avoid vehicle damage. Visitors are requested to stay on defined tracks and observe directional and warning signs.

> ↩ **Let's Stay Here**
> **Pinnacles Beach Backpackers,**
> *91 Seville St, Cevantes,* ☎ *9652 7377,* ▤ *www.wn.com.au/ pbbackpackers* Located about 10 minute walk from the shops and close to the beach. New and brilliant with facilities including a fully equipped kitchen, laundry, comfy lounge and very clean bathrooms. *Dorms ✪$20 ; double/twin $55*

Moora

Located on the Midlands Road, 190km (118 miles) north of Perth via New Norcia, or 175km (109 miles) via Mogumber.

Visitor Infomation is in the Moora Shire Office, *34 Padbury Street,* ☎ *(08) 9651 1401.* Moora is recognised as the heart of the wheat district of the Midlands, and is on the banks of the Moore River. The town stretches across the clay flats deposited by an ancient waterway, and the area in its virgin state was a large salmon gum forest. Pioneer, Walter Padbury opened up more land in the area than anyone. He was a great philanthropist and Western Australia's first millionaire.

Attractions include: **Watheroo National Park**; **Jingamia Cave**; the **Mill Museum**; **Waddi Farms**; and the **Australian Flower Farm at Coorow.**

Morawa

Morawa, 100km south west of Geraldton, is the centre of a well established district. It was settled about 1905 and declared a townsite in 1912. It has a population of around 1350, and the area is based on wheat and wool growing. Prater Airport

Pinnacles

Swan Bells Tower, Perth

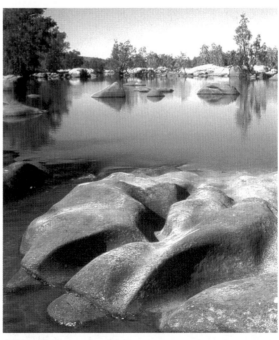

Ashburton River

which accommodated Dove and DC3 aircraft, is now a regular port of call for light aircraft. A fully illuminated strip allows for night landing of the flying doctor and courier planes.

Visitor Infomation is available from the Morawa Shire Council, ☎9971 1204.

Attractions include: **Koolanooka Springs; Bilya Rock Reserve; old mine sites; Mingenew Coal Seam; the Historical museum; Holy Cross Church;** and wildflowers. Facilities for sports include golf, football, basketball, badminton, squash, rifle shooting, tennis, bowls, swimming, gliding and flying.

Outlying Attractions
Mullewa

Situated 100km (62 miles) east of Geraldton, Mullewa is the gateway to the Murchison pastoral and old goldfield area. The most direct route is along the Geraldton Highway to Mingenew, then along the Mingenew/Mullewa Road. Visitor Infomation is in Mullewa Shire Council, *Jose Street,* ☎*(08) 9961 1007,* email ✉admin@mullewa.wa.gov.au, internet 💻*www.mullewa.wa.gov.au*

Attractions include: **Murchison Goldfields; Tenindewa Pioneer Well; Glacier Bed; St Andrew's Anglican Church; Pallottine Mission;** and **Tallering Peak and Gorge.**

Northampton

Northampton, 52 km north of Geraldton, has one of the richest histories in the State of Western Australia, and is situated 52km (32 miles) north of Geraldton.

The hills of the town, drained by creeks with permanent pools attracted game and proved a haven for Australian Aborigines. Evidence of their ancient culture can be seen in cave paintings at the Bowes River turnoff. Shepherds gradually moved into the area, and one of them, Thomas Mason, discovered copper at Wanneranooka in 1842. The copper mine which subsequently developed was the first in the State.

Lead was discovered in 1848 and the Geraldton mine was developed. The labour shortage, acute throughout the State, was relieved to some extent by the continuation of the transportation of convicts. A convict hiring station was established at Port Gregory 1853-1856.

The Northampton Tourist Bureau is on the *North West Coastal Highway,* ☎*(08) 9934 1488,* and they will advise of the attractions, which include: **Chiverton House Museum, Gwalla Cemetery and Church; Wanneranooka Copper Mine; Original Miner's Cottages; Alma School House; Warribano Chimney;** and **Port Gregory.**

Kalbarri

Kalbarri is one of the fastest growing holiday resorts in WA, and is 591km (367 miles) north of Perth, 167km north of Geraldton. The climate is suitable for all year round swimming and fishing, and the scenery is unique. The town is on the mouth of the Murchison River and it is the river gorges which provide much of the unique scenery in the area, not to mention spectacular coastal scenery south of the town. Fishing from the beach or from boats is first class, and the town's main activity, along with tourism, is the rock lobster industry. Abundant and beautiful flora is just another attraction.

The history of Kalbarri is fascinating, though violent, as its treacherous coastline has resulted in many shipwrecks. Australia's first white settlers arrived here in 1629, though probably with a degree of reluctance. Commodore Pelsaert marooned two conspirators here for their activity in the 'terrible' Batavia mutiny. Visitor Infomation is available from the Kalbarri Tourist Bureau in *Grey Street,* ☎*(08) 9937 1104.*

🔖 **Let's Stay Here**
Kalbarri Backpackers YHA, *52 Mortimer St,* ☎*9937 1430,* 💻*www.kalbarribackpackers.com.au* Located not far from the Murchison River. Facilities includes laundry, kitchen, TV lounge, internet access, swimming pool and a nice, shady barbecue area. Free use of boogie boards and snorkel gear are available for guests. Bike and car hire can also be arranged. Parking available. *Members dorm* ◐*$18 ($19 non members); single $44 ($46 non members); double $46 ($48 non members) BC MC VA EFTPOS*

Carnarvon
Population 6,700
Carnarvon is situated 902km (560 miles) north of Perth and 481km north of Geraldton, at the mouth of the Gascoyne River.

Climate
Average temperatures: January max 40C (104F) - min 35C (95F); July max 25C (77F) - min 16C (61F). Average annual rainfall: 127mm (5 in).

Characteristics

Carnarvon, often described as 'the sun's winter home', is the commercial centre of the Gascoyne district. It is a friendly town, with a tropical, relaxed atmosphere, and an abundance of fish and tropical fruit.

How to Get There
By Bus

Bus Australia and **Greyhound** have daily services to Carnarvon from Perth.

Visitor Infomation

Carnarvon District Tourist Bureau is in the Civic Centre, *Robinson Street,* ☎ *(08) 9941 1146.* Send emails to ✉cvontourist@wn.com.au

↪ Let's Stay Here

The Tourist Bureau has a full list of the accommodation available, but here we have a selection of budegt accommodation which should be used as a guide only. The telephone area code is 08.

Carnarvon Backpackers, *97-99 Olivia Terrace,* ☎ *9941 1095.* Basic lodging and facilities catering mostly for working travellers. Set in two old houses and has a nice games room area. There is also a barbecue area outside. Parking available. *Dorms* ✪*$20 ; double $47*
Port Hotel, *Robinson Street,* ☎ *9941 1704.* 17 rooms (private facilities), swimming pool, barbecue ✪*$40.*

Carnarvon Hotel, *Olivia Terrace,* ☎ *9941 1412.* 27 units (private facilities) ✪*$65.*

Caravan Parks
Wintersun Caravan Park, *Robinson Street,* ☎ *9941 8150.* (No dogs allowed) - *powered sites* ✪*$19 for two, on-site vans $50 for two.*

Norwesta Caravan Park, *cnr Robinson and Angelo Streets,* ☎ *9941 1277* (No pets allowed) - *powered sites* ✪*$14.50 for two, on-site vans $30-45 for two.*
Plantation Caravan Park, Robinson Street, ☎9941 8100. (No dogs allowed) - *powered sites* ✪*$18 -19 for two, cabins $22 for two.*

Carnarvon Tourist Centre *Caravan Park, Robinson Street,* ☎ *9941 1438* (No pets allowed) - *powered sites* ✪*$17 for two, on-site vans $34-56 for two.*

There are also several guesthouses in Carnarvon, and it is also possible to stay at farms and stations in the area. The Tourist Bureau are the people to see about these.

Let's Eat
Most of the hotels and motels have restaurants, either licensed or BYO, and there are many outlets specialising in the local fish, cooked to perfection. The Tourist Bureau has a full list, and you can be guided by their recommendations. If you're in the mood for Chinese, head for the **Dragon Pearl** at *18 Francis St,* ☎ *9941 1941.*

Points of Interest
Plantations extend along both banks of the Gascoyne River for about 15km (9 miles), and some welcome visitors to buy their mangoes, pawpaws, bananas, oranges and grapefruit.

The **Gascoyne River** usually flows below the surface of the river bed, with irrigation channels pumping the water to the plantations along the river flats. Occasionally, after heavy rains upstream, the river can be seen, and levee banks have been built to protect low-lying areas during floods.

The most obvious landmark in Carnarvon is the '**Big Dish**', a 26.5m (87 ft) diameter reflector which was of major importance to global communications from 1966 to 1987. It closed down in May of that year, but is open to visitors. The site also provides a magnificent view of Carnarvon and the plantations.

The building adjoining the **Tourist Bureau** has a museum with exhibits from the NASA base, a large collection of shells and some local artefacts.

Pioneer Park, in *Olivia Terrace,* contains a number of relics of the town's history, including the two whale bones which form the arch over the entrance. The park is a popular picnic spot, and has coin operated barbecues and swings for the kids.

Jubilee Hall, in *Francis Street,* was opened in 1887 and for years served as Council Chambers and Shire Offices. The first 50 pounds received for the construction of the hall was donated by Queen Victoria!

St George's Church of England, in *Francis Street* opposite the Shire Offices, was erected in 1907. The first Bishop of North-West Australia was enthroned here on July 4, 1910. It is the most westerly parish in

Australia, and part of the largest Anglican diocese in the world.

Chinaman's Pool is a great picnic area and swimming spot in the Gascoyne River, between *Marmion* and *Saw Streets*. It was originally a watering hole for the township, and now attracts many varieties of birdlife, especially in the early morning or evening.

One Mile Jetty, on **Babbage Island**, actually stretches 1,493m (4,898 ft) out into the bay. It was built in 1904, and widened in 1912, and was used by ships until 1966. The jetty end was burnt by vandals in 1985, but the locals raised the funds to have it rebuilt. In the lighthouse keeper's cottage there is a museum which is run in conjunction with the Gascoyne Historical Society.

Just before you get to the One Mile Jetty you'll come to **Dwyer's Leap**, a water ski area that is usually sheltered from the wind.

The Blowholes near the town are spectacular, as the trapped water is forced out through a hole to a height of 20m (66 ft). Nearby is a good beach where people go for oysters, fish and crayfish.

Cape Cuvier, 30km (19 miles) north of the Blowhole is a deep port where ships load salt for Japan. It is fascinating if you are there when they are loading, although not if you are too close. The port is situated beneath a 60m (197 ft) cliff and they simply bulldoze the salt over the cliff onto a conveyor below.

The **HMAS Sydney Memorial Cairn** was erected near High Rock, Quobba Station, to commemorate the tragic battle between the *Sydney* and the German raider *Kormoran* off Carnarvon on November 19, 1941.

The **Fascine** is the bay formed by the South Arm of the Gascoyne River. The name is derived from the Latin word meaning 'bundle of sticks', because in the old days bundles of sticks were placed on the foreshore to help prevent erosion during the major river flows. Now the waterway is lined with stately palms. The area is a favourite spot for a picnic, or an evening stroll.

Pelican Point is a popular swimming and fishing spot about 5km out of town. **Bibbawarra Bore** is 16km (10 miles) north of Carnarvon. The Bore was originally worked for coal in 1905 to a depth of 914m (3000 ft), and now produces a continuous flow of hot water around 65C (145F). Be very careful with children and pets, as many have been scalded.

Bush Bay and **New Beach** are both excellent for swimming and fishing. They are reached from the *Geraldton Road.*

Festivals

The **Carnarvon Rodeo** is held in July; **Sandhurst Run**, a rock concert, is held annually in August; **Dry River Regatta** is held between July and September, depending on the weather; and the **Yachting Regatta,** from Denham to Carnarvon is also held every year. The Tourist Bureau can advise the dates.

Facilities

There are sailing, surfing, fishing, windsurfing, waterskiing, snorkelling, boating, swimming, and tours, both local and further afield.

Outlying Attractions
Shark Bay

Shark Bay is an historic area.

Dirk Hartog, the Dutch navigator landed on the island which now bears his name, in 1616, and nailed that famous pewter plate to a post. In 1696, another Dutch navigator, William de Vlamingh, removed Dirk's plate and took it back to Holland, and put his own plate in its place. That plate was in turn removed by a Frenchman, Captain Freycinet, in 1818. He took it back to France, and for 40 years no one knew where it was. In 1947 the plate finally turned up and was presented to the Western Australian Museum, where it has pride of place.

The French named many places in the area - Hamelin, Peron, Faure, Lesueur, Freycinet, Heirisson, for example, but Shark Bay was given its name, albeit a in a different form, by William Dampier, who visited in 1699. He called it 'The Bay of Sharks'.

The only town in Shark Bay is **Denham**, the westernmost town in Australia. It has a permanent population of around 400, and has excellent recreational facilities - lawn bowls, tennis courts, mini golf, trampolines, golf course, charter boats and tours.

The Shark Bay Tourist Bureau, *71 Knight Street, Denham,* ☎ *(08) 9948 1253,* has accommodation details, and information on sightseeing and the *Shark Bay Heritage Trail,* a 130km (81 miles) features sites of historical interest and the unique natural environment.

There are only two beaches in the world made completely of sea shell that has been washed up on the shore for thousands of years and compacted by nature. One of them is close to Denham, and locals have cut blocks of shell from the beach to build along the foreshore. **Shell Beach** is a natural wonder which still has scientists intrigued.

Hamelin Bay, on the way into Denham, has another scientific mystery. In the clear shallow waters of the Bay, stromatolites dating back millions of years, can be seen. They are one of the world's two oldest living fossils.

Monkey Mia

Some 260km south of Carnarvon and about 25km (16 miles) from Denham across the peninsula, is Monkey Mia, where friendly bottlenose dolphins visit, apparently just to interact with people. The local *Dolphin Information Centre* has loads of information on these creatures ☎ *9948 1366.*

Monkey Mia is also an excellent spot for fishing, boating, or lazing on the clean white beaches.

↳ **Let's Stay Here**
Shark Bay and Monkey Mia Bay Lodge YHA,
95 Knight Terrace, Denham, ☎ *9948 1278,* ▄ *www.yha.co m.au* Located right in front of the beach. Numerous water activities are very close by. Fully self contained units with air condition, bathroom, TV and kitchen. Other facilities includes TV lounge, internet access. Highlights would probably be the heated swimming pool and barbecue area. There is also a free shuttle bus service that takes you to Monkey Mia daily to see the dolphins. Parking available. *Members dorm* ❂ *$20; single $20; double $50 BC MC VA EFTPOS*

Monkey Mia Dolphin Resort YHA,
Monkey Mia Rd, ☎ *9948*

1320, ▄ *www.monkeymia. com.au* Located right next to the well known Monkey Mia Beach where dolphins visit. You can feed them during certain hours of the day at your leisure. Facilities kitchen, TV lounge, laundry, internet access, swimming pool and barbecue area. Canoes and bikes are available for hire. Buses stops right in front of the hostel and they also offer a shuttle bus to the airport. Parking available. *Members dorm* ❂ *$16.65 ($18.50 non members); single $30.60 ($34 non members); double $43.20 ($48 non members) BC MC VA EFTPOS*

Gascoyne Junction

About 13km (8 miles) north of Carnarvon is the turn-off for Gascoyne Junction, which lies a further 164km (102 miles) to the east, at the junction of the Gascoyne and Lyons Rivers. It is the only town in the Shire of Upper Gascoyne, which covers an area of 57,146km2 (22,058 sq miles). There are huge sheep stations in the area which produce an annual wool clip of over 1.5 million kilograms (3,307,000 lbs). After the long drive on the gravel road, which incidentally is well formed and graded, you will welcome the site of the **Gascoyne Junction Hotel,** a real bush pub made of corrugated iron, which seems to have stepped out of the past. Further along the road you will pass **Minnie Creek,** and the **Kennedy Ranges** which have Aboriginal caves and rock paintings. The Ranges are known for the semi precious gem stones to be found there, so you might like to take some time out for fossicking.

Mount Augustus

The Mount is a rock. In fact it is the largest rock (monocline) in the world. It is not as famous as that other one in Central Australia, but by its geological formation it should be, and it is well worth the trip through the rugged bush country.

Mount Augustus is 289km north west (180 miles) from Gascoyne Junction, and accommodation is available at: **Mount Augustus Outback Tourist Resort,** via Carnarvon, ☎ *(08) 9943 0527.* The Mount was of significance to the Aborigines, so there are plenty of rock paintings, and at the pools close to the rock, ornithologists catalogued more than 100 species of birds in just two days!

Coral Bay

Located 250km (155 miles) north of Carnarvon, and 150km (93 miles) south of Exmouth, Coral Bay is situated in a lagoon formed between the Ningaloo Coral Reef and the coastline. The Reef is the longest continuous and most accessible reef complex in Western Australia, extending from north of Point Murat, round North West Cape, and south to Amherst Point, a distance of about 260km (162 miles). Coral Bay is a blue-water paradise, that has yet to be commercialised. There is only one small hotel and several caravan parks, and the beach and bay area provide a perfect place for beachcombing, fishing, swimming and exploring. Offshore the occasional humpback whale, dolphin and dugong can be seen, and in summer, if you are lucky, you may see turtles lumbering up from the sea to lay their eggs.

Then, of course, there is the

reef, considered one of the most beautiful in the world, with its abundance of Spanish mackerel, tuna, marlin and sailfish. Fishing tours and charter vessels can be arranged, and for diving contact **Coral Dive, ☎** *(08) 9942 5940.* **Bay View Caravan Park** has a glass bottom boat tour ☎ *9942 5932,* and **Sub-Sea Explorer** has a semi-submersible craft for viewing the reef ☎ *9942 5955.*

↵ Let's Stay Here

Coral Bay Backpack-ers, *Robinson St,* ☎ *9942 5934,* Located very close to the beach Part of the Ningaloo Reef Resort/Coral bay Hotel chain. Great for the guest who have access to all their facilities including the bar, swimming pool and games room. Dorms are small. Facilities includes a kitchen, swimming pool and barbecue area. Parking available. *Dorms ❂$16.50*

Ningaloo Club,

46 Robinson St, ☎ *9948 5100,* ▣ www.*ningalooclub.com* Just a new developed hostel making everything spick and spam with excellent facilities. Facilities includes a kitchen, TV lounge with pool table, swimming pool and barbecue area outdoors. There's also a cafe on site. Parking available. *Dorm ❂$18-10 bed, $21-6 bed, $23-4 bed; twin $30 pp ; double $60*

Exmouth

Located 155km (96 miles) north of Coral Bay, and 400km (249 miles) north of Carnarvon, Exmouth is one of the newest towns in Australia. It was founded in 1967 as a support town for the US Naval Communications Station, and now has a population of around 3000.

Exmouth is the home of the big fish, and draws many people eager to experience the feel of a taut line. To date, 13 world and Australian game fish records have been landed at Exmouth, as well as the largest sailfish ever caught. The town has six large charter vessels, an offshore rescue group, and a variety of accommodation houses and caravan parks. The Exmouth Tourist Bureau, *cnr Murat Road* and *Truscott Crescent,* ☎ *9948 1176* is ⊕open daily 9am-5pm, and they have details of all accommodation and sightseeing.

The town is situated on a peninsula surrounded by Ningaloo Marine Park, and the reef is accessible by small boat.

Surrounding Exmouth is some of Australia's best bush country with its wildlife and flora. On a scenic drive through **Cape Range National Park** and **Ningaloo Marine Park's** perimeter, there are many rugged gorges and canyons for you to explore.

For details of the many wonders of the Cape Range National Park, visit the Milyering Visitor Centre, about 52km (32 miles) from Exmouth in the heart of the Cape Range National Park.

↵ Let's Stay Here

Excape Backpackers, *Corner Payne St and Maidstone Cres,* ☎ *9949 1200,* ▣ www.*potshotresort.com* Located on the northern part of town. This hostel is part of the Potshot Hotel complex. Expect the basic accommodation at the blue building. Facilities in-

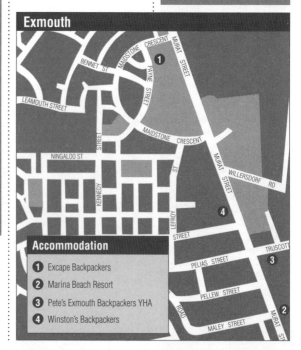

Exmouth

CRESCENT · MURAT STREET · MAIDSTONE · BENNET ST · PAYNE STREET · ❶ · LEAMOUTH STREET · STREET · MAIDSTONE CRESCENT · NINGALOO ST · MURAT STREET · WILLERSDORF RD · KENNEDY · ST · LEFROY · ❹ · STREET · TRUSCOTT · PELIAS STREET · ❸ · PELLEW STREET · ROAD · MALEY STREET · MURAT ST

Accommodation

❶ Excape Backpackers

❷ Marina Beach Resort

❸ Pete's Exmouth Backpackers YHA

❹ Winston's Backpackers

cludes a swimming pool and a good bar. There's a $20 key deposit when you check in. *Dorm* ✪ *$22; single/double $59*

Marina Beach Resort,
50 Market St, ☎ *9949 1500,* 🖳 *www.ningaloochase.com.au*
Located south, right on the beach, which is great location compared to the other hostels in town. It's quite a distance from town though. But the 25-minute walk along the beach is a must. The hostel is styled like a resort, with dorms in raised tent-like cabins with balconies at the front and doubles in safari tents. Your standard facilities including a kitchen, swimming pool, TV lounge and bar. Look out for the observation deck which is fantastic for whale watching. Parking available. *Dorm* ✪ *$24; double/twin $24 pp*

Pete's Exmouth Backpackers YHA,
Corner Truscott Cres and Murat Rd, ☎ *9949 1101 or 1800 621 101,* 🖳 *www.exmouthdiving.com.au* Winner of the State Tourism award in 1994, 1996 and 1998. Part of the Exmouth Cape Tourist Village. Accommodation in air conditioned port cabins with air condition and en suite. A definite highlight of this hostel is their offered services of courtesy bus to beaches, turtle tours and fresh fish BBQs. Don't miss the Village Dive shop which offers the likes of scuba diving, fun activities like abseiling and rock climbing and other courses. Facilities includes kitchen, laundry, TV lounge, internet access, swimming

pool and barbecue area. Bike and Suzuki car hires can be arranged. Parking available. **Recommended.** *Members dorm* ✪ *$20 ($22 non members); single $32 ; double $52 ; BC MC VA EFTPOS*

Winston's Backpackers,
Murat Rd, ☎ *9949 2377 or 1800 652 665* Located just in town, right across from the Visitor Infomation Centre. Part of the Ningaloo Caravan Park. Quite a clean place with a camp kitchen, swimming pool and barbecue area. Parking available. *Dorms* ✪ *$18.50 ; single $55; double/twin $55*

Port Hedland
Population 15,000
Port Hedland is 1763km (1096 miles) north of Perth, at the junction of the North West Coastal Highway and the Great Northern Highway, on the shores of the Indian Ocean.

Climate
Average temperatures: January max 36C (97F) - min 25C (77F); July 26C (79F) - min 12C (54F). Number of days per year with temperature over 30C (86F) - 259; number of days per year with temperature over 40C (104F) - 29. Average annual rainfall: 304mm (12 ins); wettest six months - January to June.

Characteristics
Port Hedland is the biggest port by tonnage in Australia, and the world's biggest ships visit its wharves to collect the Pilbara's most valuable commodity - iron ore. Almost everything in the town revolves around mining and iron ore.

The town has an airport that provides a gateway for international visitors.

How to Get There
By Bus
Greyhound Pioneer have daily services to Port Hedland from Perth.

Visitor Infomation
Port Hedland Tourist Centre is at *13 Wedge Street, Port Hedland,* ☎ *(08) 9173 1711.* There is another outlet at South Hedland, in *Leake Street,* ☎ *(08) 9172 5177.*

↩ Let's Stay Here
There is not a lot to choose from, but here is a selection, with prices which should be used as a guide only. The telephone area code is 08.

Dingo Oasis Backpackers,
59 Kingsmill St, ☎ *9173 1000* The waterfront location makes this a choice to stay at. Exceptional accommodation with a separate annex building catering for travellers of the easy rider bus. Good facilities. Don't miss the hammocks outdoors that overlooks the sea. Parking available. *Dorm* ✪ *$20; single/double $50*

Frogs Port Hedland Backpackers,
20 Richardson St, ☎ *9173 3282* Located at the very centre of town close to the bus depot and tourist centre. Small hostel with friendly staff. Ocean-view fronts on the verandah. Air conditioned accommodation. Facilities includes kitchen, laundry, internet access, TV/video lounge and a swimming pool. Also off street parking. *Dorms* ✪ *$18; double $45*

Caravan Parks

Port Hedland Caravan Park, *Great Northern Highway,* ☎*9172 2525.* (Dogs allowed on leash) - *powered sites* ✪*$20 for two, on-site vans $35 for two.*

South Hedland Caravan Park, *Hamilton Road,* ☎*9721 1197.* (No pets allowed) - *powered sites* ✪*$20 for two, cabins from $60 for two.*

Cooke Point Holiday Park, *Athol Street,* ☎*9173 1271.* (No pets allowed) - *powered sites* ✪*$20-22 for two, no on-site vans.*

Let's Eat

Most of the hotels and motels have licensed restaurants, and there are a few takeaway outlets. Some places you might like to try are:

Bruno's Pizzeria and Ristorante, *7 Richardson Street,* ☎*9173 2047.*

Oriental Galley Chinese Restaurant, *19 Edgar Street,* ☎*9173 1272.*

Shell Restaurant, *Wilson Street,* ☎*9173 2551.*

The Copper Pot, *Shop 4 Keesing Street,* ☎*9173 1363.*

Points of Interest

Port Hedland was named after Captain Peter Hedland, who discovered the entrance to the shallow bay in 1829. The first sheep station in the Pilbara was started on the nearby De Grey River in 1864.

In the 1870s, pearls were found along the coast, and Port Hedland became the home base for the pearling luggers. Inland, gold was discovered, and that brought new settlers. When the gold ran out, the town declined and in 1946 the population was 150. The 1950s saw some activity with the commencement of small tin, copper, gold and manganese outfits that used the town as a base. Then in the 1960s, the embargo on iron ore was lifted, and the modern industry was born. Port Hedland is now the major centre of Western Australia's iron ore industry, and one of the largest mineral ports in the world. The population of the town includes the two satellite towns of South Hedland and Finucane Island. Tours of the port are available and allow you to see the iron ore being loaded onto some of the biggest ore carriers in the world. The Visitor Infomation Centre has details.

The Don Rhodes Mining Museum, *Wilson Street,* has relics of the early mining days, and there are barbecue facilities.

Lion's Park, in *Anderson Street,* is a good picnic area, with lots of shade and lawn.

The tides in the area range up to 8m (26 ft), and create good fishing spots and chances to collect shells. Note the patterns formed on the tidal flats by the outgoing tide.

Cemetery Beach is a great fishing spot at high tides, and nearby is a children's playground. **Pretty Pool** is also good for fishing and picnics. Due to the dangers of stonefish, blue-ringed octopus, sea snakes and sharks, it is not recommended that you swim in the ocean or the creeks, but there is an olympic pool, with a wading and diving pool in the town, and in South Hedland there is a big aquatic centre.

There are several Heritage Trails in and around the town, and the Tourist Centre has full details. **The Old Port Hedland Trail** is a 2.25km walk retracing the development of the early port township, taking in the historical buildings and sites. It commences at the Tourist Centre. **The Port Trail** is a 1.8km walk combining the port's history with more recent developments. It commences at the Port Authority Offices and takes about one hour. **The Sutherland Trail** begins at the Tourist Centre, and its 9km route is an easy 45 minute drive. **The Out and About Trail** begins at Pretty Pool, covers about 85km (53 miles) exploring South Hedland's natural, Aboriginal and historic sites, and takes about half a day.

Facilities

Car Hire - Budget Rent A Car, Airport, ☎9140 1229; Hertz Rent A Car, Airport, ☎9140 1555; WK Motors, Anderson Street, ☎9173 1729.

Sporting facilities include swimming pools, tennis, basketball, golf, horse racing, rifle and pistol shooting, yachting and hot rods.

Outlying Attractions
The Pilbara

Many people think of this region as one huge mine, and it is because of the mining industry that much of the Pilbara is now accessible to the visitor. Natural wonders such as **Wittenoom Gorge**, the **Hamersley Range**, and other places where 200 years of white inhabitation becomes nothing when compared with the eons it has taken to shape the landscape, are now within easy reach.

Roebourne

Situated 201km (125 miles) west of Port Hedland, Roebourne was the first capital of the North-West, and has many old stone buildings. The town is about 14km (9 miles) from the coast on the Harding River, and was established in 1864, making it the oldest town on the north-west coast of WA.

The Tourist Bureau is in the **'Old Jail'**, *Queen Street*, *(08) 9182 1060*, and they can advise on accommodation and attractions both in Roebourne, and nearby Cossack and Point Samson.

From the top of **Mount Welcome,** behind the town, there is a panoramic view of the coastal plains and rugged hills which surround Roebourne. You can see the railroad from Cape Lambert weaving its way through the hills to Pannawonica in the south, and the pipeline carrying water from Millstream to Wickham and Cape Lambert.

Picnic spots are found at the **Harding River Dam**, on the *Cooya Pooya Road*; **Python Pool** on the **Wittenoom Road**.

The **Emma Withnell Heritage Trail** begins in Roebourne and travels 52km (32 miles) tracing the development of the early settlement of the eastern corridor of the Shire of Roebourne, including Cossack and Point Samson, and the modern industrial town of Wickham.

Cossack

Nearby is the first place settled on the north-west coast (1863), Cossack was a bustling seaport with a colourful multi-racial population in its heyday. Pearling was its main source of income until the industry moved to Broome. Then the wharf facilities were removed and it became a ghost town. The old graveyard and the **Courthouse**, which is ☺open daily 10am-3pm, are the only man-made attractions, but the ocean and river scenery make a visit worthwhile.

Karratha

In the same area is Karrathe meaning 'good country', so named because of the area's natural supply of food sources enjoyed by the local Aborigines. Today, the inhabitants enjoy the same resources along with the modern shopping centres and facilities.

Karratha is about 230km (143 miles) west of Port Hedland on the North West Coast Highway, and the Tourist Bureau is in *Karratha Road*, ☎*(08) 9144 4600*. They have all the details on accommodation, tours, car hire, diving establishments, and fishing and charter vessels.

Around the town there is much

evidence of early Aboriginal life, and on the **Jaburara Heritage Trail**, a 3.5km walk, you can see Aboriginal carvings, shellfish middens, grinding stones, artifacts and spiritual taboo sites. In the **Burrup Peninsula** area there are 10,000 petroglyphs (Aboriginal etchings) which are thousands of years old, showing wildlife such as turtles, fish, kangaroos, and a Tasmanian Tiger! One of the etchings is of a man in uniform, who some say is William Dampier, the English buccaneer, explorer and naturalist, who visited the coast aboard the *Cygnet* in 1688. He returned in 1699 in the *Roebuck*, and anchored in a bay in what is now known as Dampier Archipelago. He decided that the place was completely inhospitable, undoubtedly influenced by the fact that he couldn't find any water, and his disparaging reports to his superiors in England discouraged further exploration for over a century.

> ↰ **Let's Stay Here**
> **Karratha Backpackers,**
> *110 Wellard Way,* ☎*9144 4904* Expect basic accommodation and facilities in this hostel. Atmosphere is good though. *Dorm* ○*$20; double/ twin $50*

Dampier

Dampier is really a small satellite town of Karratha, about 17km (11 miles) to the west. It is a well-kept town, and the bay and sound area is almost picture-like with the vivid blue and earthy colourings. The town overlooks Hampton Harbour, and was built in the 1960s by Hamersley Iron to export the iron ore from the mines at Tom Price and Paraburdoo. Dampier Salt also uses the shipping facilities to export salt from the nearby pans. Fishing is a great pastime for locals and visitors alike, and the waters abound with popular game and reef fish. The **Dampier Archipelago** incorporates the only coral reefs found in a tropical arid setting within Australia, and they are home to more than 200 species of living coral.

Onslow

Situated on Beadon Bay, 83km (52 miles) from the turn off the North West Coastal Highway, which in turn is 456km (283 miles) south-west of Port Hedland, Onslow is said to have more potential as a tourist retreat than any other coastal spot in the north of WA.

It has a great winter climate with temperatures of up to 30C (86F) daily, and in the waters surrounding the town you can fish for bream, whiting, catfish, mullet, reef fish, flathead, pike, kingfish, gold skipjack, whitefish and nor' west salmon.

The laid-back atmosphere of the town encourages just lazing around, or you can visit the site of the old township, about 45km (28 miles) out of town, which was abandoned in 1925-26. Everything that was transportable was moved to the new site, but there are still the stone and cement buildings, mostly owned by the State Government, for you to explore.

The Tourist Centre is on *Second Avenue, Second Avenue,* ☎ *(08) 9184 6644.*

Tom Price - Paraburdoo

The two mining towns of Tom Price and Paraburdoo, in the heart of the rocky Pilbara country and on the edge of the Hamersley Range gorge area, were built to service the iron ore industry.

Paraburdoo is 394km (245 miles) south-east of Onslow, and Tom Price is 79km (49 miles) north-east of Paraburdoo, on sealed roads. The Tom Price Visitor Infomation Centre is in *Central Road,* ☎ *(08) 9188 1112.* Information on Paraburdoo can be obtained from the Ashburton Shire offices in Ashburton Avenue, Paraburdoo, ☎ *(08) 9189 5402.* Mining activities and mining tours are major attractions for the traveller, and the magnificent mountain scenery is worth the long drive. This is the high country of the Pilbara. Tom Price is the highest town in WA at 747m (2450 ft) above sea level, and is accordingly called Top Town. From the summit of **Mt Nameless,** 1128m (3701 ft) above sea level, there are incredible views of the surrounding landscape, while on the ground the wildlife includes echidna, red kangaroo, and a variety of reptiles such as pythons, legless lizards, and the legendary bungarra. The **Nameless Festival,** which includes fireworks displays, a ball and mardi gras, is held every August.

Hamersley Range National Park

The Park is one of WA's largest, and within its borders are some of the most ancient parts of this planet. The slow process of erosion has carved an intriguing landscape in a complex ecology.

Within the ranges there are many gorges, and in most are permanent pools of clear fresh water. Some are exposed to the sun and are pleasant places to swim, whilst others are in deep, shaded areas and are extremely cold. Each gorge is different, and has its own attractions. **Dales Gorge** has sunken gardens, deep pools, ferns and waterfalls. **Joffre, Red, Hancock, Weano** and **Knox Gorges** are for those who like rock climbing.

Kalamina Gorge is easily accessible and has a clear shaded pool, ferns, tropical paperbarks and river gums. **Yampire Gorge** has magnificent rock formations, and the ruins of an old asbestos mine. **Wittenoom Gorge**, though not in the park itself, has picnic places under shady gum trees, and swimming holes.

Wittenoom

The small town of Wittenoom is in the heart of the Pilbara, and information on the town and the Range can be obtained from **Auski Tourist Village Roadhouse,** *Great Northern Highway,* ☎ *(08) 9176 6988.*

If you are travelling through Wittenoom, you are advised to keep in mind that there was an asbestos mine nearby, and although it closed in 1966, it still poses a health problem. It is considered that, while the risk of cancer from inhaling asbestos fibres to short term visitors and tourists is minimal, the following precautions should be taken:
• Keep to main roads in the town and gorge areas.
• Camp only in areas set aside for that purpose. Camping is not allowed in the Wittenoom Gorge.

Newman

Newman is often described as an 'oasis in the wilderness' and was built in recent times for workers at the world's largest open cut mine, **Mt Whaleback.** It is 416km (258 miles) south of Port Hedland and 238km (148 miles) south-east of Wittenoom.

Tours are conducted of the world's largest open cut mining operation. For more information ☎9175 3502.

The **Newman Visitor Infomation Centre and Museum Gallery** can be found in *Fortescue Avenue* ☎ *(08) 9175 2888,* ✉newmanvc@bigpond.com

Marble Bar

Marble Bar has the reputation of being Australia's hottest spot, earned in 1923-24 when the town experienced 160 consecutive days of temperatures over 38C (100F). In those days it was said that a beer at the town's hotel, **The Iron Clad,** was worth more than its weight in gold, as there was more gold in the town than beer.

With this in mind, if you intend to visit Marble Bar, wait until the winter (July-August), when the temperature is around a pleasant 25C (77F). Then you will have the energy to fossick for alluvial gold, or explore the natural geology of the town. The town gets its name from the bar of jasper marble across the **Coongan River,** and all visitors are directed to the spot. Other places to visit are **Chinaman's Pool, Miles House** and the **State Government Offices,** which were completed in 1895.

Broome

Population 13,000
Broome is 223km (138 miles) south-west of Derby and 624km from Port Hedland, on a peninsula bounded by Roebuck Bay, stunning Cable Beach and the Indian Ocean. It is a colourful old pearling port, and its cosmopolitan population adds to the atmosphere of the town. Many of the old pearl divers were Japanese, Malays, Koepangers and Filipinos, and each year their descendants remember their ancestors in the **Shinju Festival,** which is held in August. Broome Tourist Bureau is on the corner of *Bagot Road* and *Broome Road*, and is ☉open Easter to October, Mon-Fri 8am-5pm, Sat 9am-1pm, Sun 9am-5pm, ☎ *(08) 9192 2222.* They have excellent local brochures, and information on attractions in the town, such as the **Historical Museum, Captain Gregory's House, Streeters Jetty, the Court House,** the half submerged flying boats, and the **Japanese Cemetery**. Two popular drawcards are the **Broome Crocodile Park,** *Cable Beach Road,* ☎*9192 1489*, and the **Willie Creek Pearl Farm,** ☎*9192 6500*.

Broome is not short of natural attractions either, and a must is a visit to **Gantheaume Point** to see the dinosaur's footprint, estimated to be 130 million years old. **Cable Beach,** with its 24km (15 miles) of clean, white sand, is 6km from Broome, and opposite the beach is the **Cable Beach Club,** a multi-million dollar development. Nearby are the **Pearl Coast Zoological Gardens** and the **Broome Crocodile Farm.**

On the web, go to Nebroome. com/tourism or email the Bureau at ✉tourism@broome.wt.com.au

↶ Let's Stay Here
Broome's Last Resort YHA,
2 Bagot St, ☎*9193 5000 or 1800 801 918*

✉www.*yha.com.au* Located not far from the airport, town centre and the bus station. Tropical laid back setting with a nice swimming pool and plenty of atmosphere. Other facilities includes a TV lounge, laundry, internet access, games room with a pool table and jukebox and a barbecue area. Cafe on site and meals are served. There are also organised activities including theme nights, parties, BBQs and pool competitions. Also offers the best bar in town. Parking available. **Recommended.** *Members dorm* ✪*$21 ($22 non members); BC MC VA EFTPOS*

Cable Beach Backpackers,
33-37 Lullfitz Dr, Cable Beach, ☎*9193 5511 or 1800 655 011,* ✉www.*cablebackpackers.com* Located minutes away from Cable Beach. It has a nice laidback atmosphere. Facilities includes a kitchen, swimming pool, basketball and barbecue area. There's also a bar with a pool table. Caters a lot for the beach lovers. Surfboard, body board and bikes can be hired here. They also offer a shuttle bus to the town centre. Parking available. *Dorms* ✪*$22; double $60*

Kimberley Klub,
62 Frederick St, ☎*9192 3233,* ✉www.*kimberleyklub.com* Situated nicely where everything is only minutes away by walking. Fantastic hostel with a really good feel atmosphere. Everything is purpose built in a tropical resort style and aesthetically beautiful. With lush gardens and tropical plants, with a swimming pool and

beach volleyball court on the premises. Other facilities includes a big kitchen and TV lounge with a pool table. The bar on site is a good hang out. Ask for the dinner vouchers. Be warned that they can get a little commercialised, with prices on the likes of air condition and the book exchange etc.. **Recommended.** *Dorms ✪$23 - 10 share, $25 - 4/5 share;*

Roebuck Bay Backpackers, *Napier Terrace,* ☎*9192 1183* Part of the Roebuck Bay Hotel and situated at the heart of town. Facilities includes a kitchen, TV lounge, swimming pool and barbecue area, but not on par as the other hostels in town. Off street parking. *Dorms ✪$15 - 12 share, $16 - 8 share, $18 - 4 share*

Derby
Population 5,000
Derby is situated at the southern end of King Sound, 2354km (1463 miles) north of Perth, and is the Gateway to the Kimberley Gorges.

Climate
Average temperatures: January max 33C (91F) – min 26C (79F); July max 29C (84F) – min 14C (57F). Number of days per year with temperature above 30C (86F) – 279; number of days per year with temperature above 40C (104F) – 44. Average annual rainfall: 627mm (25 ins); wettest six months – December to May.

Characteristics
Derby is one of the best known towns in the Kimberley region. The narrow channels between the islands off Derby have strong rips and currents, as well as an 11.6m

(38 ft) variation between high and low tides.

How to Get There
By Bus
Greyhound Pioneer have daily services between Derby and all major centres in WA and the Northern Territory.

Visitor Infomation
The Derby Tourist Bureau is located at *2 Clarendon Street, Derby,* ☎*(08) 9191 1426.* They have a website at 🖳*www.*derbytourism. com and can be emailed at ✉derbytb@co mswest.net.au

↩ **Let's Stay Here**
Here is a selection of budget accommodation available in Derby, with prices that should be used as a guide only. The telephone area code is 08.

Spinifex Hotel, *Claredon St,* ☎*9191 1233* Located just above the pub in the centre of town. Just your basic accommodation in four-bed dorms. Buses stops outside. *Dorm ✪$20 ; double with enuite $50*

Caravan Parks
Kimberley Entrance Caravan Park, *Rowan Street,* ☎*9193 1055.* (Dogs allowed on leash) - *powered sites ✪$21 for two, no on-site vans.*

Let's Eat
Derby is not the gourmet capital of the world, but the motels have restaurants. A couple of places you might like to try are:

Lwoy Chinese Restaurant, *Lot 269 Loch Street,* ☎*9191 1554;*

Wharf Restaurant and Take Away, *Main Jetty,* ☎*9191 1195.*

Points of Interest
Derby is half surrounded by tidal marsh, and boab trees line the main street. Boab trees are ridiculously shaped trees resembling a bottle, and one, about 7km south of the town, is hollow with a girth of 14m (46 ft). According to legend, policemen bringing in prisoners used the tree as an overnight cell before the final trek into Derby.

Nearby is **Myalls Bore** with one of the largest cattle troughs in the southern hemisphere. It is 120m (131 yds) long and 1.2m wide.

The **Cultural Centre** in Derby houses a regional museum, library and art gallery. It is built of Kimberley colourstone from Mt Jowlaenga, south-west of Derby.

Other attractions include: the **Wharfinger Museum, Derby Library, Botanic Gardens** and **King Sound.**

Outlying **Windjana Gorge** and **Tunnel Creek** can be seen with Kimberley West Tours ☎*9193 1442,* operating out of Derby. Tours cost $90 per person.

Scenic and charter flights are available over the spectacular **Kimberley** coastline, the **Napier** and **Leopold Ranges,** and **Horizontal Fall.** Contact Scenic Air Tours on ☎*1800 066 132* for bookings. They are located at Hangar 3, Derby Airport.

Festivals
The **Country Music Festival** is held in July, as is the **Boab Festival.**

Facilities
Almost all popular Australian sport is played in Derby – cricket,

football, golf, tennis, basketball, squash, horse and car racing – and shooting clubs have been organised. Darts, lawn bowls and swimming are also very popular. The swimming pool is open all year round. The outdoor cinema screens films on Friday and Saturday nights.

Tours
There are many half and full day tours and longer safaris available in Derby, and the Tourist Bureau has full information. Here we have listed some, to give an idea of what is available

West Kimberley Tours, ☎9193 1442, have a Town Tour. It visits the Prison Tree, longest trough, crafts, art gallery and the town jetty. They also have a full day tour to Windjana Gorge/Tunnel Creek National Parks – features include the best exposed fossil reef in the world, Cave of Bats and the story of the outlaw Pigeon. Their day visit to Cockatoo Island ⊕departs on request daily from May through September, and includes a 35 minute flight over the Buccaneer Archipelago, luncheon and a short island tour. Bushtrack Safaris, ☎9191 4644, ⊕depart from Mt Elizabeth Station, 360km (224 miles) from Derby along the Gibb River Road. Kimberley Getaway Safaris, ☎9192 7436, offer: a 5 day King Leopold Safari, featuring tours of the Mornington and Bell Gorges, swimming, fishing and photography; a 6 day Bungle Bungle Safari, featuring Geikie Gorge cruise, Wolfe Creek Crater and Bungle Bungle mountain area; a 10 day Mitchell Plateau Safari, featuring gorges of the Gibb River Road, Mitchell Falls, Windjana Gorge and Tunnel Creek. Buccaneer Sea Safaris, ☎9191 1991, offer: a 4 day Cone Bay/Strickland Bay Safari; Walcott

Inlet/Yampi Sound; Walcott Inlet Sea and Land Safari, with 6 days at sea then travel by 4WD.

The Gorges
There is a loop road from Derby via Kimberley Downs, Windjana Gorge on the Lennard River, and Tunnel Creek National Park on Tunnel Creek. The road then re-joins the great Northern Highway west of Fitzroy Crossing.

Fitzroy Crossing is small mining town 223km from Derby. This is a great stop to explore the surrounding areas including the gorges of Geikie and Windjana. The Tourist Bureau is in *Forrest Road*, ☎ *(08) 9191 5355*, for more information on accommodations and places to see.

The **Windjana Gorge**, about 140km (87 miles) east of Derby, is also called Devils Pass. It is about 5km long, and the limestone cliffs vary between 30m and 90m (98 ft and 295 ft) in height. During the wet season the Lennard River becomes a ranging torrent through the gorge, but it dries out in the dry season to form a string of picturesque pools in a spectacular setting. On the north-western cliff face, near the carpark, is **Pigeon's Cave**, which was the hideout of the Aboriginal outlaw of the Leopolds who terrorised police and settlers from 1894 to 1897.

Tunnel Creek is 30km (19 miles) east of Windjana Gorge, and has eroded a tunnel through the limestone 750m (820 yds) long and up to 12m (39 ft) high, and 10m (6 yds) wide in places. It is possible to walk right along the tunnel, but care should be taken and a strong torch should be used. Don't wear your best shoes as some of the floor is under water. Cave paintings can be seen near

the north entrance to the tunnel, and the black dolorite and basalt rocks at the other end were used by the aborigines to make stone axes.

Geikie Gorge was formed by the Fitzroy River cutting through the limestone formations of the Geike and Oscar Ranges, and is about 19km (12 miles) north of Fitzroy Crossing. The ranges are part of a fossilised coral reef which is thought to be one of the best preserved fossil reefs in the world. There is a 3km walk along the west bank of the river to the west wall of the gorge.

Most of the park is suitable for experienced bushwalkers only, as the terrain is rugged and inhospitable. Walkers must contact the Ranger before commencing their walks, and walking is not permitted on the east bank. The distinctive change in colour on the rock face of the gorge marks the high water level during the wet season. ⊕Between November and April there are twice daily cruises on the River.

The rock pools are ok to swim in. There are toilets, showers and barbecues in the gorge, and hotel accommodation at Fitzroy Crossing.

The Gibb River Road to Wyndham passes many of the West Kimberley gorges.

Garnett Gorge, Galvan's Gorge, Adcock Gorge and **Manning Gorge** should satisfy most travellers' desire to hike and explore the rugged rocks. At **Mt Barnett Station** you can camp or stay in a caravan, and visit the nearby **Manning Gorge.** There are some beautiful waterfalls about 10km (6 miles) upstream.

Halls Creek
Situated on the Great Northern

Highway, 555km (344 miles) east of Derby, is near the old town of Halls Creek, the site of Western Australia's first gold rush. Today it is a cattle centre, but remnants of the old town remain. Near here an almost vertical quartz vein projects above the surrounding rocks to form a startling white stone wall, which is known as the **Great Wall of China.** A major attraction in the area is 133km (83 miles) north near Carranya Station, the **Wolf Creek Meteorite Crater,** which is 835m (913 yds) wide and 50m (164 ft) deep.

The **Bungle Bungle National Park** is within Halls Creek Shire and scenic flights can be taken from Halls Creek to view this incredible sight from the air.

There are a number of motels and caravan parks in the area which Visitor Infomation Centre might be able to help you out with.

Kununurra

A rich green oasis amid the rugged land of the Kimberleys, Kununurra is in the centre of the **Ord River Irrigation Scheme,** about 1057km (657 miles) east of Broome. As a result of the Ord River Scheme, a wide variety of crops are now grown, eg rice, sugar cane, peanuts, sorghum, fodder crops, sunflower and high protein beans, as well as fruit and vegetables.

Lake Argyle, which was formed as a result of damming the Ord River in the Carr Boyd Ranges, has many tranquil bays, inlets and islands, and the irrigation canals are a fascinating feature of the district. A panoramic view of the Ord Valley can be obtained from Kelly's Knob, 2.5km from town.

Hidden Valley, 3km away, has some interesting rock formations and birdlife. Among unusual rock formations on the way are some Aboriginal rock paintings.

South of Kununurra is the huge **Argyle Diamond Mine** with a visitors' centre at the site.

Kununurra has all the facilities you would expect and it is also on the Perth/Darwin Greyhound Pioneer route.

The Tourist Bureau is in *Coolibah Drive,* ☎ *(08) 9168 1177* or ✉email kununurratb@bigpond.com

Wyndham

In the old days, crocodiles were attracted to Wyndham because of the meatworks, which were kept busy by the thousands of cattle on the vast Kimberley stations. They scented blood and used to come up to the aptly-named **Blood Drain.** Now that a **Crocodile Lookout** has been built, crocodile-sighting is not such a blood-curdling exercise.

Wyndham, a port established originally to land hopeful prospectors heading for the goldfields of Halls Creek, is now used for exportng produce from irrigated areas around Kununurra. The town stands on Cambridge Gulf, with its fast running tides, and the best views of both the town and the Gulf beyond are to be had from the **Bastion,** which is higher than Uluru.

The Grotto, near Wyndham, is a pleasant pool surrounded by rocks and boulders, with plenty of trees providing shade.

The Visitor Infomation Centre is at Kimberley Motors, **Great Northern Highway,** ☎ *(08) 9161 1281.*

NB Many roads in this area become impassible during the wet season (December to March). Even during the dry season it is best to first check with the Visitor Infomation or the Police, about the condition of the roads, before venturing off on your own.

Also, keep a watchful eye out for salt water crocodiles in the north of the Kimberley region, and don't forget box jellyfish are prevalent in the ocean north of the Tropic of Capricorn during the summer months (October to March).

↵ Let's Stay Here

Kimberley Croc Backpackers YHA,
Corner Konkerberry Dr and Tristania St, ☎ *9168 2702* ✉*www.yha.com.au* Set in a tropical atmosphere closest to the town centre. Close to the foodstore. Rooms are big and air-conditioned but basic. Features a swimming pool, barbecue area and TV lounge outdoors, laundry facilities and a kitchen. Parking available. *Members dorm ✪$18 - 8 share ($19 non members), $21 - 4 share ($22 non members); single $24 ; double $48 BC MC EFTPOS*

Kununurra Backpackers Adventure Centre,
22 Nutwood Cres, ☎ *9169 1998 or 1800 641 998* ✉*www.adve nture.kimberley.net.au* Caters for both working travellers who opt to stay for long periods and your run to the mill day stayers. Rooms are air conditioned. Good facilities includes a kitchen, good TV lounge, internet access, swimming pool and barbecue area. Very helpful staff to guide you about the area and canoe safaris can be organised. Free bus pick ups. Parking available. *Dorm ✪$19; twin $24pp; double $48*

South Australia

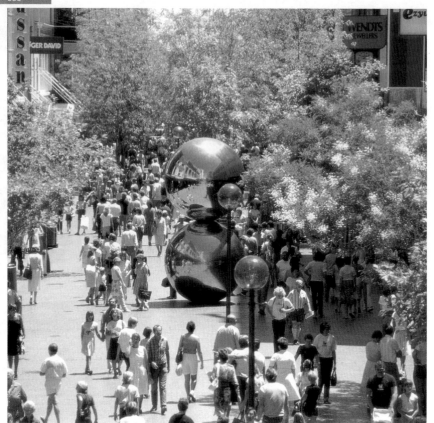

Adelaide

Population 1,675,000

Adelaide, the Capital City of South Australia, is situated on a narrow plain bounded on the west by the waters of St Vincent Gulf, and on the east by the rising slopes of the picturesque Mount Lofty Ranges. It is 660km (410 miles) from Melbourne, 988km (614 miles) from Canberra, 1,196km (743 miles) from Sydney, 1967km (1222 miles) from Brisbane, and 2216km (1377 miles) from Perth. The River Torrens flows through the city.

Climate

Adelaide has a mediterranean type climate with warm dry summers and cool winters. Average annual rainfall is 530mm (21 ins), and it generally falls between May and August. Average temperatures: January max 30C (86F) - min 16C (61F); July max 15C (59F) - min 7C (45F). Water temperature: January 19C (66F); July 14C (57F).

Characteristics

Colonel Light planned Adelaide to be a city of broad streets and handsome terraces. He dotted it with spacious squares, and bounded it on all sides with a broad band of natural parkland. Today it is a vibrant, sophisticated city enjoying the fruits of Colonel Light's planning.

How to Get There
By Air
Adelaide International Airport, ☎ *8308 9211*, is served by Air New Zealand, British Airlines, Cathay Pacific Airways, Japan Air Lines, Malaysian Airlines, Philippine Airlines, Qantas, Singapore Airlines, Thai International and United Airlines. The Airport is about 6.5km (4 miles) out of the city centre, and a Transit Airport City Bus operates 7 days a week

between the international and domestic airport terminals and the major accommodation houses in Adelaide City.

Qantas has services to Adelaide from the other capital cities in Australia.

By Bus
Greyhound Pioneer and **McCafferty's** have services from the other capital cities.

By Rail
The **Indian Pacific** stops at Adelaide on its Sydney to Perth run. The **Overland** has an overnight service from Melbourne to Adelaide.

Visitor Information
The South Australian Visitor and Travel Centre, **18 King William Street, Adelaide,** is ⊕open Mon-Fri 8.30am-5pm. Contact them on ☎1300 655 276 or email at ✉informationandbookings@south australia.com The website to explore is ▣www.southaustralia.com

↪ Let's Stay Here
Adelaide has a large range of accommodation to suit every budget, and for full details it is best to enquire at the Travel Centre. Here is a selection of budget accommodation in the city, which should be used as a guide only. The suburbs of Adelaide also offer good accommodation, and as with any city, the further from the city centre, the lower the rates. The telephone area code is 08.

Adelaide Backpackers Inn,
112 Carrington St, ☎8223 6635 or 1800 247 725 www.tne.net.au/~abackinn

Conveniently located less than ten minutes walk from the city centre and only a few minutes away from the Central Markets and Shopping Centre. Features 2 kitchens, laundry and on site travel agent. They offer a lot of free stuff like fruit, apple pie, ice cream, rice and custard every night to make you feel at home. Pick up and drop off service from bus and train station or from the airport. Parking available. *Dorms ✪$20; single $44; double $50; twin $55*

Adelaide Central YHA,
135 Waymouth St, ☎8223 6007, www.yha.com.au Situated nicely at the heart of the city overlooking the Light Square and is close to the bus station. Rooms are fully air conditioned. Quite a new hostel with excellent facilities. This includes a large kitchen, dining room, laundry, internet access, several TV rooms and lockers in every room. Bike hire and parking are available. Look out for the waterproof covering on the mattresses. *Dorms from ✪$20; twin from $29.50pp (from $36 with en suite) BC MC JCB VA EFTPOS*

Adelaide City Backpackers,
239 Franklin St, ☎8212 2668 www.citybackpackers.com.au Adelaide's original bed and breakfast. Located at west side of Franklin St, built in a 136-year-old historic building. Their balcony overlooks the street and a bar. Rooms have electric blankets and are fully heated and cooled. Facilities

includes kitchen, laundry and TV lounge. Home cooked meals are offered. *Dorms ✪$16; double/twin $55* (prices includes continental breakfast)

Backpack Australia,
128 Grote St, ☎8231 0639 or 1800 804 133 Located not far from the bus station, just on the corner. Quite cosy and has a homely feel to it. The rooftop terrace with the views of the city is quite a highlight and is the only hostel in Adelaide that has it. Facilities includes a laundry, cable TV and kitchen. **Recommended.** *Dorms ✪$15; single $30; twin $36* (prices includes free breakfast)

Backpack Oz,
144 Wakefield St, ☎8223 3551 or 1800 633 307, www.backpackoz.com.au Located at the heart of the city. Free dinner is offered every Wednesday nights. Facilities includes pool table and a nice huge TV lounge with free videos. **Recommended.** *Dorms ✪$20; single $45 ; double $50* (prices includes breakfast)

Cannon St Backpackers,
11 Cannon St, ☎8410 1218 or 1800 804 133, www.cannonst.com.au Bright and newly painted hostel from a transformed warehouse. Features a TV lounge with cable, internet access, laundry, kitchen and games rooms that boasts of ping-pong and pool tables and a pinball. Offers free apple pies and ice cream every evening.

Adelaide

Accommodation

1. Adelaide Backpackers Inn
2. Adelaide Central YHA
3. Adelaide City Backpackers
4. Backpack Australia
5. Backpack Oz
6. Cannon Street Backpackers
7. East Park Lodge
8. Nomads Brecon Inn
9. Nomads Tatt's Inn the City
10. Sunny's Backpackers Hostel

Bar is also on site. Free activities are offered once and a while. *Dorms from ❂$17; single $50; double/twin $50* (prices includes breakfast)

East Park Lodge,
341 Angus St, ☎8223 1228, www.eastparklodge.com.au Located in the quiet residential area on the east of Angus St, and minutes walk away from the city centre and the eateries at Hugh St. This lodge used to be the Salvation Army building, with large verandas in the front and a nice courtyard. The only hostel in Adelaide with a swimming pool and sauna. Other facilities includes laundry, dining area, large kitchen, internet access and TV lounge with pool table. *Dorms ❂$22; double/twin $51* (includes light breakfast)

Glenelg Beach Resort,
1-7 Moseley St, Glenelg, ☎8376 0007 or 1800 066 422, www.glenelgbeachreso rt.com.au Not your off-the-shore beach resort. Located at the back terraces blocks a few streets down. Features cable TV lounge downstairs. The management occasionally organises live entertainment ranging from jazz bands to karaoke. Quite a party atmosphere also occurs downstairs at the bar each night. *Dorms from ❂$20; single $55; double/twin $33pp* (prices includes breakfast)

Kings Head Hotel,
357 King William Street, ☎8212 6657. 8 rooms ❂$45.

Nomads Brecon Inn,
11-13 Gilbert St, ☎8211 8985 or 1800 990 009, www.breconinn.com.au Out of the three Nomad's hostels in Adelaide, this must be the favourite. Located in the southern end of the city centre. Facilities includes a fully equipped kitchen, laundry, TV lounge, internet access and lockers in the room. The ever rare 'gym' is one of the few seen in hostels and which this hostel should boast. *Dorms from ❂$18; single $40; double/twin $55*

Nomads Tatt's Inn the City,
17 Hindley St, ☎8231 3225 or 1800 133 355, www.hosteladelaide.com Fantastically located right at the very heart of the city. You won't miss the huge balcony that overlooks Hindley Street. Features a laundry, kitchen, common room with open fire, internet access and a pool table. A bar is also on site. *Dorms from ❂$19; double $55*

Sunny's Backpackers Hostel,
139 Franklin St, ☎8231 2430 or 1800 SUNNYS or 1800 BAKPAK, www.sunnys.com.au Situated close to the bus station in an old building. Facilities includes a kitchen, TV lounge room and has internet access. There are also some nice picnic tables at the front. Travel agency on the premises. Parking is available. *Dorm ❂$17; double/twin $45* (breakfast included)

Caravan Parks
Adelaide Caravan Park, *Cnr*

Richmond and Bruton St, Hackney (3km east of city), *☎8363 1566.* (No pets allowed) *powered sites ❂$23-26 for two, on-site vans $39-46 for two.*

Levi Park Caravan Park, *69 Landsdowne Terrace, Walkerville* (5km north-east of city), *☎8344 2209.* (No pets allowed) *powered sites J $21-23 for two.*

Woodcroft Park Caravan Park, *Lot 1 Bains Rd, ☎8325 1233.* (No pets allowed) - *powered sites ❂$17 for two, park cabins from $50 for two.*

Adelaide Shores Caravan Resort, *1 Military Road, West Beach* (8km west of city), *☎8356 7654.* (No pets allowed) - *powered sites ❂$26-29 for two, on-site vans $45-60 for two.*

Local Transport
Bus
All metropolitan buses **(STA)** leave from the main city shopping areas: King William Street, Grenfell Street, North Terrace, etc. For all enquiries about timetables, destinations, and faresaver deals, *☎8210 1000* or go online to 🖥www.adelaide metro.com.au. A free inner city bus service is run by the STA called the **BeeLine Bus.** The bus number is 99B, and every five minutes buses travel along a set route and make ten stops for passengers to get on and off. The route is from Victoria Square along King William Street, left into North Street, left into George Street, right into Hindley Street, right into West Terrace, right into North Terrace, right

King William Street, Adelaide

Glenelg, Adelaide

Port Elliot

Lighthouse near Whyalla

Cactus Beach

into King William Street, back to Victoria Square. ☼The service operates Mon-Thurs 8am-6pm, Fri 8am-9pm, Sat 8am-12.15pm.

Rail

All suburban trains depart from the Adelaide Railway Station, *North Terrace*, ☎8410 1488.

Tram

The Glenelg Tram Service operates from *Victoria Square* and terminates at *Mosely Square, Glenelg*. The trams are of 1929 vintage and the trip takes about 30 minutes.

Taxi

Taxis are available in the city and metropolitan area 24 hours a day, seven days a week. They can be hailed in the street, or booked by telephone:

AAA, ☎13 1008;
Taxi About Town, ☎13 2227;
Taxi Adelaide, ☎13 2211;
Access Cabs (wheelchair taxis), ☎1300 360 940.

Car

Most major car rental firms can be found in Adelaide. They offer a wide selection of vehicles. Car rental firms require a current driver's licence and a deposit. International credit cards are acceptable. If you are under 25 years of age, check minimum age requirements.

The **Royal Automobile Association of SA**, Hindmarsh Square, offers a complete service to its members and also to members of all automobile associations within Australia, ☎8202 4600; Emergency Road Service, ☎13 1111. Petrol stations are usually ☼open 7am-6pm, but some are open

24 hours. Most stations are self service, but some do offer driveway service.

O-Bahn Busway

A unique Adelaide experience is a ride on the O-Bahn busway system, ☎8210 1000. At 12km (7 miles) in length, the O-Bahn guideway is the longest in the world. You can board a bus and travel through the city onto the O-Bahn track for a smooth 100kph cruise to Paradise Interchange or Tea Tree Plaza shopping centre. The trip crosses the River Torrens ten times, passing parklands and reservoirs.

Let's Eat

Adelaide has an abundance of fine restaurants, and due to its cosmopolitan population, there are many different cuisines from which to choose. If you are looking for takeaway to eat in one of the parks, start around Hindmarsh Square. If you prefer to eat in a reasonably priced restaurant, then try *Hindley Street*. Here are a few selections.

Bangkok Restaurant, on the first floor of *217 Rundle Street*, ☎8223 5406, is a popular Thai restaurant with good service and prices that won't strain your travel budget.

Hindley Pasta Palace at *100 Hindley St*, ☎8231 9500. It is ☼open for lunch Mon-Fri and dinner Mon Sun, is fully licensed, and has authentic Italian cuisine.

Jerusalem Sheshkabab House, *131B Hindley Street*, ☎8212 6185 which is licensed and BYO, and has inexpensive Lebanese and Middle Eastern food, ☼open daily noon-midnight.

Zapata's Mexican Restaurant, at the northern end of *Melbourne Street (no 42)*, *North Adelaide*, ☎8267 4653, is one of the most charming of Adelaide's restaurants and is fully licensed.

Red Ochre Grill, *Ebeneser Place*, ☎8212 7266 is a licensed restaurant specialising in native Australian flavours. It is open seven days, accepts all major credit cards.

Stanleys The Great Aussie Fish Cafe, *76 Gouger Street*, ☎8410 0909, attracts locals and visitors alike to its central location in the CBD. The main cuisine here is, you guessed it, seafood, but meat-lovers are also considered.

Entertainment

Most of the nightspots in Adelaide focus around **Hindley Street** and **North Adelaide.** You'll find nightclubs, discos, restaurants and coffee lounges, many of which are open until the wee small hours. Then there is the casino.

Skycity Adelaide, *North Terrace*, ☎8212 2811, is in a classic sandstone railway station building that blends elegance, history and tradition. You're unlikely to find any of these three attributes inside the casino, but it does offer the usual entertainment. It features 98 gaming tables on two floors, five bars and a restaurant and carvery, and is ☼open Mon-Thurs 11am-4am, and on the weekends it is open Fri 11am and closes Mon 4am.

Many hotels, motels and restaurants have regular dinner dances or discos. Some also feature floor shows by local and international artists. Details are available in the local press. Adelaide takes its arts seriously and is proud of its many fine theatres. Programmes cater for a multitude of cultural tastes, ranging from children's and experimental theatre to full scale national and international productions. We suggest you check for details in the entertainment pages of the daily press.

Shopping

Adelaide is a shopper's paradise, and here are the most popular shopping venues.

Rundle Mall is the city's central shopping district, with large department stores, chain stores, boutiques, specialty shops and eateries.

Rundle Arcade, is beneath the Gawler Place Car Park, and is accessed from between *Stephens Place* and *Gawler Place*, behind David Jones.

The **Gallerie Australis**, off *Gawler Place* has three floors with over 55 individual shops.

The **Renaissance Centre**, off Rundle Mall, is a patchwork of arcades, walk-throughs, flyovers and multi levels.

City Cross, accessed from Rundle Mall, *James Place*, *Grenfell Street* and *Gawler Place*, has over 60 well appointed specialty shops.

Southern Cross Arcade, between *James Place* and *King William Street*, is on the site of the former Southern Cross Hotel, and has two levels of specialty shops.

Regent Arcade runs from Rundle Mall through to *Grenfell Streets* and houses the **Hoyts Cinema** complex. It also has over 30 specialty shops.

Adelaide Arcade, between Rundle Mall and *Grenfell Street*, was built in 1885, and has over 100 shops and two levels.

City Centre Arcade, cnr Rundle Mall and *Pulteney Street*, has fashion shops, an international food hall, and a licensed restaurant.

John Martin's Plaza, was built in 1983, and is situated between The Link and John Martin's Store, and linked to the latter's ground and first floors. The arcade has 18 specialty shops.

Suburbs

Unley - **Metro** shopping complex on *Unley Road*, has some of the city's top designer shops, and antiques.

Hyde Park - *King William Road* has many specialty shops and boutiques.

North Adelaide - **Melbourne Street** has boutiques, specialty shops and restaurants.

Glenelg - the main shopping area is in **Jetty Road**.

St Peters - **Jam Factory and Craft Centre,** *169 Payneham Road*, ☎ *8362 4542*, was once a jam factory but it is now a large shop featuring the best in SA contemporary craft.

Modbury - **Tea Tree Plaza,** *North East Road*, has 150 retail outlets including large department stores. It is connected to the city by the O-Bahn Busway.

Markets

The **Central Market,** *Grote Street, Adelaide*, has been the culinary inspiration of Adelaide for 120 years and still provides a dazzling array of fresh foodstuffs. ☼open Tues 7am-5.30pm, Thurs 11am-5.30pm, Fri 7am-9pm, Sat 7am-3pm, ☎ *8203 7494*.

Brickworks Leisure Markets,

36 South Road, Thebarton, is a 6ha (15 acres) site with a permanent variety of leisure activities and an air-conditioned main market area. ☼open Fri-Mon 9am-5pm, and right through school holidays, ☎ *8352 4822*.

Junction Market, *Prospect Road, Kilburn,* has about 150 stalls including an international food hall, a produce section and a full range of variety and specialty stalls. ☼open Sat-Mon 9am-5pm, ☎ *8349 5866*.

Reynella Markets, *255 Old South Road, Reynella,* has over 200 variety stalls under the main roof, plus an international food hall. ☼open Fri-Mon, 9am-5pm.

Adelaide Sunday Market, *East Terrace,* between Rundle and Grenfell Streets, is based on the famous Paddy's Market in Sydney, and has around 300 stalls all under cover. ☼open 9am-4.30pm.

Points of Interest
City

A walk along Adelaide's wide and gracious streets allows you to see much more than you do when driving. There are suggested walks to allow you the chance to see many facets of the city.

North Terrace

Adelaide Gaol, *Gaol Road,* western end North Terrace, is more than 147 years old and marks the transformation of early Adelaide into a permanent settlement. The gaol complex is an example of 19th century gaol architecture although it was used as a place of confinement as recently as February 1988. Special features include the **Hanging Tower,** the original bell and honeycomb brickwork. ☼open the first and third Sunday of each month with guided tours between 10am and 3.30pm.

Newmarket Hotel, *1 North Terrace,* ☎*8216 5216,* was erected in 1884 and has a magnificent freestanding spiral staircase.

Lion Arts Centre, *cnr Morphett Street* and *North Terrace,* is the home of the biennial **Fringe Festival.** The centre occupies the site of old factories, and incorporates the **Lion Factory** building, ☉open Mon-Fri 9am-5.30pm.

Holy Trinity Church, *cnr Morphett Street* and *North Terrace,* on the other side of **Morphett Street Bridge** underpass, is the state's oldest Anglican Church. The tower houses the original, now restored clock, made in 1836 and shipped from London. ☉open Mon-Fri 9am-4.30pm, Sat-Sun from 8am, Sunday services from 8am.

Adelaide Plaza Complex comprises the **Adelaide Convention Centre, Exhibition Hall, Hyatt Regency Adelaide, Adelaide Casino** and the adjacent **Festival Theatre.**

The **Adelaide Convention Centre,** *North Terrace,* ☎*8212 4099,* is Australia's first multi-purpose convention centre, and can be transformed to accommodate sporting events, conventions of up to 3,500, or as an entertainment venue.

Festival Centre, *King William Road,* is the home of the biennial **Adelaide Festival.** The centre comprises a multi-purpose concert hall and lyric theatre, a drama theatre, experimental theatre and an open air amphitheatre. An interesting feature is the 1.2ha (5 acres) of open plaza and terrace surrounding the complex. There is also a Bistro overlooking the river. ☉open daily from 9.30am (excluding Public Holidays) and guided tours are available, ☎*8212 7849.*

Old Parliament House, *North Terrace,* was built in 1855 as South Australia's original Legislative Council Chamber. It is now a museum of political history and has displays and audio-visual programmes, and a courtyard restaurant. ☉open Mon-Fri 10am-5pm, Sat-Sun noon-5pm.

Parliament House, *cnr King William Road* and *North Terrace,* is constructed of Kapunda marble on a foundation of granite. It was commenced in 1883 and completed in 1939. When Parliament is sitting there are public viewings from 2pm.

Government House, *cnr North Terrace* and *King William Road,* ☎*8203 9800,* is the Governor's residence, and is the oldest surviving Regency building in Adelaide. Tours of the garden are advertised in daily newspapers. Continue your walk past the Prince Henry Gardens and note the commemorative plaques laid in the footpath naming outstanding contributors to South Australia's first 150 years.

National Soldiers' War Memorial, *cnr Kintore Avenue* and *North Terrace,* features a student, a farmer and a young girl, watched over by an armed angel representing the **Spirit of Duty.** The memorial was unveiled in 1931, and commemorates those who died in World War I.

Royal South Australian Society of Arts, *59 King William Street,* houses many interesting and historic paintings in its permanent collection. ☉open Mon-Fri 11am-5pm, Sat-Sun 2-5pm.

Migration Museum, *82 Kintore Avenue,* ☎*8207 7580.* South Australia's living history is here to explore at the Migration Museum. The building was the old Destitute Asylum. ☉open Mon-Fri 10am-5pm, Sat-Sun 1-5pm.

State Library of South Australia, *cnr Kintore Avenue* and *North Terrace,* ☎*8207 7250,* is an Angaston white marble building. ☉open daily from 9.30am, closed public holidays.

South Australian Museum, **North Terrace,** ☎*8207 7500,* is a treasure-trove of objects. Collections include Ngurunder, an Aboriginal Dreaming, and the Egyptian Room. The Museum has its own shop and information centre. It is ☉open daily 10am-5pm, except Anzac Day 1-5pm.

Art Gallery of South Australia, *North Terrace,* ☎*8207 7000,* has a comprehensive collection of Australian, European and Asian Art. ☉open daily 10am-5pm.

Museum of Classical Archaeology, first floor, *Mitchell Building,* in the grounds of Adelaide University, *North Terrace,* ☎*8303 5638.* The museum has some 500 objects, many dating back to the 3rd millennium BC. ☉open Mon-Fri noon-3pm, closed school holidays.

Scots Church Adelaide, *237 North Terrace,* ☎*8223 1505,* was opened in 1851, the second oldest church in the city. Extensive renovations to the building and church organ place this National Heritage Building on everyone's sightseeing agenda. Special features include the 19th century stained glass windows, the original organ, the pulpit and the font.

Elder Hall, *North Terrace,* was built in 1900, and is one of

Australia's finest concert venues. It has a spectacular pipe organ built by Casauant Feres of Quebec in 1979. Concerts are often held and a calendar is available free at the hall.

Ayers House, *288 North Terrace,* was designed by Sir George Kingston and took nearly 30 years to build. The central one-storey section was built in 1846. Sir Henry Ayers, seven times elected Premier of South Australia, later added the bow window, dining and drawing rooms. The building has been restored and houses two restaurants. It is also headquarters for the **State Branch of the National Trust**. ⊕open Tues-Fri 10am-4pm, Sat-Sun 2-4pm, ☎8223 1234.

Tandanya Aboriginal Cultural Institute, *253 Grenfell Street,* is the first major cultural facility of its kind and scale in Australia. Some facilities within the institute are a performing arts area, a museum gallery, a visual gallery and art/craft workshops. Tandanya is the only Aboriginal multi-arts complex in Australia and is owned and managed by Aboriginals. It is ⊕open Mon-Fri 10.30am-5pm, Sat-Sun noon-5pm, ☎8224 3200.

King William Street

King William Street starts at the corner of North Terrace. One of the city's widest boulevards, it is the main street of Adelaide.

Edmund Wright House, *59 King William Street,* is an elaborate renaissance-style building designed by Edmund Wright in 1876 for the Anglican Bishop of South Australia. The building is now the office of the Registry of Births, Deaths and

Marriages. There is a lunchtime musical performance to be seen here every Wednesday, ⊕12.10-1.10pm.

General Post Office, *cnr King William* and *Franklin Streets.* The foundation for the present GPO was laid in November 1867, and the building completed in 1872. ⊕open Mon-Fri 7.15am-6.15pm, Sat 8.30am noon, Sun 12.30-5pm, public holidays 9am-noon for stamps and postal parcels only.

Adelaide Town Hall, *cnr King William* and *Pirie Streets,* was built from designs by Edmund Wright, Mayor of the City, in 1859. The foundation stone was laid on May 4, 1863, by the then Governor of South Australia, Sir Dominic Daly, and the opening ceremony took place on June 20, 1866. The entire front of the building and Albert Tower is constructed of freestone.

Old Treasury Building Museum, *cnr King William* and *Flinders Streets,* parts of which date back to 1839, has a collection of exploration, surveying, drafting and computing instruments and artifacts. The major theme of the display is the history of land settlement and development of South Australia since 1836. ⊕open Mon-Fri 10.30am 3.30pm.

Victoria Square has some noted examples of early Adelaide architecture. The fountain was designed by Adelaide sculptor John Dowie, and has as its theme three of the rivers of South Australia - Torrens, Onkaparinga and Murray.

Supreme Court, *cnr Gouger Street* and *Victoria Square,* was built in 1869 of Tea Tree Gully sandstone, and features a three

arched entrance, cast-iron gates and ionic columns.

Cathedral Church of St Francis Xavier, *cnr Wakefield Street* and *Victoria Square,* was built in three sections, the central part in 1858, with additions in 1886 and 1926. The cathedral is the centre of Roman Catholic life and worship in Adelaide, and celebrates five Masses a day. ⊕open every day.

North Adelaide

A short distance from the heart of the city, north of the River Torrens, is North Adelaide, one of the oldest parts of the city. Away from the shopping districts of O'Connell Street and Melbourne Street, North Adelaide abounds in gracious and grand old homes.

Popeye Motor Launch, Elder Park, River Torrens, leaves from near the **Festival Theatre** and cruises along 6km of winding waterways, stopping at the Zoo landing. Departure times vary. Call ☎8295 4747 for information.

Light's Vision, Montiefiore Hill on *Montiefiore Road,* is a tribute to Colonel Light who planned the city of Adelaide. The statue of him points the way to a spectacular view of the city and hills.

St Peter's Cathedral, *King William Road,* took seven years to build and was completed in 1876. The towers and spires were built and consecrated in 1902. The Cathedral has the heaviest and finest bells in the southern hemisphere. ⊕open daily 7.30am-5.45pm, and conducted tours are available on the second Sunday of each month at 3pm.

Carclew, *11 Jeffcott Street.* 'The Home on the Hill' dates back to the late 1890s, and has a tower in the style of the German Rhine castles. Since the early 1970s,

Carclew has been a centre for the arts for young people, from which the Youth Festival **"Come Out"** emanates biennially in May, ☎*8267 5111*.

Parklands

Adelaide and North Adelaide are completely surrounded by extensive parklands. In many there are barbecue and picnic facilities.

Adelaide Botanic Garden, State Herbarium and Conservatory, *North Terrace,* ☎*8222 9311*, has numerous heritage buildings and subtropical and Mediterranean plant displays. The **Bicentennial Conservatory** is the largest in the southern hemisphere and features between 3000 and 4000 plants from Australasia and Malaysia, including 15 to 20 medium sized rainforest trees with associated understorey and ground vegetation. Free guided tours are available Tues and Fri at 10.30am from the kiosk. The garden is ⏰open Mon-Fri from 7am, Sat-Sun from 9am. The Conservatory is ⏰open daily 10am-4pm, and there is a small admission charge, ☎*8232 2745*.

Adelaide Zoo, *Frome Road,* is beautifully landscaped with grassy-moated enclosures, walk-through aviaries, a new reptile house, and a licensed restaurant. ⏰open daily 9.30am-5pm, admission is ✪$13 adults. ⏰Feeding times: seals 11.45am and 3.45pm daily; big cats 3.15pm Tues, Thurs, Sat and Sun; penguins 2.45pm daily; pelicans 2.30pm daily.

The **North Parklands** are on either side of the River Torrens, and they also surround North Adelaide. **Bonython Park** (Port Road entrance) has miniature lakes, children's adventure playground and a round pond for model-boat sailors. The Municipal Golf Links has two 18-hole courses, a fine club house and public restaurant. There is also a Par 3 (pitch and putt) Golf Course of 18 holes.

Elder Park, *King William Road,* is on the slopes of the south bank of Torrens, and is the site of the **Festival Centre**. The **Rotunda** in Elder Park was erected in 1882.

The **Eastern Parklands** combine natural and planned landscaping. To the east of *Rundle* and *Grenfell Streets* is **Rymill Park**, which has a boating lake, a rose garden, barbecue and picnic areas. Nearby are children's playgrounds, a wading pool and the **Adelaide Bowling Club**. The National Fitness Council's "sweat track" is in the East Parklands. The 600m course starts at the eastern end of *Halifax Street*, and is sign-posted.

Veale Gardens is a feature of the **South Parklands** and has lawns, flower beds, rose gardens, winding streams and weirs, grottoes and fountains, and a conservatory.

Adelaide Himeji Garden, *cnr Hutt Road* and *South Terrace*, was built to symbolise the bonds of friendship between the City of Adelaide and the Himeji Region of Japan. ⏰open 7.30am-4pm, Sat-Sun 8am sunset.

Linear Park has evolved into a beautiful park that graces the banks of the River Torrens. It spans the length of the river from the hills to the sea, a distance of approximately 30km (19 miles). It can be accessed at any point of the river, and provides many recreation opportunities for cyclists, walkers, joggers, bird watchers, picnickers and fishing enthusiasts. For a pleasant way to view the park, contact Linear Park Mountain Bike Hire, in Elder Park, on ☎*8223 6271*.

Suburbs
St Kilda

St Kilda Mangrove Trail, *Fooks Terrace*. You can discover the marine life of a mangrove forest along a 1.7km boardwalk. Mangroves and mudflats are the remains of a sensitive coastal wetland system which is a valuable feeding and breeding area for marine life. Guided walks are available (subject to tides) ⏰Sat-Sun, public and school holidays 10am-3pm, phone ☎*8280 8172* for more information.

Tramway Museum, *St Kilda Road,* preserves some of the vehicles which served the city from 1909 to 1959. ⏰open Sun and public holidays 1-5pm, Wed during school holidays 1-5pm, ☎*8280-8188*.

Port Adelaide

Situated 25 minutes from the centre of Adelaide, Port Adelaide has undergone a renaissance in recent years, and here are some the attractions:

Port Dock Station Railway Museum, *Lipson Street,* has 26 locomotives on various track gauges and a re-created "break of gauge" railway platform. Two steam trains take visitors around the museum grounds. ⏰open Sun-Fri 10am-5pm, ☎*8341 1690*.

Port Dock Brewery Hotel, 10 Todd Street, is an historic hotel first licensed in 1855. The building is registered with both the National Trust and State Heritage, and award winning beers and ales are brewed on the premises. ⊙open daily, ☎8240 0187.

South Australian Maritime Museum, *Lipson Street,* is a living, working Maritime Museum in the Port. There are four restored historic buildings, an 1869 lighthouse, the museum wharf. The historic vessels moored at the wharf house a large collection of maritime artifacts. ⊙open Sat-Wed 10am-5pm, and daily during school holidays, ☎8207 6255.

Sailmaker Gallery, *117 Lipson Street,* behind the Maritime Museum's shop, features Australian paintings and crafts. ⊙open afternoons until 5pm.

The **Port Waterfront Markets,** at the end of *Commercial Road,* next to the red lighthouse, has over 100 stalls selling foodstuffs, plants and crafts. ⊙open Sun 9am-4pm.

Falie Charters, *3 Divett Street.* This 46m steel hulled twin masted ketch was built in Holland in 1919, and was used as a cargo vessel for 60 years, and as a guard boat in Sydney Harbour during the Second World War. She was the Flag Ship of the Jubilee 150 celebrations. ⊙Cruises on the Falie operate from 9.30am and 5.30pm, ☎8341 2004 for information and bookings.

One and All, *Queens Wharf,* ☎8447 5144, is a centreboard brigantine built of timber. She has been built to operate a Sail Training programme in SA waters. Day trips, half day trips and twilight cruises are available.

Aviation Museum of South Australia, *Ocean Steamers Road,* in the historic Lion flour mill, has a collection of aircraft and artifacts from Australia's

colourful civilian and military air past. ⊙open Sat-Sun and public holidays 10am-5pm, ☎8240 1230.

Largs Bay/North Haven

Fort Largs was built as the northern battery of the SA coast defence about 1882, and is now a police training college. Landmarks include the **Largs Pier Hotel** and the old **Post Office**, now a coffee shop. North Haven has Australia's largest man-made harbour, with marina docks, ten lane trailer boat launching ramp and cruising yacht club, and a 9-hole golf course.

Semaphore

In its hey-day, Semaphore was a popular seaside resort, and holiday makers enjoyed huge carnivals, side-shows and picture palaces. In the early days of sail and steam it was also an important signal station and recorded information on all ships entering and leaving St Vincent's Gulf. Today, Semaphore is rich with historic landmarks, buildings, and antique shops. **Fort Glanville,** *Military Road, Semaphore South* was South Australia's first fortification, dating back to 1878. It was built to combat the Russian scare. The fort has been restored and its re-creation of colonial life of the 19th century includes cannon firings, rifle drills, parades and sentry changes. ⊙open the third Sunday of each month 1-5pm, with additional openings during December and January. Details are printed in the local press.

West Lakes

West Lakes provides facilities for water sports including sailing, canoeing, windsurfing and swim-

ming. There are several indoor centres in the area, and West Lakes is the location of **Football Park**, home of the SA Football League.

MV Foxy Lady Scenic Cruises, *145 Brebner Drive,* have cruises of the West Lakes, ⊙departing Mon-Sun 1.45pm and 3pm, ☎8242 3933.

West Beach

West Beach Reserve has numerous playing fields, two golf courses, a boating lake and a large modern caravan park. The nearby Adelaide Airport is the site of a memorial building to the pioneer aviators Sir Ross and Sir Keith Smith. It houses the **Vickers Vimy** aircraft they flew from England to Australia in 1919.

Glenelg

Known as *The Bay*, Glenelg is the State's Birthplace. On December 28, 1836, the Province of South Australia was first proclaimed beside the **Old Gum Tree**, now in *MacFarlane Street, Glenelg North.* **Jetty Road**, the shopping strip, is in the heart of the town, and, with the arcades running off it, there are over 400 outlets.

Shark Museum, Town Hall, *Moseley Square,* has a 30-year collection of displays, photographs and film of sharks, amassed by Rodney Fox. ⊙open Wed-Sun 11am-5pm, admission is ❸$4.50 adults, ☎8376 3373.

HMS Buffalo Nautical Museum, *Adelphi Terrace,* is a magnificent replica of the HMS Buffalo, built on site between 1980-82 using the original Admiralty plans, at a cost of $1.5 million. The museum houses illustrations and extracts from the old log books, original diary notes, sketches and photographs, and a host of other pieces that tell the story of the original ship's voyage from Portsmouth to Holdfast Bay (off Glenelg) in 1836. There is also a restaurant and an aquarium devoted to species of fish found in South Australia. ⊕open Mon-Sat 6.30pm-9pm, Sun 12pm-2pm. Admission is ✪$2.50 adult.

Wayville
Royal Adelaide Showgrounds, *Goodwood Road*, host the **Royal Adelaide Show** in September each year. At other times the Showground hosts Expo, the Motor Show, Home Show, Caravan and Camping, Pools and Spas and the Christmas Earth Fair. Call ☎8231 6565 for event information.

Woodville
The **Brocas Historical Museum**, *111 Woodville Road, Woodville*, is in a classified house built in 1840 for an early pioneer, John Newman. The house is furnished with period furniture and contains documents, artefacts, photographs, Services memorabilia, and a large scale model of **Captain Cook's Endeavour**. ⊕open Sun 2-5pm, ☎8347 3810.

Festivals
February - **Adelaide Fringe Festival,** a biennial festival run in conjunction with the **Adelaide Festival of Arts**. The Fringe maintains its position on the cutting edge of Australian cultural development in creating an environment which encourages new, innovative and experimental art forms alongside traditional art, ☎8100 2000.
March - **Adelaide Festival of Arts,** Australia's major cultural event. The programme includes music, drama, ballet, opera, dance, art exhibitions and light entertainment, ☎8216 4444.

May - **Adelaide Cup Carnival**, South Australia's major horse racing event held at Morphettville Racecourse.

August - **Royal Adelaide Show**, a week-long family event featuring showbags, livestock, fireworks and staged events.

Facilities
Whatever sport you are into, you'll find it in Adelaide. For information on sporting facilities, matches and associations, contact the Sports Institute, ☎8416 6677.

Adelaide Oval, *King William Road*, was established in the 1870s and is the premier venue for international and interstate cricket matches. It is also hosts local Australian Football in the winter months. The Oval is ⊕open to visitors Mon-Fri, and organised tours can be arranged by telephoning ☎8300 3800.

Memorial Drive Tennis Club, *War Memorial Drive*, was established in the 1920s, and is set in parklands. The courts have played host to international players since 1929, and every year hosts tournaments attracting big names. Visitors can book courts, coaching and hire equipment, ☎8211 8706. There are grass courts (in summer only), Rebound and synthetic ace courts.

The **Aquatic Centre**, *Jeffcott Road, North Adelaide*, has a new leisure pools dimension. It is a world of warm activity pools, cascading water, fountains, bubble beaches, river rapids and other features in a tropical landscape setting. For further information and opening times, ☎8203 7203.

Mt Thebarton Snow and Ice, *23 East Terrace, Thebarton*, has the world's first indoor artificial ski slope, designed for beginners but great fun for all. There is also an olympic size and beginners skating rink, and all equipment available for hire. ⊕open Mon-Fri from 9.30am, Sat-Sun from 12.30pm, ☎8352 7977.

Outlying Attractions
The Adelaide Hills
If there is one feature that characterises Adelaide's landscape it is the rim of hills along the city's eastern country. Within a half an hour of the city centre is another world - a world of tranquility and greenery. In the summer it is a refuge from the heat; in winter, a touch of Europe.

⤸ Let's Stay Here
Geoff and Hazel's,
19 Kingsland Rd, ☎8339 8360, *www.geoffandhazels. com.au* A fantastic place to stay who caters well for backpackers. Located about half an hours away from Adelaide. Very close to shops, pubs and cinema. Rooms have balconies. Features a nice lounge and kitchen and there are some hammocks out in the back for a quiet nap. *Double* ✪*$50* (breakfast included)

Morialta Walks YHA,
Moores Rd, adjacent Morialta Conservation Park, Norton Summit, ☎8414 3000, *www.yha.com.au* Beautifully timbered bush hostel with fantastic views of Adelaide

from the balcony. Purpose-built in the 1960s it boast of a conservation pit that surrounds the gas heater. Facilities includes a gas stove, fridge, heater and toilets. Be warned, there are no showers. Pre-booking is essential. Parking available. *Dorms from ⊘$20 BC MC JCB VA EFTPOS*

Mt Lofty Cottage YHA, *Summit Rd, ☎8414 3000, www.yha.com.au* A beautiful stone cottage erected in 1880. Located at the quiet Cleland Conservation Park, across the Cleland Fauna Park with great panoramic views of the city of Adelaide. Find yourself walking with kangaroos and emus alike. Facilities includes electric stove, microwave and fridge. Pre-booking is essential. Parking available. *Dorms from ⊘$20 BC MC JCB VA EFTPOS*

Mylor Conservation Park YHA, *Whitehead Rd, Mylor, ☎8414 3000, www.yha.com.au* This hostel is built like a modern bush-style house, fully surrounded by farms and horse studs. Facilities includes a kitchen with electric stove and oven, dining, microwave and fridge. There are also very comfy living areas with heating. Pre-booking is essential. Parking available. *Dorms from ⊘$20 BC MC JCB VA EFTPOS*

Hahndorf
The people who settled Hahndorf were emigrating from the eastern provinces of Prussia to escape the religious persecution they were suffering because of their staunch Lutheran convictions. Their ship, the *Zebra*, under the command of Captain Hahn, arrived at Holdfast Bay on December 28, 1838, and Port Adelaide on January 2, 1839. Captain Hahn had been so impressed with his passengers that he was determined to see them settled together on land they could farm. He finally decided on the spot, and the grateful people named their village after him. **Founders Day** is held on the Sunday of the Australia Day Long Weekend holiday in January. Hahndorf is 28km (17 miles) from Adelaide, and there is a regular bus service from/to Adelaide, call ☎8391 2977 for further information.

The Adelaide Hills Information Centre is at *41 Main Street,* ☎8388 1185, and is open seven days. Some of the town's attractions are: the **Pioneer Memorial Gardens,** *Main Street,* opened in January 1939, to mark the centenary of the town; **St Michael's Lutheran Church,** *cnr Balhannah* and *Church Streets,* built in 1859 (the foundation stone had been laid on September 29, St Michael's Day, hence the name of the church); **Hahndorf Oval,** in *Pine Avenue,* was established in 1936 to mark the State Centenary.

Early each year it is the venue for the colourful **Schutzenfest** (Shooting Festival), which derived in the provinces of Germany. Traditional costumes, steins, German style foods and beverages, together with music and dancing, make this annual event very spectacular.

The **Historic Old Mill** (Wittwer's Mill) was built in 1864 by Mr F.W. Wittwer, and first used as a flour mill. Today it is a restaurant, motel and convention centre, ☎8388 7888.

German Arms Hotel, ☎8388 7013, was the first hotel built in Hahndorf, and its publican's licence was issued in 1839. The site of the first hotel is now a grocery store, and the present Hotel was built during the late 1860s.

Hahndorf's favourite son is Sir Hans Heysen, who was born in Germany in 1877, emigrated to Adelaide in 1883, and moved to Hahndorf in 1908. The success of various exhibitions of his water colours in Melbourne enabled him to purchase **The Cedars,** a property on the outskirts of Hahndorf in 1912. He lived there until his death in 1968. Many of the old barns, cottages and trees that he painted can still be seen in and around Hahndorf. Some of his original works are on display at the **Hahndorf Academy Public Gallery and German Migration Museum,** *68 Main Street,* ☎8388 7250.

Torrens Gorge
The North East Road from Adelaide leads to the semi rural setting of **St Agnes,** and a few minutes further on at **Tea Tree Gully** is the 100 year old **Angoves Winery.** 2km further on, into *Range Road North* to Upper Hermitage, on the Ansteys Hill to **Gawler Scenic Tourist Drive** there are panoramic views of the city, northern suburbs and Adelaide Plains and across the Gulf of St Vincent to Yorke Peninsula. On the way to Gawler, you can go to **Para Wirra National Park** or go up over the mountains to Kersbrook.

Glenara Wines, *126 Range Road North, Upper Hermitage,* ☎*8380 5277,* has a picnic area and barbecues are available to customers at their cellar door sales in the heart of the vineyard.

The next town is **Inglewood,** about 30 minutes from the city, with the **Historic Inglewood Inn,** one of only three Historic Inns in South Australia. **Old Inglewood Cottage,** next to the General Store, was in 1860 the local blacksmith shop, but now it sells locally produced handcrafts and produce.

Cudlee Creek is home to **Gorge Wildlife Park,** which covers an area of approximately 6ha (14 acres). The park is privately owned and has a large collection of animals, including big cats, deer and plenty of koalas. **Gumeracha** is one of the oldest settled areas of South Australia, dating back to 1839. Two historic buildings are the **Baptist Church** and **Randell's Mill**. The town also has the **Biggest Rocking Horse in the World** at the Toy Factory, ☺open daily, ☎*8389 2206* or ☎*8389 2332.*

Other towns in the Gorge include **Birdwood, Mt Pleasant, Keyneton, Springton, Mt Torrens, Charleston, Tungkillo** and **Lobethal.**

Onkaparinga Valley

The Heart of the Hills is a beautiful valley, and the small river which gives this valley its name meanders through orchards, rich pasture and meadow land, flanked by the Mount Lofty ranges.

Verdun is the beginning of the Onkaparinga Valley, and other towns that are in the valley include **Balhannah, Oakbank, Woodside, Lenswood** and **Forest Range.**

East Torrens

The East Torrens area is a nature wonderland with its many parks sheltering the native wildlife and birds. The winding roads, breathtaking views, cool waterfalls, bubbling creeks, pear, apple, cherry and plum orchards, make a trip here a memorable experience. The parks in the area are **Black Hill Conservation Park, Morialta Conservation Park, Horsnell Gully Conservation Park, Ferguson Conservation Park, Waterfully Gully, Cleland Conservation Park** and **Montecute Conservation Park.**

Marble Hill, located 6km beyond Norton Summit on the *Ashton* to *Cherryville Road,* was a residence built as a summer retreat for early Governors. The site commands wide views overlooking the plains and out to the sea. Built in 1878-79, it was surrounded by a large area of garden. Marble Hill was totally burnt out on Black Sunday (January 2, 1955). In 1967 it was offered to the National Trust and is being partially restored. ☺open Sat, Sun, Wed and public holidays (closed during August).

The waterfalls of **Morialta** are its best known feature, but there are also walking trails and picnic areas in this park. The dark wooded contours of **Black Hill** are easily seen behind Adelaide's north-eastern suburbs. At the base of the hill are picnic areas and gardens. Towns in East Torrens include **Norton Summit, Ashton, Basket Range** and **Summertown.**

Mt Lofty Area

In 1802 Mt Lofty was sighted and named by Captain Matthew Flinders from Kangaroo Head on Kangaroo Island. Conservation and Recreation Parks in the area include **Mt Lofty Summit Lookout, Mt Lofty Botanic Gardens, Mt George Conservation Park, Beechwood Gardens, Loftia Park, Sturt George Recreation Park, Scott Creek Conservation Park, Brownhill Creek Recreation Park, Belair Recreation Park, Mt Bold Reservoir** and **Cleland Conservation Park.**

Mount Lofty Summit Visitor Centre and Gift Shop, *Crafers Court, Summit Road, Crafers,* ☎*(08) 8370 1054,* ☺open 7 days.

Blackwood Hills District

The Wittunga Botanic Gardens, *Shepherd Hills Road, Blackwood,* have two lakes and a sand-plain garden. There are dazzling displays of Australian and South African plants. ☺open Mon-Fri 10am-4pm, Sat-Sun 10am-5pm, ☎*8370 8370.*

The **Coròmandel Valley** is located between Blackwood and Clarendon, and has stands of large trees, streams and gullies.

Old Government House, in *Queen Jubilee Drive, Belair,* is a must for anyone with an interest in cultural history, historical architecture, antiques or cottage gardens. The house and gardens are open for viewing, and guided tours on Sunday and public holiday afternoons.

Mt Barker Area

Mt Barker is the largest town in this area of the Adelaide Hills, and is a service centre for the surrounding rural district. One of the town's best known landmarks is the historic steam flour mill. It has been restored and is now **The Flour Mill Tea and Coffee Shop** and gallery. Other towns in the area are **Clarendon, Meadows, Macclesfield, Wistow** and Nairne.

Fleurieu Peninsula

From the Main South Road to the McLaren Vale turn-off, there's detour for a tour of the **Southern Vales**. **McLaren Vale** is the centre of the wine coast with 45 wineries, and the McLaren Vale and Fleurieu Visitor Centre on *Main Road, McLaren Vale,* has a map and opening times for all of them, phone ☎ *(08) 8323 9944,* or ✉email information@visitorcentre.com.au

Port Elliot

Situated on Horseshoe Bay, Port Elliot was originally selected as the site for the ocean port for the Murray River trade, but it was a poor choice as it was unprotected. Several shipwrecks followed and the port was transferred to the lee of Granite Island at Victor Harbour. Today Port Elliott is a popular tourist resort, and **Boomer Beach** on the western edge of the town is a gathering point for the surfing fraternity.

↵ Let's Stay Here
Arnella By The Sea YHA,
28 North Terrace, Port Elliot, ☎*8554 3611, www.yha.com .au* Arnella by the Sea YHA is the oldest heritage building (1851c) in Port Elliot. Located 4km from Victor Harbor. Swimming and surfing beaches only minutes away. Facilities includes large fully equipped kitchen, laundry, spacious dining and living areas, TV lounge and a courtyard with a barbecue area. Parking available. *Dorms from* ✪*$20; sin-*

gle from $30; double/twin from $25pp BC MC VA EFTPOS (price includes complimentary breakfast)

Victor Harbour

Victor Harbour is a delight coastal resort, and the largest of the resort towns on **Horseshoe Bay.** It was an old whaling base and much of its early history has been preserved at Whale Centre, *2 Railway Terrace,* ☎*8552 5644.*

An old horse tram runs out to **Granite Island** which has colonies of wallabies and fairy penguins. At night you can spot the penguins in their rookeries. One of the best known landmarks on the south coast is **Rosetta Head**, also called the **Bluff.** It is a natural rock formation which dominates the skyline just west of the town. There is a magnificent view from the top, but the climb is demanding.

Just out of town is the **Urimbirra Wildlife Park**, *Adelaide Road,* ☎*8554 6554*, with a good collection of Australian animals, and **Greenhills Adventure Park,** ☎*8552 5999,* with a giant waterslide and roller sled.

↵ Let's Stay Here
Grosvenor Hotel,
40 Ocean St, ☎*8552 1011* Situated above a pub. Lovely old building with balconies that overlooks the streets. Basic accommodation but well maintained. Amenities includes a TV lounge and fridge. *Dorm* ✪*$25; single $25;* (price includes breakfast)

Cape Jervis

The cape, 109km (68 miles) from Adelaide, is mostly known as a jumping off place for

Kangaroo Island. A car ferry takes passengers to Kangaroo Island from its moorings nearby, ☎*8553 1233.*

The **Heysen Walking Trail** begins at Cape Jervis and goes all the way to the northern Flinders. You can explore the rugged coastline around Cape Jervis, or fossick around the nearby **Talisker Mine** which dates back to 1862.

↵ Let's Stay Here
Cape Jervis Station,
Main Rd, ☎*8598 0288, www.capejervisstation.co m.au* Situated about 3km from town. A range of accommodation from the expensive 41/2 star luxury rates to the backpackers rates. The Shearer's Quarters houses the backpackers which are self contained stone cabins with a wood fire, kitchen and a veranda at the front. Bathrooms are outside. Shared facilities includes a games room with pool tables and ping-pong. There are also croquet, badminton, tennis courts and a golf range. Caravans with powered sites and camping available. *Dorms/double from* ✪*$20*

Kangaroo Island

When Matthew Flinders discovered Kangaroo Island in 1802 it was uninhabited. However, the island had been inhabited by Aboriginal people, about whom little is known. Stone tools have been found in some areas, indicating their presence probably over 10,000 years ago. Kangaroo Island is not small, as most people expect, as it is approximately 145km (90 miles) by 60km (37 miles). To fully explore all that it has to offer takes a minimum of five days. Package tours including travel and accommodation are available, and you should enquire at your local travel agent. There are no foxes, dingoes or rabbits on the Island, but there are wild pigs, which are thought to have been released by the French explorer Nicholas Baudin, as a food source for shipwrecked sailors. The main towns on the island are **American River, Kingscote** and **Penneshaw,** and they all have hotels, motels, licensed restaurants, coffee shops and delicatessens.

The Kangaroo Island Gateway Visitor Information Centre is in *Howard Drive, Penneshaw, ☎(08) 8553 1185,* ✉email tourki@ kin.on.net, ◷open Mon-Fri 9am-5pm, Sat-Sun 10am-4pm. The National Parks and Wildlife Service also has an office in *Dauncey Street, ☎8553 2381.*

The island is home to many **Fairy Penguins,** who come ashore at night to roost or feed their young, and can be seen on the foreshore at Penneshaw and Kingscote. There is no public transport covering the island, however there is a bus service between Penneshaw, American River and Kingscote. You can fly to Kangaroo Island with **Whale Air, ☎8555 4075,** or sail across.

⤏ Let's Stay Here
Kangaroo Island Central Backpackers,
19 Murray St, ☎8553 2787
Placed in the middle of town. Very basic accommodation. Check in at the service station. *Dorm ❍$22.50; double/twin $36.50pp*

Penguin Walk YHA, *33 Middle Terrace, ☎8553 1344* Formerly a motel. Location overlooks the eastern coast bay of Kangaroo Island and best hostel in the island. A minute walk to the beach and two minutes away from the ferry. There is a nice lawned garden outside that has sea views. If you're lucky you might spot a penguin in the garden. Facilities includes a laundry, kitchen and TV lounge. Parking is available. *Dorms from ❍$19; double/ twin from $33pp BC MC VA EFTPOS* (price includes complimentary breakfast)

Penneshaw Youth Hostel, *43 North Terrace, ☎8553 1284* Situated close to the shops, restaurants and ferry. Basic accommodation including kitchen, TV lounge and a small courtyard. *Dorms ❍$18*

Murray Bridge
Situated about 80km (50 miles) east of Adelaide, Murray Bridge is the favoured haunt of water skiers - the river between **White Sands** and **Willow Banks** provides a special paradise for them. **Puzzle Park** in the town has Australia's largest maze, 4.5km of passage ways, mini golf, and the **Murray River Fish Aquarium, ☎8532 3709.** As with many South Australian towns, Murray Bridge has great parks, and the town is also the base for trips down the Murray River.

Mount Gambier
Population 23,000
Mount Gambier is located 451km (280 miles) south-east of Adelaide, on the slopes of an extinct volcano.

Climate
Average temperatures: January max 25C (77F) - min 11C (52F); July max 13C (55F) - min 5C (41F). Average annual rainfall: 708mm (28 ins).

Characteristics
Mount Gambier has two famous attractions, the Blue Lake and the Cave in the centre of the city. As a consequence the town is known as 'Blue Lake City' or the 'City Around A Cave'. The lake is famous for its change of colour from winter grey to intense blue in November each year. It remains blue until late March, and aside from its beauty, is the City's source of domestic water. The open cave is set in attractive gardens, well renowned for their roses, and was the original source of the water supply.

How to Get There
By Bus
Bonds Adelaide - Mount Gambier Coach departs daily via Coorong (Highway 1) and via Naracoorte (inland route).

By Rail
There is a regular service between Adelaide and Mt Gambier via Warrnambool or Ballarat.

Visitor Information
The Lady Nelson Visitor and Discovery Centre, *Jubilee Highway East, ☎(08) 8724 9750* or toll-free *☎1800 087 187* is ◷open seven days, 9am-5pm, with extended hours over school holiday periods. You can contact them by ✉email thelady nelson@mountgambier tourism. com.au or check out the comprehensive website at ▣ *www.mount gambiertourism. com.au*

Alternatively, Limestone Coast Tourism is in the Old Town Hall Building, *Commercial Street East*, ☎*(08) 8723 1644*, with email at ✉tourism@thelimestone coast.com and a website at 🖥*www*.thelimestonecoast.com

⤶ Let's Stay Here

Mount Gambier has motels, hotel/motels, hotels and caravan/camping parks. Here is a selection, which should be used as a guide only. The telephone area code is 08.

Blue Lake Motel,
Kennedy Avenue, ☎*8725 5211.* 24 units, licensed restaurant (closed Saturday and Sunday) *from* ✪*$50.*

Le Cavalier Court Motel,
37 Bay Road, ☎*8725 9077.* 10 units, licensed restaurant (closed Monday) ✪*$55.*

The Jail YHA,
25 Margaret St, ☎*8723 0032, www.jailbackpackers.com* What used to be a jail prison is now converted into a hostel. Accommodation is in the former cells which opens into exercise yards. Dorm rooms are in the jail keepers residence. Features a kitchen, laundry and a huge exercise yard. There is also a restaurant and bar. Parking available. **Recommended.** *Dorms from* ✪*$22 ; single from $30 ; double/twin from $24pp BC MC VA EFTPOS*

Caravan Parks
Mt Gambier Central Caravan *Park, 6 Krummel Street,* ☎*8725 4427.* (No pets allowed) - *powered sites* ✪*$15 for two, on-site vans $31 for two.*

Jubilee Holiday Park, *Jubilee Highway East,* ☎*8723 2469.* (Pets allowed on leash) - *powered sites with en-suite* ✪*$11 for two, cabins $39-49 for two.*

Blue Lake City Caravan Park, *Bay Road,* ☎*8725 9856.* (Pets allowed on leash) - *powered sites* ✪*$20 for two, on-site vans $32-47 for two.*

Pine Country Caravan Park, *Port MacDonnell Road,* ☎*1300 720 115.* (Pets allowed on leash) - *powered sites* ✪*$16 for two, cabins $33-49 for two.*

Let's Eat

As will be seen in the accommodation listed in this section, many of the motels have restaurants, and there are the usual number of takeaway outlets. Following are some restaurants you might like to try:

Golden Chopsticks Chinese Restaurant, *95 Commercial St East,* ☎*8725 3935,* is ⏰open for dinner Tues-Sun and lunch Thu-Fri.

Le Cavalier Restaurant, *37 Bay Road ,* ☎*8725 9077,* have an a la carte menu for lunch on Tue, Fri and Sun and are ⏰open for dinner every night except Monday.

Mandarin Restaurant, *68 Commercial Street West,* ☎*8723 2100,* are ⏰open Wed-Mon and serve Chinese a la carte.

The Mt Gambier Hotel, *2 Commercial Street West,* ☎*8725 0611.* Has a reasonably

priced smorgasbord, and also a la carte in the atrium.

The Barn Steakhouse, *Nelson Road* (8km out of town), ☎*8726 8250,* have very reasonable prices, and an extensive wine cellar.

Points of Interest

The 197m (646 ft) deep **Blue Lake** is the premier tourist attraction. In the area, an obelisk marks the spot where the poet Adam Lindsay Gordon made a famous leap on horseback over a fence on to a narrow ledge overlooking the lake.

The Cave in the centre of town is probably next in importance, and its sunken gardens are worth a visit.

Facing the Cave Gardens is the modern **Civic Centre**, which houses the offices of the City of Mount Gambier, Council Chambers, City Library and the Sir Robert Helpmann Theatre - a modern 528 seat theatre which is host to local and visiting artists.

The Lady Nelson Visitor and Discovery Centre on *Jubilee Highway East,* is a major historical and social interest Jubilee 150 Project, which commemorates the sighting and naming of Mount Gambier on December 3, 1800 by Lt James Grant, from the deck of The Lady Nelson, a small survey brig.

The major feature of the complex is the full scale replica of the brig, which is cut in half through the longitudinal cross-section, and forms part of the structure of the building. The complex provides displays and information on the area encompassing the south-east of South Australia and the south west of Victoria.

Adjacent to the Blue Lake is another volcanic crater with the **Valley** and **Browne's Lakes** and the former **Leg of Mutton Lake,** which no longer contains water but is a pleasant wooded area. The Valley Lake is used for aquatic sports and is dominated by the Centenary Tower on the summit of the mount.

Umpherston Sinkhole, with its terraced gardens and barbecue areas, is an ideal spot for a picnic, and the cave is floodlit at night.

Many historic buildings line the streets of Mt Gambier. Of particular note is **Jens Hotel** which was the original site of the town's first hotel, the **Town Hall** built in 1862, and the **Post Office** built in 1865. To guide visitors to the more interesting historic sites, a heritage walk has been devised, and the pamphlet is free from the Visitor Centre.

Visitors can walk through one of the huge timber mills, or a cheese factory, or tour the **Blue Lake Pumping Station** and view the Lake from the pontoons on the surface. There are also museums and galleries – including the **Port MacDonnell and District Maritime Museum** – and several parks and gardens. The Visitor Centre will be able to advise on these.

Festivals

The **Blue Lake Festival** is held in November each year and incorporates the **Christmas Pageant** and **Generations in Jazz.**

The **Mt Gambier Gold Cup Racing Carnival** is held in June.

Facilities

Tennis, flying, racing, trotting, cycling, go-kart racing, ten-pin bowling, squash, rifle range, gun club, stock car racing, pistol shooting, speedboating, lawn bowls, golf and health studios.

Outlying Attractions
Port MacDonnell

Situated 28km (17 miles) south of Mt Gambier, Port MacDonnell is Australia's most southerly port. Originally it was busy with freight from the early settlers being sent to Adelaide and Melbourne, but now it is a base for a large fleet which fishes the Southern Ocean for lobster between the months of October and May.

The township has retained the atmosphere of a small fishing village, and is a peaceful place to visit.

2km from Port MacDonnell is the former home of well-known poet and horseman **Adam Lindsay Gordon**. The cottage dates back to the 1860s and has been restored. It contains some of Gordon's belongings.

The lighthouse at **Cape Northumberland** sits above one of the most rugged sections of the coast, and the scenic drive to the lighthouse passes a petrified forest. Near Cape Northumberland are the **Frog, Dinosaur and Camel rocks** and the **Map of Australia reef**.

Piccaninnie Ponds Conservation Park is 27km south-east of Mt Gambier off the *Nelson Road*, and its main feature is a large reed swamp. The area is well known as a popular cave diving spot.

North of Port MacDonnell is **Mt Schank** volcano, which was sighted and named by Lt Grant as he sailed by in the Lady Nelson in 1800. From the top of the mount there are spectacular views of the countryside, and walking tracks have been built on the outside and inside of the crater for the energetic.

Little Blue Lake, 3km on the opposite side of the road from Mt Schank, is a popular spot for experienced swimmers, and changes colour like its large cousin in Mt Gambier.

For local information, stop in at the Port MacDonnell and District Council Office in *Charles Street*, ☎*(08) 8721 0444*. They are ⏰open Tue-Thu 9am-4pm.

Penola

Centrally located, 51km (32 miles) from Mt Gambier, Penola is the South-East's oldest town, and a joy for anyone interested in history. The many remaining slab and hewn cottages erected in the 1850s depict the lifestyle of the early settlers, and **Yallum Park,** built in 1880 shows life on a grander scale. Many famous names are associated with Penola - poets Adam Lindsay Gordon, John Shaw Neilson and Will Ogilvie spent time here, and it was here, in 1866, that Mother Mary MacKillop, Australia's first Saint, established the first school in Australia which catered for all children regardless of income or social status. The **Mary MacKillop Interpretive Centre,** *Portland Street*, tells the story of the history of the district and Mary's life, and has an audio-visual show. It is ⏰open seven days 10am-4pm and costs ⊙$3.50 adult.

The Visitor Information Centre in *27 Arthur Street*, ☎*(08) 8737 2855*, has details of all attractions.

Coonawarra

The Coonawarra grape growing and wine producing area now occupies a significant position in the Australian Wine Industry. It came into being when John Riddoch of Yallum Park, established a fruit colony on 2000 acres of his property. Grapes figured prominently among the fruit grown, and thrived in the rich soil, so in 1893 Riddoch built the first winery in **Coonawarra**.

Coonawarra is 10km (6 miles) north of Penola, and now has 22 wineries open seven days a week, with tastings and cellar door sales. Information on the various wineries can be obtained from the Visitor Information Centre in *Penola, ☎(08) 8737 2855*.

Naracoorte

Situated 39km (24 miles) north of Coonawarra, Naracoorte is one of the region's larger commercial centres. Its history dates back to the 1840s when the first hotel and store were built by William MacIntosh. The name Naracoorte, by the way, means 'running water'.

The town's main claim to fame now, though, is the **Naracoorte Caves Conservation Park**, ☎*8762 3412*. The park is 12km (7 miles) south-east of the town on the way to Penola. There are approximately 60 known caves along a 25km (15 miles) range, and many are within the park itself. Visitors can take guided tours to a range of underground caves, including the **Alexandra, Blanche** and the **Victoria Fossil Cave**. If you intend to take one of the Special Adventure Cave tours on offer, make sure you wear sneakers and take a change of clothes, as they involve crawling and climbing. The Park has a camping ground, picnic areas, interpretive centre and kiosk facilities.

🛏 Let's Stay Here
Naracoorte Backpackers YHA,
4 Jones St, ☎*8762 3835,*

www.yha.com.au Right at the heart of the town. Only minutes away from all major shopping malls and bus station. A large looking cottage house with plenty of space. Facilities includes two fully equipped kitchens, TV lounge, internet access, laundry, games room with pool table and a barbecue area outside. *Dorms from ◑$20; double/ twin from $25pp*

Millicent

Millicent is 40km (25 miles) west of Mount Gambier, in the centre of the South-East. The town was named after Millicent Glen, wife of one of the early pioneers and daughter of the first Anglican Bishop of Adelaide. Millicent was a rural centre at the beginning of this century, but the development of a pine plantation and the establishment of a sawmill and two paper mills saw a change of identity, and a large increase in population.

The **Tantanoola Caves** are 19km (12 miles) east of *Millicent*, in the **Tantanoola Caves Conservation Park**, ☎*8734 4153*. They are unique in that there are no stairs in the caves, and a pathway allows wheelchair access. When you visit the caves stop off at the **Tantanoola Hotel** in the township, and ask about the legend of the **Tantanoola Tiger**, who apparently prowled the area in the late 1800s.

Millicent Visitor Information Centre is in *1 Mount Gambier Road, Millicent,* ☎*(08) 8733 3205*.

Beachport

35km (22 miles) west of Millicent is Beachport, which was first settled as a whaling station by the Henty Brothers in the 1830s. It is now a quiet seaside town involved in the lobster and fishing industries.

Robe

Robe is 50km (31 miles) from Beachport, and the road there passes **Lakes George, St Clair** and **Eliza**. The Port of Robe was proclaimed in 1847 and gradually grew, exporting wool and horses. An unusual import at the time was over 16,000 Chinese, heading for the Victorian goldfields, who landed in South Australia to avoid the ten pounds poll tax imposed by the Victorian Government.

By 1864 Robe had become South Australia's third most important port, then the shipping trade declined and only the fishing fleet remained.

The Visitor Information Centre is located in the **Library** on *Mundy Terrace,* ☎*8768 2465*, and they will point out the museums and historic buildings. They will also have information on the tours available in nearby **Little Dip Conservation Park,** 4km to the south. ◷opening hours are Mon-Fri 9am-5pm and Sat-Sun 10am-1pm.

🛏 Let's Stay Here
Robe Long Beach Holiday Park YHA,
70-80 The Esplanade, ☎*8768 2237, www.yha.com.au* Located so close to the stunning Long Beach. Has a very spacious setting with lawns and gardens. Self contained units with kitchen, TV, fridge and heater. A new games room and a barbecue area is also on site. Parking is also available. *Singles from $30; double/twin from $24 BC MC VA EFTPOS*

Kingston

The entrance to the town of Kingston is guarded by a 17m (56 ft) lobster named **Larry**, letting everyone know that this is lobster country. Situated 44km (27 miles) north of Robe, Kingston was named in 1858 after being established in 1856 by the Cooke Brothers who took up Government Land Grants near Maria Creek.

There are many fine old buildings in Kingston, including the **Post Office**, the **Colonial Tea Rooms and Gallery,** the **Court House** and the original **Gaol and Police Station**, which now houses an antique shop. The **National Trust Museum**, built in 1872 as a timber mill, contains general folk items including gowns and nautical items. **Cape Jaffa Lighthouse** was originally erected on **Margaret Brock Reef** in the 1860s, but was moved to its present position as part of the town's heritage, in the 1970s when the erection of an automatic light left it redundant.

Visitor Information is found in the **Big Lobster Complex** on the *Princes Highway*, ☎*(08) 8767 2555.*

Barossa Valley

The Barossa is about 50km (31 miles) north of Adelaide.

Climate

Average temperatures: January max 29C (84F) - min 14C (57F); July max 13C (55F) - min 3C (37F). Average annual rainfall: 633mm (25 ins).

Characteristics

The Valley is the vineyard of the nation, producing nearly 60% of Australia's wine, and exporting more than 6 million litres

of fine, quality wine a year. In 1842, Pastor Kavel lead a group of Lutherans to the valley, and they brought not only their vine cuttings, but also their building techniques and culture.

How to Get There
By Bus

Greyhound Pioneer stop at Nuriootpa on their Brisbane/Adelaide routes.

Visitor Information

The Barossa Wine and Visitor Information Centre is at *66-68 Murray Street, Tanunda*, ☎*(08) 8563 0600* or by ✉email info@ barossa-region.org. ⏰opening hours are Mon-Fri 9am-5pm, Sat-Sun 10am-4pm. The website to explore is 🖥*www*.barossa-region. org

---

⤵ **Let's Stay Here**

Some of the wineries and homesteads in the valley offer accommodation, and the Information Centre has all the details. The telephone area code is 08.

Barossa Gateway Motor Inn, *Kalimna Rd,* ☎*8562 2788.* Ensuite, air conditioning, TV, fridge, laundry, spa and barbecue. *Dorms from* ✪*$55*

Caravan Parks
Barossa Valley SA Tourist Park, *Penrice Rd,* ☎*8562 1404.* (Pets on leash) 200 sites. Showers, laundry, kitchen, kiosk, tennis courts, barbecue area and playground. *Powered sites* ✪*$19; unpowered site $15; cabins with ensuite $36-59; park cabins from $52.50*

Let's Eat

Most of the hotels and motels around town have licensed restaurants, and each town has the usual amount of coffee lounges and takeaway outlets. The Visitor Information centres in each town have a complete list of eateries, and many are mentioned in the Points of Interest section.

Points of Interest
Gawler

Gawler was the second country town to be created in South Australia (Port Adelaide was the first), and its official birthday is January 31, 1839. Many of the buildings reflect the architectural design and influence of the late 19th and early 20th centuries, with beautiful stonework. Most were constructed of local stone, and the nearby hills show the scars of the excavation of the bluestone used for the **Town Hall** and **churches**, the **Post Office** and the **Old Telegraph Station**.

The Gawler Visitor Centre is at *2 Lyndoch Road,* ☎*8522 6814,* and they have information and maps for walking, cycling and driving tours of historical sites. You can email them at ✉visitor.centre@gawler. sa.gov.au or visit the website 🖥*www*.gawler.sa.gov.au The Centre is ⏰open 9am-5pm seven days and can organise wine tours and other activities for you.

Stroll down **Murray Street** for a place to dine out. Here you will find the **Gawler Palace Chinese Restaurant,** the **Bamboo Hut Bistro**, **Cafe Nova**. If none of these suit you, try The **Wheatsheaf Inn** in S*unnydale Road,* ☎*8522 5762,* or **Zeebous** in *Calton Road,* ☎*8522 3621.*

From Gawler, the main road to

the **Whispering Wall Reservoir** turns off to the right in **Sandy Creek,** passing the village of **Cockatoo Valley,** with its general store. Near here are the remains of the old **Barossa Goldfields** along *Goldfields Road*, and a converted miner's cottage which offers accommodation, ☎ *8524 6213*.

Further on is the **Barossa Reservoir,** built in 1898 and the largest in South Australia. The retaining wall has an unusual acoustic effect so that a person standing on one side can hear whispers from the other side of the dam - hence the name **Whispering Wall**.

Rosedale is on the western side of the *Barossa Valley Highway*, driving from Sandy Creek north to Lyndoch, and in the district there are many beautiful old buildings and a farm cottage that has been converted to provide accommodation.

↗ **Let's Stay Here**
Barossa Valley Farmhouse YHA,
Sandy Creek Conservations Press, ☎ *8414 3000*, *www.yha.com.au* Beautifully renovated farmhouse. Situated in a magnificent bushland with plenty of native animals and plants to see. Barossa wineries nearby. Facilities includes self-contained kitchen with electric oven, microwave and fridge and a nice living area. Dining area has a great view of the bush. Great for bush walk lovers. Pre-booking is essential. Parking available. *Dorms from ❂$20 BC MC VA EFTPOS*

Gawler Caravan Park, *Main North Road*, ☎ *8522 3805*. (No pets allowed) 82 sites, playground, barbecue, good facilities - *powered sites ❂$16 for two, on-site vans $32 for two, cabins $50 for two.*

Hillier Park, *Hillier Road*, ☎ *8522 2511*. (No pets allowed) 270 sites, barbecue, swimming pool - *powered sites ❂$15 for two, cabins $50 for two.*

Lyndoch
The town was named by Colonel William Light in 1838 to honour Lord Lynedoch, under whom he had served in the Napoleonic Wars. The present name came from a spelling mistake.
The first settlers arrived in 1839 and farming was the main early industry. In late 1847, a group of Germans settled at Hoffnungsthal (or Valley of Hope) in the hills behind Lyndoch. The valley basin formed a lake during wet seasons, and the village was destroyed by floods in 1853, the only remnants now being the foundations of a church and a plaque.

Vineyards were established in the early years and the first winery was set up in 1896 in a converted flour mill. Today there are ten wineries in the immediate area, all family owned, ranging in size from very small to one of the largest in the Barossa.

Visitor Information is available at **Kies Family Wines,** *Barossa Highway*, ☎ *8524 4110*, and they can provide a map pinpointing the location of the various wineries, and a pamphlet outlining a walking tour of the town.

↗ **Let's Stay Here**
Barossa Caravan Park,
Barossa Valley Highway, ☎ *8524 4262*. (No dogs allowed) 50 sites, good facilities, barbecue - *powered sites ❂$15 for two, on-site vans $25 for two.*

Let's Eat
Eating places in the town include the **Lyndoch Bakery and Restaurant,** ☎ *8524 4422*, fully licensed and serving home-cooked German meals, and the **Lyndoch Hotel,** ☎ *8524 4211*, also with home-cooked style offerings.

Wineries
Wards Gateway Cellar, Barossa Highway, ☎ *8524 4138*, has a good range of interesting wines, and is ⊕open for tasting and sales daily 9am-5.30pm.
Burge Family Winemakers, Wilsford, ☎ *8524 4644*, is ⊕open seven days, and is a must for quality wine enthusiasts. Limited output is available ex-vineyard only.
Charles Cimicky Premium Wines, ☎ *8524 4025*, is a small winery renowned for premium boutique-style wine making. There is a Cellar Bistro offering lunch, and the winery is ⊕open for tastings and sales daily 10am-4pm.
Chateau Yaldara, ☎ *8524 5637*, is ⊕open for tasting and sales 7 days a week, and has conducted tours of the winery and the Chateau Collection. There is also a Garden Bistro serving lunch and morning and afternoon teas.
Kies Estate Cellars, ☎ *8524 4110*, have premium dry and sweet table wines, and are ⊕open Mon-Fri 9am-5pm, Sat-Sun 10am-5pm. There is ample parking, and a children's playground in the grounds.
Kellermeister Wines Pty Ltd, ☎ *8524 4303*, are ⊕open every

day 9am-6pm, and have award winning wines for tasting in an historic building.
Barossa Settlers, ☎8524 4017, was established by descendants of Barossa pioneers in an historic stable, and there is a collection of artefacts and implements. Award winning wines are available at the cellar door only. The winery is ⊙open Wed-Sat and Mon 10am-4pm, Sun 1-4pm.

Rowland Flat

Johann Gramp began commercial wine making at Jacobs Creek in 1847, and Rowland Flat was also the home of one of South Australia's earliest potters, Samuel Hoffmann. Today, the town is well known for the large winery complex, and the souvenir and craft shops in its grounds.

Driving towards Tanunda there are four wineries along **Krondorf Road,** running from **Hallett Valley,** on the western side, to the foothills of **Kaiser Stuhl** on the east. There are many typical valley buildings, many of which have been restored and offer farm-style accommodation. A nearby road gives access to the **Heysen Trail**, and the high country of the **Barossa Ranges**. In **Hallett Valley** there is a keg factory where coopers carry on their traditional craft, and ⊙welcome visitors Mon-Sat 8am-4.30pm, ☎8563 3012.

Wineries
Miranda Wines, Barossa Highway, ☎8524 4537, is ⊙open for tastings and sales Mon-Fri 8.30am-4.30pm, Sat-Sun 10am-4.30pm.
Orlando Wines, ☎8521 3111, have a picnic and barbecue area, and staff who are very proud of their products. The complex is

⊙open daily.
Grant Burge Wines, Barossa Valley Highway, Jacobs Creek, ☎8563 3700, have excellent wines and tasting facilities, and cellar door sales ⊙daily 10am-5pm.
Rockford Wines, have full bodied Australian wine styles in a restored 1850s cottage and farm buildings. hTastings and sales daily 11am-5.30pm, ☎8563 2720.
Charles Melton Wines, Krondorf Road, ☎8563 3606, specialise in premium Barossa reds, and are highly acclaimed for quality and presentation. ⊙open daily 11am-5.30pm.
Liebuchwein, ☎8524 4543, have reds, whites and fortified wines, and are ⊙open daily 11am-5pm.

Bethany

Situated near Tanunda, Bethany was the first German settlement in the Barossa. In 1842, a group of Silesian families settled near the Tanunda Creek, and named their village after the biblical Bethany.

The town has many lovely old stone houses, farms and cottage gardens, and many of the old buildings have been tastefully restored. Some are still used as houses, while others have been transformed into art galleries, a restaurant and Australia's smallest motel, the **Landhaus, ☎8563 2191**, which also has a very good restaurant.

Of interest in the town are the **Pioneer Cemetery** and the **Lutheran Church**.

Winery
Bethany Wines - Bethany Road, ☎8563 2086, is ⊙open Mon-Sat 10am-5pm, Sun 1-5pm. The Winery selects grapes from the Schrapel Family vineyards, and commands the best views of the Barossa Valley.

Tanunda

Tanunda was originally the village of Langmeil, the second German settlement in the Barossa in 1843. A drive through the back streets of Tanunda on the western side of the main street, takes you through **Goat Square** and **Langmeil Road** where many of the early stone buildings can still be seen. Goat Square was the site of the first town market, and many of the bordering cottages have now been classified by the National Trust. Restored buildings in the tree-lined main street include the hotel, the museum and the old institute.

Visitor Information is available at the **Barossa Wine and Visitor Information Centre**, at 66-68 Murray Street, ☎(08) 8563 0600, and they can advise on the many attractions in the town, which include **Story Book Cottage** and **Whacky Wood**, Oak Street, ☎8563 2910; and **Norm's Coolie Sheep Dog Performance, ☎8563 2198**. They also have a pamphlet on a walking tour of the town, which visits all the important sites.

Eating places include the fully licensed, or BYO, **Park Restaurant**, 24 Murray Street, ☎8563 3500, ⊙open for lunch and dinner seven days, and serving German and Australian meals; **Cafe Heidelberg and Art Gallery**, 8 Murray Street, ☎8563 2151, ⊙open Wed-Mon 10am-10pm (children welcome); and **Tanunda Hotel**, 51 Murray Street, ☎8563 2030, with an a la carte bistro and restaurant.

↪ Let's Stay Here
Tanunda Caravan and Tourist Park, Barossa Valley Way, ☎8563 2784. (Pets allowed on applica-

tion) 276 sites, excellent facilities - *powered sites ❖$17 for two, on-site vans $35 for two.*

Wineries

Tanunda Cellars, Murray Street, ☎8563 3544, specialise in premium and museum wines. ⊙open Mon-Sat 9am-6pm, Sun 11am-6pm.

Basedow Wines, Murray Street, ☎8563 0333, were established in 1896, and have tastings of premium tables wines in an underground cellar. There are picnic grounds, and the winery is ⊙open Mon-Fri 10am-5pm, Sat-Sun 11am-5pm.

Langmeil Winery, cnr Para and Langmeil Roads, ☎8563 2595, is set on the river bank, and has picnic facilities and barbecues. It is ⊙open for tastings and sales daily 11am-5pm.

Chateau Tanunda, Basedow Road, ☎8563 3888, featuers an historic French-style chateau surrounded by gardens. Tastings, gourmet snacks and premium wines are available ⊙daily 10am-5pm.

Peter Lehmann Wines, ☎8563 2500, is also on the banks of the North Para River, and has a full range of premium Barossa varietals. ⊙open Mon-Fri 9.30am-5pm, Sat-Sun 10.30a 4.30pm, and there are picnic facilities and barbecues.

Barossa Valley Way

It only takes about five minutes to drive between Tanunda and Nuriootpa, through the vineyards that stretch across the valley to the Barossa Hills. There have been some new developments along the road in recent years, as well as the continuation of long established businesses.

You can wander through a fascinating private museum, or enjoy the history of **Dorrien** contained in murals at the old Seppelt winery building which is on the corner of *Seppeltsfield Road*. The village of **Siegersdorf** was also in this area, and the name was one of those changed during World War I (to Bultawilta) and restored in 1975. Just past the Dorrien corner on the *Seppeltsfield Road* there is an old cemetery, **Seppelt's Mausoleum**, and from the corner Siegersdorf Road takes you to **Angaston**.

Along Barossa Valley Way and also on *Seppeltsfield Road* and *Research Road,* are a number of wineries, some long established and others recent enterprises. Accommodation in the area is available at the travellers' hostel, a guest house, and in some imaginatively converted railway carriages. Visitor Information is available in the **Rohrlach Kev Museum**, ☎8563 3407, which is ⊙open daily 10am-5pm. The Museum has a kiosk, and can advise on eating establishments.

Wineries

Chateau Dorrien Winery, ☎8562 2850, has wine and mead tastings ⊙daily 10am-5pm, and don't miss the murals on the original wine tanks.

Tarchalice Schmidt Family Winery, Research Road, Vine Vale, ☎8563 0667, have picnic facilities under the vines and tastings of their complete range of wines.

Mildara Blass, ☎8562 1366, have tastings of premium red and white table wines at their Medlands winery, Seppeltsfield Road, Dorrien, ⊙on Fri and Sat 10am-5pm, and Mon-Sat during school holidays.

Marananga

Marananga, which is Aboriginal for 'my hands', was settled in the mid-1840s and originally named Gnadenfrei, meaning 'Freed by the Grace of God', by the pioneers who had gained freedom from religious persecution in Silesia.

The original **Gnadenfrei Church** was begun in 1857, and there are many other interesting old buildings including the old school house.

Visitor Information is available in the **Gnadenfrei Estate**, which is on *Seppeltsfield Road*, ☎8562 2522.

For good restaurants, try the **The Hermitage of Marananga Restaurant** on *Seppeltsfield Road*, ☎8562 2722, which is fully licensed, or BYO, and is ⊙open for lunch Wed-Mon, and dinner Thurs-Sat, with bookings taken for other nights.

Wineries

Heritage Wines, a small family winery on Seppeltsfield Road, ☎8562 2880, which is ⊙open daily for tastings and sales. Gnadenfrei Estate Winery, ☎8562 2522, ⊙open for tastings and sales daily 10am-5.30pm. They have picnic areas, and provide picnic baskets.

Seppeltsfield

The town was established in 1851 when Joseph Seppelt, his family and workmen arrived to run a dairy and grow tobacco and wheat in the valley. The tobacco grew too rank, so Joseph started to experiment with winemaking. Soon Seppelts became the largest winery in the colony, and the cellars and stores were described in the London Gazette 1892 as 'the most modern in the world'. They have been maintained in their original condition. Close by the winery is the old Seppelt family house, which has been restored and provides accommodation. There are also holiday units in the town.

The winery to visit here is **Seppelt's**, and they have tastings of their award winning wines daily, ☎8568 6200. You can explore the extensive grounds and the preserved buildings, and picnic and barbecue facilities are available. They are ☾open Mon-Fri 10am-5pm, Sat-Sun 11am-5pm and conduct daily tours.

Greenock

Situated on the western edge of the Valley en route to the mid-north, Greenock is home to one of the Barossa's famous bakeries, and the local hotel dates back to the 1870s. It is a pretty place for a picnic, or you can call into the **Greenock Creek Tavern** in *Kapunda Road* for a counter lunch Mon-Sat, or dinner Fri and Sat, ☎8562 8136.

Nuriootpa

The North Para River winds through the town of Nuriootpa, at the northern end of the Barossa Valley. The name is Aboriginal for 'a meeting place', and it was an important tribal centre for bartering. Now, Nuriootpa is the commercial and service centre of the region, with a number of government agencies' regional offices.

William Coulthard laid out the first town acre in 1854, and the town grew around his red gum slab hotel. The building is no longer there, but his home at the other end of the main street (*66 Murray Street*), has been preserved. The The Barossa Wine and Visitor Information Centre in Tanunda have information on a walking tour of the town, which visits about 20 sites. They can also advise on restaurants, but you might like to try the **Shangri-**

La Thai Restaurant, at *31 Murray Street*, ☎8562 3559.

⤳ Let's Stay Here

Barossa Bunkhaus, *Barossa Valleyt Way, Nurioopta*, ☎8562 2260 Located 2km south of Nurioopta. Set among vineyards, a place of choice to stay at for troopers opting to stay for longer periods to get a better feel of the valley. Relaxing atmosphere with well maintained facilities including a kitchen, swimming pool and a TV lounge. Bikes are available for hire. *Dorms ✪$15 ; double $50 ($44 per night for longer stays)*

Barossa Gateway Motel, *off Sturt Highway*, ☎8562 1033. 23 units, basic facilities. *From ✪$55.*

Barossa Valley SA Tourist Park, *Penrice Road*, ☎8562 1404. (Pets allowed on leash) 176 sites, tennis, barbecue, excellent facilities - *powered sites $18 for two, cabins $35-55 for two.*

Wineries

Penfolds Wines - Nuriootpa, is the largest winery complex in the Valley, and is the home of Kaiser Stuhl and Tollana wines. ☾Tours are held Mon-Fri at 10am, 11am, 1.30pm, 2.30pm, and tasting and sales are available Mon-Fri 9am-5.30pm, Sat 10am-5pm, Sun 1-5pm. The winery is on the Barossa Highway, ☎8568 9408. Elderton Wines, on the corner of Murray Street and New Road, ☎8562 1058, is a family winery with award winning wines at reasonable prices. Available are vineyard tours, bike rental, moke rental and picnic grounds.

Wolf Blass Wines International, on the Sturt Highway, ☎8568 7311, have tastings of the full range of award winning wines in picturesque surroundings. They are ☾open Mon-Fri 9.15am-5pm, Sat-Sun 10am-5pm. The Willows Vineyard, ☎8562 1080, has tastings of varietal wines made from fruit grown on the Scholz Family's historic property, and are ☾open daily 10.30am-4.30pm. Drive through the vineyard to Huldas Cottage for the tastings.

Stockwell

Situated at the northern approach to the Valley, the peaceful village of Stockwell is dominated by the **Lutheran Church** and the old flour mill group of buildings, both of which have played an important role in the town's history. The mill still produces a variety of high quality flours.

The hotel and the small winery offer a change to experience the days gone by.

The historic **1865 Gaol House** was converted to a boutique winery with a fine selection of 15 year old liqueur fortifieds and Barossa table wines.

Stockwell Hotel, established in 1857, is ☾open daily for counter meals, with the dining room open Fri and Sat evenings and Sun lunch, ☎8562 2008.

Angaston

The town is named after George Fife Angas, a prominent figure in South Australia's history, who took up large land holdings in the Barossa Ranges and Valley in the 1830s. Angas himself settled Lindsay Park, near the present town, in 1851. Angaston is the centre of a rich pastoral district, with viticulture and fruit growing playing an important part in the local economy.

Visitor Information is available at **Angaston Abbey**, *18 Murray Street*, ☎*8564 2648*, a 125-year-old former church, now an art and craft exhibition. It is ⏰open Thurs-Mon 10am-5pm. Another information place is the **Collingrove Homestead** on *Angaston Road*, a former home of the Angas family. The homestead offers casual accommodation, morning and afternoon teas, light lunches, and formal dining on Fri and Sat nights. It is ⏰open daily 10.30am-5pm, ☎*8564 2061*.

For fine food, try the **Brauhaus Hotel**, *41 Murray Street*, ☎*8564 20144*, home of the renowned 'Brauhaus Pepper Steak' or get takeaway from **Angaston Chicken Shop**, in the heart of town, ☎*8564 2552.*

Gawler Park Fruits (Mariani Australia), *29 Valley Road*, ☎*8564 2021*, are ⏰open Mon-Fri 9am-4.30pm for sales of quality glace fruit and table raisins; and **Angas Park Fruit Co Pty Ltd**, *cnr Murray* and *North Streets*, ☎*8564 2052*, are ⏰open Mon-Sat 9am-5pm, Sun 11am-5pm, for sales of quality nuts and dried fruit related products.

➥ Let's Stay Here
Vineyards Motel,
cnr Stockwell and Nooriootpa Roads, ☎*8564 2404*. 22 units, heated swimming pool, spa, undercover parking, barbecue *from* ✪*$55.*

Barossa Brauhaus Hotel,
41 Murray Street, ☎*8564 2014*. 7 rooms (no private facilities), basic accommodation, licensed restaurant. ✪*$55* (prices includes breakfast.)

Wineries
Saltram Winery, ☎*8564 3355*, was established in 1859, and is one of the oldest wineries in the Valley. It is ⏰open for tastings and sales Mon-Fri 9am-5pm, Sat-Sun noon-5pm.
Yalumba Winery, is in an old marble building with clocktower facia, and is even older, having been established in 1849.
⏰Cellar door sales are in the Old Bond Store, Mon-Fri 8.30am-5pm, Sat 10am-4pm, Sun noon-4pm, ☎*8561 3200*.

Keyneton
Keyneton is a small village 10km (6 miles) south-east of Angaston in the Barossa Ranges. In the early 1900s, there were five wineries, all with large vineyards, located in the Keyneton area. The one remaining today, **Henschke**, is noted for the quality of its wines and old stone buildings. Henschke is owned by the fifth generation of winemakers, and was established in 1868. They are specialist makers of an exclusive range of premium quality red and white estate bottled table wines, and are ⏰open Mon-Fri 9am-4.30pm, Sat 9am-noon, ☎*8564 8223*.

Eden Valley
Situated south of Keyneton, Eden Valley is home to **Eden Springs Wine Estate** and the **High Eden** vineyard which produces classic regional wines. Tasting is available in an old Melbourne tram. There are picnic and barbecue areas, nature walks, and on Sunday a Lamb Spit Lunch. The estate is ⏰open daily 10am-5pm, ☎*8564 1166*. In the town there is also an historic hotel, which serves meals, and a general store which offers delicious Devonshire teas.

Springton
At Springton is the historic **Herbig Gum Tree**, where pioneers Caroline and Friedrich Herbig began their married life and had two of their sixteen children! The original old stone blacksmith shop is now a small winery and cafe, and the old store and post office has been restored and is now an art and craft gallery.

South of the town is the **Merindah Mohair Farm**, in *Springton Road, Mt Pleasant*, ☎*8568 2043*, where you can buy hand knits, or yarns and patterns to knit your own garments. The farm is ⏰open daily 10am-4pm.

Wineries
Craneford Wine Co and Zilm's Cafe has full flavoured regional wines, and cellar door tasting and sales are available ⏰daily 11am-5pm. The restaurant provides lunches Wed-Mon 12.30pm-3pm, and dinner Fri and Sat, ☎*8564 0003*.
Robert Hamilton and Son - Sprinton Wine Estate, 3km east of Springton, ☎*8556 2222*, are 6th generation winemakers. Wine tasting and sales are in an historic bluestone building, which is ⏰open daily 10am-4pm.

Festivals
The **Barossa Valley Vintage Festival** is a biennial event beginning on Easter Monday – with a week of activities.

The **Angaston Show** is in February. The **Tanunda Show** is in March, as is the **Essenfest (Eating Festival)**.

The **Tanunda Christmas Parade** is in December.
Facilities
Bike Hire - Barossa Valley Tourist Park, ☎*8562 1404*; Bunkhaus, *cnr Barossa Valley Highway and Nuraip Road, Nuriootpa*, ☎*8562*

2260; Elderton Wines, *Nuriootpa,* ☎*8562 1058;* Keil's Gift Centre, *63 Murray Street, Tanunda,* ☎*8563 2177.*

Ten pin bowling - Barossa Bowl, *Menge Road, Tanunda,* ☎*8563 3177.*

Squash and Rollerskating - Barossa Valley Recreation and Fitness Centre, *cnr Menge Road and Magnolia Street, Tanunda,* ☎*8563 2766.*

Golf - Gawler Par Three Golf Course, ☎*8522 3060.*

Ballooning - Balloon Adventures, Nooriootpa, ☎*8562 3111.*

Helicopter Rides - Barossa Helicopters, Lyndoch, ☎*8524 4209.*

Renmark

Population 7,750
Situated on the Murray River in the centre of the Riverland, Renmark is the first major town in the state when entering South Australia from the Eastern States along the Sturt Highway.

Climate

Average temperatures: January max 31C (88F) - min 15C (59F); July max 15C (59F) - min 5C (41F). Average annual rainfall: 312mm (12 ins).

Characteristics

Renmark is recognised as the River Holiday Centre of Australia, offering a wide range of river holiday experiences from luxury cruising on the grandiose Paddle Steamer Murray Princess, self-drive houseboats, daily river cruises, dining aboard the cruising restaurant MV Barrangul, relaxing in picturesque riverside caravan parks, or simply skiing, boating, canoeing or trying to catch one of the River Murray's 'tasty' fish, such as callop.

How to Get There
By Bus

Greyhound Pioneer stop at Renmark on their Sydney/Adelaide routes. **Stateliner** has a service from Adelaide to Renmark.

Visitor Information

The Renmark Paringa Visitor Information Centre is at *84 Murray Ave,* ☎*8586 6704,* email ✉tourist@riverland.net.au. It is ⏲open Mon-Fri 9am-5pm, Sat-Sun 9am-4pm.

⤴ Let's Stay Here

Following is a select of available budget accommodation which should be used as a guide only. The telephone area code is 08.

Caravan Parks
Renmark Riverfront Caravan Park, *Riverfront,* ☎*8586 6315.* (No pets allowed) 300 sites, playground, barbecue - *powered sites* ❍*$15-18 for two, on-site vans $30 for two, cabins $35-60 for two.*

Riverbend Caravan Park, *Sturt Highway,* ☎*8595 5131.* (No pets) 60 sites, kiosk, barbecue - *powered sites* ❍*$17 for two, on-site vans from $40 for two.*

Houseboats

Renmark is now firmly established as the Houseboat Hiring Centre of Australia, and there are over 55 houseboats available for hire, ranging in size from two to ten berth, and offering from standard to luxury facilities. For information about bookings, contact the Tourist Centre, or try Liba-Liba, ☎*8586 6734.*

Let's Eat

There is a good selection of restaurants, cafes and takeaway outlets, and here are some names and addresses.

Ashley's Restaurant, *210 Renmark Avenue,* ☎*8586 6854,* ⏲open 7 days from 6pm.

Renmark Club, *Murray Avenue,* ☎*8586 6611.* Thursday - family economy; Friday - smorgasbord; Saturday - a la carte, 6.30-8.30pm. Visitors welcome.

Riverland Golden Palace Restaurant, *Renmark Avenue,* ☎*8586 6065.* Chinese cuisine, closed Monday, ⏲open Tues-Thurs noon-2pm, 5-9.30pm, Fri-Sat noon-2pm, 5-10.30pm, Sunday 5-9.30pm.

Points of Interest

Bredl's Reptile Park and Zoo, 5km from town on the *Sturt Highway,* has over 400 species of reptiles, birds and animals. The largest collection of live reptiles in Australia includes deadly taipans, cobras, death adders, tiger snakes, pythons, boa constrictors, crocodiles, monitor lizards. There is a kiosk with a large range of souvenirs. ⏲open daily, with the snakes being fed every Sunday 2-3pm, ☎*8595 1431.*

Olivewood (Chaffey House), was the original home of the Chaffey brothers, who founded the original settlement here in 1887. It is a National Trust of South Australia House on the heritage list, and has a museum, ⏲open Thurs-Mon 10am-4pm, Tues 2-4pm, closed Wednesday, ☎*8586 5745.* It is located on the corner of *Renmark Avenue* and

Twentyfirst Street, with admission ✪$4 adults.

David Ruston's Rose Garden is a 6ha (16 acres) reserve with over 30,000 rose bushes, a large collection of flowering trees and shrubs, and many varieties of iris and day lilies. A viewing tower gives a chance for some great photographs. ☺open daily from October 1 to May 31, ☎*8586 6191*.

The **PS Industry** was built in Goolwa, SA, and commissioned in January 1911 as a workboat for the South Australian Engineering and Water Supply Department. It played a major part in keeping the river open for traffic by removing snags. It is located on *Murray Avenue*, and can still be seen chugging down the river.

Harding's Folklore Gallery, *Murtho Street*, has a large ceiling mural depicting colonial Australian bushrangers, and a good collection of Australian art and weapons of the colonial days. The gallery is ☺open most days, ☎*8586 6972*.

Ozone Gallery, ☎*8586 6368*, has arts and crafts mostly by local people, with around 355 paintings on display. The gallery is run by volunteer help, and is ☺open at these hours: Mon-Thurs 9.30am-5pm, Fri 9.30am-6pm, Sat 9am-12.30pm, Sun 1-4pm. Another gallery in town is **Zenith Art Gallery**, ☎*8586 6274*.

River Cruises - 1.5 hour day cruises, luncheon, dinner and sunset cruises are available from several companies, and the Visitor Centre has all the necessary information:

Wineries

Angove's, makers of St Agnes Brandy, Marko Vermouth, Stones Ginger Wine and Angove's Varietal Table Wines, have winery tours ☺Mon-Fri 10.30am, cellar sales and tastings Mon-Fri 9am-12.30pm, 1.30-5pm (no tours over the two weeks of the Christmas-New Year period), ☎*8580 3100*.
Renmano Wines, , ☎*8586 6771*, ☺open Mon-Sat 9am-5pm for tasting and sales. Winery tours are by arrangement only.

Facilities

Three bowling clubs, lawn, all-weather and indoor tennis courts, olympic swimming pool and waterslide, football, indoor/outdoor cricket, hockey, basketball, volleyball, rollerskating, badminton, gymnasium, table tennis, golf, rifle club, horse and pony club.

Outlying Attractions
Berri

Situated on the Murray River, 18km (11 miles) from Renmark and 238km (148 miles) from Adelaide, Berri was originally settled as a pastoral area. When irrigation commenced in 1908, it became a major fruit growing area specialising in grapes for wine and drying, stone fruits and citrus. Large industries grew to process these fruits, examples being **Berri Estates Winery, Berri Company Co-operative Ltd,** and **Berrivale Orchards Juice Plant and Food Processing Plant.** Now Berri has a population of around 7000, and is a pretty town with many parks and gardens along the town riverfront.

The Berri Visitor Information Centre is in *Vaughan Terrace*, ☎*8582 5299*, and they can advise on attractions, and arrange houseboat bookings, and all accommodation.

The **Berri Estates Winery,** on the *Sturt Highway* towards *Glossop*, is the largest single winery and distillery in Australia, and is ☺open for sales Mon-Fri 9am-5pm, Sat 9am-4pm, closed Sunday, ☎*8582 0340*.

The **Riverland Big Orange**, *Sturt Highway* at the Monash/Morgan turn-off, is the largest orange in the world, and has excellent views of the River Murray. Here you can buy local produce, wines, souvenirs, or take an orchard tour. ☺open daily 9am-5pm, ☎*(08) 8582 4255*.

⤵ Let's Stay Here
Berri Backpackers, *Sturt Highway*, ☎*8582 3144* A hostel that caters for travellers opting for work on the orchards and vineyards. Well equipped with the facilities comprising of a kitchen with large ovens, internet access, swimming pool, saunas and tennis court. There is also free use of bicycles and canoes. Saturday nights are set for a BBQ too. Parking available. *Dorms/doubles $20*

Loxton
256km (159 miles) from Adelaide, and about 30km (19 miles) from Berri by river, Loxton was settled in 1895 as a farming community, and the **Historical Village** on the riverfront, ☎*8584 7194*, has many early buildings, and a replica of William Charles Loxton's pine and pug hut. They also have a large display of early farming equipment and machinery - ☺open daily 10am-4pm, and during holiday periods also Wed 7-9pm.

The Visitor Information office is

at *45 East Terrace*, ☎*847 919*, and has details of accommodation and attractions.

The **Loxton Visitor Information and Arts Centre** is in *Bookpurnong Terrace,* ✉email loxtour@riverland.net.au, ☎*(08) 8584 7919*. ⏰opening times are Mon-Fri 9am-5pm, Sat 9.30am-12.30pm and Sun 10am-4.15pm. They open for early-birds from 7.15-7.45am Mon-Sat.

On Wednesday night, the **Murray Princess** pulls into Loxton on her cruise down the Murray, and a good time is had by all, with Village Minstrels and true riverboat celebrations.

Barmera

Barmera is situated on the shores of Lake Bonney, a freshwater lake whose source is the Murray River through Chambers Creek. Joseph Hawdon discovered the lake in 1838 whilst overlanding cattle from NSW to Adelaide, and named it after his companion Charles Bonney. The surrounding area was first taken up with pastoral leases until 1922 when they were divided into irrigation blocks for growing grapes, stone fruits, citrus and vegetables. Today, as with other Riverland towns, Barmera has been developed along community and co-operative lines.

The ideal climate, combined with the swimming, yachting,water skiing, speed boating, wind surfing and fishing that the lake provides, makes Barmera an ideal place to spend some time. The Visitor Information Centre is in *Barwell Avenue,* ☎*8588 2289*.

↪ **Let's Stay Here**
Barmera Backpackers YHA, *6 Blice St,* ☎*8588 3007* Lo-cated at the very centre of town, just next to the supermarket and right in front of all the other shopping facilities. Quite famous for it's friendly and relaxed atmosphere along with hospitable locals. Facilities includes a well equipped kitchen, internet access, TV lounges and a barbecue area. Bikes can be hired. Parking also available. *Dorms from* ✪*$16.50 ; twin from $22 BC MC VA*

Waikerie

Situated on the Murray River, 175km (109 miles) from Adelaide, Waikerie was settled in 1894, and is a well-planned, pretty town with award winning gardens. Street names bear evidence of a strong German heritage. The town is acclaimed as a glider's paradise, and also has the largest citrus packing house in Australia, the Waikerie Co-op Producers Ltd.

Although the Sturt Highway by-passes the outskirts of Waikerie, it is well worth a side trip for closer examination. Apart from its natural flora and fauna, the town also has several pleasant eateries, wineries and shops specialising in locally made goods. Visitor Information is available at **The Orange Tree** on the *Sturt Highway,* ☎*(08) 8541 2332*. It is ⏰open Mon-Fri 9am-5.30pm and Sat-Sun 10am-4pm.

Morgan

The township of Morgan is on the Murray River, 166km (103 miles) from Adelaide. The site of the town was passed by Charles Sturt on his voyage down the Murray and back in 1830. Known originally as **North West Bend, the Great Bend,** or **the Great Elbow**, it became a point for overlanders, on their way to Adelaide with stock, to leave the Murray and make for Adelaide. In 1878 the town was proclaimed, and the Kapunda to Morgan railway officially opened.

Changing times forced the closure of the railway service in 1969, but relics of this era remain with the original **Station, Station Master's Residence, Turntable** and **Rest Rooms**, all in excellent condition.

Morgan Visitor Information Centre is at *11 Railway Terrace,* ☎*(08) 8540 2354*, and the local people are very friendly and will give all the advice you need to see the local attractions.

Blanchetown

Blanchetown is your first port of call in the Riverland if you are travelling the 134km (83 miles) from Adelaide, or the last if you are travelling from the eastern States. The town was laid out in 1855 and declared a port in 1863. It is the start of the River Murray lock and weir system for water quantity control. The lock was completed in 1922, and is an impressive sight from the lookout at the **Blanchetown Bridge**.

Blanchetown is a popular holiday resort with many holiday homes lining the river banks, and good fishing and skiing areas nearby. You can grab a hearty meal at the *Blanchetown Hotel,* ☎*8540 5017,* the hub of this tiny town.

Flinders Ranges

The foothills of the Flinders Rangers begin at the northern end of St Vincent's Gulf, and stretch north for approximately 800km (497 miles) into the dry outback region.

Climate

Semi-arid climate which leads to dry-country vegetation, including saltbush and light timber. In spring the area is alive with wild flowers, making it an ideal time to visit. Winter days can also be pleasant, however the nights are very cold; summer is very hot with temperatures ranging from 30-40C (86-104F); autumn has much the same temperatures as spring.

Characteristics

Granite mountain ranges with towering peaks, razor backed quartzite ridges, slashed by precipitous gorges, and creeks with cool, deep waterholes framed by stately gums. The whole area is an artist's or photographer's delight. The colours and shadows change continually depending upon the time of day and the season of the year.

How to Get There
By Bus

Premier Stateliner service towns to Hawker and Quorn. For details of timetables phone ☎ *8415 5555.*

By Rail

Australian National operates regular air-conditioned services from Adelaide, Coonimia near Port Pirie, Port Augusta, Whyalla and Peterborough.

Visitor Information

The Flinders Ranges Visitor Information Centre is at *3 Seventh Street,* ☎ *(08) 8648 6419,* email ✉tourism@flindersrangescouncil .sa.gov.au

Alternatively, Wilpena Pound Visitor Information Centre is at the *Wilpena Pound Resort,* ☎ *(08) 8648 0048.* It is ⏲open 8am-6pm seven days.

You might also wish to visit theuseful website ■*www.*flinders .outback.on.net

↵ Let's Stay Here

For information and Camping Permits for the various National and Conservation Parks in this region, contact the National Parks and Wildlife SA, Hawker branch, at *60 Elder Terrace,* ☎ *8648 4244.*

Let's Eat

The majority of hotels and motels in the area have restaurants, and general stores and petrol stations usually sell takeaway food.

Points of Interest
Quorn

Situated 334km (208 miles) from Adelaide, the old railway town of Quorn is an ideal holiday base. The town has many historic buildings reflecting its former importance as a railway junction. Nowadays, the only railway sounds are when the old steam trains (Afghan Express, Pichi Richi Explorer and Barwell Bull) run to through **Pichi Richi Pass** to **Woolshed Flat** and **Stirling North.** Trains are scheduled to run on certain days from Easter to October, and timetables are available from Information Outlets, by calling ☎ *8658 1109* or visiting the site ■*www.prr.org.au* online. Bookings can be made at the Railway Station on the day of travel, or on the number mentioned above. There are also guided tours of the railway workshops throughout the year, and on days when the train runs.

Only a short distance from town are the **Wankerie Falls, Warren, Buckaringa** and **Middle Gorges.**

About 14km (9 miles) south of the town is **Mt Brown** (900m - 2953 ft), the highest point in the area. Nearer town are **Devil's Peak** and **Dutchman's Stern**, both of which are richly coloured and have walking trails to the summit.

Quorn has retained much of its old world character, and the **Mill**, built in 1878 as a flour mill, has been restored and houses a restaurant. Other galleries with local art and craft are: **Junction Art Gallery, Quandong Cafe and Art Gallery** and **Sue's Art Studio Gallery.**

North of the town are the historic **Kanyaka** ruins and graveyard, all that remains of the homestead which once supported 70 families for about 20 years from the 1850s. Located near the ruins is the **Death Rock waterhole.**

Local 4WD tours are available from Quorn, contact **Ozzies Bush Track Tours,** ☎ *8648 6016,* for details.

Apart from the Flinders Ranges Visitor Information Centre, Visitor Information is also available at the **Flinders Ranges Council** at *1 Seventh Street,* ☎ *8648 6031.*

↵ Let's Stay Here

Andu Lodge YHA, *12 First St,* ☎ *8648 6655 or 1800 639 933, www.headingbush.com* Offers a high standard but cheap accommodation in historic sandstone buildings. Close to shops. Well equipped facilities includes a large kitchen, laundry, internet access and TV lounge. Free BBQ Tuesday nights. Bikes are available for hire. Ask the friendly and helpful staff for info about the surrounding region. Parking available. *Dorms from* ⊙*$20; single from $35; double from $25pp BC MC VA EFTPOS* (prices includes breakfast)

Quorn Caravan Park, *Silo Road,* ☎*8648 6206.* (Pets allowed on leash) 110 sites, barbecue, good facilities - *powered sites* ⊙*$18 for two, on-site vans $35 for two, cabins $55-60 for two.*

Transcontinental Hotel, *15 Railway Terrace,* ☎*8648 6076.* 19 rooms, licensed restaurant, basic accommodation ⊙*$55-60* (price includes breakfast)

Wirrabara Old Schoolhouse YHA, *Forest Rd,* ☎*8414 3000, www.yha.com.au* Take a part of Australian rural history

when you stay at what used to be the local community school house built in 1880. Modern features includes a electric stove and oven, microwave, heating, showers and toilets. Pre-booking is essential. Parking available. *Dorms from* ⊙*$20 BC MC JCB VA EFTPOS*

Hawker

A typical outback town, Hawker is the hub of the Flinders Ranges, being the junction of roads from Port Augusta, Orroroo, Leigh Creek, Marree and Wilpena/ Blinman. It is 374km (232 miles) from Adelaide, and was a thriving railway town before the line was relocated in 1956. Hawker is now an important tourist centre in the Flinders, and a Town Heritage Walk has been developed to take you through the town's pioneering history.

The Visitor Information Centre is at **Hawker Motors,** *cnr Wilpena* and *Cradock Roads,* ☎*8648 4014.*

A walking trail and scenic lookout have been established at **Jarvis Hill,** 5km south-west of Hawker. The lookout provides a spectacular panorama of the surrounding countryside.

Easy day trips from Hawker include to Quorn and Pichi Richi Pass, Wilpena, Brachina and Parachilna Gorges, Leigh Creek coalfield and Aroona Dam.

Yourambulla Caves, south of the town, have a number of Aboriginal paintings as well as another good view.

There are many scenic drives available from Hawker, and one of the most popular is the **Moralana Scenic Drive** joining *Wilpena* and *Leigh Creek Roads.* It offers good scenery, particularly from the **Black Gap Lookout.** A more rugged drive, through Yappala and past Middle and Buckaringa Gorges to Gordon, provides a mixture of outback pastoral country, rugged hills, creeks, flora and fauna. It is advisable to check local road conditions before setting off on one of these drives.

↪ Let's Stay Here
Flinders Ranges Caravan Park, *Hawker-Leigh Creek Road,* ☎*8648 4266.* (Pets allowed on leash) 100 sites, excellent facilities - *powered sites* ⊙*$18 for two, on-site vans $35-40 for two, cabins $50-70.*

Hawker Caravan Park, *Chaceview Terrace,* ☎*8648 4006.* (No dogs allowed) 120 sites, playground, barbecue area - *powered sites* ⊙*$19 for two, cabins $65-100 for two.*

Quorn

PARK TERRACE

Accommodation

1 Andu Lodge YHA
2 Transcontinental Hotel

STATION ROAD

RAILWAY TERRACE

FIRST STREET

SECOND STREET

PITAL RD

TERRACE
WEST STREET
FOURTH STREET
THIRD STREET
FIFTH STREET
SIXTH STREET
SEVENTH STREET
EIGHT STREET
EAST TERRACE

SOUTH TERRACE

Wilpena Pound

Situated 54km (34 miles) north of Hawker, the Pound is probably the best known feature of the Flinders Ranges. It is an oval bowl 16km (10 miles) long and 10km (6 miles) wide, surrounded by high quartzite cliffs. The only route to the Pound is over **Sliding Rock** along the edge of **Wilpena Creek**. Aboriginal legend says that the rim is formed by the bodies of two serpents. Enough rain falls on the higher walls of the range to keep the inner gorges and valleys green for at least part of the year, making it an oasis in the dry heart of Central Australia. Handsome red rivergums line the watercourses. The whole of the Pound has been grazed at some time - some parts as recently as 1970. Sheep have removed most of the saltbush, and the plants which flower gaily each spring are generally introduced weeds. Nevertheless, in most people's eyes, this does not detract from the beauty and majesty of the oasis. There are several walking tracks from Wilpena to gorges and parks. These range from easy to difficult, taking from an hour to a day. The walk to the top of St Mary's Peak (1164m - 3819 ft), the highest point in the range, takes a whole day, but the view from the top is worth it. The walk should only be attempted after checking with the ranger, and only if you are fit. For those who haven't the time, the fitness or the inclination to attempt it, scenic flights are available (bookings at the resort, ☎8648 0004).

Rawnsley Park is 20km (12 miles) south of Wilpena on the *Hawker* to *Wilpena Road*, located in a beautiful natural setting at the foot of **Rawnsley Bluff** (the southern rampart of Wilpena Pound). The area has marked walking tracks, and saddle and pack horse treks are available from **Rawnsley Park Station**, ☎8648 0008.

⤳ Let's Stay Here

Parachilna Overflow, *Corner High St and West Terrace, Parachilna,* ☎8648 4814 Accommodation consists of prefabricated units with air condition. Features basic swimming pool and barbecue area. A nice common room is also reserved for Adventure Tours and Oz experience customers which has internet access, pool table and a kitchen. *Dorm* ➊*$25; single $30; double/twin $25pp*

Rawnsley Park Station, *Wilpena Road,* ☎8648 0008. (No pets) 300 sites, basic facilities - *powered sites* ➊*$21 for two, on-site vans $42 for two, cabins $55 for two.*

Wilpena Pound Camping and Caravan Park, ☎8648 0004. (No dogs) 300 sites, basic facilities - *powered sites* ➊*$20 for two.*

Blinman

Situated 60km (37 miles) from Wilpena, and 485km (301 miles) from Adelaide, Blinman was once a bustling copper mining town, and some of the old mine machinery can still be seen. There is one hotel and a small caravan park. Access is via the *Blinman Road* from Wilpena and the Leigh Creek road through the scenic **Parachilna Gorge,** or from Parachilna through the spectacular **Glass's Gorge,** noted for its show of wild hops in good seasons. East of Blinman, the road winds through the scenic **Eregunda Valley** to **Chambers Gorge,** a rugged area with sparkling rock pools and Aboriginal carvings.

North of Chambers Gorge is **Big Morot Gorge** with numerous rock pools and cliffs, while to the south, on the *Wilpena Road* is the extensive and prominent rocky outcrop called the **Great Wall of China.**

The **Blinman Pools,** which are near Angorichina, are fed by a permanent spring even in the heat of summer. They offer one of the most beautiful and secluded spots in the Ranges.

⤳ Let's Stay Here

Blinman Campground, *Mine Road,* ☎8648 4867. (Pets allowed on leash) 8 sites, barbecue, pool - *powered sites* ➊*$10 for two.*

Leigh Creek

The new town of Leigh Creek is 13km (8 miles) south of the original township, and has excellent facilities. The town was moved when the first site was needed for further coal mining. Opened in 1981, the new town is in slightly hilly country, and has pleasant views of the Flinders Ranges.

Leigh Creek's brown coal deposits were first mined for power generation in 1943, and since 1948 it has been operated by the Electricity Trust of SA. It produces about 2.3 million tonnes of coal annually for the Port Augusta power stations. The brown coal deposits here are Triassic (200 million years old) and are the remnants of deposits laid down on a Pre-Cambrian basement. Open cut methods are used to extract the coal, and part of the workings can be viewed from the visitors viewing area, 2.7km from the turn-off to the **Leigh Creek Coalfields**, on the *Hawker* to *Marree Highway*.

If you need to quench your thirst or rest tired eyes, the **Leigh Creek Tavern** is in *Black Oak Drive* and has accommodation ☎ *8675 2025*.

Marree

Once known as Hergott Springs, Marree was the staging post for the camel trains that transported supplies and heavy loads to the Outback. Marree is Aboriginal for 'possum', and the town is the beginning, or the end, of the infamous Birdsville Track.

The **Birdsville Track** links Marree and Birdsville in Queensland, and was developed in the 1880s as a stock route for drovers bringing cattle from the rich grazing country of south-west Queensland to the railhead at Marree. The track skirts some of the driest areas of Australia, passing between the **Simpson Desert** and **Sturt's Stony Desert.**

Since being upgraded for beef cattle transports, the track is usually in a fair condition, but as with all Outback driving, care must be taken. Please check with Visitor Information Centres for advise on precautions when taking this track. Check with the police at Marree, or Birdsville if you are travelling from there, before departure to make sure the road conditions are favourable.

Habitation is limited to scattered and remote homesteads and not all of them are close to the Track. Fuel supplies are available at the **Mungerannie Roadhouse,** ☎ *8675 8317,* near **Mungerannie Homestead**, 204km (127 miles) north of Marree.

↩ Let's Stay Here
Marree Caravan and Campers Park, *cnr Birdsville and Oodnadatta Tracks,* ☎ *8675 8371.* (Pets allowed on leash) 120 sites, barbecue - *powered sites* ✪ *$16 for two, cabins $30 for two.*

Arkaroola

Situated in the rugged northern Flinders, 660km (410 miles) from Adelaide, Arkaroola is a 61,000ha (150,670 acres) wildlife sanctuary. It can be reached by road from Copley, Blinman or Yunta, and all these roads are unsealed, though usually well maintained. Many tours include this resort as a focal point, and there are two airstrips, one at Arkaroola and one at Balcanoona.

The area is rich in minerals and evidence abounds of early exploration. The old Cornish-style **Bolla Bollana Smelters,** erected in 1861, stand as a reminder of miners of the nineteenth century.

The nearby **Gammon Ranges National Park** is an extensive wilderness area, and other attractions include **Nooldoonooldoona, Barrarranna and Bola Bollana waterholes, Echo Camp, Dinnertime Hill, The Needles, Sitting Bull** and the **Pinnacles.**

Paralana Hot Springs, 27km (17 miles) north of Arkaroola, are radioactive and are believed to be the last remaining evidence of volcanic activity in Australia. The area is an Aboriginal ceremonial site.

↩ Let's Stay Here
Arkaroola-Mt Painter Sanctuary Resort, *Wilderness Sanctuary,* ☎ *8431 7900.* (No pets) 150 sites, playground, pool - *powered sites* ✪ *$17 for two, bunkhouses from $30.*

Whyalla

Population 27,500

Whyalla is situated on the western side of Spencer Gulf, 394km (245 miles) north-west of Adelaide by road, and 241km (150 miles) by air.

Climate

Average maximum temperature is 29C (84F); minimum is 7C (45F) in winter and 19C (66F) in summer. There are 301 days of sunshine every year, and the average annual rainfall is 268mm (11 ins).

Characteristics

The Gateway to the Eyre Peninsula, Whyalla is the largest regional city in South Australia, and the third largest steel producer in Australia. It is an industrial city with a difference as it is also an extremely popular venue for tourists because of its ideal, sun-drenched climate. In fact, it's booming, with top-class attractions drawing tens of thousands of annual visitors.

How to Get There
By Bus

Stateliner have six services daily from Adelaide, and connect with **Greyhound Pioneer** services from other states.

Visitor Information

Whyalla Tourist Centre is on the *Lincoln Highway* ☎ *(08) 8645 7900* or ☎ *1800 088*

589 and can be emailed at ✉tourist.centre@why alla.sa.gov.au. They are ⊙open Mon-Fri 9am-5pm, Sat 9am-4pm and Sun 10am-4pm. The website ▇www.epta.com.au has further information.

↴ Let's Stay Here

The city has motels, hotel/ motels, hotels and caravan parks. Here is a selection of budget accommodation which should be used as a guide only. The telephone area code is 08.

Sundowner Hotel/Motel, *Cowell Road,* ☎8645 7688. 24 units, licensed restaurant (closed Sunday), swimming pool, barbecue. ✪$34.

Spencer Hotel, *Forsyth Street,* ☎8645 8411. 30 rooms (private facilities), licensed restaurant ✪$32.

Caravan Parks

Whyalla Foreshore Caravan Park, *Broadbent Terrace,* ☎8645 7474. (Pets allowed at manager's discretion) - powered sites ✪$17 for two, on-site vans $28 for two.

Whyalla Airport Caravan Park, *Malaquana Road,* ☎8645 9357. (Pets allowed on leash) - powered sites ✪$16-18 for two, cabins $52-54 for two, on-site vans $28 for two, park cabins $40 for two.

Let's Eat

Most of the hotels and motels have licensed or BYO restaurants, and there are many takeaway outlets, and others which have takeaway or eat in. Here are a few restaurants you might like to try.

Oriental Inn Chinese Restaurant, *83 Essington Lewis Avenue,* ☎8645 4630.

Parkview Restaurant, *23 Essington Lewis Avenue,* ☎8644 2100.

Spagg's Mediterranean Cafe and Restaurant, *30 Patterson Street,* ☎8645 2088.

Tavern In The Town, *1 Kelly Street,* ☎8644 2255.

Points of Interest

Whyalla Maritime Museum, *Port Augusta Road (Lincoln Highway),* is a unique $1.3 million attraction at the northern entrance to the city. It features the 650 tonne corvette the Whyalla, now resting 2km from the sea. Originally named *HMAS Whyalla*, and later the **Rip**, it was the first vessel built in 1941 at the former Whyalla Shipyard. It has been restored, and there are guided tours of the ship. The nearby **Tanderra** building traces the city's important shipping past through models and artefacts of BHP's shipbuilding days (1941-1978), wartime memorabilia of the Whyalla, a scale model of the **Santos plant** at nearby **Port Bonython**, audio visual presentations, and other interesting displays. Also in the Tanderra building is the largest "OO" gauge model railway in Australia. The complex is ⊙open daily 10am-4pm, with ship tours on the hour from 11am-3pm. Entry is ✪$7 for adults.

Tours of the **Steelworks** are operated by Whyalla's Steel City Coaches ⊙on Mon, Wed and Sat, departing from the Tourist Office at 9.30am. The costs are ✪$9

for adults. For more information contact the Visitor Centre on ☎8645 7900.

The **Whyalla Art Group** has its own gallery in *Darling Terrace*, just a block and a half from the City Plaza. It has a display of oil paintings, watercolours, acrylic, pen and wash, covering local scenes, the Flinders Ranges and sea and landscapes. Two major exhibitions are held each year in Autumn and Spring. ⊙opening times are weekdays noon-4pm and weekends 2pm-4pm and entry is free.

Hummock Hill Lookout was developed by BHP, and overlooks the eastern end of Whyalla, the foreshore and marina, across Spencer Gulf to the Southern Flinders Ranges, nearby **Point Lowly Lighthouse**, the Santos plant at Point Bonython, and westward towards the iron ore rich **Middleback Ranges**. **Hummock Hill** was the site of the first settlement at the turn of the century. During World War II it saw service as a gun battery and observation post.

Ada Ryan Gardens are located between *Cudmore* and *Watson Terraces*, and are linked to the **Whyalla Foreshore**. It was the first major park established in the city and named after the wife of the chairman of the original City Commission, the local government before a City Council was established. It is an ideal spot for a picnic lunch.

Whyalla Foreshore and Marina. The modern Foreshore Centre has a cafeteria, change rooms and toilets, lifesaving and rescue facilities and has had extensive landscaping, with lawns, barbecues and a playground. The beach offers

Yaldara Winery

Riverland Vineyards

Murray River Princess, Murraylands

Umpherston Cave

Wilpena Pound, Flinders Ranges

safe swimming in shallow water, while a nearby fishing jetty is well used by locals after tommy ruffs, garfish, squid, blue swimmer crabs and some species of whiting. At low tide in summer, you can walk out to the blue 'line' in search of a feed of sea fresh crabs. The marina here provides boat owners with a superb four-lane launching ramp, and a small launching fee applies to assist with on-going maintenance. Access to the launching area is controlled by a boom gate which is activated by tokens available from **Foreshore Cafe**, ☎ *8645 0340* (open 7 days). A new beach has resulted from the marina development, at the extreme eastern end, and it is less affected by low tides.

Mount Laura Homestead Museum in *Ekblom Street, off Nicolson Avenue*, behind the Westland Shopping Centre, is a National Trust Museum housed in a former sheep station homestead. It has a collection of yester-year household items, relics and many old photographs of the city. In the grounds is a fully restored and furnished cottage, originally built near Hummock Hill in 1914 and transported to the museum in the 1970s. There is also an engine shed which has a comprehensive range of more than 60 stationary engines, all fully restored and in working condition. An 80-year-old locomotive used to haul ore from Iron Knob stands next to the homestead, as does Whyalla's first lock-up. The Museum is ☺open Sun, Mon and Wed, 2-4pm, and Fri 10am-noon, other times by appointment. Entry is ✪$5 adults.

The **Whyalla Health and Leisure Centre**, off *Racecourse Road*, near the junction of *Nicolson Avenue*, has a 25m indoor heated swimming pool, squash and racquetball courts, sports hall, gymnasium, weightlifting facilities and a picturesque courtyard. There is also an outdoor sweat track comprising a commando-style course, and a tennis area. Known simply in town as the Rec Centre, visitors are welcome, and if you haven't brought your sporting gear, you can hire it all on the premises. ☺open daily, except public holidays, as follows: Mon-Fri, pool 6am-8.45pm, all other areas 6am-10pm; Sat-Sun all areas 9am-5pm (pool closes at 4.45pm).

Whyalla Wildlife and Reptile Sanctuary, on the *Lincoln Highway*, near the airport, is one of the largest parks of its type in an arid climate. There are all kinds of Australian fauna, a reptile house, a walk-through aviary with about 200 birds, and a children's section where the favourites can be nursed and fed. The Park has barbecue and picnic facilities, and offers a bush walk through the main vegetation communities within the area. An added feature is a **Nocturnal Walk Guided** tour every Wednesday at 9pm in summer months, 7.30pm in winter - bookings are essential. The complex is ☺open daily 10am-6pm (Nov through March), 10am-4.30pm (other times). Entry is ✪$7 adults, and for further information ☎ *8645 7044*.

Information and maps for a self-guided walk, called the **Historic Town Trail**, and a Tourist Drive through Whyalla are available at the Visitor Centre.

Facilities

Whyalla has shopping centres in the city, and there is a theatre, cinema, etc. Check with the Visitor Centre for information on other entertainment. Sporting facilities include gliding, golf, roller skating, squash, swimming, yachting, and diving.

Outlying Attractions
Port Bonython

The Port is home to the **Santos Fractionation Plant**, and although tours do not operate over the plant, it can clearly be seen from the roadside and shoreline vantage points.

The products of the plant, such as the crude oil and condensate is sold to Australian petroleum refineries, while the LPG is sold to both domestic and export markets. Port Bonython has been operating since 1984.

Point Lowly

The **Point Lowly Lighthouse**, oldest building in the Whyalla area (1883), is 2km past the Santos Plant, and about 34km (21 miles) from Whyalla. There are often dolphins in the area, and plenty of people fishing. Facilities include toilets, playground and picnic area.

From the Point there are good views of the gulf and the southern Flinders Ranges. The lighthouse is an unmanned station.

Scenic Drive

16km (10 miles) along the all-sealed Point Lowly/Port Bonython road is the turnoff to **Fitzgerald Bay**, and the start of a scenic drive to the holiday spot of **Point Douglas**, about 20km (12 miles) further on. The first section from the turnoff to Fitzgerald Bay is a sealed road, and the rest is a well maintained gravel surface. Along the road there are many picnic areas and opportunities for beach and bush walks.

Iron Knob

The township of Iron Knob is 52km (32 miles) north west of Whyalla on the Eyre Highway which links Port Augusta with Western Australia. Flora of the area is mainly low, stunted growth of mallee scrub and saltbush. Sheep grazing is the major local primary industry. Mining began in 1899, the ore being used as a flux in the smelters of **Port Pirie**. At one time the Iron Knob and Iron Baron mining operations supplied the iron ore for all BHP blast furnaces.

The Iron Knob Tourist Centre, ☎ *8646 2129*, have details of inspections of the open cut mines, which are undertaken in your own car. The Tourist Centre has been developed by BHP as a mining museum, with displays of old mining equipment, mineral specimens, photographs, and a theatre which presents the story of mining and steel making. The grounds of the centre are ideal for a picnic lunch.

Iron Knob has good facilities for a small town, and they include a nine-hole golf course, a registered race club, lawn bowls, tennis, basketball and netball, football and swimming clubs.

South of Whyalla

The coast to the south is a succession of serene villages and resorts, set on crescent-shaped bays with charming names like **Tumby Bay, Arno Bay** and **Lucky Bay**. The beaches are long and deserted, broken by low, occasional headlands, and the whole area affords good fishing.

Cowell

Situated on the sheltered **Franklin Harbour**, which is more like a large lagoon, is the sleepy village of Cowell. It is a safe fishing and boating resort, with night crabbing in the shallows a special attraction. Jade is mined at nearby **Mt Geraghty**, and is brought to the factory in Cowell where it is cut and polished. Visitors are welcome to watch the large diamond saws cutting the stone.

The **Franklin Harbour Historical Museum** is in the old Post Office, and preserves memorabilia from the town's past, ☎ *8629 2032*. **The Cowell Area School Fauna Park** is home to a range of native Australian Wildlife, ☎ *8629 2150*.

Port Lincoln

Had it not been for the lack of a permanent water supply, Colonel Light may well have selected Port Lincoln as the capital of the State of South Australia. Now it is a blue water paradise and the holiday centre of the peninsula. It is 270km (168 miles) south of Whyalla, on Boston Bay which is ideal for sailing, swimming, water skiing, fishing and skin-diving.

Port Lincoln was first settled in 1834 and has many old buildings, including the **Lincoln Hotel** in *Tasman Terrace*, which first opened for business in 1840.

The Port Lincoln Visitor Information Centre, *66 Tasman Terrace*, ☎ *(08) 8683 3544*, has information on the many attractions of the town. The Centre is ☉open 9am-5pm seven days and can be emailed at ✉plvic@dove.net.au

Highlights of the town and surrounds include the **Mayne and Arteyrea galleries, Mill Cottage Museum, Alex Stenross Maritime Museum, Glen-Forest Animal Park, Railway Museum, Apex Wheelhouse, Rose-Wal Shell Museum, Mikkira Station and Koala Park,** and the **impressive Constantia Designer Craftsman tour.**

From **Winter's Hill lookout,** 5km from the town, there is a very good view of York Peninsula, and short trips can be made to **Sleaford Bay, Lincoln National Park, Whaler's Way** and **Flinder's Well.**

Elliston

The trip to Elliston, about 140km (87 miles) up the coast, passes **Sheringa Beach**, **salt lakes**, the **Old Hamilton Eating House**, and you can detour to **Locks Wells**, a favourite with fishermen and photographers.

The little fishing village of Elliston is nestled between some small hills and Waterloo Bay, and there are spectacular stretches of rugged cliffs rimming the coast. Flinders Island is 35km (22 miles) off the Elliston coast.

Visitor information is available from the **District Council** on *Beach Terrace*, ☎ *8687 9177*, ☉open Mon-Fri 8.30am-5pm.

Ceduna

The town is a popular overnight stop for the east-west traveller, but is gaining a reputation as a holiday destination in its own right. From here there are scenic drives to **Decres Bay, Laura Bay,** the **Davenport Creek** wilderness area and **Denial Bay.** Ceduna is well known for its fabulous fishing and for seafood lovers, a visit to **Denial Bay Oyster Farm** is a must. The Ceduna Visitor Information Centre, *58 Poynton Street,* ☎*8625 2780,* has details on this and other attractions.

Further along the coast, near Penong, is **Cactus Beach**, regarded as having one of the best surf breaks in the world.

⤴ Let's Stay Here
Nomads Shelly Beach Caravan Park, *178 Decres Rd,* ☎*8625 2012* Located about 3km out of town. Facilities includes a laundry, kitchen and barbecue area. *Powered/ unpowered sites $18-19.50; park cabin ensuite from $60*

Port Augusta
Population 15,300
Port Augusta lies on saltbush plains between Spencer Gulf and the Flinders Ranges, which are about 20km (12 miles) to the east.

Climate
Average temperatures: January max 32C (90F) - min 19C (66F); July max 17C (63F) - min 7C (45F). Annual rainfall: 243mm (10 ins).

Characteristics
Known as the Crossroads of Australia and Gateway to the Outback, Port Augusta was surveyed in 1852, and has a number of historical places of interest. It is an ideal base for access to the attractions of the Flinders Ranges, Eyre Peninsula and the Outback of South Australia.

How to Get There
By Bus
Stateliner and **Greyhound Pioneer** stop here on their Adelaide/ Perth and Adelaide/Darwin routes.

By Rail
Trains arrive in Port Augusta from Perth, Alice Springs and Sydney.

Visitor Information
The Port Augusta Visitor Information Centre is in the **Wadlata Outback Centre** complex, *41 Flinders Terrace,* ☎*(08) 8641 0793.* It is ☺open daily, Mon-Fri 9am-5.30pm, Sat-Sun 10am-4pm. The centre contains the Interpretive Centre, souvenirs, the Outback Tuckerbox and toilet facilities. Contact can also be made by email at ✉wadlata@port augusta.sa.gov.au

⤴ Let's Stay Here
Here is a selection of budegt accommodation with prices which should be used as a guide only. The telephone area code is 08.

Blue Fox Lodge,
Corner Trent Rd and National Highway One, ☎*8641 2960, www.bluefoxlodge.com* Small and quaint hostel that houses only 20 people. Basic facilities includes a small kitchen, a TV lounge and a barbecue area. A bar is also on site. *Dorm ◯$17*

Port Augusta East Motel, *Highway One,* ☎*8641 1008.* 15 units ◯*$59.*

Port Augusta International Backpackers Hostel,
17 Trent Rd, ☎*8641 1063* Situated in the main highway on the way to town. Very

cheap and oldish, with basic facilities of a kitchen and TV lounge. *Dorm ◯$14*

Caravan Parks
Port Augusta Big 4 Holiday Park, *cnr Highway 1 and Stokes Terrace,* ☎*8642 2974.* (No pets allowed) - *powered sites ◯$20 for two, cabins $30-40 for two.*

Shoreline Caravan Park, *Gardiner Avenue,* ☎*8642 2965.* (Dogs allowed at managers discretion) - *powered sites ◯$18 for two, park cabins $50 for two, cabin $39-50 for two, on-site vans $33 for two.*

Port Augusta Caravan Park at Stirling North, *9 Brooks St, Stirling North,* ☎*8643 6357.* (Pets on leash) - *powered sites ◯$17 for two, on-site vans $28 for two, park cabins $42-47 for two, cabins $38 for two.*

Let's Eat
Most of the motels and hotels have restaurants, and there are two clubs offering dining rooms.

Barnacle Bill Family Seafood Restaurant, *78 Commercial Road,* ☎*8641 0000.*

Cooinda Club, *Flinders Terrace,* ☎*8641 0166.*

ETSA Club, *Hannagan Street,* ☎*8642 5853.*

King Po Chinese, *88 Carlton Parade,* ☎*8642 5851.* Licensed restaurant.

For coffee shops and takeaway food outlets, there is more variety, and the Visitor Information Centre will have information.

Points of Interest

The Visitor Information Centre has organised a **Heritage Walk,** which commences, naturally enough, at the Wadlata Outback Centre where their office is located. The centre was originally **St Joseph's Convent**, which opened in 1927. The Walk then takes visitors to 32 other places of interest, including many classified by the National Trust or State Heritage, including the **Old Railway Station**, and the **Curdnatta Art and Pottery**.

Homestead Park Pioneer Museum in *Elsie Street*, features the only original log station homestead in SA. It was transported from its original site to Port Augusta and rebuilt as part of the museum. The 126-year-old **Yudnapinna Homestead** is fully furnished in period style. For further information ☎ *8642 2035*.

The museum adjoins a park with large shady trees, a playground and barbecue facilities, as well as kangaroos and other animals. There is also a kiosk with cold drinks, ice creams and tea and coffee.

McLellan Lookout, *Whiting Parade* at the end of *Edinburgh Terrace*, has a stone cairn marking the spot where Matthew Flinders stepped ashore on March 10, 1802. The lookout was named after Alan McLellan, an early settler of the area, and from it there are good views of the **Gulf**, the **Northern and Thomas Playford Stations**, and the picturesque Flinders and Bluff Ranges.

Red Cliff Lookout at the very end of *McSporran Crescent*, off the *Woomera Road* on the Westside, provides an excellent view of the head of the gulf and the Flinders Ranges. The adjacent area is the site of the **Australian Arid Lands Botanic Gardens**, which, when completed, will be a unique attraction.

The first stage of **Port Augusta's Playford Power Station** was opened in 1954, powered by coal railed from Leigh Creek, and the second stage opened in 1960. The adjacent **Northern Power Station** has two generators that will each produce 259 megawatts. Ultimately the new and old power stations will consume up to 4 million tonnes of coal annually. Tours of the Northern Power Station are ⊙conducted weekdays (except public holidays) commencing 10am, 11am and 1pm. Strong footwear should be worn. Turn off *Highway One* at **Truckers Tucker**, approximately 5km each of Port Augusta. For further information, ☎ *8642 0666*.

The **Royal Flying Doctor Service Base** at *4 Vincent Street*, has tours for visitors on weekdays ⊙at 10am, 11am, 2pm and 3pm, ☎ *8642 2044* for large group reservations.

The **School of the Air**, at the eastern end of *Commercial Road*, in the grounds of the Central Primary School, has ⊙conducted tours on school days at 10am. A small entrance fee is charged.

Festivals

The **Australia Day Festival** is held in January, the **Apex Trade Fair** in March, and **Race Week** in June each year.

Facilities

Boating, lawn bowls, croquet, fishing, golf, greyhound racing, horse racing, horse riding, sailing, squash, swimming (beach and pool), tennis, trotting, cinemas.

Outlying Attractions
Port Pirie

Port Pirie is 95km (59 miles) south of Port August, and 229km (142 miles) north of Adelaide, and has a population of around 15,500. In 1889 three smelters were built near Port Pirie to refine the ore being railed from Broken Hill. Today it is the largest lead smelter in the world, and produces lead, zinc, gold, cadmium, antimony and copper by-products, and sulphuric acid. Lead is South Australia's biggest single-produced export income earner. Conducted tours of the smelting works are available, and the Visitor Information Office at *3 Mary Elie Street,* ☎ *(08) 8633 0439*, ✉tourism@ppcadc.sa. gov.au), has information on times and costs.

The **Railway Museum** in Port Pirie has detailed pictures, documents and memorabilia of early days, and another specialist museum is **Carne Brae**, with a collection of over 2500 dolls, superb stained glass windows and a lifetime's collection of silverware and fine china.

The **Northern Festival Centre** is the cultural heart of the north and combines live theatre, art exhibitions, visiting entertainers and social happenings under the one roof.

Port Pirie has all the facilities you would expect for a city of its population, including fishing, golf, greyhound racing, horse racing, sailing, squash, swimming (beach and pool), tennis, trotting and water skiing.

Peterborough

Situated 162km (100 miles) south

east of Port Augusta and 252km (156 miles) north of Adelaide, Peterborough is one of only two known towns in the world where three different rail gauges meet. Peterborough is the gateway to the Flinders Ranges for travellers from NSW, or from Adelaide via the historic mining town of Burra. The Visitor Information Centre is located in a restored **1917 Railway Car** on *Main Street*, ☎*8651 2545*, and is ☉open daily 10am-3pm. You can also email ✉cwoodman@iweb.net.au

The **Steamtown Peterborough Railway Preservation Society** officially commenced operations during Easter 1981, almost 100 years to the day since the first railway to reach Peterborough was opened. The Society runs steam passenger trains at specified times on the narrow gauge line from Peterborough to Orroroo, and the view enjoyed by passengers is one that shouldn't be missed. Timetables for this attraction can be obtained by phoning ☎*8651 3355*.

Amelia Park, 11km (7 miles) east of Peterborough, has a picnic and barbecue area, and playground. **Victoria Park** has a lake, an island and a large barbecue area. **Tank Hill lookout** gives a panoramic view of the town.

Burra

Nestling in the **Bald Hills Range**, 157km (98 miles) north of Adelaide, and approximately 90km (56 miles) south of Peterborough, is Burra, where copper was discovered in 1845. The mines closed down in 1877, but the era of the mining days has been preserved in the unique old buildings around **Paxton Square,** the nearby **Bon Accord Mining Mu-**

seum, the 10 metre timber junker which transported the huge boiler for the mine's engine house, the ruins of the mine buildings, and the restored **Morphetts Engine House**. Other interesting places to visit are the **Redruth Gaol**, the courthouse and the underground **Unicorn Brewery**. The movie Breaker Morant was filmed in the hills around Burra, and Redruth Gaol was used to portray Fort Edwards in the film.

The Burra Visitor Information Centre is at *2 Market Square*, ☎*(08) 8892 2154*.

Clare

The historic township of Clare is 135km (84 miles) north of Adelaide, and approximately 43km (27 miles) south-west of Burra, and is set in a thriving agricultural district, known especially for its wines. Each of the 31 wineries in the district produce wines with a special character, and offer cellar door tastings and sales of internationally acclaimed vintages.

Special events in the valley are the **Clare Valley Easter Festival**, and the **Gourmet Weekend** in mid-May. Both events provide the opportunity to sample a range of the regions finest wines, while top restaurateurs complement the new vintages with plates of their best fare.

Full details of all wineries can be obtained from the Visitor Information Centre Clare Valley, *229 Main North Road, Clare,* ☎*(08) 8842 2131* or ☎*1800 242 131*. It is ☉open daily 9am-5pm (except Sun when it opens at 10am). Browse 🖳*www.*clarevalley.com.au for more information.

Moonta

Moonta is situated on the Yorke Peninsula, 167km (104 miles) north-west of Adelaide.

Yorke Peninsula is part of a copper heritage that is uniquely South Australian. It was copper that saved the young colony and gave the place a distinctive Cornish heritage in the triangle of mining towns at the top of Yorke Peninsula. The many thousands of Cornish miners, who came to mine the precious metal during the 60 year boom, left a legacy which is now celebrated in the biennial festival of **Kernewek Lowender**. It is held over the long weekend in May in every odd-numbered year, in the copper triangle towns - **Moonta, Kadina** and **Wallaroo**.

Moonta is virtually a monument to mining, its architecture belonging to a by-gone era. Of particular note is the gothic-influenced **Uniting Church**. Nearby at the mines site, there are mine buildings and relics to explore, and at **Moonta Mines Museum**, ☎*8825 1944*, in what was once a school, there are exhibits of the life of the miners, and some typical cottages. The deepest shaft in the area is **Taylor's Shaft** at 767m (2516 ft).

The Yorke Peninsula Visitor Information Centre is in the old **Moonta Railway Station**, *Moonta*, ☎*(08) 8825 1891* or ☎*1800 654 991*. It is ☉open 9am-5pm seven days and can be reached be email at ✉tourism@yp-connect.net

Outback South Australia

There are only four main routes through the Outback, each with an individual character and history. There's the famous **Birdsville Track**, along which stockmen once drove herds of cattle south from Queensland. And there's the **Strzelecki Track,** through remote sand dune country of the **Moomba Gasfields** to **Innamincka** on the **Legendary Cooper Creek.** Either way crosses the famous '**dog fence**' - the world's longest protective wire fence, extending more than 3000km (1864 miles) across the centre of Australia to keep wild dingoes from entering the southern pastoral zones.

Following the *Stuart Highway* or the *Oodnadatta Track* takes visitors into opal country and three of the world's most prolific opal mining areas - Coober Pedy, Andamooka and Mintabie.

Let's Stay Here
Woomera Tourist Village, *Old Pimba Rd,* ☎*8673 7800, www.woomera.com* Quite a large place, that has an army barracks feel to it. Plenty of room to move about. All backpackers rooms contains fridge and hand basin. Some rooms are air conditioned. *Dorm* ✪*$22-25; double/twin $55-66; camping $9*

Andamooka
Andamooka is 287km (178 miles) north of Port Augusta (597km [371 miles] from Adelaide), to the west of Lake Torrens. It is an opal field which although far smaller than Coober Pedy is famous for the quality of the gemstones. The opal was discovered by two drovers in 1930, but activity has been declining over recent years.

The mining is concentrated around the edge of the town on the broad flat spurs formed by Opal Creek and its tributaries, and extends about 5km to the Lunatic

Hill workings north of the town.

Facilities in the town include a hotel/motel, motel, guesthouse, caravan park, camping areas, restaurant, hospital, general store, garage, post office, public phone, swimming pool and an airstrip.

The **Opal Gleam** dugout home may be inspected, and a local landmark is the unique **Duke's Bottlehouse,** built from discarded beer bottles. A petrified plesiosaur measuring 9m in length has been found in the diggings, and is on display. Historical cottages have been restored and are used as tea rooms in the cooler weather. At nearby **White Dam** is the late Bill McDougall's famous **Ettamoggah Pub,** a great place for a cooling ale. The road from Woomera to Andamooka passes the turn-off to **Roxby Downs Township,** which was established as a centre for the employees of the **Olympic Dam Mining Project.** Roxby Downs grew at a rate of 1000 persons per year, and was one of the two newly developed townships in the north of the state during the 1990s. The other was Leigh Creek.

Coober Pedy
South Australia's biggest and oldest mining town, Coober Pedy is 610km (379 miles) north-west of Port Augusta, and 850km (528 miles) north-west of Adelaide. The town was established in 1915, and the name is thought to be derived from the Aboriginal words Kupa (white man) and Piti (waterhole, or hole).

To put it mildly, Coober Pedy is very hot and very dry, and the early miners very intelligently decided the best place to live was underground. But the so-called dugouts lack nothing in

comfort and furnishings, and a tour through one of those open for visitors is a must. It is also possible to stay in underground accommodation in the town, for example at the **Underground Motel,** ☎*8672 5324.* If this doesn't appeal to you, there is a hotel/motel and a camping ground above ground. Apart from the opal shops vying for your patronage, there are a few other places to visit. The underground churches are unique, and really beautiful, and the water desalination plant interests some people. There are plenty of local companies offering tours, and for information on these contact the Visitor Information Centre, **Council Offices,** *Hutchison Street,* ☎*(08) 6725 298.* The office is ☺open Mon-Fri 9am-5pm. Visit ▪*www.opalcapitalofthe world.com.au* For further information, ☎*8672 5298* or ☎*1800 637 076* (free call).

If you are feeling lucky, you can try 'noodling' for opal. This means that you must not be on a pegged claim, and must not use a pick, shovel or any digging device. It must be remembered, though, that there is a great danger of unprotected mine shafts on the opal fields, and you really have to look where you are walking.

Let's Stay Here
Bedrock Backpackers, *Hutchinson St,* ☎*8672 5028, www.opalcavecooberpedy.com* Basic underground hostel with TV lounge room and a small equipped kitchen. Bathrooms are located outside next to the spaceship. Opal Cave next door. Parking available. *Dorm* ✪*$17; double $52.50pp* (continental breakfast available)

Joe's Backpackers,
Corner Brewster and Oliver Sts, ☎*8672 5163* Another underground hostel with internet access, TV lounge, bar and pool table. *Dorms* ✪*$19*

Radeka's Backpackers Inn,
Corner Hutchinson and Oliver Sts, ☎*8672 5233* Longest running hostel in town. Accommodation all underground. Amenities includes a internet access, huge kitchen, TV lounge room, pool table, and an above ground common area with laundry. There is also a bar on site. **Recommended.** *Dorms* ✪*$22; double/twin $52-60*

Riba's Underground Camping,
William Creek Rd, ☎*8672 5614* Located 5km south of town centre. You have the option of camping above or underground. No dorms, just camping. Facilities includes a TV room all underground and an outdoor kitchen. They offer an opal mine tour which includes a night of free camping. *Dorm* ✪*$15 (above ground), $9 underground*

Oodnadatta

One of the few centres with real outback character, Oodnadatta was an important railhead between 1891 and 1929 when the rail link to Alice Springs was completed. Before then, camels were used to transport freight from Oodnadatta to Alice Springs. The railway has now been replaced by a new line 100km further to the west, but the sandstone railway station built in 1890 remains. 'Utnadata' means 'Blossom of the Mulga'.

The town has a hotel, caravan park, general stores, post office, public telephone, mechanical repairs, police station, medical services and an airstrip. There is also good swimming in some of the nearby permanent waterholes. North of Oodnadatta lies the **Witjira National Park** which surrounds the **Dalhousie Mound Springs**. However, some tracks in the Park are not maintained and their condition can change rapidly. The area is recommended for **4WD vehicles only**, and visitors are advised to enquire at **Oodnadatta Police Station** in *Oribee Avenue* before setting out, ☎*8670 7805.*

⤷ Let's Stay Here

Maree Drover's Rest Tourist Park, *Corner Oodnadatta and Birdsville Tracks,* ☎*8675 8371* Air conditioned cabins. *Powered sites* ✪*$12; unpowered $8; rooms $20.*

Oodnadatta Caravan Park,
Oodnadatta Track, ☎*8670 7822* Located next to the easy-to-spot Pink Roadhouse. *Powered sites* ✪*$14.50; unpowered $9.50; rooms $38.*

William Creek Hotel,
Oodnadatta Track, William Creek, ☎*8670 7880* Accommodation is located at the back of the pub. The pub with so much character is usually the highlight here. *Dorm* ✪*$19 with linen.*

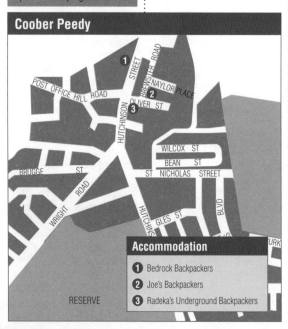

Coober Peedy

STREET
BREWSTER ROAD
POST OFFICE HILL ROAD
NAYLOR PLACE
OLIVER ST
HUTCHINSON
WILCOX ST
BEAN ST
ST NICHOLAS STREET
BRUGGE ST
WRIGHT ROAD
HUTCHINS
GLES ST
BLVD
URK
RESERVE

Accommodation
❶ Bedrock Backpackers
❷ Joe's Backpackers
❸ Radeka's Underground Backpackers

Victoria

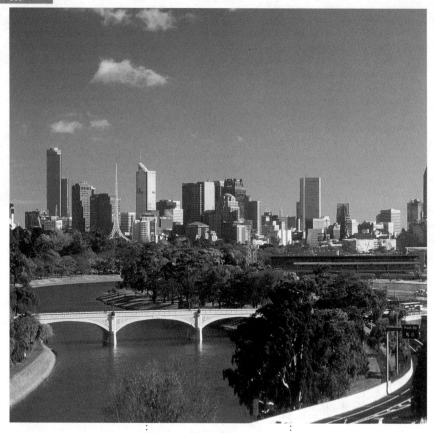

Melbourne

Population 3,000,000

Melbourne, the capital of Victoria, is situated on the shores of Port Phillip Bay. The Yarra River flows through the city.

Settlers in Van Diemen's Land (Tasmania) had known for years that there was good grazing land in the Port Phillip area, but had been refused permission to settle there. In 1835, John Batman ignored the ban, landed with a party, and 'bought' 600,000 acres of land from the local Aborigines for a few axes and other trade goods. He then returned to Launceston and formed the Port Phillip Association. (On the north side of Flinders Street, between Market and William Streets, there is a small plaque in the pavement marking the place where Batman stood when he declared that it was a good place for a village.)

In 1836, Governor Bourke vetoed Batman's purchase, and appointed Captain William Lonsdale as resident magistrate of the rapidly-growing settlement. Bourke visited the site in the following year, named the place Melbourne, had a street plan drawn up, and offered lots for sale.

The Australian Colonies Government Act was passed in August 1850, and constituted the Port Phillip district as a separate colony, with La Trobe as its first Lieutenant-Governor. Soon after, gold was discovered near Ballarat, and people came from all over the world seeking their fortune. The consequent Eureka Uprising gave the new government its first major challenge.

Climate

Melbourne's climate is midway between maritime and continental, and is very changeable. Average temperatures: January max 26C

(79F) - min 14C (57F); July max 13C (55F) - min 6C (43F). Average annual rainfall: 656mm (26 ins). The driest months are June to August.

Characteristics

Victoria is called the Garden State, and its capital city certainly does its share to live up to that reputation. Melbourne has tree-lined boulevards, acres of parkland on the banks of the Yarra River, and parks and gardens galore in the suburbs.

How to Get There
By Air

Melbourne International Airport, at Tullamarine, is serviced by over 20 international carriers. The domestic lines of **Qantas**, ☎ 13 1313, have regular services from other cities in Australia.

The airport is about 20km (12 miles) out of the city, and the **Skybus** operates between Tullamarine and the terminal at 58 Franklin Street, ☎ 9335 3066 or ☎ 9662 9275. The **Frankston and Peninsula Airport Shuttle**, ☎ 9783 1199, takes passengers to that area, and there are also shuttle buses for the eastern suburbs.

By Bus

Greyhound Pioneer, ☎ 13 2030, and **McCaffertys**, ☎ 13 1499, have regular services to/from Melbourne and Sydney, Adelaide, Canberra, Newcastle, Coolangatta, Brisbane, Alice Springs, Townsville, Perth, Cairns and Darwin.

By Rail

There are rail services from Sydney and Adelaide, with connections from other capital cities, ☎ 13 2232. The country and interstate terminal is Spencer Street Station.

V/Line

Rail and coach services operate from country Victoria to Melbourne daily. They also travel as far as Adelaide, Canberra and the Sapphire Coast of NSW. For further information, ☎ 136 196.

Visitor Information

The Victoria Visitor Information Centre is in the Melbourne Town Hall on the corner of *Swanston Walk and Little Collins Street*, ☎ (03) 9658 9955. It is ☺open Mon-Fri 8.30am-5.30pm and weekends and public holidays 9am-5pm. They can be emailed at ✉visitor@melbourne.vic.gov.au

There are information booths in Bourke Street Mall, between Elizabeth and Swanston Streets, and Flinders Street Station, on the corner of Flinders and Swanston Streets.

The Victorian Tourism Operators Association is on *Level 2, Rialto North Tower, 525 Collins Street*, ☎ (03) 9614 8877 or email ✉vtoa@vtoa.asn.au

Tourism Victoria is on *Level 6, 55 Collins Street*, ☎ 132 842.

City of Melbourne, is in Melbourne Town Hall, *Swanston Street*, ☎ (03) 9658 9955.

The Travellers' Aid Society of Victoria is on the *2nd Floor at 169 Swanston Street*, ☎ (03) 9654 2600. They are ☺open Mon-Fri 8am-6pm and Sat-Sun 10am-4pm. They also have a Rail Room at *Spencer Street Railway Station*, ☎ (03) 9670 2873.

Melbourne also has an Information Line available 7 days a week from 8am-6pm - ☎ 13 28 42.

The following websites will give you a detailed insight into the city of Melbourne, outlying regions and potential itineraries for travel

around Victoria:
- ▤ melbourne.citysearch.com.au
- ▤ www.melbourne.org
- ▤ www.tourism.vic.gov.au
- ▤ www.theage.com.au
- ▤ www.victrip.vic.gov.au

⤳ Let's Stay Here

For a complete list of accommodation, contact one of the Tourist Offices above or explore the web pages. As with any big city, accommodation is usually cheaper in the outer suburbs, and that is obviously where you find the caravan parks. Here is a selection of city and inner suburban budget accommodation, which should be used as a guide only. The telephone area code is 03.

City Centre
All Nations,

2 Spencer St, ☎ 1800 222 238, ▤ www.allnations.com.au Located in a shaby area within walking distance of popular sites and the clubs in King Street. Right next to the Yarra river and the Crown casino. Free city tram is just on their door step. If you judge the cover then it looks old, but the inside is nice with a good feel to it. Three storeys high and the bed have new amenities. Facilities includes a small kitchen (there's free bread), laundry, TV lounge and common room with internet access. There is also an on-site bar and Seven 11 is just next door. Free Pickups from the airport, the bus station or the nearest town. Check out their website to find out 'what's on' at All Nations like

their Monday movie nights. Parking available. *Dorms from* ✪*$15;*

Elephant Backpackers,
250 Flinders St, ☎ *9654 2616,* 🌐 *www.elephantbackpackers.citysearch.com.au* Located nicely at the heart of the city, close to the cafes and adjacent from Flinders Station. Very good value for money. New amenities and the bunks have real nice mattresses. Facilities includes a small kitchen, laundry, common room, internet access and a big TV lounge. **Recommended.** *Dorms* ✪*$20; single $35; double/twin $25pp ;*

Exford Hotel,
199 Russell St, ☎ *9663 2697,* 🌐 *www.exfordhotel.com.au* Located above a pub, but has more common rooms than usual. Old looking but provides a very good atmosphere, and is quite colourful. Accommodation is really good with secured lockers. Facilities includes a good kitchen, laundry and TV lounge. **Recommended.** *Dorms* ✪*$19; single $56; double/twin $56;*

Flinders Station Backpackers,
35 Elizabeth St, ☎ *9620 5100,* 🌐 *www.flindersbackpackers.com.au* Centrally located and stands tall boasting it's 11 floors. 24 hour supermarket is conveniently across the road. Facilities includes an equipped kitchen and laundry which are scattered all over the place. There is a common room situated upstairs on the third floor which has three TV lounges,

internet access and games area which has the usual pool table and video games. There's also lockers and the ever rare gym. *Dorms* ✪*$19; double/twin $56 ;*

Friendly Backpackers,
197 King St, ☎ *9670 1111 or 1800 671 115,* 🌐 *www.friendlygroup.com.au* Quite a popular hostel due to their high rating facilities and well cared for environment. Secured lockers in rooms. Facilities includes a well equipped kitchen and dining area. Other facilities can be found either on top or bottom floors. Pool table is downstairs and the TV lounges and reading rooms are on the upper levels. They can also help you look for jobs. Free internet and e-mail access. **Recommended.** *Dorms* ✪*$23;* (includes free breakfast)

The Greenhouse Backpacker,
228 Flinders Lane, ☎ *9639 6400 or 1800 249 207,* 🌐 *www.friendlygroup.com.au* You won't find a hostel in the city quite like this one. Though the facilities quite match the other hostels, it's the little added touches that makes and breaks this from the rest. It's well maintained and very clean. Accommodation is superb with air conditioned rooms, secured lockers and reading lights in all the beds. The rooftop garden is a highlight, including the fully equipped kitchen, massive laundry, cable TV and pool tables. The staff will go to all lengths to assist you in your queries about the city and makes sure that you enjoy your stay. They also organise a lot of activities like pubcrawls,

excursions and 'Neighbours' tour. Watch out for the free barbecue and pancake nights. **Highly recommended.** *Dorms* ✪*$24; single $45; double/twin $30pp*

Hotel Bakpak,
167 Franklin St, ☎ *9329 7525,* 🌐 *www.bakpak.com* A large sized hostel with a great feel to it and loaded with things to do. Includes your normal facilities like the 24 hour laundry plus a cafe, employment agency, travel agent and internet access situated at the ground floor. There is also a bar in the basement which is brilliant and usually has different theme nights and live bands. They have enough equipment in the bar to keep you occupied for a few hours like a ping pong table, foosball, pool tables and video games. Need a work out? The ever rare gym is also accessible which has a swimming pool, sauna and spa. Plus there's a cinema and TV lounge with cable TV and video. Upstairs is a rooftop with great city views. **Recommended.** *Dorms from* ✪*$24; single $55; double/twin $30pp*

Melbourne Connection,
205 King St, ☎ *9642 4464,* 🌐 *www.melbourneconnection.com* This newly renovated hostel is a choice for a place to stay. Small, friendly hostel, situated in Melbourne's city centre catering for backpackers and other budget conscious travellers who may be visiting Melbourne for study, work, a sporting event or just a weekend away. Rooms have air conditioning/heating. Great

facilities including a fully equipped kitchen, dining area, laundry, TV room and has internet access. They also offer employment assistance and 24 hour access with security. **Recommended.** *Dorms from ✪$20; double/twin $30pp*

Melbourne International Backpackers,

450 Elizabeth St, ☎9662 4066 Another huge establishment located at the very heart of the city. Very close to the Queen Victoria Market and the Melbourne Central shopping centre and just opposite the Greyhound Bus Station. Newly furnished accommodation and well secured lockers in rooms. The common room includes a kitchen, massive dining area, a TV lounge and a courtyard. *Dorms from ✪$18; double/twin $30pp*

Stork Hotel,

504 Elizabeth St, ☎9663 6237, ▇www.storkhotel.com This is a budget accommodation located above a pub, and has been established here since the gold rush days. Top choice for budget stayers. Pretty good quality accommodation with rooms lathered in themes and supplied with linen and towels. Mostly double rooms and caters a lot for couple backpackers. Facilities includes a limited small kitchen/TV room. A cafe and a good bar is located downstairs. **Recommended.** *Dorms ✪$25; single $43; double/twin $58*

Toad Hall, 4

41 Elizabeth St, ☎9600 9010, ▇www.toadhall-hotel.com.au

Quite a classy hostel and appeals mostly to couples and mature backpackers. Conveniently located, the hostel is only minutes away from Victoria market, cinemas, theatres and major shopping precincts. Facilities includes a kitchen, laundry, courtyard and a barbecue area. The two TV lounges with cable TV are separate and the one at the basement has a better atmosphere. Tours and car hire is also available. Parking available. **Recommended.** *Dorms ✪$25; single $60; double $35pp; twin $30pp;*

Other Areas

Bev and Mick's Backpackers,

575 Spencer St, West Melbourne, ☎9328 2423 Located at the heart of West Melbourne. Newly renovated. A few blocks from station. Facilities includes a fully equipped kitchen, laundry, games lounge room with ping pong tables, basketball ring and a barbecue area. Licensed bar on site. Free bike hire and free Barbecue on Thursdays. *Dorms ✪$15*

Boutique Backpackers,

337 Highett St, Richmond, ☎9428 7821 Located about 25 minutes walk to the city centre, in a nice street lined with trees. This newly renovated place has a warm atmosphere. Quite popular with working travellers. Facilities includes a kitchen, lounge room with TV and offers internet access. *Dorms from ✪$20* (but mainly does weekly booking s only)

Carlton College Hostel,

95 Drummond St, Carlton,

☎9664 0664 or 1800 066 551, ▇www.carltoncolleg e.com.au Situated close to the Melbourne Museum, the Royal Exhibition Buildings and fantastic restaurants. Very close to most attractions. Housed in a huge terrace house, and caters often to large school groups. Facilities includes a kitchen, TV lounge and an internet access. *Dorms from ✪$15; single $40; double/twin $48;* (prices includes breakfast)

Central Accommodation,

21 Bromham Pl, Richmond, ☎9427 9826, ▇www.centra laccommodation.net Located about 20 minutes walk away from the city centre, in a quiet residential area. Caters a lot to working travellers and long term budget stayers with friendly and welcoming staff. Can help you with employment. Has a lot of warmth. Facilities includes a small fully equipped kitchen, TV lounge and offers internet access. Weekly rates apply. *Dorms from ✪$15; single from $22 a day; double/twin $36 a day*

Chapel St Backpackers,

22 Chapel St, Windsor, ☎9533 6855, ▇www.csbackpacke rs.com.au You can find this hostel at the cheaper end of Chapel Street's busy shopping strip, just across the Windsor Station. Newly renovated and most rooms have en suite. Rooms are small and cozy with secured lockers. Facilities includes a small kitchen and dining, common room, TV lounge and internet access.

Accommodation

1. All Nations
2. Elephant Backpackers
3. Exford Hotel
4. Flinders Station Backpackers
5. Friendly Backpackers
6. The Greenhouse Backpacker
7. Hotel Bakpak
8. Melbourne Connection
9. Melbourne International Backpackers
10. Stork Hotel
11. Toad Hall

Melbourn Tram

Kings Domain

Dorms ○*$23; double $35;*
twin $25; (prices includes all-you-can-eat breakfast)

Chapman Garden YHA,
76 Chapman St, North
Melbourne, ☎ *9328 3595,*
▆ *www.yha.com.au* Located
with easy access to the city
centre, in a quiet residential
street, north near Royal Park.
A small and friendly city
hostel close to trams. Facilities
includes a kitchen, laundry,
TV lounge, internet access
and a barbecue area. There is
a nice gazebo and garden in
the backyard. They also offer a
tour booking service and free
swimming passes and videos.
Bike hire and parking available.
Members Dorm ○*$24; single*
$48; double $58; twin $25pp
BC MC VA EFTPOS (if you
intend to stay longer ask about
their specials)

City Scene Backpackers,
361 Queensberry St, North
Melbourne, ☎ *9348 9525,*
▆ *www.cityscene.com.au.*
Quaint and homely. Located
close to Queen Victoria market
and the trams. Rooms have
central heating. Just your basic
facilities including a small
modern kitchen, TV lounge and
a barbecue area outdoors. Free
membership to health club
for the length of stay. *Dorms*
○*$14; double $38 (with fridge*
and TV); twin $33;

College Lawn Hotel,
36 Greville St, Prahran, ☎ *9510*
6057, ▆ *www.collegelawnhot*
el.com.au Located just above
a nice pub in a quiet strip just
minutes away from Chapel St.
All dorms have lockers and

most have their own fridge.
Facilities includes a minimally
equipped kitchen and laundry.
On site lounge bar, restaurant,
bar and bottle shop. *Dorms*
○*$15; single $30; double $50;*

Court House Hotel,
86 Erroll St, North Melbourne,
9329 5394. If you're after
the nicest accommodation
that's situated above a pub,
then you've found the place.
Located very close to the local
shops. Small and basic accommodation, but very clean
and offers a good atmosphere.
Minimal facilities includes a
small kitchen and a cosy TV
lounge. There is also a sundeck on the small rooftop. The
bar downstairs is known to
offer really cheap meal deals
and there's also a pool table
and cable TV. *Dorms* ○*$17*

Gunn Island Hotel,
102 canterbury Rd, Mid-
dle Park, ☎ *9690 1882,*
▆ *www.gunnisland.com.au*
Situated above a pub that was
just renovated. Located just in
between the city centre and St
Kilda, with the shops, trams
and beach close by. Facilities
includes a small kitchen,
laundry and a common
room with a nice TV. On site
brasserie, street cafe, bar and
brewery. *Dorms* ○*$19; sin-*
gle $38.50; double/twin $55;
(complimentary breakfast on
Mondays - Fridays)

Hotel Claremont Nomads,
189 Toorak Rd, South Yarra,
☎ *9826 8000,* ▆ *www.hotel*
claremont.com/ A uniquely
restored 1886 Victorian
building, now a budget hotel

and guesthouse, located in
the heart of Melbourne's
most chic and trendy suburb
of South Yarra. Facilities
includes a kitchen, laundry,
games room, swimming
pool and a barbecue area.
Recommended. *Dorms*
○*$30; double/twin $36pp;*
(breakfast included)

Lord's Lodge,
204 Punt Rd, Pra-
ran, ☎ *9510 5658,*
▆ *www.lordslodge.com.au*
Minutes away from everything
in Prahran and South Yarra
area. Housed in an old 1870s
building with a really good
feel to it. Beach and city
only minutes away. Double
and twin rooms located in
bungalows in the backyard
with a nice barbecue area.
Facilities includes a small
kitchen, internet, TV and video
lounge with open fireplace,
garden with barbecue area.
They also offer employment
assistance. Parking available.
Dorms ○*$20; single $45;*
double/twin $58 ; (girls only
dorm available)

New Terrace Inn,
418 Murray Rd, Preston,
☎ *9470 1006* Situated about
10 mins by train from Melbourne. Facilities includes a
kitchen, laundry, games room
and two TV lounges. Parking
available. *Dorms* ○*$15.40*

Nomad's Market Inn,
115 Cecil St, South
Melbourne, ☎ *9690 2220,*
▆ *www.marketinn.com.au*
Located just right across
the road from South
Melbourne Market. The bright

interiors should start off the atmosphere. Look out for the 1950s style furnishings. Facilities includes a small kitchen, dining area, internet access, TV lounge and a barbecue area outside. There's also a licensed bar on site with a pool table. Free beer on arrival. Bicycle and car hire is also available. *Dorms from ✪$19; double/twin $58; (breakfast included)*

Queensberry Hill YHA,
76-86 Howard St, North Melbourne, ☎9329 8599, 🖳*www.yha.com.au* Located not far from the city centre and major attractions, adjacent to the church. Offers a lot of things and is well facilitated. Facilities includes a kitchen, laundry, common room, TV lounge, internet access and a barbecue area. Licensed cafe, in-house travel agency for tour bookings, international and interstate travel and also a foreign currency exchange all in the premises. Free bike hire and swimming passes offered. Parking is subject to availability. **Recommended.** *Members Dorm ✪$23; single $58 ; double/twin $34pp ($40.50pp with en suite); BC MC VA EFTPOS (if you intend to stay longer ask about their specials)*

Railway Hotel Backpackers,
291 Albert St, Brunswick, ☎*9380 1483,*🖳*www.therailw ay.com.au* Quite a popular above the pub accommodation especially for the working travellers. This hostel is located a few kilometres north of the city but very close to the shops and

restaurants. Public transport is very accessible and a huge Safeway supermarket is right across the road. Facilities includes a kitchen, a big common room with a TV and pool table. There's also an internet access and an on-site 24 hour bar. Parking available. *Dorms from ✪$18*

Royal Derby Hotel,
446 Brunswick St, Fitzroy, ☎*1800 777 052,* 🖳*www.derbyhotel.com.au/* Located at the heart of Fitzroy, close to shops and entertainment.Tram lines are just at the door. Facilities includes a kitchen, laundry, cable TV, internet and pool table. On site bar and beer garden plus cheap meals. *Dorms ✪$16; twin $18pp (breakfast included)*

Spencer City Central,
475 Spencer St, ☎*9329 7755 or 1800 638 108,* 🖳*www.hotelspencer.com.* Situated about 10 minutes away from Spencer Street Station. The hostel is in an old building with a good feel, a renovated top floor and some views of the city and the docklands. The staff are wonderful and helpful. Facilities includes a kitchen, laundry, a TV room and internet access. A bar and restaurant is attached on-site downstairs, but food can be pricey. Parking available. **Recommended.** *Dorms ✪$22; single $55; twin $27.50 ($37.50 with en suite)*

The Nunnery,
116 Nicholson St, Fitzroy,

☎*9419 8637 or 1800 032 635,* 🖳*www.bakpak.com/nunnery* This hostel used to be the Nunnery. Set in an old building with plenty of character. There is also a guesthouse next door which is more grand and a lot more quiet with a great atmosphere. Facilities includes a kitchen, laundry and TV lounge. The rooftop deck has the barbecue area. *Dorms from ✪$23; single $55; double/ twin $35pp (prices includes breakfast)*

Wild Bunyip Backpackers,
153 Hoddle St, Richmond, ☎*9428 5932* Another working travellers hostel and is situated on a busy street. Clean and newly painted. Might as well stay in your room where there's the TV, fridge and handbasins. Very minimal facilities including a tiny kitchen and a semi-outdoors TV lounge. Parking available. *Dorms from ✪$15; single $45; double/twin $23pp ;*

Caravan Parks
Ashley Gardens Holiday Village, *129 Ashley Street, Braybrook,* ☎*9318 6866.* (No pets allowed) 106 sites, tennis, heated pool - *powered sites ✪$23, cabins from $35pp for two.*

Melbourne Holiday Park,
265 Elizabeth Street, Coburg, ☎*9354 3533.* (No pets allowed), 120 sites, heated pool - *powered sites ✪$23 for two, cabins $45pp for two.*

Sylvan Caravan Park, *1780 Hume Highway, Campbell-*

field, ☎ 9357 0009. (No dogs or cats) 101 sites - powered sites ۞$20 for two.

Local Transport

The Met, Melbourne's public transport system, covers trains, trams and buses, and is operated by the Public Transport Corporation. Melbourne is divided into three zones and your ticket type depends on which zone you are going to travel in, and for how long. Two-hour, daily, weekly, monthly or yearly tickets are available.

The routes of the various forms of transport are indicated on the Met map, available from railway stations, newsagencies and some book shops. Further information is available from the Met Transport Information Centre, *589 Collins Street*, ☎ *13 1638* (⊙open 7am-9pm), or from The Met Shop at *103 Elizabeth Street*.

Melbourne's metropolitan public transport website for **Bayside Trains** is ▣ www.met.vic.gov.au Victoria's official public transport site, containing timetables and fares for trams, buses and trains, is ▣ www.victrip.com.au

Trams

Trams are just about the 'symbol' of Melbourne, and are a big draw-card for visitors. These vehicles, some old-fashioned and some sleek and new, continue to provide transport for thousands of commuters.

They are an interesting, reliable and efficient way to see the city. The Visitor Centres can provide you with a brochure outlining the routes, stops, zones and fares, with explanations to assist your reading of tickets (Metcards) and timetables.

Here are a few hints: remember to take coins with you, as this is the only form of currency which ticket vending machines accept. You can purchase a daily ticket for ۞$4.40, allowing you unlimited travel in Zone 1, which covers the city and immediate surrounds. Keep an eye out for retailers displaying the Metcard Sales Flag, because daily tickets must be pre-purchased. In the city centre, there is a free tram service, the Free City Circle, which skirts the rectangular perimeter of the CBD and may be useful for reducing your legwork while shopping or sightseeing.

Taxis

These can be hired off the street, at taxi ranks, major hotels, or by phoning one of the taxi companies.

Initial flagfall is ۞$2.60 and the meter clicks over at ۞$1 per kilometre, or at 41.6 cents per minute if the speed of the vehicle drops below 25km/h. There is a booking fee of $1 and also a late night surcharge of $1. Be aware that City Link tolls will be added to the fare if you choose to travel on certain roads - both the Western and Southern Links are ۞$2 for taxis.

Following are some of the companies operating in Melbourne:

Arrow Taxi Service, ☎ *13 2211;* Astoria Taxis, ☎ *9347 5511;* Black Cabs Combined, ☎ *13 2227;* Embassy Taxis, ☎ *13 1755;* Frankston Radio Cabs, ☎ *9786 3322;* North Suburban Taxis, ☎ *13 1119;* Regal Corporate Cars, ☎ *9326 6600;* Silver Top Taxi Service, ☎ *13 1008;* West Suburban Taxi, ☎ *9689 1144;* Yellow Cabs, ☎ *13 19 24.*

Water taxis include: River Yarra Water Taxis,

☎ *0416 06 8655;* and Melbourne Circle Water Taxis, ☎ *9686 0914.*

Car Hire

There are plenty of car rental agencies, and they accept current international licences.

Airport Rent A Car, ☎ *9335 3355;* All Cheap Car Rentals, ☎ *9429 6999;* Atlas, ☎ *9633 6233;* Avis, ☎ *9330 4011;* Budget, ☎ *1300 - 362 848;* Crown, ☎ *9682 2266;* Delta, ☎ *9330 6122;* Hertz, ☎ *13 3039;* Murphy, ☎ *9602 2265;* National, ☎ *9696 9000;* Pacific, ☎ *9347 9600;* Thrifty, ☎ *1300 367 2277.*

When driving in Melbourne, there are a few rules about the trams. Drivers must not obstruct trams, and there are yellow lines on roadways indicating streets in which drivers must keep clear of the tracks when trams are approaching. Drivers must also stop when a tram is picking up or setting down passengers, if there is not a central traffic island. Making a right hand turn can sometimes be dicey in the city centre. If the intersection has a 'hook turn' sign, the turn has to be made from the left-hand lane when the lights change, to leave the centre of the intersection clear for trams.

Bicycle Hire

Melbourne has quite a few bike tracks, and to hire a bike it is best to get in touch with **Bicycle Victoria**, *19 O'Connell Street, North Melbourne*, ☎ *9328 3000:*

Let's Eat

Melbourne has over 3200 restaurants representing 70 national cuisines. The most plentiful choice of Asian restaurants is found in Chinatown's Little Bourke Street; for Italian food, try Lygon Street,

Carlton; for Greek, Lonsdale Street; and for Vietnamese, Victoria Street, Richmond. South Yarra is another restaurant centre. Here is a selection of highly recommended restaurants.

Asian

Bamboo House, *47 Little Bourke Street,* ☎*9662 1565.* Licensed. Peking duck and spicy seafoods are specialties. Open daily from 5.30pm and for lunch Mon-Fri.

Empress of China, *120 Little Bourke Street,* ☎*9663 1833.* Open for dinner 6 days and lunch on Sundays.

Isthmus of Kra, *50 Park Street, South Melbourne,* ☎*9690 3688.* Gernerally considered one of the finest Thai restaurants in Melbourne. Licensed, wonderful wine list, varied menu, open for dinner 7 days and lunch Mon-Fri.

King of Kings, *209 Russel Street,* ☎*9663 2895.* Inexpensive meals of a good quality, open daily 11am-2.30am.

Mask of China, *117 Little Bourke Street,* ☎*9662 2116.* Licensed, excellent seafood and wine list, dinner served daily from 6pm, lunch on Sunday from midday.

European

2bc, *177 Greville Street, Prahran,* ☎*9529 4922.* Busy and trendy establishment that serves Mediterranean-style meals at reasonable prices. It is licensed and open for lunch 7 days and dinner Mon-Sat.

Akvavit, *Ground Level 3a, 2 Southgate, Southbank,* ☎*9699 9947.* Swedish restaurant with

views of the river and city. Licensed or BYO, open daily for lunch and dinner. Two people can escape here paying around $40 for meals plus drinks.

Austria Haus Edelweiss, *419 Spencer Street,* ☎*9329 5877.* Licensed, open 7 days for lunch and dinner, with Viennese Sunday luncheon.

Bonum, *2 Collins Street, City,* ☎*9650 9387.* Licensed, up-market restaurant with inventive and exotic dishes at prices around $25 for a main course. Open for dinner Mon-Sat and for lunch Mon-Fri.

Casa Di Iorio, *141 Lygon Street, Carlton,* ☎*9347 2670.* Italian cuisine restaurant and pizza house, plus takeaway.

Da Salvatore, *29 Gratton Street, Carlton,* ☎*9663 4778.* Pizza, pasta and steaks, quick service, open 7 days for lunch and dinner.

International

Abla's, *109 Elgin Street, Carlton,* ☎*9347 0006.* Considered to be the best Middle Eastern restaurant in Melbourne. Set menu with a variety of complementary flavours. Open Thu-Fri for lunch and Mon-Sat for dinner.

Becco, 11-25 Crossley Street, ☎*9663 3000.* Efficient service, strong wine list and an extensive menu. Open daily 9am-11pm.

Blakes, *Ground Level, 2 Southgate, Southbank,* ☎*9699 4100.* Extensive menu offering a variety of unique flavours. Wonderful views of the Yarra and city. Open daily for lunch and dinner.

Harvey's, *10 Murphy Street, South Yarra,* ☎*9867 3605.* Predominantly Asian and Italian flavours. Open daily for lunch and dinner, from 7am Mon-Fri.

O'Connels, *407 Coventry Street, South Melbourne,* ☎*9699 9600.* A changing menu that ranges from North American to Middle Eastern cuisine. Licensed, open for lunch and dinner 7 days.

Theatre Restaurants

Dirty Dick's Medieval Madness Restaurant, *45 Dudley Street, West Melbourne,* ☎*9325 3999.* Licensed, medieval banquet.

Dracula's Theatre Restaurant, *169 Exhibition Street, Melbourne,* ☎*9663 1754.* Comic Transylvanian theme. Centrally located in the city.

Hofbrauhaus, *18-24 Market Lane, Melbourne,* ☎*9663 3361.* Bavarian beerfest. Affordable lunch menu. Licensed, open daily midday to midnight.

The Comedy Club, *380 Lygon Street, Carlton,* ☎*9348 1622.* Open 9am-5pm Mon-Fri. Fully licensed, cabaret environment, dinner and show packages available.

Witches in Britches, *84 Dudley Street, West Melbourne,* ☎*9329 9850.* Bar, three course meal and a two-hour show to follow. Open 7pm-1am 7 days.
At the other end of the scale, **KFC** is at *201 Bourke Street and 37 Swanston Street.* **Pizza Hut** is on the *corner of Elizabeth and Bourke Streets* (☎*13 1166* for delivery). There are no less than 11 **McDonalds** branches, with *4 on Bourke*

Street, *2 on Collins Street, 2 on Elizabeth Street,* and *one each on Lonsdale, Swanston* and *St Kilda.* Of course, the suburbs are represented by additional branches of each of the above.

You will find many other types of fast food outlets in the city centre. Going hungry in Melbourne is almost impossible, except in cases when you remain indecisive for hours, overwhelmed by the wide choice of venues. But this seldom occurs.

Entertainment

Melbourne's nightlife conjures up images of excitement, colour, action and entertainment. There is a comprehensive range of nocturnal activities to select from including discos, wine bars, concerts, theatre, cinema, live bands, nightclubs and much more.

Here is a selection of entertainment venues in the city.

Cinemas

Hoyts Cinema Complex, *140 Bourke Street,* ☎ *9663 3303.*
Village Centre, *206 Bourke Street,* ☎ *9667 6565.*
Chinatown Cinema, *200 Bourke Street,* ☎ *9662 3465.*
Crazy Horse Cinema, *34 Elizabeth Street,* ☎ *9654 8796.*
Greater Union, *131 Russell Street,* ☎ *9654 8235.*
Kino Cinemas, *45 Collins Street,* ☎ *9650 2100.*
Lumiere Cinemas, *108 Lonsdale Street,* ☎ *9639 1055.*
Moonlight Cinemas, *Level 10, 140 Bourke Street,* ☎ *9663 9555.*

Theatres

The **Half-Tix** kiosk is in the Bourke Street Mall, ☎ *9650 9420.*
Princess Theatre, *163 Spring Street,* ☎ *9662 2911.*
Victorian Arts Centre, *100 St Kilda Road,* ☎ *9281 8000.*
Athenaeum Theatre, *188 Collins Street,* ☎ *9650 1500.*
Comedy Theatre, *240 Exhibition Street,* ☎ *9209 9000.*
Playbox Theatre Company, *113 Sturt Street, South Melbourne,* ☎ *9685 5111.*
Melbourne Theatre Company, *129 Ferrars Street, Southbank,* ☎ *13 6166.*
Her Majesty's Theatre, *219 Exhibition Street,* ☎ *9663 3211.*
Forum Theatre, *154 Flinders Street,* ☎ *9299 9700.*
Princes Theatre, *163 Spring Street,* ☎ *9299 9800.*
Regent Theatre, *191 Collins Street,* ☎ *9299 9860.*
Sidney Myer Music Bowl, *Kings Domain,* ☎ *9281 8360.*

Bars and Pubs

Gin Palace, *191 Little Collins Street,* ☎ *9654 0533.* Characterised by an eclectic mix of furniture fashions and cocktail concoctions (try an 'Industrial Revolution', for example!). ☺open daily 4pm-3am.

Hairy Canary, *212 Little Collins Street,* ☎ *9654 2471.* An inviting complement of food is on offer for those who feel that they need something to wash down with their drink. ☺open 7.30am-3am 7 days.

The Bullring, *95 Johnston Street, Fitzroy,* ☎ *9416 0022.* Lively atmosphere with music and dance of Latin American derivation. ☺open from 6pm-late, entertainment begins at 10.30pm. ☻$5 cover charge.

Up Top Bar, *First Floor, 163 Russell Street,* ☎ *9663 8990.* ☺open from 4pm until late the following morning Wed-Sun. Nostalgic '50s decor revised in trendy style. Impressive list of alcoholic beverages. Entry is free.

Walters Wine Bar, *Upper Level, Southgate, Southbank,* ☎ *9690 1211.* Popular after-dark venue with stunning city views across the Yarra River. Good meals also available. ☺open midday every day and closes Sun-Thu at 1am and Fri-Sat at 3am.

Music Venues
Rock

Central Club Hotel, *246 Victoria Street, North Melbourne,* ☎ *9329 7482.*
Wayside Inn, *466 City Road, South Melbourne,* ☎ *9699 8469.*

Jazz

Dizzy's Jazz Bar, *90 Swan Street, Richmond,* ☎ *9428 1233.* A deservedly famous centre for jazz lovers. ☺open Thu-Sat 8pm-1am. Cover charges are ☻$8 on Thursday and $10 on Friday and Saturday.

Moylans, *384 Flinders Lane, Melbourne,* ☎ *9629 1030.* Smoke-free environment, and a magnet for talented jazz musicians.

Ozcat, at the Parkview, *cnr Scotchmer Street and Georges Road, Fitzroy North,* ☎ *9489 8811.* This venue will be used only for special concerts, while the main features of the Australian Catalog of Independent Artists will be played at Moylans (see above).
Rhythm and Blues

The Next Blue, at the Crown Casino, *8 Whiteman Street, South-bank,* ☎ *9292 7007.*

Shopping

Melbourne is Australia's fashion

capital, and has an enormous selection of clothes and accessories boutiques.

Collins Street has many designer label boutiques, and is linked to **Bourke Street** by a network of arcades and alleys with boutiques and specialty shops. Explore the sidewalks along Collins Street between Swanston and Spring Streets for some exclusive up-market clothing stores.

234 Collins, located at that address, is a complex dedicated to fashion.

Australia on Collins is another fashion mecca. It joins **Collins** and **Little Collins Streets** and boasts an elaborate food court.

The 19th century **Block Arcade**, with its high domed ceiling and mosaic tiled floor, runs from *282 Collins Street* to *Little Collins Street*, or you can enter from Elizabeth Street.

The **Royal Arcade**, the oldest arcade in Melbourne, links *Little Collins Street* and *Bourke Street Mall*, and also has an entrance in Elizabeth Street.

The **Galleria Plaza** is a centre for fashion and also a good place to find gifts. It is on the corner of *Elizabeth* and *Little Collins Streets*.

The **Bourke Street Mall** in the heart of the city, between *Swanston* and *Elizabeth Streets*, offers very good shopping, and is dominated by David Jones and Myer Department Stores. Other arcades running off the Mall are the **Centrepoint Mall** and **The Walk**. Although the Mall is classed as a pedestrian area, trams do run through its centre.

Midtown Plaza is on the corner of *Bourke* and *Swanston Streets*.

If you are searching for duty free shopping, head to the stretch of **Elizabeth Street** between *Bourke* and *Lonsdale Streets*.

The bazaar-like character of: the **Queen Victoria Market**, *cnr Victoria and Elizabeth Streets;* the **Prahran Markets**, *Commercial Road,* just off Chapel Street; **South Melbourne Markets**, *York Street, off Ferrars Street*; and the **Victorian Arts Centre Sunday Markets**, *100 St Kilda Road, South Melbourne,* each offer an alternative and entertaining shopping experience.

Toorak Village, in *Toorak Road* from *Punt Road* to *Williams Road* has restaurants, boutiques and expensive furniture stores.

A little further out in Campbellfield at *400 Mahoneys Road,* just off the *Hume Highway,* is the **Pipeworks Fun Market**, ☎*9357 1155*, with 600 shopping stalls, fun rides, live entertainment, mini-golf and bungee jumping.

Many shopping tours are available to factory outlets. Here are a few of the options:

Shopping Spree Tours, *2/77 Asling Street, Gardenvale,* ☎*9596 6600.* **8.30am-5pm daily, ❂$50 a head.**
Special Buying Tours, *198 Cotham Road, Kew,* ☎*9817 5985.* **9am-5pm Mon-Sat, ❂$15-40 a head.**
Melbourne Shopping Tours, *7 Almeida Crescent, South Yarra,* ☎*9826 3722.*

Points of Interest

City Explorer Bus. Taking a tour on the City Explorer Bus is a good way to get your bearings. This red and white double-decker leaves from *Swanston Street,* just outside the Visitor Information Centre, on the hour between ⊙10am-4pm and visits most of the main city attractions with its 16 stops. There are discounts on entry into nominated venues and other perks that might appeal. The costs are ❂$22 adults. For additional information, ☎*9650 7000.* Enquire also about the evening City Lights Tour or the Half-Day Tours which include Australian Wildlife, Shrine of Remembrance and Botanical Gardens and All Around Melbourne.

Melbourne Museum. The Melbourne Museum replaced the Museum of Victoria, formerly in *Swanston Street,* which is now closed as a result. This $263 million project places Victoria's newest museum to the north of the Royal Exhibition Building in Carlton Gardens, off *Nicholson Street.* Its exhibits focus on the natural environment and new technologies. Among the many facilities are an **Aboriginal Centre, a Forest Gallery**, a Mind and Body Gallery, Technology Exhibitions and a Science Gallery, ☎*8341 7777.* Adults ❂$12. Apart from the attractive garden surrounds, an **IMAX Theatre**, off *Rathdowne Street,* opened on the site in 1998, ☎*9663 5454.* The nearby **Royal Exhibition Building,** built in 1880, is itself worth a visit for its history and architecture, ☎*9270 5000* for enquiries.

Immigration Museum. The museum is located in Old Customs House, on the corner of *400 Flinders Street and William Street,* ☎*9927 2700.* This museum takes visitors through a cultural tour using interactive computer displays and permanent physical exhibits. Personal stories are recounted by immigrants themselves, providing insights into the emotions and memories of immigration experiences. The museum is ⊕open between 10am and 5pm and admission is ✪$7 adults. The best method of transport is the **Free City Circle** tram, which passes nearby on *Flinders Street* between 10am and 6pm.

Hellenic Antiquities Museum. Located on the second floor of Old Customs House, this museum is designed to host periodical exhibits of ancient Grecian and Byzantine treasures, and is a joint venture of the Victorian and Greek governments. It shares opening times and entry fees with the Immigration Museum on the ground floor, ☎9927 2700 for current and upcoming showcases.

Scienceworks Museum. Scienceworks is a short 10 minute drive from the city centre, and occupies the futuristic cylindrical building in *2 Booker Street, Spotswood*, which cannot be missed. Exhibitions include a detailed exploration of the human body and its mechanics (Stayin' Alive), and a 'behind-the-scenes' look at producing special effects for movies and television (The Sequel). Also included in the complex is the fascinating *Melbourne Planetarium*. Admission is ✪$8 adults, and the museum is ⊕open 10am-4.30pm, ☎9392 4800 for more details.

State Library. The oldest public library in Australia, established in 1856, is on the corner of *Swanston and La Trobe Streets*. It contains over one million books and periodicals, as well as overseas manuscripts, maps, microfilms, a multimedia catalogue, paintings and photographs. The **La Trobe Library** is located in a special

wing opened in 1965. It is ⊕open Mon-Thurs 10am-9pm, Fri-Sun 10am-6pm, ☎9669 9888.

Rialto Towers. An excursion to the top of Rialto Towers, *525 Collins Street,* ☎9629 8222, is absolutely imperative for any visitor. The magnificent panoramic vista, completely unobstructed from mountain to ocean and everything in between, is undoubtedly the best way to see Melbourne and its surrounds. At 253m in height, it is the tallest office building in the Southern hemisphere. The **Observation Deck** is accessible ⊕Sun-Thu 10am-10pm and Fri-Sat 10am-11pm, adults ✪$7.

Old Melbourne Gaol. The National Trust has preserved one remaining cell block as a penal museum, which has a unique collection tracing the story of transportation, convicts, and the development of Victoria's penal system. It is believed that 104 hangings were carried out at the gaol, including that of Ned Kelly on November 11, 1880. The gaol is located in *Russell Street, near Victoria Street*, and ⊕opens daily 9.30am-4.30pm, with admission ✪$9 adults, ☎9663 7228. For ✪$15 adults, shows are conducted on Wednesday and Sunday nights - but some may consider them to be suggestively violent in nature.

Chinatown. Chinatown is in *Little Bourke Street,* and extends from *Exhibition Street* to *Swanston Street*. It contains many restaurants from the most economical to the extremely expensive. **The Chinese Museum** is in *22 Cohen Place*, and is one of the best small museums in Melbourne. It is ⊕open Sat midday-4.30pm, Sun-Fri 10am-

4.30pm, and entry fees are ✪$5 adult, ☎9662 2888.

Fire Services Museum Victoria. The museum, on the corner of *39 Gisborne Street and Victoria Parade, East Melbourne,* was once the Eastern Hill Fire Station. Now it has displays of restored fire fighting equipment used by fire brigades throughout the city. The museum is ⊕open Fri 9am-3pm, Sun 10am-4pm, with admission ✪$5 adults, ☎9662 2907.

Parliament House. The State Houses of Parliament in *Spring Street,* at the top of Bourke Street, were built in stages between 1856 and 1930, and have never actually been finished as the dome and facades to the side and rear were never added. Guided tours of this Victorian construction are available at 10am, 2pm and 3pm Mon-Fri when Parliament is in recess, ☎9651 8911.

The Old Treasury. This fine public building was restored, converted to a museum and re-opened in 1994. It is situated in *Spring Street*, at the top of *Collins Street,* ☎9651 2233. There are three permanent exhibitions which encompass the past history and contemporary life of the city, its art, culture and architecture. The layout of the museum is designed for self-guiding, but guided tours are offered at 1pm and 3pm. The Treasury is ⊕open 9am-5pm Mon-Fri and 10am-4pm on weekends and public holidays. Admission is ✪$5 adults.

St Patrick's Cathedral. This Gothic Revival cathedral is in *1 Cathedral Place*, which runs off Lansdowne Street, East Melbourne, and is constructed of Footscray bluestone. It was completed in 1897, except for the spires, which were added in 1936. There is a statue in the churchyard of the great Irish liberator, Daniel O'Connell, which is a replica of that which stands in O'Connell Street, Dublin. The Cathedral contains many beautiful works of art and is ☉open 9am-5pm Mon-Fri, ☎9662 2233.

Fitzroy Gardens. Bounded by Albert, Clarendon, Lansdowne Streets and Wellington Parade in East Melbourne, Fitzroy Gardens are delightful nineteenth century gardens. The gardens contain **Cooks' Cottage**, ☎9419 4677, which was transported to Australia in 1934 and rebuilt block by block. It was originally built in the mid-eighteenth century by Captain James Cook's father. The cottage is ☉open daily 9am-5pm. Also in the garden are the famous Fairy Tree and the miniature Tudor Village replica. Next to Fitzroy Gardens are the **Treasury Gardens** containing the John F Kennedy Memorial.

Australian Gallery of Sport and Olympic Museum. The museum is outside the member's entrance to the Melbourne Cricket Ground in Yarra Park, Jolimont, and is Australia's first multi-sport museum. The three level building has priceless collections of memorabilia, which are displayed graphically in exhibitions aimed at entertaining and educating. **The Australian Gallery of Sport** now incorporates the Olympic Museum, which traces the history of the Olympics, from the ancient Greek games to the Modern Summer Olympics from 1896-1992. The museum is ☉open daily 10am-4pm, ☎9657 8879. For tours of the adjoining MCG, which depart every day on

the hour between 10am and 3pm, ☎9657 8879.

Queen Victoria Gardens and Kings Domain. These were originally the site of a gold-rush shanty-town, and were proclaimed public parkland in 1854. The area contains Australian and English trees, and one of the most attractive sections of the Kings Domain is a garden of rockeries, tiny paths and waterfalls which commemorate the Pioneer Women of Victoria. The **Myer Music Bowl**, ☎9281 8360, venue for many of Melbourne's most popular entertainment events, is in the Kings Domain.

The **Shrine of Remembrance**, also in Kings Domain, is dedicated to the sacrifice made by Victorian men and women in the two World Wars. A feature is the Stone of Remembrance, the centre of which is illuminated by a shaft of sunlight at exactly 11am on Armistice Day, November 11 each year. It is ☉open every day between 10am and 5pm. There is no charge, but a donation box is located out the front if you wish to support the volunteers who give their time to conduct tours and answer your questions. For more information, ☎9654 8415.

The well-known **Floral Clock**, whose floral design is changed four times a year requiring the planting of over 30,000 flowers, is in the Queen Victoria Gardens.

La Trobe's Cottage. The Cottage, on the *corner of Birdwood Road and Dallas Brooks Drive*, in the *Domain, South Yarra*, was the colony's first Government House. La Trobe brought the house with him in the ship Fergusson, along with his family and possessions. The National Trust supervised the re-creation

of the buildings, and they contain many of the original furnishings. The Cottage is ☉open 11am-4pm Mon, Wed, Sat and Sun, ☎9654 4711.

Victorian Arts Centre Complex. On the banks of the Yarra River, at *100 St Kilda Road*, the Centre comprises the theatres, the **Melbourne Concert Hall**, the **Performing Arts Museum** and the **National Gallery of Victoria**. As well as the performance and exhibition spaces, the **Victorian Arts Centre** has several restaurants. The George Adams Gallery has an extensive collection and is ☉open Mon-Sat 9am-11pm, and Sun 10am-5pm, ☎9281 8194. The **Performing Arts Museum** has regularly changing exhibitions, free entry and is ☉open Mon-Sat 9am-11pm, Sun 10am-5pm, ☎9281 8000. Guided tours of the Centre are available at limited times, ☎9281 8198.

Princes Bridge. The bridge is Melbourne's oldest and grandest, and is located at the point where *Swanston Street* becomes *St Kilda Road*. It was built around 1886, replacing a wooden bridge that had been opened by La Trobe in 1850.

Young and Jackson's Hotel. Also known as Princes Bridge Hotel, the pub is at *1 Swanston Street*, ☎9650 3884. Its claim to fame is that the upstairs lounge is home to the infamous painting 'Chloe' which caused a scandalized public outcry when it was first hung in the Melbourne Art Gallery in the 1880s. She may have caused a stir then, but now she hardly manages to raise an eyebrow.

St Paul's Cathedral. This Gothic Revival Anglican cathedral is on the *corner of Swanston and Flinders Streets*, on the site of the first official church service in Melbourne. The Cathedral was completed in 1891, and the spires added between 1926 and 1931. The doors are ☉open Mon-Fri 9am-5pm, ☎*9650 3791*.

Capitol Theatre. The astonishing ceiling of the theatre, at *113 Swanston Street*, was designed by Walter Burley Griffin, the architect of the city of Canberra. Entry is ✪$8 adults.

Melbourne Town Hall. The Town Hall, in *Swanston Street Walk*, ☎*9658 9779*, was built between 1867 and 1870, and the portico added in 1887. It is worth going inside the main hall to see the chandeliers, murals and organ and the rest of its recently restored interior. The Town Hall was one of the main venues for concerts before the advent of the Concert Hall in St Kilda Road.

Polly Woodside Maritime Museum. The baroque Polly Woodside, in *Lorimer Street East, Southbank*, is a deepwater, square-rigged, commercial sailing ship built of riveted iron in 1885. Seventy years ago, she was one of the fast fleet of windjammers, today she is fully restored and is the centrepiece of a display of Australia's maritime history. ☉open 7 days 10am-4pm, admission ✪$7 adults, ☎*9699 9760*.

Melbourne Exhibition and Events Centre. At *28 Clarendon Street, South Melbourne*, ☎*9205 6400*, this complex is the largest and most modern of its kind that Australia has to offer, and plays host to a wide range of exhibitions throughout the year. Its unique exterior design is worth a glance.

Crown Entertainment Complex. The complex is often described as 'the city under one roof', and indeed its restaurants, theatres, cinemas, **Crown Towers Hotel**, bars, nightclubs, showrooms, cocktail lounges, cafes, ballrooms, shopping boutiques and unabated gambling opportunities at the **Crown Casino**, do give the impression of a mini metropolis. The complex is in Southbank, and the Casino is at *8 Whiteman Street*, ☎*9292 8888*.

Melbourne Aquarium. This Aquarium, situated on the *corner of King Street and Queenswharf Road, City*, ☎*9620 0999*, is a very sophisticated and impressive way to view ocean creatures. It has the enormous Oceanarium viewing tank, modern computer interactions, aquatic feeding facilities and a simulator. The complex is ☉open daily 9am-6pm (until 9pm during summer), and costs adults ✪$17.50.

Suburban Attractions

Royal Botanic Gardens. The Royal Botanic Gardens are in *Birdwood Avenue, South Yarra*, and have 41ha (101 acres) of lawns, gardens and ornamental lakes. The Gardens are regarded as one of the finest examples of landscape gardening in the world. Their development commenced in 1846 under the direction of the then Superintendent of the Colony, Charles Joseph La Trobe, and now features 12,000 plant species. Brochures are available on special seasonal walks through the Gardens. **Como House, Como Park**, is an elegant colonial mansion, built in 1847, which has been classified by the National Trust and is ☉open for inspection daily 10am-5pm, ☎*9827 2500*.

St Kilda

St Kilda is Melbourne's equivalent of Sydney's Kings Cross, only more so. Developers would like to move in and restore the area to the fashionable and wealthy resort it once was, but they are meeting resistance from long-established residents. From Swanston Street, there are many trams that run to St Kilda, including Tram 16 from Swanston Street, and from Bourke Street, Tram 96 goes through South Melbourne to St Kilda. From Richmond, take Tram 79, which travels along Church Street, and Chapel Street in Prahran, then continues on to St Kilda Esplanade. The Esplanade runs along the beach, which is not very inviting, and leads to the **St Kilda Pier**, which has a kiosk built in 1904 at the corner. The St Kilda hot sea baths are nearby, and are very popular. **Luna Park** is in *18 Lower Esplanade*, next door to the Palais Theatre, and has been run as a fun palace since the 1920s. There is a restaurant behind the Palais that was originally a bathing shed. Rides such as the Mad Mouse, the Ghost Train and the Scenic Railway have been entertaining young ones for years. Entry is free into the Park but rides are priced at around ✪$2 or $3. It ☉opens 11am daily and closes at 5pm Mon-Thu and Sun and 11pm Fri-Sat. **Rippon Lea**, *192 Hotham Street, Elsternwick*, is a brick mansion built between 1868 and 1887, and has 33 rooms, iron carriage gates and a conservatory. It is set in a beautiful garden with a lake, and is one of the National Trust's pride and joys. It is ☉open Tues-Sun 10am-5pm, ☎9523 6095. Ripponlea Railway Station is a fine example of early twentieth century architectural style.

↪ Let's Stay Here

Coffee Palace,
24 Grey St, ☎ *9534 5283,*
💻 *www.coffeepalace.com.au*
Huge hostel with plenty of atmosphere. Facilities includes a kitchen, dining area which has a pool table and a barbecue area upstairs on the small rooftop. Internet access and tour booking desk located on the ground floor. There is also weekly barbecues and some wine and cheese nights done by the staff. *Dorms* ✪ *$15; double/twin $50 ($45 private with bunkbeds); (breakfast included)*

Enfield House,
2 Enfield St, ☎ *9534 8159,*
💻 *www.bakpak.com/enfield*
Set in a big old building with a happening atmosphere. This is one of Melbourne's longest running backpackers. Facilities includes a fully equipped kitchen, two TV lounges (one with a log fire) and internet access. Parking available. *Dorms* ✪ *$23-24; single $49; double/twin $32.50pp; (prices includes breakfast)*

Jackson's Manor,
53 Jackson St, ☎ *9534 1877,*
💻 *www.jacksonsmanor.co m.au* A magnificent heritage homestead designed and built in 1847, just a short walk from the most popular beach in Melbourne. Right in the heart of the hip café and night-life precinct, surrounded by the city's best bars and restaurants. Great atmosphere, with stained glass windows and Persian rugs. Rooms have heating and cooling. Facilities includes

St Kilda

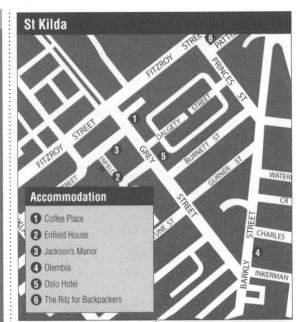

Accommodation

1. Coffee Place
2. Enfield House
3. Jackson's Manor
4. Olembia
5. Oslo Hotel
6. The Ritz for Backpackers

a fully equipped kitchen, laundry, TV lounge, a common room with a pool table, internet access and a barbecue area. Parking available. *Dorms from* ✪ *$19-24; single $58; double/twin $30pp;*

Olembia,
96 Barkly St, ☎ *9537 1412,*
💻 *www.olembia.com.au*
Quite a chic and upmarket looking hostel. Very charming and located just in the beachside suburb of St.Kilda. This is a good choice for those looking for a more quieter place to stay. All our rooms are centrally heated and have a vanity basin. Facilities includes a fully equipped kitchen with free tea and coffee, dining, laundry, communal area with comfortable lounge room, an open fireplace and TV room. Free off-street parking and a bike shed to lock

your bicycles available. **Highly Recommended.** *Dorms* ✪ *$22; single $46; double/twin $37pp*

Oslo Hotel,
38 Grey St, ☎ *9525 4498 or 1800 501 752,*
💻 *www.oslohotel.com.au*
Basic compared to the other flashier hostels in town. Quite eclectic in feature where you'll find areas with funky rugs and shaby old furnishings and other rooms that are quite nice. Facilities includes a kitchen, laundry, TV lounge with a pool table and there's also internet access. The highlight would be the rather nice view from the balcony. *Dorms* ✪ *$16; single $44; double $55;*

Pint on Punt,
42 Punt Rd, ☎ *9267 7718, 9510 4273 or 1800 424 444,*
💻 *www.pintonpunt.com.au/*

index.htm Located more on the Windsor side than St Kilda Junction on the east. Not that far from St Kilda though, it being only about 10-15 mins walk. Situated above a British pub with good clean accommodation, many with their own TVs in their rooms. Their facilities includes a small kitchen and a TV lounge. On site bar and restaurant offering discounts for backpackers. *Dorms ☻$20; double/ twin $25;*

The Ritz for Backpackers, *169 Fitzroy St, ☎ 9525 3501,* 🖳*www.*backpackerscentre.com */ritz/index* Situated just above the Elephant and Wheelbarrow pub with a feel good atmosphere. Just a short walk from the beach and entertainment. Accommodation is in self-contained cabins. Facilities includes a kitchen, games room with foosball and a pool table and TV lounge. There's also free wine and cheese and internet access. **Recommended.** *Dorms ☻$16; double/twin $46;* (breakfast included)

Parkville

Parkville is a student area with colleges, halls of residence and student flats set amidst fashionable homes, office buildings and Victorian terraces. Its main attractions are the Melbourne Zoo and the nearby University of Melbourne.

The **Melbourne Zoo** is in Elliot Park, ☎*9285 9300.* It has a lion park, walk-through aviary and native fauna park, and a butterfly enclosure. More than 350 species are represented here in Australia's longest-standing

zoo (since 1862). The Lakeside Restaurant serves 'meals with a view', looking out to Gibbon Island. Standard opening times are ☉daily 9am-5pm, but some exhibits and special events have alternative times. It is recommended that you allow at least four hours to fully appreciate this attraction, and you can phone the above number for feeding times and other points of interest to better plan your visit. Admission is adults ☻$14.50.

The **University of Melbourne,** *Gratton Street, ☎ 9344 4000,* dates back to the 1850s, and contains, among other interesting buildings, The **Grainger Museum,** *Gate 13, Royal Parade, ☎9344 4270,* which is ☉open Mon 10am-1pm, Tue 10am-4pm and Wed-Fri 10am-4pm.

Flemington

Flemington Racecourse is one of the most beautiful courses in the world, and is worth a visit even if you are not into betting. Unfortunately, it is only open to the public on race days, but the crowds add to the atmosphere anyway. The daily papers have details of race meetings in the sports pages. The famous **Melbourne Cup** is run here on the first Tuesday of November.

Tours

The Visitor Information Centre has details of all tours that are available in and around Melbourne. Try these:

Melbourne Discovery Pass Duration: ☉12pm-5pm daily. Attractions: Lunch at Rialto Towers, cruise on the Melba Star past Southbank and the Royal Botanic Gardens, Como Historic House, afternoon tea and return.

Cost: ☻$45 Operator: Rialto Towers Observation Deck, ☎9629 8222.

City Tour Duration: ☉9am-12pm daily. Attractions: City, Chinatown, Parliament House, Fitzroy Gardens, Captain Cook's Cottage, Melbourne Cricket Ground, National Tennis Centre, Albert Park, Westgate Bridge, Botanic Gardens, Shrine of Remembrance and return. Cost: ☻$45. Operator: Gray Line, ☎9663 4455.

Melbourne Highlights Duration: ☉1.30pm-5.30pm daily Attractions: City, Chinatown, Shrine of Remembrance, South Yarra, Toorak, Dandenong Ranges, Sher-brooke Forest, Mt Dandenong and return. Cost: ☻$46. Operator: Gray Line, ☎9663 4455.

Additional tours of the Great Ocean Road, Grampians, Murray River and extended trips to Phillip Island are also available, and the Visitor Information Centre will supply you with details of all of them.

The National Trust (Victoria) produces a brochure which you can pick up at the Visitor Information Centre. It outlines buildings of particular historical significance and includes all the relevant details for visiting them.

Apart from their regular city service, the City Explorer Bus offers a number of different tours in the Melbourne area and to outlying regions, ☎*9650 7000* to enquire further.

Cruises on the Yarra are also available. Here are a few companies which operate such services:

Melbourne River Cruises, Vault 18, Banana Alley Jetty, ☎9614 1215.

City River Cruises, 3 Princes Walk, Melbourne, ☎9650 2214. Southgate River Tours, Southgate, Southbank, ☎9682 5711.

Festivals

The **Moomba Festival** is held in March each year.

A parade is held before the Grand Final of the **AFL** competition in September.

The **Melbourne Cup** is held on the first Tuesday in November each year.

Sporting Facilities

In summer, many **International Tests**, one day **International and Sheffield Shield Cricket** matches are played at the Melbourne Cricket Ground (MCG), *Yarra Park, Jolimont.*

Australian Rules Football (AFL) is played every Saturday during the season (March to September) at various grounds around the city, including the MCG.

Soccer's main venue is Melbourne Park, *Swan Street, Melbourne,* ☎9286 1600.

The **Australian Tennis Open** is held each year at the National Tennis Centre in *Batman Avenue, East Melbourne,* ☎9286 1600.

Calder Park Thunderdome, *Calder Highway, Keilor,* is Australia's only super speedway. For information on race meetings, ☎9217 8800.

The **Australian Motorcycle Grand Prix** is held at the Phillip Island Motor Racing Circuit, *Back Beach Road,* ☎5952 9400.

The **Formula One Grand Prix** is held at Albert Park in March, ☎9258 7100 for more information.

Melbourne has facilities for every type of sport, and venues and clubs are listed in the Yellow Pages telephone directory.

Outlying Attractions
Phillip Island

Phillip Island is 129km (80 miles) from Melbourne, and is the home of the fairy penguins. At dusk, the famous penguins emerge from the surf, completely ignoring the thousands of curious onlookers. The Island has a **Phillip Island Nature Park,** which is divided into a number of outlets for wildlife viewing and information, including koalas, fur seals, pelicans, mutton birds, and the famous fairy penguins.

There are more than fifty places to stay in **Cowes** alone, the main tourist centre of **Phillip Island.** The districts of **Newhaven**, **Rhyll** and **San Remo** offer several alternatives. All types of accommodation are available.

The **Penguin Parade Visitors Centre,** off *Ventnor Road,* ☎5956 8300, is open daily from 10am and you can view the seasonal nightly pilgrimage of the cute creatures as they waddle their way onto the beach and up the sand dunes. It costs adults ✪$11.50.

The **Koala Conservation Centre** is located at Fiveways on *Phillip Island Road,* ☎5952 1307. It ⊕opens at 10am 7 days a week and costs ✪$5 adults.

Churchill Island, accessed via Newhaven, off *Phillip Island Road,* is popular for its tranquil gardens and stunning array of bird life. Costs are ✪$5 adults.

The **Seal Rocks Life Centre**, Penguin Reserve, *The Nobbies,* ☎9793 6767, has amazing educational displays and panoramic views. Entry is ✪$10 adults.

A **Four Park Pass** gives access to all four attractions listed above for the one price: ✪$25 adults.

At the **Australian Dairy Centre**,

Phillip Island Road, Newhaven, there is a museum explaining the history of the dairying industry, and a cheese factory with sales section and tastings. The cafeteria sells dairy-based light meals and snacks, ☎5956 7583.

Other attractions include great surfing beaches and restaurants.

French Island National Park, which can be reached by ferry either from Cowes at Phillip Island or from Stoney Point on the Mornington Peninsula, is larger than Phillip Island although less developed.

In Korumburra, on the South Gippsland Highway east of Phillip Island, is **Coal Creek Heritage Village**, a re-creation of an 1890s coal mining/railway town, with 40 buildings, including a mine, blacksmith, printer, stores, and a saw mill, ☎5655 1811.

For more information on Phillip Island attractions, contact the Phillip Island Information Centre, ☎5956 7447, or drop into their outlet at Newhaven on *Phillip Island Tourist Road.* It is ⊕open 7 days a week, 9am-5pm.

You can take advantage of the comprehensive web page at ▣www.phillipisland.net.au, or the Centre's accommodation booking service on ☎1300 366 422. Contact them via email at ✉info@phillipisland.net.au

Another good website for planning and attractions details is ▣www.penguins.org.au which includes an email form at ▣www.penguins.org.au/trip/index.html

⤹ Let's Stay Here

Amaroo Park YHA Hostel, *97 Church St, Cowes,* ☎5952 2548, ▣www.yha.com.au Located closely to the beach, main shops and only walking distance to wildlife and nature parks. Placed within a caravan park. Fully facilitated hostel. This includes a kitchen, dining area, laundry, common room, TV lounge, internet access, a swimming pool and a barbecue area. Licensed bar on site. Daily tours arranged. Bike hire and parking available. *Members Dorm* ❸*$19.50; single $33; double/ twin $25 BC MC VA*

Tynong

Tynong is a town on the *Princes Highway*, and can be visited on the way to Melbourne from Sale. Here you will find **Victoria's Farm Shed**, Australia's leading farm animal theatre featuring parades, milking, shearing and sheep dog displays. Show times are 10.30am and 2pm daily. For more inform-ation, ☎*5629 2840.*

Also at Tynong is **Gumbuya Recreation and Leisure Park**, a 174ha (430 acres) recreation park with toboggan slide, minicars, pony coach and trail rides, mini golf, adventure playground, water slide, half court tennis, barbecue and picnic areas, and a restaurant, ☎*5629 2613.* The park is ⏱open every day 10am-6pm (rides in operation 11am-4pm) and admission is ❸$6 adults.

Bass

Bass is located on the Bass Highway and can be visited on the way to Phillip Island from Melbourne.

The **Giant Worm Museum,** on the Bass Highway, is a unique attraction and education facility. They do actually have giant worms (including one you can walk through!), and many other historical and hands-on displays, ☎*5678 2222.*

Mornington Peninsula

The Nepean Highway follows the eastern shore of Port Phillip Bay for 97km (60 miles) to the seaside resort of Portsea. On the way it passes picturesque peninsula beaches such as **Dromana, Rosebud** and **Sorrento.**

At Dromana, the **Arthur's Seat Scenic Chairlift** ride offers great views of Melbourne, Port Phillip Bay and the Mornington Peninsula. It ⏱opens at 11am daily September-April, and only on weekends and holidays during winter, ☎*5987 2565.*

The **MV Peninsula Princess,** a car passenger ferry, operates every day linking the Mornington and Bellarine Peninsulas, from Queenscliff to Sorrento.

Ashcombe Maze, *Red Hill Road, Shoreham,* ☎*5989 8387,* is a large hedge maze believed to be the only significant one of its type in Australia. There are tea rooms surrounded by extensive gardens. It is ⏱open from 10 am every day and costs ❸$6 adults.

The Visitor Information Centre for Peninsula Tourism is at *359B Point Nepean Road, Dromana,* ☎*5978 3078.* For web information 🖥*www. melbour ne.citysearch.com.au* includes the Mornington Peninsula region.

↘ Let's Stay Here

Queenscliff Inn YHA, *59 Hesse St,* ☎*5258 4600,* 🖥*www.yha.com.au* Located very close to the water on this historic seaside town, an hour and a half away from Melbourne. A stylish guest house with a classy feel to it and plenty of atmosphere. Foodstore is just next door. The warmth of their hospitality is added by their luxurious

---

open fires. Rooms are large and spacious. Other facilities includes a kitchen, laundry, and an internet access. You can also find pot pourri lying everywhere while listening to music. Downstairs is a drawing room where you'll find some board games and a selection of books, newspapers and magazines for reading. Enquire about a mid-week group booking. *Members Dorm* ❸*$20; single $45; double/twin $25.50pp BC MC VA EFTPOS*

Dandenong Ranges

The Dandenongs are only 35km (22 miles) east of Melbourne, and the area is ideal for picnics, bushwalks and wildlife observation. It is an extremely popular destination with Melbournians and tourists for both daytrips and weekend escapes. Mt Dandenong (630m - 2067 ft) offers a panoramic view of Melbourne from its strategic lookout points.

One of the most popular attractions is **Puffing Billy,** *Old Monbulk Road, Belgrave,* ☎*9754 6800,* an historic narrow gauge train that runs through 13km (8 miles) of mountain scenery between Belgrave and Lakeside (Emerald Lake) in the Dandenong Ranges every day of the year, except Christmas Day. Return fares are adults ❸$17.50. The line opened in 1900, and it is the ideal way to view the Dandenongs at close range. The suburban trains from all stations connect with Puffing Billy at Belgrave, one hour's easy drive from Melbourne.

The famous **William Ricketts Sanctuary,** *Mt Dandenong Tourist Road,* ☎*13 1963,* is set in the lush surrounds of the Dandenong

Ranges and comprises the inspired sculptures of one artist. Encapsulating the spirituality of Aboriginal culture and expressing an affinity with nature, these startling images bear a powerful mystique. The Sanctuary is ☉open daily 10am-4pm and entry is ✪$5 adults.

The Dandenongs are covered in ▇www.melbourne.citysearch.com.au

↪ Let's Stay Here
Emerald Backpackers,
2 Lakeview Cres, Emerald, ☎*5968 4086,* ▇*www.emeraldbackpackers.com.au/home.html* Quietly situated near Emerald Lake, and little over a kilometre from the centre of Emerald itself. The hostel is comprised in several buildings, with many of the accommodation en suite. There's your basic kitchen facilities, a games room and a barbecue area out the back. Travellers are known to work in the nearby farms and nurseries. **Recommended.** *Dorms* ✪*$19; double $21;*

Lakes Entrance
Population 5,500
Lakes Entrance is at the gateway to the Gippsland Lakes, Australia's largest inland water system. It is 360km (224 miles) east of Melbourne, 840km (522 miles) south of Sydney and 429km (267 miles) south-west of Canberra.

Climate
Lakes Entrance has a temperate climate. The average maximum temperature in summer is 33C (91F), in winter 21C (70F). There is some rain in July and August,

and occasional overnight showers in summer.

Characteristics
The largest town on Ninety Mile Beach, Lakes Entrance is a popular holiday destination. It has a spectacular hinterland with mountains (snow in winter), rivers and forests. Wildlife in the area includes dolphins and water birds, kangaroos, wombats, koalas and bush birds.

How to Get There
By Bus
Greyhound Pioneer, ☎*13 2030,* provides interstate connections.

By Rail
V/Line, ☎*13 6196,* offer a road and rail combination to Lakes Entrance.
By Air
Flying is not the preferred method of access to this area, but regional connections can be made throughout the district and the Visitor Information Centre will be able to advise on the timetables and routes that suit your itinerary.

Visitor Information
The Lakes Entrance Visitor Information Centre is on the corner of *Marine Parade and The Esplanade,* ☎*(03) 5155 1966.* They are ☉open 9am-5pm daily. Contact them over the internet at ✉lakes@lakesandwilderness.com.au or simply explore the web page at ▇*www.lakesandwilderness.com.au*

↪ Let's Stay Here
As mentioned, Lakes Entrance is a popular holiday spot, so there is plenty of accommodation from which to choose, in fact over 60 places

in the town. The Information Centre has a complete list, but here are a few examples, with prices, which should be used as a guide only. The telephone area code is 03.

Albatross Motel, *661 Esplanade,* ☎*5155 1779.* 8 units, heated swimming pool, barbecue - *from* ✪*$50.*

Golden Beach Motor Inn, *607 Esplanade,* ☎*5155 1666.* 29 units, swimming pool, unlicensed restaurant - *from* ✪*$55.*

Lakes Central Hotel, *321-333 Esplanade,* ☎*5155 1977.* 16 units, licensed bistro, swimming pool, spa, barbecue - *from* ✪*$55.*

Lakes Seaview Motel, *12 New Street,* ☎*5155 1318.* 11 units, barbecue - *from* ✪*$40.*

Lakeside Motel, *164 Marine Parade,* ☎*5155 1811.* 27 units - *from* ✪*$45.*

Riviera Backpackers YHA, *5 Clarkes Rd,* ☎*5155 2444,* ▇*www.yha.com.au* Located just right by the lake, close to a foodstore, cinemas and restaurants and about 1km out from town. Rooms are big. Facilities includes a kitchen, laundry, common room, TV lounge, internet access, a swimming pool and a barbecue area. Bike hire and parking available.
Members Dorm ✪*$17.50; single $28; double/twin $37 ($50 with en suite) BC MC VA*

The Esplanade Motel, *251 Esplanade*, ☎*5155 1933*. 40 units, car wash, heated swimming pool, spa, barbecue - *from ✪$40*.

Caravan Parks

Echo Beach Caravan Park, *33 Roadknight Street*, ☎*5155 2238*. (Pets allowed under control) 25 sites - *powered sites ✪$18-32 for two, cabins from $45*.

Lakes Haven Caravan Park and Flats, *3 Jemmeson Street*, ☎*5155 2254*. (No pets allowed) 17 sites, barbecue - *powered sites ✪$17-28 for two, cabins $40 for two, holiday flats from $45-105 , on-site vans from $30*.

Lakes Entrance Tourist Park, *127 Princes Highway*, ☎*5155 1159*. (Pets by arrangement) 100 sites, barbecue, heated pool - *powered sites ✪$18-30 for two, cabins from $35*.

Riviera Country Caravan Park, *29 Palmers Road*, ☎*5155 1236*. (No pets allowed) 62 sites, barbecue - *powered sites ✪$17-26 for two, on-site vans from $35, cabins from $40*.

Silver Sands Tourist Park, *33 Myer Street*, ☎*5155 2343*. (No pets allowed) 37 sites, spa, pool, barbecue - *powered sites ✪$18-30 for two, on-site vans from $30*.

Let's Eat

There is the usual range of takeaway outlets, and most hotels serve counter meals. Local seafood is often the specialty on the menu. Some of the motels

have restaurants, but here are the addresses and phone numbers of other restaurants you might like to patronise.

Egidio's Wood Oven, *573 The Esplanade*, ☎*5155 1411*. Licensed, Italian menu.

Ocean Dragon, *601 The Esplanade*, ☎*5155 1349*. Chinese cuisine.

Pinocchio Inn, *569 The Esplanade*, ☎*5155 2565*.

Shang Hai Garden, *215 The Esplanade*, ☎*5155 2602*.
Skippers, *481 The Esplanade*, ☎*5155 3551*.

The Scallop Pot, *221 The Esplanade*, ☎*5155 1555*.

Tres Amigos, *521 The Esplanade*, ☎*5155 2215*. Authentic Mexican flavours.

McDonalds is at *359 The Esplanade*. Although there are no KFC or Pizza Hut branches here, you will find an abundance of alternative fast food outlets along *The Esplanade*.

Points of Interest

The artificial entrance of the lakes to the ocean was completed in 1889, and there are still visible signs of the equipment used to bring logs and rocks from inland for the construction.

A short walk across the footbridge brings you to the **Entrance and Bass Strait**, with Ninety Mile Beach stretching away into the distance. A section of the beach is patrolled by the Surf Lifesaving Club during the holidays.

Nyerimilang Park on Lake King, *Kalimna West Road, Nungurner,* overlooks **Rigby, Fraser** and **Flannagan Islands.** It has bullock driving demonstrations and field days, and there are bushwalks, as well as barbecue and picnic facilities, ☎*5156 3253*. Nyerimilang is Aboriginal for Chain of Lakes.

Kinkuna Country Fun Park and Zoo, *Princes Highway*, ☎*5155 3000* has waterslides, a toboggan ride with electronic timing, kiosk, sou-venirs, crafts and games room. It is ☾open daily from 10am (weather permitting) and the entry fee includes barbecues, toddlers' pool, the jumping castle and wildlife area. The lions are hand-fed (not fed hands) at about 1pm on most days. Entry is ✪$4.50 adults.

Griffiths' Sea Shell Museum and Marine Display, *125 Esplanade*, ☎*5155 1538*, also has a gift shop and a model railway display. Over 90,000 shells from around the world are featured, and there is also a model railway room for locomotive enthusiasts. The complex is ☾open daily.

The **Lakes Entrance Aboriginal Art and Crafts**, *239 The Esplanade*, ☎*5155 3302*, has genuine Aboriginal artifacts on display and for sale. ☾open 9am-5pm daily.

Festivals

Here are a few of the major events in the East Gippsland area:
January - the **Metung Regatta**, and the **New Year's Eve fireworks** at Lakes Entrance.
February - the **Canni Creek Race**s near Buchan, the **Cattlemen's Cup** (every year in the high country, once every four years at Omeo).
March - the **Marlay Point**

Overnight Yacht Race and the **Bairnsdale Festival**.
Easter - **Rodeos** at Omeo and Buchan, the **Kinkuna Festival** and **Blessing of the Fleet** at Lakes Entrance.
June - the **Wildtrek** at Dinner Plain.
November - the **Flat Water Classic** (windsurfing) at Paynesville.

Facilities

Boat cruises from Lakes Entrance, Metung, Lake Tyers, Paynesville. Sail and motor boat hire, daily or longer term, from Lakes Entrance, Metung, Paynesville, Lake Tyers, Johnstonville. Fishing from jetties, shoreline, from hired boats, or on organised fishing trips. Swimming in lakes and sea. Viewing the hot pools at Metung. Rafting and canoeing on rivers. Horse-riding - full day and extended trail rides. 4WD tours, bushwalking, tennis, lawn bowls, golf.

The Visitor Information Centre has all the information on times and locations, ☎(03) 5155 1966.

Outlying Attractions
Mallacoota

Reached via Genoa on the NSW/Vic border, Mallacoota is surrounded by the Croajinolong National Park. Mallacoota is situated in one of Victoria's most remote and peaceful lakeland settings. There are many walking tracks through the **Croajinolong National Park**, which has prolific birdlife.

If you wish to explore the natural wonders here, contact the Park Office, *Genoa Road, Mallacoota*, ☎(03) 5158 0263 or the Information Centre in nearby Cann River, ☎(03) 5158 6351.

Orbost

Orbost is the railhead for East Gippsland, and is situated on the Snowy River 16km from the coast. It is the gateway to Marlo where the Snowy meets the Brodribb River and where a sandbar allows the rivers to reach the sea. Scenic drives and walks are the main attraction of this stunning region. Cape Conran, reached via Marlo, has camping, picnic and walking facilities.

For ideas on the best places and routes to explore, the Snowy River Visitor Centre in *Lochiel Street* can be contacted on ☎(03) 5154 2424 or emailed at ✉orbost@lakesandwilderness.com.au

Omeo

Omeo is on the way to the snowfields at Mt Hotham, about one-and-a-half hours drive from Bairnsdale. The town's history lies in timber, gold and cattle, and the town is like the backdrop for a movie set in the 1880s. Omeo is an ideal place to stop for a meal and to hire skis and chains during winter, and even close enough to stay in the town and visit the snow of Alpine National Park daily. Many people visit Omeo for trout fishing, bushwalking and canoeing.

Buchan

In the foothills of Snowy River Country, 56km (35 miles) from Lakes Entrance, lies the town of Buchan which is probably best known for its limestone caves.

The limestone caves were discovered in 1907, and the reserve surrounding them has picnic facilities, barbecues, and lots of kangaroos. There is also a swimming pool fed by

an extremely cool underground stream. The rangers conduct tours through the caves during the day.

The Visitor Centre in Lakes Entrance produces a very good pamphlet detailing activities and attractions in the area, including a comprehensive driving map, ☎5155 1966.

Bairnsdale

Bairnsdale, just over 30km west of Lakes Entrance, was the port for its pastoral hinterland in the days before road transport. Now it supports a number of secondary industries.

St Mary's Roman Catholic Church, ☎5152 2942, built in 1913 and extended in 1937, has unique murals by Frank Floreani, an incredible painted ceiling and other works of art.

The Court House, built in 1893 and classified by the National Trust, has delightful architecture, but it can only be viewed from the street.

The **Historical Museum**, *Macarthur Street*, has some interesting memorabilia on display, ☎5152 6363. It is ⏴open Wednesday, Thursday and Sunday 1-5pm.

The Visitor Infomation Centre is at *240 Main Street*, ☎(03) 5152 3444, and they have brochures and details of all attractions. You can email them at ✉bairnsdale@lakesandwilderness.com.au

Paynesville

Known as the boating capital of the Gippsland Lakes, Paynesville is 18km (11 miles) south-east of Bairnsdale, with a well-marked turn off the Princes Highway. **McMillan Strait, Newlands Arm** and canals provide sheltered moorings for many pleasure and commercial fishing boats.

From Paynesville there are many places to go by boat - the **Lakes National Park**, with its picnic grounds and kangaroos, the beautiful **Duck Arm**, and three of Victoria's best bream rivers: **Mitchell, Nicholson and Tambo.** There is also a ferry that runs from Paynesville to Raymond Island, which is inhabited by kangaroos, koalas and water and bush birds.

Stratford

Stratford is a town located on the Avon River 17km north of Sale. A **Shakespearean Festival** is held here in April every year. For more details, ☎5145 6133, email ✉dmccubb@netspace.net.au or visit the website at Nhome. bicnet.au\-shakes

Gippsland

In general terms, the Gippsland area stretches from the east of Bairnsdale to Phillip Island, and north of Morwell and Traralgon down to Wilsons Promontory and Ninety Mile Beach on the southern coast, taking in just about everything in between. It covers the beautiful landscapes of fertile countryside and is full of various natural wonders from mountains and forests to rivers and beaches.

The best way to explore the Gippsland is by driving through it at a leisurely pace and absorbing its scenic qualities.

Plenty of touring material is produced covering the Gippsland region. There are detailed maps, driving routes, accommodation listings and current news and events. Two information outlets are:

Gippsland Country Tourism Information Centre, *Shop 1,*

Southside Central, Princes Highway, Traralgon, ☎5174 3199 or ☎1800 621 409 (toll free).

South Gippsland Visitor Information Centre, *cnr South Gippsland Highway* and *Silkstone Road, Korumburra,* ☎5655 2233 or ☎1800 630 704 (toll free).

For online information visit ▆ *www.*gippslandtourism.com.au or email ✉information@gippsland tourism.com.au

Sale

Situated on the Melbourne side of Lakes Entrance, Sale is the operations centre for the nearby Bass Strait oil fields of Esso-BHP. There is also a large **RAAF** training base located here.

Cullinen Park, off *Foster Street,* is the site of the historic Port of Sale where, in days of yore, steamers tied up after their long trip from Melbourne. From Sale there are roads leading to the southern end of **Ninety Mile Beach.**

Apart from the historical interest of the town centre, including the **Gippsland Art Gallery,** *68 Foster Street,* ☎5142 3372 and the **Historical Museum,** *Foster Street* ☎5144 5994, Sale is surrounded by attractive natural areas which include a **Wildlife Refuge** and **the David Morass State Game Reserve.**

The Central Gippsland Visitor Information Centre can be found in *8 Foster Street,* ☎*(03) 5144 1108.* Email them at ✉toursale@i-o.net.au

Healesville and the Yarra Valley
Population 10,000
Healesville is 62km (38 miles) east of Melbourne, in the foothills of the Great Dividing Range.

Climate
The climate can be brisk in winter, with snow on the higher peaks.

Characteristics
Healesville is the gateway to towering ash forests, waterfalls and fern bowers. The township is surrounded by high mountains, and one of Victoria's most picturesque mountain highways climbs from Healesville to Marysville over the Black Spur through forests of mountain ash, beech and wattle.

How to Get There
By Rail
From Melbourne's Flinders Street Station, take a train to Lilydale, which connects with a **V/Line** coach to Healesville.

Visitor Information
The Yarra Valley Visitor Information Centre is in The Old Courthouse, *Harker Street,* ☎(03) 5962 2600, email ✉info@yarraval leytourism.asn.au, online at ▆*www.*yarravalleytourism.a sn.au

a guide only. The telephone area code is 03.

Caravan Parks

Ashgrove Tourist Park and Holiday Units, *322 Don Road,* ☎ *5962 4398.* (Pets allowed by prior arrangement) - *powered sites* ⊘*$20-22 for two, no on-site vans.*

Badger Creek Caravan and Holiday Park, *419 Don Road,* ☎ *5962 4328.* (No pets allowed) - *powered sites* ⊘*$20-24 for two, no on-site vans.*

Let's Eat

Some of the motels have BYO restaurants, and the hotels have licensed restaurants or bistros. Here are a few others you might like to try.

Ming Gardens Restaurant, *271 Maroondah Highway,* ☎ *5962 5067*

Montiverdi Pizza Restaurant, *335 Maroondah Highway,* ☎ *5962 4455* - BYO and licensed, eat in or takeaway.

Mount Rael Restaurant, *Healesville/Yarra Glen Road,* ☎ *5962 4107* - BYO, Australian cuisine.

Strathvea Country House, *Myers Creek Road,* ☎ *5962 4109* - BYO, Australian cuisine.

Points of Interest

One of the most popular attractions is the **Healesville Sanctuary** in *Badger Creek Road,* ☎ *5957 2800.* The sanctuary is the only place where the platypus has been bred in captivity, and they are on display here ⊕between 11.30am-3.30pm. There are also koalas, wombats, kangaroos and emus, and a Nocturnal House with some of Australia's least seen animals such as the Leadbeater possum, kowari, sugar gliders and potaroos. The Reptile House has a selection of Australia's venomous snakes, and in another area there are lyrebirds, that have also been successfully bred here. The Sanctuary has a catering centre for picnic lunches, a licensed bistro, and a gift shop. ⊙open daily 9am-5pm.

Hedgend Maze, at *163 Albert Road,* is a giant hedge carved into a maze, with cryptic messages to solve on the way to help you get through. The grounds make for a pleasant picnic setting. It is ⊙open daily from 10am, ☎*5962 3636.*

Maroondah Reservoir is a popular place, and is set in a landscaped park of exotic and native trees, shrubs and flowers. Badger Weir and Donnelly's Weir also provide beautiful bushland walks and superb picnic-barbecue areas. For the more energetic, walking tracks explore local National Parks and Forests.

Queen's Park, in the centre of the township, is ideal for picnics, and has a sports oval, tennis courts, children's playground and swimming pool.

11km (7 miles) west of Healesville is the township of **Yarra Glen,** and the Yarra Valley Tourist Railway winds between the two towns. A group of volunteers are in the process of making the railway a premier tourist attraction. Trolley rides can be taken from **Healesville Station** through a 100m old, brick-lined tunnel. Just out of Yarra Glen is the historic **Gulf Station,** which is worth a visit.

Toolangi, about 30km (19 miles) north of Healesville, was the home of C.J. Dennis, author of The Sentimental Bloke. Arden, the **'Singing Garden'** he and his wife Biddy created, is ⊙open daily 10am-5pm. The 1.5ha rhododendron gardens are a delight, and there are Tea Rooms where you can spend some time admiring them, and enjoying a light lunch. Across the road is **Toolangi Pottery,** where master potter David Williams produces and displays his stoneware and crystalline pottery. His work has been exhibited in the National Gallery of Victoria.

Wineries

The Yarra Valley has many wineries, and here they are listed, with the cellar door hours.

Yarra Burn Vineyard, Settlement Road, Yarra Junction, ☎5967 1428 - ⊙open daily 10am-6pm.
McWilliams Lillydale Vineyards, Davross Court, Seville, ☎5964 2016 - ⊙open daily 11am-5pm.
Five Oaks Vineyard, Aitken Road, Seville, ☎5964 3704 - ⊙open daily 10am-5pm.
Kelly Brook Winery, Fulford Road, Wonga Park, ☎9722 1304 - ⊙open Wed-Sat 9am-6pm, Sun 11am-6pm, Mon 9am-6pm.
Bianchet Winery, Victoria Road, Lilydale, ☎9739 1779 - ⊙open Mon-Fri please phone prior to visit, Sat-Sun 10am-6pm.
Warramate Vineyard, Maddens Lane, Gruyere, ☎5964 9219 - ⊙open daily10am-6pm.
St Huberts Vineyard, St Huberts Road, Coldstream, ☎9739 1118 -⊙Mon-Fri 9.30am-5pm, Sat 10.30am-5.30pm, Sun 11.30am-5.30pm.
Eyton On Yarra Winery and Restaurant, cnr Maroondah Highway and Hill Road, Coldstream, ☎5962 2119

- ⏲daily 10am-5pm.
Fergusson's Winery and Restaurant, Wills Road, Yarra Glen, ☎5965 2237 - ⏲Mon-Fri 9am-5pm, Sat-Sun 11am-5pm.
De Bortoli Winery and Restaurant, Pinnacle Lane, Dixons Creek, ☎5965 2271 -⏲daily10am-5pm.
Shantell Vineyard, Melba Highway (60km post), Dixons Creek, ☎5965 2155 - ⏲Thu-Mon 10.30am-5pm.
Broussard's Chum Creek Winery, Cunninghams Road, Healesville, ☎5962 5551 - ⏲Sat-Sun 10am-6pm.
Long Gully Estate, Long Gully Road, Healesville, ☎9510 798 - ⏲Mon-Fri please phone prior to visit, Sat-Sun noon-5pm.

Festivals

The **Yarra Valley Expo**, celebrating the regions wine, food and farmlife, is held in March.

Facilities

Lawn bowls, swimming, tennis, golf, fishing, greyhound racing, horseracing, harness racing and squash. There is a cinema on the highway.

Outlying Attractions
Marysville

Situated 36km (22 miles) north-east of Healesville, Marysville is high in the Great Dividing Range, 500m (1640 ft) above sea level. It has great forests and tree-fern gullies, and is a cool and welcome retreat. In winter, nearby Lake Mountain offers one of the best cross-country ski areas outside Scandinavia.

Steavenson Falls, the tallest in Victoria, cascade 82m (269 ft) in three leaps and are floodlit at night.

Accommodation is available in guesthouses, holiday lodges, cabins and motels, as well as a camping and caravan park beside the Steavenson River. For more information on Marysville, contact the Visitor Information Centre, *11 Murchison Street,* ☎*(03) 5963 4567.*

Eildon and Alexandra

These towns are the gateways to **Lake Eildon** and **Fraser National Park.** Both have facilities for fishing, bushwalking, camping, water skiing, swimming, sailing, cross country skiing, golf, tennis, squash and bowls, and accommodation is plentiful.

Alexandra is 69km (43 miles) north of Healesville, and Eildon is 26km (16 miles) east of Alexandra.

There are quite a few attractions - art and craft shops and galleries; fauna parks with native animals, deer and camels; **The Timber Tramway and Museum** at the old railway station, Alexandra, ☎*5772 2392*; and the Visitor Centre at *45a Grant Street, Alexandra,* ☎*(03) 5772 1100* will assist with further enquiries.

Bright and the Victorian Alps
Population 3,500

Bright is situated on the Ovens River, in the foothills of the Victorian Alps. It is 310km (193 miles) from Melbourne, 700km (435 miles) from Sydney, 940km (584 miles from Adelaide, 74km (46 miles) from Wangaratta, and 116km (72 miles) from Albury.

Characteristics

Bright is truly a town for all seasons. In Summer, there is the river for safe swimming and fishing, and horseriding and bush walking are very popular. In Autumn, the European and Asian trees left by the pioneers become a blaze of gold, orange, red and yellow, and the town celebrates with the Autumn Festival. Winter brings snow to the mountains surrounding Bright, and the skiers arrive in their thousands for the slopes in the three close alpine resorts. And in Spring, the elms, poplars, wattles, fruit trees, etc, create the brightest Bright of all.

How to Get There
By Bus

Greyhound Pioneer travel to Albury-Wodonga from Sydney and Melbourne, and connect with a local bus service to Bright.

By Rail

Regular train services run from Melbourne and Sydney to Wangaratta, and then **V-line** buses to Bright.

Visitor Infomation

The Bright Visitor Infomation Centre is at *119 Gavan Street,* ☎*(03) 5755 2275* or ☎*1800 500 117,* ✉email bright@dragnet.com.au
Two websites to visit are 🖥*www. brightdistrict.com.au* (for limited local information) and 🖥*www. alpinelink.com.au*

⤵ Let's Stay Here

Bright's main industry is tourism, so there is no shortage of accommodation. Here we have a selection which should be used as a guide only. The telephone area code is 03.

Bright Hikers Backpackers,
4 Ireland St, ☎*5750 1244,* 🖥 *www.brighthikers.com.au*
A really good hostel situated just across the post office and not far from the bus stops. Facilities includes a fully equipped kitchen, laundry, TV

lounge and internet access and barbecue area. There is also bike hire and a nice verandah that looks out to the main street. *Dorms ✪$19; single $29; double/twin $42 ;*

Caravan Parks

Alpine Cabins and Caravan Park, *1 Mountbatten Avenue,* ☎*5755 1064.* (No pets allowed) - *powered sites ✪$20-25 for two, cabins from $57.*

Bright Caravan Park, *Cherry Avenue,* ☎*5755 1141.* (No dogs allowed Christmas, January and Easter) - *powered sites ✪$17-25 for two, park cabins (en-suite) from $50 for two, park cabins (standard) $40 -56 for two.*

Bright Riverside Holiday Park, *4 Toorak Avenue,* ☎*5755 1118.* (No pets allowed) - *powered sites ✪$17-26 for two, cabins $25-33 for two.*

Green Hills Caravan Park, *Great Alpine Rd,* ☎*5750 1218.* (Pets allowed on leash) - *powered sites ✪$16-22 for two, on-site vans $29-41 for two.*

Let's Eat

Many of the hotels and motels have dining rooms, and there are the usual amount of takeaway outlets for a holiday town. Here are some you might like to try:

Golden Bright Chinese Restaurant, *108 Gavan Street,* ☎*5750 1155.*

Simone's Restaurant, *cnr Ovens Highway and Ashwood Avenue,* ☎*5755 2022.*

Ned's Rstaurant and Bar, *13-17 Gavan Street,* ☎*5755 1244* - licensed, country-style dining - ⏰open Tue-Sat for dinner.

Poplars, *8 Star Road, Bright,* ☎*5755 1655* - BYO and licensed, a la carte and seafood - ⏰open daily from 6.30pm.

The Cosy Kangaroo, *Gavan Street,* ☎*5750 1838* - good value family restaurant.

Tin Dog Cafe and Pizzeria, *94 Gavan Street,* ☎*5755 1526.*

Points of Interest

The pretty village of Bright sparkles against its backdrop of dark green-clad hills, and is one of Australia's longest established holiday destinations, having welcomed visitors for more than a century. Bright's first guide book was published in 1887, and included maps of walking tracks and bridle paths, specially marked and graded according to degree of difficulty. These are still popular today, and current maps are available at the Visitor Infomation centre. Some of the most popular walks are to the **Clearspot, Huggins** and **Mt Porepunkah lookouts,** which offer a panoramic view of the village.

The **Historical Museum of Bright** has been established in the town's disused railway station. It is ⏰open 2-4pm Tue, Thu and Sun during school holidays and festivals, and 2-4pm Sun from September to May.

The **Bright Art Gallery and Cultural Centre,** *28 Mountbatten Avenue,* ☎*5750 1660,* has a comprehensive art collection and a gem and rare mineral collection, as well as the largest cuckoo clock in Australia. It is ⏰open

Mon-Sat 1-5pm, Sun 9am-5.30pm, and daily during school holidays.

Gallery 90, *90 Gavan Street,* ☎*5755 1385,* has original paintings, pottery, leather, handpainted clothing, jewellery, handpainted porcelain, traditional cottage crafts, and much more. The gallery is housed in a restored local granite and bluestone cottage that dates back to 1881, and is ⏰open Mon-Sat 9.30am-5.30pm, Sun 11am-5.30pm. During the **Autumn Festival** the hours are extended to 9am-5.30pm daily.

Walks around Bright are marked by sign posts and yellow track markers fixed to trees and posts. Maps and guides are available from the newsagent and the Visitor Infomation Centre for walks further afield, and if venturing up in the hills you should remember to take some warm clothing, as it will be colder there than down in the valley. The climb to **Mt Buffalo** commences at the Park entrance and climbs through 11km (7 miles) of varied scenery, to arrive at the oval below the Mt Buffalo Chalet.

For the less energetic, there is a wide variety of tours, both half and full day, to various attractions around Bright and the high country. For further information and bookings, contact the Visitor Infomation Centre. If you are in Bright in the winter, enquire about ski packages and snow trips.

Festivals

The **Bright Autumn Festival** is held during the last week of April and the first week of May each year, and one of the main features is Gala Day with street processions and stalls. The entrants for Miss Autumn Festival are received at the Presentation Ball and the judging and crowning takes place.

Among the many events that are part of the Festival are: the opening of the Autumn Art Exhibition; conducted tours of tobacco farms; gold panning exhibitions; historic tours of Wandiligong and surrounding districts; tours of the forests by the Forest Commission; a Family Picnic; an Old Time Music Hall; and wine and cheese tastings.

The Springtime in Bright Festival is held during October and November, and co-ordinates a whole range of events and activities.

Outlying Attractions
Porepunkah

The small town of Porepunkah is 6km (4 miles) from Bright, at the junction of the Buckland and Ovens Rivers, and the turnoff to Mount Buffalo National Park. Originally named Port Punka, the area was part of a cattle station which reached from Eurobin to Bright. During the gold mining era, the township site was known as The Ovens Crossing. It is a quiet, peaceful spot, and has a hotel, post office, petrol station, general store, several riverside caravan parks, and a growing number of flats and motels. The two rivers provide excellent fishing for trout.

The Snow Country

The major ski centres are **Falls Creek, Mt Buffalo** and **Mt Hotham.** The website ▄www.ski.com.au gives the latest information about the weather and skiing conditions at all the Victorian ski resorts. Ski pack-

ages and snow trips to the three resorts can be arranged thorugh various outlets, and the Tourist Centre can provide you with a list of operators and prices.

Mount Buffalo

The mountain is 32km (20 miles) from Bright, and 320km (199 miles) from Melbourne. Accommodation on the slopes is available at Mount Buffalo Chalet and Lodge, and inclusive packages are offered.

Operating only 3 poma lifts and 2 chairlifts, Mt Buffalo is a small, sheltered ski field that focuses on laid-back family enjoyment. It is comprised mainly of gentle downhill slopes. Serious skiers looking for a challenge should head elsewhere, although cross-country ski trails are available here in **Mt Buffalo National Park.**

Lift ticket prices are $39 adult; $180 adult for 5 days; and $199 for a season pass.

Dingo Dell

Ski runs are 6km (4 miles) south of the Chalet, and are ideal for beginners and family groups. There are two poma lifts and a portable beginners' lift. Amenities and services include the large car park within easy walking distance of the slopes; ski instruction; **Keown Lodge**, a visitor centre which is used as a day lodge and provides takeaway and eat-in meals, changing rooms, toilets and first aid facilities.

Cresta Valley

Ski runs are 4km (2 miles) south of Dingo Dell, and are around the Mt Buffalo Lodge and Alpine Resort, ☎5755 1988, at about 1525m (5003 ft) above sea level. There are eight runs served by

5 lifts catering for beginner, intermediate and advanced skiers. The degree of difficulty of a slope can be identified by the coloured markers at the runs. Easiest runs are marked by green circles and are served by the Gully Poma and Novice Poma. More difficult runs are marked with blue squares and suit intermediate skiers. The Valley and Cresta Chairlift runs are in this category. The most difficult runs are marked by black diamonds and are reached by riding the Cresta Poma.

The Cresta Day Visitor Centre houses the resort management office, ski school, ticket office, National Park information area, medical centre and a cafe offering takeaway.

Cross Country Trails are graded Beginner and Intermediate, with access to Cresta Valley graded Intermediate to Advanced. Lift Tickets: Ticket boxes have single ride, half-day and full day; Cresta Office has a season pass (photo required); and The Chalet and Tatra Inn have 1-day, 2-day, 3-day, 5-day and 7-day packages.

Falls Creek

▄www.fallscreek.com.au
Falls Creek is 62km (39 miles) from Bright, 32km (20 miles) from the township of Mount Beauty, and 356km (221 miles) from Melbourne. There are many guest houses to choose from, and several offer ski packages.

Falls Creek has snowmaking machines, and the system covers 10ha (25 acres). It is installed on **Towers Duplex, Panorama, Playground, Tom Thomb** and at the top of **Eagle, Halley's Comet** and **Scott Chairlifts.**
Following is a brief description of the ski runs -

Novice

Nursery Pomas/Dogpatch Pomas - in the bowl area, near the Ski School. Ideal for beginners. Saddle Linklift - an easy T-Bar for skiers of all standards. Also gives access to the Ruined Castle area.

Headwater Poma, Playground Pomas, Tom Thumb - gentle and have easy access via the Eagle Chair and Halley's Comet Quad Chair, returning via the Broadway Hometrail and the Wombat's Ramble Home-trail.

Halley's Comet Quad Chairlift - a fast access lift from the carpark to the slopes of Sun Valley. Novice skiers return via the Wombat's Ramble Hometrail and intermediates return via the Last Hoot Hometrail. At the top of Halley's Comet is the Cloud Nine Restaurant with bar, dining and restroom facilities.

Intermediate

Gully Triple Chairlift - an access lift from the carpark to the bowl. Gully slopes are not suitable for novices.

Village T-Bar - forming part of the sheltered bowl, these runs are ideal for easy intermediate skiing.

Panorama Poma, Towers Duplex T-Bar, Lakeside Poma, Scott Quad

Chairlift, Ruined Castle Poma - these five lifts offer a variety of intermediate skiing. The valley holds a good cover of dry snow on interesting gullies and lightly wooded trails.

Eagle Triple Chairlift - a fast access lift from the bowl to the slopes of Sun Valley. Return via the Broadway Hometrail.

Advanced

Big Dipper Duplex T-Bar - a good length run for intermediate skiers.

However, on the right-hand side is a large cornice with deep soft snow.

Summit T-Bar - known traditionally as the advanced skier's paradise, the finest bumps run in Australia.

International Poma - a fast lift providing challenging skiing for advanced skiers. Also provides access to the Bowl, the Summit, and the slopes of Sun Valley.

Lift Tickets

A full range of lift tickets is available early in the morning at Bogong Ski Centre, Kiewa Valley Highway, Mt Beauty, and at JD's Mountain Sports, *cnr Burke* and *Anderson Streets, Bright.* They can also be purchased in the Sun Valley area. Passport type photographs are required for Season and 4, 5, 6 and 7 day lift, and lift and lesson packages. Instant photos can be taken at Cumings, The Hub, Gebi's, Snowland and The Creek Photo Service. 4, 5, 6 and 7 days lift, and lift and lesson tickets can be purchased after 4pm on day prior to the first day of use. Approximate prices are: Half day - $56 adult; 1 day - $75 adult; 2 day - $144 adult, $74 child; 3 day - $212 adult; 4 day - $273 adult; 5 day - $328 adult; 6 day - $383 adult; 7 day - $420 adult,

Season tickets cost between $400 and $900, depending on the time of purchase - the earlier the better.

A one day lift and lesson package costs $105 adult. Ski hire is available.

↰ Let's Stay Here

Below is a selection of what is available in the heart of Falls Creek. All have outstand-

ing views of the surrounding mountains.

Alpha Lodge,
☎5758 3488, from $23 for shared rooms and $41 for a single room, per person.

Alpine Woodsmoke,
☎5754 1138, ▇ *www.wo odsmoke.com.au,* apartments from $200 per night.

Attunga Alpine Lodge and Apartments, ☎ *5758 3255,* from $50pp for a double room, including breakfast.

Mount Hotham

▇ *www.*mthotham.com.au
Mount Hotham is 55km (34 miles) from Bright, and 354km (220 miles) from Melbourne. It is Australia's highest alpine village at 1750m (5741 ft), and all accommodation is only minutes from the ski runs. The runs are classified as 27% beginner, 36% intermediate and 37% advanced.

More information can be obtained from the Mount Hotham Alpine Resort Management Board, *Great Alpine Road, Mount Hotham,* ☎*5759 3550,* email ✉mhar@ mthotham.com.au

There are over 40 marked and groomed runs on the slopes, and the ski school, ticket sales, ski shops and ski hire are all in easy walking distance from the car parks, and one short step from the slopes.

Above the Village

Summit - a high altitude slope of south-easterly aspect, and a reliable beginners' area. Served by the Summit quad chairlift, and on the summit is the Doppelmayr T-Bar.

Big D - at the southern end of Mt Hotham village, with reliable snow and gentle beginners' slopes.

Below the Village

Sun Run - opposite the Summit, the Sun Run is for skiers progressing to intermediate. Served by a T-Bar lift.

Basin - a sheltered bowl opposite the main day car-park offering skiing for beginners and intermediates. Served by a Doppelmayr platter lift.

Playground - several trails for intermediate and advanced skiers down to Swindlers Creek.

Heavenly Valley

The Heavenly Valley quad chairlift provides access to vast areas of skiing terrain for confident intermediates and advanced skiers.

Blue Ribbon - served by a Doppelmayr triple chairlift, offers sustained and sheltered fall line skiing for intermediate and advanced skiers.

Mt Hotham Village offers a range of shops and services including ski hire, ski shop, licensed restaurants (Italian, international and modern Australian), pizzeria, a supermarket, bistro, post office, nightclub and information desk.

Lift Tickets

Lift passes are available from the Mount Hotham Skiing Company, ☎5759 4444, which has an office on the mountain.
The following are prices for lifts only. Half day - $56 adult; 1 day - $75 adult; 2 day - $144 adult; 3 day - $212 adult; 5 day - $328 adult; 7 day - $420 adult; Season - from $870 adult.

Myrtleford

Situated 29km (18 miles) northwest of Bright on the Ovens Highway, Myrtleford is at the foot of Mount Buffalo. The district's main industries are timber, hops, tobacco and cattle.

The town has 3 hotels, 2 motels, a caravan park, 2 camping reserves, bunkhouse and lodge accommodation. There are facilities for swimming, tennis, golf, bowls, bocce, croquet, fishing (trout and redfin), horse riding, hang gliding, bush-walking, and of course, skiing.

Shepparton

Population 32,000

Shepparton is located in the Lower Goulburn Valley in the northern 'centre' of Victoria, 178km (111 miles) north of Melbourne.

Climate

Average temperatures: January max 30C (86F) - min 14C (57F); July max 13C (55F) - min 4C (39F). Average annual rainfall: 502mm (20 ins). Shepparton averages more than 7 hours of sunlight per day.

Characteristics

Shepparton was declared The Solar City by the Solar Council in 1986, due to the large amount of sunshine it averages, and the city has a solar heated swimming pool (in summer), some solar powered street lighting in areas, a solar powered telephone outside the Visitor Infomation Centre, and some solar powered parking meters. It is the major city of the Goulburn Valley, one of the food bowls of the nation. The area produces enormous quantities of fruit, vegetables and dairy products, as well as cereal crops, grapes, wine, beef, wool and lamb.

How to Get There
By Rail

V/Line Trains have services Mon-Fri from Spencer Street Station in Melbourne, ⊙leaving at 9.10am and 6.15pm. On Saturday the trains leave at 9.10am and 6.10pm, and on Sunday at 9.50am and 6.05pm.

By Bus

Greyhound Pioneer stop at Shepparton on their Melbourne/Brisbane service. **V/Line** coaches have services from Melbourne daily except Saturday.

Visitor Information

The Visitor Infomation Centre, Victoria Park Lake, *534 Wyndham Street,* ☎*(03) 5831 4400* or ☎1*800 808 839*, is ⊙open 10am-3pm daily. Further information is available online at ▣*www.*shepparton.vic. gov.au and you can email ✉visitor@ shepparton.vic.gov.au

Caravan Parks

Pine Lodge Caravan Park, *cnr Midland Highway and Orrvale Road,* ☎*5829 2396.* (No pets allowed) - *powered sites* ✪*$19-22 for two, no on-site vans.*

Shepparton Riverview Caravan Park, *Melbourne Road (Goulburn Valley Hwy),* ☎*5823 1561.* (Dogs allowed at manager's discretion) - *powered sites* ✪*$16 for two, no on-site vans.*

Strayleaves Caravan Park, *cnr Mitchell Street and Old Dookie Road,* ☎*5821 1232.* (No dogs allowed) - *powered sites* ✪*$16 for two, on-site vans $29 for two.*

Let's Eat

Cellar 47 Restaurant, 166 -170 High Street, ☎5831 1882, is ⊙open for lunch Tues-Fri noon-2pm, dinner Tues-Sat from 6pm.

Aloi Thai Restaurant, *630a Wyndham Street,* ☎*5831 6613.*

Calzoneys Restaurant, *30 North Street,* ☎*5831 3578.*

Casablanca Pizza Restaurant, *125 High Street,* ☎*5821 1115* - takeaway available.

La Porchetta, *264 Maude Street,* ☎*5821 0800* - Italian and pizza.

New China Restaurant, *55 Fryers Street,* ☎*5831 1166.*

Parklake Motor Inn Cafe Bar Restaurant, at the Parklake Motor Inn, *481 Wyndham Street,* ☎*5821 5822,* is ⊙open for dinner nightly from 6pm, and has a dinner dance on Saturdays.

Riviera Pizza Restaurant, *117a Wyndham Street,* ☎*5821 4402.*

Shepparton Family Restaurant, *City Walk,* ☎*5821 3737,* specialise in Chinese and Australian smorgasbord - ⊙open for lunch Mon-Sat 11.30am-2.30pm, dinner every day 5.30-9.30pm.

Pizza Hut is at *525 Wyndham Street,* ☎*5822 2111,* and **KFC** has two outlets in *Wyndham Street* at *nos 620 and 465.*

Points of Interest

Victoria Park Lake, near where the Visitor Infomation Centre is found, has picnic, barbecue, water skiing, windsurfing and cycling facilities. It is the leisure centre of the city.

The **Eastbank Centre** in *Welsford Street,* which houses the town hall, art gallery, theatre and municipal offices, is one of the most outstanding in any rural city in Australia. It was designed by architecture students from the University of Melbourne.

The **Shepparton Art Gallery,** in the Eastbank, has an extensive collection of ceramic works by well known artists, and around 150 paintings including pieces by McCubbin. It is ⊙open 10am-4pm seven days, and admission is free, ☎*5832 9861.*

The **Historical Museum,** *cnr Welsford and High Streets,* is ⊙open on irregular Sundays 1-4pm *(*☎*5831 4400),* and has exhibits of local memorabilia from Aboriginal and European heritage to current events.

The **Telecommunications Tower** in *Fraser Street, West Walk* of the Maude Street Mall, has an observation platform which allows 360 degree views of the district. At the base of the tower is a **Human Sundial,** which accurately tells the time when you stand on the point corresponding to the day's date.

Maude Street Mall is in the heart of the city and is a shopping centre with many features including entertainment areas, loads of trees and flower beds, and plenty of parking.

Shepparton Preserving Company (SPC), *Andrew Fairley Avenue,* has a sales outlet ⊙open Mon-Fri, and factory tours during the canning season, January-April.

Driver Education Centre of Australia (DECA), *Wanganui Road,* ☎*5821 1099,* has courses for people of all ages, and tours of the complex are havailable Mon-Fri 8am-5pm.

In the **Shepparton Sports Stadium,** near McEwan Reserve, is a Maze which will keep all the family involved for a while.

Radio Australia in *Verney Road, Lemnos,* is home of the international broadcasting station. Tours are by appointment only, ☎*5829 9202.*

The **Dookie College of Agriculture and Horticulture,** is midway between Shepparton and Benalla. The buildings are situated at the foot of Mt Major, on the fringe of the Goulburn Valley, and have excellent accommodation, conference and seminar facilities, ☎*5833 9200.*

Festivals

The **Sun City Festival** is held over seven days in March/April, and the **Shepparton Show** is in October.

Kialla West Strawberry Festival is held in November.

Facilities

Sporting facilities include horse-racing, trotting, greyhound racing, tennis, squash, lawn bowls, golf, and water sports. There is a cinema, *cnr Maude and Stuart Streets*, and a Drive-In Theatre in *Melbourne Road, South Shepparton*.

Outlying Attractions
Numurkah

Situated 35km (22.miles) north of Shepparton on the Goulburn Valley Highway, Numurkah has a population of around 3000, and is on Broken Creek. The town is surrounded by mostly irrigated farmland, with a wide range of crops. There is also wool and beef production, and a large dairying industry.

The town is about the same distance from the Murray River, and its attractions include the **Barmah Forest, Monichino Wines** (☎*5864 6452*), **Brookfield Historic Farm** (☎*5862 2353*), and of course, the **Murray River beaches**.

The Numurkah Visitor Information Centre is at *25 Quinn Street*, ☎*(03) 5862 3458*.

Tocumwal

This is the first New South Wales town on the Newell Highway, and is situated on the banks of the Murray River. It offers a blend of old with new, from Federation era buildings with stained glassed windows to modern licensed clubs, business and accommodation developments.

The town has a population of around 1400, but this is regularly swelled with visitors stopping off on their north or south journeys. There is a golf club and a bowling club with first class facilities,

restaurants, and being in New South Wales - poker machines. The main street of the town and the river are divided by parklands with camping sites, water skiing, swimming, boating, sailing and fishing facilities, and houseboat cruises departure points. About 2km from town there is a wartime aerodrome where **Sportavia Soaring (Gliding) Centre** offers year-round gliding, ☎*5874 2063*. The Visitor Information Centre is in *Foreshore Park*, ☎*(03) 5874 2131*.

Benalla

Benalla is 61km (38 miles) south-east of Shepparton, at the junction of the Hume and Midland Highways. The Visitor Information Centre is at *14 Mair Street*, ☎*(03) 5762 1749*.

Benalla was the base of operations in the 1870s for the Kelly Gang, and many mementos of the Gang can be found in the **Kelly Museum** in *Bridge Street*. Enquire at the Visitor Centre about opening times.

Benalla is also famous for its roses, and from late October until early April the **Benalla Gardens** provide the finest display of that bloom in the State. **The Rose Festival** is held each November.

The **Benalla Art Gallery**, in the Benalla Gardens, ☎*5762 3833*, has an impressive collection of Australian art, including several paintings from the Heidelberg School by Roberts, Streeton and McCubbin.

Mansfield

Situated 63km (39 miles) south of Benalla, at the terminus of both the Maroondah and Midland Highways, Mansfield is the gateway to the Mount Buller alpine resort.

The town is also close to the north arm of Lake Eildon, and to Lake Nillahcootie, so in summer is a popular spot for fishing, sailing, water skiing and white water canoeing. In winter the skiers move into town. This area was the setting for the classic The Man From Snowy River movies, and that beautiful scenery was not trick photography, as visitors soon discover.

Call in at the Mansfield Visitor Information Centre at the Railway Station on the *Maroondah Highway*, ☎*(03) 5775 1464*.

⤴ Let's Stay Here

Mansfield Backpackers Inn, *112-116 High St*, ☎*5775 1800*, 🖥 *www.itchy-feet.com.au/vic/vichostels/mansfield.html* A very good hostel with nice facilities. Located about a km to the bus station and supermarkets and eateries. It's small but has a good atmosphere and is kept clean. Excellent dorms and bathrooms. Your facilities includes the kitchen, laundry, a lounge containing a TV and piano, internet access, and a barbecue area. Parking available. *Dorms from ✪$17*.

Mount Buller

🖥 *www.mtbuller.com.au*
The ski village is 47km (29 miles) from Mansfield, and is situated at 1600m (5249 ft), with the highest lifted point at 1788m (5866 ft). There are 5 Poma, 8 T-bar, 4 Triple chair and 7 Quad chair lifts, with a capacity of 38,500 people an hour.

The downhill skiable area is 162ha (400 acres), and is graded 24% Beginner, 34% Intermediate and 42% Advanced, with the longest run 2500m (2734 yds).

The Cross-Country areas are Village Loop (Beginner) and Corn Hill (Beginner), with total trails of 10.9km (7 miles).

Lift Tickets: Day - adult $70; Half day - adult $60; Five day - adult $300; Seven day - adult $420; Season - adult $1000.

Violet Town

Situated 13km (8 miles) west of Benalla, Violet Town is on Honeysuckle Creek and at the foothills of the Strathbogie Ranges. It is the oldest surveyed inland town in Victoria, having been surveyed in 1838, but there was no permanent settlement until 1846. There is a caravan park, hotels, a swimming pool, and many sporting facilities.

Head out to the **Stonecrop Fine Art Gallery** on *Harry's Creek Road*, ☎*5798 1444*, ⏰between 11am and 5pm any day, and enjoy their dispays and garden surrounds.

Euroa

Euroa is 45km (28 miles) west of Benalla. The Euroa district is steeped in history from the time of early settlement in the 1800s, prospering from people heading for the goldfields. The first flock of Saxon Merino sheep in the State was driven overland from New South Wales to Euroa, and since that time wool has played the major part in the development of Euroa.

Seven Creeks winds through the town with parkland on both banks, and the "Seven Creeks Run" has been established, a project depicting the history of the wool industry. International shearing competitions are conducted in Euroa, and **Wool Week** has become an event known through-

out Australia.

The surrounding district, which includes **Forlonge Memorial** and **Strathbogie Ranges**, appeals to the trout fisherman and the bushwalker.

Seymour

Situated at the northern foothills of the Great Dividing Range on the Goulburn River, Seymour is 84km (52 miles) south of Shepparton, and only one hour's drive from Melbourne. The **Panyule Fauna Park** and Visitor Infomation Centre, on the corner of *Seymour-Tooboorac and Pyalong Roads*, can be contacted on ☎*(03) 5799 0043*.

A short distance to the north of the town is **Mangalore Airport**, originally built as an alternate airport for Melbourne. It is now the headquarters of the **Australian Sport Aviation Council**, and the **Mangalore Air Spectacular Show** is held annually over the Easter weekend.

Attractions in the area include: **Trawool Valley** has been classified by the National Trust for its scenic beauty. There is an international standard resort, and tea rooms and a gallery. The century-old former **Trawool Chool** is an art gallery, ☎*5792 3118*. **Riddy's Trawool Valley Tours,** ☎*5792 1654*, is one way to see the area in full.

Avenel is a small township on Hughes Creek, some 20km (12 miles) from Seymour. It has a number of historical buildings, four of which have been classified by the National Trust, and the grave of Ned Kelly's father. Look out for the old **Harvest Home Hotel**, built in the 1860s and now a restaurant, ☎*5796 2339*.

Puckapunyal Army Camp is

13km (8 miles) west of Seymour, off the Hume Freeway. The camp has the **Royal Australian Armoured Corps Tank Museum,** which may be viewed 10am-4pm daily, ☎*5793 7285*.

Nagambie

The gateway to the Goulburn Valley, Nagambie is 28km (17 miles) north of Seymour. The township was founded in the mid-19th century and has a number of important historical buildings, seven of which are classified by the National Trust. The eastern shore of Lake Nagambie abuts the main street, with grassy picnic areas on its banks. Buckley Park, at the southern entrance of the town has a shady picnic area, boat launching ramp, and swimming area.

Lake Nagambie was created by the construction of the Goulburn Weir, which was built with manual labour in 1890. The River and Lake combine to offer over 40km (25 miles) of waterways for boating, and there are many picnic areas. The Nagambie Lakes Visitor Information Centre is at *145 High Street*, ☎*(03) 5794 2647* or ☎*1800 444 647*, and they have information on the many wineries in the area.

Bendigo

Population 59,936

Bendigo is almost in the centre of Victoria, at the junction of the Calder, McIvor, Northern and Loddon Valley Highways. It is 151km (94 miles) from Melbourne, 661km (411 miles) from Adelaide, 892km (554 miles) from Sydney and 653km (406 miles) from Canberra.

Climate

Average temperatures: January

max 29C (84F) - min 14C (57F); July max 12C (54F) - min 3C (37F). Average annual rainfall: 550mm (22 in).

Characteristics

Bendigo was once one of the richest gold mining towns in Australia. It is proud of its mining history and has preserved relics of the period for present and future generations. The most tangible of these is a complete mine in working condition, in the town - the Central Deborah Mine.

How to Get There
By Bus

Greyhound Pioneer stop at Bendigo on their Melbourne/Mildura routes. A mini-bus service operates between Ballarat and Bendigo.

By Rail

A regular daily service operates between Melbourne and Bendigo, and the journey takes two hours. Bendigo is also linked by rail to Echuca, Cohuna, Swan Hill and Charlton.

Visitor Infomation

The Bendigo Visitor Information and Interpretive Centre is located inhe Historic Post Office, *51-67 Pall Mall*, ☎*(03) 5444 4445* or ☎*1800 813 153*. It is ⊕open seven days a week 9am-5pm. Email them at ✉tourism@bendi go.vic.gov.au or visit the website ▦*www.*bendigo tourism.com Another website, for the wider region, is ▦*www.* goldfields.org.au, but it is less detailed.

⤻ Let's Stay Here

There are 24 motels, 7 hotels, 10 caravan parks and a youth hostel. Here is a selec-

tion which should be used as a guide only. The telephone area code is 03.

Buzza's Bendigo Backpackers YHA,
33 Creek St South, ☎*5443 7680,* ▦*www.yha.com.au* Located very close to the shops, art precinct, cafes and Rosalind Park. Art-deco styled hostel with landscaped gardens and sitting areas outdoors. Facilities includes a big kitchen, laundry, TV lounge with open fire, internet access and a barbecue area. Enquire about their 'Hot n Steamy/Gold'n Dreamy' package which includes 4 night accommodation and entry to some attractions around the area. Bike hire and parking available. *Members Dorm* ✪*$17; double/twin $44; BC MC VA EFTPOS*

Calder Motel,
296 High Street (Calder Hwy), Kangaroo Flat, ☎*5447 7411.* 12 units, swimming pool, barbecue - *from* ✪*$50.*

Nomad's Ironbark Bush Cabins, *Lot 2, Watson St,* ☎*5448 3344,* ▦*www.bwc.com.au/ironbark* This hostel is almost your horse riding ranch with it's fascination with horses and the fact that it's part of a horse riding complex. Hiking trails are also nearby. Situated about five to ten minutes drive from north Bendigo. Accommodation are in self contained cabins with en suite bathrooms, TV, fridge and the rare clock radio. Facilities includes a kitchen, laundry,

games room, swimming pool and a barbecue area. *Dorms* ✪*$20; double/twin $55;*

The Elm Motel, *454 High St,* ☎*5447 7522.* 15 rooms (private facilities) - *from* ✪*$55.*

Caravan Parks

Ascot Lodge, *15 Heinz Street, White Hills,* ☎*5448 4421.* (No pets) - *powered sites* ✪*$20-22 for two, cabins (en-suite) from $30pp, cabins (standard) $45-55 for two.*

Robinley Caravan Park, *Calder Hwy, Maiden Gully,* ☎*5449 6265.* (No pets) - *powered sites* ✪*$15-20 for two, on-site vans $35-40 for two.*

Central City Caravan Park, *362 High Street (Calder Hwy), Golden Square,* ☎*5443 6937.* (Dogs allowed on leash) - *powered sites* ✪*$17 for two, on-site vans $35 for two.*

Let's Eat

There's a good range of restaurants and cafes in Bendigo, offering various types of cuisine. Pub lunches are widely available and usually represent good value. They range from the humble ploughman's lunch to hearty steak and vegies. Good restaurants include:

Bazzani, *Howard Place,* ☎*5441 3777* - licensed - ⊕open 7 days.

Cafe Tram, *76 Violet Street,* ☎*5443 8255* - licensed - bookings essential - ⊕open for dinner Fri and Sat, lunch on Sun.

Fortunes Restaurant, *171 McIvor Road,* ☎*5443 8166* - open 7 days

- a la carte - lunch and dinner
- licensed.

Malayan Orchid Restaurant, *157 View Street,* ☎ *5442 4411* - Thai, Cantonese and Malaysian curries - ☉open Mon-Fri 12-2pm, dinner seven days.

Whirrakee Restaurant, *17 View Point,* ☎ *5441 5557* - overlooks Alexandra Fountain - licensed - modern Australian cuisine.

There is also a **Pizza Hut** on the corner of *High and Violet Streets,* ☎ *5443 2122,* and **McDonald's** is at *63 High Street.*

Points of Interest

The heart of Bendigo is well worth exploring on foot, with much to see and admire in the busy shopping area and nearby parks. The **Vintage Talking Trams** will take you to many other places of interest. A **Bendigo Heritage Walk** leaflet is available from the Information Centre.

Bendigo has been described as, architecturally, the most interesting and integrated provincial city in Australia. Solidly built with the wealth that gold gave it, the city has some of the best preserved Victorian-era buildings and street-scapes to be found anywhere.

Pall Mall is Bendigo's main boulevard, and has some of the city's grandest Victorian buildings. Take note of: the Italianate post office (1887) and law courts (1896); the Shamrock Hotel (1897); Alexandra Fountain (1881); the Beehive Store (1872); National Bank (1887) and Grand United HBS building (1886). Other buildings nearby include: the Bendigo Town Hall (1885);

Bendigo Gaol (1864); Old Police Barracks (1859); St Paul's Cathedral (1868); Goldmines Hotel (1857); Specimen Cottage (1856).

View Street begins at the Alexandra Fountain, and also has some impressive 19th century buildings: Atkinson Building (1877); Bendigo Trades Hall (1885); Bendigo Art Gallery (1890); Capital Theatre (1874); Dudley House (1858); National Australia Bank (1863); Old Fire Station (1899); Rifle Brigade Hotel (1887); Sandhurst Trustees (1891).

Alexandra Fountain is situated at the head of Bendigo's Pall Mall, Charing Cross. The fountain was a gift from George Lansell 'the quartz king'. Designed by W.C. Vahland and erected in 1881, it is made from 20 tones of Harcourt granite and features seahorses and nymphs.

Chinese Joss House, *Finn Street, Emu Point,* ☎ *5442 1685.* The original Chinese temple was built in the 1860s of handmade bricks and timber, and painted red, the traditional Chinese colour for strength. To get there, follow the tram tracks towards Echuca, then turn at Lake Weeroona. The Joss House is operated by the National Trust, and is ☉open daily 10am-5pm. Admission is adults ✪$3.

Golden Dragon Museum and Chinese Gardens, *5 - 13 Bridge Street,* ☎ *5441 5044.* Trace the history of Chinese influence in Bendigo, going right back to the gold rush days, in this impressive setting. Entry is ✪$7 adult, and the complex is ☉open daily 9.30am-5pm.

Central Deborah Gold Mine, *76 Violet Street,* ☎ *5443 8322.*

The last deep-reef goldmine in Bendigo - sunk in 1909, closed in 1954 - has been restored and is open for inspection. It is 411m (135 ft) deep with 17 levels. The tourist level at 61m (200 ft) includes a 350m (383 yds) circuit which illustrates the various geological features of the Bendigo region, and the machinery used in the gold retrieval process. Above ground there are many exhibits to be inspected. The mine is ☉open daily 9.30am-5pm, the tour takes about 1.5-2 hours, and there is an admission charge.

Vintage Talking Trams, *1 Tramways Avenue,* ☎ *5442 2821.* The Bendigo Trust has a collection of 34 vintage trams, and they are one of Bendigo's most popular tourist attractions. They run through the city centre, via Pall Mall, and along the 8km route between Central Deborah Mine and North Bendigo. A recorded commentary highlights more than 50 features along the way, and a stop at the **Tram Museum** in *Tramways Avenue,* ☎ *5442 2821,* is included in the tour. The trams ☉depart from Central Deborah Mine Mon-Fri 9.30am, 1 and 2pm, hourly on weekends and school and public holidays from 9.30am-4.30pm. The tour takes approximately one hour.

Hargreaves Mall is a retail shopping area in the city centre, and has a wide selection of specialty shops and boutiques.

Lake Weeroona, *cnr Midland Highway and Nolan Street,* is a delightful ornamental lake close to the city centre. Surrounded by trees and gardens, there are boat hire, picnic and barbecue facilities.

Discovery and Science

Technology Centre, *7 Railway Place,* ☎*5444 4400,* has hands-on exhibits and a vertical slide. Admission is ❂\$7.50 adult it is ◷open daily 10am-5pm.

Within a few minutes drive from the city centre there are many interesting places to visit :

Bendigo Pottery, *Midland Highway, Epsom,* ☎*5448 4404,* ◷open daily 9am-5pm, with guided tours at 10.30am and 2.30pm. Admission is free.

Bendigo Market Place, *116 - 120 Mitchell Street, Bendigo,* ☎*5441 6906,* ◷open daily.

Kennington Reservoir, *Reservoir Road, Bendigo* - swimming, boating, windsurfing and canoeing. Barbecue and picnic grounds.

Espsom Market, off *Midland Highway* at *Epsom* past the Bendigo Pottery, ☎*5448 8411,* ◷open every Sunday 8.30am-3pm. Country Victoria's largest undercover market.

Eaglehawk, an historic town 8km north-west of Bendigo, and the site of a gold rush in 1852.

One Tree Hill Lookout, 8km south of Bendigo - from the Fountain follow *Mitchell Street,* then *Carpenter Street,* into *Spring Gully Road.* Continue south and the turn-off is just before Tannery Lane.

Wineries in Bendigo include:

Balgownie Vineyards, Hermitage Road, Maiden Gully, (8km west), ☎*5449 6222,* closed Sunday; Chateau Leamon, Calder Highway, Big Hill, 10km south of Bendigo, ☎*5447 7995,* closed Tuesday; Chateau Dore Vineyard, 8km south-east of Bendigo at Mandurang Valley, ☎*5439 5278,* closed Monday.

For information on other wineries in the surrounding districts, contact the Visitor Information Centre.

Festivals

The **Easter Fair** has been staged for more than a century. The ten day festival commences with a street carnival on Easter Saturday; a 'waking of the dragon' ceremony takes place on Easter Sunday when a small lion wakes 'Sun Loong' with fireworks. **Sun Loong** is 100m long and is the largest known ceremonial Chinese dragon in the world. It is a colourful feature of the major procession on Easter Monday.

Facilities

Lawn bowls, ten-pin bowling, ice skating, roller skating, golf, tennis, swimming, croquet, indoor cricket, squash, horse racing and trotting and greyhound racing.

Outlying Attractions
Castlemaine

Nestling in a dip of the Great Dividing Range 38km (24 miles) south of Bendigo, Castlemaine is another gold mining town.

Attractions in and around town include nineteenth-century **Buda Historic Home and Garden** in *Hunter Street;* **Skydancers Butterfly Sanctuary** on the *Midland Highway, Harcourt;* **Kyirong Emu Farm** on *Strathlea Road, Strathlea;* and **Maldon Porcupine Township,** a recreation of life in early Victoria, *cnr Bendigo and Allan Roads, Maldon,* ☎*5475 1000.*

The Castlemaine Visitor Information and Interpretive Centre is in *Market Building, Mostyn Street,* ☎*5470 5566* or ☎*1800 171 888.*

Echuca-Moama

Population 10,500 and 3,500 respectively. Echuca-Moama is located near the junction of the Murray, Campaspe and Goulburn Rivers, 205km (127 miles) from Melbourne.

Climate

Average daily temperatures: January max 32C (90F) - min 17C (63F); July max 15C (59F) - min 4C (39F). Average annual rainfall: 451mm (18 ins).

Characteristics

More than 130 years ago two ex-convicts, Henry Hopwood and James Maiden established the twin towns of Echuca-Moama on opposite sides of the Murray River. For about 40 years, from 1860 to 1900, Echuca was a busy port with hundreds of paddlesteamers and barges carrying supplies to stations along the Murray, Darling and Murrumbidgee Rivers. Much of the romance of this era was captured in the television mini-series All The Rivers Run.

The name Echuca is Aboriginal for 'meeting of the water'.

How to Get There
By Bus

V/Line have a service from Melbourne on Tues, Wed, Thurs and Sat. **Greyhound Pioneer** stop at Echuca on their Sydney/ Adelaide run.

Visitor Infomation

Echuca-Moama District Tourism is at *2 Heygarth Street, Echuca,* ☎*(03) 5480 7555* or *1800 804 446.* They can be emailed at ✉emt@origin.net.au and the website is 💻*www. echucamoama.com*

↪ Let's Stay Here

Echuca-Moama has motels, hotel/motels, a guest house, caravan parks, and self-contained unit accommodation. Here is a selection of budget accommodation with prices, which should be used as a guide only. The telephone area code is 03.

Big River Motel, *317 High Street*, ☎*5482 2522.* 15 units, barbecue - *from* ✪*$60.*

Echuca Gardens YHA, *103 Micthell St, Echuca,* ☎*5480 6522,* ✉*www.echucagardens.com* or ✉*www.yha.com.au.* This building used to be a worker's cottage from the Victorian period restored into a hostel. Located behind a two-storey log cabin and less than two kilometres off town. Relax in the gardens during the day and the saunas and spas at night. Other facilities includes a kitchen, laundry, TV lounge, open fire, internet access and a barbecue area. Bike hire and parking available. **Recommended.** *Members Dorm* ✪*$19; double $43; (discount weekly rate available) BC MC VA EFTPOS*

Fountain Motel, *77 Northern Highway,* ☎*5482 3200.* 13 units, swimming pool, barbecue - *from* ✪*$55.*

Highstreet Motel, *439 High Street,* ☎*5482 1013.* 11 units - *from* ✪*$60.*

Nomads Oasis Backpackers, *410-424 High St,* ☎*5480 7866,* ✉*www.backpackersech*

uca.com/index2.htm. A huge place with very good facilities located in the city centre. This hostel caters a lot for those travellers who wants to work on nearby farms to pick fruits. They organise transport to farms. Facilities includes fully equipped kitchen, TV and lounge room, internet access, laundry, and a barbecue area. Note that alcohol is not permitted, but will gladly provide free drinks vouchers for the pub that they also run. **Recommended.** *Dorms* ✪*$22; double $46;*

Pastoral Inn Hotel Motel, *100 Sturt Street,* ☎*5482 1812.* 15 units, licensed restaurant - *from* ✪*$55.*

Caravan Parks

Echuca Caravan Park, *Crofton Street (Victoria Park),* ☎*5482 2157.* (No pets allowed) - *powered sites* ✪*$15-20 for two, on-site vans $35-45 for two.*

Rich River Caravan Park, *Crescent Street,* ☎*5482 3658.* (No pets allowed) - *powered sites* ✪*$15-25 for two, cabins from $52 for two.*

Riverlander Caravan Park, *48 Pianta Road,* ☎*5482 2558.* (No pets allowed) - *powered sites* ✪*$17 for two, cabins from $47.*

Yarraby Caravan Park, *River Avenue,* ☎*5482 1533.* (No dogs allowed) - *powered sites* ✪*$15-20 for two, cabins (en-suite) from $53 for two, cabins (standard) $40-53.*

Let's Eat

You can enjoy surprisingly fine dining in Echuca-Moama. The Tourism Centre has information on all the dining establishments in Echuca-Moama, and here we have a few names and addresses:

Fiori, *554 High Street, Echuca,* ☎*5482 6688* - licensed - Italian. Cock 'n'Bull Restaurant, 17 Warren Street, Echuca, ☎5480 6988 - modern Australian - licensed - ⏲open 5.30pm Tue-Sat.

Giorgio's on the Port, *527 High Street Echuca,* ☎*5482 6117* - open every night for dinner - award-winning - authentic Italian food.

Oscar W's Wharfside, Red Gum Grill and Deck Bar, *101 Murray Esplanade, Echuca,* ☎*5482 5133* - popular and highly recommended restaurant, described by critics as Echuca's best. **Radcliffe's,** *Radcliffe Street, Echuca,* ☎*5480 6720* - Mediterranean cuisine, licensed.

Top of the Town, *High Street, Echuca,* ☎*5482 4600* - excellent quality fish and chips available from this take-away shop - ⏲open seven days.

Wistaria Tea Rooms, *51 Murray Esplanade, Echuca* ☎*5482 4210* - licensed - lunch, morning and afternoon teas, children welcome.

Points of Interest

The Port of Echuca, ☎*5482 4248*, was once Australia's largest inland port, and the wharf, river boats, barges and century-old buildings have been restored. The Port is open daily and tickets for the Port Tours cost $10 adult. A full ticket ($20 adult), allows you to board the Pevensey (better known as the Philadelphia from All The Rivers Run) or the Alexander Arbuthnot which carries passengers during holiday periods and the last Sunday each month. The Adelaide, an historic logging boat, gives demonstration runs monthly, towing the D26 barge. Other features include a 10 minute film telling the Port story, an escape tunnel from the former cellar bar in the Star Hotel, the Paddlesteamer Gallery and the upstairs gallery in the Bridge Hotel.

The **Historical Society Museum**, opposite the Hopwood Gardens, has old River Charts, photographs, etc., and is ⊙open weekends, Mon, Wed, public and school holidays 1-4pm, or by appointment, ☎5480 1325.

Echuca also has the World in **Wax Museum**, Australia's largest collection of wax figures by international artists, situated in the High School. ⊙open daily 9am-5pm, ☎5482 3630.

There are one hour cruises on the **PS Canberra**, ☎5482 2711, and **PS Pride of the Murray**, ☎5482 5244. **MV Mary Ann** is a cruising restaurant that offers two hour luncheon and 3-4 hour dinner cruises. Also available is a river cruise for 2 day/nights aboard the **PS Emmylou**, ☎5482 4248.

Sharps Magic Movie House and **Penny Arcade**, opposite the Wharf, Bond Store, *Port of Echuca*, ☎5482 2361, have 30 penny arcade machines to play, the largest collection in Australia. You can also watch the old time movie shows dating from 1890. ⊙open daily 9am-5pm.

The **Murray River Aquarium**, *640 High Street*, ☎5480 7388, has fish and reptile displays.

Njernda, the Aboriginal

Cultural Centre, is in the Old Court House in *Law Place*, ☎5482 3904, and has displays of local and traditional artifacts and videotapes/language tapes of the local area. For sale are traditional crafts by people descended from the Yorta Yorta and Wemba Wemba tribes. The Centre is ⊙open daily, 10am-4.30pm.

Tisdall Winery is ⊙open daily for tastings and cellar sales, Mon-Sat 10am-5pm, Sun 11am-5pm, ☎5480 1349. It is in *Murray Esplanade*, one block down from the Port of Echuca.

Visitors can enjoy a 'flutter on the pokies' (play the slot machines) at one of the 4 licensed clubs in Moama, which also have dining facilities.

Festivals

The **Rotary Steam, Horse and Vintage Rally** is held over the Saturday and Sunday of the Queen's Birthday weekend in June. It features working exhibits of Clydesdale horses, vintage and veteran vehicles and steam traction engines, allowing everyone to experience the sights and sounds of a by-gone era.

The **Port of Echuca Heritage Steam Festival** is staged over a weekend in late October. It involves a cavalcade of riverboats and a fireworks display.

Facilities

Boating, bowls, bush walking, croquet, fishing, golf, horse racing, horse riding, sailing, swimming, trotting, water skiing, bingo, and bicycle and canoe hire are available.

Outlying Attractions
Kyabram

Situated only 31km (19 miles)

south-west of Echuca, Kyabram is becoming well known as an Arts and Crafts centre.

The **Kyabram Fauna Park**, *75 Lake Road*, ☎5852 2883, is set in 55ha (128 acres) of pleasant natural surroundings, and has hundreds of Australian animals and birds which roam freely around the park. It also has a miniature railway, playground and kiosk, and is ⊙open daily 9.30am-5.30pm.

The Barmah Forest

The Forest is a 20 minute drive from Moama, and the Visitor Information Centre in Echuca has leaflets giving directions.

The **Dharyna Centre**, *Sandridge Road, Barmah*, ☎5869 3302, is a visitor centre which also provides live-in educational opportunities for groups in the Barmah Forest, the largest Redgum Forest in the Southern Hemisphere.

Rochester

The town of Rochester is 24km (15 miles) south of Echuca on the Northern Highway. It is the Hub of the North, and has palms, peppercorns, quaint shops and sleepy streets. **Random House**, situated in on the Campaspe River in *Bridge Road*, is a stately 19th century homestead that has been restored to its former glory. It is ⊙open for morning and afternoon tea, Wed, Thurs, Fri and Sun. Meals and accommodation can be arranged by phoning ☎5484 1792.

The huge facility in the middle of town is the **Devondale** complex owned by the Murray Goulburn Co-operative Company. It is a major employer in the district, and has a retail store where you can sample and buy some of their products.

Ballarat

Population 83,000

Ballarat is the main centre of the Victorian Central Highlands, which have a decidedly Scottish flavour to them. Ballarat was made famous through the Eureka Stockade, the bloody miners' rebellion in 1854.

The city is 113km (70 miles) from Melbourne, 985km (612 miles) from Sydney, 637km (396 miles) from Adelaide, and 747km (464 miles) from Canberra.

Characteristics

Over the years Ballarat has been known as 'The Goldfields', the 'Garden City', the 'City of Statues' and the 'Historical City', and it is all these and more.

The city is one of the best preserved in Australia, and also one of the most fascinating. Steeped in history, it is a monument to the pioneering adventurers who left their distant homelands in search of prosperity in the gold rush of the 1850s.

Incidentally, is it Ballarat or Ballaarat? The original spelling came from the aboriginal 'Balla-arat', meaning 'elbow place'. Over the years the second 'a' was dropped for convenience. In early 1990 the Ballaarat Council officially re-adopted the original spelling and it is now officially the City of Ballaarat, although for commercial or other purposes either spelling is acceptable.

How to Get There
By Bus

Greyhound Pioneer stop at Ballarat on their Melbourne/ Adelaide/Perth and Melbourne/ Adelaide/Alice Springs routes. **V/Line** buses run from Melbourne to Ballarat, and the trip takes about two hours.

By Rail

There is a regular service Melbourne-Ballarat.

Visitor Infomation

Ballarat Visitor Infomation Centre is at *39 Sturt Street (cnr Albert Street)*, ☎ *(03) 5320 5741* or ☎ *1800 446 633.* For further information email them at ✉tourism@ ballarat.vic.gov.au or see the website 🖥 *www.ballarat.com*

↵ Let's Stay Here

Victoria's largest inland provincial city has a wide range of accommodation, and here we have a selection, which should be used as a guide only. The telephone area code is 03.

Sovereign Hill Lodge YHA, *Magpie St,* ☎*5333 3409,* 🖥*www.yha.com.au.* Part of the Sovereign Hill Goldmining Township which is a re-creation of the 1850s town. Located about 3kms south from the bus and train stations and the city centre. Facilities includes a kitchen, laundry, TV lounge and a barbecue area. Enquire about their 'Hot n Steamy/ Gold'n Dreamy' package which includes 4 night accommodation and entry to a variety of attractions. Parking available. *Members Dorm ✪$19; single $28; twin $48 ($55 with en suite) BC MC VA EFTPOS*

Caravan Parks
Ballarat and A Welcome Stranger Caravan Park, *Cnr Water St and Scott Parade,* ☎*5332 6818.* (No pets allowed) - *powered sites ✪$20*

for two, cabins (en-suite) $31pp, cabins (standard) $50-60 for two.

A Ballarat Windmill Caravan Park, *Avenue of Honour, Western Highway, Alfredton,* ☎*5334 1686.* (No dogs allowed) - *powered sites ✪$25-30 for two, on-site vans $44 for two, cabins from $60 for two.*

Shady Acres Caravan Park, *Melbourne Road (Western Hwy),* ☎*5334 7233.* (No dogs allowed) - *powered sites ✪$18 for two, park cabins (standard) $25-35 for two.*

Ballarat Goldfields Holiday Park, *108 Clayton Street,* ☎*5332 7888.* (No pets allowed) - *powered sites ✪$21 for two.*

Let's Eat

As with any city of its size, Ballarat has a wide choice of restaurants, as well as those in the motels and hotels. Here are some names and addresses.

Boatshed Restaurant, *27 Wendouree Parade,* ☎*5333 5533* - open seven days - situated beside Lake Wendouree.

Europa Cafe, *411 Sturt Street,* ☎*5331 2486* - dishes in a variety of flavours - dinner Thu-Sat, breakfast and lunch daily - licensed.

Golden Crown Chinese Restaurant, *cnr Main Road and Barkly Street,* ☎*5332 2169* - ⏰open for lunch and dinner seven days - licensed and BYO - takeaway available.

Lillian's Restaurant, at the Sundowner Motor Inn, *312 Main Road,* ☎*5331 7533* - modern Australian - good value - licensed.

Mexican Terrace Restaurant, *71 Victoria Street,* ☎*5333 1435* - mexican, steak, vegetarian and children's menus - ⏰open Tue-Sun from 6pm - licensed.

Pancake Kitchen, *Grenville Street,* ☎*5331 6555* - BYO, family atmosphere.

Peter Lalor Hotel, *331 Mair Street,* ☎*5331 1702* - licensed, full a la carte menu and smorgasbord - ⏰open daily for lunch noon-2pm and dinner 6-8pm.

Robin Hood Family Bistro, *33 Peel Street,* ☎*5331 3348* - licensed, a la carte - ⏰open seven days with piano bar on Thurs, Fri and Sat nights.

The Ansonia, *32 Lydiard Street, South Ballarat,* ☎*5332 4678* - international cuisine - licensed - breakfast, lunch and dinner available.

The Bonshaw, *cnr Tait Street and Ross Creek Road,* ☎*5335 8346* - licensed, seafood/steak in candlelit atmosphere - mains under $20 - ⏰open Tues-Sat.

There are also two branches of **McDonald's** in Ballarat.

Points of Interest
The Eureka Stockade Centre, *cnr Rodier and Eureka Streets,* ☎*5333 1854,* opened in March 1998 and cost $4 million to build. It involves a modern, interactive re-retelling of the story of the miner's brief but bloody uprising in 1854 Ballarat. The exhibition is well done, and should be your first port of call to understand the city's past. It is ⏰open daily 9am-5pm, and entry is ✪$8 adult.

Opposite the exhibition is the **Eureka Memorial and Park,** near where the events actually occurred.

The **Ballarat Fine Art Gallery,** *40 Lydiard Street North,* has the remains of the original Eureka Flag, depicting the Southern Cross, displayed in its own gallery alongside a changing display of related work. The flag was given to James Oddie, the gallery's founder and president, in 1895, by the widow of John King, a trooper who had taken part in the attack on the Stockade. The gallery was the first provincial art gallery to be established in Australia. The foundation stone for the present building was laid in 1887. It is ⏰open daily 10.30am-5pm. Admission is ✪$4 adult.

Historic Montrose Cottage, *111 Eureka Street,* was built in 1856 and is the oldest remaining bluestone miner's cottage in Ballarat. Classified by the National Trust of Australia (Vic), the Cottage is also on the Australian Heritage List. It is ⏰open daily 9am-5pm, as is the adjacent **Eureka Museum,** which gives an insight into life on the goldfields, with an array of personal and household items dating from the 1850s. Outside is a cottage garden featuring old roses, herbs and other aromatic plants, and next door is **Priscilla's Cottage,** offering morning and afternoon teas and snacks. This is Ballarat's oldest attraction and a multi-award winner.

Ballarat Wildlife Park, *cnr Fussel and York Streets,* ☎*5333 5933,* is set in 15ha (37 acres) of parkland, and attractions include a large collection of Australian animals, barbecue and picnic areas, children's adventure playground, tropical reptile house, large salt water crocodiles, kiosk and wildlife souvenir shop, a cafe and takeaway food shop. The Park is ⏰open every day from 9am-5.30pm. Admission is ✪$13.50 adult.

Sovereign Hill, in *Bradshaw Street,* ☎*5331 1944,* offers a trip back in time to the period of Ballarat's gold rush days. It is a re-created gold mining town complete with a Main Street, busy with people in olden day dress and horse-drawn vehicles; a blacksmith; coach-builder; tinsmith; potter; furniture maker; Clarke Brothers' Grocery; the Apothecaries Hall; Spencer's Sweetshop; and the Hope Bakery. You can pan for gold, or take a guided tour of the underground mine, play bowls at the Empire Bowling Saloon, or be photographed in period costume. There is something for everyone at Sovereign Hill, and plenty of places to eat or be entertained. The complex is ⏰open daily 10am-5pm. Entry is ✪$25 adult.

Blood on the Southern Cross is described as a "Night-time Sound and Light Spectacular". It is an unique and engaging re-creation of the Eureka Stockade, a turning point in Australia's history, which takes place on Soveriegn Hill - ☎*5333 5777* for booking and information.

The **Gold Museum** is opposite Sovereign Hill in *Bradshaw Street,* and is run by the Ballarat Historical Society. The museum has a collection of rare gold coins, including a ducat, a denarius and a doubloon, and an exhibition of Chinese bronze and porcelain, watercolours, jewellery and clothing. There is also an historical pavilion with Aboriginal artefacts, relics of the wool industry, old signs and store fronts, bric-a-brac, and memorabilia of both Ballarat and Victoria. The Museum is ⊙open 9.30am-5.20pm daily.

The **Central Business District of Ballarat** is a treasury of architectural elegance - *Lydiard Street* has the 1872 Alexandria Tearooms, Old Colonists Hall (1887-89), former Mining Exchange (1888), Reid's Coffee Palace (1886 - now a private hotel), and the George Hotel, originally built in 1853 but the present building dates from 1903.

Sturt Street has the **Post Office** (1863-1885), the **Town Hall** (1870), and a pagoda-like pavilion that was erected as a memorial to the bandsmen who played as the Titanic went down.

The Visitor Infomation Centre has information on other buildings of architectural merit.

At the western end of Sturt Street *(Western Highway)* is an unusual war memorial - the **Arch of Victory** and the **Avenue of Honour.** The Arch is across the highway, near the golf club, and is floodlit by night. Immediately west an avenue of around 4000 trees reaches to **Lakes Burrembeet** and Learmonth, each one bearing a name honouring one of the fallen.

The **Botanical Gardens** in *Gillies Street* are noted for the many specimens of mature trees ranging in age to over 120 years. About 46 of them have been registered on the National Trust register of Significant Trees. There is an informative free brochure on the gardens, that is available at most tourism outlets and accommodation, which lists the various attractions such as: **Adventure Playground**, the **Avenue of Prime Ministers**; the **Begonia display** (best in March); **Lake Wendouree**; and the **Tram Museum**.

Lake Wendouree was originally called Yuille's Swamp, named after Archibald Yuille, who in turn had named his run Ballaarat after the local Aborigines. The Lake is the focus of recreation in Ballarat, with its beautiful gardens, boat sheds, shady trees and picnic spots. It was used in 1956 for the rowing events of the Olympic Games. There are ducks, swans and other water birds, and, as is the way these days, plenty of joggers. The swans are exceptionally friendly at most times, but can become quite feisty when they have cygnets with them, so take care.

The **Ballarat Tramway Museum** is operated by a volunteer group over an original section of track. The 1.3km of track began in 1887 as a horse-tramway, then the route was electrified in 1905 and officially closed in 1970-71. Rolling stock at the depot/museum includes 10 tramcars and horse tram No 1, and there is a photographic display. The trams run hevery weekend, public holidays and school holidays from noon-5pm, ☎5334 1580.

The **Dinosaur World Fun Park and Fossil Museum**, *Midland Highway, Creswick*, ☎5345 2676, is set in 12ha (30 acres) of bushland. 18 life-size dinosaurs and Model Land are features inside the complex. Ouside there are 36 picnic tables (many under cover), 16 barbecues, a takeaway kiosk, and plenty to see and do ⊙every day 9.30am-5pm.

The **Tuki Fishing Complex**, "Stoney Rises", *Smeaton*, ☎5345 6233, is about 25 minutes from Ballarat, and you can hire all the necessary equipment and catch your trout for lunch. There are eight ponds and two lakes, all brimful with fish, and from the complex there are panoramic views over the Loddon Valley. ⊙opening hours are daily 11am-6pm.

Kryal Castle is 8km (5 miles) east of Ballarat, off the *Western Highway*, and is ⊙open daily 9.30am-5.30pm, ☎5334 7388. The castle occupies 2.4ha (6 acres) within a walled area, with 73 buildings, displays, museums, facilities and services. The castle opened in 1974, and is well worth visiting. There are gothic towers, turrets, parapets, battlements complete with moat, drawbridge, porticos, keep, tavern, craft shops, stables and dungeons. Live exhibitions include the 'Hanging of the Villain', 'Whipping of the Wench', and various changing shows. Whatever you do, don't miss the graveyard, and make sure you read the headstones. The Castle also has the Golden Eagle Tavern, where you can wine and dine like the knights of old. Entry is ✪$12.50 adult.

Festivals

The **Begonia Festival** is held over 10 days in March, and is one of the best known in Victoria.

The **Ballarat Agricultural Show** is held on the Friday, Saturday and Sunday of the second weekend in November.

Facilities

Lawn bowls, croquet, fishing, gold panning, golf, greyhound racing, horse racing, rowing, sailing, squash, swimming, tennis and trotting.

Outlying Attractions
Clunes

Situated 40km (25 miles) north of Ballarat, Clunes was the first place where gold was discovered in Victoria. A small rush followed but no permanent development occurred until 1856. Commercial development began in 'Lower' Fraser Street in the 1860s, and by the 1870s, many of the fine civic buildings you see today were constructed. Mining ceased in the 1890s and a tree planting programme began, creating one of the prettiest small towns in Victoria.

The town has a museum, a motel, hotels, historic buildings, a supermarket, and a golf course. For more local information, contact the **Clunes Museum** on ☎5345 3592.

Daylesford

John Egan first discovered gold at a site known as Wombat Flat Diggings, in August 1851. The township of Daylesford was surveyed and laid-out in 1854. A settlement, including Chinese market gardens, remained at the diggings site until 1929, when the area was flooded to create **Lake Daylesford.**

You will find the Daylesford Regional Visitor Information Centre in Vincent Street, ☎(03) 5348 1339.

Hepburn Springs

John Hepburn was credited with discovering the area in 1837, and he said it was the loveliest spot he had seen in his travels. He established an extensive sheep squat on Smeaton Hill (now Kooroocheang). The springs were known to the Aborigines of the area, and discovered by early settlers, but the true worth of their presence was overshadowed by the mining boom. However, when the gold ran out, the quality of the waters was found to equal that of Europe's famous health resorts, and soon attracted growing numbers to drink and bathe in the springs.

The Hepburn Spa Resort, *Mineral Springs Reserve*, has hot mineral water, herbal, mud, bubble and sinusoidal electric baths, and these are becoming the tourist mecca they were at the turn of the century, ☎5348 2034.

⤳ **Let's Stay Here**

Wildwood YHA,
42 Main Rd, Hepburn Springs, ☎*5348 4435,* 🖳*www.yha.com.au*
This old guesthouse was built in the 1920s with a bush setting that overlooks the Doctor's Gully and the old gold mining area. Foodstore is close by. There is an in-house massage and activities for childrens and pets. Other facilities includes a kitchen, laundry, common room, TV lounge, a barbecue area and an open fireplace. On-site kiosk. Also enquire about their 'Hot n Steamy/Gold'n Dreamy' package which includes 4 night accommodation and entry to some attractions around the area. Bike hire and parking available. *Members Dorm* ❁*$20; single $32 ; double $48 ($30 pp with en suite) BC MC VA*

Maryborough

Situated 88km (55 miles) from Daylesford, Maryborough has a population of 8,500. It was occupied by graziers until 1854 when there was a gold rush to nearby White Hills, 5km to the north. By 1856, Maryborough's main street was a thriving thoroughfare serving some 50,000 diggers. By 1918, the gold had petered out, and secondary industry took over, making it one of the most highly industrialised towns in Australia. A town tour will give an insight into the town, and its historical attractions.

For more information, get in touch with the **Central Goldfields Shire Office**, *2 Neill Street, Maryborough,* ☎*(03) 5461 0610,* 🖂*email mail@ cgoldshire.vic.gov.au* or visit 🖳*www.centralgoldfields.com.au*

Avoca

This is another former mining town in the foothills of the Pyrenees Range at the junction of the *Sunraysia and Pyrenees Highways*, on the banks of the Avoca River. Its quiet hills teem with black wallabies and grey kangaroos, and there is a growing colony of koalas. The Pyrenees Tourist Association is at *122 High Street,* ☎*(03) 5465 3767.*

Wineries around Ballarat

Yellowglen Winery, Whites Road, Smythesdale, *5342 8617* - ⏲open Mon-Sat 10am-5pm, Sun noon-5pm.
Mount Avoca Vineyard, 45 minutes along the Sunraysia Highway from Ballarat, *5465 3282* - ⏲open Mon-Sat 10am-5pm, Sun from noon.
Redbank Winery, at the 200km post on Sunraysia Highway, *5467 7255* - hopen daily 9am-5pm.

The following wineries are open weekends and public holidays. For other times phone *53687209*. Chepstowe Vineyard, Fitzpatricks Lane, Carngham, *5344 9412*. Leura Glen Estate, 260 Green Gully Road, Glenlyon, *5348 7785* Whitehorse Wines, 4 Reid Park Road, Mt Clear, *5330 1719*.

Ararat and The Grampians

Population 12,000

Ararat is situated near the Hopkins River, 203km (126 miles) north-west of Melbourne, in the central highlands of Victoria. It is the gateway to the Grampians.

Characteristics

The Ararat district was founded and settled around 1839-40 and gold was discovered in the area in 1854. Evidence of the extensive mining in the surrounding district still exists for the interested to see. The Municipality was declared a Borough in 1858, became a Town in 1934 and was declared a City in 1950.

Ararat is an important service centre for a rich farming and wine growing area. It boasts some of the finest agricultural and wine growing land in Victoria, and produces the State's top fine Merino wool, and has the largest sheep production in Australia.

Many visitors to the region use Ararat as a base to explore the magnificent natural resources in the Mount Cole Forest Ranges and the popular Grampians National Park.

How to Get There
By Bus
Greyhound Pioneer call into Ararat on their Melbourne/Adelaide runs.

By Train
Ararat is connected by rail with Geelong, Portland, western, north western and central Victoria.

Visitor Infomation
Ararat and Grampians Visitor Information Centre, *91 High Street*, ☎ *(03) 5355 0281* or ☎ *1800 657 158*. Email ✉tourinfo@ararat.vic.gov.au or visit ◼*www.ararat.asn.au* There is also the Ararat Visitor Infomation Centre in *Barkly Street*, ☎*(03) 5352 2096*.

⤴ Let's Stay Here

Ararat has motels, hotels and caravan parks. Following is a selection, with prices, which should be used as a guide only. The telephone area code is 03.

Brambuck Backpackers, *Dunkeld Rd, Halls Gap,* ☎*5356 4250* Situated right across the Brambuck Cultural Centre and about 3km from Halls Gap. Very good hostel. All rooms have en suite bathrooms and are clean. Facilities are good which includes a well equipped kitchen and a large deck with barbecue area. **Recommended.** *Dorms* ✪*$22; single $55; double/ twin $55;*

Chalambar Motel, *132 Lambert Street,* ☎*5352 2430*. 10 units, barbecue, playground - ✪*$45*.

Grampians YHA Eco-Hostel, *Corner Buckler St and Grampians Rd, Halls Gap,* ☎*5356 4544,* ◼ *www.yha.com.au* What's special about this eco-hostel is that it has many fea-

tures that helps protect and complement the natural environment of the Grampians. These includes many state-of-the-art processors that conserve water and energy. This also includes solar powered electricity. There is a kitchen, laundry, TV lounge, internet access, a swimming pool, a barbecue area, an open fireplace, a herb garden and fresh eggs everyday. Parking available. **Recommended.** *Members Dorm* ✪*$20; single $48 ; double/twin $25pp BC MC VA*

Mount Ararat Motor Inn, *367 Barkly Street,* ☎*5352 2521*. 9 units, barbecue, playground - ✪*$60*.

Tim's Other Place, *42 Garmpians Rd, Halls Gap,* ☎*5356 4288,* ◼ *www.timsplace.net* What you'll find is a small looking house which is old, but is clean. Accommodation is situated at the back on the extra buildings, which is also small. Facilities includes a the normal stuff and internet access. Bike and car hire available. *Dorms* ✪*$22; single $40; double/twin $50;*

Caravan Parks
Acacia Caravan Park, *6 Acacia Avenue,* ☎*5352 2994*. (Pets allowed by arrangement) - heated pool, *powered sites* ✪*$16 for two, on-site vans $33-42 for two, cabins (en-suite) from $55 for two, cabins (standard) $35-50 for two.*

Pyrenees Caravan Park, *67 Pyrenees Highway,* ☎*5352 1309.* (Pets allowed at manager's discretion) - *powered sites* ➋ *$16 for two, on-site vans $30-50 for two, cabins from $55.*

Let's Eat

There is not a wide range of choices in Ararat, but the following provide good meals at reasonable prices, and will give you an idea of what is on offer.

Ararat RSL Club, *76 High Street,* ☎*5352 2794.*

Man Hing Chinese Restaurant, *190 Barkly Street,* ☎*5352 3311* - BYO - lunch Mon-Sun 12-2pm, Dinner Sun-Thurs 5-10pm, Fri-Sat 5-11pm.

Noble Garden Restaurant, *204 Barkly Street,* ☎*5352 2019.*

Sicilian's Bar and Restaurant, *102 Barkly Street,* ☎*5352 2627.* **Statesman Motor Inn,** *Western Highway,* ☎*5352 4111.*

Vines Cafe and Bar, *74 Barkly Street,* ☎*5352 1744.*

Points of Interest

The town was named by the first settler, Horatio Spencer Wills, who set off in a covered wagon with 5,000 sheep from the Murrumbidgee area in NSW, to a grazing site near the Grampian Mountains. After 11 months of travel, in March 1840, Wills rested on a large bald mountain, noted that he was only one day's travel from his destination, and called the mountain 'Mount Ararat' for as he said, "Like the Ark, we rested here".

Ararat has many historical buildings classified by the National Trust, and the Visitor

Infomation Centre has a brochure setting out a City Area Walk which takes in the splendid architecture of yesteryear. It commences at the Art Gallery, on the corner of *High and Vincent Streets,* ⊙open Mon-Fri 11am-4pm, Sat closed (except school holidays 12-4pm), Sun 12-4pm. You then visit the **Town Hall**, which incorporates the **Arts Centre**; the **Shire Hall**; the **Langi Morgala Museum** (⊙open Sat-Sun 2-4pm); the **YMCA**; the **Mural** by Artist Hugh Anderson in *High Street*; **Pyrenees House**; the **Old Gaol**; **Alexandra Gardens**; the **Old Post Office** and **Sub Treasury**; the **Court House**; the **Edith Cavell Memorial**; and a **Grapevine** that has survived since 1856 when it was planted by G.W.H. Grano. The walk can take from 1/2 hour to 2 hours, depending on how much time you spend at each stop.

The Information Centre also has three Driving Tours from Ararat, which travel a bit further afield, and apart from the places visited on the walk, visit the following: **One Tree Hill scenic lookout**; **McDonald Park** approximately 4km from city centre; **Copes Hill** scenic view; **Cathcart Ridge Winery** ☎*5352 1997*; **Carrol's Cutting** with views to the Grampians; **Pinky Point** where gold was first found; **Norval Dam** for fishing, swimming and yabbying; **Montara Winery** ☎*5352 3868.*

Green Hill Lake, 4km from the city centre, is stocked with perch, trout and yellowbelly. There are gas barbecues, shade shelters, adult playground equipment and a boat ramp. The lake also has canoe channels and islands.

Alexandra Gardens have a Fernery and Glass House, which is used for growing orchids, and

in fact, Ararat is known as the orchid centre of the west and has an annual orchid display in the town hall during October.

Ararat has eight district wineries, with most open for cellar sales and tastings. The **Seppelts** guided tour is a highlight of a visit to the area. Tours are Mon-Sat 10.30am, 1.30pm and 3pm and the cellar door is ⊙open 10am-5pm Mon-Sun, ☎*5361 2239.*

Festivals

The **Great Western Vintage Races** are held on the Australia Day weekend in January.

Ararat Highland Sports, featuring the Ararat Gift (foot race) are held on the Labour Day Weekend in March.

Golden Gateway Festival is over ten days in October.

Facilities

Lawn bowls, croquet, horse racing, trotting, swimming, tennis and squash.

Outlying Attractions
Mount Cole Forest

The Forest straddles the Great Dividing Range about 20km (12 miles) east of Ararat. Mount Cole and Mount Lonarch Forests are excellent examples of forests resulting from multi-use management, and in area total about 12,150ha (30,010 acres). They produce a steady supply of high quality milling timbers to local sawmills, while providing wildlife habitat and recreational opportunities. The area also has another important value as its timbered slopes act as catchments for the streams that supply water to neighbouring towns. Road surfaces throughout the forest are good, but narrow, and allowances for slower speeds should be made.

Mount Cole Forest has become one of the most popular spots in Australia for Hang Gliding enthusiasts to practise. There are three sites used for take-off – **Ben Nevis, Mt Buangor** and **Mt Langi Ghiran**. While you might not be interested in jumping off a mountain yourself, it is exciting to watch others risking life and limb.

For those interested in nature, the things to look out for are: wildflowers, including Rare Grevillea; kangaroos and wallabies; platypus (experts guarantee they are around in the streams, but don't get your hopes too high); echidnas, koalas, deer, tree ferns and waterfalls.

Grampians National Park

The Grampians became Victoria's largest National Park on July 1, 1984.

The start of the Park is about 25km (15 miles) from Ararat, west of the township of Moyston. There are several ways to enter the Park from Moyston, through Pomonal to Hall's Gap, or west from Moyston to Mafeking and Mt William. The Park consists of 167,000ha (412,490 acres) and has a rich variety of native flora, wildlife, and Aboriginal rock art sites. The eastern slopes of the Grampians present some of the most beautiful scenery in the area with an abundance of heath, wildflowers and the tall eucalypt forest with the red gum woodland in Victoria Valley a special feature.

The Park supports over 860 native plant species. Kangaroos, koalas, echidna, possums and gliders are common, and over 200 bird species have been recorded.

More information on the Grampians is available from **Parks Australia**, ☎ *131 963* or by dropping into the information centre on **Dunkeld Road** near *Halls Gap*, ☎ *5356 4381*.

West of Moyston, about 20km (12 miles) is the **Mafeking Reserve** where the 'discovery of gold' Cairn is located depicting the site of the 1900 gold rush to the area. It is reported that over 7000 miners were in the area then, and today you can still see the sluiced gullies and disused shafts. Special care should be taken in the area, as the shafts can be dangerous.

The **Mount William** picnic area on the eastern slopes of the Grampians is a delightful spot, with the **Kalymna Falls** a short walking distance away.

The main wildflower season is in Spring (September-November), but Autumn is also a popular time to visit.

Great Western

Midway between Ararat and Stawell is the little township of Great Western, which gives its name to fine wines, including the champagne-style Great Western Special Reserve, which matures in the cellars beneath the sloping hills of Seppelts vineyards. There are many wineries in the town, all offering cellar door sales and tastings, and information can be obtained from the Visitor Infomation Centre in Stawell.

Stawell

A former gold mining town 30km (19 miles) west of Ararat, Stawell is probably better known now for the **Stawell Gift**, the world's richest professional foot running race. It is held for 3 days over the

Easter break, and is a handicap race over 120m (131 yds). Since 1986, the carnival has been open to professional and amateurs, and attracts top Australian and international competitors. In *Lower Main Street* is the **Stawell Gift Hall Of Fame**, with videos, photographs and equipment covering over a century of history, ☉open Wed-Sun 10am-4pm, or by appointment, ☎ *5358 1326*.

The Stawell and Grampians Tourism Information Centre is at *54 Western Highway*, ☎(03) *5358 2314*, and is ☉open Mon-Fri 9am-5.30pm, Sat-Sun 9.30am-5pm. From the office you can get a brochure which shows visitors the attractions of Stawell.

The Walk starts in Stawell's '**World in Miniature**' in *London Road*, ☎ *5358 1877*. This Tourist Park features a unique presentation of world cultures, and Australian and local history displayed in dioramas and working models, both indoor and outdoors in landscaped gardens. You might also like to stroll through the **Historic Precinct**, and the Visitor Centre will guide you.

Halls Gap

Halls Gaps is the heart of the Grampians National Park in the picturesque Fyans Valley. The township offers a variety of accommodation, a comprehensive shopping centre and facilities including tennis courts, swimming pool, restaurants, horse riding, walks, scenic 4WD tours, golf course, fun park, nurseries, nearby wildlife park, winery and National Park visitor centre, ☎ *5356 4381*.

The sandstone ranges of the Grampians National Park surround

Halls Gap, providing views of rugged escarpments and a tranquil atmosphere. The ridges and valleys are filled with Australian fauna, wildflowers, treefern gullies, strange rock formations, Aboriginal rock art, crystal clear rock pools, and many waterfalls, such as the **McKenzie Falls**.

Mildura

Population 50,000

Mildura is situated on the Murray River at the junction of the Sturt, Silver City and Calder Highways. It lies 560km (348 miles) from Melbourne, 398km (247 miles) from Adelaide, 1068km (664 miles) from Sydney, and 780km (485 miles) from Canberra.

Climate

Mildura has a dry, mild winter climate and 400 hours more sunshine each year than Surfers Paradise in Queensland. The average summer temperature is 32C (90F) with most days around 29C (84F).

Characteristics

The north-west of Victoria is known as Sunraysia, and Mildura is the main town. It is a great place to relax as well as being the threshold of the great outback, which begins just beyond the far banks of the Murray. Mildura is called 'The Oasis in the Desert', with mile upon mile of lush, productive vineyards and orchards, in the midst of dry, harsh Mallee country.

How to Get There
By Air

Mildura has a budy regional airport, ☎5022 2777 for information on flight services and schedules.

By Bus

V/Line and **Greyhound Pioneer** have daily services from capital cities.

By Rail

The **Vinelander** from Melbourne daily except Saturday (overnight 10 hours). **V/Line** services the region daily.

Visitor Infomation

The Mildura Visitor Information and Booking Centre is located at *180 -190 Deakin Avenue,* ☎*(03) 5021 4424* or ☎*1800 039 043* (bookings). Additionally, you can email them at ✉*tourism@mildura.vic.gov.au* or explore the website at 💻*www.milduratourism.com*

↪ Let's Stay Here

Mildura has plenty of motels, hotels guest houses, serviced apartment buildings and caravan parks/camping grounds. Here is a selection, which should be used as a guide only. The telephone area code is 03.

Juicy Grape
Backpackers Nomads,
Block 446 Sunnycliff, ☎*5024 2112,*💻*www.nomadsworld.com.* This unique hostel is in a class of its own and attracts only the best backpackers. Sitting comfortably in the heart of luscious vineyards, it caters for working travellers. Work is available 12 months of the year in the vineyards. Owners are former backpackers so they understand and meet the needs of their happy travellers. Facilities includes a fully equipped kitchen, laundry, internet cafe and a barbecue

area with weekly Barbecues and roasts. They do pick ups from bus station, organised tours and transport to jobs provided. *Dorms ✪$17; double/twin $40;*

Mildura Park Motel,
250 Eighth Street, ☎*5023 0479.* 28 units, barbecue, swimming pool - *from ✪$50.*

Mildura Riverboat Bungalow,
27 Chaffey Ave, ☎*5021 5315, users.mildura.net.au/bungalow/*Your average facilities. But the friendly atmosphere should make up for the rest. Parking available. *Dorms ✪$18.*

Orana Motor Inn,
2101 Calder Highway, Irymple, ☎*5024 5903.* 12 units, swimming pool - *from ✪$50.*

Caravan Parks
Golden River Caravan Gardens, *Flora Avenue,* ☎*5021 2299.* (No dogs allowed) - *powered sites ✪$20 for two, cabins (en-suite) from $50 for two, cabins $50 for two.*

Cross Roads Holiday Park,
cnr Deakin Avenue and Fifteenth Street, ☎*5023 3239.* (No pets allowed) - *powered sites ✪$19-20 for two, cabins (en-suite) from $50 for two.*

Sunraysia Holiday Park,
cnr Walnut Avenue and Sturt Highway, ☎*5023 1914.* (No pets) - *powered sites ✪$15 for two, cabins $40-60 for two.*

Desert City Tourist and Holiday Park, *Calder Highway,*

☎5021 1533. (No pets allowed) - *powered sites ✪$15-22 for two, cabins (en-suite) from $40 for two, cabins (standard) from $40.*

House Boats

For a holiday with a difference, get a few friends together and hire a houseboat, to cruise down the mighty Murray. The boats range from 6 berth to 12 berth units, from budget price to luxuriously equipped top of the range. For further information on this alternative accommodation, contact the Mildura Visitor Information and Booking Centre, ☎*(03) 5021 4424,* or one of the following:

Adventure Houseboats, *Sturt Highway, Buronga,* ☎*5023 4787.*
Mildura Holiday Houseboats, *842 Fifteenth Street, Mildura, 3502,* ☎*5021 4414.*
Sunraysia Houseboats, *48 Wentworth Street,* ☎*5027 3621.*
Sunseeker Houseboats, *189 Game Street, Merbein, 3502,* ☎*1800 035 529* **(free call).**

Let's Eat

Whether you prefer French, Italian, Mexican, Chinese or Vegetarian, a la carte, bistro, or casual, Mildura has the restaurant to suit your taste, and your pocket. Here is a selection:

Barneys Seafood Restaurant, *360 Deakin Avenue,* ☎*5021 2166.*

Belvue Restaurant, at the Commodore Motor Inn, *cnr Deakin Avenue and 7th Street,* ☎*5023 0241.*

Bel-Jardin Restaurant, *376 Deakin Avenue,* ☎*5023 7377.*

Doms Tavern Restaurant, *28 Langtree Avenue,* ☎*5021 3822* - open Mon-Sat, 6-30pm till late. Upstairs is the Carlyle Night Club, open Thurs, Fri and Sat, 9pm-3am.

Dragon Tower Chinese Restaurant, *29 Langtree Avenue,* ☎*5023 1925.*

Fasta Pasta, *30 Langtree Avenue,* ☎*5022 0622.*

Marias Pizza and Pasta Palace, *210a Deakin Avenue,* ☎*5023 7713.*

Mildura Settlers, *110-114 Eighth Street,* ☎*5023 0474* - open Mon-Wed 8.30am-midnight, Thu-Sat 8.30am-2am - modern Australian - licensed.

Regal Chinese Restaurant, *224 Deakin Avenue,* ☎*5021 3688.*

Wirraway Bistro, *130 Madden Avenue,* ☎*5023 1187.*

And, of course, we can't forget **McDonald's.** The local branch is at *395 Deakin Avenue,* ☎*9222 544.*

Points of Interest

In 1885, Alfred Deakin, the then Premier of Victoria, persuaded Canadian brothers, George and William Benjamin Chaffey to help plan Mildura. It was laid out in an American grid pattern, and most of its streets were given numbers instead of names. The Chaffeys installed pumps to lift water from the Murray, and after some initial problems with salt pollution, the area became well known for its fruit. Much of Mildura's history is preserved in the **Museum of Local History**, which is housed in *Rio Vista,* the stately home of W.B. Chaffey in **Cureton Avenue** - open 6 days. Also there is the **Mildura Arts Centre,** one of the best provincial galleries in Australia, ☎*5018 8330.*

Dolls on the Avenue is a collection of hundreds of dolls from every decade, and is ☼open daily 10am-4pm. It is in *Benetook Avenue,* ☎*5025 7113.*

Golden River Zoo, 4km from Mildura on the banks of the Murray River is a fine privately owned zoo. Open daily 9am-5pm on *Flora Avenue,* off *11th Street.* For information on animal show times ☎*5023 5540.* Entry is $12 adults.

Woodsie's Gem Shop is Australia's largest jewellery manufacturing complex, and one of Mildura's top attractions. It comprises: a workshop open to visitors; a spectacular showroom where finished items are for sale; an **Aladdin's Cave** full of glowing rocks and glittering crystals; a **Crazy Maze** with 100 different species of creepers over an acre of land to test your skill; and a Cave-Inn Cafeteria. The complex is on the corner of *Morpung and Cureton Avenues, Nichols Point,* 6km from Mildura, ☎*5024 5797.* It is ☼open daily 9am-5.30pm, and there is a modest admission fee to the Cave and Maze Section. The rest of the complex is free.

Orange World, 7km from Mildura on the *Silver City Highway,* is a fully operational citrus property with: ☼Tours on Tractor Train, 10.30am and 2.30pm; Citrus Tour; Red Emperor Tour, including a tour of Stanley Winery, 11.30am. Tours run daily, with extra tours during school holidays. For further information ☎*5023 5197.*

River Cruises

You can experience the old river boat era when you sail down the Murray on a paddleboat, and there are plenty of day and half-day cruises available. Details of current sailings are provided on noticeboards on Mildura Wharf, but here are a few examples.

PS Melbourne, ☎*5023 2200,* the only original steam driven Paddle-steamer (built 1912) ⊕departs Mildura Wharf 10.50am and 1.50pm for a 2 hour cruise, which goes through Lock 11.

PV Loyalty, ☎*5027 3224,* has daily cruises (except Saturdays) on the Darling River, ⊕departing from behind Wentworth Services Club at 1.45pm (returns 3.45pm).

PV Rothbury specialises in day cruises, including lunch. Cruise to the Golden River Zoo hleaves 9.50am on Wednesdays, and returns 3pm. Cruise to Trentham Estate Winery, leaves 10.30am Thursdays and returns 3.30pm. There are additional cruises during school holidays. The boat is also available for charter day or night cruises, ☎*5023 2200.*

Facilities

Olympic swimming pool, *12th Street*; putt putt golf course, cnr *7th Street and Orange Avenue*; ten pin bowling, *King Avenue;* old time dance at Nichols Point Hall, ☎*232 208,* Saturday 8pm-midnight; tennis, golf, lawn bowls, squash, skating, boating, water skiing, fishing, croquet, and badminton.

Outlying Attractions
Red Cliffs

15km (9 miles) south of Mildura along the *Calder Highway* on the way to Melbourne, lies the town of Red Cliffs which is currently enjoying a surge in development. The town gets its name from the nearby striking red cliffs which dominate the Murray River. In the early 1890s, George Chaffey bought 6060ha (15,000 acres) of rich mallee land above the cliffs to grow vines, but the cliffs proved too steep for pumping irrigation water, and it was not for another 30 years that prosperity reached the town. That was when more than 700 soldiers were re-settled in the area after World War I, and today the area is an important part of the citrus and dried fruits industries.

Using Red Cliffs as a base, the visitor has a great variety of attractions to see, ranging from the huge **Southcorp Karadoc Winery,** to various handcraft, art and gemstone displays. In the heart of the town, in *Barclay Square,* is **Big Lizzie,** the largest traction engine ever built in Australia, which took two years to make the journey from Melbourne.

Hattah-Hulkyne
National Park

Murray-Kulkyne National Park This vast Mallee park is about 70km (43 miles) south of Mildura and provides striking contrasts teeming with birdlife, kangaroos, emus and colourful wildflowers. The park information centre can be reached from the Calder Highway turn-off at Hattah (look for the store) - also enter through Nangiloc/Colignan, ☎*13 1963.*

Mungo National Park

The Park contains the unique **Walls of China,** a range of dunes up to 46m (150 ft) high shaped by erosion into a barrier 27km (17 miles) long, leaving a foreground likened to a lunar landscape, or part of the Sahara Desert. Many geological and archaeological discoveries have been made in the area, and Aboriginal ovens can be seen. There is also an old shearing shed, built by Chinese labourers more than a century ago. The site is about 110km (68 miles) north-west of Mildura, on a dry weather road. Phone ☎*5029 7292* for more information.

Wentworth

The historic town of Wentworth NSW, is situated where the Darling River joins the Murray, and is a 20 minute drive from Mildura. The Wentworth Visitor Infomation Centre, *66 Darling Street,* ☎*5027 3624,* is ⊕open seven days a week (9.30-4p, Mon-Fri and 10am-2pm on weekends), and will provide details of scenic attractions. You can email them at ✉tourism@wentworth.nsw.gov.au or visit the website ■ *www.*wentworth.nsw.gov.au

One site that you must not miss is the **Old Wentworth Gaol,** 1879-1927, in *Beverley Street.* It was designed to serve a vast outback region, and now stands as a vivid reminder of those harsh and uncompromising days when Wentworth stood on the edge of the lonely Australian inland. Classified as essential to the preservation of Australia's heritage, the gaol is a tribute to the craftsmanship of the pioneer builders and to the unfortunate inmates. The gaol also houses the Nanya Exhibit, dedicated to the courage and ingenuity of a remarkable man, and the beautiful Morrison collection. ⊕open daily 10am-5pm, ☎*5027 3337.*

A walk through town will take

Loch Ard Gorge

Countryside near Coryong

Mckenzie Falls

you pass quaint and notable buildings, some of which are heritage listed. After visiting the Old Wentworth Gaol, stop in at the **Museum**, also in *Beverly Street*, for its fascinating fossil collection.

Wineries

Capogreco Wines, Riverside Avenue between 17th and 18th Streets, South Mildura. ⏱Tastings, sales and inspections Mon-Sat 10am-6pm, *5022 1431*.
Southcorp Winery, Karadoc. Guided tours Mon-Fri 11am, 2pm and 3.3-pm. ⏱Tastings and sales Mon-Fri 9am-5pm, Sat 10am-4.30pm, *5051 3333*.
Mildara Blass Winery, Wentworth Road, Merbein. ⏱Guided tours Mon-Fri aa1m, 2pm, 3.30pm. ⏱Tastings and sales Mon-Fri 9am-5pm, Sat 11am-4pm, Sunday noon-4pm, *5025 2303*.
Buronga Hill Winery, Silver City Highway, Buronga. ⏱Tastings and sales Mon-Fri 9am-5pm, Sat 10.30am-4pm, Sun noon-4pm. Winery tours by appointment, *5022 5100*.
Trentham Estate Winery, Sturt Highway, Trentham Cliffs. ⏱Tastings and sales Mon-Fri 9am-5pm, Sat-Sun 10am-5pm, ☎*5024 8888*.

Warrnambool

Population 29,500
Warrnambool is situated on the coast, 263km (163 miles) south-west of Melbourne, where the Princes Highway meets the Great Ocean Road.

Climate

Average temperatures: January max 23C (73F) - min 13C (55F); July max 14C (57F) - min 6C (43F). Average hours of sunshine: summer 8, autumn 4, winter 3, spring 5. Wettest six months May-October.

Characteristics

Warrnambool was popular with the old whalers and sealers, as they could repair their boats and process their catches on its wide beaches. Due to reduced hunting, Warrnambool is now visited each year by a herd of the rare Southern Right whales, and a viewing platform has been erected at Logan's Beach to enable visitors to obtain a better view of the whales, which usually remain in the area for several weeks.

How to Get There
By Bus

Greyhound Pioneer, ☎ *13 2030*, stop at Warrnambool on the Melbourne/Adelaide coastal route.

By Rail

There is a regular **V/Line** service between Melbourne and Warrnambool, ☎ *13 6196*.

Visitor Information

The Visitor Infomation Office is at *600 Raglan Parade*, ☎*(03) 5564 7837*, and it is ⏱open daily 9am-5pm, or you can email the manager at ✉nan_adams@wcc.mav.asn.au The website to visit is 💻*www. warrnambool.org*

In addition, Shipwreck Coast Tourism can be found at *174a Timor Street*, ☎*5561 7894*.

↪ Let's Stay Here

Here is a selection of accommodation, with prices for a double room per night, which should be used as a guide only. The telephone area code is 03.

Backpackers Barn (Victoria Hotel),
90 Lava St, ☎*5562 2073* Accommodation located above the Victoria Hotel pub. A little run down but maintains a clean atmosphere. Facilities consists of your basic kitchen and lounge room with a piano and TV. Parking available. *Dorms* ✪*$20; double $40; (note: there's a $20 key deposit)*

The Stuffed Backpacker,
52 Kepler St, ☎*5562 2459*,💻 *www.stuffed.axs.com.au* Located centrally in town built within an old building. Just your basic facilities including a kitchen, a pool table and a TV room. The balcony also overlooks the street. Hang out for the free apple pie and ice cream every night. Parking available. *Dorms* ✪*$20; single $30; double $45;*

Warrnambool Beach Backpackers,*17 Stanley St*, ☎*5562 4874, www.beachbackpackers .com*. Located only about 10 minutes away from the beach and the town centre. Well maintained and just newly renovated. There is a great range of facilities including a kitchen, laundry, internet access and clean bathrooms. There is an on-site licensed bar and free bike hire is available. The hostel organises trips to see the penguins every night during summer. They also offer a free pick-up service from the train and bus stations. Bike hire and canoes are available. **Recommended.** *Dorms* ✪*$20; double $50-55 ;*

Caravan Parks
Ocean Beach Holiday Village, *Pertobe Road,* ☎*5561 4222.* 58 sites, 26 cabins, no pets, barbecue, heated pool - *powered sites* ✪ *$22-30 for two, cabins from $60 for two.*

Warrnambool Holiday Park, *cnr Raglan Parade and Simpson Street,* ☎*5562 5031.* 17 sites, 17 cabins, no dogs, barbecue, heated pool - *powered sites* ✪ *$20-26, cabins from $60.*

Fig Tree Holiday Village, *33 Lava Street,* ☎*5561 1233.* 72 sites, 23 cabins, no pets, barbecue - *powered sites* ✪*$17-30 for two, cabins from $55.*

Caravarna Lodge, *81 Henna Street,* ☎*5562 3376.* 42 sites, 4 cabins, barbecue, heated pool - *powered sites* ✪*$14-17 for two, on-site vans $25-40 for two, cabins $30-50.*

Let's Eat
There are over 50 places to have a meal in Warrnambool, from cafes to quality restaurants, and the Visitor Infomation Office will have details. Here is a selection.
Balenas Cafe, *158 Timor Street,* ☎*5562 0900.* Contemporary Australian cuisine as well as seafood and steaks with Italian, Mediterranean and International influences. Open 7 days.

Beach Babylon, *72 Leibig Street,* ☎*5562 3714.* Seafood with Mediterranean and Australian flavours. Open every day.

Bojangles, *61 Leibig Street,* ☎*5562 8751.* Award-winning Italian restaurant offering wood-fire pizzas and pastas as a specialty. Licensed, open for dinner only.

Breakers, *79 Banyan Street,* ☎*5561 3088.* All types of seafood served in an Australian style.

Clovelly, *cnr Banyan and Merri Streets,* ☎*5561 1415.* A-la-carte menu with seafood, steak and pasta.

Dragon Inn, *219 Lava Street,* ☎*5562 1517.* Chinese cuisine.

Freshwater, *78 Leibig Street,* ☎*5561 3188.* Licensed restaurant serving modern Australian and International cuisine and offering local wines.

Images, Liebig Street, ☎*5562 4208.* Licensed restaurant with a family atmosphere.

Jukes Cafe Restaurant, *525 Raglan Parade,* ☎*5562 3866.* A-la-carte menu with entertainment on Saturday evening. Licensed, open seven days for breakfast and dinner.

Mahogany Ship, *91 Merri Street,* ☎*5561 3866.* Australian seafood steak and pasta is served in this Scottish themed restaurant. A-la-carte dining with sea views.

Oriental Restaurant, *80-82 Liebig Street,* ☎*5562 7079.* BYO, Chinese and Australian fare, lunch and dinner, open 7 days.

Restaurant Malaysia, *69 Liebig Street,* ☎*5562 2051.* Also has Thai, Indian and Chinese dishes, BYO, open 7 days, noon-2pm, 6pm to late. Yum Cha, Sun noon-2pm.

The Blues, *142 Timor Street,* ☎*5562 2033.* Family oriented dining with live local music. Australian seafood and steaks.

Points of Interest
Flagstaff Hill Maritime Museum, *Merri Street,* ☎*5564 7841,* recreates the atmosphere of an early Australian coastal port. The lighthouse and associated buildings, and the 1887 fortifications are the original features of the site, and around them the village has been created. The story of shipping and the sea unfolds for visitors as they tour the village. Each building portrays an important aspect of port life in the last century, whether it be the role of the Ship Chandler or the function of the Mission to Seamen Church. Among the relics on display there is the Loch Ard peacock: an 1851 Minton porcelain statue which was washed up (still in its packing case) in Loch Ard Gorge after a shipwreck. The museum is ⊙open daily 9.00am-5.00pm, adults ✪$9.50.

Lake Pertobe Park has causeways, walking tracks, a maze, a flying fox, paddle boats and a well-equipped Adventure Playground behind the surf beach of Lady Bay.

Fletcher Jones Gardens, *cnr Flaxman Street and Raglan Parade,* are a colourful advocate for Victoria's claim as the Garden State of Australia. Thousands of visitors come each year to see these gardens.

The Performing Arts and Conference Centre, *185 Timor Street,* is a modern-style building situated in landscaped grounds in the heart of the business and restaurant district. It has three main venues suitable for stage presentations, conventions, dinners, cabarets, exhibitions, lectures, classes and meetings. Check the daily newspapers for programmes, or ☎5564 7904.

Warrnambool Art Gallery, *165 Timor Street,* has a permanent collection of 19th and 20th century Australian and European paintings and graphics - ⊙open daily noon-5pm, ☎5564 7832.

The **Warrnambool Botanic Gardens** are on the corner of *Botanic and Queen Streets.*

Tower Hill State Game Reserve, 14km (9 miles) from Warrnambool, is the remains of a volcano whose crater walls collapsed inward during its dying stages 6000 years ago. They blocked the 3km wide crater, which later filled with water. There is a sealed road leading to the main island, from where bushwalks radiate. There is also a **Natural History Centre,** ⊙open 9.00am to 4.30pm daily, which conducts tours, ☎5565 9202.

Hopkins Falls, are 13km (8 miles) from Warrnambool, near Wangoom. Thousands of tiny eels (elvers) make their way up the falls to the quiet waters beyond, to grow to maturity before returning to the sea to breed.

There are several recommended heritage walks through the town and nearby regions, and the Tourist Centre can provide you with maps and other details.

Warrnambool also has a mystery! There have been several reported sightings of the wreck of a mahogany ship in the windswept sandhills west of the city. The last was in 1980, and several artefacts have been found in the area. It is said that the ship foundered 400 years

ago with a complement of Dutch and Spanish sailors. If there is any substance to the story it means that Europeans set foot on Australian soil long before Captain Cook. In 1980 the City Council formed a Mahogany Ship Committee to compile all the known information, which is being fed into a computer in an endeavour to solve the mystery.

Festivals
February - **Wunta Fiesta**
May- **Racing Carnival**
Melbourne - **Warrnambool Cycling Classic** - October.

Facilities
Aerobics, badminton, basketball, volleyball, bingo, boating, lawn bowls, indoor cricket, croquet, golf, greyhound racing, horse racing, swimming, mini golf, scuba diving, skin diving, squash, speedway, surfing, swimming, table tennis, tennis, ten pin bowling, waterskiing, windsurfing and yachting.

Tours
Regular tours on the new **Sprit of Warrnambool**, lasting from 1-1.5 hours return. ⊙open 10am-6pm with nighttime charters available. Adults ✪$10.

Southern Right Charters and Diving, ☎5561 6222 or ☎5562 5044, offer fishing charters, diving charters, whale watching tours and scenic tours.

Seeall Tours, 1*3 Barham Avenue,* ☎5562 5795, have six tours through various locations, costing between ✪$10 and $50.

Warrnambool River Cruises, *2 Simpson Street,* can be contacted on ☎5562 7788.

Outlying Attractions
Great Ocean Road
The spectacular Great Ocean Road follows the coastline for much of its 250 kilometre (156 miles) length from Torquay to Peterborough. In some parts it is the only thing separating the mountains from the surf beaches.

The road was built by 3000 First World War veterans, and was ded-icated to the memory of all those who fought in that war. Using picks and shovels, the men commenced work in 1919 and the road was opened in 1932.

Fully sealed, though narrow in parts, it wends its scenic route through some of Victoria's most popular resorts. Pretty coastal towns like **Lorne, Apollo Bay** and **Port Campbell** swell to capacity in the high season. But it is in the winter, when massive breakers crash into the limestone cliffs, that the challenge which confronted the captains of the small coastal vessels can be understood. In the period to 1920, some 80 major shipping disasters were recorded between Port Fairy and Cape Otway. Of these the best known are the Loch Ard and the Schomberg, relics of which can be seen in the **Flagstaff Hill Maritime Village** at Warrnambool.

The road also passes through some of the richest forests in Australia. The **Angahook Forest Park,** the **Otway National Park** and the **Lorne Forest Park** are all extensive forest systems with prolific fauna.

Start your trip along the Great Ocean Road from Lorne, which is less than 2 hours' drive from Melbourne, and 218km (135 miles) from Warrnambool.

As an additional resource, the website that

covers the general area is
🔲 www.greatoceanrd.org.au

⤳ Let's Stay Here
Torquay
✜Nomad's Bells Beach Backpackers,
51-53 Surf Coast Highway,
☎*5261 7070* A pretty laidback surf atmosphere can be expected from this hostel. It's clean and offers a good range of facilities. This includes a kitchen, laundry, internet access and a TV lounge. Expect a beach volleyball court outside along with sundecks. Plenty of things available for hire, such as surf and boogie boards, bikes as well as cars. Parking available. *Dorms* ✪*$22; double $45;*

Anglesea
Anglesea Backpackers,
🔲*40 Noble St,* ☎*5263 2664, home.iprimus.com.au/ angleseabackpacker* A small backpackers place, but is kept clean and well maintained. Located just 10 minutes from the beach and close to the golf course. Just your basic facilities including a kitchen, laundry, internet access and TV lounge. They also have surfboards, wetsuits and mountain bikes for hire. Parking available. *Dorms* ✪*$22;*

Pointbreak Backpackers,
185 Addiscott Rd, ☎*5261 5105,* 🔲*www.pointbreakba ckpackers.com.au* Located well away from town towards Anglesea. It's within cycling distance from Bells Beach. A pretty good hostel with facilities like a kitchen, a big common room with a ping pong

table, a TV lounge and a log fire. Outside you'll also spot a volleyball court and a barbecue area. A shuttle service runs to the beach and makes trips to town. *Single* ✪*$20;*

Lorne
On the Erskine River, surrounded on three sides by forest ranges, and to the south by the Southern Ocean, Lorne was the first place declared an area of Special Significance and Natural Beauty by the Victorian Government.

On a bay named after Capt Louttit, who sought shelter there around 1840 while retrieving cargo from a shipwreck, Lorne was first settled by William Lindsay, a timber-cutter. Subdivision began in 1869 and the town was named after the Marquis of Lorne. Much of its colourful history is preserved in the gracious homes which remain.

Lorne's attractions include **Lorne Angahook State Park, Erskine Falls, Pennyroyal Valley,** as well as numerous bushwalks leading through lush fauna to beautiful waterfalls.

The Lorne Visitor Information Centre is at *144 Mountjoy Parade,* ☎*5289 1152.* It is ⌚open daily 9am-5pm. They can provide you with excellent information on absolutely everything you need to know to about this area, from where to stay and eat, to what to see and do. If you wish to contact them by email, the address is ✉lornevic@primus.com.au The web page to explore is 🔲*www. surfcoast.vic.gov.au*

⤳ Let's Stay Here
Erskine River Backpackers,
6 Mountjoy Pde, ☎*5289*

1496 Quite a good hostel, which is well kept and clean. Some rooms have en suite bathrooms. Consists of your usual facilities including the kitchen, laundry, games room and TV lounge. A highlight is the balcony that overlooks the river. *Dorms* ✪*$20; double $60;*

Great Ocean Road Backpackers YHA,
10 Erskine Ave, ☎*5289 1809* A popular hostel at this part of town. A bush setting just beside the river. Situated close to the foodstore and bus stop. Facilities includes a kitchen, laundry and internet access. Nice outdoors settings includes a balcony, a deck and a barbecue area. Free use of bikes and boogie boards. Parking is available. *Members Dorm* ✪*$20; double/twin $50; BC MC VA*

Apollo Bay
Apollo Bay was first visited in 1840 by the Henty Brothers, founders of Portland and Mount Gambier. They established a small whaling station on what is now the golf course. One of the three major centres along the Great Ocean Road, it has all facilities to offer the visitor - motels, hotels, holiday flats, lodges and caravan parks; several restaurants and take-away food places.

There are also many guest houses, BBs and cottages in Apollo Bay, so if you prefer these cosy kinds of accommodation, the Information Centre can give you an idea of what is on offer. The Visitor Information Centre is on the *Great Ocean Road,* ☎*(03) 5237 6529.*

Apollo Bay is an ideal touring centre for the **Otway Ranges Forest Park, Otway National Park,** and **Melba Gully State Park.**

↪ Let's Stay Here
Apollo Bay Backpackers,
47 Montrose St, ☎ *5237 7360,* 🖳 *www.apollobaybackpackers. com.au.* Nice and quiet and is located not far from the Great Ocean Road. Facilities includes a kitchen, laundry, TV lounge and internet access. There is also a nice outdoor area with a barbecue. *Dorms* ✪ *$20; double/twin $50;* (complimentary breakfast included)

Surfside Backpackers,
Corner Great Ocean Rd and Gambier St, ☎ *5237 7263 or 1800 357 263,* 🖳 *www.totaltravel.com/ travel/vic/greatoceanroad/ appollobay.* Quite still a rundown old building, but still immerses with a warm atmosphere. What's really going for it is the great ocean views of Appollo Bay. Close to town and the beaches. Facilities includes a kitchen, games room and internet access. Outside are a number of verandas that surrounds the hostel and a barbecue area that once again overlooks the ocean. *Dorms from* ✪ *$17; double/twin $50;*

Princetown
Situated on the La Trobe Creek near Gellibrand River, the surrounding limestone cliffs contain interesting fossils and formations. Gemstones can sometimes be found along the coastline, and the area is rich in flora and fauna. Princetown was named after Prince Alfred and

was proclaimed in 1885. Safe swimming, boating, fishing and water skiing are all features of this tiny settlement.

Given its location between the western boundary of the Otway National Park and the eastern boundary of the Port Campbell National Park, Princetown is ideal as a base for touring both.

Port Campbell
At the heart of one of Australia's most famed and photographed natural attractions, Port Campbell is a very popular resort. Situated on Campbell's Creek, and named after Capt. Alexander Campbell, a Scotsman in charge of the Port Fairy whaling station, it began as a small fishing port with surrounding pastoral runs. In 1964, 700ha (1729 acres) around Port Campbell was set aside as a National Park, and in 1981 the park was extended from Princetown through to Peterborough. Port Campbell is roughly at the centre of the park.

The town is a crayfishing port near the mouth of the river and has a safe, sandy beach ideal for family swimming. Restaurants and take-away foods are available and fresh local crayfish is the specialty.

Of course the Port Campbell National Park itself is the attraction (see entry overleaf), but whilst in Port Campbell you can take a trip to the old cemetery on the northern edge of the town. It has many old graves of interest, including that of Captain Scott and some of his crew, shipwrecked off the coast in the barque Newfield in 1892.

A look-out on the western side of the river offers a scenic panorama of the town and

coastline.

The Port Campbell Visitor Information Centre, is in *26 Morris Street,* ☎ *5598 6089.*

↪ Let's Stay Here
Mathieson House,
Lord St, ☎ *5598 6305* Hostel that offers basic accommodation. Expect the very least. *Dorms* ✪ *$21*

Ocean House Backpackers,
32 Cairns St, ☎ *5598 6223,* 🖳 *www.portcampbell.nu/ oceanhouse.* Small and cozy and located just across the sea. Built in an old house with hardwood floors, but offers new furnishings. Offers your usual facilities of a kitchen, TV lounge etc... Their veranda overlooks the ocean which is nice. It's managed by the Port Campbell National Park Cabin and Camping Park, just near the tourist information centre, where you can check in if there's no one in the hostel. *Dorms* ✪ *$20*

Port Campbell YHA,
18 Tregea St, ☎ *5598 6305,* 🖳 *www.yha.com.au*
A huge hostel with a relaxing atmosphere. They take pride in being professional with a proper reception area and quality facilities. All rooms are heated. Facilities includes a modern kitchen, laundry, common room, TV/video lounge, internet access and a barbecue area. Restaurant/ kiosk on site. Bike hire and parking available. *Members Dorm* ✪ *$18; double/twin $44, $60 self contained cabins for 2; BC MC VA EFTPOS*

Port Campbell National Park

Recognised as one of Australia's most scenic sections of coastline, the 1750ha (4323 acres) Port Campbell National Park stretches 32km (20 miles) along the Great Ocean Road.

The best known features are the **Twelve Apostles, Loch Ard Gorge** and **London Bridge**. In early 1990 a span of London Bridge collapsed into the ocean, vividly demonstrating the ongoing erosion of wind and sea on the limestone cliffs of the park.

Gorges, arches, islands, blowholes and stark outcrops create a dramatic foreground to the stormy Southern Ocean which stretches to the Antarctic. Here and there a sandy beach glistens in sharp contrast to the sheer cliffs and deep inlets which offer some of the most interesting scenery and photography subjects you will find.

Further information on the park can be acquired by calling ☎ *13 1963.*

Peterborough

Situated at the mouth of the Curdie's River, Peterborough is a popular summer holiday town where you can get away from it all. River or beach swimming, and fishing for bream, mullet or crayfish are among the main pastimes, while the shipwrecks in the area provide good diving and aqualunging.

Port Fairy

The pretty town of Port Fairy is 29km (18 miles) from Warrnambool. The first stop for all visitors should be the Visitor Information Centre in *22 Bank Street,* ☎ *(03) 5568 2682,* as this historic town

has many attractions. Over 50 buildings have been classified by the National Trust, and there many art, craft and antique shops, picnic and barbecue areas, and facilities for golf, tennis, squash, lawn bowls and boat trips. There are heritage buildings outlined in brochures available from the Visitor Centre, and the **Port Fairy History Centre** in *Gipps Street* should satisfy anyone interested in nineteenth-century memorabilia.

High on the list of attractions is the **Mutton Bird Rookery** on Griffiths Island. The bird gets its name from early settlers who utilised its fatty flesh for food, and as an oil source, but it is really the short-tailed shearwater (puffinus tenuirostris). They are not much to look at, but their lifestyle is fascinating. They arrive at Griffiths Island within three days of September 22 each year, returning to the nest burrow they had the previous year, with the same partner. They spend a few weeks renovating their homes, mate in early November, then fly out to sea for a couple of weeks. They return to Port Fairy about November 25, immediately lay their eggs (one per family), then both parents share in the incubation until the egg hatches in mid-January. After two or three days, the parents leave the chicks and forage at sea for food.

⤵ Let's Stay Here
Port Fairy YHA,
8 Cox St, ☎*5568 2468,*
🖥*www.yha.com.au* Formerly the home of the town founder and its boasts as one of the oldest heritage buildings in Port Fairy. Located close to the shops, beaches, the rivers and wharf. Very friendly

owners. Facilities includes a large kitchen, laundry, open fireplace, TV/video lounge, games room with pool table, internet access, gardens and a barbecue area. Offers free use of boogie boards and fishing gears. Bike and canoe hire and parking available. *Members Dorm ✪$18; single $37; double/twin $46 BC MC VA*

Eumeralla Backpackers,
High St, Yambuk, ☎*5568 4204,* 🖥*www.backpacker.faithweb.com* Located quietly in town, 18km west of Port Fairy. This hostel once used to be an 150 year old school house. It's a nice old building with hardwood floors and plenty of character. There's a kitchen, TV room and a barbecue area outside. *Dorms ✪$16.50 ; double/twin $33;*

Geelong
Population 221,357
Geelong is on the shores of Corio Bay, south-west of Melbourne.

Climate
Average temperatures: June max 25C (77F) - min 13C (55F); July max 14C (57F) - min 5C (41F).

Characteristics
Geelong is Victoria's premier regional city and, in fact, was a more important commercial centre than Melbourne in the 1840s. It is the natural gateway to the richest wool and wheat areas of the world. The city has many antique and arts and crafts shops.

How to Get There
By Air
Geelong has its own regional

airport which can be contacted on ☎ 5264 1273.

By Rail
Trains run frequently between Melbourne and Geelong, ☎ 13 1368.

By Coach
V/Line services Geelong frequently, ☎ 13 6196.

Visitor Information
The Geelong and Great Ocean Road Visitor Infomation Centre is in Stead Park on the *Princes Highway*, ☎ *(03) 5275 5797*. More information can be found at the **Wool Museum** on *Moorabool Street*, ☎ *5222 2900* or ☎ *1800 620 888* (free call).

The website to visit is 🖳 *www*.greatoceanrd.org.au (there are no email contact facilities).

The Melbourne website 🖳 *www*. melbourne.citysearch.com.au also lists information on Geelong.

If you are wandering around the city, keep in mind that there is an information outlet in the Market Square Shopping Centre in Moorabool Street. Another can be found on the corner of *Princes Highway* and *St Georges Road, Corio*.

⤵ Let's Stay Here
Following is a selection of budget accommodtion. Please use this as a guide only. The telephone area code is 03.

Irish Murphys,
30 Aberdeen St, ☎ *5222 2900* Situated just above this Irish pub with your basic accommodation. Shared facilities includes a kitchen, TV lounge and common room. *Dorms* ✪*$19.*

National Hotel,
191 Moorabool St, ☎ *5229 1211* Another one of your basic accommodation just above the pub. Location is brilliant though, right at the heart of town. *Dorms* ✪*$19.*

Caravan Parks
Barwon Caravan and Tourist Park, *153 Barrabool Road*, ☎ *5243 3842*. (No pets allowed) 191 sites, barbecue, playground - *powered sites* ✪*$20-25 for two, cabins from $55 for two.*

City Southside Caravan Park, *87 Barrabool Road*, ☎ *5243 3788*. (No dogs allowed) 90 sites, barbecue, playground - *powered sites* ✪*$18 for two, cabins from $55 for two.*

Billabong Caravan Park, *59 Barrabool Road*, ☎ *5243 6225*. (No pets allowed) 97 sites, barbecue, playground, pool - *powered sites* ✪*$18-20 for two, cabins from $55 for two.*

Sherwood Forest Caravan Park, *70 Bailey Street*, ☎ *5243 1068*. (Pets allowed at owner's discretion) 120 sites, pool, playground - *unpowered sites* ✪*$17 for two, cabins $40-45 for two.*

Other areas: Queenscliff and the Bellarine Peninsula
Queenscliff Inn YHA, *59 Hesse St*, ☎ *5258 4600*, 🖳*www.yha.com.au* Located very close to the water on this historic seaside town, an hour and a half away from Melbourne. A stylish guest house with a classy feel to

it and plenty of atmosphere. Foodstore is just next door. The warmth of their hospitality is added by their luxurious open fires. Rooms are large and spacious. Other facilities includes a kitchen, laundry, and an internet access. You can also find pot pourri lying everywhere while listening to music. Downstairs is a drawing room where you'll find some board games and a selection of books, newspapers and magazines for reading. Enquire about a mid-week group booking. *Dorm from* ✪*$20 ($ non-members); single $45; double/twin $25.50pp BC MC VA EFTPOS*

Let's Eat
Geelong has a good selection of restaurants, with all nationalities represented. Also remember that some of the motels have restaurants serving reasonably-priced meals. Recommended restaurants are:

Bamboleo, *86 Little Malop Street*, ☎ *5229 2548*. Licensed restaurant with Spanish cuisine.

Koaki, *Bell Parade*, ☎ *5272 1925*. Traditional Japanese food.

Mexican Graffiti, *43 Yarra Street*, ☎ *5222 2036*. All types of Californian-style Mexican food available. Fully licensed. Open from 11am daily.

Mei Ling, *169 Malop Street*, ☎ *5229 7505*. Chinese food with dine-in, take-away or home delivery options.

Pastels by the Bay, *13 The Esplanade*, ☎ *5222 3499*. Fully licensed, bay views, open daily for lunch and dinner.

Pearl of China Cafe, *154 Ryrie Street,* ☎*5229 8895.* Take-away, home delivery or a-la-carte.

Sirinda, *93 Ryrie Street,* ☎*5221 5797.* Thai restaurant.

Samraat, *137 Pakington Street, Geelong West,* ☎*5229 7995.* Indian cuisine.

McDonalds have branches on the corner of *Ryrie and Yarra Streets, Geelong; 400 Melbourne Road, Geelong North;* and *230-236 Autumn Street, Geelong West.*

Points of Interest

Geelong was first settled in the 1930s and has several historic buildings within walking distance of the city centre. The Information Centre has details of a Heritage Walk that starts from the Post Office on the corner of *Ryrie and Gheringhap Streets.*

The **National Wool Museum,** *cnr Moorabool and Brougham Streets,* ☎*5227 0701,* is housed in a bluestone wool store and traces the story of wool from the sheep's back to the finished garment. Wool auctions are still held here. ⊙open daily 9.30am-5pm, and admission is ✪$7 adults.

Geelong Art Gallery, *Little Mallop Street,* ☎*5229 3645,* has some fine examples of early Australian painters and a good contemporary collection. ⊙open Mon- Fri 10am-5pm, Sat-Sun 1-5pm. Admission is free.

Port of Geelong Maritime Museum, *Eastern Beach Road,* ☎*5277 2260,* has displays depicting 150 years of shipping in

Corio and Port Phillip Bays. The museum is ⊙closed on Tuesdays and Thursdays, and opens from 10am-4pm every other day of the week. Entry fees are ✪$2 adults.

The **Ford Discovery Centre,** on the corner of *Gheringap and Brougham Streets,* ☎*5227 8700,* features the history of car design and engineering, and offers insights into the impact of global influences and environmental change on automobiles in the future. It is ⊙closed on Tuesdays but opens 10am-5pm every other day.

Gabbinbar Animal Wildlife Park, *654 Torquay Road,* ☎*5264 1455.* Many types of animals, both native and foreign, can be found in the park ⊙open daily 10am-5pm.

⚓ Beaches

Apart from the stillwater beaches in Corio Bay-Eastern Beach and St Helen's - there are the nearby still-water beaches of Port Phillip Bay - **Portarlington, Indented Head, St Leonards, Queenscliff** and **Barwon Heads.** Then you come to the ocean beaches of **Point Londsdale, Ocean Grove, Torquay, Jan Juc, Anglesea, Point Addis, Airey's Inlet, Fairhaven, Lorne,** and the famous surfing mecca, **Bell's Beach.**

Festivals

The **Springding Festival** is held in November.

Facilities

There are facilities for over 150 sports, including football, basketball, horse racing, greyhound racing, golf, tennis, and all water sports.

Portland

Population 10,000

Portland is situated on the coast of Victoria at Cape Sir William Grant, and is the only deepwater port between Geelong and Adelaide.

Climate

Average temperatures: January max 22C (72F) - min 13C (55F); July max 12C (54F) - min 8C (46F). Average rainfall: 840mm (33 in); wettest 6 months May - October. Average hours of sunshine: summer 8; autumn 4; winter 3; spring 5.

Characteristics

Portland was the first permanent settlement in Victoria, and is filled with historic buildings from the 1840s. The Henty Brothers settled here with their flocks of sheep in 1834 before Victoria was proclaimed a separate State. Portland has become an important port serving a vast hinterland including the Mallee, Wimmera, Western District and the southeast of South Australia. It is also the site of the giant Portland Aluminium Smelter.

How to Get There
By Bus

There is a daily bus service to/from Mount Gambier which takes approximately 90 minutes.

By Rail

There is a rail service from Melbourne with a coach connection to Portland.

Visitor Infomation

The Portland Maritime Discovery and Visitor Information Centre can be found in *Lee Breakwater Road,* ☎*(03) 5523 2671.* They are ⊙open daily 9am-5pm.

⤵ Let's Stay Here

No shortage in this department in Portland. Here is a selection with prices which should be used as a guide only. The telephone area code is 03.

Admella Motel,
5 Otway Court, ☎5523 3347. 10 units, barbecue - ✪$57.

Bellevue Backpackers,
☎5523 4038 Located on minutes drive from town and walking distance to the beach. The accommodation consists of two caravans that offers very basic facilities and not much in terms of privacy. Quite overpriced for a hostel. Dorms ✪$20; single $20pp; double/twin $20pp ;

Mariner Motel,
196 Percy Street, ☎5523 2877. 12 units - from ✪$55.

Melaleuca Motel,
25 Bentinck Street, ☎5523 3397. 16 units, unlicensed restaurant (closed Sunday) - ✪$55.

Portland Backpackers Inn,
14 Gawler St, ☎5523 6390 Located nicely in the centre of town. It's cheap, but everything also feels cheap. Not on par with your usual hostels. Facilities a small TV lounge and a barbecue area outside. Dorms ✪$15;

Caravan Parks
Centenary Caravan Park, 184 Bentinck Street, ☎5523 1487. (No dogs allowed) - powered sites ✪$18 for two, cabins $18 for two.

Claremont Holiday Village,
37 Percy St, ☎5521 7567. (No dogs allowed) - powered sites ✪$18-20 for two, cabins from $40 for two.

Dutton Way Caravan Park,
Dutton Way, ☎5523 1904. (Pets allowed at manager's discretion) - powered sites ✪$13-16 for two, on-site vans $30-33 for two.

Henty Bay Caravan Park, Dutton Way, ☎5523 3716. (Dogs allowed under control) - powered sites ✪$15-25 for two, on-site vans $25-40 for two.

Portland Haven Caravan Park,
76 Garden Street, ☎5523 1768. (No dogs allowed) - powered sites ✪$14-16 for up to four, cabins $33-55 for up to four.

Let's Eat
Here are a few reasonably priced eateries you might like to try:

Middle Kingdom Chinese Restaurant, 31 Henty Street, ☎5523 3666.

Poon's Restaurant and Cafe, 121b Percy Street, ☎5523 5071.

Sandilands Restaurant, 33 Percy Street, ☎5523 3319.

The Canton Palace BYO Chinese Restaurant, 7 Julia Street, ☎5523 3677.

Counter meals are available at **Richmond Henty Hotel,** 101 Bentinck Street, ☎5523 1032; **Mac's Hotel,** 41 Bentinck Street, ☎5523 2188; and **Gordon Hotel,** 63 Bentinck Street, ☎5523 1121.

Points of Interest
There are around 100 historically-important buildings in the city, many classified by the National Trust, and all giving parts of Portland an old world charm. Some buildings from the Henty era are the bluestone mansions '**Burswood**' and '**Claremont**' built in the 1850s, the Customs House and the Court House. There are five important old inns dating from 1842 and an **Historical Museum** is in one of them, the **Caledonian Inn**. The **Portland Club** and the Visitors Centre are from the same period.

The **Cottage** in the **Botanic Gardens**, built in 1858, has been the home of six different curators over the years. It has now been restored and furnished in the period style of 120 years ago. The Cottage will be opened for inspection if you arrange an appointment, ☎5523 3820.

History House, the Old Town Hall, houses a collection of historical items, including the Henty plough. It contains, as well as large framed pictures of former mayors and prominent officials who were well known in the early days of the town, a fine collection of photographs and records of the early history of Portland. It's ⊕open at 10am-noon and 1-4pm every day, ☎5522 2226.

The 250km (155 miles) **Great South West Walk** provides an excellent introduction to the fascinating variety of scenery and wildlife in South-West Victoria. The walk begins and ends at the Visitor Centre and traverses forest, woodland, the **Lower Glenelg National Park,** the magnificent beaches at **Discovery Bay**, and the high limestone headlands at **Cape Bridgewater and Cape**

Nelson. The walk is not solely for the hardy long distance walker, it can be undertaken in easy stages by young and old alike. A 2km section at Cape Grant has been sealed for the disabled.

Cape Bridgewater, is the home of the Petrified Forest, a tangle of weird tree forms fashioned by wind and water from the old root systems of the native scrub. The enormity of the rugged coastline can be experienced from cliff walks with the powerful ocean pounding the rocks below, and occasionally shooting up through blowholes.

Festivals

The **Portland Summer Festival, Apex Fishing Carnival** and **Country and Music Festival** are held in January. The **Dahlia Festival** is held in March.

Facilities
Boating, lawn bowls, bush walking, croquet, fishing, golf, horse riding, sailing, surfing, swimming (pool, river, beach) tennis, water skiing.

Outlying Attractions
Heywood
Situated 25km (16 miles) north of Portland, Heywood is a rural centre with hosts of apple orchards. The main attractions in the town are the **Bower Bird Museum,** ☎ *5527 1660*, the **Cave Hill Gardens**, and **Lake Condah Aboriginal Mission.**

Hamilton
Known as the Wool Capital of the World, Hamilton is 58km (36 miles) north of Heywood in the heart of fine wool grazing country. The Visitor Infomation Centre is in **Lonsdale Street,** ☎ *5572 3746* or ☎ *1800 807 056* (free call), and they have information on the town's attractions, which include the **Hamilton Art Gallery** ☎ *5573 0460,* **Hamilton Historical Museum** ☎ *5572 4933,* the **Pastoral Museum** ☎ *5571 1595,* **Lake Hamilton** and nearby **Nigretta** and **Wannon Falls.**

Macarthur
34km (21 miles) south of Hamilton, and 11km (7 miles) south of Byaduk Caves, Macarthur is also within easy reach of Mt Napier and its volcanic surrounds. Only a few kilometres south-west of the town is the **Mt Eccles National Park,** where you'll find **Lake Surprise**. There are two first class walks around the crater of Mt Eccles, and camping and picnic facilities are available.

Nelson
Nelson is 70km (43 miles) west of Portland, and is a picturesque fishing hamlet at the mouth of the Glenelg River. It is a popular resort and has numerous bushwalks. A regular boat service takes visitors to the **Margaret Rose Caves**, which are ☉open daily for inspection, ☎ *8738 4191.*

Tasmania

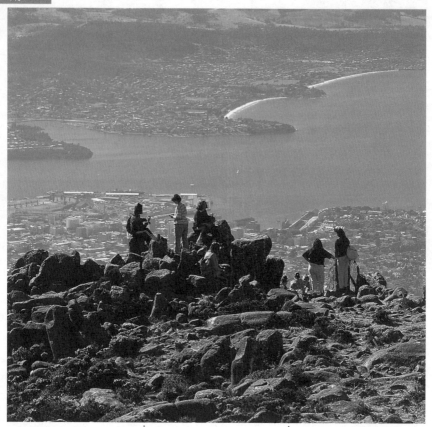

Hobart

Population 189,444
Hobart is situated on the Derwent River Estuary at Stormy Bay, at the foot of Mt Wellington, which is snow capped in winter.

Climate
Average Temperatures: January max 22C (72F) - min 12C (54F); July max 11C (52F) - min 4C (39F). Average rainfall: 635mm (25 ins). Driest months January to March.

Characteristics
The suburbs of Hobart spread along both banks of the river and into the foothills of Mt Wellington, which is 1,354m (4,442 ft) high. The central part of the city is very attractive. Hobart is the second oldest capital city in Australia, founded very soon after Sydney. Its architecture reflects its age, with beautifully preserved sandstone buildings unsullied by pollution, and clean, clear streets. It is a great place for a holiday and is well served by many hostels, motels, caravan parks and camping places.

How to Get There
By Air
Hobart Airport is 16km (10 miles) from the city centre and **Redline Coaches,** ☎*6233 9466*, operate a regular service to the city. Taxis are readily available.

By Bus
Redline Coaches have a service

to/from Launceston/Devonport/Burnie/Wynyard/Smithton and to Queenstown, ☎6233 9466.

Hobart Coaches have a Hobart/Swansea/Bicheno service, ☎6233 4232.

Peninsula Coach Service operate a Hobart/Port Arthur Service, ☎6250 3186.

Visitor Information

The Hobart Visitor Information Centre is in *Davey Street, ☎(03) 6230 8233*, email ✉*tasinfo@ discovertasmania.com*, and the website is ■*www.discovertas mania.com.au*

⤴ Let's Stay Here

The prices for accommodation vary considerably depending on the standard offered and the season. Here we provide a selection of budget accommodation which should be used as a guide only. The telephone area code is 03.

Adelphi Court YHA,

17 Stroke St, New Town, ☎6228 4829, ■www.yha.com .au Located closely to a lot of main attractions in North Hobart. Comprises of an old building with the reception and the buildings at the back has the accommodation. Has a warm atmosphere. Facilities includes a kitchen, laundry, a huge games room, and a barbecue area at the courtyard. Breakfast available. There is also and on site food store and parking available. **Recommended.** *Dorms from* ✪*$20; singles from $49 ($59 with en suite); double/twin $56 ($32.50pp with en suite)* BC MC VA EFTPOS

Allports Hostel,

432 Elizabeth St, North Hobart, ☎6231 5464, ■www.tassie.net.au/~allports Huge accommodation complex with really great facilities and great rooms. There's an extension at the back that has houses more dorms. Facilities includes a fully equipped kitchen, laundry, common rooms, internet access, TV lounge and games room with ping pong and pool table. Parking also available. **Recommended.** *Dorms* ✪*$20; single $35; double/twin $50*

Central City Backpackers,

138 Collins St, ☎6224 2404 or 1800 811 5507, ■www.ce ntralbackpackers.com.au Another big complex set in an old building. Located nicely at the heart of city. Features a fully equipped kitchen, laundry and a TV lounge with heater. During the busy periods of the year, the bar is open and there are pools tables that can amuse you and during summer there are bar snacks and meals. Bike hire available. *Dorms from* ✪*$18; single $36; double $48; twin from $24pp*

Metro Backpackers ,

16 Brisbane St, Launceston, ☎6334 4505, ■www.yha.co m.au Located at the heart of Launceston, close to everything and just newly started. Fantastic atmosphere. Rooms have heating. Facilities includes a kitchen, laundry, TV lounge, games room with a pool table, internet access and a barbecue area. There is also a roof terrace with a view. Bike hire and parking available.

Dorms from ✪*$20; double from $50* BC MC VA

Montgomery's Private Hotel and YHA Backpackers,

9 Argyle St, ☎6231 2660, ■www.yha.com.au Not too far from the ferry port and Hobart's waterfront. Museum and Gallery just across the road. Everything's brand new and all rooms have their own reading lights. Facilities includes kitchen, laundry, common room, TV lounge and internet access. Budget meals and bike hire is also available. *Dorms from* ✪*$18; double/twin from $55 (from $42.50 with en suite)* BC MC VA EFTPOS

Narrara Backpackers,

88 Goulburn St, ☎6231 3191 Located only a couple of blocks away from the city centre. Really great atmosphere. Kept clean and well maintained. Features a fully equipped kitchen, laundry, common rooms and a TV lounge. There are a few freebies such as free tea and coffee and free email access. Bike hire and parking are also available. *Dorms* ✪*$17; single $40; double/twin $44*

The Pickled Frog,

281 Liverpool St, ☎6234 7977, ■www.thepickledfrog.com This used to be an old pub that was converted into a hostel, located centrally in the city. Female dorms available. Good facilities including an industrial kitchen, laundry, a huge common room with pool tables, games, TV and videos and internet access. On site

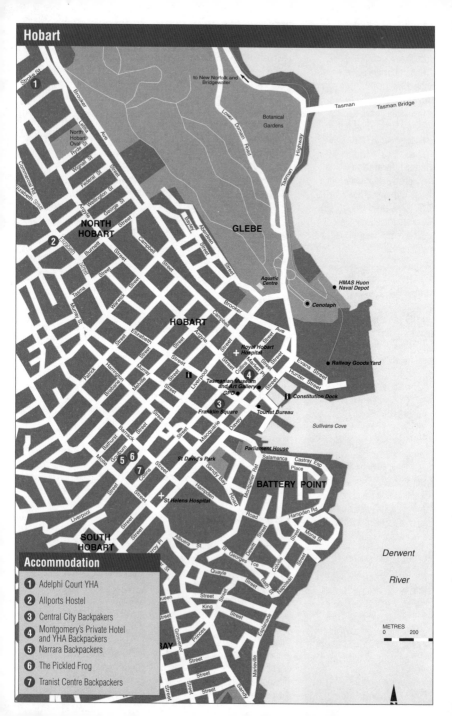

bar and cafe. *Dorms ❂$19; single $30; double/twin $48* (price includes breakfast)

Transit Centre,

1st Floor, Hobart Transit Centre, 199 Collins St, ☎*6231 2400,* 🖳*www.salamanca.com.au/ backpackers* Located closely to movie theatre and city centre and just ten minutes from Salamanca Market. Situated just above Redline Coach Terminal. Facilities includes a modern kitchen, laundry and lounge room with a pool table and TV and internet access. 'No alcohol' rule applies. *Dorms ❂$18*

Waterfront Cottage,

153 Risdon Rd, New Town Bay, ☎*6228 4748,* 🖳*www.waterfrontnew townbay.com* Situated 4km from Hobart's waterfront and CBD, set in a heritage property. Walking distance to local shops and supermarket. All rooms have their own kitchenette including microwave and fridge as well as lockers. There are also newly refurbished motel en suite rooms available. Other facilities includes laundry, an outdoor swimming pool, a spa and a barbecue area. Breakfast and parking available. **Recommended.** *Deluxe dorms from ❂$15; en suite motel rooms from $59*

Caravan Parks

Sandy Bay Caravan Park, *1 Peel Street, Sandy Bay,* ☎*6225 1264.* 181 sites - powered sites ❂$19 for two, park cabins $66 for two, on-site vans $44.
Treasure Island Caravan Park, *235 Bass Highway,*

Burnie, ☎*6421 1925.* 73 sites - powered sites ❂$9 for two, on-site vans $38 for two.

Let's Eat

Hobart caters for all tastes, and like any major population centre, its food outlets vary from quick takeaway to the more sophisticated of the restaurants listed below. Generally speaking, the fish dishes in the Hobart restaurants are something about which the city can boast.

Anatolia, *321 Elizabeth Street, North Hobart,* ☎*6231 1770* - authentic Turkish flavours - BYO - dinner Tue-Sun.

Concetta's Pizza and Restaurant, *213 Elizabeth Street, Hobart,* ☎*6234 9901* - pizza and Italian - open daily.

Marti Zucco's, *364 Elizabeth Street, North Hobart,* ☎*6234 9611* - Italian - open seven days for dinner, Thu-Sat for lunch - licensed and BYO.

Mit Zitrone, *333 Elizabeth Street, North Hobart,* ☎*6234 8113* - modern Australian dishes prepared with flair and moderately-priced - an award winner - open for dinner Wed-Sun, lunch seven days - BYO.
Thai Hut, *80 Elizabeth Street,* Hobart, ☎6234 4914 - licensed.

Local Transport

The **Metropolitan Transport Trust** buses depart from the central business district for the outer suburbs. Day Rover tickets are available for ❂$3.40 and may be used between 9am-4.30pm and after 6pm on weekdays, and all day on weekends.

Bicycle Hire

Derwent Bike Hire, *Regatta Grounds, Queens Domain,* ☎*6268 6161.*

Points of Interest

Hobart has more than 90 buildings which have been classified by the National Trust, 32 of them are in *Macquarie Street* and 31 in *Davey Street*, but apart from those there are numerous other well maintained buildings still in use today. They are some of the city's most attractive features.

The **National Trust** has regular walking tours of the city on Saturday mornings. They ❂start at 9.30am and last 2-3 hours.

If you are not in Hobart on a Saturday some of the more interesting buildings are:

Parliament House, part of which was originally the Customs House built between 1835 and 1840. The stone for the building came from what is now a lake in the grounds of Government House. The cellars, once the bonded store, still display broad arrows on the brickwork. The Legislative Council chamber has housed that body since 1856. The House of Assembly chamber is housed in a wing built in 1939. Parliament House is situated at the lower end of *Murray Street* opposite the wharves and is fronted by spacious lawns and gardens.

Government House, ☎*6234 2611,* is built in Tudor Gothic style. It has 70 rooms and 50 chimneys, and took from 1840 to 1858 to complete.

The **Theatre Royal** in *Campbell Street* - Australia's oldest theatre is built in the regency style and is a reminder of a more gracious era.

Mount Wellington

Hobart

Hunter Street Historic Buildings

The **Customs House Hotel**, *cnr Morrison and Murray Streets*, ☎*6234 6645*, was first licensed in 1846. This was the prototype for the hotels of the old Hobart waterfront of the 19th century.

Battery Point, save for the modern hotels, looks much the same as it did a century ago. Houses and cottages are packed into a jumble of narrow streets and lanes which gives the area a maritime atmosphere. The oldest building is the **1818** signal station which was used to relay messages from another station on Mt. Nelson. There is a fine terrace of Georgian sandstone warehouses on one side of **Salamanca Place** which now house restaurants, galleries and some offices. Open-air markets are now held on the other side, where the "New Wharf" used to be, every Saturday in summer. In winter the markets move into one of the warehouses. St George's Church stationed nearby has Australia's oldest Classical Revival spire.

Other interesting churches include **St. Mary's Cathedral**, *Harrington Street*, **St. David's Anglican Cathedral**, *cnr Macquarie and Murray Streets*, the **Holy Trinity Church**, *North Hobart* and **The Scots Church** and the **Uniting Church** (formerly Congregational), *New Town*. All of these churches were built in the fine architectural tradition of the great cathedrals of Europe and Britain. The imposing St Mary's was built on the site of St. Virgilius, the first Catholic Church to be built in Tasmania. Much of St. Mary's sandstone work had to be rebuilt as the original foundations were faulty. St David's is an example of the Gothic Revival style. It's solid silver altar

vessels were presented by King George III in 1803. Scots Church was first knows as St Andrews, and the 1830 building is notable for its heavy battlements. The New Town church was built in 1842 in Romanesque style.

The historic home **Runnymede** in *Bay Road, New Town*, was built in 1844. It was a family home from that time until the 1970s. It is now owned by the National Trust, and is open for inspection daily 10am-4.30pm, except Good Friday, the month of July and Christmas Day. An admission fee of ○$7.70 adults, ☎*6278 1269*.

Penitentiary Chapel and Criminal Courts, *cnr Brisbane and Campbell Streets*, were built in the early 1830s. Inspection is daily 10am-2pm, except Good Friday and Christmas Day. An admission fee of ○$7.70 adults, ☎*6231 0911*.

Hobart's main shopping area is around the **Cat and Fiddle Arcade**, which has an animated clock that is activated every hour on the hour. You will see the cat, fiddle, dog, dish, cow and spoon!

The **Tasman Bridge** is one of the main landmarks of the city, and spans the Derwent Estuary just to the north of the city centre. In 1975 it was struck by a ship, causing part of the roadway of the bridge to collapse, killing 12 people. The bridge was closed for over a year, effectively creating two population centres. The only way over the Estuary was through a winding temporary bridge floated on pontoons.

The **Royal Tasmanian Botanical Gardens**, ☎*6234 6299*, and **Queen's Domain**, where you can relax after a hectic morning or afternoon sightseeing, are near Government House. If you

are hungry, there is a pleasant restaurant in the Garden grounds, ☎*6234 4849*.

The **Wrest Point Casino**, ☎*6225 0112*, is Hobart's other landmark. It was Australia's first legal casino, and is as well known as a convention centre.

Anglesea Barracks is the nation's oldest military establishment. Some of the buildings date back to the early 1800s and the guns outside the gate were cast before 1774. It is open daily, and guided tours are held on Tuesday morning at 11am.

Hobart's city centre is very close to the harbour. From certain vantage points, it often appears that boats are moored in the streets. Most of the waterfront is recreational area which is frequented by locals and visitors alike. The annual blue water classic, The **Sydney to Hobart Yacht Race** begins on Boxing Day, and finishes at Constitution Dock right in the heart of the city.

There are quite a few interesting museums in Hobart.

The **Tasmanian Museum and Art Gallery** is housed at *5 Argyle Street*, and has an emphasis on Tasmanian Aborigines and early colonial activities. It is open daily 10am-5pm and admission is free, ☎*6211 4177*.

The **Allport Museum and Library of Fine Arts** is in the State Library in *Murray Street* - open Mon-Fri 9.30am-5pm, admission free, ☎*6211 4177*.

The **John Elliott Classics Museum** is at the University of Tasmania at *Sandy Bay*, ☎*6226 2235*.

The **Lady Franklin Museum**, in *Lenah Valley*, is built like a Greek temple, and is the headquarters of the Art Society of Tasmania. It has a display of paintings by Tasmania's leading artists and a library of art books. Open Sat-Sun 1.30-4.30pm, and admission is free, ☎*6228 0076*.

The **Maritime Museum of Australia** is housed in Secheron House, *Secheron Road, Battery Point* - ⏰open daily 10pm-5pm with free admission fee, ☎*6234 1427*. The collection dates back to the time of Abel Tasman, 1642.

The **Tasmanian Transport Museum** is in **Anfield Street, Glenorchy** - ⏰open Sat-Sun and Public Holidays, 1-4:30pm. Closed Christmas Day and Good Friday. Admission is ❂$5 adult, ☎*6272 7721*.

Narryna at *103 Hampden Road, Battery Point,* is one of Hobart's oldest colonial homes. Well worth a visit, an admission fee is charged - ⏰open Mon-Fri 10am-5pm, weekends and Public Holidays 2pm-5pm, closed Christmas Day, Good Friday and Anzac Day, ☎*6234 2791*.

Shot Tower on the *Channel Highway,* is 10km south from the centre of Hobart. It is here that shot for rifles was made. It affords an excellent view of the Derwent Estuary.

On the opposite side of the Derwent, near Risdon Cove, are the Bowen pyramids in **Bowen Park**. It was the site of the first European settlement in Tasmania. These house historic exhibits including Tasmanian Aboriginal artefacts.

The **Bellerive Battery** also across the Derwent, was built in the 1880s when a Russian invasion was feared. From the Fort you have excellent views of the Derwent Estuary and Mt Wellington.

If you like chocolate then you may be interested in visiting the **Cadbury/Schweppes Factory** at *Claremont*. Tours can be organised by phoning ☎*6249 0333*. Inspections take places on ⏰Tues, Wed, Thurs at 9am, 9.30am, 10am. The factory is closed at certain times during the year because of annual leave by employees, so check before you visit. Children must be accompanied by an adult.

The old **Cascade Brewery** is a striking relic of colonial times, and is set picturesquely beside a stream in the shadow of Mt Wellington. Guided tours are available, ☎*6221 8300*.

Mt Wellington, 1270m (4,167 feet), has many walking tracks and offers a superb view of Hobart, but it can get cold up there even in summer. In winter it is often dusted with snow.

Facilities
Hobart has all the facilities you would expect of a capital city - horse racing, car racing, lawn bowls, golf courses, squash and tennis courts, swimming pools, cricket and football ovals, convention facilities etc..

Outlying Attractions
The Derwent Valley
Granton is where you can see the **Bridgewater Causeway** which was built by convict labour.

Boyer is 32km (20 miles) from Hobart. The news-print mills here supply about half of Australia's news-print.

New Norfolk, which is a few kilometres further on, could almost be a village of England with its quaint old buildings. It is classified by the National Trust as a historic town. It is possible to get to New Norfolk by launch from Hobart. Hops are grown in the surrounding countryside.

Plenty, where brown and rainbow trout are raised at the 'Salmon Ponds', is 11km (7 miles) from New Norfolk.

Mt Field West National Park is 73km (45 miles) from Hobart and well worth a visit. It consists of a high plateau dotted with high peaks and tarns (lakes). The National Parks and Wildlife have huts for hire up in the Park, ☎*6288 1526*. They are rudimentary but are a great to use as a base for day long hiking excursions to various tarns and outcrops. The paths are well marked, but I would only advise this sort of activity during the summer months. For winter, there are a number of ski lodges up here and a number of tow bars. Nearer to the entrance, and easily accessible, are the attractive **Russell Falls** whose rock formation is in a series of levels over which the water tumbles.

South of Hobart

Kingston-Blackmans Bay is south along the coast and one of Hobart's fastest growing outer suburban areas. It has attractive beaches (little surf) and picnic areas. Blackmans Bay has a small blowhole, and lookouts at **Doughty Point** and **Piersons Point** offer superb views of **Bruny Island** and **Storm Bay.**

Margate, which is 19km (12 miles) from Hobart, has a motor museum and an unusual market. The market has its headquarters in Tasmania's last passenger train. The converted carriages house toymakers, glass blowers, woodworkers, artists and other creative pursuits.

Snug, a few kilometres further south on the *Channel Highway*, is an aptly named village, and a little further on some 34km (21 miles) south of Hobart is **Kettering**. The terminal for the Bruny Island vehicular ferry is here.

Bruny Island is a popular holiday destination for campers, although I would not be too keen camping here during winter. The main township is **Adventure Bay** on the east coast of South Bruny Island. The island has a narrow neck, and on North Bruny there is an aero club and airstrip with a memorial to some of the country's early navigators. At **Fluted Cape** at the southern end of Adventure Bay on South Bruny Island is the spot where Captain Cook landed in his voyage down the east coast of Tasmania. There is also a **Museum** of that cruel and talented British seaman, Captain Bligh, on this part of the island. For more information, contact Bruny D'Entrecasteaux Visitor Centre, *Ferry Road, Kettering,* ☎*(03) 6267 4494.*

Huonville is south and inland from the areas mentioned above. It is 37km (23 miles) south of Hobart and is the commercial centre of the area. It is a pretty area which has pleasant rural and seascape scenery. The Huon Valley was a large apple exporter before Britain joined the EEC. There is an apple industry museum here, as well as a motor museum and a couple of hotels. The population is a little over 1300 people. A cruise on the 'Huon Pride' is a good way to see the area. Information is available at the centre on the Esplanade, ☎*(03) 6264 1838.*

The Huon Valley

The Huon Highway (A6) follows the Huon River until Surges Bay, where it crosses overland to Dover. It is a lovely drive, with rolling hills and steep green paddocks, and stands of tall gums and pines. The section between Glendevie and Dover is especially picturesque. As you drive along, you can see the striking silhouette of **Hartz Peak**, looking a bit like Mount Fuji.

⤵ Let's Stay Here

Huon Valley Backpackers, *4 Sandhill Rd, Cradoc,* ☎*6295 1551,* 🖥*www.nomadsworld.com/ country.asp?country=AUST RALIA* Centrally located in Tasmania's magnificent Huon Valley, just 45 minutes from Hobart. Caters a lot to backpackers who are in a working holiday. Kept clean and well maintained. Facilities includes a kitchen and dining, laundry, TV lounge, common areas, an internet access and a barbecue area. There is also a sun deck outdoors where you can witness the great views of the Huon Valley. Friday pizza night and harvest work is offered. *Dorms* ✪*$17; double/ twin $40*

Geeveston

This timber town is further 31 km south of Hounville and is a base for visits to the Hartz Mountains National Park and the rugged valleys of the Huon and Picton Rivers.

The main attraction around here is the **Tahune Forest Air Walk** and the Visitor Centre. The 597m long Air Walk is up to 38m above the Huon River and offers visitors a magnificent view of the environment. It is built to withstand winds up to 180kph.

The **Tahune Forest Reserve** was chosen as the Air Walk site because of its location at the confluence of the two rivers, and has surrounding eucalypt forest. The attached Visitor Centre sells local produce, and during summer it also offers a smorgasbord barbecue. ✪Admission is adults $9.

At the end of *Avre Road* from Geveston is a 102 hectare reserve, with picnic facilities on the banks of the Huon River, tall forest and rainforest walks with 1000 year old Huon pine and 500 year old celery top pines. Amongst other sights is the **Big Tree**, a swamp gum 87m tall and 21m around at the base and small Huon Pine trailing their branches in the river. At **Keogh's Creek** there is a level walk through rainforest. Much of this area is logged but carefully managed by Tasmania's Forestry Commission. It is interesting to see how quickly the forest regenerates after being cleared.

Hartz Mountains National Park is reached through Geeveston. It has some of the wildest and most spectacular scenery in the world, and is said to resemble the Canadian Rockies. For information on fees and road access, contact the Parks and Wildlife Service in nearby Dover on ☎6298 1577.

Dover is a further 21km (13 miles) south of Geeveston on the coast. It is the last petrol stop for motorists heading into the lonely and rugged country towards South-East Cape. There are two fish processing factories there.

Southport is another 21km (13 miles) further south from Dover. Nearby is the **Hastings Thermal Pool**, which is 27C (80F) all year round, and **Fairy Caves** - ☎6298 3209. There are daily tours of the caves and a restaurant nearby, although there is no accommodation available.

Lune River is a popular place with gem collectors. A tramway still operates taking tourists for a 6km trip through bushland from the township to **The Deep Hole** across the bay from Southport.

> 🔖 **Let's Stay Here**
> **Geeveston Forest House,**
> *24 Arve Rd, Geeveston,*
> ☎62971102, 💻 *www.tassie*
> *.net.au/~Idillon/* Adjacent to
> the World Heritage areas of
> Hartz Mountains and the South
> West Wilderness of Tasma-
> nia, 50 minutes from Hobart.
> Located just in town close to
> a lot of things. An old hostel
> which is small and offers basic
> accommodation. Homely feel
> with a kitchen, laundry and TV
> room. *Dorms ✪$14*

North of Hobart

Richmond is as elegant today as it was in the 1820s when it was an important military post and convict station linking Hobart with Port Arthur. Situated only 27km (17 miles) north of Hobart on the Coal River, its village green is shaded by leafy green trees, and its old stone buildings house galleries, tea shops, craft boutiques and museums. **Old Hobart Town**, *cnr Henry and Bridge Streets*, is a stunning model re-creation of the convict-built town of the 1820s, which you can stroll through at your leisure. **The Maze and Tea Rooms**, *13 Bridge Street*, are ☉open daily 10am-5pm, ☎6260 2451. The **Richmond Gaol** is ☉open daily 9am-5pm except Christmas Day and Good Friday, ☎6260 2127. The bridge spanning the Coal River is convict built, as are most sandstone buildings in this town. **St John's Catholic Church**, just up from the bridge, was built in 1836. It is the oldest Catholic Church in Australia, as up until the 1830s public worship in the Catholic faith was outlawed.

The telephone area code is the same as Hobart - 03.

> 🔖 **Let's Stay Here**
> **Richmond Cabin and Tour-
> ist Park**, *48 Middle Tree
> Road*, ☎6260 2192 - pow-
> ered sites ✪$16-18 for two,
> on-site vans $35-45, cabins
> $45-55.*

Tasmania's Holiday coast extends from **St. Helens**, with the **Bay of Fires** slightly to the north where many trekkers camp, through to Orford in the south off which is

Maria Island, now a National Park. The island is serviced by a ferry in the summer. In winter, check before you leave, ☎6257 1589. The coast has sheltered beaches, rocky coastline, terrific surf and great fishing. For those used to balmy water temperature, such as most 'mainlanders' (a term used by Tasmanians to describe the rest of Australia) then you will be surprised to find that even in summer the water temperature is cold. You cannot stay in for too long. Cramps are common.

Continuing north, there's **Sorell**. **Orford**, another town, boasts at least 8 decent motels and other guest houses.

> 🔖 **Let's Stay Here**
> **Old Penitentiary,**
> *Darlington, Maria Island,*
> ☎6257 1420, 💻 *www.tasmani
> aoutdoors.com/* This used to
> house 400 convict prisoners
> in histories past but is now
> converted into a hostel, set
> up by the Parks and Wildlife
> authority. Facilities includes
> a wood fire heater which can
> alternately be used for cook-
> ing and a barbecue area.
> Toilet and laundry facilities
> nearby. Book ahead of time.
> **Recommended.** *Dorms from
> ✪$8.80; penitentiary unit $22*

Swansea

Situated 137km (85 miles) from Hobart and 51km (32 miles) north of Triabunna, Swansea is a pretty seaside town which has 2 caravan parks, more than 10 home host accommodation outlets, and 3 motels (around ✪$60-90 double).

To get to Coles Bay, a very popular tourist spot inundated with Tasmanians camping during the summer, you have to travel 32km (20 miles) north before turning south along 32km (20 miles) of partly dirt road. Coles Bay is in the vicinity of Freycinet Peninsula which is a very scenic spot.

↪ Let's Stay Here

Gumleaves,
Swanston Rd, Little Swanport, ☎6257 3439 Located about 25km north of Triabunna. A huge 400 acres of land and bush settings. Quiet and secluded. Mainly caters for group bookings. Your normal facilities of kitchen and lounge rooms plus the added bonus of rare features such as mini golf, basketball, tennis and volleyball courts. There is even a lake and a deer park. *Dorms* ✪*$25*

Triabunna YHA,
12 Spencer St, Triabunna, ☎6257 3439, 🖥*www.yha.com.au* Set in 11 acres of land, a km off Triabunna and the nearest bus stop. Basic facilities including a kitchen, laundry and lounge area with open fire. Fresh egg and produce available. On site foodstore. Bikes and camping equipments available for hire. There is also parking available. *Dorms from* ✪*$16; single from $18; double/twin from $18*

Freycinet Peninsula and Coles Bay
The Freycinet Peninsula (pronounced fray-sin-nay) is a place of captivating pink granite cliffs, dazzling blue seas and long white sandy beaches. It is now the most popular national park in Tasmania. (The Tasmanian poet

James McAuley wrote a whole book of poems about the area.) Much of the park is coastal heathland with brilliant wildflowers in the spring.

There are large shell middens in the park, relics of its long occupation by Aborigines of the Oyster Bay tribe. **Moulting Bay Lagoon** is a wetland of international importance with many black swans. Two or three hour easy bushwalks are well worthwhile. The road south ends at a car park from which you can climb 20 minutes to a lookout over **Wineglass Bay**, one of the most photographed spots in the State, with an unspoilt white beach stretching in a perfect curve along the clear blue water. A three hour walk to the top of **Mt Amos** gives some spectacular views.

For the really adventurous, try **Schouten Island**, a seldom visited section of the national park, just off the tip of the peninsula. There is no jetty, but the walks are very interesting...a true desert island.

Nearby Coles Bay has accommodation for tours of the Freycinet Peninsula. Demand is very high during the holiday season and we advise you to book ahead. To get to Coles Bay you have to travel about 30 km north from Swansea before turning south onto 30 km of partly dirt road.

↪ Let's Stay Here

Coles Bay YHA,
Freycinet National Park, Coles Bay, ☎6234 9617, 🖥*www.yha.com.au* A small and well secluded hostel that looks over the beach. Very basic hostel with facilities such as stove and fridge and a barbecue area. Note that there is no hot water system and you might think about bringing

your own food due to the fact that the nearest foodstore is miles away. Book way ahead of time too for a chance of vacancy. There is parking though. *Room min 2 people from* ✪*$10; single from $45*

Iluka Holiday Centre YHA,
The Esplanade, Coles Bay, ☎9257 0115, 🖥*www.yha.com.au* Located close to the beach, just in town. Features a kitchen, TV lounge and a barbecue area. Meals available. There is also a tavern, bistro and bakery on site. Parking available. *Dorms from* ✪*$18.50; single from $50; double/twin from $26pp BC MC VA EFTPOS*

Bicheno
The town of Bicheno is 43km (27 miles) north of Swansea, and is a very attractive spot. The beaches are covered in an incredibly soft silver sand that is unique to the area. Off the main beach is **Diamond Island**, home to the fairy penguin, which can be reached at low tide. Keep an eye on the time and tide because the behaviour of the penguins can be very absorbing, and you may find that you have to swim back to the beach. Bicheno was a whaling station, and is now a popular fishing and boating spot. There is a sea life centre, and **East Coast Natureworld** (☎6375 1311, admission ✪$11 adult, nearby. The surfing off **Cape Lodt** is usually very good.

↪ Let's Stay Here

Bicheno Backpackers Hostel,
11 Morrison St, ☎6375 1651 Located closely to the town centre. Set in a wooden build-

ing. Features a kitchen, laundry, a TV lounge and a barbecue area. Parking available. *Dorms* ✪ *$17*

Bicheno Caravan Park, *52 Burgess Street,* ☎ *6375 1280, powered sites* ✪ *$14 for two.*

Seaview Accommodation Centre,
29 Banksia St, ☎ *6375 1247,* 🖳 *www.users.bigpond. com/Seaview_Accom* Winner of the Micro Business Network's Annual Award 2002. Overlooks the seaside town of Bicheno on the East Coast of Tasmania. A well equipped hostel that caters mostly to school and church groups. Rooms only provide blankets. Facilities includes a small kitchen and a huge games room with pool tables and ping pong tables. Outside is also a nice sun deck with unbelievable views of the sea. *Dorms from* ✪ *$15; bunks with en suite $35; double $35*

Other places:
Seaview Farm Lodge,
686 german Town Rd, St Marys, ☎ *6372 2341,* 🖳 *www.seaviewfarm.com. au* Located 8kms away from St Mary's and set in 400 acres of rural land with fantastic sea views. Electric blankets can be found on all beds and double rooms have en suite bathrooms. Facilities includes a kitchen, common lounge rooms with open fire and a barbecue area in the garden. *Dorms* ✪ *$18;*

St Helens
This bayside town is on Georges Bay, a further 37km (23 miles) north. It is a popular holiday and commercial fishing centre, and the most northern town on the east coast. From here the road swings westwards towards **Scottsdale** through some beautiful mountainous country. The permanent population of St Helens is 2000 people, but this swells during the summer. It has a variety of clubs - bowling, sailing, and golf with facilities for boating, water skiing, and surfing, although you get good surf further to the north on the **Bay of Fires** around **Binalong Bay**. If you are staying overnight maybe camp here on the beach.

We found that if you want to swim every day and go to see a few sights and not rush yourself, but take in the feel of the east coast- seeing the fairy penguins, having a delightful lunch in one of the pubs in the towns along the coast - the trip takes two days. You can leave Hobart in the morning, go to Port Arthur for the day and then head north stopping overnight in either Swansea or Bicheno. Next day you can take your time until you get to St Helens, and stay there for the next night. The following day you can head towards Launceston.

⤳ Let's Stay Here
Prices of accommodation vary considerably depending on the standard and the season. Here's a selection, with prices which should be used as a guide only. The telephone area code for St Helens is 03.

Anchor Wheel, *61 Tully Street,* ☎ *6376 1358.* 7 units, licensed restaurant (closed Sun), barbecue - *from* ✪ *$50.*

Bayside Inn, *2 Cecilia Street,* ☎ *6376 1466.* 27 units, licensed restaurant, indoor heated pool - *from* ✪ *$50.*

St Helens YHA,
5 Cameron St, ☎ *6376 1661,* 🖳 *www.yha.com.au* Located at the heart of town, close to food store and bus stop. Very warm atmosphere. Basic facilities includes a kitchen, laundry, TV lounge and a barbecue area. There are also some nice views. Parking available. *Dorms from* ✪ *$16; double from $38*

Caravan Parks
Hillcrest Caravan Park,
Chimney Heights Road, ☎ *6376 3298.* (No pets) 80 sites, playground, barbecue - *powered sites* ✪ *$15 for two, cabins from $50.*

St Helens Caravan Park,
2 Penelope Street, ☎ *6376 1290.* (No pets) 100 sites, excellent facilities - *powered sites* ✪ *$17-22, on-site vans $25-40, cabins from $40.*

Other Areas:
Merlinkei Farm YHA,
524 Racecourse Rd, Winnaleah, ☎ *6354 2152,* 🖳 *www.yha.com.au* Situated in a farm surrounded by very green rural land. Very homely atmosphere. Good facilities includes a kitchen, laundry, TV lounge room with open fire, internet access and a barbecue area. Pool tables are in the dorms. Meals and bike hire available. They also offer cow milking experience if you'd like. Parking on site. *Dorms from* ✪ *$17*

Port Arthur and the Tasman Peninsula

Population 1,500

Port Arthur is 95km (60 miles) south-east of Hobart on the Tasman Peninsula. The Settlement is joined to the main island by Eaglehawk Neck, a narrow strip of land only 200m across, thus making it an ideal location for a penal colony.

Climate

The average annual rainfall is 1031mm (40.6ins). The wettest six months are from May to October. It has 8 sunshine hours per day in summer, 7 in spring, 5 in autumn, and 4 in winter.

Characteristics

This old penal settlement was home to 12,500 convicts who served in a rehabilitation/punishment station and lived under the threat of the lash, and an experimental isolation system that often drove them to madness. Escape was rare and many remained to be buried in mass graves on the Isle of the Dead. Today, Port Arthur rests in peace amidst English oaks and expansive green lawns that roll down to the water's edge.

Getting There
By Bus

You can take one of the organised tours from Hobart (enquire at the Visitor Information Centre) or you can catch **Hobart Coaches**' service which ☉leave Hobart Mon-Fri at 4pm, and leave Port Arthur at 7.45am, ☎6233 4232.

Visitor Information

There is an information centre at the Port Arthur Historic Site,

☎(03) 6251 2371, and the staff are happy to provide you with any information you need.

↪ Let's Stay Here

There are quite a few hostels on the road to Port Arthur, and as it can be visited in a day from Hobart there is no problem ensuring you have a bed for the night. The accommodation varies depending on price. Here we have a selection which should be used as a guide only. The telephone area code is 03.

Eaglehawk Neck Backpackers,

94 Old Jetty Rd, Eaglehawk Neck, ☎6250 3248. Friendly atmosphere. Features your basic facilities like the kitchen and TV lounge and old furnishings. The hostel also overlooks the sea at Eaglehawk Neck. *Dorms ✪$15; double $60.*

Roseview YHA,

27 Champ Street, ☎6550 2311, ✉ www.yha.com.au Set in an old house built in the 1890s which use to be a guesthouse. The Port Arthur historic site is in full view from here. Facilities includes a kitchen, laundry, TV lounge room, internet access and a barbecue area. On site foodstore. Parking available. *Dorms from ✪$18; double/twin from $42 BC MC VA EFTPOS*

Port Arthur Caravan and Cabin Park, *Garden Point, Port Arthur,* ☎6250 2340 Set in natural bushland backdrop not far from Port Arthur. Has

bunkhouse accommodation. *Dorms ✪$15; double from $32.50pp*

Let's Eat

There are four restaurants where you are sure to have a pleasant meal: **Bush Mill Grill,** ☎6250 2221, **Commandant's Table Restaurant,** ☎6250 2101, **Red Fox Restaurant,** ☎6250 2217 and **Felons Restaurant,** ☎1800 659 101.

Points of Interest

The whole of the Tasman Peninsula can be seen as "convict country" although, like most country areas, it also has farms, orchards and small industry, with State Reserves and holiday homes near the beaches.

Port Arthur is the pre-eminent symbol of Australia's 19th century convict system. One which we would regard today as being anything but enlightened. Some believe that out of such a system there emerged many national characteristics especially the Aussie attitude to freedom and authority. Some claim mateship as well, but the author prefers to ascribe this theory to life and survival in the bush, and its further forging in the hell of wars.

The settlement operated from 1830 to 1877, as a timber producing "sawing station", and later as an industrial prison. Many of the convicts were recidivists, others were political prisoners, and they were therefore treated harshly. Towards 1877, with fewer convicts in Tasmania being sent for secondary punishment, life in the prison became less austere.

After closure, most of the land and buildings were auctioned off, with new residents renaming it

After the Sydney to Hobart Yacht Race

Currie Harbour

Port Arthur Jail

Carnarvon township. Bushfires virtually destroyed Carnarvon in 1895 and 1897 - only two out of perhaps 300 wooden buildings are left, together with brick and stone ruins and officer's houses.

What is left of the old penal settlement is atmospheric and following recent restoration, Port Arthur today is Tasmania's premier historic site.

The whole township area is maintained by the National Parks and Wildlife Service.

The $4.5 million Visitor Centre at the Port Arthur Historic Site opened in 1999. The **Interpretation Centre** has an imaginative and interactive method of imparting information on the site's convict heritage. In the complex is a restaurant, gift shop and cafe.

The Museum in the old Lunatic Asylum contains displays, an audio-visual theatre, a scale model of Port Arthur up to the 1870s, and a shop.

Officers' houses, newly restored, are open for inspection. The **Commandant's residence** shows details of 1800s construction practices, and furniture and furnishings from the period. **Smith O'Brien's cottage** gives an insight into the history of Irish and political prisoners. The Medical Officer's house reflects 1850s living. In 1985 this house was awarded - The Museum of the Year.

In the **Model Prison**, the solitary confinement cells can still be seen, and anyone who has experienced, even for a few minutes, the claustrophobic darkness of the cells, can well understand why one of the larger buildings in the prison complex was the **Lunatic Asylum**.

Other ruins include the **Penitentiary**, the **Church** (which is perhaps the most famous of the buildings as it is featured in most tourist literature), the **Guard Tower** and the **Paupers Mess**. These are perhaps the most evocative of convict life at the settlement.

Point Puer, the boys' prison, is across the bay. Here lads between the ages of 8-18 served after being convicted of crimes in Ireland or England. The ruins of the bakers' ovens and the old school are all that remain today.

The **Isle of the Dead**, the Port Arthur cemetery, is just off *Point Puer*. It can be reached by regular ferry. Here, in 0.7ha (1.7 acres), lie 2,000 convicts and free, an indication of the harshness of this convict prison.

The **Museum of Records** has actual records of the transportees sent to Tasmania (a long list of prisoner names, their crimes and punishment). The minimum term of transportation was seven years, which was imposed for such offences as stealing a lamb, a sheep, a pig. One prisoner, Joseph Parker, was transported for life for stealing a silk handkerchief. On another list, several men and women were sentenced to transportation for life for theft of articles of little value. In one case, the sentence of death for stealing 24/- was commuted to transportation for life. Even children received long gaol sentences.

Guided tours leave all day on the half hour, or you may wish to hire a tape recorder for an individual tour and ramble around Port Arthur. Entry fee to the site is ✪$20 for adults.

Facilities

You can swim in the beautiful bays, fish, go canoeing, boating and bushwalking.

Outlying Attractions

There were several subsidiary establishments on the peninsula, the **Coal Mines**, the **Saltwater Agricultural Station**, timber mills at Premaydena and Koonya together with the guard posts at Eaglehawk Neck and Dunalley. Semaphore stations were located on line-of-sight around the Peninsula and up to Hobart.

Cascades Cottage, *Koonya*, is privately owned, as are many of these outstations now. Accommodation is offered at the here in 4-star comfort.

Coal Mines Historic Site is an interesting place to explore, and is near a camping area in the north-western part of the peninsula. The Mines in the convict days served a dual purpose. They provided fuel for use in the colony, and were used as a punishment centre. In producing 80 tons daily the convicts were basically worked to death here. Cells were even built into the mine galleries. After 1848 the Coal Mines were privately operated, and were abandoned in 1877 after an underground fire.

Eaglehawk Neck is the narrow strip of land joining the Tasman and Forestier Peninsulas. During convict times, several dogs were chained close to each other along the Neck making escape virtually impossible. Nearby are several coastal formations - the **Devil's Kitchen**, **Tasman's Arch** and **Blowhole** as well as the **Tessellated Pavement** which looks like well-laid large pavers. These natural formations are well worth a visit. They are unique in Australia. Just keep your kids away from the edge; some have been known to try to find a way down into the Devil's Kitchen.

Dootown is nearby. It is a picturesque group of holiday homes, and almost all the houses have names incorporating Doo, e.g. Much-a-Doo, Didgeri-Doo, Doo Little. I suppose that is one approach to life.

Remarkable Cave is another blowhole which, unlike the Devil's Kitchen formation, is accessible at low tide. This is 7km (4.4 miles) south of *Port Arthur*, and an after-dinner walk there reveals spectacular coastal scenery and 300m high sea cliffs. Large binoculars have been placed at the car turning circle. The scenery at **Cape Raul** is quite spectacular as years of weathering have caused the rock to split vertically, creating an organ pipe effect.

Nubeena, on the shore of *Parson Bay*, is the largest town on the Tasman Peninsula, and is a popular resort. In convict days, timber cut from the hinterland was shipped to England from nearby Wedge Bay.

Launceston
Population 98,160
Launceston is Australia's largest inland port, and Tasmania's second largest city. It is situated at the head of the Tamar River at the junction of the north and south Esk, in the central northern region of Tasmania.

Climate
Average temperatures: January max 21C (70F) - min 13C (55F); July max 13C (55F) - 5C (41F). The average rainfall is approximately 750mm (29.5 ins)

with the wettest period being from May to October. The Sunshine hours are Summer 7, Autumn (Fall) 4, Winter 3, Spring 6.

Characteristics
Known as the 'garden city' because of its abundance of well established beautiful public and private gardens, Launceston nestles in a wide river valley amid lush green countryside. It has given rise to the description of Tasmania as 'this other England'.

Getting There
By Sea
Spirit of Tasmania passenger/car ferry operates between Melbourne and Devonport, *9206 6211*.
Tasmania's Own Redline coaches operate a service from Devonport to Launceston, *(03) 6336 1446*.

The **DevilCat Express** catamaran passenger/car ferry operates *Port Welshpool, Gippsland, Victoria* to *George Town* with a coach to Launceston daily return during peak season (summer) and 5 times a week during off season (not Tues and Thurs).

By Bus
Tasmania's Own Redline coaches operate a Hobart/Launceston and Launceston/Devonport, Burnie, Wynyard and Smithton service.

Visitor Information
The Gateway Tasmania Visitor Information Centre is on the corner of St John and Paterson Streets, *(03) 6336 3133*. It is open Mon-Fri 9am-5pm, Sat 9am-3pm, Sun and Public Holidays 9am-12pm.

↪ Let's Stay Here
Launceston, with many hostels and motels, boasts of

moderate budgets. Prices vary considerably depending on the standard of accommodation and the season. Here we have a selection of places which should be used as a guide only. The telephone area code is 03.

Hotel Tasmania, *191 Charles Street*, ☎*6331 7355*. 25 rooms, licensed restaurant - ✪*$45*.

Irish Murphys, *211 Brisbane St*, ☎*6331 4440*, ✉*www.irishmurphys.com.au* Accommodation located above an Irish pub situated not too far from the Museum and Gallery. Your basic facilities including a kitchen and TV lounge. Drinks and meals available in the pub. *Dorms* ✪*$17; double $35*

Launceston Backpackers VIP, *103 Canning St*, ☎*6334 9779*, ✉*www.launcestonbackpackers.com.au* Set in a one hundred year old federation home that has been tastefully renovated. Located not too far from the main city attractions off the road from a park. Kept clean and well maintained. Facilities includes a large kitchen, TV lounge room and a common room with a piano. *Dorms* ✪*$17; single $38; double $40; twin $38*

Launceston City Youth Hostel, *36 Thistle St, South Launceston*, ☎*6344 9779* Located in the south from the city centre not too far from shops. It has the traditional boarding school feel to it. Features a

big kitchen, TV lounge and games room with a pool table and ping pong. *Dorms* ✪*$15; single $20*

Metro Backpackers, *16 Brisbane St*, ☎*6334 4505*, 🖳 *www.backpackersmetro.com.au* Located nicely in the heart of town close to everything with a really great atmosphere. Kept clean and well maintained. Facilities includes a nice modern kitchen, laundry, a number of TV lounges, internet access and a barbecue area in the terrace. Bike hire and parking available. *Dorms* ✪*$23; double $55 ($47.50pp with en suite)*

No. 1 Backpackers, *1 Tamar St*, ☎*6331 1938* Located just at the northern end of the city centre overlooking the North Esk River. Situated just above the Tamar Bridge Hotel. Your very basic accommodation with laundry facilities, a small common room and pool table. There's a nice view from the balcony that overlooks the river. *Dorms* ✪*$16*

Caravan Parks
Treasure Island Caravan Park, *94 Glen Dhu Street*, ☎*6344 2600. Powered sites* ✪*$17 for two, on-site vans $38-40 for two.*

Let's Eat

Launceston has over 40 restaurants and many additional takeaway outlets. Below we have listed some restaurants that cater specifically for certain dishes. Most restaurants are BYO and those that are licensed have a corkage charge if you bring your own.

Arpar's Thai Restaurant, cnr *Paterson and Charles Streets*, ☎*6331 2786.*

Calabrisella Pizza Restaurant, *56 Wellington Street*, ☎*6331 1958* - Italian, BYO - open Wed-Mon.

Fu Wah Chinese Restaurant, *63 York Street*, ☎*6331 6368.*

Plate of the Art, *185 Wellington Street*, ☎*6334 3220* - modern Australian - open for dinner Tue-Sun, lunch Fri - good selection of wines.

Terrace Restaurant, at the *Country Club Casino*, ☎*6335 5775* - refined setting, excellent service - dinner Tue-Sat.

Points of Interest

There are many quaint malls and shopping centres in the city such as the **Quadrant Mall** and **Yorktown Square**.

The **Queen Victoria Museum and Art Gallery** in *Wellington Street* has a unique collection of Tasmanian fauna and Aboriginal artifacts, a Planetarium and a reconstructed joss-house. ⏲Open Mon-Sat 10am-5pm, Sun 2pm-5pm, ☎*6331 6777.*

The **Umbrella Shop**, in *George Street*, is built entirely of Tasmanian Blackwood and is preserved by the National Trust, ☎*6331 9248.*

The **City Park**, ☎*6323 3610*, is spacious with well laid-out gardens amid old elm and oak trees. It contains a small zoo and houses the **John Hart Conservatory** which is noted for its displays of begonias, cyclamen and many other hot house blooms.

The **Design Centre of Tasmania**, cnr *Brisbane and Tamar Streets*, ☎*6331 5506*, is ⏲open Mon-Fri 10am-6pm, Sat 10am-1pm, Sun 2pm-5pm. It has displays by Tasmania's best designers and craftsmen, some available for purchase.

The **Penny Royal World**, in *Paterson Street*, is an imaginative man-made development. It depicts early nineteenth century gunpowder mills, cannon foundry and arsenal in a landscaped setting with streams and waterfalls. Within the complex there is a canal system and lake complete with a fleet of vessels, two of which fire and proof their guns daily. A scale model railway system runs the 700m (766 yards) from the **Gunpowder Mill** to the **Penny Royal Watermill** complex. (the Penny Royal Watermill is a motel) Besides visits to the various Mills, and a ride on the train, cruises operate from here. ⏲Open daily 9am-5pm.

The **Country Club Casino**, at Prospect Vale besides accommodation mentioned above, has various gaming tables and offers live entertainment.

Franklin House, 7km (4.3 miles) south, is an early settler's home furnished in the colonial style. It is owned by the National Trust - ⏲open for inspection daily 9am-5pm, ☎*6344 7824.*

Tamar Knitting Mills, *Hobart Road*, are ⏲open daily 9am-4pm, ☎*6344 8255.* The mills have been operating since 1926, and you can purchase woollen garments there after touring the operation.

The **Cataract Gorge** is quite a place, and it is only a few minutes by bus from the city. A 1.6km (1 mile) walk along the face of the cliff ends in the **Cataract Cliff Grounds Reserve** from where a chair lift crosses the gorge. Manicured gardens, complete with strutting peacocks, merge with native flora on the upper bank, whereas on the city side, gardens surrounding a swimming pool extend to the lake over which you pass in the chair lift.

National Automobile Museum of Tasmania, *cnr Cimitiere and Willis Streets*, ☎ *6334 8888*. Showcasing a selection of international cars, some in pristine condition and others undergoing restoration, this museum is ⏰open 9am-5pm seven days.

Cruises on the Tamar River can be taken on either the **Tamar Odyssey**, a 14.9 metre Cougar Cat (☎ *6334 9900*) or the Lady Stelfox, a paddlesteamer operating every hour between h10am and 3pm daily (☎ *6331 6699*).

Festivals

There are a number of local food, wine, racing and agricultural shows scheduled throughout the year, and the Visitor Centre can provide details of specific events.

Facilities

As with all cities of a reasonable size, all sports such as lawn bowls, golf, squash, water sports, horse and greyhound racing, cycling and the various football codes are catered for.

Outlying Attractions

In Launceston many tours - half day and full day - and a variety of travel packages, are offered to see the sights of the **Tamar Valley** and the area surrounding Launceston. Contact the Visitor

Centre in *Paterson Street*, ☎ *(03) 6336 3133*, for information.

South
Hadspen

Located some 13km (8 miles) south-west, the village of Hadspen is often referred to as being very much like England. Here **Entally House**, which is built like an English farmhouse, is ⏰open daily 10am-12.10pm, 1pm-5pm, ☎ *6393 6201*.

Liffey Valley

Around 60km (37 miles) south-west via Carrick and Bracknell, are the **Liffey Falls**. It is a popular destination for bushwalkers and fishermen. There is a large fernery located here which sells a large variety of ferns. The Falls are in the Reserve and drop into a beautiful rainforest.

Ross

The town of Ross on the Midland Highway, is famous for its elaborately carved convict-built bridge of 1836. 75km (47 miles) south of Launceston and on the banks of the Macquarie River, Ross is classified by the National Trust. It is well worth a stop on your way to or from Hobart. There are many interesting buildings in the village - **1836 War Memorial, Sherwood Castle Inn, Macquarie Store, Old Barracks Building** (now a wool craft centre) - and information can be obtained at the Visitor Information Centre. They are located in the tearooms, which were originally **St John's Anglican Church.**

North
Exeter

24km (15 miles) north-west

along the Tamar River, Exeter is the centre of a fruit growing area, and even the local school has its own farm. At the mouth of the **Supply River** are the remains of Tasmania's first water driven flour mill. The Visitor Information Centre is on *Main Road*, ☎ *(03) 6394 4454*.

Batman Bridge

The bridge spans the Tamar River another 30km (19 miles) downstream at **Whirlpool Reach**. It was one of the world's first cable-stayed bridges. Dominated by a 100m (328 ft) high steel A-frame inclined 20 degrees from the vertical, it leans out 30m (98 ft) across the river and carries almost the entire weight of the 206m (676 ft) main span. The bridge was opened in 1968.

George Town

The town is the residential and commercial centre for **Bell Bay**, but offers little in the way of accommodation. It has a beautiful **Georgian mansion**, The Grove, *25 Cimitiere Street*, that has been restored and is open for inspection ⏰daily 10am-5pm, ☎ *6382 1336*. It is the port for the Catamaran ferry service to Port Welshpool in Victoria. There is an information centre on *Main Road*, ☎ *(03) 6382 1700*.

⤿ Let's Stay Here
Traveller's Lodge YHA, *4 Elizabeth St*, ☎ *6382 3261*, 🖳 *www.yha.com.au* Set in an old cable cottage house built in the 1890s, situated at the heart of town close to a lot of things. Features a fully equipped country kitchen, lounge room with open fire, TV room, the rare piano and a barbecue area.

Bike hire and parking available. *Dorms from ✪$18; double from $50; twin from $55*

Other Areas:
Bridport Seaside Lodge,
47 Main St, Bridport, ☎*6365 1585,* 💻*www.yha.com.au*
Situated closely to the beach, the river estuary and everything else. It has nice oak floors and huge windows that catches the spectacular views. This purpose-built hostel features a kitchen, laundry, TV lounge and a barbecue area. Canoe hire and parking available. *Dorms from ✪$16; double/twin from $19pp BC MC VA*

West Scottsdale
Scottsdale, with a population around 2800, is 70km (43 miles) north-east of Launceston, and is the centre of a large market garden area. A food processing factory specialising in deep freezing and dehydrating vegetables is located here. Oil poppies are grown in the area, and when they bloom in January and February the countryside is a blaze of colour. Lavender is grown around Nabowla, 13km west of Scottsdale. It blooms in late December through January pervading the air with its perfume. The **Bridestow Estate Lavender Farm** is at *296 Gillespies Road, Nabowla,* ☎*6352 8182.*

Ben Lomond National Park
The Park is 48km (30 miles) south-east of Launceston, and reached via White Hills. It boasts of spectacular mountain scenery, as do all national parks in Tasmania. It is Tasmania's leading ski resort. Access is by a very steep and winding mountain road through precipitous gorge and across the mountain plateau. In winter it is often covered with heavy snow. Contact the Visitor Information Centre in Launceston about bus timetables and departure points.

↩ Let's Stay Here
Creek Inn,
1 High St, Alpine Village, Ben Lomond National Park,
☎*6390 6199*
Backpacker accommodation is allocated in the further back of this hotel complex. Book early to avoid the complications during ski season. *Dorms from ✪$20; double from $40*

Devonport
Population 25,000
Devonport is situated on the north coast of Tasmania, where the Mersey River enters Bass Strait.

Climate
Average temperatures: January max 21C (70F) - min 13C (55F); July max 13C (55F) - min 5C (41F). Average annual rainfall: approximately 800mm (31 ins). The wettest six months are May-October. Hours of sunshine are: Summer 7; Autumn 4; Winter 3; and Spring 6.

Characteristics
Devonport, the fourth largest city in Tasmania, is the gateway for the car and passenger ferries from the mainland. It was originally two towns that voted to amalgamate in 1893 - Formby on the west bank of the river, and Torquay on the east bank.

Devonport had its beginnings as the centre of a rich agricultural and orchard area. Today, the Mersey Valley remains one of Tasmania's main orchard districts, but is now also famous for its mushrooms.

Getting There
By Bus
Tasmania's Own Redline coaches connect Devonport to Launceston, Burnie and Hobart, with a connection to Queenstown from Burnie.

By Sea
Spirit of Tasmania passenger/car ferry operates between Melbourne and Devonport, ☎*9206 6211.*

Visitor Information
Devonport Visitor Information Centre is at *92 Formby Road,* ☎*(03) 6424 8176.*

Showcase Info, *Best Street,* ☎*(03) 6424 8176,* apart from being a tourist attraction in itself, has complete information about all the things to see and do in Devonport and the North West Coast. It is open seven days a week.

↩ Let's Stay Here
Following is a selection of budget accommodation with prices which should be used as a guide only. The telephone area code is 03.

Devonport YHA - MacWright House,
115 Middle Rd, ☎*6424 5696,* 💻*www.yha.com.au* Located at the southern area of town set in an big, old house. Comfortable and spacious, with a pleasant outdoor environment. 1km to the nearest food store. There are buses that stops in front of the hostel. Features a kitchen, laun-

dry, TV lounge and a barbecue area at the back. Note the no alcohol rule. Parking available. *Dorms from ❂$13; single from $19; family room from $29*

Formby Road Hostel,
16 Formby Rd, ☎*6423 6563,* ▤*www.devonport.tco.asn. au/formby* Set in a Federation old styled mansion located in between Bass Highway and the town centre. Situated in an industrial area, but there's a view of the Mersey River that may just make up for it. It has a feel good vibe and there are a lot of common areas to hang out in. Your normal facilities. **Recommended.** *Dorms ❂$16; double $36*

Molly Malone's Irish Pub,
34 Best St, ☎*6424 1898* Centrally located Irish pub that has your basic accommodation but kept clean. Shops are nearby and it is close to the Mersey River ferry. Basic facilities includes a kitchen and TV room. Meals and drinks available downstairs. *Dorms bed ❂$15; double $50; twin $30*

Tasman House,
114 Tasman St, ☎*6423 2335,* ▤*www.tasmanhouse.com* This is one of those hostels that looks and feels like a school boarding house, but is a real value for money. Set in 11 acres of land, it's a huge hostel. Located not far from the supermarket and just at the centre of town. There are great facilities that features a fully equipped kitchen and dining, laundry, games with 8-ball and a ping pong table, TV room with a fire place, entertainment lounge, library and a barbecue area. There are also pub nights. Also offers transport from the airport. *Dorms from ❂$12; double $39; twin from $14pp*

Caravan Parks
Devonport Vacation Village,
20 North Caroline Street, East Devonport, ☎*6427 8886.* (No pets allowed) - *powered sites ❂$17 for two, cabin section from $45.*

Abel Tasman Caravan Park, *6 Wright Street, East Devonport,* ☎*6427 8794.* (No pets allowed) - *powered sites*

❂*$16 for two, on-site vans $33-40 for two.*

Lakeside Caravan Park,
Lakeside Road, Eugenana, ☎*6427 2343.* (Pets on application) - *powered sites ❂$16 for two, cabin section $55 for two.*

Let's Eat
Devonport has a good selection of restaurants, and several hotels have counter meals. Coffee shops abound, as do takeaway outlets. Here are a few you might like to try.
China Garden, *33 King Street,* ☎*6424 4148.*

El Mecciko, *24 King Street,* ☎*6423 5455.*

Golden Panda Restaurant, *38 Formby Road,* ☎*6424 9066* - open Sun and Tues-Fri noon-2pm, Sun-Thurs 5-9pm, Fri 5-10.30pm, Sat 5-11pm.

Rendevous, *142a William* Street, ☎*6424 7157* - restaurant and coffee lounge.

Renusha's, *153 Rooke Street,* ☎*6424 2293* - Indian cuisine.

Devonport

Accommodation
1. Molly Malone's Prish Pub
2. Tasman House
3. Abel Tasmans Caravan Park

Nelson Falls

Queenstown

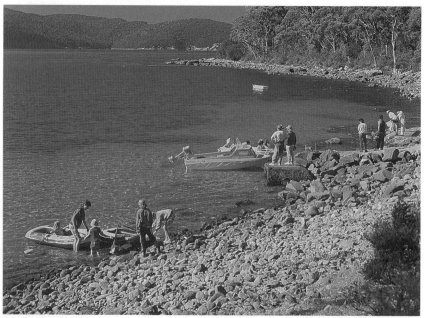

Fortescue Bay

Tooska Restaurant, *19 Steele Street*, ☎*6423 5456*.

KFC, *26 William Street, Devonport*, ☎*6424 2285*. **Pizza Hut**, *132 William Street*, ☎*6424 9344*. **McDonalds**, *1 Best Street*, ☎*6424 9400*.

Points of Interest
The **Victoria Bridge** connects East Devonport to Devonport, and it is 2km downstream from the Abel Tasman Terminal. To get to the bridge follow *Formby Road* along the river bank.

Walking and bicycle tracks circle the city and are found along the eastern shore. Bicycles can be hired at Mersey Bluff during the season, and the **Showcase** can advise of places at other times.

Mersey Bluff is one of only thirteen major sites where rock carvings by the Tasmanian Aboriginals can be viewed.

Tiagarra Tasmanian Aboriginal Culture and Art Centre at the Bluff headland has dramatic dioramas of the way of life of these people. It is open daily, except for July when it is closed for renovations, ☎*6424 8250*. The Tasmanian Aboriginals were physically different from their mainland counterparts. Some scientists believe they were originally an African or Polynesian people who drifted to Tasmania on primitive rafts, but a more plausible explanation is that their ancestors crossed over from the mainland when Tasmania was still joined to it. An unfortunate part of Australian history began when the first European settlers reached the Derwent in 1803. They began wiping out the Aboriginals, and by 1876 the entire race of full-blooded Tasmanian Aborigines

had disappeared.

The **Devonport Maritime Museum**, *Gloucester Avenue*, was formerly the Harbour Master's residence and Pilot Station, built early 1920. It now has exhibits of Devonport and North West Coastal Maritime History, with fine detailed models from the days of sail and steam to the modern passenger ferries, ☎*6424 7100*.

Devonport Gallery and Arts Centre is in the middle of the city at *45-47 Stewart Street*. The lovely old converted church has the latest exhibitions, and is ☺open Tues-Fri 10.30am-4.30pm, Sat 9.30am-noon, Sun 2.30-4.30pm, ☎*6424 8296*.

Victoria Parade is a scenic garden walk which follows the river and sea to Mersey Bluff. There is a good swimming beach, children's playground, kiosk and public toilets.

Taswegia, *57 Formby Road*, ☎*6424 8300*, is an Historic Printery and Craft Gallery, and is ☺open daily 10am-5pm. It has one of Australasia's largest heritage collection of print technology dating from 1852, and all in working condition. Taswegia specialises in the production of early colonial charts, convict documents, paintings, maps and paraphernalia. It also has an exclusive range of gift ware including printed linen, fabrics, wood-crafts, ceramics, pottery, posters, books and many other interesting and decorative items.

Home Hill, *77 Middle Road*, was the family home of Prime Minister Joseph Lyons and Dame Enid Lyons, Australia's first woman member of the House of Representatives, and the author of several books. Dame Enid

passed away in 1981, and the home is now operated by the City Council in conjunction with the National Trust. Home Hill is as Dame Enid left it and contains many interesting and historic mementoes. Phone ☎*6424 8055* for opening times.

The **Don River Railway**, ☎*6424 6335*, off *Bass Highway* (road to Ulverstone) is an operating railway museum, and is open daily throughout the year with steam trains running hourly every Sunday and public holiday afternoons. The museum has the largest collection of steam locomotives in Tasmania, dating from 1879 to 1951, and the largest collection of passenger carriages dating from 1869 to 1961. There are many other interesting exhibits, a souvenir shops, and a refreshment outlet.

Festivals
January - **Devonport Cup Carnival**.
February - **Food and Wine Frolic**. **Dahlia Show**.
March - **Mersey Valley Festival of Music**.
October - **Annual Show** of the Devonport Orchid Society.
November - **Agricultural and Pastoral Society Show**.

Facilities
There is ample scope for skin diving and sea, river and lake fishing. Angling for trout is popular in the Mersey, Forth and Leven Rivers.

A tennis centre is situated near Mersey Bluff, and there are also courts at *Wright Street, East Devonport*.

At the western end of *Steele Street* there is an aquatic recreation centre with an olympic pool and water slide set in natural parklands.

Other sports catered for are lawn bowls, golf, greyhound racing, trotting, horse-racing and squash.

Outlying Attractions
Ulverstone

Situated in the centre of Tasmania's Holiday Coast, Ulverstone is a seaside town on the Leven River, 18km (11 miles) west of Devonport. It is in rich agricultural country reaching south from the sea to the mountains. Safe and extensive beaches and river, woodlands, parks and mountain resorts provide ideal conditions for people to stay a while.

The town is the **Woodchopping Centre of Australia**, and the sport had it beginnings here in 1870 when two bushmen got into an argument in a local pub about who was the best man with an axe. With a wager of ✪$50 at stake, they adjourned to a nearby paddock to settle the matter and the sport was born. In 1974, the world championship was held in Ulverstone.

In the main street there is a large unusual **War Memorial**, which consists of 17m pillars joined by bronze chains.

Caves and Gunns Plains and the spectacular **Leven Canyon** at Nietta are some of the chief attractions of the Ulverstone district. A round trip to **Gunns Plains**, which is the site of a new hop industry, also traverses magnificent rural, mountain and river scenery.

Your first stop should be the Ulverstone Visitor Centre, *Car Park Lane*, ☎ *(03) 6425 2839*.

Penguin

The town of Penguin, 12km (7 miles) further west, is situated on three bays which provide safe beaches for bathing and picnicking.

A feature of the Penguin Municipality is the ambitious **Penguin Sports Club Dial Regional**, ☎ *6437 2767*, catering for most sports, plus bushwalking. Visitors are most welcome.

Sheffield

The town is the gateway to the Mersey-Forth Hydro-Electric Power Development with seven power stations and seven man-made lakes, including Lake Barrington, a venue for rowing events.

The lake is accessible by bitumen road which goes through some of Tasmania's most rugged mountain scenery. If you have your own equipment, **Lake Barrington** is ideal for a range of water sports including rowing, water skiing, power boating, canoeing and model yachting. There are launching ramps on both sides of the lake. It is necessary to book the rowing course with the ranger. The recreation area of the park is open daily from 8am until dusk, and facilities include a large day visitor shelter with wood barbecues, seats and tables, and a kiosk which is only open on weekends throughout the summer season.

Standing guard over Sheffield and dominating the skyline is 1231m (4039 ft) **Mt Roland**.

Cradle Mountain/
Lake St Clair National Park

The Visitor Information Centre is just inside the northern boundary of the Park, and is ☉open daily 9am-5pm, and after hours for special events, ☎ *(03) 6492 1133*. The Centre has a model of the Cradle Mountain, children's exhibits, maps, books, posters, registration for day walks and Overland Track, toilets, electric barbecues and picnic shelters. Other day visitor facilities are a day-use hut and toilets near Waldheim, fire sites by Ronny Creek, and toilets at Lake Dove. Walkers are requested to enter details of any walk in the walker registration book, and to de-register at the end of their walk, which is just as important.

Visitors should not forget that this beautiful area is a mountain wilderness where the weather can change abruptly and without warning. For people without experience and the right equipment, it can be a dangerous place in which getting lost is all too easy. Hiking clubs throughout Australia arrange parties to walk through the National Park to Lake St Clair, along the 85km (53 miles) Overland Track from Waldheim, and unless you are a very experienced hiker, you should go with one of these parties. For those who haven't the time or the inclination to hike, charter flights are available from Devonport, and you should enquire at the Information Centre.

which has a fully equipped kitchen, an open fire and there's a barbecue area outside. A foodstore, internet access and parking also available. *Dorms from ✪$18 BC MC VA EFTPOS*

Deloraine

The township of Deloraine is on the Bass Highway, 45km (28 miles) from both Devonport and Laun-ceston. It is nestled in a valley surrounded by Quamby Bluff (1226m - 4022 ft) and the Western Tiers. Historical and natural features mingled with rich farmlands make Deloraine a worthwhile stopping place.

Among the many attractions in the district are the **King Solomon and Marakoopa Caves** near Mole Creek. These world renowned limestone caves are open every day, but you will need to be book with the Mole Creek Guest House, Pioneer Drive, Mole Creek, ☎(03) 6363 1399. Inspection times are -

King Solomon Cave - ◷10.30am, 11.30am, 12.30pm, 2pm, 3pm and 4pm.
Marakoopa Cave - ◷10am, 11.15am, 1pm, 2.30pm and 4pm.

There are several walking tracks in the area catering for both the well equipped and experienced walker, as well as those desiring more relaxed yet equally scenic walks.

For further information, contact the Deloraine Museum and Visitor Information Centre, 98 Emu Bay Road, ☎(03) 6362 3471.

⤷ Let's Stay Here
Highview Lodge YHA,
8 Blake St, ☎6362 2996,
🖳 www.yha.com.au

Situated in town just a km from the nearest foodstore and bus depot. Your very basic normal facilities of kitchen and a sitting area. Highlight of this place would have to be the beautiful view of the Great Western Tiers and Quamby Bluff from the verandah. Parking available. *Dorms from ✪$18; double from $40*

Port Sorell

The port is 19km (12 miles) east of Devonport on the picturesque Rubicon River estuary. It is a popular holiday resort with prolific native flora and fauna, and good swimming and boating are available at nearby Hawley Beach.

Burnie

Population 20,000
Burnie is on the north-west coast of Tasmania on the shores of Emu Bay.

Climate
Average Temperatures: January max 21C (70F) - min 13C (55F); July max. 13C (55F) - min 5C (41F). Average annual rainfall approximately: 900mm (354 in); wettest six months - May - October. Sunshine hours: Summer 7, Autumn 4, Winter 3 and Spring 6.

Characteristics
A thriving industrial centre and deep water port which handles more than 2 million tons of cargo each year. It is the terminal for ANL sea road vessels, and trades directly with more than 40 overseas ports. Burnie is in the centre of lush dairying area and is surrounded by a wide forest belt that runs parallel with the coastline, about 50km (31 miles)

inland. About 22 million super feet of quality timber is produced each year from this area.

How to Get There
By Bus
Redline offer a service from Hobart connecting Oatlands, Launceston, Abel Tasman, Devonport, Burnie, Wynyard to Smithton four times a day, with special services between Wynyard and Burnie another 4 times a day.

Visitor Information
The Visitor Information Centre is in the **Burnie Civic Centre Precinct (Museum)**, *Little Alexander Street,* ☎*(03) 6434 6111.*

⤷ Let's Stay Here
Treasure Island Caravan Park, *253 Bass Highway, Cooee,* ☎*6431 1925. Powered sites ✪$16 for two, onsite vans $42.*

Let's Eat
You can have a decent night out at one of Burnie's restaurants. Listed below are a few with their specialities.

Fortuna Garden Chinese Restaurant, *68 Wilson Street,* ☎*6431 9035.*

Mandarin Palace, *63 Wilson Street,* ☎*6431 7878* - Chinese, licensed, open daily.

Renusha's Indian Restaurant, *28 Ladbrooke Street,* ☎*6431 2293.*

Rialto Gallery Restaurant, *46 Wilmot Street,* ☎*6431 7718* -

Points of Interest
The **Pioneer Village Museum** in

High Street, Civic Centre Plaza, is Burnie's premier attraction. It is close to the centre of the city, and the entire village is under one roof. It has more than 30,000 individual items on display. There is an inn, newspaper office, general store, blacksmith shop, and many authentic replicas of a commercial centre of the 1890-1910 period - ⊙open Mon-Fri 10am-5pm, and Sat-Sun 1.30pm-5pm. Admission ✪$4.50 adult, ☎6430 5746.

Burnie Park is only a few minutes walk away. It has shady trees, a rose garden and the old **Burnie Inn** which was first licensed in 1847. It is the oldest building in the city, and is open daily for inspection during the summer. They only sell light refreshments and Devonshire Teas - a little different from days of yore. There is also an animal sanctuary.

The **Civic Centre and Regional Art Gallery** in *Wilmot Street,* ⊙open Tues-Fri 10.30am-5pm, Sat-Sun 2.30pm-4.30pm, are also worth a visit. Admission is free, ☎6431 5918.

The **Australian Paper,** *Marine Terrace,* ☎6430 7777, has free guided tours at 2pm Tues-Fri of the processing of wood into paper. Children under the age of 12 are not admitted, and women are asked to wear slacks and low heeled shoes. Booking is essential.

The **Lactos Factory,** *Old Surry Road,* has cheese tasting ⊙Mon-Fri 9am-5pm, Sat-Sun 10am-4pm. Admission is free, ☎6433 9255.

Round Hill Lookout, 6.5km on the *Stowport/Natone Road,* and **Fern Glade** are only 3km from town and well worth a visit.

Facilities

The city and district caters for lawn bowls, boating, fishing, sailing, swimming (pool or sea), golf, bike and horse riding, as well as squash, the various football codes and cricket.

Outlying Attractions
Helleyer Gorge

The Gorge is 52km (32 miles) from Burnie on the Waratah Highway, which links the north-west with the west coast. The gorge itself is older than time, and is a scenic reserve. Nearby are glorious white sandy beaches, tidal inlets, freshwater streams and pools where campers can pitch their tents in near solitude, and enjoy nature in an undisturbed and timeless area.

Wynyard

16km (10 miles) from Burnie with a population of around 4500 people, Wynyard is a pretty town, and is almost more English than England. The town is located on the Inglis River, and the airport for Burnie is found here.

It is a major gateway to the north-west coast and offers superb panoramic views, while **Fossil Buff** (just beyond the Wynyard Golf Course) is a unique area rich in rare and ancient fossils. Among the important finds made here is that of a whale bone some 2 million years old.

The waters around the town are popular with divers and underwater photographers because of their clarity. Equipment for scuba diving can be hired in town, ☎6442 2247.

7km (4 miles) south is the **Oldina Forest Reserve** which contains a virtual museum of superb trees. At the Reserve are spacious lawns and picnic facilities.

30km (18.6 miles) east from Wynyard is **Rocky Cape National Park**. Some of its geological formations are 700 million years old, and some Aboriginal remains found there indicate that the area was occupied at least 9000 years ago, before Bass Strait was formed. There are also some interesting caves, and several bushwalks in the park. The walk from **Sisters Beach** to **Rocky Cape** is noted for its spring displays of wildflowers.

Tasmanian Scenic Flights, ☎6442 1111, out of Wynyard Airport, offer daily scenic flights to **Cradle Mountain** in the south over incredible gorges, farmland and various peaks, and shorter duration flights along the north coastline.

Boat Harbour

On the way to Boat Harbour from Wynyard is the **Shannondoah**

Cottage, ☎ *6445 1141*, that is essentially a craft centre, but also has tea rooms. Built in an old family homestead, it stocks Tasmanian craft items - patchwork, applique wall hangings, etc...

Boat Harbour's permanent inhabitants number about 300, but that number swells during the summer. Only 16km (10 miles) from Wynyard, it is a popular holiday resort with beautiful beaches, facilities for boating, fishing, water skiing and is close to a number of national parks.

Boat Harbour Beach Caravan Park, ☎ *6445 1253*, on the beachfront has powered sites ✪*$18 for two*. There are various flats and guest houses which can be booked through Tasbureau in Burnie.

Stanley

Only a one hour drive from Wynyard Airport, Stanley is an historic town as it was the site of the first settlement in north-west Tasmania. It has changed very little since its early days.

Its most distinctive feature is **'The Nut'** which rises 152m (500 ft) sheer on three sides, and is on the end of a 7km (4.3 miles) long isthmus. This landform has a 35ha (80 acres) summit that dominates the landscape, and affords a superb view of the countryside. If you wish to climb it, there is an easy walking track which begins opposite the post office and ends at the summit cairn. Alternatively, you can take the chair lift that operates from the rear of the Nut Shop Tea Rooms, ☎ *6458 1286*

There is good fishing in the bay and along the coast around Stanley.

Smithton

The administration of the Circular Head Municipality of the far north-west is based at Smithton. It has a large modern butter factory as well as a bacon factory, a large piggery and several saw mills. The district has an ideal climate for growing peas, and the town boasts of a pea freezing factory.

Lacrum Dairy Farm, ☎ *6452 2653*, is 6km (4 miles) west of Smithton. Visitors are welcome to this 275ha (679 acres) property, where they have a Wombat Tarn, picnic and barbecue facilities, bush walks, and milking between 3pm-5.30pm every day from October to the end of June. There is an admission fee, and groups of 10 or more should book.

Driving directly south, you can visit **Allendale Gardens** at Edith Creek (botanical gardens in miniature), **Balfour Track Reserve**, **Julius River Reserve**, **Lake Chisholm**, **West Beckett Reserve** and **Milkshake Hill Forest Reserve**. You would have to do this independently, though, as there are no guided tours to these parts.

Montagu is some 20km (12 miles) north-west of Smithton, and is the site of the Van Diemen's Land

Co which was founded in 1825 by Royal Charter of King George IV. This historic cattle and sheep property provides access for visitors seven days during summer months and 10am-2pm on weekends in winter. They have a multitude of displays, activities, walks, and refreshments are available.

Marrawah

Situated at the western end of the Bass Highway, 48km (30 miles) from Smithton, and very close to **Green Point** on the west coast, the settlement of Marrawah is well worth a visit, as wildflowers and native fauna are plentiful. There are several important Aboriginal rock carvings at **Mt Cameron** a little to the north. The carvings of circles and bird tracks are similar to ones found in the deserts of the Australian mainland.

King Island

The island is a region on its own. 64km (40 miles) long and 27km (17 miles) wide at its widest point, it has 145km (90 miles) of coastline. In addition to its wildlife, the island is very famous on the mainland for its cream, which causes queues in some Sydney shops when it becomes available.

There are two main towns on the island - Currie on the west coast and Grassy in the south-east. **Currie** (population 700 approx.) is the administrative centre, and has the **Bass Caravan Park**, ☎ *6462 1260* - on-site vans ✪*$45 for two*.

Grassy (population 600) is a deepwater port, and the site of the scheelite mine. The island would appeal to travellers and those who enjoy skin diving, surfing and shooting. The pheasant shooting

The Nut, Stanley

Table Cape

season is in June; the duck shooting season in March and April; and mutton-birding takes place in the autumn.

For more information about King Island, visit 🖳 *www.kingisland.net .au*

Queenstown
Population 3,715
Queenstown is located on the rugged west coast of Tasmania, in the midst of a wilderness area.

Characteristics
Queenstown is firstly and lastly a mining town. After seeing so many trees, your first glimpse of Queens-town may come as a shock because the hills around the town are denuded of greenery. This has been caused by a combination of tree felling, sulphur, fire and rainfall.

As the Lyell Highway descends steeply into Queenstown via the Linda Valley, there is a panoramic view of naked hills strewn with multi-coloured boulders which reflect the sun's rays. In the evening, the setting sun causes the mountains and hills to change from shades of brilliant gold to hues of deep pink. It is an unforgettable sight.

Climate
The area averages only 1750 hours of sunshine in a year, while it rains on an average of 320 days per year. The annual rainfall is over 3000mm (118 ins).

How to Get There
By Bus
Tasmania's Own Redline
Coaches have services between Hobart, Burnie, Strahan and Queenstown.

Visitor Information
Visitor information can be obtained the Galley Museum, *cnr Stitch St and Cutten St,* ☎*(03) 6471 1483.*

🔁 Let's Stay Here
Following is a selection of budget accommodation with prices that should be used as a guide only. The telephone area code is 03.

Mountain View Holiday Lodge,
1 Penghana Rd, ☎*6471 1163*
This used to be a historical singlemen's quarters converted into a one and two bedroom motel style units. Situated just on the A10 Highway not far from the town centre. All rooms have en suite plus TV, tea and toast making facilities, phone, fridge, electric blankets and heating. There's also the basic kitchen and dining, laundry and a barbecue area. There is also an on site bistro that serves breakfast and dinner. Parking available. *Dorms* ☎*$15; motel style double $35pp*

Caravan Park
Queenstown Cabin and Tourist Park, *17 Grafton Street,* ☎*6471 1332. Powered sites* ☎*$20 for two, on-site vans $40 for two.*

Let's Eat
You may want to try one of the restaurants below.

Gerry's Bistro Restaurant, *1 Penghana Road,* ☎*6471 1163.*

Maloneys, *Orr Street,* ☎*6471 1866.*

Miners' Crib Room, *10 Orr Street,* ☎*6471 1152.*

Points of Interest
In November 1883, Steve Karlson and Mick McDonough, who had only arrived in the Linda Valley the day before, discovered a strange iron outcrop which rose about 25 ft above the surface. This was the famous **Iron Blow**, where mining of the riches of Mt Lyell began. About two weeks later, the diggers pegged out a fifty acre lease, in the centre of which was the *Blow.* They suspected that the Blow was the source of the gold they washed in the creek below the outcrop. The Blow was worked as a gold mine for ten years, with everybody ignoring the millions of pounds of copper in it.

The **Mount Lyell gold mine** was bought by Bowes Kelly in 1891, and he formed the Mt Lyell Mining Company in Melbourne. But in that year gold mining at Mt Lyell came to an end, although it has always remained a welcome by-product. The directors of the company brought Edward Dyer Peters, a world authority on copper smelting, from the USA, and he conducted a successful smelting trial at the Argenton smelter, four miles south of Zeehan.

The present **Mt Lyell Mining and Railway Company,** one of the oldest mining companies in Australia, was formed in 1893, after the previous company had been dissolved for financial reasons. The new company failed to raise enough money for an extensive development programme, and mining at the Blow nearly came to a stop. Then an incredulously rich silver seam with an average of over a thousand ounces of silver to the ton was discovered by Dr Peters. This lucky discovery helped the young company out of its financial difficulties.

In 1895, Robert Carl Sticht, another American, but this time a metallurgist, was given a free hand by the directors of the company to design the first Mt Lyell smelters. His pyritic smelting process, which represented an important advance in the technology of copper smelting, became famous and was copied in many countries.

By 1891, the little shanty town of Penghana had sprung up around the smelters, but in 1896 it was wiped out by fire. The refugees set up home in a newly planned town on the banks of the Queen River, and called it, appropriately enough, Queenstown. In the same year the **Queenstown Hotel** was built.

An historic tour walk has been mapped out around the town, and information plaques have been erected at places of interest.

No stay in Queenstown would be complete without a visit to the **Mt Lyell Mine**. Guided tours are available and depart from Farmer's Store in *Driffield Street,* ☎*6471 2388.* Tours are of approximately two hours' duration, and include viewing the mine workings and the **Mining Museum**.

The **Eric Thomas Galley Museum**, *cnr Driffield and Sticht Streets*, features displays of old photographs dealing with the West Coast, as well as items of household equipment and personal effects in use during the early days. The museum is ⊕open daily, except Saturday mornings, and a small admission

fee is charged, ☎*6471 1483.*

Miners Siding in *Driffield Street* is a Queenstown Centenary Park Development, and incorporates the Miners Sunday Sculpture by Stephen Walker. The sculpture is made of bronze and Huon Pine, and depicts an early miner and his family on the day of rest, and the changes that transformed a rough miners' camp to a town and community. Part of the Miners Siding Park has been developed as a rainforest, with many species that occur mainly in Western Tasmania. Also in the Park is a restored ABT Locomotive, which was part of the system that was the only transport link between Queenstown and the outside world until 1932.

Iron Blow, the original gold mine, is situated north of the town at *Gormanston*, 2km off the *Lyell Highway*. The site has been developed as an area of historic and scenic interest, and offers excellent panoramic views over the mountains and **Linda Valley**.

The *Crotty and South West Access Road* turns off the *Lyell Highway* 10km (6 miles) north of the town, and was once the railway line for the North Lyell Copper Co. It provides access to the **Darwin Meteorite Crater, the Franklin River, Fincham Park, Kelly Basin, the King Power Development** and **Crotty Camp.**

Lake Margaret, north of *Queenstown*, was one of Tasmania's first hydro electric schemes and was built and owned by the Mt Lyell Co in 1914. The station and village remain as they were in the 1900s, with the original machines still working. A 2134m (7000 ft) wooden stave pipeline still delivers water from the lake to the Penstock, and a walk up the

hill provides unparalleled views of the rugged West Coast.

On the *Zeehan Highway*, 14km (9 miles) from Queenstown, there is a **balancing rock** which gives an insight into the unique geology of the area. The parking area here offers views over the glacial valleys of the **Henty** and **Yolande Rivers.** There are information plaques, and sign-post to the rock.

Facilities
Swimming pool, golf course, gem fossicking and gold panning.

Outlying Attractions
Zeehan
Zeehan is 33km (21 miles) north of Queenstown, and the town boomed when rich silver-lead deposits were discovered in 1882. By the turn of the century it was a town of 5000, and an entertainment 'capital' - Dame Nellie Melba and Enrico Caruso performed here. But, the ore ran out and the town declined before the beginning of World War I. A number of buildings have survived from its boom time including the **Gaiety Theatre, St Luke's Church** and the **Post Office.**

The **West Coast Pioneers' Memorial Museum** is housed in the old School of Mines, and is divided into five main categories of exhibits - a mineral collection; historical items relating to the West Coast; modern mining on the West Coast; locomotives and tracked mining equipment; and exhibits of Tasmanian animals and birds, with artefacts of the extinct Tasmanian Aborigines.

Places to visit around Zeehan include **Trial Harbour** (20km - 12 miles), **Heemskirk Falls** (19km

Gordon River

Canoeing in Freycient National Park

Tasman Peninsula

- 12 miles), **Granville Harbour** (40km - 25 miles), and the **Lower Pieman Dam** (50km - 31 miles). Both harbours are popular with fishermen seeking crayfish and abalone.

Strahan

Situated on Macquarie Harbour, 36km (22 miles) south-west of Queenstown, Strahan dates back to the convict days when it was a dreaded place. Many of the convicts who were sent to Sarah Island in Macquarie Harbour found life there was hell on earth, and death was seldom from natural causes.

The closure of many mines on the West Coast, and the building of the railway line from Zeehan to Burnie led to the decline of Strahan, and today it is a fishing port, holiday village, and a base for trips into the wilderness area around the **Gordon River**.

From Strahan you can take a flight on a sea plane over the peaks of **Frenchmans Cap National Park,** majestic **Lake Peddar**, the rapids and gorges of the **Franklin River**, and then land on the tranquil **Gordon River**. For further information contact Wilderness Air, ☎*6471 7280.*

Another adventure is a half-day scenic cruise on a motor launch which will take you from **Macquarie Harbour** to the Gordon River, pull into Heritage Landing to walk through a rainforest on an elevated walkway to view a 2000-year-old Huon Pine, and return to Strahan via the infamous **Sarah Island** and **Hell's Gates**, the notorious entrance of Macquarie Harbour. For further information contact Gordon River Cruises, ☎*6471 4300.*

The interesting Strahan Visitors Centre is on the *Esplanade*, ☎*6471 7622*, and in addition to local Visitor Information they have details of the history and heritage of the region.

↪ Let's Stay Here
Strahan YHA,
43 Harvey St, ☎*6471 7255 or 1800 444 442,* ▇ *www.yha.com.au* Bush area setting, located not far from the centre and close to the beach. Cabins have heating. Features basic facilities like kitchen, laundry and TV lounge. Outside are some picnic tables. There is also an on site foodstore and parking is available. *Dorms from* ✪*$20; single from $24; double from $50; twin from $44 BC MC JCB VA EFTPOS*

Frenchman's Cap

The mountain is part of the **Wild Rivers National Park**, and the *Lyell Highway* passes close to the northern edge of the park. There are several bushwalks in the area. You can take a short walk to view the white quartz dome of the Cap and look out over the **Franklin River**, or if you have more time, you can walk right into the rainforest.

For more information, contact the Parks and Wildlife Service in Queenstown, ☎*(03) 6471 2511.*